Advanced Praise for Margo Komenar's *Electronic*

CW00602523

*It's all here. Margo Komenar has written and assembled a won...
plete, well-written, thoroughly useful treasure of facts and imp...
Electronic Marketing is a must read for ALL marketers, whether ...ey are
currently using electronic selling tools, or they just hope to keep up with the
rest of the world. I guarantee that those who read this book will use it for the
rest of their careers.*

—LYNN UPSHAW, AUTHOR OF *BUILDING BRAND IDENTITY*
AND FORMER MANAGING DIRECTOR OF KETCHUM INTERACTIVE

*Competitive distinction for your company means giving your clients instant
access to information. It's about transforming mundane data into useful
information. . . . Electronic Marketing teaches the principles of turning your
data "inside-out" and targeting it properly. Individualism, speed, and accuracy are the calling cards of today's "customer-centric" enterprise. This book
shows you how to do it.*

Read it and survive.

—ED MARGULIES, VICE PRESIDENT, FLATIRON PUBLISHING, AUTHOR OF SIX BOOKS ON
COMPUTER TELEPHONY AND INVENTOR OF AN ARTIFICIAL INTELLIGENCE CONVERTER SYSTEM

*I found it to live up to its billing: comprehensive, practical information!
    Perhaps the thing that struck me most, however, was the applicability of
this information beyond just marketing. It is, in fact, really about building
relationships with customers using the new communications technologies
available. Thus, the techniques, approaches, case studies, and reference
information are equally valid to building, say, an electronic customer support system as an electronic marketing vehicle.*

—GARRY HORNBUCKLE, DIRECTOR, DEVELOPER TECHNOLOGY SERVICES, APPLE COMPUTER

*A must read in a new era of marketing. . . . the professionals involved in the
case studies are truly the pioneers of electronic marketing.*

—ANNIE VAN BEBBER, VICE PRESIDENT, ATTITUDE NETWORK/HAPPYPUPPY.COM

ELECTRONIC MARKETING

MARGO KOMENAR

WILEY COMPUTER PUBLISHING

John Wiley & Sons, Inc.

New York ◆ Chichester ◆ Brisbane ◆ Toronto ◆ Singapore ◆ Weinheim

Publisher: Katherine Schowalter
Editor: Tim Ryan
Assistant Editor: Kathryn Malm
Assistant Managing Editor: Carl Germann
Text Design & Composition: North Market Street Graphics

Designations used by companies to distinguish their products are often claimed as trademarks. In all instances where John Wiley & Sons, Inc., is aware of a claim, the product names appear in initial capital or ALL CAPITAL LETTERS. Readers, however, should contact the appropriate companies for more complete information regarding trademarks and registration.

This text is printed on acid-free paper.

This publication is designed to provide accurate and authoritative information in regard to the subject matter covered. It is sold with the understanding that the publisher is not engaged in rendering legal, accounting, or other professional service. If legal advice or other expert assistance is required, the services of a competent professional person should be sought.

Library of Congress Cataloging-in-Publication Data:
Komenar, Margo, 1945–
    Electronic marketing / Margo Komenar.
       p.   cm.
    Includes bibliographical references (p.).
    ISBN 0-471-15553-5 (paper : alk. paper)
    1. Internet marketing. I. Title.
  HF5415.1265.K66   1996
  658.8'00285'467—dc20   96-35527
                      CIP

Printed in the United States of America
10 9 8 7 6 5 4 3 2 1

CONTENTS

CREDITS

Preface
John Petrillo

Introduction
Margo Komenar

Chapter 1—Defining Your Market
Solange Van Der Moer

Chapter 2—Designing Your Presence
Margo Komenar

Chapter 3—Making It Legal
Dianne Brinson and Mark Radcliffe

Chapter 4—Supporting Your Presence
Margo Komenar

Chapter 5—Interactive Advertising
Margo Komenar

Chapter 6—Fax-On-Demand
William Austad and Paul Probst

Chapter 7—The SmartCard Game
Margo Komenar
Debit Card information contributed by Shirley Ah Sing

Chapter 8—Interactive Kiosks
Margo Komenar

Chapter 9—Marketing on the Commercial Online Services
Margo Komenar and Irene Graff

Chapter 10—The Internet: Marketing & Business Opportunities
Claudia Brenner and Tim Pearson

Chapter 11—How Businesses Use Electronic Marketing
Margo Komenar
Womanhood, Inc.—The Solutions Network for Business Women on the Web, Case Study written by Kathryn Swafford

Chapter 12—Industry Leaders: The Road Ahead
Margo Komenar
Contributions by Eric Nee, Editor in Chief, Upside *Magazine*

Dedicated to:

My Dad and mentor:

Irving A. Fields, MD

My Inspiration: Marc, Jill, and Michelle

ACKNOWLEDGMENTS

Special Thanks to
Irene Graff—Audrey Graff—Mary Bull—Brian Cooke
Jeff Najar—Natalie L. Wood—Ruby Yeh

Editing
Mary Bull

Assistant Editing
Brian Cooke
Christine Zibas

Transcribing
Maryann Woodruff
Renea Norton

Interview Contributions
Claudia Brenner
David Canja
Brian Cooke
Cimeron Dunlap
Irene Graff
Jeff Najar
Tim Pearson

Research Contributions
Shirley Ah Sing provided the Debit card information in Chapter 7.
Matt Chanoff
Brian Cooke
Paul Emhoff
Irene Graff

Kathryn Swafford provided the Womanhood, Inc. case study in Chapter 11. Eric Nee, Editor in Chief of *Upside* Magazine provided valuable contributions to Chapter 12.

Glossary
Infostreet

Administrative Contributions
Elaine Bulloch
Irene Graff
Dawnde Wallen

Contributing Companies
Research Studies
Forrester Research, Josh Bernoff, Senior Researcher
Jupiter Communications, Yvett DeBow, Editorial Director
Interstellar's Cyberatlas, Michael Tchong, Management Consultant
SIMBA, Karen Burka, Editorial Director
The Gartner Group, Scott Nelson, Research Director

Advertising and Multimedia Production
21st Century Media
CD Direct
CKS/Interactive
HyperMedia Group
Ketchum Interactive
Medius IV
New Order Media
Newsweek Interactive
Planet Interactive
Red Sky Interactive
Saatchi & Saatchi
Softbank Interactive Marketing
Spiral West
Studio Archetype (Clement Mok designs)
Symantec
Team One Advertising
True North Technologies (Foote, Cone & Belding Advertising)
Vivid Studios

Online Services
America Online
AT&T
Bloomberg Financial Markets
CompuServe
Micrsoft Network
Prodigy

Internet Related Companies
Attitude Network
Golf Web
Hawaii's Best Espresso Company
I-Chat
IBM
Internet Shopping Network
I/PRO
NetGravity
Net Objects
Sabre Interactive
Spider Technologies
Sun Microsystems
Travelocity
Worldview Systems Corporation

Public Relations
Janal Communications
Ketchum Communications
Niehaus Ryan Group Public Relations
Oakridge Public Relations
On Target Public Relations
Pat Meier Associates PR
Phase Two Strategies
Torme & Kenney Marketing and Public Relations

Debit Cards
Partners in Communication

Smart Cards
CardTech/SecurTech
First Union Bank
Gemplus International

Giesecke & Devrient
MICRO CARD Technologies
Mondex
Schlumberger SmartCard Systems
SmartCard Forum
VISA International

Case Studies & Other Contributions

1-800-FLOWERS
2 Market
3PCO
American Airlines
Bank of America
Capp Records
Computer Express
Datasel
Electronic Gourmet Guide
Fabrik Communications, Inc.
Fragrance Counter
Great Escapes
Information Access Company
Infostreet
Idea Cafe
KidSoft
Paul Frederick
Quarterdeck
Reebok
SBT Software
Some Like it Hot
Southwind Enterprises
Symantec
Trans-Act Training
Windham Hill
Womanhood, Inc.
Yinspire, Inc.

PREFACE

John Petrillo, Executive Vice President, Strategy and Service Innovation, AT&T

The Genius of Electronic Marketing—Serendipity at Work

It's not widely known, but AT&T invented electronic marketing. Unfortunately, at the time, we didn't have a clue as to what we were doing. Like many great inventions, it was pure serendipity.

Almost 30 years ago one of my colleagues, Roy Weber, who is now a key executive at AT&T Labs, was trying to find a way to reduce the cost of operator-handled calls. Roy and his fellow researchers invented and patented a way to have the telephone network automatically reverse the charges, that is, to bill the party being called, rather than the person making the call. Thus was invented the 800 number.

The 800 number certainly reduced operating expenses for the telephone companies, but it was their customers who thought of great new ways to exploit the new capability of "toll-free calling." Over the years, merchants, advertising agencies, and entrepreneurs worked with us to develop new features, and, in the process, 800 service transformed their marketing and customer care operations. Today, 800 service truly is the way America shops—to the tune of more than $100 billion a year. It's also the way American businesses care for their customers; 800 numbers are featured not only in ads, but on packaging, instruction booklets, even on the sides of trucks.

New Forms of Electronic Commerce

In the pages that follow, creative marketers tell how they are continuing to develop new forms of electronic marketing and commerce. The merger of the communications and computing industries has created an electronic platform on which marketers can create new value for their businesses. Indeed, it has created a new "mega industry," which is transforming the way the world works, sells, gets its information, and plays.

Some have called this a revolution, but I think it is more an *evolution* at a rapidly escalating rate of change. I find it ironic that the mainspring of much of this change was created not in the laboratories of this mega industry; rather, the phenomenon we call the Internet is the creation of all the individuals who use it. Through their interactions on the Internet, users have legitimized a set of standards that has become the underpinning of a new wave of innovation that is transforming our society. The Internet offers a special advantage that eluded all of the movers and shakers in our industry—it's a democratic set of standards developed and agreed upon by its very users.

By contrast, standard setting for more "mainstream" data networks has been like dancing in a full-body cast. Further, the Internet—because it is a global network—provides a very attractive worldwide platform for new forms of electronic commerce and other applications.

Kevin Kelly, executive editor of *Wired* Magazine, calls this phenomenon the "hive mind," a collective wisdom that exceeds the capabilities of the individuals. In his book, *Out of Control*, Kelly suggests that the Internet has become biological, both because it has a growth rate that is analogous to growth in living organisms, and because it has developed the ability to sustain itself.

The Internet has clearly reached critical mass. It already contains more than 70,000 interconnected networks. Monthly user growth rates are in the double digits. And many analysts are predicting a billion users by the end of the century. But there are really two Internets: the physical Internet and the virtual Internet. The physical Internet consists of those 70,000 networks, the backbone routers, the domain name servers, and the backbone that interconnects them.

The virtual Internet consists of the Internet's 40 million or more TCP/IP addresses. I submit that the physical Internet will become less important, as will the well-known business limitations that we associate with the physical Internet—such as holdup times, navigation, reliability, and security. That's because AT&T and other carriers are building networks with access to both the Internet and to each other. So the virtual Internet becomes a sophisticated superset of networks linked by a set of open standards.

As the virtual Internet grows, it will be less often necessary for a packet to traverse the Internet backbone to reach its destination. It will become more common for packets to go from, say, one access provider to another without ever going over the Internet's physical backbone, proving Metcalfe's law that the value of a communications system is proportional to the number of end points that it can use.

Building a New Market

A recent survey of MIS managers estimated that over 60 percent of businesses will be using Internet access services within a year. Almost 46 percent of the respondents plan to market products or services over the Internet. But for all its growth, as I write this, the Internet is used primarily by technically proficient individuals who tend to access it mostly from work. For example, roughly 33 percent of American homes have PCs and almost 75 percent of those home PCs have modems. That means one quarter of all U.S. families have the electronic equipment (and likely the disposable income) to access online services or the Internet if they choose to. Yet only about 6 percent of these families do, and usually only one member of the household goes online. Although the mix is changing, 70 percent of Internet users are men between the ages of 25 and 39.

People equipped with PCs and modems who do not use the Internet or online services explain that they find the experience of accessing these services overwhelming. They are not sure how to get started. They find the process of going online laborious. Once they are online, finding content of any significant interest to them is a challenge. Fear that their credit card will be used without authorization makes them reluctant to participate in electronic commerce transactions. They wonder about the privacy of their Internet usage, and many are concerned about some of the content that could find its way into their homes.

There is a tremendous opportunity to expand the Internet's reach by making it easier for new users to get online in the first place and by giving them compelling reasons to go online at work, at home, and on the road. Simply put, that's AT&T's goal: to make the Internet as universally accessible and as easy to use as the telephone, and to make the Internet as useful for commerce as 800 service.

Global Marketing to a Segment of One

All this technology boils down to an exciting new business capability. Today, with a relatively simple Web site, even the smallest business can have a global presence. More important, it can do what the biggest companies have had difficulty doing: it can customize its offerings to a market segment of one.

CCTC, a virtual corporation that uses a network application to link retailers, customers, and suppliers, for example, discovered that a lot of women are happy to pay more for jeans that really fit. They've developed freestanding kiosks for retail clothing stores that allow women to order custom jeans. By using the kiosk, a customer can look at the various styles of jeans available, input measurements, provide payment information, and complete the transaction electronically.

In a very real sense, the network is CCTC's business. It enables the company to deliver a custom product for just $10 more than off the rack. And since it eliminates a lot of costs, such as carrying an inventory of finished goods, margins are very healthy.

Today, CCTC uses a combination of networks, but in the future, similar applications could be developed entirely on the Internet. In fact, I predict we will see many such examples as intelligent agents deliver individualized information and services to users. New forms of "digital money" will make transactions on the Net easier and more secure. Competition will spur those of us providing access services to upgrade our network infrastructure to improve reliability and—because this is now an industry driven by users—to fill screens faster and to support such bandwidth-eating applications as desktop video.

The creativity of the Net will spawn services we haven't imagined yet. They will become the global malls, marketplaces, and communities of the future. Boundary-less colleges and universities, for example, will push the limits of learning. But, most of all, we will have an opportunity to collaborate in creating a world that is richer and more fulfilling for all of us.

INTRODUCTION

Margo Komenar

The expanding global electronic marketplace has triggered an evolution with powerful implications. The introduction of interactive media and the online environment has made real-time, customized one-to-one advertising, marketing, and commerce possible. Interactive multimedia can no longer be considered an afterthought or a luxury when developing an integrated marketing campaign. The opportunities opened up by the Internet and sophisticated database mining are yet to be fully realized.

This book explores the realm of electronic marketing from the perspectives of three key groups: advertising agencies, multimedia production firms (and their clients, the advertisers and marketers), and the companies building the infrastructures for the new electronic marketplace. In order to provide the reader with the highest-possible quality of information on each topic area, several experts and researchers were selected to gather and present specialized chapter content. In addition to assembling and coordinating this team, the author conducted more than 70 interviews with industry leaders, pioneers, and subject matter experts. Interview excerpts are incorporated throughout the book along with information contributed by a number of the most highly respected research firms.

Strategic electronic marketing can harness the power of today's technology to propel a company of any size farther into the worldwide market than at any other time in history, increasing potential profits and productivity. Some of these technology tools include software catalogs; interactive kiosks; fax-on-demand systems; digital infomercials; demos and encrypted samplers online, on CD-ROM, and on new enhanced CDs. Interactive kiosks, public installations found in places such as corporate, travel, and entertainment environments, are becoming more sophisticated and provide a consistent user-friendly way to both give information and store responses.

Online marketing is the most rapidly growing channel being explored today. Users of this expanding medium include a range of service providers; publishers and marketers of print, music, software and other products that cross an increasing number of industry lines. Such standard issues as targeting your audience, knowing how to use your competition, appropriate design, and approach all must be applied to a well-orchestrated electronic marketing plan. The online arena presents a variety of choices in such areas as marketing affiliations with the commercial online and Internet companies, cross-merchandising, PR, advertising, and technical support. All pose pressing questions for anyone including this new channel as part of their marketing plan.

This book addresses the exponential advantages to employing several electronic vehicles in marketing a company's product or service.

Chapter 1, Defining Your Market, discusses the nature of effective market research and the questions marketers and businesses should explore when preparing to launch or market products and services, especially into the new electronic marketing channels. Solange Van Der Moer, contributing author, has more than 20 years of marketing and sales experience in the computer, cable, and entertainment industries. She is also co-founder and senior partner of Infinity Marketing Group, a full-service marketing agency. Her expertise spans market research through public relations, distribution, and sales. Each of these topics is discussed here, along with real-life applications and case examples that include HotWired, KidSoft, Levi Strauss, Yahoo!, Ralph Lauren, Chrysler Plymouth, and @vantage, the Gartner Group Online.

Due diligence in defining and researching your primary and secondary target audiences, factoring in trends and fads, and positioning in the appropriate market channels are critical to the success of a business. The questions surrounding how these definitions are arrived at and how the research results are interpreted and applied bring up key issues that are addressed by Van Der Moer. This due diligence process is the first step to effectively enter or remain strong in the marketplace, electronic or otherwise. This chapter is a basic component in the foundation for the chapters that follow.

Chapter 2, Designing Your Presence, looks at creating effective visibility for today's evolving consumer-driven, interactive marketplace. Industry leaders and innovators from top design firms and advertising agencies discuss integrated marketing campaigns that incorporate traditional and new media, branding issues, creating effective content-based marketing promotions, the nature and uses of databases in designing customized one-to-one immediate response ads, and detailed design and production processes used by these firms with clients. Companies providing case examples include CKS/Interactive, Ketchum Interactive, Medius IV, Newsweek Interactive, Red Sky Interactive, Saatchi & Saatchi, Studio Archetype (formerly Clement Mok designs) and TN Technologies.

Electronic marketing has introduced a myriad of legal issues that companies would be well advised to understand. The online and digital electronic environment has made it extremely easy to copy and reprint published text and graphics. The nature of public access in the online world to such a wealth of information can lead users to believe it is there for the taking—and reusing or republishing. It is not, unless specifically stated, and this issue along with many others worthy of consideration for marketers, designers, advertisers, and consumers is presented in Chapter 3, Making It Legal, by J. Dianne Brinson and Mark Radcliffe, two top attorneys and authors in this field. Together, Dianne and Mark wrote and self-published two editions of the *Multimedia Law Handbook* and another book titled *Multimedia Contracts.* This chapter is an adapted excerpt from their June 1996 edition of the *Multimedia Law Handbook.* Topics covered include: copyright law, patent law, trademarks, trade secrets, and online marketing.

Chapter 4, Supporting Your Presence, is devoted to the role of PR in the overall marketing mix. Public relations, or PR, utilizes the press media including print, radio, television, and the online environment to get the word out and to manage the public and target audience image for client companies. PR is an often overlooked and underrated component in designing a strategic marketing and maintenance plan. Well-orchestrated PR, however, can mean the difference between success or failure of a product launch; control of a damaging incident or industry rumors; projecting the desired and appropriate portrayal of a brand and corporate and product image. Each medium needs to be approached differently, and consistent monitoring on the press media front can be a crucial asset to a company. Leading PR firms such as Pat Meier Associates, Torme & Kenney, Phase Two Strategies, Ketchum Communications, Oakridge Public Relations, and On Target Communications share their expertise and case examples.

Chapter 5, Interactive Advertising, explains and illustrates how interactive marketing media open doors in many directions for businesses. The implications are powerful, and are substantiated by extensive Gartner Group research. Interactive advertising is worth researching, experimenting with, and integrating into a marketing plan, and the examples provided in this chapter clearly illustrate a range of innovative approaches to this new technology. This is not just a passing trend; it is a permanent shift in the way business and marketing will be conducted. This chapter includes case examples and interviews with representatives from Ketchum Interactive, Newsweek Interactive, Saatchi & Saatchi, Red Sky Interactive, 21st Century Media, Hypermedia Group, CD-Direct, New Order Media, and SBT Software, as well as a detailed example of a company doing business on both sides of the firewall.

Chapter 6 looks at fax-on-demand, one of the most broadly accessible information delivery vehicles in businesses today. Bill Austad and Paul Brobst are expert consultants and authors of the books, *Fax-On-Demand, Marketing Tool of the 90s* and *How to Profit With Fax-On-Demand, a Manager's Guide to Deliver-*

ing Information by Fax. Austad and Brobst present a range of creative marketing and support applications in areas such as real estate, publishing, product promotion and support, the delivery of timely financial information, and more. The demand for custom-designed and enhanced fax systems is on the rise, and Austad and Brobst discuss features such as interactive voice response, e-mail selection, conversion, and Web linking. Standalone and networked systems, options, and costs are explored, and a step-by-step planning and delivery process is provided. A company survey is included to assist businesses in evaluating the need and possible applications for a fax-on-demand system.

Debit and smart, or chip, card technology will impact information and transaction management in reach and scope rivaling the personal computer in the years ahead. Chapter 7 explores the technologies, business promotion, and marketing potential of debit cards, stored value cards, the electronic purse, and (microcomputer) chip, or smart cards. Smart cards can store a range of information in different categories from complete health records and encrypted identification information, to loan information, personal purchasing patterns, and bonus programs. It is estimated that more than one-half of all payment cards issued worldwide will be chip cards by the year 2000, and it is further predicted that these cards may even replace money altogether. Industry leaders and case examples illustrate the current global uses of these cards and associated technologies, and their initially slower but now rapidly expanding introduction into the U.S. market through a number of pilot programs including one at the 1996 summer Olympics in Atlanta, Georgia. Companies contributing case examples and other information to this chapter include Gemplus International, Giesecke & Devrient, Micro Card Technologies, Mondex, Schlumberger Smart Card Systems, CardTech/SecurTech, First Union Bank, the Smart Card Forum, and Visa International.

Interactive kiosks offer some unique opportunities to marketers and have a surprisingly accessible entry cost. Chapter 8 provides a variety of case examples to illustrate kiosk program design, development, and applications. Examples presented include kiosk programs for Levi's 501 Jeans, Kathleen Brown's political campaign, the Missouri Botanical Gardens Online, Reebok On Tour and "through glass" (Reebok's storefront window), and multimedia telephones. With the added connectivity of the Internet, a kiosk can deliver real-time services such as transportation, theater or sports events tickets, course registrations, a variety of online information search and retrieval, and so on. It is a flexible and growing marketing opportunity that can be easily adapted to almost any market segment.

With all of the competition, collaboration, constant growth, and change in the commercial online services and major Internet sites, it is very difficult for businesses to know what advertising or marketing options exist and which ones might be most appropriate for their company's products or services. Chapter 9, co-written with Irene Graff, an accomplished industry researcher and writer, addresses this dilemma by providing a synopsis of the features, marketing, and advertising programs on the major commercial online services and a smaller niche market proprietary service. America Online, CompuServe, and Prodigy offer similar membership features, but slightly different marketing opportunities for vendors, and various business and revenue models within each venue. Microsoft's MSN is positioned as an Internet-based service that aggregates its content, but also offers a range of user services and advertising opportunities. Bloomberg Financial Markets is a high-end vertical audience service that is included in this chapter because of its unique array of multimedia components and extensive marketing opportunities.

All of these services are focusing more on the Internet, and mutually beneficial partnerships are forming at an unprecedented rate. Strategies and trends are discussed through interviews with each of the services as well as with their vendors. Advertising programs are an expanding and moving target at this point, but those most likely stay in place in the near future are detailed in this chapter, plus some that are slated to launch by the fall of '96. Case examples are provided to illustrate ways vendor companies have taken advantage of the various venues, sometimes on several services simultaneously. Vendor companies interviewed include 1-800-FLOWERS, Computer Express, Electronic Gourmet Guide, Fragrance Counter, KidSoft, and Windham Hill. The information in this chapter will assist the reader in gaining a basic understanding of the marketing and advertising opportunities each service has to offer, and the trends and strategies that are shaping the future of online marketing.

The economic power of the Internet is still a relatively untapped giant. The online marketplace is expected to reach over $1.4 billion by the year 2000, according to industry reports. Great efforts and strides are being made to make commerce safe and viable on the Net, and businesses are discovering that information gathering and database mining are only some of the great riches to be had by venturing out into cyberspace.

In Chapter 10, Claudia Brenner and Tim Pearson present an impressive wealth of information on marketing and business opportunities provided by this new channel. Ms. Brenner is the co-founder and marketing director for FutureLink, an interactive and Web marketing consultancy. Her background includes business development, strategic product and channel marketing for major high-tech corporations such as IBM, Oracle, Macromedia, and AT&T Wireless. Tim Pearson is the co-founder and director of technology and design for FutureLink. His background includes design of information architecture for interactive media and Web site design for electronic commerce. Companies interviewed for this chapter include I-Chat, IBM, Internet Shopping Network,

I/PRO, NetGravity, Sabre Interactive, Spider Technologies, Sun Microsystems, Travelocity, and Worldview Systems Corporation.

Chapter 11, presents a variety of case studies rich in useful information and experiences shared by a mix of small entrepreneurial companies and major corporate leaders. AT&T leads off with an overview of its online strategies, and follows with a detailed description of each of its new online services. Explanations of AT&T's WorldNet Service, New Media Service's Business Network, newly merged with Industry Net to form Nets Inc., AT&T's Personal Online Services, and AT&T's Easy Commerce Services are all explained with the help of six top AT&T executives. Other companies profiled include SoftBank Interactive Marketing, a company that represents the largest group of Web sites and advertising inventory on the Internet; Womanhood, Inc., a specialized resource for women on the Web; InfoStreet, a small electronic publishing and Internet marketing company (including a number of "Project Briefs" and a Web Weaving estimate sheet); Cary August Productions & Publishing, a small music publishing and band Web site production company; Great Escapes, a home-based full-service travel agency launched by two women (over 60); Southwind Enterprises, Inc., an innovative direct-e-mail company; and Yinspire, Inc., an Internet company targeting the world's *nontechnical majority* and implementing a unique business model in which both the internal team and the community can benefit from the overall financial success of the company.

The final chapter consists of interview excerpts from industry leaders who share their visions of the future. They include comments from Microsoft's Bill Gates; Institute of the Future's Paul Saffo; Michael Bloomberg of Bloomberg Financial Markets; Michael Rogers of Newsweek Interactive; SoftBank Interactive Marketing's president and COO Ted West; Michael Rogers, the VP of Post-Newsweek New Media and Managing Editor of Newsweek InterActive; Daniel Miessau, CKS/Interactive's director for Digital Multimedia; and Dave Clauson, managing director of True North Technologies.

The Contributor's Resource Directory provides a wide variety of business resources for all of the topics covered (plus a few others) in this book. The companies that have participated are the pioneers and visionaries building the electronic marketplace of today and preparing the infrastructures needed for tomorrow.

The opportunities for marketing, expanding, and building new businesses based on interactivity and sophisticated database technology are vast. The information shared by industry leaders and topic experts is intended to provide the reader with guidance and tools for educated participation in the interactive electronic marketplace.

CHAPTER ONE

DEFINING YOUR MARKET

Solange Van Der Moer

About a year ago a story appeared in my local paper that essentially denounced the Internet as not ready for prime time marketing. This was so, the author contended, because the demographics of the Internet showed that it was largely populated by males, average age of 36, who were either students or engineering types. In other words, he said, the Internet consisted mostly of nerds, thus there was little point in trying to market anything on the Internet! It showed a glaring error in judgment and failure to understand consumers. Last time I checked, students were among the largest consumers of recorded music sales, made up the highest percent of movie ticket buyers, regularly buy clothing, and many of them drive a car. Consider this: The average American college student owns five to six pairs of jeans. What the author failed to realize was that each of these students and engineering types, as he called them, undoubtedly wears clothing, eats, sleeps, drinks, and has hobbies, passions, likes, and dislikes, and ultimately *is a consumer of something.*

Unfortunately, the author was not alone in his opinion. In fact, in 1994, most businesses shared the perception that the Internet was populated by geeks, nerds, and students, and therefore was not worthy of consideration in their marketing plans. Pity for them and bully for those who quickly grasped that the Internet and commercial online services, with their discussion groups and free-flowing information exchange, are a market researcher's dream come true. Moreover, these companies overlooked the fact that the Internet offers the first cost-effective way to *directly* interact with millions of potential and existing customers. It's what I call real-time market research or *nano-marketing.* Being able to get to a personal level of marketing and responding in a nanosecond.

How times have changed. Today it seems a new Internet site goes up at the rate of one every minute. True, in most cases, the content of these sites is still

1

excruciatingly boring, and in the words of Gertrude Stein, "There's no there there." Very few companies (or individuals) have figured out how to keep the consumer coming back for more, but you have to credit those companies for at least being out there and getting their electronic marketing feet wet. Through trial and error, and most important, through direct interaction with consumers, they'll learn what works and what doesn't. Our contention is that the companies that truly do their homework—market research—will get there faster and save money in the process.

What Is Market Research?

Let's take a minute to test our assumptions of what marketing research really is by looking at a few definitions. The American Marketing Association defines Market Research as follows:

> Marketing research is the function which links the consumer, customer, and public to the marketer through information—information used to identify and define marketing opportunities and problems; generate, refine, and evaluate marketing actions; monitor marketing performance; and improve understanding of marketing as a process.

More succinctly put, it is anything that will help you understand what your customers will buy, and thus help you make better decisions when developing products and running your business. The dictionary defines research as:

1. Deep study or investigation.
2. The quest for new information through examination of source material.

It's the "deep" part that is most often overlooked by large and small companies alike. Deep study is more than asking a few friends and colleagues what they think of a product; it's more than running a quick little focus group to bask in the glow of having one's instincts confirmed. Good market research is hard work and can be time- and cost-consuming to boot. Nonetheless, it is absolutely critical to the success of any business. Granted, there are many factors that will determine the success or failure of any given business, but nothing is more basic than knowing who your customers are and what they want. The world history of commerce is littered with the bodies of those who failed to really listen to their customers.

Types of Market Research

Market research boils down to gathering information that will tell you as much as possible about who your customers are and why they buy what they buy. Fact gathering can reveal the who and what part, but the why part can be answered only by the customers themselves. This is a key distinction and is exactly where most companies fail in their market research, because in our numbers-obsessed culture, we place a far greater value on objective quantitative data. Information such as age, gender, and household income is collectively referred to as *demographic information* and is easily found. The why is much harder to quantify and requires direct interaction with the customers—interaction that focuses on why they buy looks at, what motivates them to buy a service or product, why they buy one product over another, what needs the product fulfills and how it makes them feel. In essence, this type of research addresses the psychology of buying. In market research, this is referred to as *psychographics.* Understanding the psychographics of customers is further complicated by the fact that when answering why, we are by definition dealing with perceptions, not facts. Yet, why customers buy is as important, if not more, than what they buy.

Anyone who has delved into the psychology of why their customers buy quickly understands that the best product doesn't necessarily win. The very word best is a matter of perception. Let's use the personal computer as an example. Say you have manufactured the world's fastest chip. All your tests prove that your PC is faster than any other on the market. Assuming you have priced it right and have the right distribution, you would think it would automatically outsell all slower PCs. However, to consumers who are new to computers and care only about ease of use, an easier-to-use, slower PC is the "best," because it fulfills their particular needs better.

Words like best are relevant only in the context of the customer's needs and desires. So in conducting your research and understanding who your target audience is, the key is discerning their wants and needs. It isn't enough to understand what key attributes your prospects value most. You must also understand how to position that message in such a way that you aren't using words or focusing on attributes that are already firmly associated with another company's product. For example, assume you're in the car industry and your surveys and research show that among your target audience safety is the most important attribute. Logic would dictate that your marketing campaign should emphasize and focus on the word safety, so that your product becomes indelibly linked in the consumer's mind with this key feature. However, in the car world, Volvo already owns that word association, so don't even try; you won't dislodge it from the consumer's mind no matter how much money you spend.

Just ask Mercedes Benz and GM—they've tried for years and are still failing in survey after survey.

All positioning is relative to the competition. Never forget this. Even the most sophisticated companies who do reams of research frequently neglect to interpret the data *relative to the competitive environment.* This kind of marketing arrogance has been the downfall of many a giant.

Primary Research

Simply put, primary research is any information that you collect and analyze yourself. When you create a list of questions and send it out over the Internet, you are engaging in primary research. When you ask your friends what they think of your idea, you are doing primary research. Probably the best known primary research is that done by pollsters. By constantly sticking their thermometer in the populace's psyche, politicians are the primary market researchers par excellence. In the commercial arena, you may have heard of companies such as Gallup, Roper Starch, Simmons Market Research, Data (SMRD), and others. These companies are syndicated research firms and conduct primary research on a large scale using mail, telephone, and in-person surveys. For example, Simmons uses a base of 22,000 families and individuals who are regularly interviewed from a survey booklet with more than 115 pages. Believe it or not, people willingly fill them out. The questions cover subjects ranging from what magazines they read to which brand of peanut butter they prefer, and are incredibly detailed.

Primary research can take many forms and use different methodologies. Data collected can come from mail, telephone or in-person surveys, point-of-sale information (such as scanner data collected from bar codes), focus groups, mall surveys, interactive kiosks, daily or weekly diaries, and, of course, interactive data collected online or via fax.

Gathering original data is challenging in and of itself, but the real challenge lies in building a useful database to collect all the bits of information, and then analyzing and interpreting this information so that it is meaningful to your business. It's easy to get overwhelmed by volumes of raw data, but a well-thought database design can go a long way to helping you sort the wheat from the chaff. The key to good database design lies in being very clear on what the goals of your study are. This does not mean that you should ignore interesting patterns as they emerge (and they often do), but rather that you remain focused.

Secondary Research

Secondary research is information you collect from existing research. This includes research conducted by others, information you collect by reading articles or industry reports—in other words, any data that has been gathered by someone other than you. The most commonly used secondary research is U.S.

Census information. Think of it this way: If you experienced it yourself, that's primary research; if you hear or read about an experience, that is secondary research.

In almost every instance, you will want to start with secondary research before conducting any primary research of your own. No matter how extensive your primary research, you will still need to put it in the context of what's happening in your industry and your consumer world at large; hence you start by collecting market and industry information. Here again, the growth of online services has made finding useful information much easier. By using search tools such as WebCrawler and Yahoo, you can fairly quickly find many useful chunks of information that will help you fill in the picture of your market and customers.

Suppose you want to understand how to reach the rapidly increasing number of people over 55, often referred to as seniors. Let's further suppose that you also want to gain some insight into their use of computers. You might begin your search by going to Yahoo and doing a search using the qualified phrase "seniors OR mature adults." This will likely bring you many different sources ranging from articles written for college publications to government statistical analyses. You may want to narrow your search to include only those publications that contain both the words senior and computers. You peruse these and select the data you want (be sure to always cite the original source!). Yahoo is but one example of a simple search engine. There are many search engines available online, and describing them all would be the subject of another book.

Reliability

Whenever you encounter statistical data, it is critical that you understand how the data was gathered. You don't need to delve into a dissertation on statistical analysis, but you should understand what the goal of the study was and the basic methodology employed. For example, if you were to read a study that asked teens their preferences about clothing, you would want to know how the information was gathered. Did they do a survey at a suburban mall, or did they do a telephone survey of randomly called numbers in urban areas? Each method would yield different results, since the mall survey would capture a socioeconomic group that is different from that of the telephone survey. Also, always ask to see the original survey questions.

Remember, too, that there are substantial differences between tests that determine actual usage and tests that you perform as part of your business plan to raise funding. You would think that our brethren on Wall Street and Sand Hill Road would have wised up to the vagaries of market testing by now, but time after time, funding is secured based on the flimsiest evidence of consumer interest. Many of these folks think in numbers only and are typically schooled in finance and operations. While in school they eschewed all those "soft" courses like sociology and psychology—the very disciplines critical to understanding what shapes trends and what makes consumers tick.

Why Bother with Market Research?

Because your only purpose is to create products that someone is willing to pay for. Despite your best efforts, insights, and intuition, you cannot magically divine what your consumer wants, needs, or will pay for. You probably have a good gut feel, but unless you test your assumptions with a broader audience, you are asking for trouble. Human beings are a funny lot, and we do tend to seek our own level; consequently, our friends tend to reflect our tastes and values. Moreover, it's a rare friend who will tell you your idea stinks. So be sure to cast a wider net and test your idea with lots of strangers.

Concept testing and conducting surveys and focus groups need not be expensive. Much of it you can do yourself. In fact, only you can determine what the goals of such research are, and you should be actively involved in designing the survey or focus group. However, be sure you have an objective party review the questions and actually conduct the survey, especially if it's a face-to-face focus group. No matter how disciplined you think you are, you will inevitably betray your emotions or subconsciously skew follow-up questions, thereby invalidating the results. We call this skewing *parental pollution* because the parents of an idea doesn't like to admit that their perfect child has a severe case of acne. So do yourself a favor and sit quietly in a corner. Watch, observe, and learn from your prospective customers and let someone less involved ask the questions.

Especially challenging is dealing with products or services that don't exist yet. Imagine asking a nineteenth-century consumer about air travel. To someone who has never even thought of flying, it would require a major leap of imagination, and is therefore unlikely to yield a coherent answer. That's the problem with doing research for products that are futuristic, such as interactive television. The key is not being first, but being *right.* Just ask Elisha Gray, who, like Alexander Graham Bell, invented the principle behind the telephone. Why is it Alexander Graham Bell we remember? Elisha Gray filed his patent application at the same time as Bell, but Bell saw the invention as a telephone, while Gray saw it as an improved telegraph. The rest is history.

Who Is Your Target Audience?

Frame your product in terms of what it does for the customer, rather than immediately calculating who will use it. Once you have defined what your product actually does, it becomes much easier to clearly articulate its benefits, as well as the characteristics that differentiate it from the competition. Once you understand the needs and wants your product fulfills, you can begin to talk about who your target audience is.

The people who comprise your target market are much more than demographic numbers on a census sheet (Figure 1.1). The basic facts are their age, income, gender, and location. All of these facts and figures are readily available both online and in print, and most of this information is free for the taking from the government in the form of census data. Since the information remains relatively static—that is, it does not change significantly over three to five years—you needn't worry that the data is typically two to three years old.

Beyond these demographics lie many interests and lifestyle habits. These too are available, though still mostly in print form. One of the best sources of information about your target audience are the magazines that cater to them. Most magazines regularly conduct primary research among their reader base. These are typically known as readership surveys and often contain a wealth of information about what other media the audience uses and likes, what products

---

Sample information from U.S. Census

Population information such as:
 Total Male: 121,239,418
 Total Female: 127,470,455

Breakdowns by age category: e.g.
 18–24 = 26,737,766
 25–44 = 80,754,835

By searching the Civilian Labor Force file you can find specific information such as the number of people in a specific profession:

Pharmacists (096)	114,949 Male	66,849 Female
Firefighting (416)	218,763 Male	5,998 Female

For targeted market research, the census also contains breakdowns by race, religion, marital status, income, owned versus rental housing, home values, and many other categories.

Figure 1.1   Basic demographics from a U.S. Census Sheet.

they own, what programs they are most likely to watch, the products or services they intend to buy (often down to the brand name), as well as opinion surveys on everything from politics to lifestyle (Figure 1.2).

In addition to magazines, you should check into associations. There are more than 22,633 associations in the United States, and the vast majority are conveniently listed by subject in a wonderful publication called *Gale's Encyclopedia of Associations.* Run, don't walk, to your nearest local library and find this researcher's friend (no, it's not available online). For every special interest, there's probably an association that caters to it. By their very nature associations depend on dues and sponsors to stay in business, and they cannot successfully raise these funds if they do not cater to their membership. Thus you will find most association personnel to be highly knowledgeable about their members. Some of the more cutting-edge associations now have fax-on-demand systems and an online presence, and can easily be reached by e-mail.

Age:

13–19	25%
20–29	59%
30+	14%

Sex:

Male	81%
Female	19%

Income:

$40, 770 (average HHI)

Computers:

Own home computer	64%
Online subscriber	32%
Buy entertainment SW	83%
# games in last year	5.32 average
CD ROM drive	60%

Video Games:

Own any system	85%
Super NES	36%
Sega Genesis	27%
Sega CD	8%
3DO	2%
Other	36%

Star Wars Merchandise:

Amount spent in year	$459 average
Spent over $1,000	14%

Figure 1.2 Sample information found in a magazine's survey of it's readers (*Star Wars Galaxy* Magazine, May 1995).

Why Would Your Target Audience Buy Your Product?

Armed with the preceding information, you should be getting a fairly solid picture of your target audience, but you still may not know *why* they buy, much less why they would buy *your* specific product. This is the hard part. There's only one way to find out: ask them. It is at this point when you will want to conduct primary research, be it in the form of focus groups, telephone surveys, or other means mentioned in the primary research section of this chapter. You can also learn a fair amount from secondary research about the psychographics of your target audience. Formal research programs, such as SRI's Value and Lifestyle studies (VALS), provide insight into the beliefs and lifestyle attributes of various groups. However, unless the SRI study is specifically commissioned to focus on your product category, it will only provide you with some basic insight.

Again, media such as magazines relevant to your product are excellent sources. Ask for their media kits, which usually contain a wealth of information about their readers. For example, if you offer a product aimed at recent mothers, you should collect magazine kits from *Baby, Parenting,* and *Working Mother,* among others.

Another useful exercise is to flip through the tables of contents of two to three years worth of issues of several magazines that target your audience. You'll quickly find that certain topics are consistently covered and regularly generate reader interest. Remember that magazines survive by their advertising, and advertisers will buy only if the magazine consistently delivers the right audience. Content is what delivers and holds the audience.

The letters to the editor section of print publications can provide some insight into the mind-set of a particular target audience. Now that most print publications have established some form of online presence, you should be able to find many of these via your computer. Online is a veritable smorgasbord of discussion groups, forums, and chats, some of which are banal, others which are intense and full of terrific detail. To get a solid picture, expect to spend many days, if not weeks, following these discussions. Participate if you have something to contribute, but this is not the time to jump in and announce that you're conducting research. It's best to observe quietly for a while and come back to the group later to ask whether you might pose some questions. As usual, honesty is the best policy. Be sure to offer participants as many ways to communicate with you as possible, such as online in an open forum, via private e-mail, fax, and phone.

Who Are Your Peripheral Customers?

Look at the characteristics of your target audience and learn whom they influence. These are your peripheral customers. For example, if your product is targeted at children between six and eight, it's likely that the actual purchaser will be an adult, in many cases, a parent. Much has been made of the so-called Generation X as a target audience. A straight demographic analysis of this target market suggests that it consists of young men and women between the ages of 18 and 34. In reality, however, you'll probably find that your consumer is not confined to that age group, but may include many teens who wish to emulate Gen Xers, as well as Baby Boomers who subscribe to a lifestyle that marketers associate with a much younger group.

Here's another scenario: Your product may have been very well targeted at a particular group and positioned just right. Much to your surprise, you discover an entirely new audience with completely different attributes who adopt your product in ways you had not foreseen. Such was the case with Timberland. For years, this company was a steady, rather conservative producer of hiking shoes, until the outdoor hiking look was adopted by young urban boys who liked the look and feel of these well-constructed boots. Within two years, Timberland became a fashion statement. Fortunately, the Timberland marketing beagles were paying attention and capitalized on their good fortune by ramping up a clothing line and gearing their whole campaign around rugged comfort. Today, Timberland's retail chains are highly successful and growing.

In some instances, you will find that you must consider more than your target audience. You may also want to think about who serves that target audience. For example, consider the case of a celebrity café such as the Fashion Café in New York. Three supermodels got together and created a restaurant based on the premise that the public will flock to a hip place with passable food, if the supermodels can occasionally be seen there. While the restaurant must maintain a certain standard of food quality and ambiance for all customers, it must also cater to the special needs of models (healthy foods, quick service, and a secure environment), who actually comprise a very small minority of the customer base. To stay in business, the restaurateurs must keep the models coming—however infrequently—because the other customers come *because* those models *might* be there.

The same holds true for a city. You need to prove that it's a cool place to be; provide incentives, and attract some star companies or an entire industry (like multimedia in San Francisco); then those companies will serve as the Pied Piper for others to follow. This concept is well understood by commercial developers who have built their malls across America on the principle of *anchor stores*. In the case of a trade association, you must consider not only your core constituency, but also the many service providers who will join your association because they want access to your core constituency. Take Women in Communications, or WICI. This association is targeted at professionals in the media and includes illustrious members, such as Barbara Walters and Kathleen Quinn. It also includes wardrobe and image consultants who want these luminaries as customers. WICI must serve all those constituencies, but its priority must be to meet the needs of its core constituents. If it doesn't, it will lose not only its core audience, but all those who came to attend that core audience. In the high-tech world, organizations like the Software Publishers Association (SPA) were initially formed to serve the interests of software publishers. But today, you will find that a significant number of developers, consultants, and distributors have joined the SPA because they benefit from ready access to their target audience of publishers.

What Are Some of the Trends Shaping Your (Changing) Audience?

For your business to thrive and grow you must not only pay attention to the narrow confines of what your product or service does today. You must also be aware of the myriad cultural and popular influences that help shape your audience's view of what their needs will be tomorrow.

The Difference between Fads and Trends

In this nanosecond-timed world of ours, it may seem contradictory to focus on long-term trends, but in fact, trends are usually very tenacious and tend to stick around for a decade or so. They are quite different from fads, which tend to have a fairly short life cycle and thus rarely afford companies the luxury of planning. In the beverage industry, clear drinks became the rage for a few brief years, but the overall trend toward healthy ingredients (or more accurately, the perception of healthy ingredients) has lasted for more than a decade and continues. Thus the market quickly became saturated with clear everything (not just drinks), and many companies were left with excess inventory. Health consciousness is the trend, whereas "clear" was simply a fad.

Today, another example is the explosion of aromatherapy products. This fad is nothing more than a manifestation of a long-term trend of buying ourselves small, affordable luxuries and rewards. I contend that trends are about the only thing you can be reasonably certain of (once you've identified them) in a business environment where flexibility is definitely key. So, if trends are identifiable and they stay with us a long time, then why don't more companies succeed in tapping into them?

Paying attention to trends is rather like putting a giant jigsaw puzzle together. It requires time, patience, and keen observation. Pay attention to enough different goods and services, and soon you will see patterns emerge. By this I mean, go beyond your immediate industry and look at a wide range of goods and services. For example, if you are a maker of children's software, pay close attention to what's selling in toys and books aimed at your target age category. And don't stop there; go to department stores and observe what clothing mom and dad are buying for their little tikes. Do the same with mail-order and online catalogs. Watch Saturday morning TV and go see those Disney movies. I promise, you'll learn more from close observation of these related industries than by reading every trade article written for your industry. Luckily, we live in an era when technology can greatly accelerate our ability to collect the data and analyze it. Instead of reading through stacks and stacks of magazines, you can turn to tools like Infoseek and WebCrawler and speed up the search for relevant information.

Looking *outside* your specific industry is also critical to spotting the formation of trends. Even something as mundane as determining what colors are selling well can be tracked if you pay careful attention. Don't think it's relevant? What about when you are ready to design your packaging? Won't color be a factor? Ever notice that the color schemes that originate in the fashion industry seem to migrate to automobiles next, and then to houses? It's not coincidence; it is carefully applied marketing based on research and trend analysis—plus a dash of hype. How will you know what colors are trendy? There are two organizations in the United States to help you. Every year the Color Marketing Group and the Color Association of the United States get together with leading fashion and interior designers to decide what color palettes they will concentrate on for the year.

Some Major Trends

In the next few pages let's look at some of the major trends that are influencing you and your customers. Think about products you've recently purchased and see if any of them seem to be a reflection of the following trends moving through our country.

Cocooning or Nesting—My Home Is My Castle

The mantra from Baby Boomers across the land seems to be "We're staying in tonight." Not only are they staying home at night, but more of them are working there during the day as well. And since they're spending so much time in their homes they want to feather the nest as comfortably as they can. Over the past three years, sales of home furnishings have skyrocketed. Pottery Barn, Crate & Barrel, and Pier 1 (to name a few) have all seen sales soar—both in mail order and retail. Companies like The Limited and The Gap are opening home furnishing divisions that sell everything from furniture to bath soap. When did Americans suddenly decide that rustic pine, wicker, and wrought iron were must-haves in their homes? While each company certainly carries some unique products, there is a remarkable similarity in style, materials, and price points. They all offer good quality at reasonable prices, but what they really offer is the promise of a return to simpler times and a romanticized view of "life on the farm." It's a classic case of tapping into a nostalgia for an era and lifestyle that never existed in the first place—except in Hollywood.

This trend proved highly successful for Ralph Lauren, who grasped early on that he wasn't just selling clothes, he was selling a lifestyle. Moreover, he wasn't selling a real lifestyle, rather he was offering to put consumers into the era of their dreams. Take your pick: the cowboy look—without the poor pay and harsh conditions; the English manor—without the draftiness and poor plumbing. Lauren doesn't just dress his customers in the clothes of a bygone era, through home furnishings and accessories, he convinced them that they could *live* in that era. Lauren completely understood his target market and tapped into *why* they buy.

Customization—The I in What They Buy

The blue plate special of days gone by has been replaced by the half-caf/nonfat, light foam, double latté of today. Consumers live in a paradox of obeying the herd instinct, yet wanting to feel that products are created especially for them, whether it's custom-made clothing or a newspaper tailored specifically to their interests. Technology has made it possible to comply with the consumers' wish to have customization at mass market prices. In the clothing business, Levi Strauss has come up with a new spin on an old favorite: blue jeans. Customers can now walk into select Levi stores, try on several base models, get measured and fitted, and have a custom-made pair of 501 jeans in less than a week for under $40. Levi puts the measurements into the computer, which cuts the fabric directly. The customer feels very special, the price is right, the fit is perfect, Levi has made a profit—everybody is happy.

Individual, Inc. created a market for itself by providing harried consumers with a customized fax containing news geared to their specific interests. Customers are sent a form on which they check off topics that interest them (Figures 1.3 and 1.4). Everyday, Individual scans a wide range of publications, compiles excerpts and abstracts of articles on the topics chosen by the cus-

Home Furnishings	Clothing	Entertainment	Media Topics
Warm earthy colors, plump upholstery, basic elements such as pine and wrought iron.	'50s influence Mainstream clothing, fairly conservative, subdued colors Avant-garde—back to the future ('70s)	Nature-inspired stories Remakes of classics Nickelodeon Tony Bennett	Relationship everything Country settings Education Family values

Figure 1.3   Some 1995–96 popular culture themes.

tomer, and delivers this news medley each morning to the customer via fax. It's kind of a Readers Digest version of topical news, custom made for the time-pressed society we've become.

Security/Safety—Please Fence Me In

The security trend is closely related to our newfound nesting instinct. The 1995 Oklahoma City bombing was a defining moment for America, because it seemed such an unlikely place for such evil destruction. At last the scales fell from our innocent eyes, and we realized there really was nowhere to hide any-more, to feel completely safe. It's not surprising that, in the aftermath, sales of home security devices went through the roof. While these sales are a direct manifestation of our need to feel more secure, the cocooning/nesting trend just described also accelerates, as more people retreat to the safety of the home. You can see this security trend reflected in sales increases in obvious areas, such as home security devices, guns and personal protection devices.

When California recently legalized the sale of pepper spray, most stores that carried this nefarious little device were sold out within hours. Also reflective of this trend is a highly innovative program that provides battered women with a cellular phone preprogrammed to dial 911 (and only 911).

Small Luxuries—The Affordable $2 Chocolate Truffle

After the '80s, decade of gluttony and greed, the '90s seem pretty sobering by comparison. We have tightened our economic belts and declared that "flaunt-ing it" is out, sometimes by choice, often by necessity. Unless we are willing to live the life of a Trappist monk, however, we do feel the need to reward our-selves. So we've devised ways to do this with little luxuries, small doses of the very best. We buy a single perfect chocolate truffle, a cake of luxurious soap, a beautiful flower, or just one incredibly rich cookie.

Companies like Mrs. Fields, The Body Shop, and Starbucks Coffee are all founded on the principle of creating a "perfect" product in a very narrow prod-uct niche—and then selling volumes of it, while making customers feel they're getting a special treat. If we ever sat down and figured out what those little $1 and $2 treats add up to, we would be aghast at the cost; but in a single serving, it doesn't feel like an extravagance at all. Affordable luxuries is a product and service category that continues to grow steadily.

Entertain Me!—From Spinachware to Edutainment

No matter what age, consumers seem to be seeking more entertainment in all its myriad forms. In a word, we want to have *fun,* no matter what we're doing. In some malls, shopping is no longer simply a matter of schlepping from store to store; it has been turned into a mini-amusement park, complete with food

INDUSTRIES AT A GLANCE

Automotive	1	Environmental Services	6
Banking	1	Finance & Real Estate	6
Business Management	1	Healthcare	7
Computer Hardware	2	Insurance	8
Computer Services	3	Interactive Media/Multimedia	8
Computer Software	3	Mass Communications & Media	9
Consumer Electronics	4	Semiconductors	10
Cross Technology & Industry Specific IT	4	Telecommunications	10
Data Communications & Networking	4	Transportation & Distribution	11
Defense & Aerospace	5	Travel, Hospitality & Gaming	11
Energy & Other Natural Resources	6		

Figure 1.4 Some of the Topics from Individual, Inc.'s Topic Selector.

emporium, gaming machines, and live entertainment. It's a long way from elevator Muzak.

The same trend is evident in fitness training. Where we used to live by the maxims "feel the burn" and "no pain, no gain," now the approach is more moderate, and, above all, it must be fun. Even in the halls of academia there is a slow realization that Mary Poppins was right after all when she suggested that a spoonful of sugar makes the medicine go down. More schools are turning learning into play (not just in elementary school) in hopes that students will retain more of what they need to know. Even one-time stodgy corporations are turning to games and role-playing to train their workers. Check out Riddler.com and you'll find a company that has turned advertising on the Internet into a game for consumers. It builds games and riddles for its advertisers so that consumers are funneled to particular sites, and then rewarded by an entertaining experience. Companies that can successfully give their products a fun and entertaining edge stand to win big with consumers.

The Entrepreneurial Itch—My Way or Bust

One of the fundamental changes in our society is the mutual breakdown in loyalty between employer and employee. After a decade of constant downsizing, it's a rare individual who feels any job security. Consequently, we have finally realized that each of us is responsible for his or her own success. When there is no security in the corporate world, the notion of being an independent entrepreneur suddenly doesn't seem quite as risky as it used to.

Then there's the middle road—telecommuting: still employed (with bene-fits!), but with more time and freedom for the employee and less overhead costs for the employer. The home office products explosion is a direct result of this trend. In addition, this country has always had a reverence for the lone wolf, the independent, and now we seem to have entered an era when the entrepre-neur reigns supreme. It's no coincidence that most of the recent heroes of U.S. culture have been successful entrepreneurs. It's highly doubtful that we will ever return to the old lifelong employment contract between companies and employees. Thus products and services that cater to the needs of small busi-nesses and entrepreneurs are likely to continue to grow.

Instant Everything—The Need for Speed

Stress! It's the disease of our era and everybody seems to feel pressed for time. We're expected to work, eat well, exercise, spend quality time with the chil-dren, run errands—all at breakneck speed. No wonder we gravitate toward any service or product that gives us what we want *now,* preferably while driving through. All those annoying errands that we have to do: dry cleaning, grocery shopping, oil changes, and so on: If it is good enough for hamburgers, why not oil changes? Jiffy Lube, dry cleaners in office buildings, services that run your errands for you—these are all manifestations of our need to save time. Espe-cially with two-income families, there is an ever-increasing desire for these products and services. This trend has some interesting side effects that you might not expect. For instance, teenagers now routinely do at least a portion of the household shopping, since they're home before their parents and tend to have more leisure time. As a result, they have a much greater voice in product selection. This has not been lost on manufacturers who are now aiming some of their marketing at the 29 million teens who control a portion of the family's spending.

What Electronic Marketing Approaches Are Being Tried?

What could be more illustrative of our times than a tool that promises to feed our need for speed and give us instant gratification? The World Wide Web. Granted, at present it often feels more like the World Wide Wait, but as the speed of transmission improves, it certainly has the potential to provide us with customized information on demand and in the safety of our own home or office. Now that we've looked at some major trends, let's look at how some busi-nesses are using electronic marketing tools to tap into these major trends and satisfy their customers.

Chrysler Plymouth

Chrysler Plymouth, with the help of Shamrock Communications, was one of the first major manufacturers to use both online and offline media to more effectively reach specific consumer segments. To create greater awareness of the NEON car brand among 18 to 34 year old males, Shamrock created an innovative partnership among computer magazines, leading game publishers (such as LucasArts), and Chrysler Plymouth. Shamrock produced a CD-ROM that showcased the NEON car and contained LucasArts action games. The CD-ROM was then bundled with leading computer game magazines. The result was that Chrysler got its message in front of a highly targeted audience in precisely the cutting-edge fashion this audience demands.

Since then, Shamrock has gone on to create for Chrysler Plymouth a hybrid CD-ROM and online product called the Virtual AutoPlaza. Of particular importance to Chrysler Plymouth is the potential for a one-on-one customer relationship through the use of an online function within the CD-ROM. At the click of a button, an 800 number connects the consumer to an online server. This connection allows consumers to express their preferences and desires directly to the manufacturer, while—not so incidentally—registering to win a new car. The Virtual AutoPlaza collects information from the consumer by recording preferences selected on the vehicle options screens; electronic mail and registration provide critical demographic information. In addition to standard demographics, the software can be used to measure audience response to promotional campaigns, graphic designs, advertising campaigns, the company, and the company's policies.

One of the implications of this campaign is the ability to create the ultimate focus group, not of a hundred or so consumers, but potentially of millions. Focus group participants can be selected by virtue of their media consumption and enticed to participate by the empowering notion that their input will actually impact how a product or service is designed. Shamrock and Chrysler Plymouth chose to use a direct 800 number connection, rather than the Internet, because they wanted consumers to feel secure in the knowledge that the information they provide Chrysler Plymouth is completely confidential.

HotWired

HotWired, the Web site that is the Internet sibling of *Wired* magazine, offers advertisers a way to customize their advertising by site type and geographic location. By tracking whether a Web user lives in Britain versus the United States, or is logging on from an educational site versus a business site, HotWired offers advertisers the ability to tailor their ads accordingly. While today this technology is used for simple customization, such as using the geo-graphically correct brand name, the implications clearly go beyond that.

@vantage (Gartner Group Online)

Gartner Group is a leading research and consulting firm in the high-tech indus-try. Traditionally, the firm was paid an astronomical sum of money per year for which the client received excellent research and access to an analyst by phone when needed. Gartner has recently created a business-to-business online service that provides real value at a lower price than its conventional research service. While its traditional research is sold primarily on an "all-or-nothing" basis (you must subscribe to the full service), the online service allows individuals, includ-ing nonsubscribers, to purchase research piecemeal. Moreover, it provides the information anytime, anywhere, instantly. It is an easy way to have industry pro-fessionals partake of, and, in effect, contribute to their for-profit research. Gart-ner has greatly broadened its customer base by providing a service that is no longer the exclusive province of large, well-heeled companies.

KidSoft

KidSoft is a hybrid publishing and distribution company based in Palo Alto, Cal-ifornia. It provides subscribers (children and their parents) with both a printed magazine and a CD-ROM containing reviews and samples of children's interac-tive software titles, games, contests, and articles (written by or for kids). The CD-ROM presents kids with a cozy room environment that they can explore. Clicking objects in the room triggers product demonstrations, information, and reviews, as well as fun activities, whimsical sounds, and animation. Parents can order soft-ware right off the CD-ROM. KidSoft tests its products on both children and par-ents, and the company's close attention to its customers shows. It has created an entertaining magazine and CD-ROM for kids, while giving parents the security of knowing what they're buying in advance. Some of the more subtle emotional needs KidSoft has tapped into include the need for parents and children to have a shared experience, the desire on the parents' part for a product endorsement prior to purchase, and the child's desire to feel empowered.

What Are the Key Elements of Success?

In Chapter 2 you will get some excellent guidelines on designing your elec-tronic presence, but first let's review some often overlooked basics.

Understand Who Your Customers Are and Never Stop Challenging Your Assumptions

Many companies do a reasonably good job of initially understanding who their customers are. The danger is in assuming that once they do a thorough analysis up front, they're done. The smartest companies constantly check their assumptions by keeping in close contact with their customers and maintaining a regular dialog. In the past, this has often been a time-consuming and expensive task, requiring mass mailings, intrusive telemarketing tactics, and multiple focus groups. Happily, we are now in an era in which we can reach people electronically. Not only is such communication dirt cheap, but it has the key attribute of allowing customers to decide if and when they wish to respond—without interrupting dinner.

The most successful businesses find a way to take what they have learned about their customers' habits, likes, and dislikes, and create activities and environments that result in an ongoing dialog with those customers. Despite the popular myth that Internet consumers value their anonymity, most human beings have a basic need to make their mark, and Internet surveys have consistently demonstrated consumer willingness to participate. This shows up in the form of registration forms, guest books, and other means by which consumers willingly give their names, addresses, and all sorts of details. As a businessperson, just remember to be fair; you're getting very valuable information, and today's consumers are very savvy about that value, so be sure to give your customers and prospects something valuable in return.

Create a Compelling Environment That Stimulates Customer Participation in the Evolution of That Environment

There are a number of ways that you can significantly increase the odds of your customers becoming willing and positive contributors to your ongoing market research. Once again, the key is knowing as much about them as possible. Armed with what you know about their preferences, you must build a presence that appeals to your audience, and, of course, key the content to their interests. This presence may take the form of a Web site on the Internet, a fax-on-demand system that periodically polls and updates customer preferences, or an annual user meeting. Whichever vehicle you choose, your presence must be keyed to the lifestyles of your audience. Better still, have them help you build your ongoing customer communication vehicles. Let's look at a few electronic vehicles.

Web Sites

It may require extra work, but you will do your audience a great favor if, when building your Web site, you make linking to other sites of interest easy by providing so-called hot links to those sites. Better still, provide hot links within the articles you post; this is particularly appreciated in articles that require the reader to have some basic knowledge of underlying principles. For example, if you provide technical information and products that deal with networking computers, you would be well advised to include as many useful links as possible to related sites, such as Novell's home page, LAN Times magazine, and MIT's public research area. Within an article you might provide hot links to areas that explain how basic networking works or to a glossary of computer terms. Not only does this linking make your site that much more useful to the consumer, it also allows you to request reciprocal links from larger companies with established traffic.

Kiosks

Interactive kiosks are finally coming into their own. While expensive to set up, the payback can be swift if they are used appropriately. They are particularly efficient at disseminating frequently requested information, such as travel directions or descriptions of points of interest. Most major car rental companies now have kiosks at their rental locations, providing everything from directions to cross-promotions with hotels. Having kiosks perform these tasks frees the reservation agent to process more customers. For many years, Phoenix, Arizona, has equipped municipal buildings with kiosks that provide civic information, such as schedules of community events, and direct access to the city supervisors' calendars. As a result of its constituent services, the city has garnered many awards and is perceived to provide some of the best service in the country. Kiosk applications are broadening, from offering bridal registries at department stores to helping customers design custom kitchens in do-it-yourself home improvement stores.

CD-ROM

Although the speed and bandwidth of online connections are rapidly increasing, it is likely to take some years before the average consumer will have sufficient bandwidth to enjoy all the multimedia possibilities of the World Wide Web. In the interim, CD-ROM is an excellent vehicle for providing rich graphics, sound, and video for marketing products. Where possible, it's still a good idea to have a back-end capability that links customers to an online site or 800 phone number for direct interaction and ordering. With today's database technology, you should always ensure that any CD-ROM that goes into the marketplace has the capability to capture customer information to a database. By building this in, and then providing an online link, you can ensure that critical customer data is captured on a regular basis. Be honest with customers about what you're doing, and tell them what's in it for them: better products, better service, and so on. You'll find that they are very willing to provide information and feedback—and be sure to keep your end of the bargain, and deliver better products and services that reflect customer input.

Do What You Say You're Going to Do

This may seem basic, but it is amazing how often companies fail to honor their promises. I remember a particular Web site that promised its customers detailed information about earthquake safety measures. As you might imagine, many Californians logged on, only to find a three-page brochure behind some lovely graphics that made up the home page of this company. The company led consumers to believe that they would find real information about a subject near and dear to their hearts, but delivered glib generalizations instead. Not only did this company fail to deliver, but it broke a promise, thereby destroying any trust the consumer might have had in its products. When you are selling a life-saving device, especially, the first requirement is that the customer trust you. By contrast, Moon Publications, a publisher of travel guides, established a Web site that was modeled after travel magazines. It not only provided its readers with loads of well-organized travel information free of charge, but invited them to contribute their own tips and stories. In addition, Moon made it simple for the consumer to buy its products by posting the names and addresses of retailers where their books could be bought.

Avoid Pigging Out on a Banquet of Technical Gimmicks

Technology for technology's sake is a syndrome that many electronic marketers fall prey to. Just because it's possible to put a five-minute video on the Net does not mean it's a good idea to do it. In fact, given today's communication infrastructure, you are more likely to annoy your customers than please them by putting time-consuming, endless downloads in their path. The key is to gear your choice of technological tools to your audience. If your product is highly complex, you are perhaps better off giving your audience reams of plain old text with the information they want, rather than some voice-over graphics that do not answer all their questions or fully educate them.

Be Generous with Your Links to Other Sites

If you build a Web site and nobody comes, does it exist? I'm not a Buddhist, so I don't know the answer, but I do know that if nobody knows you're there, no one will come. With the number of Web sites growing at a clip of one new site per minute, it becomes increasingly difficult for the consumer to find the proverbial needle in the haystack; your job then is to make it easy for them to find you. If you've done your homework on who your target audience is and what they like and dislike, you should be able to build a list of likely sites that would be of interest to them. You then need to approach these companies and individuals and create a reciprocal link from their home pages to yours. Yes, many companies are now charging for this "privilege" with fees ranging from $25 to $30,000, but unless you have a killer brand name, I suggest you refrain from greed and focus on building traffic to your site. Once you have built up a steady roster of subscribers or visitors (and you can prove it!), then you can consider charging for links to your site. In addition, you should aggressively pursue companies that provide search tools, such as Yahoo, to be included in their search universe. Treat your Web site as you would any other new product: publicize its existence any way you can. Thus you need to create a marketing plan for your Web site that includes a well-defined strategy for advertising, public relations, and cross-promotion of your site both online and offline.

How Can You Make the Most of Your "Competitor's" Presence in the Electronic Marketplace?

If "Know thy Customer" is the first commandment of business, then "Know thy Competitor" is surely the second. Shame on the company that claims to have no competitor—they are always wrong and history usually proves them so. Fortunately the proliferation of the Internet, reference CD ROMs, and ever more sophisticated database tools are making competitive intelligence easier to come by.

The Fine Art of Lurking

Other than citing the Freedom of Information Act, I can think of few better resources than the online world to check out what your competition is up to. It is a very efficient and cost-effective tool for learning and, yes, spying. The online world permits you to read discussion groups without participating in them, a practice known as *lurking*. Thus it is possible to preserve your anonymity while freely roaming through cyberspace. Be aware, though, that what you do unto others can of course be done to you. While I certainly encourage people to learn as much as possible about their competitors by lurking, I draw the line at posting negative comments in a competitor's support forum. Not only is it unethical, it can get you into legal trouble.

Observe Your Competitors; Positioning and Marketing Techniques

By paying close attention to your competitors' electronic presence, you will learn a great deal about how they are positioning themselves in the marketplace. The very fact that they have a Web site suggests that someone in their organization is at least paying attention to current technology. You may find that they are offering special promotions or cross-promoting their product with a complementary product from another vendor. For example, if you saw that Mattel was comarketing its Barbie doll with a perfume manufacturer, you could either approach Mattel with a similar offer; or, it might at least get you thinking about who to approach for a similar online promotion of your product. Observing your competitors online is no different from paying careful attention to your competitors in other media—you collect, read, and analyze their marketing collateral and clip every article about them. It's just a lot faster and easier online.

Online Support Forums

If you have a technical product, support forums provide a rich source of product information, including strengths and weaknesses, and of insight into the attitudes of your competitors' customers, as well as the way your competitors relate to their customers. Some companies have built firewalls around their support forums in order to keep snoopers out, but the vast majority, particularly on commercial services, are open.

Online Discussion Groups

Topic-specific discussion groups are a rich source of information. Discussions can sometimes go on for months on a single topic and can provide diligent researchers with lots of insight into how a particular group feels about a topic, product, or service. I once spent four months tracking a discussion among a group of mothers on the subject of nutrition. It was fascinating to see the level of detail these women got into and the passion with which they defended their positions. Many brands and companies were discussed in the process, and if I were a less scrupulous sort, I could have sold the information for a great deal of money. Rest assured that the companies being discussed regularly spend a large amount of time and money to find out the feelings these women were discussing for free online. Interestingly, one of these companies has yet to stick so much as a toe in the online waters. When I called the company to ask about its online plans, its marketing people (who should know better) told me they didn't think their target audience were online users. So much for knowing your audience.

TABLE 1.1   Information You Need to Reach Your Target Audience

Type	What Can You Learn?
Associations	Think about which associations you might contact to obtain mailing lists, detailed information about your target audience, etc.
Books	What were the top selling books in your audience category? Make a list, and contact the authors/publishers.
Catalogs	Can you identify which catalogs reach your audience?
Clubs	Which clubs cater to your audience's special interest? Do they have a newsletter? A Web site? Regular meetings? Chapters all over the country? If yes to the latter, shouldn't that give you insight into where interest is particularly high and target those first?
Competitors	Who are your major competitors? Don't just list the ones with the same/similar products. What about companies that meet similar needs? For example, remember that a book and a video about the same subject compete with one another for both time and money. If that is the case, consider teaming up and bundling them as complementary products or cross-promoting them.
Complementors	What products/services can you identify that complement yours? (*See comments on competitors.*)
Digizines	Is your audience techno-savvy? If so, remember to include the digizines that cater to them and include them in your public relations and advertising plans.
Education	Check out both college and extension university catalogs to see whether a course is taught that closely relates to the benefits of your product. Find out who the leading professors/lecturers are and include them in your resource list. Sometimes they will simply serve as fountains of knowledge about your target audience, and sometimes they may even become key endorsers.
Events	What special events/conferences might your audience attend? What else goes on there? Who performs, sells, promotes, etc. there?
Housing patterns	Where does your audience tend to live? If you depend on retail, this is obviously key information, but it is also critical when it comes time to plan your PR and advertising coverage.
Leisure activities	How does your audience spend their leisure time? This is another way of asking: how do they spend their discretionary income? How leisure time is spent tells you not only about lifestyle preferences, but also where else you might reach your audience (how about in-flight magazines for an audience that travels a lot?).
Media consumption	Identify the magazines, radio stations/formats, and television programs that cater to your audience. Get their media kits, read/listen/watch their content. Sooner or later you'll need this information anyway for your public relations and advertising plans, so you may as well get it now and take advantage of the audience knowledge that the content creators have about your target market.
WWW sites	What Web sites are likely to attract your audience? What are the most common links that these sites point to? Can they provide you with specific audience information? (Caution: Unless they are audited by an indepenent service, I would take the numbers with a large dose of salt!)

Coopetition

Coopetition is a term used to describe those situations when it is wiser to cooperate with your competitors than to fight them. For example, if you are a small company that has a novelty food product, you may find it almost impossible to get on grocery shelves in the large chains, distribution you need in order to survive. Rather than giving up to the giants, you might instead approach one of them and offer to private-label your product for them. In effect, you become a supplier to your competitor and sell your product under that brand name.

In small service businesses it is common for erstwhile competitors to form an alliance whereby they share projects. Each service may have 80 percent of its skill set in common, but each one offers a specialty that the other does not have. By pooling their skill sets and each contributing what it does best, they can often secure projects that they would not have been able to secure individually. On a larger scale, in both the record and software industries, large companies often "rent" their distribution channels to smaller companies. This is known as *affiliate label publishing,* and is a form of coopetition, since the large publisher's products compete for shelf space with the smaller company's products. On the other hand, the small record label or software publisher might never get any shelf space without the clout of the larger company. It used to be that if you couldn't beat them, you joined them; today, it's often more appropriate advice to at least date them for a while.

Getting the Picture

Table 1.1 is intended to get you thinking about who your target customers are, what activities they engage in, what they read, where they shop, what other products they buy, and more. Try to fill out each category as thoroughly as possible. Once you've completed this profile to the best of your ability, you will begin to form a well-rounded picture of who your audience really is, how they spend their time, and where they spend their income.

I think you'll find that once you have such a detailed profile, you will begin to notice patterns and linkages you probably had not thought of. Equally important, you will end up identifying who your logical marketing partners are, and find new ways of getting your message to your audience.

This is by no means a complete list, but it will get you thinking in ways that most traditional marketing planning doesn't. My aim is to get you to look beyond the confines of a narrow industry niche, to instead consider about what makes up the daily lives of your audience. The farther you look, the more you'll be able to connect the dots. Experience has taught me that most companies are pretty lazy in their audience research, and the person who does his or her homework comes out ahead.

CHAPTER TWO

DESIGNING YOUR PRESENCE

Margo Komenar

The *kind* of knowledge and understanding you have of your target audience is perhaps your most valuable asset when designing an effective marketplace presence. Traditional *demographics* tell you who, where, and how old your audience is. It is *psychographics,* however, which tell you how they think, feel, and behave, that today's technology makes possible and demands. Designing to this new marketing paradigm is a formidable challenge. Advertising and design firms must adapt images and messages to a wide range of consumer profiles and venues, while incorporating the continuous and varied feedback from an audience that demands customized attention *now!*

Mass-Micromarketing

By segmenting audiences through the use of highly sophisticated consumer databases, one-to-one *mass* marketing, or *mass-micromarketing* is made possible along with the shift from demographics to psychographics as a key targeting tool. Tim Smith, president and CEO of Red Sky Interactive, describes the shift this way:

> *In the whole new world of narrow casting, it's no longer mass marketing, it's micro marketing on a massive scale, which is a very subtle distinction. So you've got to get into the psychographic of who you want to talk to and forget about the demographics because they may be in Taiwan. They may be demographic groups you haven't even thought about in third world countries. They still might be in your market but you just haven't anticipated it. Figure out what about your product really appeals to them and sell that and categorize that and market that.*

Instead of the age group, say, of the single white male between 30 and 35, which may or may not be the prevalent group on the Web, we think in terms of Gen X or the senior person in a technical industry, which could be any age group, any sex. We're much more interested in that. That's getting back to not putting them into a statistical group but putting them into an emotional group. What pulls their strings? Because that's how you're going to get them, and it's not necessarily going to follow any demographic group.

The Customer-Centric Relationship

The ability to market directly to the individual results in a customer-controlled or customer-centric relationship between buyer and seller. The consumer now controls pricing more immediately and more directly than ever before. The Gartner Group, one of the leading information technology advisors to business professionals, states: "Mass-marketing and micromarketing paradigms are being augmented by new customer-centric relationship marketing strategies."

In its 1996 Interactive Marketing Strategic Analysis Report the Gartner Group states the following trends are all negatively impacting traditional marketing:

- less product differentiation
- increasing competition
- rising consumer expectations
- splintering mass markets
- diminishing effectiveness of mass media
- heightened consumer privacy and security concerns

"These trends do not mean that traditional marketing will disappear, but that it must be supplemented by new relationship-oriented strategies that interactive marketing enables. Every organizational process and function must become closer to the customer and be defined by how it adds value to the customer relationships."

The Gartner report further states that with the diminishing return from traditional marketing and the increase in the complexity of information management and the marketing process, automation will be essential for survival. The group warns, however, that technology alone is not a panacea. The key will be to achieve a competitive advantage from effective relationship marketing. A "strong vision and deep organizational commitment" will be essential for success as the necessary changes in culture, technology, and process are implemented. Figure 2.1 compares traditional and technology-enabled marketing implications.

Marketing Area	Traditional Marketing	Technology-Enabled Marketing	Implication
Segmentation	Demographics	Behavioral	Database
Advertising	Push	Pull	Interactive
Promotions	Mass	Tailored	Reemergence
Pricing	Set by Firm	Set by Customer	Tailored Pricing
Sales Mgmt.	Data with Sales	Data Shared	Mktg. and Sales Are Partners
Distribution Channels	Intermediaries	Direct	Multichannel
New Products	Constrained	Customer Driven	Mkt. Expansion
Monitoring	Share, Profit	Retention, Value	New Metrics

Figure 2.1 Implications of traditional versus new marketing methods. (*Source: Gartner Group, based on a framework developed by John Deighton, Harvard Business School, and Robert Blattberg, Northwestern University's Kellogg School of Management*)

Due to increased competition for a customer's attention, traditional marketing methods are proving less effective, and the issue of return on investment is coming under tighter scrutiny. According to Gartner's report, *Interactive Marketing: A New Business Landscape for Marketing Professionals,* the result is that marketing departments are being forced to measure and examine activities and allocate resources to those with the best potential for an acceptable return. "As a result, most enterprises are finding that to achieve the same results, they have to spend more money on marketing, sales, and advertising. However, the cumulative effect of more messages being sent out by more enterprises competing for the same consumer budgets is that each additional marketing dollar achieves fewer results." Figure 2.2 illustrates media effectiveness by cost per activity.

Dave Clauson, managing director of True North Technologies, Inc., interactive production arm to the advertising agency, Foote, Cone & Belding, explains:

> . . . agencies have been talking about highly integrated campaigns for years. Most big agencies have fallen flat on their faces in doing it. More midsized and smaller agencies have had better success with integration because they did more of the work for those clients as entities. But now, in having to strike this balance between one-way and two-way media, it's forcing marketers and their agencies to come to grips with how to make it all work, because the one thing that we know is true is that clients' marketing budgets are not increas-

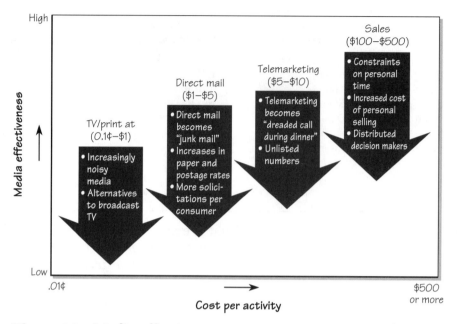

Figure 2.2   Media effectiveness versus cost per activity. (*Source: Gartner Group*)

ing. In fact, they're going the other way. So it behooves clients to ask that question again: "Where can I get the most effectiveness? What should I do and in what order? How am I using the CD-ROM environment, the Web environment, the kiosk environment to complement what I'm doing in the television environment, the print environment, the in-store environment, et cetera?"

The complexity of the new interactive marketing model creates new management challenges. Figure 2.3 illustrates the basic steps of this new marketing cycle. A complete understanding of these steps is necessary in order to design an effective campaign that covers all of the relationship bases, and thoughtfully addresses the idiosyncratic needs of each.

According to the report in this new model, a customer may receive a marketing contact in various ways, including a page on the Web, a TV ad, or a piece of direct mail. If this contact comes in a way that the customer prefers, it will evoke a response. The vehicle or venue of that response may be different from the contact venue. For example, a Web site may generate a return phone call; a TV ad may precipitate an e-mail response. The key is that the customer controls the time, place, and process of the response. The customer deals with the enterprise when, where, and how he or she likes.

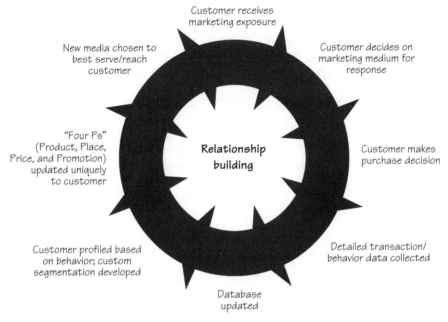

Figure 2.3   The new marketing cycle. (*Source: Gartner Group*)

The customer makes a purchase decision based on exposure to the marketing message. Because the customer controls the flow of marketing information, this step may be difficult for marketers to control. However, the customer's purchase decision generates detailed behavioral data that the marketing organization can, and should, capture, including contact medium, response vehicle, purchase location, and so on. This information is fed into a comprehensive marketing database (updated in real time or daily-batched, as monthly or quarterly updates are no longer sufficient), and the customer's profile is re-created using these up-to-the-minute facts.

The new profile may conform to an existing segment classification or generate a new classification. In either case, future marketing contacts with the individual are based on his or her most recent behavior. The four Ps—product, place, price and promotions—have been uniquely updated for this customer. Future marketing venues are selected based on the individual's demonstrated preferences for receiving and responding to the marketing message. With this model, effective marketers will not waste money on media that a particular customer does not respond to. This cycle is repeated over and over again (see Figure 2.3). A complete cycle may occur in the course of a single day.

Connecting with Your Customers

Ketchum Communications, a full service agency, outlines a process that it implements when working with clients to design a strategic campaign. There are five essential elements of a successful customer connection:

Uncovering the Brand Essence

- Reveals the underlying nature of the brand among the key customer group(s).
- Divines leverageable brand characteristics based on personal perceptions and feelings.

Discovering the Buying Motives

- Determines why customers really buy brands by understanding their inner thoughts, emotions, desires, beliefs, and impulses.
- Creates communications that connect leverageable brand characteristics to personal motivations.
- Crystallizes customer insights by stimulating their personal reaction to ideas.

Formulating the Creative Brief

- Delineates the most compelling strategy in an inspiring way.
- Focuses the strategy into a single word.
- Provides a focal point for the thorough creative exploration.

Developing the Creative Connection

- Explores and refines creative concepts based on customer reactions.
- Verifies the power of the key selling idea to meaningfully connect with the target.

Validating the Market Impact

- Verifies the overall impact of the communication program in the marketplace.
- Continuously monitors personal reactions to ensure an ongoing, successful, customer connection.

Branding

Most companies lead their efforts for visibility in the marketplace with their name or brand identity. A brand is more than a name, a logo or even an identification. It is the currency in the emotionally defined relationship between buyer and seller. If it is designed well and backed up with reliable, responsible and responsive performance, a brand can become a lifestyle choice and in some cases an integral part of the consumer's personal lifestyle identity. Pete Snell, general manager of CKS/Interactive, a division of CKS Advertising, a respected integrated marketing communications firm, explains:

> *Often when people first hear about a brand or see it, they see it in terms of a logo or the identity treatment. What also builds a brand is the way in which the company communicates that brand both through marketing communications and more importantly how it interacts with the consumer. . . .*
>
> *What's the quality of their products and services? How well do they treat their customers? How are they treated on the phone if there's a problem after the sale? That's what builds the brand, and what a marketer or marketing communications company can do is help communicate about that brand and reinforce some of those characteristics, some of those essential cultural values of that company, one of which might be quality. Communications and how a company deals with its customers are the two biggest ways you build a brand.*

All businesses with a name or logo technically have a brand, even though some may not have created much of an identity around it. Some brands are not promoted intentionally. When you go to a hardware store to get supplies, you do not find most of the building materials, such as lumber or nails, sold by brand names. The only person those brands are important to is the buyer who depends on that vendor for stocking purposes. The buyer will usually make purchasing decisions based more on pricing and reliable delivery service than on brand identity. In fact, going with a lesser-known brand can often mean lower prices and greater flexibility in an effort by the smaller vendor to establish a long-term relationship. Nevertheless, since these are key components to building brand credibility and popularity, over time even these brands will gain recognition within their own market segment.

According to Brand Consultant Lynn Upshaw, of Upshaw & Associates and former managing director of Ketchum Interactive, there is a latent brand in everything. "It doesn't pay, for some businesses, to spend a huge amount of time doing branding work if they are basically in a nonbranded or a commodity business. But for I would say the vast majority of products and services out there, it does make sense, to a minimum, to strategize about it, to think about it, and consider what you're doing. If you don't have that strategy, that overall plan about what's happening, what you want to have happen to your brand, then it's equivalent to a human being going through life without any plan at all. We can have fun, but sooner or later, we're liable to stumble, and that's going to happen with a brand too."

A perfect example of a commodity that branded itself was the Intel Pentium chip, made inseparable from the image of fast and superior-quality PC computers in the minds of the consumer. Customers would request an Intel or Pentium over the actual brand name of the computer in which the chip was housed! Upshaw elaborates on this classic example in his book *Building Brand Identity*, John Wiley & Sons (1995), in which he states, ". . . it was a brilliant move. It helped accelerate their gripping of the whole dominance of the category." This strategy elevated the Intel brand to an unprecedented level for a company of this type, and awakened others in previously latent brand categories to reconsider the leveraging possibilities.

The principles of advertising and direct marketing are the same regardless of the medium. The electronic marketplace is simply one more channel with its unique benefits and limitations. The challenge at hand is to learn as much as possible about what those benefits and limitations are and how they can optimize your overall marketing program and brand awareness. Pete Snell of CKS/Interactive relates:

> We start with a core set of messages with a look and feel, and take that into a variety of different media, and that's really what we mean by integrated marketing communications. It creates the impression that the company or the message or branding is actually much bigger than it might be in reality. . . . Just think of the brands that you know of that are so strong like Coca-Cola, McDonald's, AT&T, MCI. People think of things when you mention AT&T, Coca-Cola. It conjures up an image in their mind; it conjures up characteristics, and that's the brand. Being able to nurture and cherish and grow and create and establish a brand is a very important thing for a marketer to do.

A great deal can be learned by visiting the Web sites of these major brands and comparing the way they approach their other advertising venues. These companies have spent millions of dollars to research and develop their campaigns, and, often, parallels can be drawn by observing their strategies. Many of them may be targeting one or more of your consumer audiences, and their tactics can be very revealing, even if it is for a different product. Tim Smith of Red Sky comments:

> Now branding is a much more tenuous thing. Look at the Saturn ads. Look at ads for companies that have a high emotional content. That is a kind of branding by inference. It evokes a response internally, which is not the perception of a logo; it's a response that is the brand, which is weird. It's an emotional, tactile response that you get to a large manufacturer or product company. That is the brand.

An innovative community approach to branding was undertaken by CKS/Interactive, a division of CKS/Group, an integrated marketing communications firm. A fast food company that we will refer to as Charlie's Fish, (the real name could not be used) approached CKS/Interactive to design a localized branding program. The purpose was to localize marketing materials for franchised fast food products, currently targeted at the general U.S. English-speaking population. Charlie's Fish wanted to sell into the U.S. Chinese-speaking market directly, and adapt its promotional information and paper goods to the written and cultural language of those communities. A private network was set up over which franchises in these communities could receive information directly from the main company database. The goal was to create brand affinity with this population across the country.

By speaking to Chinese-Americans in their own language, Charlie's Fish was creating a bond and making it possible for consumers to develop a more personal relationship with the brand. CKS created an integrated database in English that would update and maintain the positioning and design guidelines, but make the information available for localization. *Localization* could account for not only language specifications, but also the way materials were presented to meet certain cultural preferences. Marketers selling the franchised Charlie's Fish product into the Chinese community would have access to this database in order to adapt it to the local consumer. Marketers could either localize the information themselves or have it done for them. The consistency of the franchise look, feel, and brand identity would be maintained. This was a highly successful endeavor, and exemplifies creative adaptation and implementation of technology to support and build brand identity through the use of electronic and on-line mediums.

Many Brands Under One "Roof"

Companies that have many different brands and varying types of audiences are faced with an interesting challenge when considering visibility in the electronic marketplace. Studio Archetype brings its expertise to these kinds of projects on a regular basis. Amanda North, chief identity architect, states:

> *Usually in the print world, a customer is not exposed to a company as a whole, but rather to a set of materials from one division or brand. The only place a consumer may find a comprehensive overview is in the annual report. However, the Internet provides another opportunity for access to broader company information. A customer can now visit a Web site where the click of a button will take the user from one brand to another, one division to another. This new level of access provides an opportunity for the marketplace to get a feeling for a company across all of its lines of business*

that they might not have been able to get previously. This also presents a
challenge, because it forces the divisions to really look at the ways in which
they appear uniformly across different levels, and at what level they want
their divisional identities to be reflected.

HarperCollins, the publishing firm, has about eight divisions, which had to consider for the first time what they wanted their overall image to be. Studio Archetype spent a great deal of time developing an illustrative style that the divisions could all agree to, and then determined how many layers down into the Web site they should go before each division would be free to tailor its look and messages to its own unique audiences.

Originally, Studio Archetype started working in the HarperCollins interactive division developing a packaging and identity system for the publisher's CD-ROM products. That was so successful that Studio Archetype was asked to create the corporate Web site. What the firm ultimately designed was a program that worked effectively across all divisions. North explains:

> *It was an interesting exercise to create HarperCollins' identity on the Web.*
> *The Web brings together the brand identities of the different divisions in one*
> *place, which is different than what happens in the print world. On the Web*
> *it is necessary to not only let the unique aspects of each division come*
> *through, but to also build a unified core brand. There are many trade-offs*
> *involved, and we spent a lot of time with HarperCollins at the beginning of*
> *the project, asking questions like: 'What degree of differentiation should*
> *each division have? What do you want the overall HarperCollins brand to*
> *look like, and what do you want to say to the marketplace?'*
>
> *They decided that they could all agree on this woodcut tradition of pub-*
> *lishing as a way of metaphorically describing all of their different busi-*
> *nesses. As you go into the site and carry this look and feel throughout, you*
> *can see that it got a little wilder as we got into the interactive area.*

You can visit this Web site at http://www.harpercollins.com (Figure 2.4).

When the Brand Is the Product

What about when the brand *is* the product? And what if it is also bundled with and hosts other brands? Microsoft approached Studio Archetype to design the introduction of the Microsoft Network. The software giant was presenting an online service for the mass market audience, and it was to be bundled with Windows 95. An initial 3 million users were expected, ranging from consumers in the home all the way up to MIS audiences in Fortune 200 companies. The

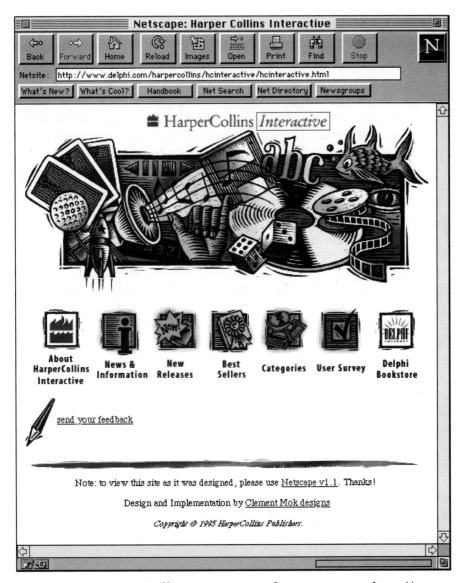

Figure 2.4   HarperCollins Interactive home page at http://www. harpercollins.com.

user *experience* was to *be* the product! It had to invite this diverse audience in, and respect the range of interests and levels of sophistication.

Cultural considerations and color and graphical depictions were all important factors. The design had to reflect simplicity balanced by graphical richness, enticing to the home user and serious enough for the business person. Although its strategy and appearance has changed a little from the original solution provided by Studio Archetype, Microsoft's home page and organizational structure still reflects Archetype's work, and the graphic symbols were carefully considered so that they spoke to a global audience. North comments:

> *The nature of our business has changed the way people view design. People used to think of design as simply a picture or an afterthought, and now it is seen more as the essence of the communication program. We recently put QVC online with Microsoft Network, (QVC Web Site: Microsoft Network (MSN), Go word: qvc). We developed the information architecture and the design, the look and feel. In this online media world, the result is very much like designing the product itself, and sometimes actually is the product, as in the case of QVC. It's the essence of a product in many cases. Particularly in this new media arena, it's all bits and bytes going out to the world. There is no tangible, physical product, so the navigation and look and feel is what it's all about.*
>
> *Since the third-party presence was an important element in the Microsoft project, part of our branding consideration in the initial strategy was to consider how Microsoft Network interplayed with Nickelodeon. They might not only be an advertiser, but actually a content provider on MSN. So one question we had to address was how the two identities worked together, and how much visibility to give one versus the other.*

Examples of many of Studio Archetype's campaigns and design work can be viewed online at http://www.studioarchetype.com.

Interactivity

Interactivity is the single most impactful element in advertising and branding today. It works on many levels simultaneously in the buyer-seller relationship. When used in an entertaining presentation, an interactive program captures and holds attention while branding images are displayed or cleverly woven into the content. The ability to gather specific and up-to-the-minute consumer feedback makes it possible to adapt messages instantaneously and respond to needs and changing requirements quickly. In the opinion of Pete Snell from CKS:

*The power of interactive media is that consumers can go in at their conve-
nience and can get a deep impression about a particular brand or company
that is unique. There's no other way that consumers can get this type of experience or this type of interaction with a company. They can't get it from passive advertisement like TV, print, or radio, or even if they're speaking with a
representative of the company. Often consumers feel that they can't trust a
company representative because the information they're getting is biased.*

According to Ketchum Interactive, consumers are rapidly coming to expect
the extraordinary from the messages they receive. They are more media-savvy
than any generation before them. They are obtaining life-or-death control over
what they see, when they see it, and how it is delivered to them. Very soon, virtually all traditional forms of marketing communications will have to be made
interactive in some way if the marketer hopes to create and hold a customer
franchise for the long term.

By the year 2000, the Gartner Group expects that "leading-edge marketing
departments will have elevated interactive marketing into the lead position in
their marketing mix." Gartner emphasizes the importance of formulating a clear
strategy for each media type within each aspect of the mix, to include specifically defined tactics for exploiting each one. By analyzing the cost to deliver
each medium, the appropriate audience segment to target with each, and the
most effective tactics to employ, the right tools will become obvious. Figure 2.5

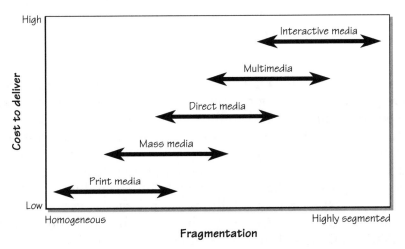

Figure 2.5 Progression of cost to deliver new media as
audience segmentation increases. (*Source: Gartner Group*)

shows the progression of cost to deliver new media as audience segmentation increases.

What Lynn Upshaw, of Upshaw & Associates, believes is so important about interactivity is that it provides the opportunity for dialog. He sees it as an advanced form of direct marketing, and explains that when the brand is skillfully integrated into the subject being presented so that it captivates and engages the consumer, greater brand involvement is accomplished. To illustrate this, he adds:

> *Pepsi used to have a test commercial it ran on the late great Interactive Network. The idea was, you'd be watching and playing Jeopardy at home and then the screen would read, "Watch the following commercial; you'll be asked questions and you'll be given a prize if you get them all right." Then a Pepsi commercial would come on and suddenly you'd be looking at a Pepsi commercial and trying to memorize things about it. You were so much more involved than if you just saw a Pepsi commercial in standard programming.*

The Web offers even greater potential for this approach to brand involvement, and it is actively being implemented by many pioneering companies. Upshaw explains that while *Launch* magazine on CD-ROM has brands pop up as you are experiencing the content, it differs from the real-time give and take of the Internet, and the nature of interactivity has a more powerful ability to create a stronger relationship. There is an active exchange of information, so more time is actually spent with the brand.

The Internet makes it possible for the consumer to interact with the brand in ways never before possible, and it is crucial that companies understand the implications of "putting themselves out there." On the Internet, a brand is like a living entity that must be constantly monitored, updated, and responsive to input. Formerly, many brands went through a third party rather than dealing directly with the consumer. This relationship has now become much more far-reaching, and requires savvy strategic planning and very well-thought interface design and response mechanisms. According to Pete Snell of CKS, it is imperative "to understand what it means to have your brand alive in an interactive medium. It's very, very different from being in a passive medium, so you need to understand the medium and how you can use it, things to avoid. . . ."

Making use of interactive media without proper understanding and strategic implementation will result in costly failures for a large percentage of businesses. According to the Gartner Group, by the year 2000, up to 60 percent of interactive marketing efforts will not succeed because of ineffective strategies and the lack of vision needed to leverage and make appropriate use of these technologies. Interactive marketing is much more than using multimedia to entertain or engage a consumer. It is a higher level of strategic marketing, enabled by sophisticated technology and intelligent databases that can respond to interactive relationships. The Internet has brought these relationships into a real-time arena, and has dramatically impacted the clout of traditional advertising. On the technology side, the infrastructure is able to capture, measure, compare, and analyze all aspects of the consumer's input into the system. This allows an intelligent sorting of information that can assist on the marketing side in strategic allocation of traditional and interactive resources.

Proper forethought and management can steer a business away from the dangers and into the great potential of the electronic marketplace. The Gartner Group illustrates some of the keys to successful interactive marketing in Figure 2.6.

Interactive media is excellent for qualifying purchases, especially in the case of high-ticket items. Although people usually make major buys in person, such media as CD-ROMs, kiosks, or online services can provide depth of information, animated demonstrations, and simulations. It is also possible to use a variety of search engines on the Internet to gather extensive current, historical, and comparative data.

Tim Smith of Red Sky relates: "When you're shopping for a new car, you get it down to three or four, and then you get those wonderful color brochures and you take them home and you lie in bed with them. This is a very "boy" thing, a very "boy" perspective. And you read every 10-point word in that brochure. . . . You know, you totally consume the product before you buy it. That's pretty typical."

Today, interactive media are created by the major auto companies on CD-ROM, floppy disk, and online, where most have a significant presence, to assist current customers in making a purchasing decision and to entice new ones. The major car companies are aggressively developing their electronic presence, making full use of the interactive environments with ad games, event promotions, prizes and giveaways, and direct mail campaigns that include floppies and CD-ROMs. They are actively engaged in building relationships with consumers, striving to contribute to their lives, to win their business and loyalty. The consumer is finally in the "driver's seat," with easy access to all of the information they need to educate themselves before even going into a dealership. Ultimately, buying a car is an emotional decision, and requires a face-to-auto experience. But the use of interactive media is becoming a more available asset in this process. Smith continues:

> It's the smell of the leather. And then you take it home and it's the 10 miles per gallon, right? It's that world, you know, jumping back and forth between your right brain and left brain. The fine print doesn't mean a thing. When they've done analyses of how people buy, it's back to the leather. The boys will read all these things about why they have to have a Landrover. . . . [The

car companies have] an expensive product that [requires] a longish sales cycle, where the consumer needs a lot of information about the product, and there still is an emotional sell. And that gets back to the companies that can really combine an emotional sell with the real analytical sell. . . . 30 seconds long, 30 minutes deep. That's where interactive can work very well."

Gartner sees today's Web site hot links, (words or pictures that you click on at someone's online site that will immediately take you to another location of interest), as a precursor to a phenomenon it calls "just-in-time marketing." It

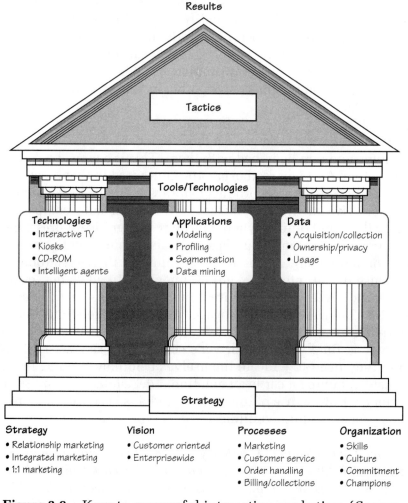

Figure 2.6 Keys to successful interactive marketing. (*Source: Gartner Group*)

will not be long before these kinds of links will deliver information that has been customized to go to the right person at the right time and in the right way. It is the challenge of businesses today to position themselves along the appropriate electronic pathways, to both provide and receive pertinent information. Gartner states:

> *Future examples of this phenomenon will include complex expert systems involving interactive information exchanges and sophisticated segmentation and classification to ensure that the right information gets to the right consumers just as they need it. This "just-in-time marketing" will be the key to using electronic channels successfully. Enterprises must first provide complete and persuasive information, and then find ways to make the consumer want more of this information.*

As the marketing paradigm shifts, it will become more critical to understand the differences between the why and how of using these technologies. Gartner offers the following key strategies for optimizing the use of interactive marketing:

- *Serve before selling:* The primary reason enterprises will fail in adopting this new marketing method is that they will use interactive marketing to sell products, not to service customers. Interactive marketing is about information—providing more information, closer to the customer and at the customer's discretion—but enterprises are already trying to determine how to close sales with interactive marketing. For many enterprises, this is the wrong use, at least for now. Enterprises that develop sales strategies instead of service strategies will fail.

  Management implication: Determine what information (especially more complex information) customers want, and plan to shift the dissemination of that information to interactive marketing.

- *Think of interactive marketing as a way to capture data:* Interactive marketing will allow for a nearly infinite segmentation of the market. The customers will decide what information they need, what problems this information will solve, and how they will react to that information. With this, marketing professionals can gather much more information about customers' behavior and attitudes, and this will benefit market research and product development. This data will be quantitative and accurate, and it will reflect customer behavior.

  Management implication: Do not neglect the database. Spend the time and money now to develop state-of-the-art, transaction-based repositories of customer information, and plan on using interactive marketing to populate these databases.

- *Learn to control information flow even though it lies with the customer:* The rules are changing. The customer will truly be "king," at least with regard to marketing programs. If enterprises continue to use the old "push" model instead of this new "pull" model, they will fail. Enterprises must learn early how information flow can be controlled when the control is no longer obvious. This will create a huge competitive advantage. Take as an example two firms that both have large amounts of information on their product available on the Internet. One exercises no control over the flow of information, causing a prospective customer to simply view some general information, then go elsewhere. The second firm guides the customer through comparative analysis, pricing justification, and a sample of how the product can solve his or her unique problems. The second company is much more likely to make the sale, even though the same information is available in both Web sites.

- *Understand how all the parts of the marketing strategy, including interactive marketing, fit together, and make each serve a unique purpose and market group:* Interactive marketing involves more than simply distributing brochures electronically. It is an entirely different marketing model. As such, it needs a unique place among marketing strategies. Shifting the entire marketing burden to interactive marketing will fail. Translating existing marketing into interactive marketing will fail. Doing something simply because everyone else is doing it will fail. The only way to succeed is to position interactive marketing as a unique effort to serve a select, important group of customers.

  Management implication: Give interactive marketing its appropriate place. To work, it cannot be viewed as a skunkworks or an extension of an existing strategy. Carve out appropriate resources and develop a comprehensive strategy, ensuring that each aspect of the marketing mix reaches a unique piece of the customer mix.

By taking educated advantage of interactive, database, and automating technologies, you can move your business to a new plateau of performance and success. The ramifications of design are far more impactful today, and it becomes obvious very quickly when something has been forgotten, inappropriately represented, or misunderstood. The ripple effect is a more global one, and the lights and cameras are on 24 hours a day, every day!

Integration

Pete Snell explains that CKS was founded on the premise of integrated marketing back in 1987 by Bill Cleary. All the senior founders, including Mark Kvamme and Tom Suiter, had worked together at Apple and were witness to the power of this strategy. He adds, "Apple was the only firm at that time that was actually doing integrated marketing communications, where whether you saw it on a logo, on a seat cushion at the Super Bowl, on a *Wall Street Journal* ad or on the outside of its packages, it was the same look, the same font treatment, and it's still being used today.

The Garamond font treatment and that whole white look is still being used today. Apple leverages it out into print mediums and TV, as well. Listen to an Apple TV or radio spot; you'll hear the same announcer. Apple was doing this in the early '80s, and Tom, Mark and Bill were all working there at that time. Bill left Apple on the premise that "We gotta take this message out; a bunch of other companies can benefit from it." That was the start of CKS.

"Now we have major brands realizing the power of integrated marketing communications, whether it's MCI, McDonalds, Time Warner, or United Airlines. They are all saying they want to have one team create these messages, but use them in a variety of different media. It has been working well for the brands that we've been working with."

Repurposing

When Time Warner Interactive (TWI) was launching Primal Rage, a very popular video arcade game, into the home market, it needed to create high consumer demand if it was to succeed. The game had been ported over from the arcade platform to players like Nintendo, Super NES, and Sega. It was necessary to create tremendous "pull" on a very conservative budget, exciting the consumers and retailers simultaneously. TWI approached CKS/Interactive to design a fully integrated campaign.

Pete Snell of CKS elaborates:

> One of the neat things about that game was that it was very visually striking and very visually appealing. We took a lot of the graphics and visual imagery from the game and created some messages around it, and ended up doing a laptop sales presentation where their salespeople went out and sold to retail buyers at places like Toys 'R Us, and CompUSA. In addition, we took that same imagery and created 30-second spots, print advertising, retail software packages, and did their retail merchandising, all from the

same digital imagery, just refocusing and reusing it. That was a very cost-
effective campaign; they got this integrated campaign and I think five dif-
ferent media for much less money than they would have paid if they had
used separate firms. It probably would have cost three or four times as
much money.

One of the great benefits of an integrated marketing campaign is that it is possible to repurpose digital media for many different formats and platforms.

Medius IV, a San Francisco interdisciplinary design firm, was faced with the
challenge of converting the information from the rather weighty *Intellectual
Law* booklet, usually distributed to clients in print, into an interesting and useful electronic presentation. The law firm came to Medius IV, requesting that it
create a floppy disk both for the booklet material and as a marketing tool with
several purposes. The real challenge was to create a product that would serve
as an educational and resource tool, while marketing the firm's services, taste-
fully promoting the preexisting equity in brand identity. Moez Rafieetary, CEO
and art director, explains:

The client used to send out a 60-page document to potential clients.
Because the firm itself is involved in the digital medium, it wanted to take
advantage of that and market itself accordingly. Unfortunately, the 60-page
booklet was so forbidding that it would often get stashed away and never be
used. The overall purpose of sending them out was lost for the department.
To address the problem, Medius IV designed an electronic medium to
replace the 60-page booklet.

As designers sensitive to multipurposing, we thought ahead. Although the
product would be used as a direct mail piece, it would also serve as a desk-
top reference tool, as it provided pertinent and useful information on a range
of topics. To keep its value foremost in mind, it was designed to be kept on a
potential customer's hard drive. Then, anytime potential customers might
need to answer a question, they could just click on the program, and easily
access the information. In-house lawyers at the firm also saw its value as a
tool for speaker support. Further, Medius IV suggested to the client that the
product could be designed in such a way that it could serve as a kiosk in its
law office lobbies around the country and internationally.

Because of the nature of the client's business, the interface was developed
to reflect a mix of contemporary and classical design. It was consistent with
the old look, and the packaging was designed to integrate easily with the
firm's other marketing materials, so that it would fit easily with already
existing collateral, and would not incur any new costs to package. The final
product was a digital floppy containing all of the information of the 60-page

booklet, which could be sent out and required only 2 megs of space. This floppy was not only a desktop reference, it also had interactivity, animation, and a quiz.

The quiz added levity to the product, yet was designed to test a potential customer's knowledge about intellectual property. The quiz's purpose was to highlight any gaps about the subject of intellectual property and emphasize the value of the law firm's expertise in this area. It also contained valuable information that was put at the fingertips of potential customers and could easily be grasped. Before potential customers met with a lawyer and got deeper into a subject, they could find cursory information about the issue they would be discussing.

This turned out to be a very successful product, and the law firm was able to secure a number of accounts though direct marketing. In addition to direct marketing, it is also used for speaker support and as a desktop reference tool, even for the legal firm's in-house lawyers. Finally, with only slight modification to the interface, the product is now used as a kiosk and is displayed in the lobby of [the law firm's] offices throughout the country.

The product was also designed in view of the future: to be displayed at [the law firm's] Web site. This aspect is currently being developed. Herein lies a valuable lesson: If a designer is able to convince a client to think ahead, and is able to leverage graphics from one medium to another, a lot of money can be saved. This is the reason it is so important for a graphic design firm to understand not only the electronic medium, but also the print medium. A well-rounded, full-service design firm can help its clients better leverage their assets.

Design "On the Fly"

CKS/Interactive ran an integrated marketing campaign that was one of the more effective applications of interactivity and media integration used in the electronic marketplace. It designed a Web site for Clinique, a women's cosmetics company, with all of its products made available for perusal. Through a brief introductory survey, the Web page can be "built on the fly," as the answers to some 10 questions on such things as complexion, skin type, and so forth are entered. The page is instantaneously designed *by the consumers,* based on their input.

Daniel Miessau, CKS/Interactive's director for Digital Multimedia, adds, "They can go in and [the survey will] qualify them and put them into a particular category. There are over 2,000 choices, and we can, through a series of 10 questions, get them down to a particular group of products where maybe they have a hundred choices to make." CKS also created a floppy disk that was mailed out, leveraging the same look and feel, and incorporating a connection to the Web site. This was a very successful integration of direct mail with truly interactive Internet marketing.

One of the important keys for Studio Archetype has been to thoroughly train its own people in how to take full advantage of this new media so that the team is able to maintain a consistency regardless of the type of project they are challenged by. Each member is a respected talent in his or her own right, and the collective and individual ability to think way beyond the box is evident in their work.

The head of marketing services for the Twentieth Century Fox Home Entertainment group came to Studio Archetype to design the Internet portion of a campaign for the final rerelease of the *Star Wars* video. The Studio Archetype team suggested to the clients that, starting six weeks prior to the launch, they update their Web site with something new each week, to reintroduce people to *Star Wars*. Amanda North, identity architect, explains, "Some people hadn't seen it since it was first released in the '70s. We had to excite them about the whole experience and drive them into the stores, so we came up with a new marketing concept to stimulate consumer interest. We integrated our online campaign with the print campaign, so images that we developed for the Web site would be printed along with the URL. It has been very, very successful."

Twentieth Century Fox's plan was to make changes in the site as the featured product changed. One of the questions Fox had to grapple and experiment with was the length of time a particular product out of their video catalog was featured. The promotions require a tremendous amount of memory to run on the Web site, but as long as a product is selling well, Fox didn't want to scale back. The rest of the site was to rotate through the catalog for past decades. This Web site can be viewed online by going to Twentieth Century Fox Home Entertainment at http://www.tcfhe.com.

North commented that one of the more interesting challenges was to work with the client to determine the best way to access the catalog. "We asked them, 'Do you want to select by director, by Academy Award winners, by anything in the '50s? How do you access this information?' And the client said yes to *all* of the options. Given the myriad of choices, we had to figure out how to make the site into something digestible. We needed to determine the key ways to access this site."

The site was designed so that different areas would be "lit up" to let people know that they were accessible. The areas that were depicted but not yet highlighted would serve as enticements so that people would return to see if they had "come to life" yet. This created a sense of anticipation and kept people coming back to see what had changed. It proved to be a very successful strategy, and kept traffic coming steadily even through the release date.

North explained that the Studio Archetype team has developed a number of valuable tricks in designing these sites with heavy graphics. One is that they only reload parts of the graphic when the user moves from page to page. It makes a big difference in speed, which is crucial to keeping people at your site. They also used navigable props and sweepstakes, and provided e-mail so that users could submit stories on how *Star Wars* impacted their lives. According to North, one respondent reported, "I named my first son Luke." They also gave Yoda dolls away that were signed by George Lucas, which North states resulted in something like 13 inquiries a minute!

Consistency

Ian Beavis, Toyota executive vice president of Saatchi & Saatchi, holds a tight rein on designs that have anything to do with this brand. He is adamant about the need for consistency and appropriate integration throughout all media that communicates the Toyota image. He states: "You have to be ruthless and relentless about synergy at every level in terms of tone of voice, visual elements, and adhering to the strategy. Don't let the interactive medium wow you to such a degree that you produce something that totally obscures the message. We often have to reel people back quite a bit. We've had instances where suppliers who don't understand marketing have produced diskettes with really neat little tricky things that totally obscure what we're trying to do. If you let the "propeller heads" run this, it'll be a mess. You have to ask what's in it for me as a consumer and stay focused on that."

The skillful use of consistency in representing brand identity across media can pay off exceptionally well. Moez Rafieetary illustrates this in a campaign Medius IV designed for a major computer monitor company, which included participation in the largest computer show of the year, Comdex, in Las Vegas. He feels strongly about the importance of clean, consistent, and well-integrated design, and believes, "Corporate and product branding have become more and more important as we get deeper and deeper into the digital medium. There is so much to see, and if people cannot at a glance relate the content to its owner, the effectiveness of the marketing message will be lost."

He goes on to describe this challenging and very successful project, explaining that the advertising agency the client was previously using did not have the expertise needed to fully integrate the message from print through to a digital interactive format. Rafieetary relates the approach taken by Medius IV:

> For the design's focus, we used their brand new product, a pivoting monitor. We designed a direct mail piece for the country's largest computer trade show, Comdex. In addition, we designed ads for magazines that reflected the

look and feel of the direct mail piece. Finally, we designed the graphics that were used in the trade show booth using vibrant colors intentionally, to capture attention, create instant recognition, and to show off the high-quality resolution of the ADI monitors we were introducing.

There are thousands of booths at Comdex, and the number of attendees approaches 200,000 people, so designing a booth that stood out from the rest was a primary goal. With the thousands of attendees at the trade show, we didn't want people to have any difficulty locating our client. To that end, we always design what we refer to as a "leverage piece," which is usually the key identity graphic, logo, or illustration that is consistently applied to all of the materials produced, to create a strong brand identity. In this case, the identity illustration was displayed in the booth so that it could be seen from over 50 feet away.

In addition to the direct mail and media advertising campaign, we also designed an interactive puzzle that was featured at the trade show booth, to create greater interest and draw people into the booth to actually use the product. The puzzle capitalized on the product that was featured, namely the pivoting monitor. It was played in one direction with one picture, and when the monitor was pivoted, a different picture would appear from the same image.

People had the opportunity to play the game at the trade show, and winners were awarded various prizes. To heighten interest in the monitor and game, these were both featured in the direct mail piece, which was sent prior to the trade show. In this way, people knew that if they came to the booth, they would walk away with something. There were more than 8,000 attendees at the booth, a lot of whom won prizes. Because not all the people who wished to play the game could not do so at the booth, the puzzle was also made available on a floppy disk, which was given to everyone who visited the booth. In this way, even those who were not able or did not have time to play the game during the course of trade show had the opportunity to play at home.

Rafieetary continues, "The puzzle was also tied into the company's Internet site, which we designed at the same time. The game was designed so that each time the game was played and won, an encrypted number was created that could be posted to the Net site. There continued to be prize drawings, which were also announced at the site. In the first three weeks, nearly 1,000 people visited. Of that group, close to 95 percent had played the game."

This is one example of the successful integration of interactive media into a comprehensive and highly focused campaign. As you can see in Figure 2.7, conceptual and graphic design, from print through digital, was consistent, as was the corporate branding. Because Medius IV had attended the trade show

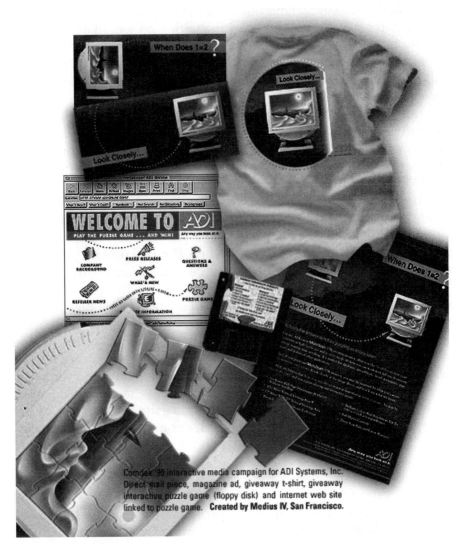

Figure 2.7 Medius IV integrated ADI media campaign. (*Source: Medius IV*)

previously, they knew the type and number of people to expect and what was necessary to make its client stand out from the crowd.

Rafieetary states that, "Although working with a project like this on the Internet was new to us, we knew the kind of experience we wanted to create. Our goal was to provide the potential customer with an incentive to visit the site; that is, to have fun and enjoy themselves and maybe even get something while they were receiving information. This approach, we believed, would provide the opportunity for our client to make their name known in the marketplace." He believes that interactive designers today must seek to create intuitive and fun interfaces, not losing sight of the importance of effectively conveying the marketing message and designing engaging content. "This is a guiding tenet at Medius IV," he concludes.

In deciding on a design for a brand, a very important question to consider is whether the brand has "permission" to "do" the screen. Pete Snell of CKS/Interactive explains that there are some brands that clearly do not have permission to be fun; they just will not work. He explains that there is a "disconnect" there, and that the brand could be compromised by engaging in a game meiliu. However, if a marketer wants to alter the image of a brand, it may be the perfect way to break or expand brand identity. Snell states, ". . . they may use the Web, and they may use the game as a way to change the brand image. The games certainly imply certain attributes and characteristics, and you want to be sure your brand has the permission to use those characteristics."

Clearly, the ADI pivoting monitor not only gave permission for a "playful" approach, but the promotion was a perfect fit; the game demonstrated the product while it was being played. It held an easily identifiable and memorable image in the player's mind through the consistent use of colors associated with the brand and the entertaining and challenging interaction with the puzzle. By using the pivoting monitor in both the portrait and landscape mode at the trade show booth, players were able to experience the advantage of having a choice.

The key question to ask is whether the path that is chosen for both design and implementation is consistent with the current or new direction in which a brand is moving. At some level, *brand essence* is a very intangible entity. It relies on an emotional, visceral response that is highly individual and subjective. Discovering the key that unlocks this kind of response from a large number of people is a real art, backed up in most cases by very tangible research. Implementing a successful campaign requires skillful integration of this "art," with in-depth understanding of the available research, artistic talent, and high-level technological capability. This combination of skills and talent are difficult to find in one company. The trend today is for large advertising agencies to either spin off their own interactive division, often as a separate company, or work with a separate design and production firm such as Studio Archetype, Medius IV, or Red Sky Interactive.

Redefining Roles

Many interactive production houses and design firms are developing relationships with their clients that move beyond the production of media for a few isolated marketing channels and into the realm of more far-reaching campaigns. Some are clearly incapable of making the leap from producer to campaign designer, while others are well prepared to design an integrated presence.

On the other hand, it is important to note that while roles are changing, comprehensive design campaigns are still not the full-service media placement and management campaigns waged by advertising agencies. For the most part, the account executives at the larger ad agencies still feel that the primary relationship with the client belongs with them, and that the smaller design firms are not really equipped to wage a complete, well-rounded campaign. Collaboration and cooperation must increase between the two camps for the benefit of clients requiring comprehensive campaigns. A greater understanding of the assets each brings to the table will only benefit all parties.

Some design and production companies prefer to maintain their autonomy and control of the client relationship. Amanda North of Studio Archetype states, "Although we are not an advertising agency, as we get into the Internet arena, some of these projects are very campaign-oriented, and the distinction begins to blur. We only work as part of a team with traditional ad agencies when we can have direct access to the clients, so we don't lose that necessary channel of communication."

According to Moez Rafieetary of Medius IV, "Most of the time, because we have direct communication with the client, we are asked to create complete campaigns for their projects. This doesn't mean that we are an advertising agency, but we are forced to play that role to some extent. This is particularly the case because of the emergence of new media (specifically, the growth of the Internet). Because of the complexity of some of the projects we work on, we would prefer direct contact with the client, and a lot of traditional ad agencies don't want to allow it. I only remember one occasion in which an ad agency put us in direct contact with the client, and that was at the client's request. As a result, we usually don't work as part of a traditional ad agency's team on a project."

Since clear and immediate communication is such a vital component in a successful design and production process, most firms demand direct contact with the end client. The results of miscommunication and delays are disastrous and costly. Interactive media is a challenge even when all circumstances are ideal. Advertising agencies need to be aware of this sentiment, as it could prove to be a significant obstacle to getting a job done well, on time and on budget.

The Power of Integration

Pete Snell of CKS/Interactive states, "We're seeing more and more companies realize the power of integrating their messages and their branding, their look, and instead of having one firm or one set of designers or one set of copywriters do different messages depending upon the medium, they're seeing the power of having one company be able to prepare all their marketing communications and do that for all the media they use. It's a very strong, growing trend."

Dave Clauson, managing director of True North Technologies, adds:

> . . . agencies have been talking about highly integrated campaigns for years. Most big agencies have fallen flat on their faces in doing it. More midsized and smaller agencies have had better success with integration because they did more of the work for those clients as entities. But, now, in having to strike this balance between one-way and two-way media, it's forcing marketers and their agencies to come to grips with how to make it all work, because the one thing that we know is true is that clients' marketing budgets are not increasing. In fact, they're going the other way. So it behooves clients to ask that question again: "Where can I get the most effectiveness? What should I do and in what order? How am I using the CD-ROM environment, the Web environment, the kiosk environment to complement what I'm doing in the television environment, the print environment, the in-store environment, and so on?

Barry Layne, who has worked as a major account executive at a large full-service agency, describes what the big agencies have to offer: "What a full-service advertising agency brings is brand stewardship . . . a relationship, a reputation, and an ear of senior management. The new media requires that advertising agencies learn some new skills, no doubt about it."

Dave Clauson adds, ". . . what is true about advertising agencies, despite what a lot of digital boutique people would like to have you believe, is that they own the relationship with the client. In many cases they've been caretakers for that client's brand for a long time, and there is a degree of intimacy, trust, and understanding that is created among the best client-agency relationships. That is not about to go away necessarily. What needs to happen is that that relationship needs to be translated or designed for the two-way media."

SIMBA reports that the most significant factor holding Madison Avenue back from fully entering the electronic marketplace is the reluctance by advertising agencies to use the new electronic vehicles. The agencies are not certain how they fit into this picture, as they watch small upstart multimedia companies usurp some of the strategic advertising functions. According to SIMBA's 1995 report on electronic marketing, some businesses think they can break away and go directly to these small multimedia companies, (and avoid the big agency fees). The companies are extending some advertising agency-type duties to many of these interactive production houses as well. SIMBA states:

> *Nearly 30 percent of CEOs in a cross-section of businesses including health care, retailing, publishing, and banking said their agencies weren't prepared for the information superhighway, according to a survey of New York-based Crain Communications. More than 27 percent said they weren't sure if their agencies could handle their interactive needs. . . . Electronic, interactive marketing, by its very nature, allows marketers to communicate directly with their customers. One of its goals should be to help companies establish a two-way dialog with the users of its products. The need for an intermediary, such as an advertising agency is diminished. Nearly half of the 360 CEOs that responded to the Crain Communications survey said they wouldn't need an agency if they could talk directly to customers through interactive media.*

Regrouping

As mentioned previously, one of the ways some of the larger agencies are addressing the interactive arena is by creating either small subsidiary or totally separate companies that act as their interactive production "divisions." This has worked well for Foote, Cone & Belding (FCB), a major agency that established True North (TN) Technologies to handle all of its interactive media needs. TN Technologies also functions as a separate entity with its own clients, and is slated to become a publicly traded company in '96, completely separate from its holding company, True North Communications, (also the holding company for FCB). Dave Clauson describes the formation and positioning of True North (TN) Technologies in relation to Foote, Cone & Belding (FCB):

> *The mission of TN Technologies is to maximize our clients' experience with digital media, in particular to ensure that our clients achieve maximum marketing value from their use of digital media. . . . Foote, Cone & Belding is an advertising agency. It's 120 years old, and it is exceedingly good at serving the needs of clients in traditional one-way based media, whether it be broadcast television, radio, prints, outdoor, any of the one to many media, as we like to describe them here. Foote, Cone & Belding is incredibly good at serving those needs.*

Where TN Technology fits is as a complement to FCB in the area of two-way or digitally driven media; that is, potentially one-to-one or markets of one that are predicated by the presence of a computer and a networked environment, whether it be Internet, a network of kiosks, or a number of computers linked in any number of different ways.

First, taking a look at large agencies, one of the things that our management realized early on is that if you try to create an interactive group within a traditional advertising agency, your likelihood for success would be relatively small. In other words, there have been relatively few examples where in-house groups created for specific opportunities have been successful within enterprises dedicated toward another objective. In other words, we have developed engines here to produce terrifically powerful creative advertising in one-way-oriented media. The minute you try and do something that runs against that grain, your chance for success has been minimized.

So I believe, as does our management, that it is far better to create a resource outside the box, if you will, whose sole function and purpose is to define, create, deploy visually driven media on behalf of clients, and then weave that organization back under the umbrella of the agency in an appropriate way. In other words, I tell people that part of my job is to obsolesce myself in 18 months, that a lot of what I'm doing now will be part of what any good agency will be doing to serve its clients. However, the place to experiment, understand, explore, define, develop the core competencies to deliver in the digital arena may not be within the confines of the traditional agency, per se, not at this point. So one way of differentiating is that we've consciously chosen to create the expertise separate and distinct from the traditional agency, so that the missions of the two are not clouded by the needs of either.

Secondly, it leaves the unit free to make its own acquisitions. In other words, we have acquired RGA, Robert Greenberg Associates, their interactive company, which is one of probably five firms in the world that are at the leading edge of what is technically possible with the use of computers within the confines of the creative experience. And to stay at the leading edge demands a high degree of focus. If you were to take a company like that and put it inside of a traditional agency and manage it with people who have come up from a very different world called "advertising," it [would] probably be a prescription for failure. But within the organizational structure of TN Technologies it's a perfect fit. It is a complementary component to what we can provide a client. And it gives us flexibility to continue to acquire, merge, develop whatever kinds of talent and infrastructure we need to deliver on our mission without having to be necessarily part and parcel of the agency as a whole.

Our mission right now is to serve the needs of FCB clients, per se, but actually it's the needs of TN clients. So you have to remember that includes agencies like Mojo, like Borders Perrin Norrander, like Publicis, a number of agencies that are part of True North Communications. Our existing clients within the confines of True North Communications are the core of our business right now, but we are free to accept assignments from whomever we choose to do so. We are continuing to add people into the TN Technologies group.

CKS is another example of a company that created a separate entity, called CKS/Interactive. Saatchi & Saatchi has successfully kept all of its production in house and has made sure the whole company is well educated and integrated into the electronic marketplace.

Following this model, Ketchum Interactive was created by Ketchum Communications, a full-service agency. Lynn Upshaw, of Upshaw & Associates, formerly of Ketchum Interactive states, "I think Ketchum is attempting to be more of a full-service provider in the sense of the full communications that it offers. Ketchum is able to do that in a more seamless way. And they are also able to get into brand building from a lot of different angles. I talk about brand contact. There are a lot of different places that a brand comes in contact with a prospective customer, and Ketchum tries to manage that more than by just simply saying, 'let's do a television commercial.' They try to take a broader view of that."

On the other hand, some large agencies prefer to work closely with an independent design or production company. Tim Smith of Red Sky Interactive states:

> *If a large, strongly branded company comes to us direct, our first question is, "Who is the agency, and to what extent do you want them involved?" We want them there, because it is the fastest road to understanding the brandedness of the company. They bring to the table materials that the client typically doesn't, because they have a very advertising focus on this product, so they get us there faster.*
>
> *We push, we push real hard. We'll say, "Okay, here's the current brandedness. Can we evolve it? How can we change it? Are we breaking any rules or can we break any rules?" So we'll push the envelope as hard as we can, but it's very helpful when we work with agencies, and we hope that as we evolve into new markets and new providers in these markets that the advertising agencies aren't threatened by production companies like Red Sky, but embrace them and use them as the tools that they really are.*

When communication is direct, clear, and consistent, regardless of the agency, design firm, or combination of the two that may have been used, these qualities are usually reflected in the final product. When communication breaks down, and competition gets in the way of clarity and responsiveness, the final product tends to reflect that as well. The companies that can use this process of regrouping as an asset will be the first to discover the inherent opportunities for innovation and new levels of creativity.

Design

A design that is well thought out, well planned, and well executed will result in a strategic advantage over your competition, and inspire your audience to take action. It is more important than ever to understand all of the subtle and blatant messages implied and communicated in your market presence. The investment you make needs to be an educated and deliberate one, as the financial and identity risks are high.

Tim Smith of Red Sky Interactive explains that he and his colleagues begin by asking their client to justify the use of the media in question from a marketing and business perspective, because, he states, "it absolutely informs how we design the project." In 1995, they won the silver medal in the New Media Invision Competition for a piece called Ready Set Dinner. Their client was Ketchum Public Relations for the National Potato Board.

Smith explains, "It manifested itself ultimately as a direct mail piece with a really nice print campaign that was associated with it, as well as in-store kiosks and a broadcast PR campaign. So there weren't spots done on it but there was some heavy television public relations that went along with the product promotion. The whole product was very heavily branded across nontraditional media, interactive media, and the traditional media. It worked quite well."

April Minnich, marketing director for Red Sky, adds, "So you could basically get this product at point of purchase, through being a part of the National Potato Board Club, as well as finding out about it in the press. Ketchum marketed it to 190 food-related trade magazines through public relations. This was really an example of a cross-platform project."

Red Sky worked collaboratively on the project with Ketchum PR. Smith explained that Joel Hladecek, their creative director, worked on the design of the disk along with Susie Watson, the creative director of Ketchum Advertising's interactive division. The disk was so successful and received so much attention that what had started out almost as an afterthought became a nationally recognized award winner (see Figure 2.8) The impact of a strong design can produce results far beyond the original concept. Innovative, quality design in the realm of new media receives extraordinary attention today, and can add considerably to the visibility of a brand. The audience can instantly grow far beyond the initial target and become recognized as a technological/artistic achievement, adding immeasurable PR value.

Moez Rafieetary from Medius IV explains:

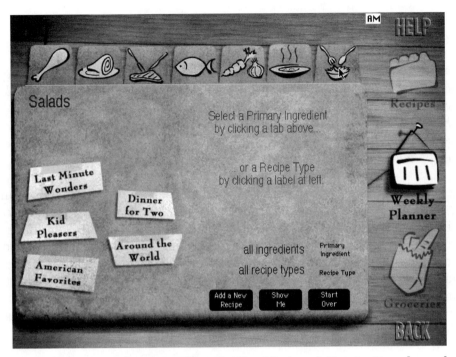

Figure 2.8 Ready, Set, Dinner: The National Potato Board used floppy disk mailers and interactive supermarket kiosks for its first venture into multimedia. (*Source: Red Sky Interactive*)

One of the issues to consider when putting a marketing campaign together is whether the look and feel of the art reflected in the print material is also reflected in the digital medium. These are the types of issues that must be kept in mind when designing for more than one medium. Because of the vast amount of information available, access to content is not necessarily the issue. Rather, it is presenting content coherently that provides the biggest challenge today, especially for designers who are used to working in the more traditional print medium.

When designing for digital media, for example, one is dealing with a small amount of real estate. There is only a small screen, and the amount of information that can be successfully employed in getting the message across is limited. What is the best way to convey the desired message, given these limitations? If the company already has a strong image, we want to take advantage of that. If the client is new to the digital medium, this does not mean they have to forgo a successful, established image. Rather, the message can

*be maintained, branding can remain consistent, and the earlier investment
can be protected.*

*Continuing to use already existing resources also helps maintain consis-
tency in corporate and product branding. Because of the wide range of types of
media, and the number of venues in which they appear, only a consistent look
will help distinguish the client's profile. Through repetition and consistency,
the total sum (the message) becomes larger than the pieces (various media) in
people's minds. So the branding, consistency, and quality that designers make
use of must carry through in the presentation of the marketing message.*

The design process has distinct phases, defined with slight variations by
firms working in the digital production arena. Three processes that will be
mentioned here are employed by expert teams of professionals who have been
experimenting with and honing these approaches in order to achieve the best
possible results when entering into the often treacherous realm of interactive
media design and production. These processes are equally suited to traditional
media production, and the fact that today more projects are completely integrated or linked makes a clearly delineated path mandatory, and this usually is
visible in the quality of the results.

The ASAP Process

The Hypermedia Group, a full service multimedia communications company,
rolled out a very powerful, branded process in 1995 that it calls ASAP, which
stands for Accelerated Specification and Prototyping Process. Ross Gillanders,
VP of Business Development, describes it as follows:

*It is a very structured, facilitated process whereby we meet in intensive daily
sessions for up to two weeks and hammer out all the issues and finally
arrive at an agreed-upon specification. In parallel, we are doing rapid prototyping behind the scenes. At the end of the ASAP, basically there is an
agreement between the client and HMG as to what we want to build. We
have looked at all of the issues concerning audience, technology, best use of
media, and we have mocked it up and prototyped it. Then, ideally, we go
ahead and implement that particular specification, or the client uses it to
put the project out to bid.*

Gillanders explains that the cost for this process depends on the size and
scope of the resources that will be needed. He adds:

*What the process really does is front-load development. So, all the first four
or five phases of a typical development project—which are content develop-*

ment, content acquisition, scripting, storyboarding and first phase of devel-opment—are rolled into ASAP. And what we're doing is real-time prototyp-ing behind the scenes during a swing shift. We have people behind the scenes taking down all the agreed-upon points from each day's session, and they begin working on what this can look like navigationally.

What we do is break it up. We have the client team and Hypermedia Group team meeting one day, and then we have a break where Hypermedia Group is working independently, presenting that first day's results in the next day's session. It's a very focused process whereby we have a lot of whiteboarding going on. We have PowerPoint jockeys that are sitting in real time at computers during the sessions and recording everything into Power-Point, and developing PowerPoint presentations on the fly. We have a data-base jockey who is recording everything into a database that has been talked about . . . to take a look at the end of the day's session.

It's a very facilitator-oriented process that keeps everybody on the beam during the day's session. It's not really new; in fact, in big software develop-ment projects, corporate America has incorporated these kinds of tech-niques for some time, but usually it's over a much longer period of time. In terms of multimedia development, it's fairly unique in our industry. We rolled it out with IBM.

It dawned on us after eight years of developing multimedia solutions that even though clients have spent significant time and money developing a specification, either internally or using outside consultants, they still don't know what they want once into the project. ASAP addresses that real issue.

What Hypermedia is providing, in fact, is a very thorough and potent front-end analysis. The company is then free to either contract with Hypermedia to carry the project through to completion, or not. Often this kind of process can serve as an extermely valuable piece of marketing research that will greatly impact the next step or direction of a product or company. It is an all-around win in that it has still provided a good solid project for Hypermedia within an efficient process and compact time frame, and the client has a tangible result.

Gillanders adds, "Ideally, our business is about building applications and feeding our factory. ASAP also serves to align the client's team with Hyperme-dia group's team in a very intense immediate way. One of the hardest things in running projects is getting decision makers to agree in a timely way to keep everything moving forward. Another impossible challenge is to get them in one place at one time. So we are really forcing the client to make the commitment, saying if this is going to work, it will only work if all of your major decision makers or anybody who really has any say in this project are here for ASAP. ASAP, by the way, is resonating extremely well with our prospects because they have been down the multimedia development road before and know all its pitfalls. So, if they are serious about a project they will make the commitment and arrive at a solution without wasting effort and time."

This process saves money and time for both parties, is an effective relationship builder, and leaves clients feeling very much in charge of their own destiny. Since venturing into this high-tech arena can be very threatening to some CEOs and marketers, a process that is respectful of time, money, and provides a quick and potent educational component is highly desirable. By breaking the steps into bite-size chunks, it also becomes very feasible, and worth the risk. While most companies go through this kind of process when developing the concept and preproduction "prototype," few have taken the time to spell it out as concisely or hone the art of implementing it.

The Archetype Process

Another process, developed by Studio Archetype, called The Archetype Process, is defined as follows:

As "Identity and Information Architects," our work often comprises corporate identity and branding projects executed across media types. Because of the often complex nature of our work, we have developed the Archetype Process in order to accurately define and execute our client projects.

This process is appropriate whether a specific project is print or new media in its execution. The Archetype Process is particularly relevant for complex projects that start with a general concept and can only be refined as the project proceeds. It also provides a vehicle for explaining the role of each individual as he or she is involved in different stages of the project.

The Archetype Process comprises four steps: define, architect, design, and implement. This segmentation is based on the natural division of information and labor that occur within most projects.

Information Architecture Methodology

Seeking to create good products and smooth procedures, Medius IV created and trademarked its own Information Architecture Methodology to help clients understand what it takes to make an outstanding interactive product. By using this methodology, Medius IV says that it has been able to eliminate a lot of wasted time and streamline coordination, thus lessening the overall difficulty of the process for both the company and the client. The Medius IV method addresses all steps of the production process.

Outlined on page 66 are Medius IV's internal steps for product development. Note that not all steps are applicable to every project.

Phase 1: Define In the Definition Phase we gather the information required to architect, design and implement the project. This information provides us with a tool to align expectations between our company and our clients. In general we will not analyze, or execute against, this information during this phase. On most projects we will require that this information either be provided or that we establish a research program through which we can gather the information.

During This Phase We Will:
1. Determine the objectives of the project: What do our clients want to accomplish?
2. Identify the project content: What do they want to sell, promote, or provide?
3. Understand the competitive scenario: Who are they, or will they be, competing with?
4. Establish the demographic profile of their customers: Who are they selling to?
5. Define desired functionality types: What kinds of features do they want (i.e. chat rooms, commerce)?
6. Identify the execution medium (or media): Is it a packaging system, a Web site, an MSN site, or other?
7. Explore the technology issues (on interactive projects): What browsers or operating systems do they want to support?
8. Determine the clients' time line: When do they want it and what is driving that date?
9. Determine the clients' budget: How much do they want to pay and how did they determine that budget?

We may receive this information in a written RFP, it may be gathered through one or more meetings with the client, or we may need to conduct extensive interviews and perform research to collect this information. Therefore, the time and budget required for this phase may vary broadly.

Deliverables from This Phase Could Include:
A proposal to architect and/or design and/or implement the project

Interview questions or discussion guides as required to conduct research or interviews

A summary of the information collected

Phase 2: Architect In the Architecture Phase we will execute against the information gathered in Phase 1. We will analyze, prioritize, categorize, and interpret

Continued

the information. Phase 2 provides the framework on which the look and feel will be built in the Design Phase.

The Architecture Phase can be as straightforward as a single brainstorming meeting to determine the hierarchy of information on the front panel of a package or an elaborate six-week mapping exercise for a large Web site. In either case, Phase 2 should provide a concise analysis of the content and a complete mapping of the information.

During This Phase We Will:

1. Assess the content:

    Define the key messages.
    Define the information types and functionality.
    Define logical relationships.
    Define links between information types.

2. Perform brainstorming and concepting.
3. Develop names or positioning platforms.
4. Provide marketing strategy consultation, including media planning.
5. Perform any required research and development related to advanced technologies.
6. Test the functionality of the information architecture and navigation.
7. Identify specialized resources required to complete the project.

Deliverables from This Phase Could Include:

A proposal and time line to design and/or implement the project

A technology platform agreement

A proposal for the creation of specialized resources such as custom programming or material prototyping

Positioning statements, naming conventions, and/or marketing plans

Maps, thumbnails, storyboards, or roughs as required to communicate the architecture

Phase 3: Design   In the Design Phase, we create the look and feel for our projects. This is not to say that this is the only phase in which we design—in Phase 2 we might brainstorm concepts and produce names and positioning platforms as well as maps and storyboards, and in Phase 4 we may also produce design variations that apply across media types—but Phase 3 is when we execute the creative that gives the project its personality. We create visual metaphors that support and enhance the architecture of the information.

Continued

During This Phase We Will:
1. Create the look and feel for the project that creates or supports the brand identity.
2. Create or supervise the creation of illustration, photography, and/or writing.
3. Perform additional customer testing if required.

Deliverables from This Phase Could Include:

A proposal to implement the project

Photographs, illustrations, animations, and copywriting

A proposal to create or supervise the creation of illustration, photography, and/or writing

Comps or prototypes

Analysis of customer research

Phase 4: Implement   In Phase 4 we apply the creative directions from Phases 1, 2, and 3. This should not be considered strictly "the production phase" even though we will produce mechanicals, HTML code, and so on. Rather, this is when we execute the architecture and look and feel across single or multiple platforms, browsers, and media types. We combine production and creative processes in this phase to the extent necessary to execute the Phase 3 design across large packaging systems, Web sites for multiple browsers and so on.

During This Phase We Will:
1. Format and implement the design from Phase 3.
2. Extend the system across multiple components or platforms.
3. Beta test our work.
4. Press check our work.
5. Proofread our work.

Deliverables from This Phase Could Include:

Styles guides

Mechanical files

HTML templates

Operational Web sites

Photographs, illustrations, animations, and copywriting (as required to extend the project)

A proposal for printing, manufacturing, or producing variations on the design

A. Preproduction

1. Write down all the ideas, organizing them into a proposal, which is later refined and revised.

2. Assemble everyone on the project in a think-tank atmosphere to analyze the proposal:

    a. Who is the target audience? Does the complexity of the presentation fit the intended audience?

    b. What stands out as the best features? Retain these aspects.

    c. What is less successful? Set those aspects aside.

    d. Brainstorm other possibilities. Keep the best; set the rest aside.

    e. Weave it all into a cohesive whole.

3. Set it aside for a few days.

4. With a fresh perspective, repeat step 2.

5. Think Tank: Analyze the proposal.

    a. Review media integration and navigation.

    b. Brainstorm other possibilities. Keep the best; set the rest aside.

    c. Weave it all into a cohesive whole.

    d. Will it work for the target audience?

6. Think Tank: Break down the presentation.

    a. What are the lowest common-denominator target platforms?

    b. Break the presentation into as many discrete parts as possible. Plan transitions.

    c. Determine where to use animation, video, still photos, and/or drawings.

    d. Determine where to use voice, music, and/or sound effects (including atmospheric sounds).

    e. Plan for required text.

    f. Allocate space on the CD (or other storage device) for animations, movies, sounds, control software, and contingency slack space.

    g. Identify anything that could pose problems in development or play. Determine how these can be solved.

B. Production (Complete on section-by-section basis.)

1. Graphics

    a. Select color palettes. If needed, select typefaces.

    b. Create sketches and storyboards as needed.

    c. Scan in all final sketches, photos, and so on.

    d. Colorize.

  2. Programming

    a. Write handlers for navigation, controls, and transitions.

    b. Port code as needed.

    c. Write installer software as needed.

    d. Comment well; plan for upgrades and/or free versions from bugs.

  3. Text-write all needed text. Revise and condense, retaining the idea that less is better.

  4. Video

    a. Cast all video parts.

    b. Assemble production team.

    c. Shoot all the footage needed.

    d. Edit. (Note: This step and the next may be interchanged.)

    e. Digitize all final video into digital movies.

    f. Adjust color and sharpness as needed.

    g. Do the movies work? Is everything visible that needs to be?

    h. Compress all digital movies.

  5. Sound

    a. Complete sound design for target platforms, planning use of bandwidths.

    b. Write, record, and digitize music.

    c. Create sound effects and atmospheric sounds. Record and digitize.

    d. Cast all spoken parts, including any narration. Record and digitize.

    e. Play designed sounds together. Is everything intelligible?

    f. Compress all sounds.

    g. Assemble each part as it is finished into the final framework.

    h. Incorporate transitional images and/or sounds. Create workarounds for any problems.

C. Postproduction

  1. Assemble everything, putting all files needed for the presentation onto one hard drive. Test to confirm that nothing is missing by running on virgin systems.

2. Test!

   a. Does everything work? Do all controls respond correctly?

   b. Does it flow smoothly? Is navigation intuitive? Test connections between all locations.

   c. Is the interface intuitive and easy to use?

   d. How does the presentation look? Is it rich and inviting?

3. Assemble distribution and mastering: Put all files needed for the presentation onto a single hard drive. Test to ensure that nothing is missing. Adjust finder windows as needed. Set all bits correctly.

These three examples of processes employed by the Hypermedia Group, Studio Archetype, and Medius IV provide a good overview of the way design firms approach multimedia projects. While they vary, they also have many basic components in common. All contain essential elements that need to be a part of the design, development, and implementation process.

Defining the Project

The uninitiated have one great miscalculation in common when they venture into the world of "multimedia." They will invariably use the only gauge with which they are familiar: the print world. When a change needs to be made in print, the cost is comparatively low and can be taken care of a lot closer to the deadline than with interactive or animated media. In contrast, changing one element in electronic media, even something as simple as a color, impacts every other aspect, and is not only costly in dollars, but in time.

Therefore, the first phase of any project must include an educational process that adequately explains what is involved, both time- and dollarwise, in making changes at each juncture of the project. This should be spelled out in writing and agreed to up front, or both parties will find themselves at an unnecessary disadvantage when inevitable changes need to be made. An educated client can have more realistic expectations, and will appreciate the clear communication of charges from the outset. The design firm must have this safeguard in place, or it runs the risk of doing the job several times over for the originally agreed-upon price, (all too common), or worse, not being able to deliver on time or anywhere close to the original budget. Better that the "sticker shock" occurs at the beginning. Relationship is everything in business, and bridges are better crossed than burned!

Amanda North explains that a lot of the people who approach Studio Archetype say, "I need a corporate Web site *next month!* I've got a major sales meeting, and I need it up!" They really don't know what it requires. North explains, "They don't know what kind of budget is needed or understand the technical limitations of the Internet. They also don't know what it can accomplish. One of our challenges has been to reign back those expectations and say, 'This is what we think you can do at this point in time. Over the next 12 months, here are the additional capabilities that are going to come online.' We often play the role of technologist. We have people here whose titles are R&D programmer, HTML programmer, executive producer, and information designer. These are not roles that you would have seen in our firm or any company a number of years ago."

Another area that requires clear definition and usually some education is platform considerations. North has a lot of clients come to Studio Archetype who will have heard about a hot new technology like Java or Shockwave and want the "coolest" Web site out there. She will then stop them and ask who their target audience is and what kind of equipment they have, and when they respond with 14.4 modems and a basic 386 or 286 machine, North says, "The fact of the matter is that they won't be able to access those features of the site [with that equipment], and it will give your users no benefit whatsoever, perhaps even frustrate them. We have to work from a lowest common denominator approach.

"On the other hand," North adds, "they may say, 'It's a corporate customer and everyone has a T1 line coming into the building, so we can use everything we've got for this project.' But that's an important thing to determine in the beginning."

North gives another example of a project in which she and her colleagues were highly successful in selecting the right mix of media to accomplish their goals. With Herman Miller," North explains:

> we produced a CD-ROM when they were introducing their Aeron chair last year ('95). This was a chair they spent five years developing. There were three prototypes of this chair in the world, and they were very expensive and very heavy, so they could not be shipped around. As Herman Miller was getting ready to launch, they wanted to introduce this new chair to their sales force and their distributors in various locations.
>
> First of all they wanted us to come up with something that captured the expression of the Aeron chair. We came up with something that is a beautiful video piece that didn't actually even show the chair; it just talked about the essence of how you feel when you're sitting in it. We used visuals of a pear and other symbolic things to convey a feeling or sensation.

What Aeron and Studio Archetype were actually selling was an experience, something that would speak to the senses, the emotions. Since most purchase decisions are based on these factors, this was a very clever and appropriate "soft-sell" approach, particularly well suited to the psychographics of the target audience. The video portrays images suggesting comfort, ease of movement, individuality, flexibility, diversity, inspiration, and sensuousness. By simply suggesting the experiences the buyer would have in this chair, room was left for the viewer to come up with his or her own "logical" reasons for needing the chair and deserving to own it. When messages are presented rather than pushed at a consumer, a pull effect results, drawing the consumer into the experience, and into actively creating reasons for wanting more.

Studio Archetype ingeniously created a total presentation package that not only catered to consumers on a sensate level, but simultaneously provided information about the technology of this chair in various degrees of detail. North explains:

> Without shipping the Aeron chair around, they needed to get some very technical information conveyed, so we did this interesting 3D animation and took approximately 16,000 digital images of the chair swiveling around (Figure 2.9a). We also developed the actual device that manipulated the chair into all of these different angles. The CD, given to the sales force for use on their portable computers in the field, illustrates various ways to get into the chair, and allows the viewer to examine the working parts from every possible angle. The viewer can look at the nuts and the bolts, zoom in and zoom out, and look at it just as if the physical product were present.

Mark Crumpacker, the CEO of Studio Archetype, adds, "The CD is done in five languages (Figure 2.9b). The user can select a voice-over option or menu commands written in French, German, English, the Queen's English, and Spanish. The interface is designed to have two levels to it. One is an expert level in which the user can navigate anywhere at any time, and the second is a prompted level, which will take an inexperienced user through a predetermined course."

This was an exceptionally challenging and successful campaign, and is a good example of a design firm truly understanding the conceptual goals of its client. The designers were able to integrate and leverage the significant benefits of electronic media, and save their clients not only a great deal of money, but actually solve a critical sales obstacle.

Dave Clauson, from True North Technologies, breaks his clients down into three basic categories. The first are clients who knows very little about interactive multimedia and want to know more about its possibilities. They usually need definitions of the different media before they can even begin considering the options. The next level are clients who have some knowledge about the dif-

Figure 2.9a and 2.9b Aeron Chair campaign. (*Source: Studio Archetype*)

ferent media, and are ready to move forward in a particular direction. The third level are those already actively involved in electronic media either as an integral part of their marketing mix or as an activity they are interested in expanding. They may already be doing online marketing or have CD-ROM products in distribution. True North will come in at any of these three levels and work with these clients to develop a very clear definition of a project.

Each level requires a very different type of approach, and understanding this on the part of the marketer as well as the design team is important. Some clients feel intimidated by the technology and overwhelmed by the process, and it is better that they ask too many questions than not enough. That goes for the design team, too. Anyone going into one of these projects with his or her eyes half closed is likely to come out with them forced wide open by the results!

Tim Smith, from Red Sky, emphasizes the need to really get to know the essence and value system of a company for which you will be designing branded media. Smith relates, "One of the first things we'll ask for in preproduction is an immersion in the client's current marketing communication, and that ranges from a couple of brochures, which may be all they've got, to a project like Lands' End which flew April and myself to the middle of Wisconsin. You don't work for Lands' End without trudging out into the snow and becoming fully immersed in their company. They integrate you into it right away, which is great, because then you live and breathe Lands' End, and get very excited about what they do. We've done it recently for a big project we're on now; we've had a couple of trips up to the company where we were preached and lectured at and toured." This kind of experience can then be translated into a powerful media communication campaign through the talent and technology brought to the table by Red Sky.

At the same time, Pete Snell of CKS/Interactive has found the education process essential in steering their clients into using the most appropriate medium for their audience rather than the one they find most exciting in the moment. He explains:

> We don't have a bias toward any medium. We will listen to what the client's objectives are and try to understand them, and we will recommend a medium for them.
>
> We had a cellular phone company come to us that only had coverage in a couple areas of the United States and wanted to go on the Web. "We want to just target these two areas of the United States." CKS said, "You really don't want to do that on the Web. There are much better ways to spend your money than creating a Web site if you truly only want to just target the people in your coverage area." They said, "Yeah, we don't want to interest people who aren't in our service area. There's nothing we can help them with."

CKS told them, "You shouldn't do a Web site. You should take your money and spend it elsewhere. Direct mail, for example."

We listen to what the clients' objectives are and what they're trying to accomplish, and we come back with a plan. Usually that plan involves multiple media, but we don't have any biases for one over another. Sometimes TV is appropriate, sometimes it's not; sometimes the Web is appropriate, sometimes it's not. It's common knowledge these days if you're raising a child, you gotta make sure that child is PC-literate. That's going to be an important asset for his/her success going forward. The same thing is true to a marketer. You need to learn about the power of interactive marketing or it's going to blow past you. You're going to limit your ability to add value to your corporation if you really don't understand the power of this medium.

Daniel Miessau, CKS/Interactive's director for digital multimedia, emphasizes how essential it is to take the time to have a clear and well-defined objective. He states, "We go back to marketing basics 101. We really want a clear and defined objective; we want to understand [our clients'] audience, number one, and then it's our responsibility to really develop the identity that would be uniform across all of the different medium, and we try to get a feel from the company of what the tone would be. So where we start is really understanding the objective, knowing the audience, and then getting a flavor or tone from a client."

But he adds that the biggest issue that comes up is around the objectives. "When we talk to clients and they don't have clear objectives, then we can't go anywhere except make sure that we redefine them and get sign-off from the client. Not only do they need to have clear objectives, but everybody in the company needs to be using the same guidelines. So it's ensuring that the clients have clear objectives; they usually know their audience, but the objectives sometimes get out of hand. And then internally make sure everybody's buying into those objectives. That's probably the biggest pitfall."

The Gartner Group emphasizes that the simple translation of collateral from paper to electronic format is nothing more than "brochureware," and offers the following guidelines for creating effective electronic advertising:

- *Keep it fresh:* This will make a customer want to return to an enterprise's electronic advertising (e.g., a Web page or CD-ROM). Nothing kills interest faster than simply transferring a paper brochure into electronic format. Mix up the look. Create new graphics. Entice the customer to take the time to see what has changed. Some of our clients even use software that does nothing but rearrange the elements periodically.

- *Make it interactive:* The greatest advantage of interactive advertising is that it is, indeed, interactive. Customers may throw away a brochure or skip an electronic page that has only static information, but they will return to media with which they can interact, if the interaction is interesting. Games, contests, and surveys are among the interactive hooks that can be used. One U.S. bank has a Web home page that lets viewers build their own bank based on their preferences, and they can answer product questions for prizes. Another client has an ongoing mystery that must be solved, with clues given progressively over time and at random intervals. While some marketing professionals consider these ideas gimmicks, these "gimmicks" are generating a sustained interest among customers.

- *Limit the number of graphics:* Many marketing departments go overboard on graphics for Web pages. Because of bandwidth limitations, this causes agonizingly slow response times, leading many consumers to avoid the enterprise's advertising. Even in other media, such as kiosks, a heavy reliance on graphics can obscure the marketing message. Designers must understand when graphics are appropriate and, more important, when they are not. Graphics are appropriate for creating interest and making the page stand out. They are inappropriate for conveying important information.

- *Develop distinct paths based on interest:* Paper-based collateral is linear—the reader begins at the beginning and ends at the end. Interactive media are free-form, which is both a disadvantage and an advantage. The disadvantage is that it is difficult to control and predict the order in which consumers will view the information. The advantage is that the viewer can be led to particular information areas based on interest or answers to questions. This enables persuasive marketing material to be used if the consumer resists some part of the message. As a result, the marketing message is much more targeted to the needs of the individual consumer.

- *Use more information, but make it look like less:* Another value of using an interactive medium is that it can contain huge amounts of information (e.g., some Web pages can link to hundreds of support pages). If wisely used, this wealth of information will make the medium more powerful than a small printed brochure. But customers can be overwhelmed, so use care in hiding the depth of the information. Carefully give data to the customer in response to his or her requests.

- *Have each part serve a purpose:* Marketing with interactive media allows for more distinct pieces of information (e.g., pages on a Web site), but each piece must be there for a reason. Simply filling a CD-ROM or building a huge Web site accomplishes nothing. Choose each page of information carefully, and make the whole message work together. Digitizing a paper brochure and placing it on the Internet is not interactive marketing. Enterprises now have the power of print, photography, movies, and interaction in one set of marketing devices. As enterprises work to understand the technology, they need to work to understand the tactics and strategies of the media.

Because many enterprises will not understand these strategies, 60 percent of interactive marketing efforts will be considered failures by the year 2000 (0.8 probability). In addition, at least 75 percent of Web sites will undergo a major revamping within 12 months of their launch (0.8 probability), due in large part to enterprises' failure to use electronic collateral effectively. Enterprises that understand the differences between paper-based and electronic collateral can avoid these failures.

Budget Considerations

What is key in making use of assets previously created for a client's printed materials is the ability to skillfully incorporate workable aspects into the digital format, adding a fresh look, while still making good use of the what has already been created. Moez Rafieetary of Medius IV brings a wealth of expertise to making the transition from print to digital media. In regards to the ADI project mentioned previously, he states:

> *One advantage to the client of translating print to digital media was that by consolidating all these ideas, the production costs went down dramatically. Utilizing the graphics created for print in the digital medium allowed us to leverage the client's budget. This is the advantage of thinking ahead and developing all of the various media at the same time. However, this is the ideal situation. It doesn't often happen like that, but if the designer is dealing with an experienced company with an identifiable look that already has value with the target market, this impact does not have to be sacrificed.*
>
> *Furthermore, clients who are knowledgeable can take those print and graphic resources already in their possession and enlarge on their investment. Capitalizing on the digital medium does not mean that companies*

*need to re-create everything. Instead, a client can take existing resources to
a new medium and create a fresh look without a huge infusion of capital.*

Very often, a client will not have considered the cost of assets needed to
design an interactive marketing product. Original material is frequently much
less expensive than obtaining rights to proprietary images, especially when
they will be broadcast over a range of electronic venues.

In addressing overall budget for a project, most design firms try to remain
flexible. There can often be much more equity in a project than direct or immediate financial benefit. Sometimes a company will add a prestigious name to
your portfolio, and other times it may be a great PR, community relations
opportunity. There obviously needs to be a balance between accepting jobs that
do not contribute to paying the rent and those that keep the doors open.

When approached with the question of accepting clients based on budget,
Studio Archetype's CEO Mark Crumpacker replied, "We evaluate all of our
incoming business propositions based on a number of criteria, one of which is
whether or not there is a budget for a project. If people come to us and say,
'We've got $10,000 and we want a Web site,' we can pretty much say, 'Unless it's
a really compelling one-page Web site, it's probably not going to fit the mix.' "

Amanda North chief identity architect at the firm adds:

> *An ongoing client of ours from the packaging world came to us with their
> corporate Web site, and they had a friend who had a friend who had a
> $5,000 site, so that was the cost that this person had in mind. We sat down
> and said, "You could do that, and here's what you probably would get. Now,
> what are you trying to accomplish?"*
>
> *I guess if we had to choose one kind of client or project we tend to look for
> it's one in which there is a major new thrust or new positioning, and we are
> requested to capture the essence of what that is and communicate it. I think
> each of us at Studio Archetype has some areas that interest us more than
> others, but the one thing that we all converge on is the excitement in indi-
> cating a new direction or a new expression of something in the marketplace.*
>
> *We would also be interested in working with a very small company that
> had a novel or new idea, or a mainstream company that's doing something
> radically different. We've done a lot of work for Motorola and Kodak, divi-
> sions that represented major new business thrusts for those companies, and
> addressed how that reflected back on the parent corporation. We asked
> questions such as, "Do they have the same identity or a different identity?
> How do you position them vis-à-vis each other?" That was fascinating from
> a strategic standpoint.*

Architecture

Daniel Miessau's group at CKS/Interactive specializes in what they call "cognitive architecture." He, too, feels strongly that people cannot just transfer their printed collateral directly to an electronic marketing format. He states:

> They have to be completely redesigned. So we have a group within our group that specializes in what we call cognitive architecture—or user experience. It's the human interaction with information. We have to completely redesign those elements and make them work interactively. It's human interaction, so basically there are pieces of information on a computer screen, and when you click on that information you go somewhere.
>
> What you want to be able to do is, number one, make it easy for people to find a path. They click on a button; and then you'll get down three or four levels in the interactive structure, and you'll want to have a way for someone to easily navigate throughout the information. And there has to be somewhere to go. Once they get down five or six levels, a lot of people don't realize where to go from there. You can't just end the sequence because you will lose that momentum. You want to be able to go to the next section easily. So it's defining the levels of the paths.

Miessau explains that it is important to provide information in a specific pattern, and that even though it's interactive, there's still a message that has to be communicated, "so you want to make sure that the message is communicated quite effectively and that people start becoming more and more engaged and get more information out of it, rather than feeling trapped so that they just escape. Because that's what'll happen. If they get down four or five levels and they realize it's harder and harder to move around, they'll just escape."

Studio Archetype's CEO Mark Crumpacker shares that philosophy in regards to the creative process. He states:

> There are an infinite number of appropriate solutions to any creative challenge. We believe that defining the technical and architectural parameters of the project in advance frees up our designers to explore whatever they want, and we hire the kind of people who are excellent creatives in and of their own right.
>
> We lay the groundwork and provide the infrastructure and parameters for individual projects so that our designers are able to meet the objectives properly. A lot of Amanda's [North] job is to help the clients figure out what their objectives are, communicate those objectives to the team; and, once

those objectives have been established, implement the Archetype Process, outlined previously.

Once the designers get the project, a lot of those questions have been answered, so they're unencumbered by issues such as technology platform. They are free to focus on the design, and we believe that gives them more creative room to explore. They're not worried about how to make it work; somebody else is doing that. They're worried about how to communicate the client's objectives through something that's really fresh and innovative.

North goes on to explain that technological constraints alone make it unwise to just throw a design made for the print medium directly onto a digital format. Studio Archetype has come up with some very useful tricks to increase access speeds and download times, such as using flat colors and creating unique ways to load an image only once, and add or repopulate with little bits of that image when moving to a new screen. Concerning navigation, North adds:

We found that people were very frustrated by going into Web sites and getting lost. So we spend a tremendous amount of time mapping the information, understanding the navigational approach, letting people know at any given time where they are in the site. To express a brand using interactive media, ease of use is as important as the look and feel.

In fact, what we do is map out the content without any look and feel, and then do a lot of user testing. We test how easy it is to go from one part to another. We're actively involved in some very robust shopping sites. We mentioned QVC. We're also working with Time Warner on Dreamshop, which they're totally refreshing. They had to understand that there were going to be two types of usage on this site. There will be the power shoppers who drill down and know instantaneously what they want, and we've got to be able to get them to that exact detail as fast as possible. There will be browsers also who just want to rummage around. We have to be able to have both kinds of experiences there for the user.

Another important variable in designing and architecting for clients is the international nature of doing business today, especially if you are planning to do business on the Internet. Crumpacker gives a good example of some of the things to think about. He describes their client, AMP, as a large company in Pennsylvania that makes the connectors on circuit boards and other kinds of connectors. He adds, "We did their Web site for them in several languages (Figure 2.10). When you're doing Web sites, most of the graphics are done in static form, which means that you can't change the language on the icons without redoing the whole image map."

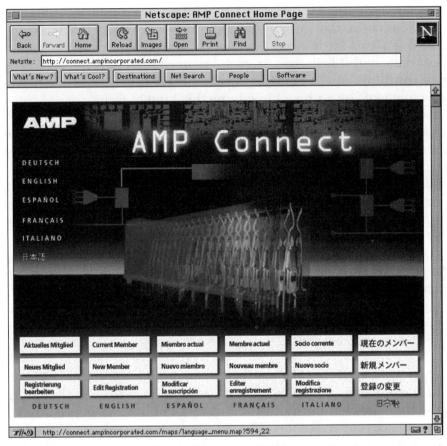

Figure 2.10   AMP Connect home page. (*Source: Studio Archetype*)

He goes on to explain that it is necessary to completely rework and often redesign the graphics due to the new font size and look, and the way it relates to the other visual elements. When these considerations are a part of the original architectural design, they can be creatively planned for and integrated smoothly.

Another very important area of consideration is the translation of colors and images in different cultures. Yellow in some Asian countries conveys anger, while in others it is considered very positive and will increase sales of products that incorporate it into their packaging. In Germany, forest green is a highly recommended color for successful products, and royal blue should be used in targeting the British consumer.

There are many books written about the translation of certain colors and images into various cultures, and it is very important to be aware of this information when designing for the global and online marketplace. Although North America dominates the online shopping audience today, this is changing almost as quickly as the Internet has changed the commerce landscape over the past few years, and it behooves anyone involved on any level—marketer, producer, or consumer—to be considering all of these issues now.

North comments on a project involving this kind of issue,

> *We were doing a project for one of the world's largest publishing companies, and one of their constraints was that its personality in the United States was very different from what it had deliberately tried to project in other countries.*
>
> *In addition, within the various publications that the company offers, there are different rules concerning advertising, and this presents interesting conceptual considerations. Some of the company's publications allowed tobacco and alcohol advertising, while others did not, so we had to address this issue on the company Web site where it's all accessible. We needed to come up with an approach that was seamless, and determine if we should design some areas that were closed off to that kind of advertising. Whether it's international or not, that has been an interesting philosophical dilemma for companies to deal with.*

It is clear that the impact of global access on design is profound. Whether you are producing media or paying someone else to do it for you, becoming well informed and educated in the cultural nuances of both your primary and secondary audiences can make the difference in your success or failure. Messages are delivered so quickly and so broadly that it is well worth the added time and preparation needed to do it "right."

Database Mining

The educated and strategic use of database information to assist in designing your presence will give you a measurable advantage in today's marketplace. Interactivity allows consumers to speak directly to the advertiser, give important feedback on how a brand is coming across, on what else they might need to get them closer to a purchasing decision. Information is the currency of today's economy, and those who know how to get it and manage it can make decisions with greater accuracy, and the information can become the company's most valuable asset.

The Gartner Group emphasizes that this consumer-driven database is perhaps interactivity's greatest contribution to marketing. They state that as each audience segment is identified, new media must be matched to the "demographics, psychographics, lifestyles, and buying patterns of that segment. In a sense, each marketing vehicle is for a segment. Because the traditional segmentation schemes cannot accommodate the complexity of the new marketing imperative, enterprises must use *database mining,* advanced data visualization and complex statistical analysis; by doing so, enterprises can have many more segments than in the past. More important, they can devise strategies and tactics for marketing to each segment.

According to the 1996 Gartner report, "Detailed transaction databases generate opportunities for behavior-modifying offers that can be used in a long-term customer retention or customer acquisition strategy. The lifetime profitability of a customer also enters the equation, enabling the use of short-term, loss-generating promotions to retain long-term profitable relationships. The key becomes one of talking to individual customers about what they really care about, and in a way that they appreciate and is appropriate to their lifestyle. This type of marketing requires extremely sophisticated marketing databases and modeling capability."

By monitoring consumer preferences, technology-enabled promotions, such as point-of-purchase coupons, can be integrated into the overall marketing strategy. Gartner refers to this as "just in time" marketing, because the consumer is marketed to at the point of making a purchasing decision. Another significant use of these "business intelligence systems," according to Gartner, is the ability to factor in the effects of competitive actions on a real-time basis. Use of these systems will make it possible to readily shift tactics, change pricing, launch defensive or offensive efforts. All of this will be impacted by the flexibility of a company's graphical presence in real-time media such as the online environment.

In addition, the Gartner report states, "Pricing will also incorporate concepts of lifetime value, letting customers worth more in a long-term relationship receive preferential pricing. This real-time interactivity will stress the abilities of most marketing departments' pricing mechanisms. In some cases, this may necessitate the creation of intelligent pricing systems tied in real time to the marketing database."

According to the Gartner Group, several studies indicate that it costs between 4 and 10 times as much to acquire a profitable customer as it does to retain an existing one. This information has resulted in a shift of focus from previous tactics aimed exclusively at acquiring new customers to relationship building in order to retain and extend existing relationships. The focus has moved from mass marketing to mass-micromarketing, and to the perceived value by individual customers every time they contact the brand as what builds a strong long-term relationship. The job of relationship building, therefore, has moved marketing out of the realm of the outer presentation and into the inner workings of an entire business entity. If service cannot back up image, the relationship is damaged or destroyed. This has always been true, but the impact has never been on so great a scale before. Therefore, when designing an identity for a company, all points of contact must be considered. Gartner illustrates this approach to relationship marketing in Figure 2.11.

The Gartner report predicts that by the year 2000:

> "Customized products, new distribution and communications channels, and multiple pricing options will drive 70 percent of enterprises to reengineer and automate their marketing process. Historically, marketing has been managed by focusing on products and their associated metrics (e.g., market share, product performance, and penetration). Today, increasingly customized products and services, new distribution and communications chan-

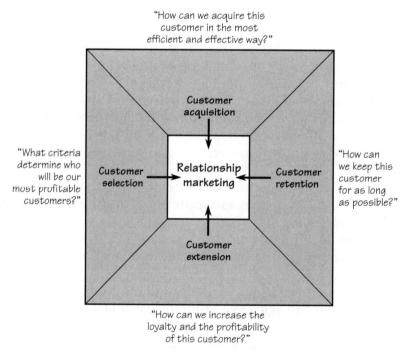

Figure 2.11   This business model calls for enterprises to differentiate themselves by consistently providing superior service at every point of contact with the customer. (*Source: Gartner Group*)

nels, and multiple pricing options are making the marketing process dramatically more complex and difficult to manage.

Traditional product-oriented marketing management will not be able to scale up to handle this vastly more complex and information-intensive environment. Already, traditional metrics are proving inadequate to measure marketing activities accurately across multiple product categories, diverse placement channels, and constantly changing price points. New fact-based metrics will let enterprises dynamically allocate marketing resources to those activities with the best ROI. Technology and automation will be key in managing these new marketing processes. However, the vast amount of detailed data that must be collected and analyzed to make effective decisions in this environment will task information systems.

Figure 2.12 illustrates the movement from a market-centric to a customer-centric marketplace.

As the use of media evolves, it is helpful to stay aware of all of the options as well as the drivers of change that are influencing the greater use of electronic vehicles. Table 2.1, provided by Gartner, gives a cursory overview of this movement.

True North Technologies, the parent and interactive company for Foote, Cone & Belding, provides an innovative service to its clients while supporting its own market research and design needs. It has integrated a highly sophisticated database with customized software that makes it possible to access and digitize a variety of media, edit it online, and transfer or download it anywhere in the world where a compatible system has been installed. True North is continuously conducting targeted market research activities and entering the results into this database. This information may include focus group findings, perti-

TABLE 2.1 The Evolution of Media

Media	Evolution	Drivers
Retail	Kiosks and Home Shopping	Immediate Service
Print Magazines	Electronic and Online Magazines	More Interaction
Print Newspapers	Online News and Advertising	Customer-Driven
Direct Mail	E-mail	Individualized
Print Catalogs	Electronic Catalogs	Improved Access
TV	Home PCs	Convenience
Cable	Interactive TV	Greater Choice
Radio	PDAs	
Telephone	Telephone	

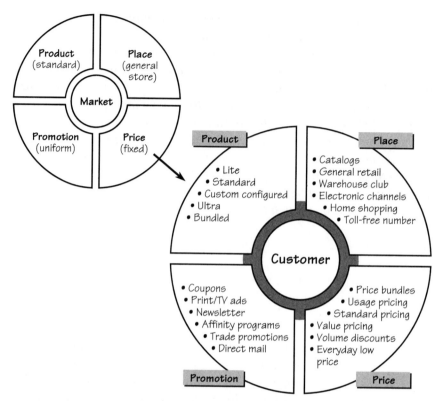

Figure 2.12 Movement from a market-centric to a customer-centric environment. (*Source: Gartner Group*)

nent articles from online news services and print publications, commercials from television and radio shows, and anything else that will keep the company attuned to the trends and pulse of consumer audiences. Some of this research is specifically geared toward particular client projects, and some is just done as part of True North's ongoing expansion of its rich database.

This system is tied into True North's Creative Partner program, in which participants, primarily clients, are set up with a customized creative partner workstation that can access this data. This also makes it possible to communicate progress on projects quickly and efficiently regardless of the physical location of the parties. Dave Clauson explains:

You can see the potential of the speed at which information can be shared. It is a critical asset to any company that wants to be successful in this mar-

ket . . . it's a store-and-forward technology, and instantly, the account direc-
tor can call up those commercials off the server and take a look.

To give you an idea of what that might mean, let's say that I'm working for
S.C. Johnson, a large multinational company. The world wide account direc-
tor at Foote, Cone & Belding Chicago, its advertising agency, wants to keep
track of what's going on competitively around the world so S. C. Johnson
can respond quickly to any competitive threat.

A complement to that, which was wholly developed inside, was our
Knowledge Network; and around the world at any point, the agency will be
doing anything from in-field analysis, telephone surveys, focus groups, mind
and mood sessions. We now have an ability to get that information online
into a server so it can be instantly shared by anyone who is authorized and
is appropriate to see that information.

There's a large software design firm in San Francisco that's looking to
develop a product uniquely suited to electrical design engineers. What have
we done around the world to understand what electrical design engineers are
doing, thinking, acting, feeling, interested in, and so on? The product makes
it possible to go into the knowledge network and quickly call up anything on
a keyword search basis, whether it be audio, video, text, data that the com-
pany has done; whether it be interviewing in the field, design engineers in
Germany, or a focus group held in Kuala Lumpur, that information is inside
the network and can be accessed by the agency, to take a look and find out
the latest information and what that target is interested in or cares about.

Clauson describes how True North spots fashion trends before they become
passé. For Levi's, they put digital cameras on the streets in various parts of the
world and upload what's hot in the fashion world of the client's primary
audience. These pictures go onto the server, explains Clauson, "and anybody
from an account planner to a creative copywriter to a producer—anyone who
might be shaping how we would send messages about the Levi's brand
around the world—would be able to access that information.

It's a way of using the technology to get the client to the window of oppor-
tunity quicker; get the message organized and focused more quickly. In
other words, instead of flying around the world and doing focus groups and
recruiting, you know, 67 people in 49 different countries, we can look at
what we have right now that will give us a quick read, and are similar but
may be slightly different, and we take a look at all of that. We look at what
other information, both traditional research-oriented, and non-, we can use
to help shape a point of view about what's going on.

True North has essentially converted its corporate library and information center in Chicago from a manual request/snail mail (as opposed to electronic transmission) response service, to a real-time online searchable database where a range of media is available on just about any topic or company that might be needed. Whether it's a brief overview of a topic or a series of TV commercials by a competitor, it is all available for viewing, editing, and downloading at the desktop.

Implementation

Most design firms and ad agencies do not want to be in the full-time business of maintaining their client's online presence, or even making minor changes to the electronic collateral they have provided. They will therefore attempt to design for self-maintenance. This too needs to be an integral part of the early planning in the design process.

Moez Rafieetary, of Medius IV, says, "One of the advantages of the electronic medium is that it can be updated remotely, particularly in regard to online design or kiosks. If you have a network of kiosks in a retail environment, for example, information can be updated via the phone line. That's a real advantage. Just imagine the cost of reprinting new materials every time. Of course, there are initially some hardware costs, but over the long term, this is a tremendous leveraging of the client's dollar."

Amanda North of Studio Archetype explains, "The degree to which we implement a project varies depending on our client's needs and desires. We're happy to provide a framework and something that can be maintained by others, whether it's a packaging system or anything else based on a style guide.

"Generally, we do maintain the client's sites on our own server for at least a month after a site has been aired, to make sure that, for any modification that is required, we can get in there easily. During the development period, we assign a secret password to our clients so they can get onto the Web site at any time and check it out. This has been very important to us, particularly with our geographically remote clients. We do meet in person regularly, but with the development of a Web site you want to get that visceral reaction frequently. We find that to be a very satisfying way of updating the communications."

Tim Smith of Red Sky comments:

Again, the distinction between discrete and continuous media, especially with continuous, is you have to teach the clients how to fish. You don't want to become a fish store for them. It becomes a very inefficient process. So we give them graphical kits they can use until they want to change the entire look and feel again. Most of the Quicken site is composed of Photoshop kits that we've developed for Intuit that allow the clients to perfectly create titles and headings, with color coordination and everything. It's very easy for them to maintain a professional looking, highly branded site. They don't call us for those minor kinds of changes and they don't need to. And if they did call us, if we hadn't provided those, we'd be doing work for them that we don't want to do, which is just rote production.

So it is designed for change. A site we're working on now is being designed for a sub-hourly change, pretty massive, based on a database. New stuff hits it on a minute-by-minute basis which has to be reflected in the Web site. It's very dynamic and very exciting. That's both graphical change as well as informational change.

While there are some firms that use ongoing maintenance as a way to "hang on" to clients, the more experienced houses are focused on doing the job they were hired to do—well. They create a solid foundation on which their client can build. Future return business comes as a result of the success, not from the maintenance and repair of a project.

Life after Implementation

One of the places where many companies fail is in the stage just following implementation. If they do not have a thorough understanding of what they have created and how to maintain and evolve it, their investment can result in an unnecessary loss. Many companies are just beginning to experiment and are reluctant to take the time to really learn about the obstacles and challenges they will be confronting. Using skilled and well-rounded talent, respecting the experience of agencies that have managed the big picture for clients, while equally heeding the knowledge and direction provided by those design firms specializing in new media development and implementation all will increase the probability of success. Making educated use of the vast resources available today and observing the successes and failures of competitors will provide a needed advantage in this electronic marketplace.

Conclusion

Interactive marketing is far more than multimedia used to entertain or engage a consumer. It is a higher level of strategic marketing, made possible by sophisticated technology and intelligent databases that can respond to interactive relationships. The Internet has brought these relationships into a real-time arena and has dramatically impacted the clout of traditional advertising. Today's technology allows us to capture, measure, compare, and analyze the consumer's input, then intelligently sort this information and strategically allocate traditional and interactive resources.

Businesses willing to balance risk with knowledge and understanding of this new electronic marketplace stand to reap great benefits. Those that don't are taking an even greater risk. This is an age of true pioneers, and the gold is in the relationships made possible through interactive technology.

CHAPTER THREE

MAKING IT LEGAL

J. Dianne Brinson and Mark F. Radcliffe

Dianne Brinson and Mark Radcliffe wear many hats. They are both attorneys, authors, and publishers. Together, Dianne and Mark wrote and self-published the *Multimedia Law and Business Handbook* (two editions) and *Multimedia Contracts.* This chapter is an adapted excerpt from their June 1996 edition of the *Multimedia Law and Business Handbook* (described in Resources). It will give the reader a basic grasp of important things to consider when producing, designing, or hiring others to develop electronic media.

Dianne has a Bachelor of Arts in Political Science and Russian; she graduated summa cum laude, from Duke University and earned a law degree from Yale Law School. She is the author of a number of articles in the intellectual property field and is a former member of the Executive Committee of the Intellectual Property Section of the State Bar of California. She has practiced law at firms in Los Angeles and Atlanta. She is a former tenured law professor at Georgia State University, and has taught at Golden Gate Law School and Santa Clara School of Law. She is now in private practice as a consultant in Menlo Park, California.

Mark F. Radcliffe is a partner in the law firm of Gray Cary Ware & Freidenrich (formerly Ware & Freidenrich) in Palo Alto, California. He has been practicing intellectual property law, with a special emphasis on computer law, for more than 10 years, and has been chairman of the Computer Law Section of the Bar Association of San Francisco and the Computer Industry Committee of the Licensing Executives Society. He is a member of the Multimedia Law Group at Gray Cary Ware & Freidenrich and represents many multimedia developers and publishers. He has a Bachelor of Science in Chemistry; he graduated magna cum laude, from the University of Michigan, and has a law degree from Harvard Law School. He is the author of the chapter on legal issues in the National Association of Broadcasters' book *Multimedia 2000.* He has been quoted in *The New*

York Times, The Wall Street Journal and the *San Francisco Examiner* on legal issues and multimedia.

In today's frenzied rush to get "up on the Web," to be at the forefront of high-tech's marketing "showbiz," companies don't always take either the time or the trouble to consider some of the legal ramifications of this new frontier. Therefore, to stave off the "morning after" legal blues, this chapter appropriately follows Designing Your Presence, not as an afterthought, but as a forethought, an integral part of planning and protecting your presence.

Legal Basics

There are four major intellectual property laws in the United States that are important for electronic marketers and multimedia publishers:

- Copyright law, which protects original "works of authorship."
- Patent law, which protects new, useful, and "nonobvious" inventions and processes.
- Trademark law, which protects words, names, and symbols used by manufacturers and businesses to identify their goods and services.
- Trade secret law, which protects valuable information not generally known that has been kept secret by its owner.

This chapter focuses on U.S. copyright law because that is the most important of these laws for most marketers and multimedia publishers. The other three intellectual property laws are discussed in less detail, as are several other relevant laws. The last section of the chapter discusses online marketing legal issues.

Copyright Law

Copyright law is a *federal* law, which means it does not vary from state to state (although the interpretation of the law may be different in different courts).

Works Protected

Copyright protection is available for "works of authorship." The Copyright Act states that works of authorship include the following types of works that are of interest to the multimedia developer:

- *Literary works.* Novels, nonfiction prose, poetry, newspaper articles and newspapers, magazine articles and magazines, computer software, software manuals, training manuals, manuals, catalogs, brochures, ads (text), and compilations such as business directories.
- *Musical works.* Songs, advertising jingles, and instrumentals.
- *Dramatic works.* Plays, operas, and skits.
- *Pantomimes and choreographic works.* Ballets, modern dance, jazz dance, and mime works.
- *Pictorial, graphic, and sculptural works.* Photographs, posters, maps, paintings, drawings, graphic art, display ads, cartoon strips and cartoon characters, stuffed animals, statues, paintings, and works of fine art.
- *Motion pictures and other audiovisual works.* Movies, documentaries, travelogues, training films and videos, television shows, television ads, and *interactive multimedia works.*
- *Sound recordings.* Recordings of music, sounds, or words.

Obtaining Copyright Protection

Copyright protection arises automatically when an "original" work of authorship is "fixed" in a tangible medium of expression. Registration with the Copyright Office is optional (but you have to register before you file an infringement suit, and registering early will make you eligible to receive attorney's fees and statutory damages in a future lawsuit).

Here's what "original" and "fixed" mean in copyright law:

Originality: A work is original in the copyright sense if it owes its origin to the author and was not copied from some preexisting work.

Fixation: A work is fixed when it is made "sufficiently permanent or stable to permit it to be perceived, reproduced, or otherwise communicated for a period of more than transitory duration." Even copying a computer program into RAM has been found to be of sufficient duration for it to be "fixed" (although some scholars and lawyers disagree with this conclusion).

Neither the originality requirement nor the fixation requirement is stringent. An author can "fix" words, for example, by writing them down, typing them on an old-fashioned typewriter, dictating them into a tape recorder, or entering them into a computer. A work can be original without being novel or unique.

> *Betsy's book* How to Lose Weight *is original in the copyright sense as long as Betsy did not create her book by copying existing material—even if it's the millionth book to be written on the subject of weight loss.*

Only minimal creativity is required to meet the originality requirement. No artistic merit or beauty is required.

A work can incorporate preexisting material and still be original. When preexisting material is incorporated into a new work, the copyright on the new work covers only the original material contributed by the author.

> *Adco's CD-ROM demo incorporates a number of photographs that were made by Photographer (who gave Adco permission to use the photographs in the demo). The demo as a whole owes its origin to Developer, but the photographs do not. The copyright on the demo does not cover the photographs, just the material created by Developer.*

Scope of Protection

Copyright protects against copying the "expression" in a work, not against copying the work's ideas. The difference between *idea* and *expression* is one of the most difficult concepts in copyright law. The most important point to understand is that one can copy the protected expression in a work without copying the literal words (or the exact shape of a sculpture, or the exact "look" of a stuffed animal). When a new work is created by copying an existing copyrighted work, copyright infringement exists if the new work is "substantially similar" to the work that was copied. The new work need not be identical to the copied work. For example, paraphrasing a short story could be copyright infringement, as could copying some (but not all) aspects of a painting.

A copyright owner has five exclusive rights in the copyrighted work:

> *Reproduction Right.* The right to copy, duplicate, transcribe, or imitate the work in fixed form.
>
> *Modification Right.* Also known as the derivative works right, this is the right to modify the work to create a new work. A new work that is based on a preexisting work is known as a "derivative work."
>
> *Distribution Right.* The right to distribute copies of the work to the public by sale, rental, lease, or lending.
>
> *Public Performance Right.* The right to recite, play, dance, act, or show the work at a public place or to transmit it to the public. In the case of a motion picture or other audiovisual work, showing the work's images in sequence is considered "performance."

Public Display Right. The right to show a copy of the work directly or by means of a film, slide, or television image at a public place or to transmit it to the public. In the case of a motion picture or other audiovisual work, showing the work's images out of sequence is considered "display."

In addition, certain types of works of "visual art" also have "moral rights" which limit the modification of the work and the use of the author's name without permission from the original author.

Anyone who violates any of the exclusive rights of a copyright owner is an infringer.

> *Marketer scanned Photographer's copyrighted photograph, altered the image by using digital editing software, and included the altered version of the photograph in an interactive kiosk. If Marketer used Photographer's photograph without permission, Developer infringed Photographer's copyright by violating the reproduction right (scanning the photograph), the modification right (altering the photograph), and the public performance or display right (using the photograph in a kiosk).*

A copyright owner can recover actual or, in some cases, statutory damages (which can be as high as $100,000) from an infringer. In addition, courts have the power to issue injunctions (orders) to prevent or restrain copyright infringement and to order the impoundment and destruction of infringing copies.

The term of copyright protection depends on three factors: who created the work, when the work was created, and when it was first distributed commercially. For copyrightable works created on and after January 1, 1978, the copyright term for those created by individuals is the life of the author plus 50 years. The copyright term for "works made for hire" (see next paragraph) is 75 years from the date of first "publication" (distribution of copies to the general public) or 100 years from the date of creation, whichever expires first.

Generally, the copyright is owned by the person (or persons) who created the work. However, if the work is created by an employee within the scope of his or her employment, the employer owns the copyright because it is a "work for hire."

> *As part of his job, Jon, an employee of Big Co., created a CD-ROM sampler of Big's products. Even though John created the sampler, Big is the author for copyright purposes and the owner of the copyright.*

The copyright law also includes another form of "work for hire" which applies only to certain types of specially commissioned works. Audiovisual works—the category into which most multimedia projects fall—can be specially commissioned works made for hire. In order to qualify the work as a "specially commissioned" work for hire, the creator must sign a written agreement stating that it is a "work for hire" prior to commencing development of the product. (Remember that this chapter deals only with United States law; most foreign jurisdictions do not recognize the "specially commissioned" work for hire, and you need an assignment to transfer rights in those countries.)

Avoiding Copyright Infringement

Current technology makes it fairly easy to combine material created by others—film and television clips, music, graphics, photographs, and text—into a multimedia product such as an interactive kiosk or CD-ROM sampler. But just because you have the technology to copy these works does not mean you have the legal right to do so. If you use copyrighted material owned by others without permission, you can incur liability for hundreds of thousands or even millions of dollars in damages. Also, the copyright owner may get a court order prohibiting you from distributing your product. For example, Delrina lost hundreds of thousands of dollars and had to recall all copies of its screen saver last fall when it lost a copyright suit. The screen saver in question displayed, on one of the 30 modules, the comic book character Opus shooting down Berkeley Systems' "flying toasters" (made famous in Berkeley's After Dark screen saver program). Berkeley Systems sued Delrina for copyright and trademark infringement. The court ruled for Berkeley Systems, prohibiting further distribution of Delrina's product and requiring recall of all of the product not already sold.

Most of the third-party material you will want to use in your multimedia product is protected by copyright. Using copyrighted material without getting permission—either by obtaining an "assignment" or a "license"—can have disastrous consequences. An assignment is generally understood to transfer all of the intellectual property rights in a particular work (although an assignment can be more limited). A license provides the right to use a work and is generally quite limited. A complete discussion of the terms of licenses and assignments is beyond the scope of this chapter (it takes up several chapters in our book).

If you use copyrighted material in your multimedia project without permission, the owner of the copyright can prevent the distribution of your product and obtain damages from you for infringement, even if you did not intentionally include his or her material. Consider the following:

> *Air Courier Company created a CD-ROM illustrating its services to send to potential clients. The CD-ROM included an excerpt from a recording of Julie Andrews singing "Climb Every Mountain." It ended with a photograph of Lauren Bacall pictured above the words, "Good luck."*

In this example, if the company did not obtain permission to use the recording of "Climb Every Mountain" or the photo of Lauren Bacall, the CD-ROM infringes three copyrights: the copyright on the song, the copyright on the Julie Andrews recording of the song, and the copyright on the photograph. Any of the copyright owners whose rights are infringed might be able to get a court order preventing further distribution of this multimedia product. (The CD-ROM also infringes Lauren Bacall's right of publicity, which is separate from copyright, by the commercial use of her image.)

There are a number of myths concerning the necessity of getting a license. Here are five. Don't make the mistake of believing them:

Myth 1: *"The work I want to use doesn't have a copyright notice on it, so it's not copyrighted. I'm free to use it."*
Most published works contain a copyright notice. However, for works published on or after March 1, 1989, the use of copyright notice is optional. The fact that a work doesn't have a copyright notice doesn't mean that the work is not protected by copyright.

Myth 2: *"I don't need a license because I'm using only a small amount of the copyrighted work."*
It is true that *de minimis* copying (copying a small amount) is not copyright infringement. Unfortunately, it is rarely possible to tell where *de minimis* copying ends and copyright infringement begins. There are no "bright line" rules.

Copying a small amount of a copyrighted work is infringement if what is copied is a qualitatively substantial portion of the copied work. In one case, a magazine article that used 300 words from a 200,000-word autobiography written by President Gerald Ford was found to infringe the copyright on the autobiography. Even though the copied material was only a small part of the autobiography, the copied portions were among the most powerful passages in the autobiography. Copying any part of a copyrighted work is risky. If what you copy is truly a tiny and nonmemorable part of the work, you may get away with it (the work's owner may not be able to tell that your work incorporates an excerpt from the his or her work). However, you run the risk of having to defend your use in expensive litigation. If you are copying, it is better to get a permission or a license (unless fair use applies). You cannot escape liability for infringement by showing how much of the protected work you did *not* take.

Myth 3: *"Since I'm planning to give credit to all authors whose works I copy, I don't need to get licenses."*

If you give credit to a work's author, you are not a plagiarist (you are not pretending that you authored the copied work). However, attribution is not a defense to copyright infringement.

Myth 4: *"My multimedia work will be a wonderful showcase for the copyright owner's work, so I'm sure the owner will not object to my use of the work."*
Don't assume that a copyright owner will be happy to have you use his or her work. Even if the owner is willing to let you use the work, he or she will probably want to charge you a license fee. Content owners view multimedia as a new market for licensing their material.

In 1993, 10 freelance writers sued *The New York Times* and other publishers over the unauthorized publication of their work through online computer services. And the Harry Fox Agency and other music publishers have sued CompuServe, an online computer service, over the distribution of their music on the service.

Myth 5: *"I don't need a license because I'm going to alter the work I copy."*
Generally, you cannot escape liability for copyright infringement by altering or modifying the work you copy. If you copy and modify protected elements of a copyrighted work, you will be infringing the copyright owner's modification right as well as the copying right.

When You Don't Need a License

You don't need a license to use a copyrighted work in three circumstances: if your use is fair use; if the work you use is in the public domain; or if the material you use is factual or an idea.

Fair Use

You don't need a license to use a copyrighted work if your use is "fair use." Unfortunately, it is difficult to tell whether a particular use of a work is fair or unfair. Determinations are made on a case-by-case basis by considering four factors:

> *Factor 1: Purpose and character of use.* The courts are most likely to find fair use where the use is for noncommercial purposes, such as a book review.

Factor 2: Nature of the copyrighted work. The courts are most likely to find fair use where the copied work is a factual work rather than a creative one.

Factor 3: Amount and substantiality of the portion used. The courts are most likely to find fair use where what is used is a tiny amount of the protected work. If what is used is small in amount but substantial in terms of importance, however, a finding of fair use is unlikely.

Factor 4: Effect on the potential market for or value of the protected work. The courts are most likely to find fair use where the new work is not a substitute for the copyrighted work.

If your multimedia work serves traditional fair use purposes—criticism, comment, news reporting, teaching, scholarship, and research—you have a better chance of falling within the bounds of fair use than you do if your work is a sold to the public for entertainment purposes and for commercial gain.

Public Domain

You don't need a license to use a public domain work. Public domain works— works not protected by copyright—can be used by anyone. Because these works are not protected by copyright, no one can claim the exclusive rights of copyright for such works. For example, the plays of Shakespeare are in the public domain. Works enter the public domain in several ways: because the term of the copyright expired, because the copyright owner failed to "renew" his or her copyright under the old Copyright Act of 1909, or because the copyright owner failed to properly use copyright notice (of importance only for works created before March 1, 1989, at which time copyright notice became optional). The rules regarding what works are in the public domain are too complex for this primer, and they vary from country to country.

Ideas or Facts

You don't need a license to copy facts from a protected work or to copy ideas from a protected work. The copyright on a work does not extend to the work's facts. This is because copyright protection is limited to original works of authorship, and no one can claim originality or authorship for facts. You are free to copy facts from a copyrighted work.

Creating Your Own Works

Naturally, you don't need a copyright license for material you create yourself. Nevertheless, you should be aware that the rules regarding ownership of copyright are complex. Do not, for example, assume that you own the copyright if you pay an independent contractor to create the work (or part of it). In fact, generally the copyright in a work is owned by the individual who creates the work, except for full-time employees working within the scope of their employment and copyrights, which are assigned in writing.

Patent Law

Certainly, copyright law is the most important intellectual property law for protecting rights in multimedia works, but you also need to know enough about patent, trademark, and trade secret law to avoid infringing intellectual property rights owned by others and to be able to take advantage of the protection these laws provide.

Works Protected

Patent law protects inventions and processes ("utility" patents) and ornamental designs ("design" patents). Inventions and processes protected by utility patents can be electrical, mechanical, or chemical in nature. Examples of works protected by utility patents are a microwave oven, genetically engineered bacteria for cleaning up oil spills, a computerized method of running cash management accounts, and a method for curing rubber. Examples of works protected by design patents are a design for the soles of running shoes, a design for sterling silver tableware, and a design for a water fountain.

Obtaining a Patent

There are strict requirements for the grant of utility and design patents. To qualify for a utility patent, an invention must be new, useful, and "nonobvious." To meet the novelty requirement, the invention must not have been known or used by others in this country before the applicant invented it, and it also must not have been patented or described in a printed publication in the United States or a foreign country before the applicant invented it. The policy behind the novelty requirement is that a patent is issued in exchange for the inventor's disclosure to the public of the details of his or her invention. If the inventor's work is not novel, the inventor is not adding to the public knowledge, so the inventor should not be granted a patent.

To meet the nonobvious requirement, the invention must be sufficiently different from existing technology and knowledge so that, at the time the invention was made, it as a whole would not have been obvious to a person having ordinary skill in that field. The policy behind this requirement is that patents should be granted only for real advances, not for mere technical tinkering or modifications of existing inventions.

It is difficult to obtain a utility patent. Even if the invention or process meets the requirements of novelty, utility, and nonobviousness, a patent will not be granted if the invention was patented or described in a printed publication in the United States or a foreign country more than one year before the application date, or if the invention was in public use or on sale in the United States for more than one year before the application date.

Scope of Protection

A patent owner has the right to exclude others from making, using, or selling the patented invention or design in the United States during the term of the patent. Anyone who makes, uses, or sells a patented invention or design within the United States during the term of the patent without permission from the patent owner is an infringer—even if he or she did not copy the patented invention or design or even know about it.

> John, working on his own, developed a software program for manipulating images in multimedia works. Although John didn't know it, Inventor has a patent on that method of image manipulation. John's use of the software program infringes Inventor's patent.

Utility patents are granted for a period of 20 years from the date the patent application was filed. Design patents are granted for a period of 14 years. Once the patent on an invention or design has expired, anyone is free to make, use, or sell the invention or design.

Trademarks

Trademarks and service marks are words, names, symbols, or devices used by manufacturers of goods and providers of services to identify their goods and services, and to distinguish their goods and services from goods manufactured and sold by others. For example, the trademark WordPerfect is used by the WordPerfect Corporation to identify that company's word processing software and distinguish that software from other vendors' word processing software.

For trademarks used in commerce, federal trademark protection is available under the federal trademark statute, the Lanham Act. Many states have trademark registration statutes that resemble the Lanham Act, and all states protect unregistered trademarks under the common (nonstatutory) law of trademarks.

Availability of Protection

Trademark protection is available for words, names, symbols, or devices that are capable of distinguishing the owner's goods or services from the goods or services of others. A trademark that merely describes a class of goods rather than distinguishing the trademark owner's goods from goods provided by others is not protectible.

> *The term corn flakes is not protectible as a trademark for cereal because it describes a type of cereal that is sold by a number of Cereal Manufacturers rather than distinguishing one Cereal Manufacturer's goods.*

A trademark that so closely resembles a trademark already in use in the United States as to be likely to cause confusion or mistake is not protectible. In addition, trademarks that are "descriptive" of the functions, quality, or character of the goods or services have special requirements before they will be protected.

Obtaining Protection

The most effective trademark protection is obtained by filing a trademark registration application in the Patent and Trademark Office. Federal law also protects unregistered trademarks, but such protection is limited to the geographic area in which the mark is actually being used. State trademark protection under common law is obtained simply by adopting a trademark and using it in connection with goods or services. This protection, too, is limited to the geographic area in which the trademark is actually being used. State statutory protection is obtained by filing an application with the state trademark office.

Scope of Protection

Trademark law in general, whether federal or state, protects a trademark owner's commercial identity (goodwill, reputation, and investment in advertising) by giving the trademark owner the exclusive right to use the trademark on the type of goods or services for which the owner is using the trademark. Any person who uses a trademark in connection with goods or services in a way that is likely to cause confusion is an infringer. Trademark owners can obtain injunctions against the confusing use of their trademarks by others, and they can collect damages for infringement.

Small Multimedia Co. is selling a line of interactive training works under the trademark Personal Tutor. If Giant Multimedia Co. starts selling interactive training works under the trademark Personal Tutor, purchasers may think that Giant's works come from the same source as Small Multimedia's works. Giant is infringing Small's trademark.

Trade Secrets

A trade secret is information of any sort that is valuable to its owner, not generally known, and that has been kept secret by the owner. Trade secrets are protected only under state law. The Uniform Trade Secrets Act, in effect in a number of states, defines trade secrets as "information, including a formula, pattern, compilation, program, device, method, technique, or process that derives independent economic value from not being generally known and not being readily ascertainable, and is subject to reasonable efforts to maintain secrecy."

Works Protected

The following types of technical and business information are examples of material that can be protected by trade secret law: customer lists, instructional methods, manufacturing processes, and methods of developing software. Inventions and processes that are not patentable can be protected under trade secret law. Patent applicants generally rely on trade secret law to protect their inventions while the patent applications are pending.

Six factors are generally used to determine whether information is a trade secret:

- The extent to which the information is known outside the claimant's business.
- The extent to which the information is known by the claimant's employees.
- The extent of measures taken by the claimant to guard the secrecy of the information.
- The value of the information to the claimant and the claimant's competitors.
- The amount of effort or money expended by the claimant in developing the information.
- The ease with which the information could be acquired by others.

Information has value if it gives rise to actual or potential commercial advantage for the owner of the information. Although a trade secret need not be unique in the patent law sense, information that is generally known is not protected under trade secrets law.

Obtaining Protection

Trade secret protection attaches automatically when information of value to the owner is kept secret by the owner.

Scope of Protection

A trade secret owner has the right to keep others from misappropriating and using the trade secret. Sometimes the misappropriation is a result of industrial espionage. Many trade secret cases involve people who have taken their former employers' trade secrets for use in new businesses or for new employers. Trade secret owners have recourse only against misappropriation. Discovery of protected information through independent research or reverse engineering (taking a product apart to see how it works) is not misappropriation.

Trade secret protection endures as long as the requirements for protection—generally, value to the owner and secrecy—continue to be met. The protection is lost if the owner fails to take reasonable steps to keep the information secret.

After Sam discovered a new method for manipulating images in multimedia works, he demonstrated his new method at an electronic marketing conference. Sam lost his trade secret protection for the image manipulation method because he failed to keep his method secret.

Right of Publicity, Libel, and Other Laws

In addition to the intellectual property laws discussed, you must also be familiar with several other areas of law that deal with the right of the individual to control his or her image and reputation. The right of publicity gives the individual the right to control his or her name, face, image, or voice for commercial purposes. For example, Ford's advertising agency tried to persuade Bette Midler to sing during a Ford television commercial. She refused. They hired her backup singer. The performance of the backup singer was so similar to that of Bette Midler that viewers thought Bette Midler was singing. On the basis of that confusion, she sued and won $400,000 in damages.

Libel and slander protect an individual against the dissemination of false-hoods about that individual. To be actionable, the falsehood must injure his or her reputation or subject that person to hatred, contempt, or ridicule. The individual can obtain monetary losses as well as damages for mental anguish.

If you intend to use preexisting material from television or film, you may also have to deal with the rights of members of the entertainment unions to get "reuse" fees. These unions include the Writers Guild, the Directors Guild, the Screen Actors Guild (SAG), American Federation of Musicians, and the American Federation of Television and Radio Artists (AFTRA). Under the union agreements with the film and television studios, members of these unions and guilds who worked on a film or television program have a right to payment if the work is reused. These payments are generally modest. However, if you are using many clips, these payments can become quite expensive.

If you use professional actors, directors, or writers in developing your product, you will also need to deal with these unions. Most of the unions have very complex contracts developed specifically for their traditional film and television work. They are still trying to understand how to deal with the multimedia industry, although both SAG and AFTRA have developed a special contract for multimedia projects. If you use professional talent, you should be prepared for the additional complexity arising out of these union agreements.

Online Marketing

Some people think that copyright law and other laws do not apply or should not apply in cyberspace, because cyberspace is a "new frontier" beyond the reach of any country's laws, or because ideas and information should flow freely in cyberspace. Don't make the mistake of thinking that the intellectual property laws discussed earlier in this chapter do not apply to online marketing. The laws *do* apply. For example:

- If you copy copyrighted graphics from a Web site and use them in your company's Web site without permission, you are opening yourself up to a lawsuit for copyright infringement.

- If you use a celebrity's photograph on your home page without permission, you could find yourself in court defending against charges of misappropriation of the celebrity's right of publicity.

- If you distribute someone else's copyrighted material over the Web or post it on your Web server without getting permission, you could be sued for copyright infringement.

- If you write an article saying unflattering, untrue things about the CEO of the company that's your main competitor and send the article to Usenet newsgroups, you will be setting yourself up to a lawsuit for defamation.

There are certainly questions about how particular laws should be applied to Internet transactions; However, if you are using the Internet, you should assume that the laws that apply to traditional transactions and traditional media apply in cyberspace—the laws discussed in this chapter and other laws, such as criminal laws and laws regulating unfair and deceptive advertising.

Myths

A lot of public domain material is available on the Net—government reports and uncopyrightable factual information, for example. But much of the material that on the Net *is* protected by copyright. There are a number of myths about how copyright law applies to copying material from the Internet and posting material on the Internet.

Copying Material from the Net

Don't make the mistake of believing these myths about copying material from the Net:

Myth 1: *"If I find something on the Net, it's okay to copy it and use it without getting permission."*
While you are free to copy public domain material that you find on the Net, generally you should not copy copyrighted material without getting permission from the copyright owner—whether you find the material on the Net or in a more traditional medium (book, music CD, software disk, etc.)

Myth 2: *"Material on the World Wide Web is in the public domain if it's posted without a copyright notice."*
Under current law, the use of copyright notice is optional. Do not assume that material is uncopyrighted just because it does not contain a copyright notice.

Myth 3: *"Anyone who puts material on a Web server wants people to use that material, so I can do anything I want with material that I get from a Web server."*

Individuals and organizations put material on a Web server to make it accessible by others. They do not give up their copyright rights by doing so. Also, remember, the person who posted the material may not own it.

Myth 4: *"It's okay to copy material from a home page or Web site without getting permission."*
Much of the material that appears in Web sites and home pages is protected by copyright. If you want to use something from someone else's home page or Web site, get permission unless permission to copy is granted in the text of the home page or Web site.

Posting Material

And don't believe these myths about how copyright law applies to putting copyrighted material owned by others on the Net.

Myth 5: *"It's okay to use copyrighted material in my Web site as long as no one has to pay to visit my Web site."*
Unless your use of the copyrighted work is fair use, you need a license to copy and use the work in your Web site even if you won't be charging people to view it.

Myth 6: *"It's okay to make other people's copyrighted material available on my Web server as long as I don't charge people anything to get the material."*
Copying and distributing copyrighted material without permission can be copyright infringement even if you don't charge for the copied material.

Myth 7: *"Posting copyrighted material on the Internet is fair use, so I don't need the copyright owner's permission."*
Under current law, there is no absolute fair use right to post someone else's copyrighted material on the Net. If copyrighted material is used on the Internet without the permission of the copyright owner, fair use will be decided by considering the four factors discussed earlier in this chapter. There is no special fair use exemption for the Internet.

Taking Material from the Net

As noted, much of the material on the Internet *is* copyrighted. If you find material on the Net that you want to use in your project, do not make the mistake of believing that you are free to use the material without going through the normal licensing process (discussed earlier in this chapter). Putting a document on the Net is not a waiver of copyright or a dedication of the document to the public domain.

When you find something on the Net that you want to use, go through the same analysis that you would if the material appeared in a more traditional medium (in a book, on a software diskette or music CD, for example). If the material is in the public domain, you are free to use it. If it is copyrighted, you need a license if your intended use of the work would, without a license, infringe any of the copyright owner's exclusive rights.

Getting permission to use material you find on the Net is complicated by the fact that some people post copyrighted material they do not own or have permission to use. If someone has posted copyrighted material in violation of the copyright owner's exclusive rights, getting the poster's permission to use the copyrighted material will do you no good. The poster has no right to authorize you to use the material. You need the owner's permission.

Be wary of people who mistakenly think they own the rights to material they have commissioned in the past.

> *Developer saw some photographs she liked in Z Company's Web Site. Developer contacted Z Company's president and got permission to use the photographs on Developer's Web site. If the copyrights in the photographs are owned by the Photographer who took them (which is likely, if the Photographer was a freelancer), Z Company cannot authorize Developer to use the photographs. Only the Photographer can.*

Developing Your Own Web Site

The following are some legal issues you should consider when developing your own Web site.

Copyright Law

Don't use copyrighted material owned by others on your Web site unless you get permission or one of the exceptions to the copyright owner's exclusive rights applies (as discussed earlier in this chapter). Copyright owners are increasingly vigilant about policing the Web to find infringers.

It is tempting to use images of copyrighted cartoon or television characters to add appeal to your Web site. Don't, unless you get a license. The owners of this type of material are particularly diligent about going after unauthorized users. For example, an individual who used a picture of Winnie the Pooh on his home page got a "cease and desist" letter from the book publisher that owns the rights to Winnie the Pooh; similarly, *Star Trek* fans who used photos from the television series got "cease and desist" letters from Paramount Pictures.

It's also tempting to use music clips to jazz up your Web site. Some people think it's okay to use three or four bars of a song without getting permission. This is a myth. Copying a small amount of a work can be copyright infringement, and there is no "safe harbor," no minimum number of bars it is safe to copy. Music licensing is especially complicated, because getting permission to use a clip of recorded music generally requires two licenses, one from the owner of the copyright in the musical composition and one from the owner of the copyright in the sound recording.

Previously Licensed Material

If you want to use copyrighted material that you licensed to use in the past, don't assume that the old license covers your use of the material on your Web site; you may need a new license. Use of licensed material in a way not authorized in the license is copyright infringement.

> *Multimedia Publisher used 10 seconds of a music clip from a recording in a CD-ROM product, Standout, after getting the necessary licenses (from the music publisher and the record company). If those licenses were limited to the use of the clip in the single product Standout, Publisher will need new licenses to use the clip in Publisher's Web site.*

Using Licensed Content on the Net

If you will be using a Web site to publicize your company's existing CD-ROM products, you will probably want to include clips of your products on your Web site. If you want to use a clip that contains licensed third-party content, be careful. Your license to use that content may not give you the right to use it on the Internet.

If you think you may be publicizing your products on your Web site in the future, your licenses to use third-party content should include language authorizing you to use a clip of the licensed content on the Net to publicize your multimedia product (in addition to language authorizing you to use the content in your CD-ROM product itself.)

Material You Own

If you own the copyright in a work, you can use the work on your Web site. An employer owns the copyright in a work created by an employee acting within the scope of employment.

> *Five year ago, Karen, a graphic designer, created a logo for Multimedia Company. If Karen was an employee of Multimedia Company and she created the logo within the scope of her employment, Multimedia Company is free to use the logo on its Web site without Karen's permission. Under copyright law's "work made for hire" principle, Multimedia Company—not Karen—is the owner of the logo.*

If you want to use material created for you in the past by an independent contractor, you will probably need the contractor's permission. In this country, a hiring party does not own the copyright in work created by an independent contractor unless the hiring party got an assignment or that work had "specially commissioned work made for hire" status.

> *High Tech Co.'s public relations department has in its files a photograph of the company headquarters taken several years ago by a freelance photographer for a company brochure. Unless High Tech Co. got an assignment from the photographer, High Tech Co. should get the photographer's permission before using the photograph in the company's Web site.*

Don't assume that because you've used a work before that you own it. The prior use may have been unauthorized, or it may have been authorized based only on a very limited license—one-time use, for example.

Other Material You Can Use

You can avoid obtaining licenses to use third-party material on your Web site if you use public domain material. You can also avoid licensing by creating your own content. You don't need a license to make fair use of copyrighted material or to copy facts or ideas, as described earlier in this chapter.

Other Laws

The laws of privacy, publicity, and defamation apply to the use of material on Web pages. Elvis Presley Enterprises is not likely to be amused if you scan an image of Elvis from a Graceland postcard and use it on your Web page. Patent law and trade secret law also apply to activities on the Internet. CompuServe caused quite a stir in late 1994 when it announced that all providers of software using the .gif format (a common data compression format for images) would have to be licensed by CompuServe due to a patent held by Unisys. The principles of trademark law also apply.

Copying Existing Web Pages

Original Web sites and original material on Web pages (logos, images, etc.) are protected by copyright. As with other copyrighted material, the copyright does not extend to ideas or facts. You are free to copy the ideas and uncopyrightable facts, but do not copy the pages as a whole or the protected expression.

> *Recycling Company's competitor, MoCo, has a Web site that consists of four components, information about MoCo, information about MoCo's services, statistics about the growing popularity of recycling in the United States, and a "request" form that users can e-mail to get more information on the company's services. Recycling Company is free to put together its own Web site with company information, service information, statistics, and an e-mail request form. It is also free to use the facts from MoCo's statistics page. However, if Recycling Company copies MoCo's graphics or Web page text and layouts, that probably constitutes copyright infringement.*

Whether you can copy an existing Web site's network of links to other Web sites is unclear. Presumably, a Web site owner cannot claim copyright protection in an individual link to another site, but the selection involved in setting up a network of links could be protected by copyright.

Pointing

Attorneys familiar with copyright law and the Net are currently debating whether you need permission from the owner of another Web site to "point" (link) to that site. The current majority view is that pointing to another site doesn't infringe the copyright on the linked site. Linking does not involve copying or displaying the pointed-at page on the Web page that contains the pointer. When someone who is browsing a Web page that includes pointers to other sites clicks on the pointer, the pointer itself is transferred to that individual's computer and sent to the source to retrieve the pointed at object.

Nonetheless, it is a good idea to ask permission before including pointers to other Web sites. Generally, permission will be granted (most other Web site owners will be happy to have the increased visibility that linking offers them).

Some owners may ask you not to point to their sites, because they don't want to be associated with your organization or products, or because they fear this will somehow result in the loss of copyright.

Don't use a graphic image from the linked Web site as a pointer to that site unless you have permission to do so. Use text instead. Copying a .gif file from someone else's Web site without permission is probably copyright infringement, even if you have permission to point to the site.

Mirroring

Some Web sites "mirror" another site by copying the other site's files and storing an exact copy of those files for users to access. Mirroring is done to minimize the load at the original site or for the convenience of the users of the Web site containing the mirrored files. Because the copying involved in mirroring could be copyright infringement, don't mirror other sites without permission from the copyright owner for that site.

Hiring a Web Developer

Many companies hire Web developers to create Web sites for them. If you will be hiring a Web developer, establish in a *written contract* with the Web developer an appropriate copyright assignment provision giving you copyright ownership. If the Web developer uses copyrighted third-party content in your Web pages, you'll need licenses to use that material. You should also get a warranty from the developer that the material he or she creates for you does not infringe any third-party copyrights or other rights.

Copyright Protection for Your Site

Although it is not necessary to use a copyright notice on your Web site, doing so may deter people from copying material without permission, and may help dispel the myth that copyright doesn't apply to material on the Internet. Although it is not necessary to register your copyright with the Copyright Office, there are advantages to doing so, as stated earlier in this chapter.

Domain Names

You may want to register a domain name for your use on the Net. A domain name is a complete description of an Internet site. Here are two examples:

> aol.com—the domain name for America Online
>
> gcwf.com—the domain name for Gray Cary Ware & Freidenrich the law firm of one of the authors of this chapter

In the two examples, the .com suffix indicates a commercial entity. Other suffixes in use are as follows:

.edu for educational institutions

.net for computers belonging to network providers

.org for miscellaneous organizations

.gov for federal government offices (in the United States only).

In a domain name, the name or initials to the left of the suffix identify the host computer (America Online in the first example, the law firm in the second one). For e-mail address purposes, a third name can be added to the domain name to identify an individual—for example, laderapres@aol.com (the e-mail address for the authors of this chapter on America Online), and mradcliffe@gcwf.com.

A domain name is the way that people can identify and find you and your company on the Internet. You don't have to get a domain name—people can reach you on the Net by sending e-mail for you to an Internet Protocol address consisting of eight numbers. However, domain names are easier for people to remember than a string of numbers.

Many companies that are generally diligent about protecting their trademark rights so far have not bothered to reserve the domain name equivalent of their trademarks. If you own trademarks, register your important trademarks as domain names. Even if you don't own trademarks, if you plan to do business on the Net, register your company name as a domain name.

How to Register

Domain name registration is under the authority of a nonprofit agency called InterNIC. InterNIC has delegated the actual registration process to Network Solutions, Inc. (NSI), of Herndon, Virginia. Generally, businesses have their Internet access providers (such as Netcom or Pipeline) register their domain name. If you want to contact InterNIC yourself to register your domain name, the phone number is (703) 742-4777, the fax number is (703) 742-4811, and the e-mail address is hostmaster@rs.internic.net. (You must have already gotten an Internet Protocol address from your Internet service provider.) The initial registration fee is $100 (for two years), and the renewal fee is $50. (This money is used to pay the cost of administering the domain name registration system.)

Most companies choose a domain name that is readily associated with the company's name—an acronym or shortened version of the name, for example, such as aol for America Online. However, the fact that you have incorporated under a name does not automatically give you the right to a domain name registration for that name—nor does the fact that you have filed a trademark application for the name.

The basic registration rule is "first come, first served"; if you apply to register a name and it has not been registered as a domain name, you'll generally be granted the registration unless another party complains that your use of the name violates his or her rights under trademark law. In your application, you must warrant that you intend to use the name on a regular basis; that your use of the name will not violate any trademark or other intellectual property right of a third party; and that you are not seeking the use of the name for the purpose of confusing or misleading anyone.

"Warehousing" of names—registering them to save them for future use or to prevent others from using them—is not permitted. The prohibition against warehousing and the warranties discussed in the preceding paragraph are designed to prevent abuse of the domain name registration system (such as standardized test preparation company Princeton Review's registration of the name kaplan.com in order to block its competitor, Kaplan Education Centers, from registering that domain name).

Important Copyright Questions to Ask

1. Will you be using copyrighted material owned by others in your project? If so, you probably need permission (a license).
2. Does your project include photographs of or refer to recognizable individuals? If so, libel law and the rights of publicity and privacy may be a concern.
3. If you have chosen a trademark for your products or services, will the mark qualify for federal trademark registration? Is the mark possibly confusingly similar to a mark already in use for similar goods or services?
4. Is it possible that your project involves the use of trade secrets owned by others—your employee's former employer, for example?
5. If your project includes film or television clips, have union reuse fees been paid and any necessary performer permissions obtained?
6. If you are hiring a Web developer to create a Web site for you, do you have a written contract with the Web developer giving you copyright ownership? Does the Web developer understand that much of the material on the Internet is copyrighted and should not be used without permission?
7. Do you own or have permission to use all the material you are using in your Web site or posting on your Web server?

8. Have you registered a domain name for your company? Have you registered your important trademarks as domain names?

The *Multimedia Law and Business Handbook* is a legal guide for multimedia developers and publishers and Internet users. An essential guide for publishers, developers, corporate trainers, video producers, educators, and attorneys, it includes chapters on licensing content, dealing with employees and independent contractors, using music in multimedia works, complying with union rules, and negotiating with publishers and distributors. Business issues covered are writing for multimedia, working with a publisher to create a title, budgeting a title, product pricing, and product planning. The book includes 22 sample contracts on disk and in hard copy form. It is available from Ladera Press (800-523-3721).

CHAPTER FOUR

SUPPORTING YOUR PRESENCE

Margo Komenar

By now the question is clearly not *why* you must support your presence, but *how* to get the job done effectively and efficiently. The principles are the same whether you are a sole proprietor or the vice president of marketing in a large corporation. You must create an ongoing relationship with your audience that fosters trust and loyalty. Just because you build it, there is no guarantee that they will come. You need to include a map with instructions on how to get there and spread a lot of goodwill along the way.

What is ironic about today's sophisticated electronic marketing capabilities is that they have given us greater access to the most fundamental and potent nontechnical marketing tool of all, the one all of the highest-paid advertising and PR agencies strive to activate: word-of-mouth endorsement. It is the interactive element of these new mediums that provides one-on-one communication and feedback on a more massive scale than has ever before been possible.

A leading PR firm, Ketchum Public Relations, a division of the full-service agency Ketchum Communications, provides clients with the following description of its approach: "In developing the media plan, we first translate our client's marketing objectives into the 'spirit of the plan,' a statement that captures the strategic mission. In developing media strategies, we conduct a comprehensive analysis of such factors as demographics, lifestyle, brand usage, and media consumption."

Getting the Word Out

Public relations, or PR, differs from advertising in that it is dedicated to getting the word out using media relations rather than by placing specific ads. In communicating with different types of media (press) about your product or service, it's important to recognize that each may need to be approached in a very specific way, as their needs vary. It is essential to monitor and maintain the consistency of how you are represented in the marketplace. The way you sound and look to your audience must remain recognizable by criteria they can understand and relate to.

According to Pat Meier, president of the San Francisco–based PR firm, Pat Meier Associates (www.patmeier.com), public relations is a "black art" to some extent. Unlike advertising, where you buy specific time and space and write the copy exactly the way you want it, PR relies primarily on media relations to get the word out. PR companies are primarily hired to create consumer recognition and loyalty. They design and communicate messages adapted to specific audiences, determine current perceptions, and decide if those perceptions need to be reinforced or changed. They handle the delivery of strategic messages through speeches, media presentations, and events. They educate company employees who interface with the media, so that consistency in image and information is maintained. They also create or increase word-of-mouth endorsement.

Given all this, businesses don't often consider how PR companies can be of use in the electronic marketplace, especially when it comes to improving customer service and customer relations. Skillful use of electronic venues can have a great impact on how you are perceived in the marketplace. Of the electronic vehicles available, PR firms generally use fax-on-demand to make client information, such as press releases, product descriptions, and other customer-oriented materials, available to the media and consumers 24 hours a day. Fax documents can be updated easily, and all businesses have access to fax machines or fax software. Many PR companies are now making this type of client information, and more, available in the online environment.

Basic Guidelines for Approaching the Media

Pat Meier Associates suggests that, before pitching your product or company to the media or hiring a PR firm to do it for you, try to answer the following key questions:

- Are you newsworthy?
- Have you developed an identity for your company and your services?
- Do you have an "audio logo" to introduce yourself and communicate your position and personality quickly and memorably?
- How would you describe your services or products?
- What makes your services or products invaluable to your customers?

- What is the significance of your company to your professional community or to families or to society at large?
- What do you expect to gain from editorial coverage?
- Is your company new, or have you introduced new or innovative services or products?
- Is your company the latest evolution in a business that has grown into the digital world?
- How do you expect to grow and expand?
- Is your distribution channel local, national, or international?
- Is your community aware of your company?
- How does your company serve the community?
- Have you employed local talent in a creative way?
- Are your products or services location-based?
- Do you have significant environmental or employee programs?
- Has a local business benefited from your expertise?
- Why is there a need for your services or products?
- What changes have occurred in your market or technology that encouraged development of products such as yours?
- Why did you personally choose this direction?
- Has the market changed since you started your company?
- How urgent is your news and how can you prove its worth?
- Do you want to emphasize that yours is a local company or do you want to make your products or services available on a national basis?
- Who is your spokesperson?

When approaching print media ask yourself:
- Who are the readers of this publication?
- What kinds of stories appear in the publication?
- Is the content solely reviews, developer or entrepreneurial profiles?
- Are the articles composed primarily of "how-to" advice or case histories?
- Are there opinion columns in which you can climb onto your soapbox and tell the world how you feel about your industry?
- Are the publications family-oriented, education-oriented, or strictly focused on another particular area?

- How often does this publication come out and what are the lead times for submitting copy?
- Is the publication local, regional, national, in cyberspace?
- Is it available at newsstands?
- Once you have made contact, how can the editors and readers find out more about you?

Approach Is the Message

It is necessary to approach PR in a strategic, systematic, and consistent manner, and to realize that the impact will build with repetition and appropriate placement over a period of time. When used reactively rather than proactively, PR efforts can prove ineffective. By maintaining an open door to the media and building a communicative relationship, you encourage the media's reliance on that relationship for accurate information.

Using this approach, eventually the media will consider you an authoritative source and spokesperson for your industry or product category. Credibility is key in communicating with the media, so it is best to be as honest as possible about questionable situations. If the story is going to be told anyway, it is better that it come from you rather than from your competitor.

CEOs and other top executives should take leading, highly visible roles in their companies' public relations process. Doing so increases a company's credibility, not only in the eyes of customers and employees, but in the eyes of the media as well. Matching a human face and voice to the image of a company goes a long way toward personalizing a company, and the CEO's involvement in this process is critical.

Oakridge Public Relations, in their Web site article "What Makes Public Relations Effective?," site the following:

In October 1991, the Public Relations Society of America presented a panel discussion called "How Important Technology News Reaches the Public." The panel featured journalists from a variety of publications, including *Fortune, Business Week,* and *The New York Times.* Repeatedly, these journalists sent the same message: The CEO is critical to successful public relations. "We look to the CEO because the CEO personifies the company," said Doug Ramsey of CNBC Business News. During a discussion of a press event announcing the alliance between Apple Computer Inc. and IBM Corp., Mr. Ramsey commented, "I was rather surprised at all the pictures we had coming in. We had John Sculley there, CEO of Apple, who's generally very available to the press and quite helpful. But not John Akers of IBM. So I was wondering, what's going on here? Why is this happening? What was he [Akers] doing that was so important that he could not be there when the CEO of Apple Computer was there? There has got to be a story there somewhere." David Kirkpatrick of *Fortune* added, "Considering they are trying to sell their alliance as significant, it was notable that [Akers] wasn't there. The media look to the CEO's level of involvement to gauge the importance of news, and they look to the CEO to embody a company's mission, values, and position.

While technical experts or marketing and salespeople may have more targeted content knowledge and understanding about a particular product, placing upper management in front of the media is part of image and brand building. Often, the vision of lower management is much narrower, and an accurate big-picture perspective is not conveyed. Therefore, the CEO needs to have a good grasp of the PR strategies, but not get involved in the tactical management of the program. Top-level executives need to be willing to take part in press tours that usually include visiting the headquarters of major publications or other kinds of media consumed by their companies' target audiences. It may also be necessary for executive management to take part in meetings with other significant influencers.

Assessing Effectiveness

It is more difficult to measure the results of a public relations effort than it is the results of an ad with a specific call to action. Oakridge Public Relations, in the Web site article "What Is Public Relations and Why Should I Care?," offered the following criteria when attempting to assess the effectiveness of a PR campaign:

Ink: The number, type, and quality of media coverage can be evaluated. Of course, this means you must have a clipping service, but this is a minimal price to pay (about $150–$200 a month) to track results. The content should be examined to see if the key messages are being picked up.

Bingos: Trade publications usually provide bingo response mechanisms to allow readers to respond directly to articles.

Direct Leads: Often, hot prospects will respond directly by phone. Your salespeople or reps need to track where leads are coming from—ads, PR, direct mail, trade shows, and the like.

Research: Performing benchmark studies periodically will help you to track changes in perception, share of mind, and market awareness.

Increased Sales: You won't be able to measure what percentage of sales is due to PR, what percentage to advertising, and so on, but if there is an increase in sales after you begin doing PR (assuming things in other areas remain relatively constant), then you can assume PR has helped. And that's about as precise as you're going to get.

Gut Feeling: Your visceral feeling about how the PR program is working is one of the most reliable indicators—although, unfortunately, not one that is readily accepted by the board of directors. You will know from talking to editors, customers, and especially the competition, whether the public relations program is effective.

Building a Responsive Infrastructure

Responsiveness is one of the most valued qualities an agency can bring to a relationship with the media. Journalists often want bylines, and need interviews scheduled within very tight deadlines. Use of the online environment makes turnaround response times quick and convenient since many journalists work outside of the typical workday schedule, and they appreciate the ability to access this information in an on-demand fashion. Public relations firms equally appreciate the ability to communicate when it is convenient for them, regardless of where their travel or other time demands take them. When unexpected events or problematic circumstances arise for a company, it is to everyone's advantage to have immediate access and control over the dissemination of information.

A San Francisco PR firm, Phase Two Strategies, relates an example of the importance of setting up responsive communications strategies. President Chris Boehlke helped to place one of the first full-service 800 customer numbers about 18 years ago, for Johnson & Johnson. It was also the first 800 number to be published on product packaging. A battery of customer service people were hired, thousands of questions and answers for their products were written, and all of the personnel who would be responding to customer calls were trained. According to Boehlke, Johnson & Johnson managers felt that, as a good consumer service company, they needed to take a leadership role in this effort. Today, companies are moving toward making this available on the Internet as well.

One of the purposes for setting up this service was to get customer feedback on products. It resulted in teaching Johnson & Johnson a good deal about their products as well as their customers. Another objective of this 800 number was to educate consumers. When the company introduced OB Tampons, for example, women were concerned that the tampons had no casing on them. Johnson & Johnson made physicians available on the phones to answer their questions and explain the benefits of the new style. This service turned out to be especially timely when the highly publicized Rely Tampon recall took place. Proctor and Gamble, also a former client of Boehlke's, put its brand name forward—an unusual step for them to take—to officially recall the product because of the level of publicity that it was generating. Johnson & Johnson, too, was flooded with calls because the real issue was Toxic Shock Syndrome, not a particular tampon product. Since J & J had done its homework with its consumer interface, it was ready.

This vehicle—well thought, appropriately positioned, and efficiently maintained—proved to be one of Johnson & Johnson's most effective PR strategies. The 800 number staffed by well-trained personnel became a powerful crisis management tool. But technological innovation and preparation were not the only factors that contributed to the success of the strategy. Johnson & Johnson's willingness to take a responsive, leadership role in the crisis situation strengthened its public image significantly. According to Boehlke, the Johnson & Johnson brand, defined in the public consciousness over many years, means, "We will do whatever is necessary to retain our customers' trust and loyalty." And that, as much as any direct advertising, is what sells Johnson & Johnson products to this day.

Phase Two uses the following quote as one of its guiding tenets: "Communication must do more than build awareness. It must strengthen each link in the circle that builds equity for your company, brand, or product."

Targeting Influencers

When asked to define the term influencers, Chris Boehlke of Phase Two Strategies explains, "There's always a small cluster of people at the very top and although there aren't that many of them, what they believe and what they say influences opinions all over the country. The Internet is a great place to reach powerful and targeted groups of influencers because [they] care passionately about things."

Phase Two had the opportunity to test Boehlke's theory about the Internet's influencers when a computer sound card company, beleaguered by scandal and financial problems, approached the firm. The company desperately needed to sell its products, despite the onslaught of negative publicity and speculation about its future. Phase Two had to move quickly and decisively. Boehlke realized that the people who care most about computer sound quality are musicians on the Internet who want people to download their music samples. She also knew that even though the company was in trouble, its sound cards were considered superior by this market segment.

Consequently, Phase Two targeted some of the better known musicians who were providing samples over the Internet and gave them sound cards for their own use. These musicians subsequently recommended the sound cards to *their* target audience, the people who listen to music samples on computers. This was a successful strategy in which the influencers were targeted and, in effect, enlisted to perform a PR function.

Torme & Kenney, a PR firm that serves a broad range of industries, has launched a strategic PR campaign in which influencers figure highly. Its client is the Walnut Marketing Board. The campaign was deemed necessary to respond to some confusing reports issued by the USDA, in which a food pyramid was used to discuss fat levels and food value. In the pyramid, nuts were lumped with a lot of other foods, so that it was difficult to tell whether nuts were good for you or not. The implication was that they were very high in fat and low in nutritional value, which made consumers wary of eating nuts, and consequently has posed a threat to the walnut industry.

The first stage of Torme & Kenney's strategy is to further the exchange of information in scientific research and nutrition in the area of nuts. Margaret Torme explains, "Some very favorable research had been done showing that polyunsaturated fats reduce blood cholesterol. It's the good fat, bad fat discussion." The PR firm decided to use the Internet to host an ongoing technological/scientific exchange on the subject. Research papers, clippings, and listings of everyone who is researching or publishing in this field are posted at this forum. The firm and its client have found that by making this accurate, up-to-date information available, the walnut and related industries have benefited. The media is also directed to this resource when any questions arise.

Once this first stage is well established, the next stage will include a much broader consumer-oriented campaign. At present, Torme & Kenney are using traditional publicity methods, along with printed materials, to send the positive message about nuts. They are fielding 30,000–40,000 customer requests for information per year. Although fax-on-demand is in place, most of this communication is currently handled by service personnel. The PR firm is experimenting with other electronic vehicles, including the online environment. Once tests have been completed, the firm anticipates using these vehicles in the next stage of the campaign. Torme comments, "Communicating a new food/health message involves many targets needing different approaches. To be effective requires being compelling to influencers and gatekeepers, as well as to consumers."

Figure 4.1 (provided by Torme & Kenney) shows how influencers, gatekeepers, and consumers in the category of food/health could be effectively targeted in a PR campaign. The message fragment indicates the specific slant to take when addressing the specified group, and the right column shows the target medium to use. This communications matrix is part of a hypothetical media plan that might run as long as 50 to 100 pages and include the entire messages for each audience, specifications for the method or mediums in which it is to be

Sample Public Relations Communications Matrix

TARGET AUDIENCE	AUDIENCE-SPECIFIC MESSAGE	MEDIUM
GATEKEEPERS		GATEKEEPERS
Nutritionists	"New research shows . . ."	Journals
Dietitians	"There are new options for patients . . ."	Internet
		Direct Mail
Medical Researchers	"Here is a rich area for future research . . ."	Meetings/Symposiums
		Advisory Councils
Physicians	"Clinical research shows patients benefit when . . ."	Mass Media
		Databases
Nurses	"Patients will be pleased to learn . . ."	Speeches/ Presentations/
FDA	"We knew you'd want to be kept up to date . . ."	Audio Conferences
USDA	"As you continue to consider dietary guidelines . . ."	
		INFLUENCERS & BUYERS
INFLUENCERS		
Medical/Health Associations	"Here's some good news for your members . . ."	Trade Publications
Health Nonprofits	"Here's a new way to help your clients . . ."	Direct Mail
		Internet
		Meetings
Health Advocacy Groups	"New research shows beneficial results . . ."	Mass Media
Nutrition Authors	"Here's some welcome news for your readers . . ."	Special Interest Media
		Newsletters
		Databases
Cookbook Authors	"Here's some recipes that are good and healthy . . ."	Books
		Monographs
Health Authors	"Here's a whole new basis for healthy eating . . ."	Speeches
		Presentations
Health Food Experts	"Sometimes health food comes in surprising forms . . ."	Presentations
		Conferences
Educators	"Conventional wisdom needs revision when it comes to . . ."	News Releases
		TV & Radio Talk Shows
Health/Nutrition Media	"Surprising new research results show hope for millions . . ."	
Food Media	"Good, and good for you . . ."	
General News/Media	"Research reveals surprising news . . ."	
BUYERS		
Retailers (Gatekeepers/ Influencers)	"Now there will be high demand for . . ."	
Consumers (Influencers)	"At last you can enjoy X without feeling guilty . . ."	

Figure 4.1   Targeting consumers in the food/health category.

delivered, and, of course, detailed contact and delivery information. A follow-up sequence might also be included in the plan.

The principals at Torme & Kenney are also spearheading another innovative approach to targeting influencers in the media. They plan to provide them with photo libraries on CD-ROM. The visuals may include foods, travel photography, charts, and graphs—anything related in some way to their clients' products. The target influencers are those who will be writing or speaking about these products. For example, a CD-ROM library might include food and recipes that promote the use of cheese walnuts, and C&W frozen foods (the California Milk Advisory Board, the Walnut Marketing Board, and C&W Frozen Foods are among Torme & Kenney's clientele) and be sent to the food editors of newspapers and magazines. Typically, in a PR campaign, influencers are given a single photo. Obviously, the CD-ROM will provide them with a lot more choices, in a format that is easy to review and reproduce. This added variety and convenience is sure to be welcomed by the media. The relationship is mutually beneficial: The media gets the information it needs, and Torme & Kenney's clients get the exposure they need.

A visionary in the field, Torme has also been instrumental in creating an international PR network called Public Relations Organization International that includes over 100 agencies. The organization plans to launch a content-rich Web site aimed primarily at serving the needs of the media. In addition, because of the depth and quality of the information to be made available, portions may also be accessible to the public. The organization is developing a list of topics and experts for every industry it serves. Subject matter will encompass legal, scientific, and environmental issues, as well as any other client- or topic-related information. Each of the member agencies is responsible for developing part of the site. Once accomplished, it will be a first.

Laddering

Within any target audience, further segmentation usually needs to be taken into account when developing a strategy. Maintaining a core consistency while addressing the needs of each of these segments begins with a process of research to determine how you are currently perceived by them. "Laddering" is a technique used by Phase Two Strategies to evaluate a client's messages from the perspective of value to the target audience:

Attributes: "My product looks like this and is capable of doing these things."

Benefits: "The attributes of my product give you the benefit of doing these specific things that will make your job/life easier and more successful."

Value: "The benefits of my product to you give you the power to accomplish those goals that are most important to you."

By determining the attributes, benefits, and values that are meaningful to your different audiences, you can deliberately and knowledgeably guide audience-specific messages through the most appropriate media channels. This is the foundation that supports all PR activities. It is important to remember that electronic marketing and technology in general has brought the consumer into a much more immediate and powerful position, demanding 24 hour access and TLC.

Contributing Something of Value

Community relations is considered one of the most potent influencers for success in business. To achieve good community relations, companies must identify with their customers, be integral to the community, and be regarded as responsible citizens by the community. Chris Boehlke of Phase Two Strategies advises, "You truly need to know your etiquette, and you need to bring something of value to the party. The Net is not a promotional environment, and this is where public relations runs the show. Either you're a good community PR representative or you're not." For example, at the time of rock legend Jerry Garcia's death, Phase Two's client, Compton's New Media, had a CD-ROM on the market called Haight Ashbury in the '60s, which included some exclusive footage of Garcia. Phase Two decided to take a few minutes of the footage and put it on the Internet, as an offering to the fans of Garcia. Making a contribution to the community instead of exploiting the tragedy by promoting its product was a wise, strategic PR move. The firm was seen as giving something of real value and "heart" to the community. This got a lot more mileage in the long run and could ultimately result in far more sales than the bad feelings or even boycotting that could have been created if they had used Garcia's death to exploit the grieving fans by pushing sales of the CD-ROM.

Educating Future Influencers

Sprint, the long-distance service provider, has been involved in a number of programs exploring such issues as distance learning, interactive education programs in a group of "wired" schools in California, and a closed system called the Silicon Valley Test Track. In the distance learning project, video conferencing was used to link schools in the United States and France. Twelve-year-old students discussed their use of technology and its importance in the future. To further the reach of these programs, Torme & Kenney also set up a simultaneous audio conference to enable the media to ask the children and teachers questions.

This project was designed with a number of goals in mind: to demonstrate the benefits of video in real time, as opposed to plain text in communication and education; to provide valuable marketing research information by exploring children's attitudes about technology; to expose the media to this communication dynamic as an alternative mode of remote news and information gathering; and to expand the perception of this tool from one that is commonly used in business for video conferencing, to one that has valuable potential for distance learning.

Another promotion for distance learning was launched by Sprint and Torme & Kenney in Pacifica, California. Sprint wired certain schools for a program it calls Video Jukebox. Computers and interactive learning materials by grade level are provided for each classroom. The Video Jukebox allows the students to select a story, a lesson, a software package, or other resource, much like choosing a song in a traditional jukebox. These jukeboxes are wired into libraries and other resource servers all across the country. This program was a first in the United States, and Torme & Kenney executed an aggressive media outreach campaign, arranging coverage by regional and national media each step of the way. The culmination occurred in the fall of '95 when Video Jukebox went completely online, and NBC's *Today Show* filmed the school environment of the future.

The Silicon Valley Test Track, which is a system built by Sprint, involves a coalition of approximately 15 companies that includes Apple, Hewlett-Packard, and Sun Microsystems. It is focused on testing various technologies that address each of their markets. The projects are targeted at both influencers and consumers of the technologies provided by all participating companies. By contributing to the community and to the education of future consumers, as well as building brand familiarity, these companies are acquiring valuable mind-share of these future consumers. The press is consistently included. The goal is to educate the press, thereby encouraging it to educate others on the benefits of these technologies.

A Potent PR Tool: The Internet

The Internet is becoming a very potent tool for PR. It enables people to "visit" a company without ever leaving their home or office. But creating a human experience with the use of technology is a critically important challenge. Chris Boehlke works with her clients to create an experience akin to a person walking into a company, taking a tour, and getting to really know the people behind the product. "We help them to set up input devices so that they can do customer research on the Web site. Using other PR and advertising vehicles, people are encouraged to visit the Web site to tell us what they think. That's very, very powerful, because somebody with a computer is going to do that before they write a letter, put a stamp on it, and send it. It's not necessarily as powerful as an 800 number yet."

Phase Two Strategies also uses the Internet in highly targeted PR campaigns. One effective campaign managed to turn potential disaster into a great success by making creative use of the Internet and other media venues. The client was Stormfront Studios, a company that produces many CD-ROM baseball games. One of its products, Old Time Baseball, is a what-if simulation game featuring every player over the past 110 years. Scheduled to ship in September 1995, well before the World Series, the product was late and didn't make it out the door until about a week before the series. "There's nothing deader than baseball after the World Series," lamented Boehlke.

Phase Two had done its homework, however, by making sure that reviewers had beta copies of the product two months early. As a result, the product reviews were not delayed. Stormfront Studios had also produced a video news release that showcased a variety of what-if scenarios, which received excellent pickup and ran during the week of the series. Phase Two also made sure that articles about the CD appeared in all of the baseball magazines. On the Internet, the PR firm identified all of the baseball venues, including every discussion forum for every team, and then staged what-if scenarios online, involving each of these forums. This gave the game great visibility. People on all of the forums really got into it, speculating on the possible outcomes. They were given something of value that they enjoyed, and at the same time they were sampling the product. Despite the late release, the game ended up selling well and the crisis was successfully averted.

Pat Meier of Pat Meier Associates describes her company as "a leading public relations agency, specializing in companies that are involved in multimedia, entertainment, interactive television, and, to a certain degree telecommunications." She adds, "We're in a unique position, because we're both a provider of online marketing services as well as a customer of those service providers." Meier is passionate about using technology to enhance human interaction, not displace it. "Our agency, no matter how large it grows, will always be a personal agency where people feel like they are dealing with people, not a machine. No matter how sophisticated we get in the services we provide, it's all about people. So one of the first [images] you see when you get into our Web sites are our account executives."

Meier provides journalists around-the-clock online access to client information, announcements, press releases, and product information. She considers this a necessary courtesy. She explains that, regardless of the high-tech marketing and PR solutions the online environment makes possible, "you're still going to have to cross-reference other media. It's imperative to list Web addresses in press releases, press kits, and business cards, both for ourselves as well as for our clients."

Chip Dehnert, account executive at Pat Meier Associates, describes the firm's Web strategy and the rationale behind it: "The bulk of our effort is to make our clients' information available to our database of journalists. Everything we have has our Web site address mentioned in it, so that the journalists, who are more or less the bread and butter of the business, know about the site, have access to it; and when they come there to look for one client, it invariably draws them in to see another one, and it may draw them to that other client's Web site."

Journalists can visit the Pat Meier Associates Web site (www/patmeier.com) any time to get information about the firm's clients. Meier elaborates, "If we're exclusively providing a client's Web site, then what we're doing is providing information to journalists on our client's behalf. And that information is mostly textual, in the form of news releases, but it's also things like tiff files, so pictures of their products can be downloaded. People can look at box shots or thumbnails of their boxes, for instance, or client personalities, head shots, and things like that."

In addition to hosting clients at its own site, the PR firm also provides links to its clients' other online locations. On the subject of hosting and linking, Meier advises, "As a marketing service provider, a company needs to look at the personality and the outreach of the site where their home page is going to be listed and find out whether there is synergy with other companies listed there."

When summing up her company's use of the Web, Meier emphasizes:

> Listing someone on the Web site is just one small part of the marketing mix. We consider it the same as sending out a news release. It's just a different delivery system. It does reflect on the style of the company, so it does require a bit more creative and design flair than simply printing text on a piece of letterhead. Really, the work we do is in writing the news releases and giving the appropriate spin. And outbound contact with journalists is still very much a people-to-people business—the Web site is a backup. Through our Web site, journalists get to know our agency. We make sure that every journalist knows who our clients are. And we become, in essence, a one-stop shop to journalists looking for multimedia stories.

Pat Meier Associates also uses the online environment in highly targeted PR campaigns. One of the agency's long-time clients, Grolier Interactive, put the first encyclopedia on CD-ROM. Grolier was the first to recognize the importance of electronic publishing, to get into the universities, and to provide online access to its entire encyclopedia. The company is now launching a full range of games and children's titles under the name 3 Prong Plug. For each of its business entities, it has created a different Web site, from which information or products can be ordered.

For one of the Grolier Interactive products, The Ultimate Challenge Golf Game, Meier's PR campaign included targeting a number of online golf sites around the world. The Internet gives Meier and her clients quick, easy, and inexpensive worldwide access, and provides an efficient, cost-effective way to publicize a product or event, and then bring people back to the larger environment, where they can find out about other products that the company offers. For example, Meier can contact a golf site in South Africa to request a link to the Grolier site. In 1996, the globalization of Grolier will be heightened by the localization of its products around the world by parent company Matra Hachette Multimedia.

On Target is a small San Francisco Bay Area company that defines itself as an electronic public relations firm, specializing in online PR and multimedia development. Mary Ann Stefanic manages the firm's campaigns, and as it makes the transition from traditional PR and advertising into the electronic arena, she incorporates all of the skills she learned in traditional media promotion. She cites the following example to illustrate a campaign across a range of media starting with print and ending up on the Web.

A networking systems company was changing its name from T3-Plus to OnStream Networks, and came to On Target to design the name-change campaign. On Target started with direct-mail trade magazine inserts, designed so that they would also fit into envelopes with a cover letter for another element in the direct mail effort. The magazine insert and letter included an offer for a free interactive demo diskette. Stefanic explained that, instead of asking the consumer to send for a brochure or request that a representative call, they read, "Send for your free demo diskette." When the diskette was mailed out, it was packaged in a jeweled case, for greater impact. The approach On Target used is called a "three flight." Stefanic explains how it works:

> We come out the first week with one insert or direct mail piece with a theme. Then, keeping the same look and feel and branding information, we change the images and wording a little, and send a second mailing out the following week. We do this three times so that by the end of the third week, we have this whole story about the company change. We send a fresh image and message as a different variation on the theme each week. It's a way to "talk" to them and begin to build recognition and the beginnings of a relationship.
>
> We ran three flights for the brochure over three months, and kept rotating it. We ran it three times for each method of outreach: three rounds in the magazine and three times in direct mail. And each time we offered the free diskette but did not mail it until the response came back.

We sent oversized postcards at the very end to tell [the consumer] about the upcoming trade show. The trade show was going to be the first one where [the company] would be using its new name. We then turned the diskette into a continuously running demo in a kiosk for use at the trade show, and added music and voice-over to it.

Now we're working on the Web site. This Web site always has our company banner on it, no matter where you go. That's where EPR—electronic PR—comes in. We're working with OnStream's PR company that manages all other media outside of the Internet, to get involved with different newsgroups, take advantage of opportunities, and constantly look for more links that would be beneficial.

Prior campaigns, according to OnStream, resulted in well under 2,000 responses. At last count, it was beginning a second manufacturing run for 2,000-plus diskettes, double highest expectations.

Budget Considerations

In addressing budget considerations, Margaret Torme of Torme & Kenney explains that it really depends on the objective: "If clients want a national campaign, I would tell them they shouldn't even think about it for less than about $300,000 for a one-year budget, to make any impact at all," whereas in a campaign that is geographically specific, such as someone trying to put up a billboard or antennae in a place that creates an eyesore and people are protesting, may take as little as $10,000 to generate a positive attitude.

Torme & Kenney lists situations in which PR will pay exceptional dividends:

New or emerging industry or category

Innovation in mature industry or category

Completely new product or service

Surprising research results

Fascinating founder, owners, or key executives

Mass market or niche market (everybody needs the product, or it meets a specific need)

Exceptional price (outrageously expensive or surprisingly inexpensive)

Remarkable remake or comeback of something old

Celebrities (sometimes)

Causes that impact the public

Controversy that involves the public

Helpful information

Health issues

Torme & Kenney bases project pricing on a set of criteria that extends beyond the confines of strict time/cost analysis: "We judge whether or not we should take on an assignment not by how much money is involved, but by how much return we can get on the effort. And the reason we do that is because that is what will bring us the referrals that build our business."

At Pat Meier Associates, to get in the door costs $5,000 a month, with a six-month minimum commitment, for which the client gets an aggressive outbound campaign, utilizing phone, mail, e-mail, and more. Meier elaborates, "We set up interviews for the client with the journalists. There's still a lot of personal contact and hand-holding. It's not just sitting back and waiting for them to come to you."

Phase Two believes that public relations should control everything and that advertising is simply one of the ways to deliver the messages. "Public relations is how you relate with your public, understand them, listen to them," states Chris Boehlke. She believes that the best way to market a company is by word of mouth, from good referrals, and that is the primary means of promotional activity used by Phase Two to market its own services.

> To that end, we spend over half (of the money we spend on marketing) on client development for providing added value. Sometimes there's a great idea and a client just can't come up with the money, and we'll say we're going to do this idea anyway. Because building our own successful cases and clients . . . is the ultimate in how we market anything. We do not advertise. We do have our own public relations program where we have somebody who places a Phase Two spokesperson in things, which is happening as we speak.
>
> Every employee has a budget to go to the industry activities they feel are best for them. They're learning, which is going to help our firm and our clients, and they're also reaching out. We have a PR outreach program for making our own company known. And the vast majority of our clients have come from having been our client somewhere else. . . . We have clients that we've had in four iterations of their professional lives. And that's exactly how we try to counsel our own clients, that performance is what creates loyalty. So that's our marketing program.

When asked why the firm is called Phase Two, Boehlke explained, "Phase one of a company is when it's just starting out and it has to get its act together and make sure it has a product or service that it can bring to market, and so on. And at the point when that's done [employees] say, okay now we need to do everything it takes to be a real grown-up company. And that's a whole new set of things they haven't thought of so far. That's when we start to get into branding issues and product lines and even internal communications. Every company goes through its own phase two situations where a market changes and it needs to change if it's going to continue to grow successfully. That requires strategic thinking through the situation, so whatever you go forth and do is based on a very sound strategy." Thus the name Phase Two Strategies.

Conclusion

Public relations is not always given its due in the midst of the frenetic excitement over glitsy new technologies and eyecatching advertising campaigns. Nevertheless, it is the backbone along which all of the branding and image messages must be built in order to be strong, coherent, and intentionally guided. Communications crises are all too common in companies today, and unless a well-defined strategy is in place and ready to be implemented, a business could find itself facing unnecessary damage, loss, and possibly even demise. The budgets for this kind of support have a healthy range, and it is even possible to hire an individual PR consultant for well below agency rates. Sometimes this is all that is needed to ensure, at the very least, awareness of potential opportunities or problems. A PR checkup is good preventative medicine, and a basic understanding of its role in the overall marketing and maintenance strategy of a company is a good place to begin.

CHAPTER FIVE

INTERACTIVE ADVERTISING

Margo Komenar

The New Face of Advertising

The face of advertising is changing quickly and dramatically. We have expanded from the passive two-dimensional world of print, TV, and radio into multimedia and online interactive marketing in a very short time. Mass marketing has traditionally consisted of utilizing a few standard vehicles to reach the greatest possible number of people, with the same message, designed to speak to the lowest common denominator audience. But with new interactive and database technology, customized one-to-one marketing is quickly moving from a considered possibility to a valued competitive strategy.

Through the use of electronic vehicles such as CD-ROM, interactive kiosks, the Internet, and interactive television, consumers are now able to self-select the advertising message. They may choose what they will look at or respond to thanks to a database that can store a range of possibilities. Marketers can now create individualized response advertisements based on a consumer's direct and immediate feedback. This is a whole new ball game for marketers, and they, as well as interactive media designers, are under great pressure to keep pace with this trend.

One-to-One Connection

Ketchum Communication's approach to successful marketing is called The One Approach. "It is centered on the belief that, to be effective, we must make an emotional connection with people, and this connection is made one person at a time, even in mass media. So we listen, personally, to people all through the communications development process to ensure this one-to-one connection is made. People don't read ads, they read what interests them. Sometime what interests them is an ad."

The principles of good communication apply to any media, anyplace, anytime. Ketchum is one of the most highly regarded full-service communications agencies today, and its vast expertise leads it right back to the most basic of strategies.

Since it is now possible to target an audience down to a "market segment of one," electronic venues such as the Internet and CD-ROMs are ideal for the kinds of highly targeted campaigns used in traditional direct marketing, according to Lynn Upshaw of Upshaw & Associates and former managing director of Ketchum Interactive. Incentive marketing, or offering the consumer points, rebates, prizes, and other benefits for spending time or money with advertisers, is another appropriate strategy that will work well in the interactive marketplace. Upshaw states that, unlike the passive experience of watching TV or listening to radio, people are drawn into interactive media, and marketers should take advantage of the consumer's desire to be an (inter)active participant:

> With interactive, you've got people who are saying when they log on or they start their CD-ROM or whatever they do, they want to do something. They want to be active. So you could take advantage of that and use their activity to get them more involved in what they're doing. For example . . . we re-created [the Bank of America] site, a thing called Build Your Own Bank. It was based on the Banking on America theme, which is based on the overall strategy of a bank that appeals to individuals, or a bank where individuals can have their financial services needs met. . . . When you log on [the first time] and you answer a few questions, the next time you log on, it will say, "Welcome to the Bank of Lynn Upshaw," and because Lynn Upshaw has two kids, it will tell you when there is a special online for student loans or for savings for college.
>
> The key thing you can do is customize these things, personalize these promotions, which you never really could do before. Even in direct mail, the most you were doing most of the time was sending [consumers] a letter with their name on it. But now you're able to say, "I know what kind of person that is because [he or she] filled out some information for me. Now I'm really going to start sending that person more targeted information." You can do that with direct mail. But you can do it so much faster with interactive.

Ross Gillanders, VP of Business Development for the Hypermedia Group, a multimedia communications company, elaborates on this move toward one-to-one marketing:

There's a real paradigm shift happening. And this notion of one-on-one marketing is on everybody's lips. It really has to do with having the ability for the first time to market directly to your customer, as opposed to a mass audience orientation. And the companies that are getting onboard and taking some risk in getting their messages out on the Web—to really understand the power of these one-on-one marketing techniques and methodologies— are going to be the winners moving into the future . . . it represents a huge opportunity so unique and so powerful.

The most popular Web site right now is Netscape's, and it surprised me that Netscape charges from $20,000 to $40,000 a month to have a banner on its sites [first quarter '96]. Hewlett-Packard has a banner on its site, and you can directly link to it. In fact, right now Hewlett-Packard has a promotion going on where [there is] a registration form if you want to sign up for a promotional contest to win a free printer; and, therefore, HP is entering all of the people who are signing up into their database, and certainly the success of these companies will probably be in how best they manage their databases.

Michael Rogers, vice president of Post-Newsweek New Media, managing editor of Newsweek Interactive, and a contributing editor to *Newsweek* explains that his company has gone through several phases in its approach to electronic advertising design since 1992. He describes the changes as follows:

The first ads we saw on CD-ROM were basically just television ads that were digitized to video. And some of the Web pages that you see today are a lot like that also, only they're just magazine pages that sit there statically.

It's very clear to me that the key to successful interactive advertising is that at the beginning of the process you have to get the viewer to incorporate something of him- or herself into it so that he or she is invested right at the start. [For example] one is a French perfume ad that was done on CD-ROM in France, and it was for a company that made five or six lines of perfume, different lines; when the ad started up, the first thing it said was: "What kind of woman is she? Is she like a spring day? Is she like a fall afternoon?" And you chose. . . . even the most sophisticated users that I saw would get hooked by this because they had invested something and now they wanted to see what the payoff was.

A similar model, I've seen a few times [are] financial service companies that played around with just putting a simple spreadsheet up and saying, "How are you doing as far as your retirement funds? Want to fill in a couple blanks here? How old are you? How much do you save? You're going to be eating cat food unless you call this 800 number and talk to one of our brokers."

Again, those really work. I think it's very clear that in the future advertising is going to have to either be of service or entertaining, and probably some combination of the two. On the Net, I think of something like the Zima site, the beer sites that have games. Perfect example. How can you advertise a commodity like beer on the Internet? Do you just go there and it talks about beer? No. The good beer sites provide games and contests, as well as lots of information about beer. So they try to be of service and they try to be entertaining.

Focus on the Internet

New Order Media is a cross between an ad agency and a software firm. Kelly Stewart, art director and producer for the company, predicts that more of the action will focus on the Internet:

> *I think we're going to see less and less of just a standalone CD-ROM or something running off of someone's hard drive, and we're going to see more and more live connections to the World Wide Web or any other sort of network-based, live system that can update information very, very quickly. Furthermore, we are going to see much more "narrowcasting" of information. Instead of television commercials and magazine ads where companies are never sure they are reaching their target audience, we are going to see information and advertisements on-demand and tailored specifically to me, my buying habits, my taste, my needs.*
>
> *Basically the Web has shown that millions of people doing unrelated work can come together and develop a sort of self-perpetuating communications vehicle that can be this continuous spider web of links. People are starting to see the value in that. So I see a day when clients will not want something standalone that is fixed. They will not be satisfied with a CD-ROM that they can't change. More immediately we're going to see combinations of CD-ROM and World Wide Web delivery where maybe higher-end media elements, such as video, are going to be on CD, but then you will have your updated information by connecting to the Web, and the two will be talking back and forth to each other.*

Stewart designs products that are modular and easy to change. He believes that the client needs to be able to adapt the media elements, and will demand more flexibility in order to be compatible with the fluidity and pace of the Internet.

The Gartner Group, a leading information technology advisor to business professionals, confirms that things are changing at a phenomenal clip:

> *Within the next three to five years, the advertising arena will be virtually unrecognizable by the standards of just a couple years ago. Although this*

change has big ramifications in its own right, it has also caused marketing to spill into such areas as custom statement design and very small press runs (sometimes runs of only one piece) to allow for marketing communications and offers highly tailored to the customer.

New advances, such as digital ad inserts (special electronic advertisements stored in a database, then accessed and inserted into a World Wide Web page as appropriate), allow enterprises to design unique, customizable, just-in-time advertising campaigns based on the situation or customer feedback. But as the media richness increases, the complexity of the marketing job will increase, too. This age of mass customization of advertising campaigns promises to swamp marketing departments not prepared.

Gartner's 1996 Strategic Analysis Report on Interactive Marketing goes into great depth on the topic of building the strong infrastructure needed to handle the growing demands of database-led interactive marketing. The report is a valuable resource for businesses looking seriously into this area.

Customized "Mass" Promotion

A different slant on electronic marketing is underway by conference planners. One example is Miller-Freeman, a major publisher of more than 70 magazines and producer of a broad spectrum of conferences. In 1995, it decided to launch a new approach to its conference promotion and registration, utilizing the Internet. Spiral West, a Northern California multimedia production company, worked with the publisher to create the site. It was a highly successful beginning. Jeff Neugebauer, owner of Spiral West, comments on this growing trend:

> *Miller-Freeman is going to continue in this direction. I believe that it's going to put the bulk of its conferences online, so all registration and everything is going to be handled electronically, and it's going to be a lot better for the user. You can see your schedule in real time online, and you know what classes you're going to get. You don't have to submit anything and register by mail or fax. You have the immediate feedback that your registration has gone through and that you have the classes that you want.*

So does all of this electronic communication save trees? Well, not exactly! One of the ironic realities of electronic marketing is that while it appears that you are obviating the need for print communication by going digital, the truth is, most people still want to receive notification and basic information by direct mail or other means. So, for now, electronic technology just means adding a channel of communication, not eliminating one. Eventually, Miller-Freeman hopes to conduct all conference registrations electronically. However, for now, people must be told where the information exists online, so the need for additional support media will continue, thus adding expense to the overall campaign. Automation does not come cheaply, and won't until critical mass is reached.

Neugebauer agrees: "I think that's going to be true for quite a while, and as the Web becomes more and more saturated with organizations trying to promote their companies, you still have to have a way to reach them, and whether it's with direct calls, direct mail, or some kind of advertisement, they're going to have to continue to use the traditional methods to tell people to look on the Internet."

New Media in the Ad Mix

Newsweek's Michael Rogers sees the changing consumer audience moving out of a hobbyist phase during which early adopters were willing to upgrade their computers so that a CD-ROM could run, or would wait for graphics to download on a slower modem connection to consumers demanding cost- and time-efficient value. He believes this second wave of electronic media and online users will be the audience from which it may be possible to actually make some money. His company is getting into position for this audience, and he believes that the most successful online publications will be highly specialized, aimed at very vertical audiences.

As businesses begin to carve out a place in their marketing plans for interactive media, they must work out strategies that incorporate both new and traditional venues. With traditional advertising like radio and television, the cost, reach, and gross rating points are measurable criteria for comparing the success of the different vehicles. The composition of the audience or the time of day an ad is run are controllable variables. In interactive advertising, a great deal of experimentation is taking place, and there are more unknowns. The variables are far more complex, the track records are short, and different venues may be used simply for branding awareness, while others may be aimed at direct sales. Incorporating the old and new media into the marketing plan requires greater risk-taking on the part of marketers since the ROI of online marketing or CD catalogs are not conclusive. This industry is in its infancy. It is certain, though, that it is very difficult to compete in today's marketplace without utilizing at least some of these venues and taking some risks.

According to research conducted by SIMBA Information, Inc., Madison Avenue has been cautious in approaching electronic marketing. Consumer product companies including Proctor & Gamble and Kraft General Foods run their marketing campaigns based on numbers of units sold on a weekly, monthly, and quarterly basis. This short-term revenue mind-set is not a compatible measurement for success in electronic marketing. This new marketplace has not yet generated a level of electronic transactions to equal the volume provided by other venues for most businesses. These major consumer product companies must sell huge quantities of their brands in order to be profitable, and the electronic marketplace cannot yet offer them the kind of volume necessary to warrant any significant shift of attention or resources.

SIMBA explains why it is just not feasible for these companies to risk much of an investment in this area: "Pillsbury, for example, has said that it needs to achieve a cost per transaction of less than one cent in order to make electronic marketing cost-effective. That being the financial reality, packaged-goods marketers like Pillsbury have limited their electronic marketing tests."

Companies with high-ticket products are using electronic media more for brand awareness and information delivery than for actual sales. It is unlikely that anyone will purchase costly appliances or automobiles that cost many thousands of dollars, sight unseen, online, but they will use that environment to gather information. Exposure to the brand identity is becoming the objective for most of these major corporations.

Approaching the Market

Once the decision has been made to use interactive media, there are several ways to improve the chances for success. Gartner suggests four tactics for marketing departments to employ once they have developed a comprehensive strategy. This strategy should include answering the questions:

> Where does interactive marketing fit in the marketing mix?
>
> Why is interactive marketing better than traditional marketing tools?
>
> Is interactive marketing the right tool for a certain product or service?

Gartner says "flooding the airwaves" is the best approach if you fall into either of these two groups:

- You are new to interactive marketing.
- You are ready to completely immerse your company in interactive marketing, which means using the entire spectrum of vehicles in a very intense campaign that literally saturates the consumer with your message.

Flooding the airwaves may be accomplished through utilizing a combination of Internet and commercial online services, interactive TV, CD-ROM, electronic catalogs, and/or kiosks. Many of the larger companies with sizable budgets will choose to support these endeavors with the traditional mix simultaneously. This is obviously very costly, but each venue is supported by all of the others, and while some may not be completely successful, together, they will guarantee maximum exposure.

Since this is so costly, Gartner says that the criteria for selecting this approach should include having a target audience that spans a broad range of customers, in some cases across a number of different industries such as airlines, automobile makers, or hotel chains. In areas such as financial services or luxury items, this method will help to wear down resistance when the sale is more difficult. And a final criterion for this approach is when you are competing against many in the marketplace.

According to the Gartner Group's 1996 Strategic Analysis Report: *Interactive Marketing: A New Business Landscape for Marketing Professionals,* selecting one new media, or two at most, and focusing all of your resources on becoming the best in that category is another potential tactic. This is especially appropriate for companies that either have one product or a single item within a brand line; the product and the marketing medium are highly compatible, such as software on CD-ROM; and the market is stable with well-established advertising patterns, such as the clothing industry.

A third tactic is to apply a different electronic vehicle to each audience segment of the market. This is achieved through the use of sophisticated databases that can identify these segments, which may fall into variously defined and refined demographic, psychographic, or lifestyle groups with specific buying patterns. Marketing in this way is less expensive than previous approaches discussed because a campaign can be rolled out incrementally, and works well within the traditional modes of advertising. According to Gartner, this method is best applied to industries in which a number of unrelated or clearly differentiated segments must be marketed to, such as the auto industry, or if the market is highly fragmented such as the software industry.

Dedicating one vehicle to one product in a mix or line of products is a fourth possible way to approach the allocation of resources for interactive advertising. Instead of lining up a product with a particular audience segment, it is lined up with a particular vehicle. This method also allows incremental rollout, and Gartner explains that this strategy "keeps the product image clean and separate, [and] makes it hard for niche players to keep up. . . ." but warns that the risk for failure is high if a bad marketing decision is made, as ". . . the tactic also places a burden on the production cycle. As a result, forecasting is critical. Because each product must have a personality, the tactic is hard to employ with products that appeal to multiple segments."

Gartner suggests that this is appropriate for products that are highly differentiated within a product mix such as in the beverage industry or with clothing brands, for those that are part of a "one-stop shopping" venue, in an aggressive market, or when the brands are disparate within a company product line.

Interactive Marketing Tools

According to the Gartner Group, interactive marketing is a multistep process that includes understanding the available media tools. Following is a list of the major electronic tools, including the trade-offs between the cost to implement and the degree to which a mass or fragmented market can be reached.

- *The Internet:* The Internet is a relatively inexpensive medium to enter into, and it appeals to a narrow slice of customer segments (upper income, young, and well-educated). However, a high degree of attention is required to use it properly (e.g., the enterprise must respond to inquiries and update Web screens).
- *Interactive TV:* This technology allows for two-way communication using a television as the medium. In coming years, it will be one of the most popular vehicles for setting up electronic marketplaces. Still in its infancy, this medium promises to have tremendous draw across a range of segments. It will be expensive, however, especially for early adopters, with early development costs approaching $5 million minimum, depending on the number of participating firms. Still, early users of this medium may build a competitive advantage that will be hard to duplicate later. Early prototypes will be rolled out in 1996, but this medium will not become significant until 1998 at the earliest (0.7 probability).
- *Online Services:* Each of the major services (e.g., America Online and CompuServe) has a unique look and feel, and provides various value-added services beyond marketing opportunities. Less expensive and less difficult to maintain than the Internet (since costs are borne by the provider), this medium appeals to a narrow slice of the market but is available to many people in that slice. These services can be a good way for enterprises to get a feel for computer-based marketing without the perils and pitfalls of the Internet, and they will appeal to more-risk-averse enterprises and those that have a broad spectrum of customers.
- *Kiosks:* Described as self-service, freestanding customer service devices, this tool is part marketing and part customer service and storefront. A medium coming into its own, kiosks have both moderate appeal and moderate cost ($20,000 to $30,000 per machine). These devices are specialized, requiring heavy-traffic outlets to be practical. In addition, kiosks provide a good degree of confidentiality.
- *CD-ROM:* This medium uses compact disk technology to transmit information (rather than music). Although it is an inexpensive medium to enter into

(desktop writable systems cost about $3,000), its appeal is still limited due to the relatively small number of consumers who have CD-ROM players. CD-ROMs can make sense if there is a natural synergy to the product, such as software distribution, or if the product is heavily dependent on photography, such as tourist advertising.

• *Electronic Catalogs:* This tool is used to distribute traditional catalogs in an electronic format. Electronic catalogs may be distributed via online services, CD-ROMs, or kiosks. They are inexpensive (usually limited to the cost of internal personnel and $1,000 in software), and make for a good transition from traditional marketing methods to new media. They have moderate consumer appeal, although they are still new and foreign to a large segment of the market. Success rates are low if the firm simply translates old catalogs to the new media, rather than understanding how to use the new media to its full advantage. An example of the latter is designing an electronic clothing catalog to let customers try different combinations of fabrics, colors and styles, enabling them to design optimal outfits.

• *Intelligent Buying Agents:* This medium enables consumers to use computer programs to find information and make purchases. Intelligent buying agents do not yet exist in the marketing or consumer realm other than in small prototypes. They have the potential, however, to be one of the mainstays of interactive marketing programs, although they will not be in common use until at least 1997 (0.7 probability). This tool will be moderately expensive ($100,000 to $200,000 due to development costs), but it will have broad appeal because of its usefulness and ease of use. Sun Microsystems' Java programming language is a likely medium for this technology.

In the past, the marketing mix consisted of television, radio, print, and point of sale. Now the mix contains interactive television, kiosks, CD-ROM, and other media with which most traditional marketers are not familiar. Enterprises that adapt to these methods early will be in a position to exploit the new technology as the market learns to accept it.

The "Right" Media

Another issue facing marketing professionals is how to decide which media is most appropriate for their needs. The Gartner Group finds that for these marketers, traditional media is familiar, and the appeal, cost versus benefit, and strengths and weaknesses are very clear-cut. Marketers who are very much at ease with "old" media have many concerns and questions regarding new media. The following, according to Gartner's Strategic Analysis Report are among the questions most frequently asked:

- What are the underlying technologies?
- Who are the vendors?
- Do customers respond?
- If so, which segments respond, at what rate, and how?
- Can the data captured be used to feed the marketing database?
- How is the new media's effectiveness measured?
- How does new media translate into more revenue?

Fear of the unknown—in this case, electronic marketing tools—keeps many marketers from moving forward into this new milieu. Eventually, they will be forced to participate if they want their businesses to succeed. A new generation of marketing has arrived. As societal, business, marketing, and technology trends converge, companies willing to take risks and begin to build the infrastructures needed to support the inevitable future will have risked success, rather than failure.

Figure 5.1 illustrates the evolution of marketing media as it passes through the '90s and is "driven" into the next millennium by higher levels of interac-

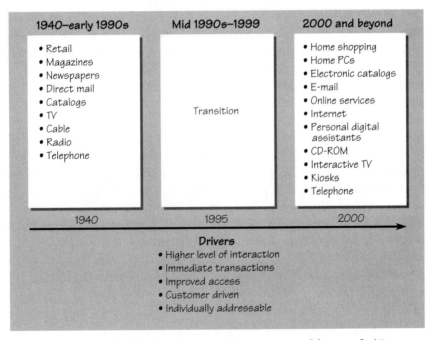

Figure 5.1   Media evolution, 1940 to 2000 and beyond. (*Source: Gartner Group*)

tivity, immediacy of transactions, improved access, a customer-driven market-place, and individually addressable promotions.

It is, however, a good idea to approach the new media with caution, because it's easy to become intoxicated by all of the animated interactive media and online hype. People often focus on the production of media rather than the production of an effective message that will translate to the most appropriate delivery vehicle. Jeff Neugebauer of Spiral West provides an example that illustrates the importance of selecting media that carefully considers the technology available to the target audience:

> It's really important to gauge your consumers and whether or not they're going to be able to view whatever it is you're creating. And sometimes traditional methods are better just because of that. A brochure is going to go a lot farther than a CD-ROM [because] if nobody can see the CD-ROM, it's really useless. Sometimes a brochure and a CD-ROM need to be done in conjunction with each other.
>
> My firm's Air Force project started out as a CD-ROM. It was for software developed to enable the Air Force to automate the acquisition process, so that proposals and requests for proposals and all that information could be sent back and forth between a vendor and the Air Force. [Personnel] wanted to eliminate the need to transport pallets full of paper documents.
>
> They found that electronic distribution was much more efficient and economical. Part of the Air Force was using it, but the majority was not on this electronic standard, [and the informed sector] wanted to inform the part of the Air Force that wasn't using this electronic tool that it existed. They decided to make a CD-ROM and send it to all these other Air Force branches, but they realized that these other groups weren't on the system because they didn't have the hardware to run it in the first place.
>
> It therefore made more sense to use videotape to get the message across, and then once the message was communicated, these branches could start to understand how it made sense to justify the equipment purchase to get on this network. In the long run, it would save them and the taxpayers money.
>
> We've actually talked people out of using CD-ROMs before because we realize once we listen to their needs and their objectives that they're trying to reach a certain audience for which a CD-ROM is a poor choice.

In contrast, Neugebauer describes a second case for which a CD-ROM was very appropriate, because the use of technology was part of the message the company was trying to communicate:

> A marketing company wanted to create an interactive brochure that would inform its clients that it was moving into the digital age and becoming pre-

pared to do not only print work but also digitally oriented brochures, floppy diskettes, or CD-ROMs. And for [this company] it was both a consulting project and a production project. As we worked with [the staff], they followed the process attentively so that as time went on they were able to do more and more of the work in house. We've found that sometimes when you're a consultant, the whole objective is to transfer those skills, even though you put yourself out of business with that client eventually, if you do a good enough job!

The Internet Channel

There is a great deal of debate as to the ultimate impact of the Internet on marketing and business activities. Some professionals think it will simply be a niche channel amidst a host of other more dominant and far-reaching media such as television and print. According to the Gartner Group, some businesspeople see the Internet as a common platform on which all of the various interactive technologies can come together to create "a new hybrid system." "This system, they believe, will be a successor in some form to the current Internet, and will act as both an inbound (customer response) and outbound (customer contact) conduit. On the other hand, some enterprises believe that the Internet will never gain widespread acceptance and will continue to be a system used by a small segment of society."

Industry shapers including AT&T and Visa—and, for that matter, the entire banking, entertainment, news, publishing, and communications industries—do not appear to have any doubts, and are moving aggressively to position themselves in the technology and marketing channels that are creating a completely new business model for the future. These leaders are taking active roles in developing and utilizing technologies that will make the Internet an integral part of their businesses. They are also investing heavily with resources and dollars to assist other businesses (their own potential customers) in setting up *intranet* (business-to-business) infrastructures. They are doing this not only to secure their own position in the revenue stream, but because they can see that this is an inevitable shift in the way business will be conducted in the future. What shape the picture will ultimately take is anyone's guess, but it is wise to follow the actions of these major industry leaders.

Michael Rogers is the vice president of Post-Newsweek New Media, managing editor of Newsweek Interactive, and a contributing editor to *Newsweek* magazine. He has been working on new media projects for Newsweek, and now the Washington Post Company, which owns Newsweek, since 1989. He has produced video disks; written, produced, and directed CD-ROMs for various platforms; and developed the company's online service on Prodigy (which has since moved to America Online). Rogers makes it clear that Newsweek is one of the aggressive leaders in the publishing industry's electronic marketing and online endeavors. It is clearly using the medium to extend brand presence. He describes his focus as follows:

> Currently I'm working on building several national Web sites. We're interested in extending our brand names, which include Newsweek, The Washington Post, *Kaplan Educational Centers, and the* International Herald Tribune. *The Post Company also owns cable and television properties that will clearly be part of the future new media mix.*
>
> *My specific focus is at longer-term possibilities, things that are hard to do now, for instance, cable modem—the sort of broadband stuff we do on CD-ROM today and hope to do online in the not too distant future.*

On this topic, the Gartner Group adds: "The Internet will become a central part of the marketing mix for most enterprises. Some of the more technologically aggressive enterprises will move to a completely Internet-based business model, incorporating sales, marketing, and back-end operations to change their way of dealing with the customer. This will produce a new model of the electronic market."

SBT Software: Business from Both Sides of the Firewall

SBT Software is a good example of a company that has utilized the full potential of the Internet to both market and run the business. It provides solutions to small and medium-sized businesses that are interested in automating electronic commerce processes and accounting transactions. SBT employees use the products they sell to run the company, so they are in a unique position in that they are their own clients first and foremost. That assures a level of quality upon which their customers can rely. When something isn't working properly or needs customization, they are already up to speed and can focus their technical team on finding and testing a quick solution. If a client wants to see how a product works, SBT is a living, working demonstration. Not many companies can claim that kind of positioning in the marketplace. SBT is its own best interactive advertisement [Figure 5.2]!

The company has two divisions. SBT Accounting Systems produces multiuser Windows applications that do tasks such as print sales and purchase orders and checks. SBT Internet Systems produces electronic versions of traditional accounting applications.

Dave Harris, president of Internet Systems for SBT, describes its products:

> *The first one is called WebStreet, and it is the hosting service. It costs $595 per year. We run all of the CGI scripts they need to do the encryption of*

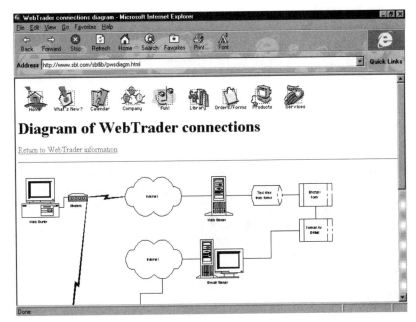

Figure 5.2 SBT site on the Internet. (*Source: SBT*) (*continues*)

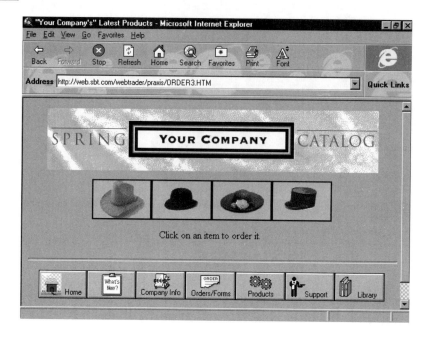

Figure 5.2   SBT site on the Internet. (*continued*)

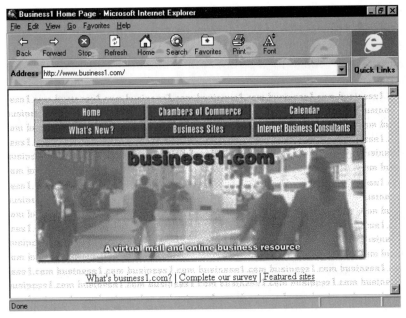

Figure 5.2 SBT site on the Internet. (*continued*)

orders and the processing of leads and e-mail and so forth. We're willing to do special services like the active database hosting.

WebTrader is an order entry and catalogue system. It basically processes orders from the Internet, whether they're point-and-click pictures or line items on a complicated sales order. It pulls the order across, encrypts it, and feeds it to the back-office system. Our third product is called WebAlert, which is an intelligent agent application that sends out mass or rifle-shot e-mails on behalf of the business. For example, it can send an e-mail to customers as soon as they become past due, or notify them that they are eligible for a promotional price. WebAlert can send details of an order confirming each line item and price along with the total of the order, and it can let the appropriate person in a company know if inventory stock is about to run out.

The fourth product is called WebPay, which will very shortly be doing direct deposit for bill paying for businesses. It's like electronic banking for businesses, except it has to handle extra things like which invoices you are paying.

SBT has been successfully selling these products since April 1995. Harris explains how SBT got into electronic commerce, and the direction in which the company has been moving:

The reason we got into the electronic commerce business is that about two years ago we saw the rise of the Internet and we realized that if we kept developing software that printed paper commerce documents, like purchase orders and sales orders, we'd be out of business by the year 2010. So we made an extremely aggressive push into the Internet, developing products, education, and actually a network of trained consultants across the United States, which now numbers about 500 independent consultants who have been trained in installing electronic commerce solutions.

After years and years of predicting the paperless office, suddenly there has been a dramatic turn of events, and that is that the Internet does some very simple things very well. Conservative projections by Morgan Stanley say that the Internet will become the post office of the world by the year 2000 with more than 200 million e-mail users using the Internet as a common clearinghouse of business communications. That's driving businesses that have been traditionally mail-based, like direct mail businesses and catalogue businesses, for example, to try new forms of communication and response.

The two things the Internet does well are, number one, it serves as a clearinghouse for me to send e-mail to you. I could be on America Online, you could be on Prodigy. I could be on Microsoft Mail in a corporation, you could be in cc:Mail in a corporation. You've got to be somebody at somewhere dot com if you're going to do business in the '90s. The second thing that it does very nicely is support World Wide Web applications, which for the most part display home pages, which are essentially like brochures for individuals or companies. Those are the two things that really made electronic commerce viable.

We run a large bank of servers here, and we're using the Microsoft Internet information server on several machines, running on the NT operating system. The reason that we use the Microsoft servers is that they come with the SSL security built into them; they are free, and they come with the NT operating system. And we find it easy to get technicians who know how to work with the graphical user interface on the NT boxes. We've experimented over the last two years with both UNIX solutions, which are very powerful but hard to use, and NT solutions, which are increasingly powerful and much easier to use. And in our analysis, reliability and ease of use won out over raw power and complexity.

So we have a fundamental suite of servers that allow us to display information and have a relationship with both our network of installers and the public at large. We can share public information. We can share private information. So the Internet works for us on a lot of different levels. One level allows us to have a kind of a company brochure, so if people want to know who we are, we can just give them the URL and say, "Check us out." And the degree to which they're interested will determine how much they pull off that site. The second level of activity that we get from our Internet site is that we pull in leads and customer requests. We call them pieces of electronic flypaper. There are little secret forms and response buttons that people hit, which cause a piece of e-mail to be generated back to our company of a viewer who has expressed some level of interest.

Marketing on the Internet is done by generating high levels of traffic and providing opportunities for people to identify themselves, answer questions, and request e-mail responses. By offering assistance in product evaluation for example, SBT was able to ask some questions of the user, and frequently ended up recommending their own products as appropriate solutions. When the volume of e-mail responses became too high to manage efficiently, SBT wrote a custom application with canned answers for every possible query generated by their survey. Some questions required five canned answers whereas others needed as many as 13.

The third level of business management SBT made use of was the Internet to expedite its customer communications. This included e-mailing newsletters to consultants, sending out statements, overdue notices, and order and shipping confirmations. Communications that formerly meant processing thousands of faxes and print mailings each month were now done automatically using e-mail. Overdue notices were accompanied by a request for a return receipt, and a service bureau was used to confirm all payments, so an appropriate use of the Internet was paired with the necessary traditional backup support. The postage saved on mailing printed newsletters alone was about $10,000 a month. The small number of customers still requesting hard copies now receive them quarterly.

SBT learned about building their presence on the Internet the hard way. When they first put up a home page, they were shocked to learn that if they wanted anyone to see it, they would have to generate the visitors. First they did the obvious and listed with all of the search engines, and then realized they already had a built-in audience of current customers, who they immediately contacted. SBT encouraged everyone to visit the site for the latest product pricing and specs and the new electronic newsletter, and asked them in turn to tell all of their own customers and friends about it. SBT made their home page a little off-beat, to grab the visitors' attention in the few seconds they were given to make an impression and interest the users in exploring the site.

One of the challenges Dave Harris of SBT warns others about is the tendency of corporate management allocating marketing dollars to revert to a very conservative corporate brochure look because it is comfortable. However, he contends that attracting and keeping a visitor on an Internet site may require a company to stretch a little beyond their comfort zone in order to design something more enticing.

SBT runs its core business behind an Internet *firewall* or barrier designed to keep both the public and any unauthorized persons from accessing its confidential databases and business operating systems. It has set up "safe" methods for customers to interact with the business by building automated order placement, shipping, billing, and other key functions into the overall system. Encryption of all communication provides for a degree of confidentiality. Harris elaborates:

My method of communicating outside the firewall is mass or targeted e-mails. Some people want to be on the bleeding edge and start to mix what is shared outside the firewall with what's on the inside of the firewall. It's a trend.

The products that are being launched by FiberSoft and Oracle and others give developers the ability to have what are called dynamic home pages; and the whole issue around dynamic home pages is, is the extra sizzle worth the extra cost or the extra risk? And so dynamic home pages are going to become the domain of slightly more sophisticated customers. They allow us to display real availability of a product or a calculated price for a particular user. We replicate a portion of the company's back-office information, like a price list or even a partial customer list, and put those two pieces of information on the Internet server and allow users to approach our home page and do a query that brings up data out of those replicated databases.

There are multiple levels of access. In order to update, or even see confidential information, you have to enter a PIN number, and that gets into a difficult area, because now all of a sudden the marketer has to not only manage a display, but proactively manage accounts. This is a large commitment and the costs of deploying and maintaining dynamic pages are substantially higher than static pages. So you've got to make sure that the application is justified.

Most of the work is done by the VARs, or Value Added Resellers of our products, but we do have a consulting service, so that any VAR can ask for help, and we will bid on a project or even do the entire project. But we will only sell those kinds of services through the VARs. So a VAR has to call us in. Basically, we want people who know what they're doing on site, who can look at the businessperson face to face and say, "I understand what you're doing; I'll do it or SBT can quote you a price."

Even though we have a hosting service, we don't sell direct to the consumer. The VAR gets a product, and he or she gets a hundred-dollar discount when he or she sells it. In our experience, the secret to rapid growth is that you allow a local consultant to make a lot of money doing customiza-

tion and the "real" client work. So everything we sell goes out at a discount, anywhere from 30 percent to 50 percent. VARs can be making $3,000 just on selling the products, and that sounds like a lot of money, and it is, but it's very hard to go out and find a business that is willing to use you as a consultant. So we have a very high reward for the VAR to actually go out and get the products installed. And that's just the beginning. The VAR makes a margin of several thousand dollars.

The VAR also provides ongoing services, which could be simple HTML or more sophisticated things, like creating a marketing survey form and helping the business process those marketing surveys. Some of [the VARs] have their own services, and they run their own businesses. We have a couple hundred that are on our server, but there are a couple hundred that use their own. Some don't want their clients to know where this magical stuff came from, so they keep a separation.

Companies want to have custom domain names because it shows that they have a substantial presence. And to us there's really no difference whether they're on one of our malls, like Business1 or Mall One, or on their own custom domain. In fact, we kind of prefer that they have their own custom domain and get the advantages of a real URL.

Business1 is one of a few malls under development. There's a domain that runs here called http://www.business1.com. If you go there, you'll see a button that reads IBC—which stands for Internet Business Consultants. And under the IBC button you'll see a map of the United States. When you click on a state, it'll take you to some of the Internet consultants that we recommend in that city or state. We've put up a couple dozen chambers of commerce, and we list 300 different ones and the memberships of most of them. We have sponsored some of them. But on Business1, we've created a mall where you can get business information.

We also have published self-study guides on how to do Internet consulting, and so if you go up to Business1 and you click on the IBC button, you'll see another button that takes you to the contents of our instructional material, and you can actually read our technical book. It's a 14-chapter book online. There's even a test that you can take. We get these Internet consultants and they think they're really hot stuff. We say, "Okay, take the test." Then they take a test online and they find out where they need to learn more. This is another example of how we've extended the processing, the training, and education. In processing new consultants who sign up with us, we've actually automated the process of letting them read the book and test out—or not—of the entry level class.

We're getting over 100,000 hits a month now, and we have a couple of clients that generate in excess of 100,000 hits a month. I haven't looked at the demographics of those hits, but the overwhelming majority of the people who hit our page bump into the topic Electronic Commerce, and say, "Oh, my God, it's happening," and then they come to our page and look around. The last time we measured, more than half were just people cruising the Net.

In regard to using the Internet for branding purposes, we found that identity is the first thing businesses are interested in. A lot of people didn't want our name involved in their server domain; they wanted to have their own name. Second, the brand names that count are the really big ones, like AT&T and Microsoft. We have come to the conclusion that the most important name that you can associate yourself with is a brand name from a Fortune 1000 company that legally gives you the right to use its symbols; in our case, we use the Microsoft logo here and there to show that we're allied with a big company. That's the same kind of thing that we recommend for small business. If you resell Nike shoes, there are rules and regulations for proper use of the Nike logo. It can appear in certain ads; it has to be a certain size, it has to be smaller than your company's name; and so on. Any logo that you can get access to is a powerful thing, as long as you have legal rights to use it, and it should be a Fortune 1000 logo.

In the final analysis, when people see your home page, they really have no idea who you are. They only know you by proxy; they only know you by who your friends are. And if your friends are Microsoft and IBM or Nike or Coca-Cola, then, wow, that gives you credibility. People are figuring out that a slick home site can be done by one guy in his garage if he's got the time, and so they want to know you're affiliated with [a company] they can trust.

The other thing about branding that we do in terms of our own business is to brand independent names. For example, we say, "Talk to one of our IBCs," or, "You need an IBC," and it takes the whole brand and proprietary software discussion out of it, and it allows you to have implied value. People feel that must be a really hot thing. The fact is, SBT is a teeny little company relative to Microsoft or IBM, and so that concept of an Internet Business Consultant is bigger than my logo.

The biggest challenge that we face is that the number of people playing in this space is going to go up by an order of magnitude in the next year, so the problem that we and our customers have when marketing on the Internet is staying clear and effective in the din that's about to come. Everybody is going to be recommending these services, and it's going to be very challenging to stay differentiated and focused.

Because so much is at stake, there'll be a lot of people declaring emergencies and wringing hands and gnashing teeth, and so setting realistic expectations during this massive, rapid expansion is the biggest challenge. I think that this market is primarily a business-to-business marketing opportunity *into '97, because it's where we are most of the time. The big hurdle is going to be to reach the consumer level. Getting all consumers online in '97 will be the big push.*

The DemoZone

A San Diego Software company called Datasel decided to take advantage of the opportunities the Internet had to offer by shifting the focus of the company from producing a variety of software applications to providing a place on the Net to find, review, and download products. The DemoZone is just that, a place to search for a range of software, try it out, and make a purchase if you find something to suit your needs (Figures 5.3 and 5.4). Jim Delappa explains his new business:

Datasel has set up a site called the DemoZone, a place where software publishers can put demo versions of their programs. We have set up a template-driven site so that consumers can come in when they're in a browsing mode and search for different software programs that might fit their needs. We started this site because we feel that the traditional distribution channel for

Figure 5.3   DemoZone home page. (*Source: Datasel*)

Figure 5.4   DemoZone software directory. (*Source: Datasel*)

software doesn't really serve the needs of the consumer or the software publisher adequately.

Our idea is to let people come in, identify the type of software they're looking for, whether they want to take a look at a particular title that they already know about or just browse a certain category. We help them narrow that focus. We have three screens of information for each product. We have a product profile, which is much like what you would find on the box at the store, but we go much further than that. We have a "frequently asked questions" (FAQ) screen for each product. The FAQ is a very popular term on the Internet, and it's popular with software developers, as well. That goes into all the more detailed information that someone might want to know about a product. And third, before people buy a product, they like to know a little bit about the company, so we always make a company profile available as part of that whole product presentation.

And then the real way we take advantage of the Internet—and this is what sets us apart from every software retailer in the country—is that upon reading that information, if [customers are] convinced that this product does what they want it to do, from the comfort of their seat, be it at home or at the office, they can click on a button and download a free demo of that software program.

[Our site is] template- and database-driven and every product is presented in the same fashion. We have a product database that has all the information in it, and we have a search engine. When people browsing the site use the search engine and identify a product they'd like to look at, then, on the fly, the HTML pages to present that information are generated. They look the same for every single product.

It is more beneficial than just creating HTML pages and being able to click through the information you're interested in because, internally, if we decide to change the look of our pages, we change it once in the template, and the database information stays the same. For example, we made some style changes the other day in the way our information was presented, and those style changes were made in less than an hour. If we had 300 products in our site, those 300 products would all be updated instantaneously or in that one-hour period, as opposed to having to go out and change all 300 of those individually. That adds a lot of benefit. As we add new products, or if a product goes away, there's a field in our database that tells whether that product should be activated for whatever reason. We can simply click it on or off, update it, and then that product will no longer be available or will now be available to people who search the site.

Incorporating the Electronic Channel

The way a business incorporates the electronic channel into its overall marketing plan should be flexible. It is important to think through the strategies for each venue, as well as how they all work together. Figure 5.5, supplied by the Gartner Group, illustrates the reach and integration of electronic channels. According to that firm: "Enterprises are rushing to the Internet as part of an interactive marketing strategy or in reaction to competitors. But no one has defined what will determine success on the Internet. Still, with each new article in the trade press, more enterprises are deciding that they, too, need to enter the "information superhighway" by setting up a Web site for marketing. These Web sites are a useful learning experience, but they are not ready to become the backbone of a marketing strategy."

Ian Beavis, Toyota executive vice president of Saatchi & Saatchi, has been very savvy and conservative about jumping onto the electronic bandwagon, and it has paid off. He sums up the strategy that has worked well for Toyota:

I think we've been significantly more cautious than anybody else. What we have done, in our normal fashion, is watch other people's successes and failures and learn from them. We didn't rush into an interactive television test like everyone wanted us to. We weren't the first on Prodigy or AOL.

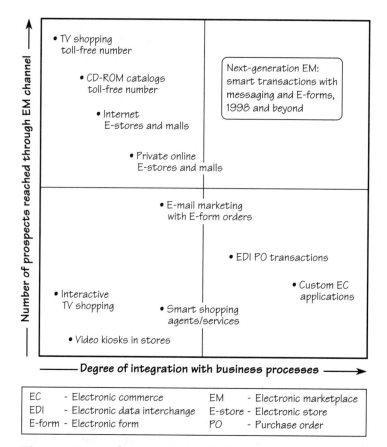

Number of prospects reached through EM channel →

- TV shopping
  toll-free number

  - CD-ROM catalogs
    toll-free number

    - Internet
      E-stores and malls

      - Private online
        E-stores and malls

Next-generation EM:
smart transactions with
messaging and E-forms,
1998 and beyond

- E-mail marketing
  with E-form orders

    - EDI PO transactions

      - Custom EC
        applications

- Interactive
  TV shopping

  - Smart shopping
    agents/services

- Video kiosks in stores

— **Degree of integration with business processes** →

EC	- Electronic commerce	EM	- Electronic marketplace
EDI	- Electronic data interchange	E-store	- Electronic store
E-form	- Electronic form	PO	- Purchase order

Figure 5.5 The reach and integration of next-generation electronic marketplace channels. (*Source: Gartner Group*)

In the case of Prodigy, we and Toyota saw it not as an advertising medium but as an owner retention tool, and designed a program for that. We've, quite frankly, learned a great deal from a lot of other people. We were probably a year behind the curve, but we had people out there talking to everybody, and we didn't spend a dollar until we were absolutely convinced it was the right thing to do.

We started off small with a little diskette. Because we have worked with the Toyota staff for over 20 years, we understand how they like to do things. Everything is plan, do, check, action. We grind people. And from this process we learned a great deal. We started with little icons and a simple home page with NBC in the early days at no cost. We didn't go into the first issue of Launch. Instead, we went into the second issue in order to see how others handled the first. We looked at their work then did something better.

Figure 5.6   Toyota media mix. (*Source: Saatchi & Saatchi*)

So we were, and continue to be, very deliberate and calculated in our approach. We didn't get emotional and then say we had to be there. I think that's probably the smartest thing we did. I come out of a strategic planning background, so no one is going to get me to do anything impulsive. We held people back, but we knew how to get it done when we finally decided to do it. And then once we decided we were going to do something, whoosh, off we went.

The following case examples illustrate Saatchi & Saatchi's use of various electronic vehicles integrated into the marketing mix.

The Toyota Strategy

The Toyota strategy incorporates the Internet with other electronic and traditional media into a highly successful program that has been carefully engineered and directed by Ian Beavis (Figure 5.6). He describes the approach as follows:

The first thing we produced was a diskette for the Toyota Avalon. We produced one for Tercel and Tacoma, and then in tandem we produced a full-line CD-ROM for Toyota. We had an Avalon airline promotion with United and American Airlines in their frequent flyer lounges where you could pick up either a Mac or an IBM PC diskette and run it on your laptop while you were on an airplane. It was an amazingly successful promotion, and it drove a lot of traffic into dealerships and gave us lots of test drives and a lot of sales.

If you called the 1-800-GO TOYOTA number, you were offered, with Avalon, a videotape, a diskette, or a brochure. At the same time, we had an infomercial running for Tercel where you could get a diskette or a brochure. One of the most amazing things with this audience of young computer-savvy adults was that we ended up with over 60 percent of the people opting for the diskette. Quite a change from 25 percent the pundits predicted.

We've been tracking our brochure usage since the introduction of the full-line CD-ROM and diskettes. Brochure usage has dropped fairly rapidly, to the point where we only do two printings of each of our brochures a year, even though sales are increasing. We're also finding—we research these things really extensively—a lot of pass-on of electronic media. Brochures don't tend to get passed on much, but diskettes and CD-ROMs do. Big time.

On the CD-ROM [there is] a spin-around of the car so you get to see it from all the angles. We've got a lot of interesting items to keep people entertained, yet we never lose sight of the content requirements. The next generation CD-ROM we're producing is truly amazing. It's going to have a photo bubble so that you can take a full look; move around the interior of a car as well as the software to go straight into our Web site. Click and you're there. So you'll have the wonderful graphic capability of the CD-ROM, and then be able to get all the updated pricing information and everything else straight off the Web site. Our CD-ROM also has a dealer locator, so you can put in your zip code and we'll tell you where your nearest dealers are, and ultimately you'll be able to go into the home page for the individual dealer, as well. It's the best of all known worlds.

We're one of the first auto companies to actually have nonautomotive information on the Web site. The average buyers trade their car every five to seven years. Obviously, we'd like them to visit our Web site more than every five years! We have to give them reasons to come back, other than cars. So, if you go to our Web site, you'll find all sorts of interesting snippets of information. We have extensive research on what our owners are interested in, and have actually targeted people's interests. We've got a living home section for instance. We've got a lot of motor sports content going into it now; we know from the Web site Toyota developed in Australia that motor sports is a very high interest area. Young males are still dominating the Internet. Team testosterone likes motor sports.

The greatest challenge for an advertising agency with interactive media is that it's always work-in-progress. The project is never finished. The project never stops. This is the content-driven medium, and we have to keep it up-to-date and we have to keep it interesting.

We aren't going to let anyone else advertise on our site. We try to get non-published materials from the magazine partners we have, other publishing groups; you name it, we put it on our Web site. We also have hot links to about 30 other Web sites. We're trying to make sure that we've got a lot of compelling reasons to be at our site. We have a large conventional media budget and leverage those dollars into interactive to our advantage.

We're on CompuServe, Prodigy, and AOL, but we don't see them adding to the process. We've been much more successful on our own Web site. We believe we have to control our own destiny. We don't like the idea of a gate-keeper. We need to control the information ourselves. It's our material, and we want to know what's being done with and to it.

Part of the problem with estimating how much we're spending on interactive is that we have a production budget and a separate media budget. Interactive is really part of the production budget because the media cost is almost nonexistent.

They say only 15 percent of Americans have ever been online. The median income of a person that buys a new car is $50,000 per year. It's broad. There are 15 million cars sold a year, so if you look at the Toyota universe, they sell a million. So it's pretty small. It's a niche within a niche. So I think if I'm saying anything about tomorrow, the Internet isn't about to replace television any time soon. You're not going to tolerate a system error while you're watching Friends *on your PC. Television has moved beyond that. There's so much hype around this thing [the Internet], it just drives me nuts. We're spending a significant amount of money, but I'd have to say that it's probably less than 2 percent of our total budget.*

The Lexus Challenge Web Event

Ellen November is the director of technology for Team One Advertising; she has been with the company since it was founded in 1987 as a division of Saatchi & Saatchi Advertising to launch the Lexus car, which at the time was still in the planning stages. She was, therefore, able to build systems from the ground floor. This project began in December 1994, when the client decided to create and promote its own golf tournament for the first time (Figure 5.7). November tells the rest of the story:

It was the Lexus Challenge hosted by Raymond Floyd, and it was held at La Quinta Resort & Club, which is located in the vicinity of Palm Springs. One

Figure 5.7   Lexus Challenge (*Source: Saatchi & Saatchi*)

of our key clients was very interested and involved in interactive media. We wanted to try to support and build on that interest, and so we said, "Well, why don't we put up a Web site to promote the Challenge!" NBC was the television sponsor of the tournament, and owned the URL golf.com, (web site location:http://www.golf.com). We spoke with the network about creating mutual hot links, since they have incredible amounts of information about golf and the players who were on the tour. And so that's how it all started. This site was "live" through February 29, and then on March 1, the Lexus corporate site was launched. Since this was event-related, it disappeared once the event was over.

Graphically, the Challenge was given the appearance of a 3D clubhouse. Instead of navigation bars, we used the furnishings in the room as links. The TV linked to NBC's golf.com. The picture of Raymond Floyd linked to information on Raymond's vision for the tournament and his career highlights. Through a window you could view the course and a Lexus parked nearby. The pin flag linked to information on great courses near Lexus dealers. And the car linked to information on Lexus vehicles. You could even review and order different clothing for the event.

The most unique thing that our site has that the other car sites don't, we believe, is something called Owners Only; a "locker room" door serves as the link. If you enter your VIN number, vehicle identification number, you can get into a section that only owners can get into, and then that plays into the Lexus branding of customer service, personalization, and so forth.

We took a survey on what other than golf interests our visitors. It was really more of a lifestyle survey. We asked about preferences in such areas as the theater, the opera, the symphony, polo, tennis, dance, and so on. This helped us to know better how to reach our target audience.

The other wonderful thing about this site is that we did a tie-in with a charity. The event supported Childhelp, which fights against child abuse and neglect. The players were committed to donate $100,000. Childhelp came away with well over $300,000 when, on the last day, some of the people just started writing checks. In the press tent, [our staff] was coached, "Whenever you're interviewed by the press, bring it back to Childhelp, and the fact that they help severely abused and neglected children." And so all of the focus kept going back to child abuse and to increasing public awareness of this issue.

A golf photographer was hired to be in the press tent to take digital photographs of the celebrities and pros, the activities, cars, scenery, and so forth. We took these images, viewed them as they came in, and posted them live on the Web in less than an hour. Within the "stars" section, we picked photos and created a gallery of pictures available exclusively to Web site visitors. We were taking advantage of the new feature in Netscape 2.0, which is called Frames. Frames allows you to have multiple viewing areas within one page . . . so that you can have one image that stays still, and on the other side you can see multiple images scrolling down.

November explained that Team One publicized the site through the NBC Web site and in print ads that included the Web site address. During the actual airing of the tournament, the Web address was shown as a "super" at the end of the ad spot.

The Yonex Screen Saver

Yonex, a high-end graphite golf club manufacturer, wanted to show its buyers that it was technologically savvy, during the PGA held in Orlando, Florida, in January 1995. Team One came up with a campaign that included the design of a screen saver product (Figure 5.8) that would show off all of Yonex's products in a 21-image slide show-type sequence, featuring the top team player Phil Mickelson. November explained the twist: "What was fun about it was that we pressed 1,000 diskettes; they were all given out, and one of them was programmed to time-bomb after 30 days. It would display something onscreen that would tell [the recipient that he or she] had won a trip for two to a PGA tournament!"

"Shoot for the Moon, Land on the Roof"

In budgeting for a multimedia project, all of the variables must be locked down before relevant numbers can be attached. Among the production houses, the steps primarily differ in what they are called and how well they are carried out, rather than in what they are intended to accomplish. Some companies add their own unique features, but the stages as defined very simply by Red Sky Interactive are preproduction (planning and prototyping), production, and postproduction.

Red Sky places a lot of importance on what it calls Joint Application Design (JAD) sessions, in which staff define the client's marketing and business objectives and the project's creative and technical parameters. This preproduction stage also includes the building and evaluating of prototypes, and the

Obviously, he's not hitting a Super A.D.X.

Figure 5.8   Yonex screen saver. (*Source: Saatchi & Saatchi*)

determination of a budget to complete the project based on the newly defined specifications.

Red Sky employees work by the motto, "Shoot for the moon, land on the roof." They "shoot" beyond the technology initially, to really explore all of the creative possibilities, knowing that if they come up with a good concept, they can fit it into the technology that is best suited to the client's needs. Tim Smith, president and executive producer of Red Sky Interactive, adds:

> *Take a floppy, for example: Someone might come to us for a direct mail floppy piece, cross-platform, Mac/Windows. We'll say the range for that will be $50,000 to $100,000. The client gets up front the range of what we'll do it for. At the end of preproduction, they'll get an answer like, "We can finish it this way for $65,000, locked. You can hold us to it." And clients know what they're getting because they get a design and specification from us, written and heavily documented. Sometimes we'll give them alternatives. "You can pick the $65,000 version or the $98,000 version, and here are the differences. This one has more video, more audio, and so forth." We can never pin it with a fixed cost up front because there are way too many variables in the multiple media we're working in.*

When the budget is very limited, Smith recommends doing one thing really well; something that makes a press-worthy statement and will get a lot of attention. He suggests putting up a page on the Web that offers the visitor a great product to download, or developing a special promotion just using one or two Web pages that will stimulate a response.

Interactive multimedia for marketing purposes can be produced for as little as hundreds or as much as millions of dollars, but the average entry range for graphical interactive floppy disks, extremely simple CD-ROMs, basic Web sites, or Internet advertising spots is around $5,000–$20,000. It is possible to spend less, especially on floppies or simple Web sites and Internet ads, but the quality and depth of the product will usually reflect the investment.

Digital Assets and Repurposing Content

There are several schools of thought on using preexisting content for the online or electronic platform. Most professionals will try to find a way to maximize the equity that a brand and previous materials might offer, but it takes skill, talent, and vision to bring those materials into a new venue and give them the appropriate look and feel. Lynn Upshaw, brand consultant for Upshaw & Associates, and former managing director of Ketchum Interactive says that while anyone can shoot a commercial and buy time on a television station or design a Web page quickly and for very little money, it takes time and money to do it well, and more important, to build the kind of strategic plan that will have a meaningful impact. He explains that there are ways to lower costs without compromising the quality of your assets:

> What you leverage, really, is the exposure, the message. The message is shared among [all venues used], hopefully so that you're saying the same thing across several different media. But in terms of cost, at this stage, the way you save money is when, for example, you're producing more than one television commercial and you get a package rate from a single production company. But when you're doing a CD-ROM here and a commercial here and a print ad here, there's not going to be much savings. . . . If you have some original artwork, you can shoot it and use it in print, and digitize it and use it in other media.
>
> If a Web site is relatively simple, you can create it for $20,000 or $10,000. I'm talking about a larger company doing it. But more likely, it's going to be minimum hundreds of thousands of dollars and, of course, there are numerous sites that cost millions of dollars to create. We're working on a site right now for a major corporation, and that site is going to be worth several million dollars, [although] the total cost to the client won't be that bad, in all things. You've got to remember that there is the creation of the site and then there's creating the back room maintenance. You have hundreds of thousands of people sending you e-mail—there has to be somebody there to answer the e-mails. It's a question of whether you include [all this] in the initial price or charge for it later, but any site worth its salt has to have a big back room to it . . . you have to maintain it. It could be thousands of dollars a month, maybe less, maybe more; it depends on what you want to do and how active you want it to be and how interactive you want it to be.

Michael Rogers of Newsweek Interactive explains that he and his colleagues do as much of the work in house as possible. They do not license their name. They create all of the digital content within the company, although they may venture out for technical services. The goal is to develop an in-house staff of what he calls "digital journalists." ". . . the days of simple repurposing are really over. You have to create original content for this medium. We like to say it's more a question now of repurposing your skills, not repurposing your material. What we've done over the past few years is explore general-interest topics ranging from the business of baseball to the health care crisis to special effects in the movies. We've done those on CD-ROM. Those were all interactive documentaries, essentially, written and produced by Newsweek staffers and then with additional video and audio that we produced in San Francisco."

The way most of the large publishers are building brand electronically is by contributing valued content, much of it free or very inexpensive, to the electronic venues, while publicizing the availability of other subscriptions and products. Rogers explains that it is very important to develop material for which you have predetermined a very specific audience/interest/technology match. He describes some of his company's projects:

> *Most recently we've gone into doing reviews. Our latest project is called the Parents' Guide to Children's Software, which is a CD that includes 50 multimedia reviews. If you're going to go to retail and make any money in the nonfiction category, you have to focus on titles that are of specific interest to people likely to own CD-ROM drives.*
>
> *Online, at the moment, we tend to use the existing material as the base. Newsweek InterActive on Prodigy, for example, has all the text of* Newsweek *but additional photos, sound clips, and we update the* Newsweek *stories with relevant stories from* The Washington Post *every day. It offers quite a bit more than the magazine, but it's based on the concept of weekly news coverage.*

Dave Clauson, managing director of True North Technologies, explains that his firm has developed a digital asset center where staff store everything they do for a client:

> *So if you're opening a Levi's store in Tokyo, you can potentially go into the digital asset center, and whether it's video, audio, poster, whatever you need, you have access to it, and you can customize it locally, instead of having to completely reshoot the thing or do it all over again.*
>
> *I have a saying in my office which is: "If you can dream it, you can do it." And that is absolutely 100 percent true. So we can take film, let's say, of a sunset that was shot for S. C. Johnson, and we can maybe put some clouds in that sunset, put a table on the beach, have a beautiful couple standing next to that table, and put in a bottle of cognac, and take that and transform it into a digital locale, all without ever leaving the computer. And as long as you have the rights to the footage, that's all you need. And our clients have a lot of stuff that they use a few times but then can never use again. But we're working with many clients to see how they can get more value out of the money they've already invested in creating these assets, these visual assets.*

The Cost to Advertise

The advertising rates in the electronic marketplace present great challenges to both advertisers and companies selling placement. Many of the online services and Internet Service Providers (ISPs) are utilizing models from other media-buying venues. On the Internet or on a CD-ROM, an advertiser is essentially buying real estate or space, which will vary in value depending upon where it is located and, therefore, the amount of traffic it receives. On a CD-ROM an advertiser is charged by cost per megabyte (space taken up), since there is a finite amount of space available. Some locations are also more expensive than others, again based on the traffic volume. For example, some ads may be located on menu screens that are used frequently.

Online venues charge in a myriad of ways. In this environment, through the use of increasingly sophisticated tracking technology, traffic is now being qualified beyond reporting that someone has simply looked at a page. Advertisers are requesting more than a "click" rate, which is the equivalent of the number of viewers of the page where your ad appears, who leave without taking any further action, such as registering, requesting more information, or ordering a product. Click rates on a site can be very deceiving because each time someone goes to a different page, it is registered as a click; thus, one person could be responsible for a large number of "clicks" but only really represent a single "visitor." Obviously, then, advertisers are less interested in click rates and more concerned with visitor rates. Some advertisers are also demanding to be charged only for follow-through visitors who take some action that is beneficial or profitable to them.

Marketers are comfortable and familiar with traditional advertising rates that are based on CMP, or cost per thousand. In this model, value has always been measured in volume. The electronic marketplace cannot even come close to the numbers provided by television, radio, newspapers, or magazines, and the online rates do not reflect a solid, comparable deliverable. This has presented marketers of advertising space with a monumental challenge. They must simultaneously educate the consumers and the advertising agencies. The two-pronged goal is to get the consumers online and technologically comfortable, and to educate the advertising agencies about the ultimate benefits of taking some risks now while the market is still developing. The companies that participate in building the electronic marketplace stand a much better chance of having a strategic position when all systems are up to speed. For many companies, the investment that is coming out of their marketing budget at these early stages of the industry might be more accurately labeled as R&D funding. However, it may be the most valuable marketing insurance investment these companies will make.

Pricing electronic advertising is a moving target, but the following examples taken from SIMBA's 1995 report on electronic marketing, and by CD Direct, a San Francisco company, paint a basic picture of this market:

> *SIMBA reports, Time Warner used the cost per megabyte pricing standard for its Full Service Network, and offered advertisers package deals in the*

$200,000 price range. That price tag seemed exorbitant to many advertisers, especially in light of the emergence of PC-based media, such as CD-ROM and the World Wide Web. Both offer multimedia capabilities and crisp, clear graphics for much less money. The CD-ROM magazine Blender, for example, targeted Generation X—the 20-somethings—with multimedia news, reviews, interviews, and features on a range of entertainment topics from music to movies.

Advertiser pricing ran about $1,000 per megabyte. There were minimum prices of $2,500, meaning each advertiser had to buy at least 2.5 megabytes of disk space. Altogether, 100 megabytes of disk space were allotted to advertising out of the disk's 650 megabyte total. About 100,000 disks were distributed through newsstands, computer stores, and record and bookstores. Consumers were charged $10–$15 dollars for the disk.

CD Direct is a multimedia advertising-company that produces CD-ROMs that contain both entertaining and informative content and advertising. The disks contain encrypted (requires access code for full use) software and music products, along with a range of other merchandise offers, which consumers can purchase online or through 800 telephone number connections. The CDs are bundled (polybagged) with magazines that are direct-mailed to targeted markets. Because the magazine publishing business is so well suited to highly refined database segmentation, it is the perfect marriage of traditional and electronic marketing. The CD adds value to the magazine, and it provides the kind of exposure that cannot yet be duplicated by electronic venues alone. In contrast, the sell-through success of products advertised on CD-ROM catalogs is not yet conclusive. This market is still "under construction," although CD Direct is building some meaningful highways.

The advertising rates published by CD Direct for 1995 are shown in Table 5.1. They demonstrate in some detail the way a rate card might look for participation in this type of media. The Standard Multimedia package provides advertisers with up to 10 electronic pages, full search capabilities, online order capture capability, and online survey capability.

Michael Rogers of Newsweek Interactive believes that the shift from the traditional advertising practice of buying huge chunks of TV time to interactive advertising where the chunks are quite fragmented will leave the veteran agency executives looking at an even greater shift in their own bottom lines.

If I were 45 years old and in the advertising business, I might just crawl under the couch and not come out until I could take early retirement. When agencies really look at the bottom line and see what they might make doing interactive advertising versus dealing with gigantic blocks of television time interactive is pretty darn scary. It will be accepted, but I believe that it's

TABLE 5.1   CD Direct 1995 Rate Card (Prices Subject to Change)

| | Electronic Entertainment Multimedia 1995 Rate Card | | | |
	1X	3X	6X	12X
Standard Package	$15,000	$13,500	$12,825	$12,184
Additional Pages				
11–100	$700	$560	$532	$505
101–200	$630	$504	$479	$455
201+	$590	$472	$448	$426
Additional Features				
Video	$500/30 sec.			
Audio	$150/60 sec. max.			
Online Order Capture	$0.75/order			
Internet Pointer	$5,000/month			
Online Registration	$0.50/name			
Electronic Software Distribution (Placement)	$5,000/month			
Standard Page Production & Insertion Cost	$300	$275	$255	$235

going to be smaller agencies that are not as dependent on passive television revenues that really will make it work.

It will be huge someday, but it won't come in big individual chunks. What we're seeing is the fragmentation of all media forms, and that means that agglomerating big audiences and getting paid lots of money for a big audience is not going to be as viable a model anymore. And it's going to hit the advertising agencies. There are decades of tradition in the advertising agencies of how to do a presentation to a client about how many impressions they got from their billboard campaign or from this or that. All that's out the window in an interactive environment. You can tell them exactly, not only how many people saw the ad, how long they looked at it, and whether the call to action worked. I mean, you are nailed if you have advertising that doesn't work. So it's a scary thing.

On the other hand, it creates some interesting new revenue models. Right now in publications we essentially just sell space. What if, in an online environment, we sold space and then took 2 percent of the transaction when somebody actually buys that Eddie Bauer sweater while he or she was watching Newsweek InterActive?

And the business model probably has to change simply because the relationship with the viewer is no longer what it was. And it raises some concerns, too. Take the example where we get 2 percent of a sale; let's extend that a little further. What if I'm reviewing books in my online publication, *and at the end of each review there's a button you can click and you can order the book, and what if I get a nickel every time a book gets ordered? Well, how much are you going to believe my book reviews? My feeling is that in an environment like that, within a few generations, you are going to find a crop of young book reviewers who like everything they see because their publishers depend on ordering books for part of their revenue stream. Negative reviews won't make them money.*

Suppose there are two competing books out there, and I'm with a magazine that's going to get a little percentage, and I can decide . . . one of them offers me quite a bit more kickback than the other one. . . . Which one am I going to recommend? So it's an area that concerns us a lot because the line between advertising and editorial has been established very clearly for a long time in the print world, and it's particularly important for a small number of publications like Newsweek, The Washington Post, *and* The New York Times. *We truly have what's called a church-state relationship. We on the editorial side are not supposed to know what pays for this thing. And those lines are really being blurred in cyberspace. Are those lines valuable anymore or should everything be sponsored? We're already moving into a world where almost everything has a logo on it. Some of our focus groups these days suggest that the public believes that everyone who talks to them is on the take somehow.*

So perhaps that's the future. Maybe that is the direction we should go. But at The Post Company, we want to maintain the ad-edit division as long as we can. It may be of no value in the next century. It may be that everything is commercialized, everything's for sale, all opinions are for sale. But we know that once we give up the high ground of journalism, we'll never get it back.

Barry Layne, a new media business consultant with Tavel/Gross Entertainment believes that the marketer has the ability to control the environment in which they communicate their message.

That means the advertiser or marketer moves from being just advertisers or marketers to creators of a media property. They've got to create—or, at least, their agency has to create—something that their target prospective consumer or customer will want to come to. Think about traditional paid advertising. What you are really getting with your media dollars is a rental. You are renting someone else's relationship with the audience you want to or need to reach. In this environment, there are, today, very few compelling places for your audience to be reached. So you need to give them one. That, in turn, elevates your relationship with that consumer to a much more inti-

mate one. And, not coincidentally, I happen to believe the same is true for
much of the linear media world, as well, and that is an opportunity too
often overlooked by advertisers and agencies.

Advertising agencies have been reluctant to enter the electronic marketplace, and this has held some of their major clients back and caused others to seek out interactive production and design firms independently. Smaller interactive production companies are stepping up to the plate to service the online and multimedia needs of some of the biggest brands, and the lines have become blurred as some of the traditional agency functions are usurped by these firms. According to SIMBA, "Nearly 30 percent of CEOs in a cross-section of businesses including health care, retailing, publishing, and banking said their agencies weren't prepared for the information superhighway, according to a survey of New York–based Crain Communications. More than 27 percent said they weren't sure if their agencies could handle their interactive needs. Nearly half of the 360 CEOs that responded to Crain Communications survey said they wouldn't need an agency if they could talk directly to customers through interactive media."

Some of the larger agencies are addressing this issue by creating either small subsidiary or totally separate companies that act as their interactive production "divisions." This has worked well for Foote, Cone & Belding, a major agency that established True North Technologies to handle all of its interactive media needs. TN also functions as a separate entity with its own clients. CKS is another company that created a separate entity, called CKS/Interactive. On the other hand, Saatchi & Saatchi has successfully kept all of its production in house, but has made sure the whole company is well educated and integrated into the electronic marketplace.

The Electronic Marketing Business Model

The electronic marketing business model is still in its infancy. The race to get onboard has not matched the pace at which electronic commerce has become profitable, profits that are being measured more in "futures" than present return on investment; and the value is steadily increasing for brand presence. Michael Rogers, of Newsweek Interactive discusses how he views the market:

Like most big media companies that are being honest, we don't quite know
what the business model is. The market, I believe, has developed more slowly
than we expected, both for CD-ROM and for online. And by market, I don't
mean the audience; I mean the ways of getting money back from them. The
Web has expanded at a tremendous rate, and it is a wonderful thing, but we
don't quite see how to make money off it yet in any of our traditional ways.

CD-ROM is a terribly expensive medium because it involves all the production values of television, yet has a tiny audience compared to television. So there are, I think, some difficulties involved in coming up with successful business models. Interestingly enough, . . . we tend to go back to basics, and believe that history repeats itself. One thing that we know is that the American public does not pay full freight for their information. We have spoiled them. The Washington Post still costs a quarter in D.C. They may think Newsweek at the newsstand is overpriced at $2.95 when, in fact, it might cost $7.00 without advertisements.

In other words, we've convinced people that information is cheap, and we've done that through advertising subsidies. We're pretty sure that there is nothing so compelling about new media, regardless of what those who love it tell you, that will make Americans dig deeper into their pockets. There is only so much money to go around in their spending on media, and they're not going to spend a whole lot more just because it's something modern.

So we have to have advertising. Advertising has to provide part of the revenue stream, and then probably some sort of subscription will provide the rest. Today in the magazine world, it tends to be, in general, 50/50; 50 percent from circulation, 50 percent from advertising. It varies, but that's a rule of thumb. So we'd love it if we could figure out some way to get to that in the online world and the CD-ROM world.

Quicken Financial Network Works

Intuit asked Red Sky Interactive to design the Quicken Financial Network site (QFN) (http://www.qfn.com). Tim Smith, Red Sky president and executive producer, describes what was so different and interesting about the various facets of this project, and why it was so successful:

[Quicken] is interesting because it's both a private service and a public service, but the more impactful part of that project was what happened when Quicken 5 was released on a CD-ROM. On the disk was a bundled licensed browser, and when you got it, you could install it, and, literally, with one click, log on to the Internet and default to the QFN site. The access was provided by Concentric Network, which was another partner in the project, and it led to private access to the Internet. It was one click to the Internet, which made it very painless; and as long as you were in the QFN site online, it was free access to the Internet.

So [in essence, it says] "here's an example of our Internet site brought to you by Intuit." Free to you, subsidized by the advertiser in other words. As long as you're here and getting all the support we offer, which is product support, other product information, access to other people using the tools, FAQs, utilities to download, and so on, it's free. As it should be.

But once you get out of Intuit's boundaries, the clock starts ticking, and that's the beauty of it, because Concentric Network then becomes the provider, by default. But that's a pretty fabulous way to put that together. You get a product that's very popular, works quite well, and is integrated with an online presence. . . . It all came together and it was made from the beginning to be pretty seamless to the user, without the intimidating, "How do I get on the Internet" stuff. It just worked.

The response has been tremendous. Intuit is doing fabulous support online, and stock zoomed up after the Web site went online. It's great for partners like Concentric who have gotten a number of subscribers through this service; and the recognition for us was pretty amazing as well."

21st Century Media: The Best Way to Sell It Is to Give It Away!

21st Century Media, an interactive marketing and production company, runs its business on a marketing model with a unique variation. It believes that advertising sponsorships, rather than the consumer, should pay for multimedia production costs. President and CEO Jim Baker launched the company on that premise.

I believe very strongly in producing CDs that are presenting information and promoting products, but that they should be free of charge [to the consumer]. It should be up to the client to pay for [the production] out of the marketing budget, or work with an interactive marketing company like 21st Century Media to bring in other sponsors of complementary products. A client may also have strategic partners with whom they can work, and we can put together a very concise, very active marketing piece that helps promote all of those people.

Initially, 21st Century developed a prototype, which was used to get sponsorship for a more elaborate product. The prototype, which showcased local recording studios, was an enhanced CD aimed at the music industry. (Enhanced CDs include music tracks that can be played on a regular CD player, as well as run on a computer.) Baker describes the evolution of the prototype:

We produced a disk called The Studio Directory [the prototype]. We wanted to put together an interactive directory of recording studios. No one had done it before. It is a video-based tour of studios with interviews, so it combines what is traditionally on a videotape, along with a very quick, easy-to-use directory that also includes graphics and text and music. It is an enhanced CD so that you can listen to music that had been recorded in the studios. Every studio has a different sound, and people can hear very quickly the individual style of output from each. We used a track-zero technology for hiding the data track, and it was one of the first track-zero disks to come out. It went into the 1995 New Media Magazine Invision Awards and was a finalist.

Not only did the prototype demonstrate how companies could benefit from becoming sponsors, it also promoted 21st Century's production skills. The sponsors of the prototype put up a nominal $200 apiece for the cost of production. The rest of the budget, an additional $20,000, came out of 21st Century's pocket—a relatively small investment for launching a company and producing its promotional materials. However, if the cost of unbilled in-house labor and other company resources were included, total production costs would have been closer to $80,000.

Based on the success of the prototype, 21st Century planned its next product, a tour of the 10 top music recording studios in the world. This product would have a much higher profile—travel costs alone were estimated to be as high as $25,000–$30,000. 21st Century decided to get one key sponsor and 10 smaller ones. The first step was to create a list of all of the companies that supply recording studios with equipment and software. They were the most obvious potential sponsors, because their products could be seamlessly included in photos and video footage, without coming across like advertisements. It took about five months to sign the sponsors, who ultimately represented the music, multimedia, and online industries. The actual production took another five months, and the product enjoyed a successful launch in March 1996. Baker describes the product:

We shot QuickTime VR at every single one of these studios, so you can have a virtual tour around these studios, and that's never been done before in the music industry. A portion of the disk is devoted to showing how we actually made the CD and the technology we used, because it's meant to be an educational piece as much as it is a promotional piece. (We are also interested in using enhanced CDs in teaching music to students, which is something that we're going to be looking at over the course of this next year.)

We have a two-minute compilation of different music that was recorded at each of the studios that you will instantly recognize and say, "Oh, so that Michael Jackson track was recorded there. Great. Interesting studio. I like that because it had great drum sound," or something like that. And, for instance, you'll get to Guillaume Tell in Paris and you'll hear this beautiful music composed by Jean Claude Petite, which he wrote for Ken Russell's movie version of Lady Chatterly's Lover. *Most studios submitted music, so we have quite varied content."*

The CD is also linked to a Web site. A game can be played between the CD and site, and the prize is a free day in one of the recording studios. Full-page, full-color ads were taken out in *Mix* magazine to promote the CD in the four months prior to its release, and it was cover-mounted on the magazine as part of the launch.

Baker lists the benefits of this kind of project:

- The sponsors get positive responses when they give the disk away, and it helps to promote their products.
- When users get onto the Internet with the CD, they visit the sponsor's Web site, and there is increased product recognition.
- The recording studios did not have to pay anything to be on the CD, and they now have a great giveaway CD to demonstrate and promote their facility.
- 21st Century Media can use the CD well into 1997 as a company promotional piece.
- The CD promotes enhanced CD technology, QuickTime VR, and integrating the Internet.

21st Century Media titles perform several functions: marketing, education, and entertainment. With its highly targeted audience, the company has succeeded at carving out a unique niche for itself. Over 20,000 disks were distributed as of April 1996, following a March 31 release date. 21st Century's next title will tour world-class video production facilities.

Because this business model was so successful from the marketing angle, Jim Baker launched a new company, studiosource, inc. with the sole purpose of publishing promotional content on CD and the Internet. Studiosource, inc. already has five new titles planned. 21st Century Media will provide the technical resources for developing these titles, while studiosource will focus on the sponsorship and marketing aspects.

21st Century Media also takes on clients who need promotional multimedia products developed for marketing purposes. It has designed a three-tiered campaign strategy called the ShowSeries that includes the integrated use of kiosks (ShowPoint), CD-ROMs (ShowRom), and the Internet (ShowNet). Media developed for the client is designed for compatibility with each of these delivery vehicles. Every disk that 21st Century produces also comes with a Web browser.

21st Century promotes the ShowSeries as a three-stage package, which is an easy concept for marketers to understand. It conveys to them the integrated, cost-effective way a project's graphical assets and other content will be used, and suggests a well-rounded, strategic approach. Categorizing the services not only assists clients, but it is valuable in the organization and allocation of the production company's resources.

Regarding the future of interactive media, Baker shares his current frustrations: "Can you imagine, back in the '50s when television was first making its appearance, what it would have been like if all of these companies had been hanging around with videotapes of TV commercials and shows, waiting for the television to be developed? Because that's how I feel right now. I'm hanging around with all these tools for interactive communication, really good technology, and there's no delivery medium with enough bandwidth. It's like that for interactive developers. We all know what we want, but the length of time it is taking to bring new delivery technologies to market is extremely frustrating."

Conclusion

Interactive advertising opens doors in many directions for businesses. The implications are powerful, and worth researching, experimenting with, and integrating into a marketing plan. The examples provided in this chapter clearly illustrate a range of innovative approaches to this new technology. Begin your venture into interactive media cautiously and with careful planning, but do begin, as this is not just a passing trend; it is a permanent shift in the way business and marketing will be conducted.

CHAPTER SIX

FAX-ON-DEMAND

William Austad and Paul Brobst

What Is Fax-on-Demand?

Fax-on-demand (FOD) is a simple and easy method of electronic information delivery. All the user needs in order to retrieve information from a document library is a phone and a fax machine or a computer with a fax board. Fax-on-demand delivers information quickly and there are few restrictions as to what can be sent, including text, spreadsheets, documents, and halftones of photographs.

The first known application of fax-on-demand was at Intel Corporation where product information was delivered to customers and prospects. Intel's goal, when it started its service in 1989, was to reduce the high cost of taking requests for product information by phone, sending the requests to a literature fulfillment house, and paying it to address envelopes, put on postage, insert lit-

> **Fax Board (Card):** A PC board that contains all the necessary facsimile hardware and software (some software is PC rather than board resident) to allow a PC to send and receive fax messages with Group 3 fax units. Some boards are send only, that is, they have no fax receive function. Most PC resident fax board software also allow printing of received fax documents on the PC graphic printer (laser, ink-jet, or dot matrix).

erature and cover letters, and mail the information. After a year of operation, a significant percentage of information requests had been shifted to fax-on-demand.

According to David Kinder, manager of the Intel FaxBACK system, the cost of sending information by fax was less than 10 percent of the cost of mailing a printed product sheet or more extensive information. This includes costs from incoming 800 number calls, system maintenance, and document preparation for the database. In addition, Intel found it could put product support instructions on the system to reduce the load on the technical support staff. The savings in time and money in a year was significant; in fact, it was such a resounding success that the original team that created the service was spun off to start a company to sell the product. FaxBack became one of the leading suppliers of turnkey systems today.

Why Use Fax-on-Demand?

In an article in *The Wall Street Journal* titled "Fax-on-Demand Provides Ready Answers," October 20, 1992, Paul Brobst, senior partner of ABConsultants, commented, "The technique (fax-on-demand) will be the marketing tool of the '90s. . . . It both provides better service for the user and saves money for the provider." Today there is a lot of hype and interest in the Internet and the World Wide Web. Many companies are scrambling to put up pages promoting their companies and products. The results, the degree of success and failure in using the Web as a marketing tool, are still not clear. On the other hand, organizations using fax-on-demand for literature fulfillment and product support almost universally claim much success and substantial savings. Fax-on-demand has proven to be an effective marketing tool. Figure 6.1 shows the growth of fax devices in the United States.

Some of the key reasons fax-on-demand is used are listed as follows:

Automatic Delivery

- Fax-on-demand automatically delivers a great variety of information for businesses, publishers, universities, government agencies, and many other organizations and associations.

Accessibility

- Information is available to customers, prospects, employees, subscribers, and associates 24 hours a day, 7 days a week.
- Only a phone and a fax are needed by a person seeking information.

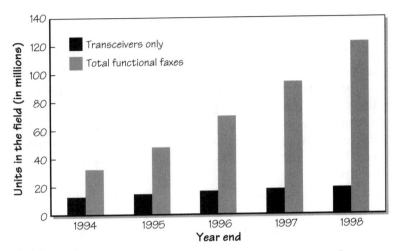

Figure 6.1 Growth of fax devices in the United States. (*Source: ABConsultants*)

Efficiency

- Fax-on-demand is a very time- and cost-efficient method for delivery of information, saving on such things as postage, paper (if sending to many recipients at once and/or using a computer to send or receive), staff, turnaround and response times.
- Most fax-on-demand systems pay for themselves within six months to a year.

Increased Quality of Service

- Fax-on-demand documents can be used to enhance voice support service.
- It gives customers an alternate source of information during peak calling periods when the technical, accounting, sales, or other support staff is difficult to reach. As an added option, a caller can be directed to the fax-on-demand system and get a directory of documents related to his or her problem and make a selection.
- In as many as half of the calls, the fax support document is sufficient for the caller to solve the problem; thus the help of support staff is not required.
- Even when callers still require assistance after reviewing the fax documents, they generally have a better understanding of their problem, often reducing the time needed for personal help.
- The caller's perceived value of service provided is higher.

How Does Fax-on-Demand Work?

A fax-on-demand system consists of a computer (usually a PC), voice boards, fax boards, and software that controls the system and provides a wide range of features. These features include voice greetings that are played back when a caller enters the system. The voice capability is used to guide the caller through a series of choices to direct them to documents they may need. At each branch point, the system prompts the caller to make choices using the telephone's Touch-tone pad. Figure 6.2 illustrates a typical voice menu, or voice tree, used in a fax-on-demand system.

One-call processing requires that the caller use the phone on a fax machine to initiate the contact. But if the caller cannot use his or her fax machine, the touch pad can also be used to enter the fax number. At the end of the selection process, the caller is directed to push the Start button on the fax machine, and the documents selected are sent to his or her fax machine during the call. The one-call mode is attractive to information providers who want the caller to pay for all of the long-distance telephone charges.

A two-call process requires the caller to enter the fax number at which the selected documents will be delivered. Then the caller hangs up and the fax-on-demand system dials the number and delivers the documents. This mode is preferred by many users because they can request the information remotely—they do not have to be at the fax machine or anywhere near the delivery site.

How Is Fax-on-Demand Used?

One of the most popular applications for fax-on-demand is distribution of product literature to prospects and customers, and this use has resulted in significant cost savings, increased sales, and improved service. Growing companies experience a rising demand for customer support as well. In the software industry, particularly, this demand has meant that companies have begun to charge for support following a brief warranty period. Fax-on-demand provides a cost-

Voice Board (Card): A PC board that contains all the necessary voice hardware and software (some is usually PC resident) to allow a PC to receive and digitize voice messages for later retrieval in a voice mail system.

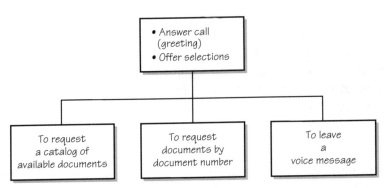

Figure 6.2   Fax-on-demand voice menu. (*Source: ABConsultants*)

and time-efficient solution, and does not usually alienate the callers—unless they don't have a fax machine or fax modem in their computers.

Although it may not be apparent at first, fax-on-demand can have educational benefits, enhancing the image of a company, organization, or institution as one that cares about its audience or topic of focus. The by-product of maintaining good community relations can come in the form of increased recognition and acceptance, even sales of a product or service; it can also bring in funding from either private or public sectors.

In addition, after-hours support in customer service operations and call centers is appreciated, especially when the support center is several time zones away. Approximately 50 percent of the time, information that is well organized will guide the caller to a solution. The obvious benefits are increased customer satisfaction, a higher level of service, and increased customer loyalty—which of course improves the chances for future sales.

Pictures of products, houses, vacation spots, and other items can be included in documents delivered by fax, although it is best to convert black and white or color photos and brochures to simulated black and white halftones. Gray scale images should not be sent directly by fax. There are programs that can do these conversions easily, and the examples that follow illustrate industries that are making good use of this faxing feature.

Where Is Fax-on-Demand Used?

From its beginning fax-on-demand has been mainly a business-to-business communications tool. It has been used in virtually every industry from health care, retailing, manufacturing, and high tech (Figure 6.3). A few applications have succeeded in consumer applications. Newspapers were early experimenters with providing information to consumers by fax. Another early innovator was Cancerfax, a system that provides information on most types of cancer to both health professionals and the general public. Wide consumer use is expected to continue to grow with the increasing number of fax machines and computer fax boards in homes and home offices.

Real Estate

The real estate industry is finding that fax-on-demand is an effective tool for delivering information to current and prospective clients. It is frequently used in conjunction with interactive voice response (IVR) to deliver:

- maps of areas of interest that identify where a property is for sale
- prices of new and used properties
- listings and brochures, including photographs and floorplans
- information on mortgage organizations
- rates and charges
- delivery specifications

Real estate offices store photographs along with descriptions of houses, and their fax-on-demand system gives callers a list of houses in locations and the price range they are interested in. If converted properly, the fax document

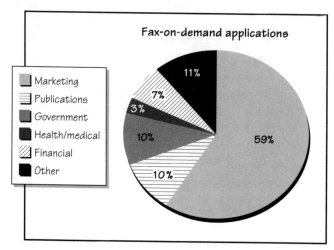

Figure 6.3 Where fax-on-demand is used. (*Source: ABConsultants*)

> **Interactive Voice Response (IVR):** IVR is the use of a telephone to retrieve information (as voice messages) from a computer system. The keys on the phone are used to communicate (to make selections or enter account numbers) usually in response to verbal instructions given by the IVR system.

delivers a good quality image of the houses comparable to halftone pictures that appear in newspapers.

MoveOrganizers, a real estate fax-on-demand service in the Twin Cities area of Minnesota, can be reached from out of state at 1-800-Fax-Home and from the Twin Cities area by dialing Call-Home. In the initial contact callers can obtain a verbal explanation of the service and receive by fax instructions and a map that can be used to select areas of interest. If they identify homes in the area and price range they want, they can call back and request brochures that provide general information on all the properties that meet their criteria. This includes price, the builder's name, address of the listed properties, a brief description, and the document number of a more detailed brochure for each listing. They then can retrieve by fax all the brochures of interest, most of which include a picture of each property and detailed specifications (see Figure 6.4).

In addition, MoveOrganizers provides information on appropriate loan and insurance companies. All services are free to the callers because builders, real estate companies, loan organizations, and insurance organizations pay for being included in the service.

Publications

Newspapers accumulate a substantial backlog of news and supportive material that is never printed because of cost and space constraints. These "news libraries" contain information valuable to the business community, the government, and consumers, and it is possible to categorize much of this information and package it for delivery by fax-on-demand.

For example, a company involved in the export of agricultural products would be interested in news that affects wheat, corn, or soybean prices. An electronic file could be set up to accumulate information on these commodities appearing in newspapers or on the newswires. Titles of related articles would then appear on a list that subscribers could access through the fax system. They would then select the titles of interest and the information would be faxed.

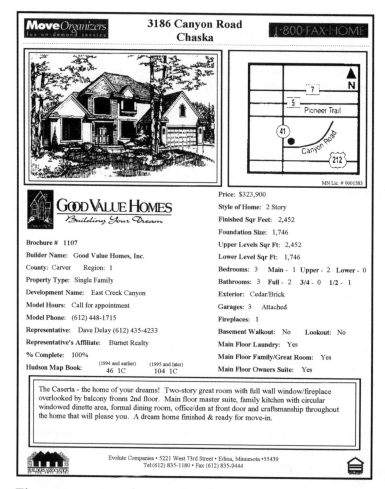

Figure 6.4   A real estate brochure by MoveOrganizers delivered by fax-on-demand. (*Source: MoveOrganizers*)

In some cases, the newspaper will not charge a subscriber but absorb the cost in order to increase circulation. The service can also be financed through space advertising that will appear on the fax documents and/or by charging advertisers for delivery of information on their products or services. When charging the subscriber, the cost is often added to the subscription fee or billed out on a per-usage basis; sometimes subscribers pay by accessing a 900 number or using a credit card.

Newspapers have also saved hundreds of thousands of dollars a year in newsprint costs by relocating listings of commodity prices to fax-on-demand.

Although commodities are followed only by a small number of subscribers to newspapers, trading results fill the major part of a financial page. Coupled with the rising cost of newsprint, some newspapers choose to move commodity prices to a free fax service for subscribers.

Advertising is another useful application. The West Coast McKlatchy newspapers use fax-on-demand to promote the names of their supermarket advertisers. They advertise a number to call through which seasonal and holiday recipes are available by fax. At the top of the recipe is a reminder that the local supermarket provided the service in cooperation with the newspaper, and that the ingredients can be purchased at that supermarket.

Literature fulfillment for organizations that advertise in a publication, delivery of article reprints, and other supplemental information are now also offered to subscribers. Some benefits to newspapers and magazines that deliver information by fax-on-demand are:

- expansion of billable services to advertisers as well as subscribers
- enhancement of advertising package
- cost- and time-efficient way to individualize information delivery for niche audiences

For years, magazines have had so-called bingo cards coded to reference numbers printed on advertisements, enabling readers to request more information. This works well, but it takes from two to eight weeks for the requested information to reach the reader. Advertisers and prospective buyers want more timely delivery. *PC Magazine* was an early adopter of fax services for readers requesting more information about advertised products. An 800 number was included in the magazine's advertisement along with a document number so that the reader could request data sheets by fax. More companies are following suit by including an 800 number and an access code in their advertisements.

Consumer Reports has a fax-on-demand service called Facts by Fax that offers reprints of articles for purchase. *Lawyers Weekly* of Massachusetts has an Automated Opinion Service that provides subscriber article reprints, court decisions, and various legal information. Registration forms are also available through the system. The *Sacramento Bee*'s BeeFax is a free information service to the Sacramento area covering sports, travel, visitor guide, entertainment, recreation, food/recipes, pet care and related subjects of interest to readers. POSTFAX, a service by the *St. Louis Post-Dispatch,* offers business and consumer information free. The costs are paid by advertisers and information providers.

The list keeps growing as information overload forces people to become more specific about what they want, and to concomitantly cut down on paper and electronic "junk" mail. Fax-on-demand systems are playing an important and growing role in addressing these issues; they can be applied creatively to almost any business where outreach to clients, customers or constituents is involved.

Travel

By the turn of the century, the number of fax machines in homes worldwide is projected to grow considerably. Already, many people have access to fax machines at work that they also use for personal business. In the foreseeable future, information on travel, sports, local and worldwide events, and other categories of interest will be accessed by the general public through fax-on-demand systems. The only obstacle to this method's wide acceptance is lack of knowledge that it exists.

Today, state and city governments use fax-on-demand to promote travel to their areas by providing information on local attractions, accommodations, restaurants, nightclubs, theater, special events, and other resources. A few examples of the use of fax-on-demand for promoting travel and tourism are presented in Table 6.1

Computer and High-Tech Industries

Fax-on-demand originated in the computer industry where its use is widespread for the delivery of product literature and customer support. Initially, the distribution of product literature was the most popular application, but with the growing demand for customer support services, providing user instructions and problem-solving information has become more prevalent.

Customers rate software companies by the quality of their customer support services. For this reason and because customer support has become increasingly costly, improved service that does not require personal contact is valued. Fax-on-demand provides support during nonworking hours and when there is a long delay in reaching a support person. Information obtained by fax often is sufficient for the customer to solve the problem and no further demands are made on the support staff. The customer receives immediate service and the technical support staff avoids a session that can last anywhere from 5 to 55 minutes.

Dell Computer provides technical product information and general product and company information through a service called TechFAX (800-950-1329). Most requests for information are from current customers who need after-sales

TABLE 6.1   Travel Industry Applications for Fax-on-Demand

User	System	Application	Number
Convention & Visitors Bureau Charleston, SC	VIS-FAX	Convention and tourist information for Charleston and surrounding area.	800-287-4329 Ext. 443
Hawaii Information Bureau	Instant Information by Fax	Tourist Information: maps, resorts by island; tours, accommodations, events calendar, sports, etc.	800-653-2962 800-OkFaxMe
Chamber of Commerce Gilroy, CA	GILFAX	Calendar of events; listings of restaurants, lodging, apartments, economic profile of the city and chamber members and services.	800-480-4329 Gilroy: Ext. 900
Chamber of Commerce Sunnyvale, CA	SUNFAX		Sunnyvale: Ext. 820

Source: How to Profit from Fax-On-Demand, ABConsultants

support. TechFAX organizes its literature into 20-plus catalogs that represent topics or product lines. Callers can request a the list of catalogs, order a catalog by number, or order documents by number. Document numbers are obtained from the catalogs, from Dell's product advertisements, or from product literature such as operator and system manuals. A key reason for Dell's reputation for good product support is attributed to the TechFAX operation.

Likewise, Merisel, a leading worldwide distributor of computer products, installed the Online Literature Library in the spring of 1992 to provide product information to its VARs, (Value Added Resellers of computer software and hardware), dealers, and other customers. The Online Literature Library, combining fax-on-demand and electronic image management technology, delivers listings and brochures 24 hours per day, 7 days a week. The system, launched in California, has been extremely successful and has been replicated in several companies worldwide.

In 1994, Merisel expanded to include an Online Lead Referral Service to provide leads to its reseller base on user contacts that Merisel makes at exhibitions, conferences, through advertising, and through its Online Literature Library Service.

Financial

Stock, bond, and commodity market data is highly time-sensitive, and customers want information regarding company performance on domestic or international trade or on their individual or business bank accounts and investments on an ongoing basis. This information is now being made available through fax-on-demand. Sometimes these services are provided by the company or organization that compiled the data, such as Dunn and Bradstreet or a commercial bank; in other cases, new service organizations have emerged as *packagers* and *resellers* of this information.

An interesting example is a service in New York City called Wall Street by Fax. This is a subscription service that provides Standard and Poor's company reports including stock charts. A demo is available for first-time callers at 800-938-5555. Wall Street by Fax gives special attention to the presentation of information, using high-quality graphics.

Types of Systems

Vendors of PC-based FOD systems have been the major force behind the development of the fax-on-demand market. Many of their products are primarily for one-function fax-on-demand systems, normally marketed as one application delivery of information for a department or small enterprise.

High-end PC-based systems provide enhanced fax functions such as broadcasting, fax mailboxes, fax forms, or fax overflow. These systems are frequently marketed as fully integrated systems sold on the corporate level for several applications, rather than solely on the departmental level as for the lower-cost ones. The demand for custom-designed fax-on-demand and enhanced fax systems, especially within vertical markets, is on the rise as fax vendors find that the fax portion of the standard system does not meet all of their customer's requirements.

Factors affecting pricing are quantity of servers, available features, and the degree of integration. A system with two voice and two fax ports may cost less than $2,000 for boards and software, while a fully integrated system with four voice and four fax ports may cost $15,000 or more. Larger high-end systems with full enhanced fax functionality generally sell for $1,500 to $2,500 per port. ABConsultants' report, *Fax-on-Demand, Marketing Tool of the '90s,* contains vendor profiles, specifications, and prices for 20-plus of the leading products.

> **Broadcast:** The dissemination of information to a number of stations simultaneously. Broadcast fax is dissemination of the same fax message to two or more fax units.

Entry-Level PC-Based Systems

Several entry-level systems are currently available. At the low end, cost is less than $1,000 for software and PC board(s), and generally has no more than one voice and one fax port, or one universal port. Most products in this category now use DSP (digital signal processor) technology so that one port on one board will provide both voice and fax operation. Several of these products enable both one- and two-call operation. The capabilities of these products are increasing, but currently most do not provide the capability to upgrade.

A related class of products are personal communicators, intended for individual workstations. They frequently provide automatic attendant voice answering, voice message recording, fax send and receive capability, fax/voice switching, fax operation, and data modem functions. These products normally incorporate phone and fax directories and other office enhancements, and usually have only one telephone port or line used for fax, data, and voice. Some current personal communicators have fax-on-demand or fax mailbox functions, and although their fax-on-demand functions are limited, they may be effective for very low-volume applications. Prices for these range from $200 to $400.

Standalone Systems

Fax-on-demand systems can be either standalone or networked. Standalone systems are small, usually supporting two to eight phone lines, and are independent from other computers or networks that may be a part of the computer environment. They also require that administration be conducted from the same PC as that used to provide the service. This means that the service must be stopped while documents are added to the library, reports are run, and other routine administrative tasks completed. Therefore, housekeeping tasks generally are performed during inactive hours, either late at night or early in the morning.

> **Automatic Attendant:** Provides automation of the switchboard capability and the tasks typically performed by a switchboard receptionist. An automated attendant answers the telephone and greets the caller, then tells the caller how to reach a particular group or individual. An option to switch to voice mail or a directory may be provided; and the caller may be given the option to talk to an operator.

Networked Systems

If the company installing the system has a LAN (Local Area Network), or expects the system size to grow to more than eight lines, a LAN setup is preferable. A LAN, or networked configuration, provides extensive flexibility in that the server can, with some additional software, operate while a separate PC is used for administration and housekeeping. The administrator can delete or add documents to the document library, prepare reports, and check the status of lines and fax queues without interfering with the operation of the fax system or stopping the service as with a standalone system.

Consequently, the administrator can more easily monitor the operation of the system when there is a LAN connected to an administrative PC. The number of ports can be expanded to 100 or more by connecting additional fax-on-demand servers. A network system also makes it easy to expand the capacity of the system, as it just requires the addition of more units (fax-on-demand servers) or PCs with the voice and fax boards and the enhanced fax software loaded.

Another advantage of a LAN setup is that PCs may be added to the network that are able to access forms faxed in and process them, and then place the resulting data in a file on the file server. A fax server can also be added to the LAN so that it is able to receive forms faxed directly into the system. They can then be logged and routed to the PC that is processing the forms. If credit card charges are made for information received by fax, a processor can be assigned to a PC to dial the credit card service organization, which will accept or reject the application for credit. The overall advantages of a LAN are clear as long as the amount and kind of traffic you are receiving warrants the additional cost.

Product Features

The differences in functionality, performance, and quality of the various fax-on-demand systems are primarily in the software and software support provided by the vendors. Typically, fax-on-demand software includes all the basic software

---

LAN (Local Area Network):   A data communications network confined to a limited geographical area (usually a building or small campus) with moderate to high data rates. Until recently (with advent of wireless LANs), all LANs were based on cable systems that provided connectivity between all devices on the network.

functions listed here. Some furnish advanced features and optional software that provides further functionality, networking operation, or improved performance.

Basic FOD Software

Most fax-on-demand systems include the following software features:

- Interactive voice response and voice messaging that allows users to record greetings, instructions, and messages.
- Programmable voice tree, password, PIN protection, and caller identification.
- Fax distribution that provides auto-redial on busy or failure, document selection, queuing, merging of cover sheet and documents, and on-the-fly conversion from ASCII to fax format.
- Capability for entry of document into a fax database from a fax machine, an image scanner, a floppy disk, or a LAN.
- Call data recording that logs calls and maintains records of calls, callers, incoming phone numbers, fax numbers, materials requested, and caller messages; and provides reporting and analysis capability.
- Diagnostics that provide remote and local troubleshooting of equipment and systems problems.
- Configuration and installation options (required with systems that allow user installation and configuration) that may allow users to select a one-call or two-call system, plus other options.

Optional and Enhancement Software

Except for some of the low-end products, most fax-on-demand systems include some combination of the following types of software functions (see also Figure 6.5):

PIN (Personal Identification Number): A special password system used by many fax-on-demand systems whereby users are given personal numbers that they must input to the system before they are authorized to use it or to retrieve information.

> **ASCII:** ASCII (American Standard Code for Information Interchange) is a coding system established by the American Standards Association used to represent alphanumeric characters in data processing systems. Documents in ASCII format do not normally provide for the various printing parameters available in today's word processing systems—such as underlining, bold type, different fonts, different type sizes.

- Fax broadcasting allows a document to be faxed to multiple locations simultaneously.

- Conversion from e-mail and PC formats to fax formats enables delivery of computer messages to a fax machine.

- Mail merge makes it possible to combine documents and a list of names, addresses, and other individual or company-specific information.

- Storage of fax documents in fax mailboxes enables recipients to retrieve at their convenience, similar to the process used in fax-on-demand.

- Multiple language support (voice tree) provides callers the option of selecting a preferred language for voice prompting to improve understanding (especially useful in international applications).

- Credit card billing provides online capture of credit card numbers. Some systems also validate the transaction online (that is, obtain approval from the bank card system). In most systems, the actual charge is accomplished later and offline. Credit card billing provides more flexibility in the charge structure (such as different prices for

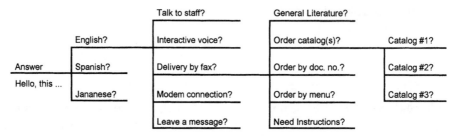

Figure 6.5 Fax-on-demand voice tree with extended options. (*Source: ABConsultants*)

E-mail (Electronic Mail):   A computer-based text system that transmits messages from PCs, workstations and larger computers to other computer systems or printers. Today's e-mail systems usually have mailbox capability whereby the system collects text messages in "mailboxes," for later retrieval.

the various types of documents and dispels some negative aspects of 900 services.

- PIN (personal identification number) and password assignments or other security measures provide privacy protection.
- Direct inward dialing makes it possible to include many telephone numbers on a group of incoming lines. Each assigned number selects a unique voice greeting and voice menu.
- Speech recognition, used with interactive voice, is available for requesting information and documents. This is important in countries where rotary dialing is still used.

Fax Forms Processing

A fax system that can read and sort answers on forms that have been filled out by your consumers can save you both time and money. With a fax form system accomplishing such tasks as filling and processing orders or gathering and sorting valuable market research information, you can really begin to maximize the marketing and management capabilities of this electronic vehicle. Fax form processing requires that your system be equipped with software that has optical character recognition (OCR) and optical mark recognition (OMR) capabili-

DID (Direct Inward Dialing):   DID provides for capture and use by the receiving telephone system of the last digits (usually the last four or five digits) in a telephone number. The receiving system is able to decode these digits and direct the call to a specific location or to use the digits for other computer-type functions. In voice-mail systems, the DID number can be used as a subscriber box number, thus eliminating the need for the caller to reenter that number.

ties for data entry and surveys. This is a relatively recent innovation in the fax world.

Some information providers and fax-on-demand vendors are using OCR and OMR for fax input as a replacement (or partial substitute) for interactive voice in their fax-on-demand applications. In order to assure high reliability, OMR should be used for the fax number, and OCR to capture vital information about the caller. Systems using OCR/OMR can capture such things as the name, address, and phone numbers of sales prospects who request information—a major benefit. A sample form is shown in Figure 6.6.

Range of Services

Service providers can introduce new customers with a basic fax-on-demand operation within a short time and offer a wide range of services. Table 6.2 shows some of the most common configurations and services available. The services are described in more detail in the upcoming list.

> **Document Preparation:** Some service providers have desktop publishing services. Typically, there is an hourly or per document fee.

> **Mail Merge:** Information of any sort can be merged into fax documents during broadcasts.

> **Database Maintenance:** Service providers offer database maintenance themselves or provide software to customers so they can do their own updating.

> **Proprietary Lists:** Some service providers build and maintain proprietary lists targeted at vertical markets.

TABLE 6.2   Fax-on-Demand Price and Features

Features	Entry	Standalone	Networked
No. of Ports	1–2	4–24	8–96
Faxes Per Day	–25	10–1,000	200–1,000+
Broadcasting	Standard	Standard	Standard
Fax Mailboxes	Optional	Optional	Optional
Fax Forms	Not Available	Optional	Optional
Faxing from the Desktop	Not Available	Not Available	Optional
Selection from E-mail/Web Page	Not Available	Not Available	Optional
Total Back-up Redundancy	Not Available	Not Available	Optional
Kit Only (Software & Board)	$600–$2,000	$2,000–$20,000	—
Turnkey System	$2,000–$3,000	$3,000–$40,000	$20,000–$60,000
Fully Enhanced System	—	$50,000+	$40,000–$150,000

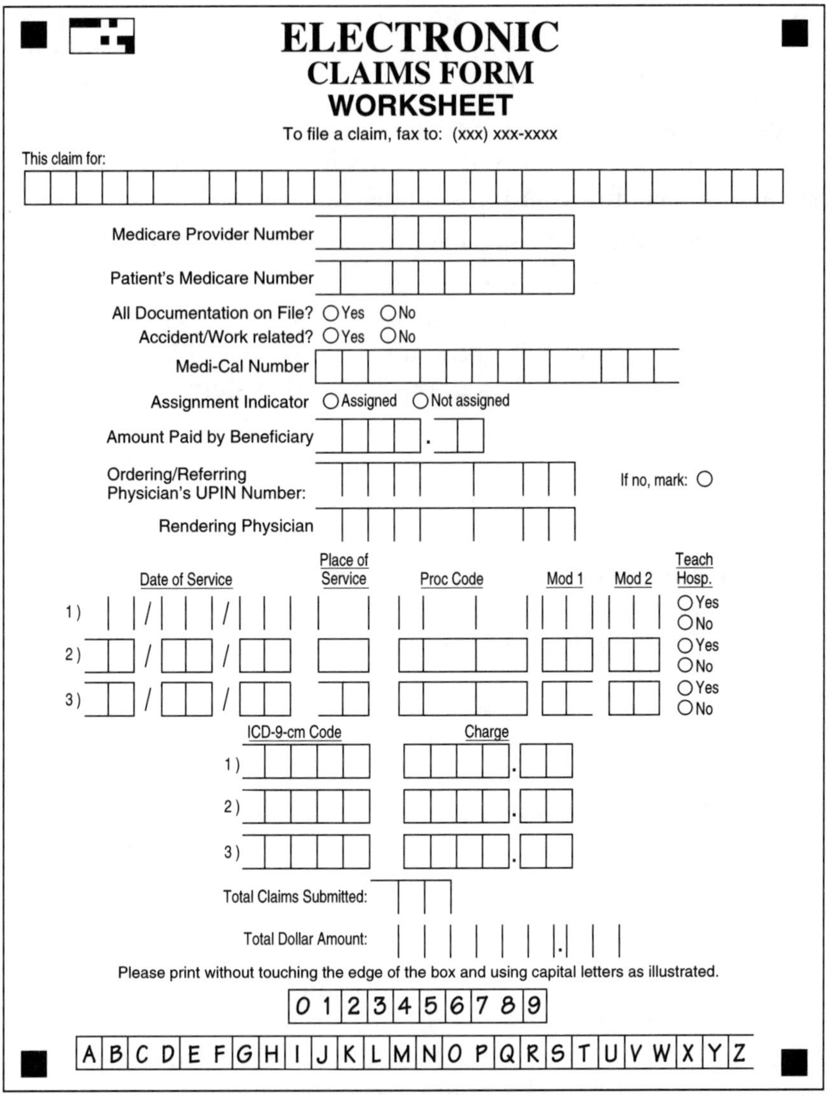

ELECTRONIC
CLAIMS FORM
WORKSHEET

To file a claim, fax to: (xxx) xxx-xxxx

This claim for:

Medicare Provider Number

Patient's Medicare Number

All Documentation on File? ○ Yes ○ No

Accident/Work related? ○ Yes ○ No

Medi-Cal Number

Assignment Indicator ○ Assigned ○ Not assigned

Amount Paid by Beneficiary .

Ordering/Referring Physician's UPIN Number: If no, mark: ○

Rendering Physician

	Date of Service	Place of Service	Proc Code	Mod 1	Mod 2	Teach Hosp.
1)	/ /					○ Yes ○ No
2)	/ /					○ Yes ○ No
3)	/ /					○ Yes ○ No

	ICD-9-cm Code	Charge
1)		.
2)		.
3)		.

Total Claims Submitted:

Total Dollar Amount: .

Please print without touching the edge of the box and using capital letters as illustrated.

0 1 2 3 4 5 6 7 8 9

A B C D E F G H I J K L M N O P Q R S T U V W X Y Z

Figure 6.6 Teleform by Cardiff Software, a fax form. (*Source: Cardiff Software*)

Fax Mailboxes: Fax mailboxes are offered to people who travel as a way of retrieving faxes while on the road. This service is most commonly promoted by local phone companies or long-distance telephone carriers.

Interactive Voice Response: Interactive voice response services are offered by a few service providers. This feature allows remote access to personal database information such as account balances.

E-mail Conversion: Some service providers convert e-mail messages to fax format and deliver them to fax machines.

E-mail Selection: E-mail users can select documents from a fax-on-demand library and send it to the fax number listed in the e-mail message without first calling the fax-on-demand system at the service provider's site.

Web Page Linking: Some service providers have linked Web pages with their fax-on-demand systems so that users can view pages on their desktop computer and have them delivered by fax.

Voice Recording: Professional voice recording services are offered by service providers. For example, ISSC Fax Information Services (a division of IBM) has a sound studio that can be used by its customers.

As this list shows, nearly any service needed to publish documents by fax-on-demand or broadcast is provided by one or more providers. The large providers such as AT&T, MCI and Sprint offer a limited range of services, leaving those that are more labor-intensive to the smaller companies.

Fax Broadcast Lists

Most service companies compile fax lists for their customers from information provided by those customers. Some do this on a routine basis, others only as part of a negotiation for a sizable broadcast. Those who routinely compile lists usually have telemarketing personnel for that purpose.

To promote list maintenance by the customer, special software is provided often without charge to encourage the customer to maintain their own lists. However, service companies will provide list maintenance if requested to do so. TCPA (Federal Telephone Consumers Protection Act) compliance is viewed as the responsibility of the customer who orders the broadcast, although service providers will assist their customers in complying with TCPA and quickly remove people who don't want to be on a list.

Custom databases are provided to customers at their request, but this is an area about which service providers are cautious because databases are expensive and time consuming to maintain. While some specialize in one or two vertical markets and use their lists to promote broadcast traffic, for the majority, mailing lists are their main business and fax lists are offered as an adjunct service.

Customer Broadcast List Creation and Maintenance

Broadcasting is a method of lead creation for companies. It is a replacement or an addition to mass mailings. In order to reach a market, a company needs a list of businesses that fit a selected profile. This profile may be by SIC (standard industry code) or by a category such as manufacturing. Lists of companies in a range of categories are offered as mailing or, due to recent demand, fax lists and are supplied as sheets of labels or on diskette. The vendors of mailing and fax lists will quote the percent of companies in their lists with fax numbers listed.

Compiling Lists

Many service companies build lists for their customers, some through in-house telemarketers. One company charges $100 per hour to call voice numbers to get fax numbers. Clearly, this is a very expensive process. One vendor uses a list on a CD-ROM to check 180,000 records, in addition to calling. AT&T will create a list only for major customers. Several service providers obtain lists from companies that develop and market fax lists, although these are considered to be less reliable sources.

List Updating and Pricing

Many service providers offer electronic updating of broadcast lists, either by modem or diskette, and most update a database from a printed list. Some charge for this service, but all will negotiate the price, if there is one, based on the volume of usage. Often, customers with large broadcast volumes are able to get service free that small volume users have to pay for.

Some service companies update lists from the *exception report* generated during a broadcast when, for various reasons, a number didn't go through. These are the same companies that create lists for customers, since resolving the problems on the exception list requires a call to the person who would have received the fax. Some service providers inactivate numbers when these appear on exception lists more than once, in which case the list owner must decide to the change or remove the number from the broadcast list. Charges vary from $0.15 to $0.55 per record to determine the reason a number was not good and to resolve the problem.

Custom Database (Vertical Market) Maintenance

Service providers offer lists to their customers for broadcast use. Sources of such lists include: National FaxList, Direct Mail Marketing Place (DMMP), and

National Registry Publications. Four types of lists are maintained by one or more of the service providers: consumer product dealers, mortgage banks, pharmacies, and travel agents. Typically, there is no charge for using a list, just for the broadcast. The cost of maintenance is small when compared to the broadcast revenue the lists generate.

The published prices offered by National FaxList, a frequent list source are:

- Price per record in basic format: $0.10 for one-time use and $0.25 for unlimited use.
- Price per record in full format: $0.25 for one-time use and $0.50 for unlimited use.
- Standard discounts are available at 10 percent for 10,000 records to 30 percent for 100,000 records. Special discounts are common.

Fax lists are available from several organizations including: American List Counsel, Am-Pro, Best Mailing Lists, Compilers Plus, Dunhill International Lists, and B&K Lists.

Fax-on-Demand and the Internet

Several approaches for marrying fax-on-demand and the Internet have been implemented variously by trendsetting vendors, service providers, and users. By combining a fax-on-demand system using a separate interactive voice server and a fax server, a bulletin board server, and an e-mail gateway on one LAN, documents may be requested by interactive voice, e-mail, and by employees from their desktop PCs. The selected documents can be automatically delivered by fax to the requester, or retrieved on the BBS or by e-mail.

World Wide Web pages are now being designed to allow retrieval of documents from fax-on-demand databases. When the title or identifying number of the document or information file is located using normal Internet and Web search techniques, the information can be downloaded to the desktop PC or sent as a document or a number of documents offline to a fax machine. This gives requesters the option to choose which location and method is most convenient, and frequently allows them to add a note to the cover page that will be used in the transmission (see Figure 6.7). This capability has been especially valuable for sending product and support information to prospects and customers. A salesperson with a portable PC, a modem, and Internet access can request that documents be sent to his or her customers. A custom cover page is also an option.

Two of the leading fax-on-demand software publishers provide retrieval of Web pages with their software (see Figure 6.8). This capability is implemented by connecting the fax-on-demand server to the information provider's Web

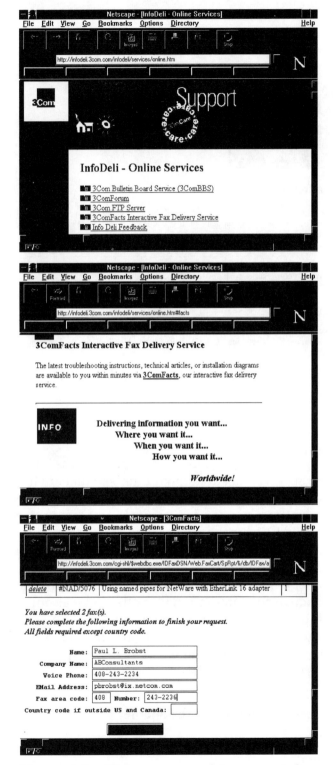

Figure 6.7 Web pages used to request fax-on-demand. (*Source: 3COM*)

Welcome to...

World Leaders in Enhanced Fax

Welcome to Ibex, the leading provider of fax-on-demand (FOD) systems. If you are not sure what fax-on-demand is, look at <u>What is Fax-on-demand</u>. If you aren't sure what FOD can do for you, you may want to look at some <u>Real-world Applications</u> .

Now, enhance your Web presence with automated fax access.

New! <u>FactsLine for the Web</u> can make *your Web pages accessible to anyone with a phone and fax machine.* Add another 100 million people to the 10-20 million that have access to the Web, using the same Web documents and effort. We invite you to try it by calling 1-800-289-9998 and requesting document 600 (this home page) or document 601 (FactsLine for the Web document). Or, check out the <u>FactsLine for the Web Press Release</u> .

Figure 6.8 A Web page delivered by fax-on-demand. (*Source: IBEX*)

server. HTML (hypertext language used to program pages for the Internet) pages on the Web server are given fax document numbers that are included in the fax-on-demand document catalog. With this feature, Web pages are available by fax from any location with a phone and a fax machine. One service provider is able to deliver World Wide Web pages by normal fax-on-demand techniques from many Web sites worldwide. Note that each level of linked Web pages require fax-on-demand call and retrieval.

Internet and other e-mail services, too, are now delivering fax messages. This is especially attractive for international traffic. Several enhanced fax service providers accept documents for a fax broadcast with an associated broadcast list via the Internet (usually from international or long-distance locations) to avoid long-distance transmission charges. The service providers then broadcast the fax using lower-cost dial-up telephone services.

Sites Integrating Fax-on-Demand with the Internet

Following is a list of some Internet sites that have integrated fax-on-demand into their Web pages.

- Octel at www.boomerang.com/webfax/octelfax.
- Sun Microsystems at www.boomerang.com/webfax/sunsoft
- Silicon Graphics at www.boomerang.com/webfax/sgifax
- Boomerang Information Services at www.boomerang.com
- Dialog at www.dialog.com (follow the path: dialog, commands feature services, ASAF, request form.)
- 3COM at www.3com.com (Path: customer support, services/information delivery, 3Com facts, interactive fax delivery)
- IBM's Microelectronics at www.chips.ibm.com (allows Web surfers to locate a product and then select several alternatives for receiving the information, including e-mail and fax delivery. This feature can be used following the path: memory, selection of any product and model (such as 11M1640BB), and request fax delivery.)
- AppleFax at www.apple.com/faxdocs/fax.html. A Common Ground Mini Viewer is required to use this feature, and access to the viewer is restricted.

Planning Information Delivery

Successful fax-on-demand systems are based on promotion of the service and maintaining an informative and worthwhile library of documents. Good PR or advertising is essential and can be as simple or elaborate as the budget allows. It is important to include your FOD number on all advertising, promotional literature, and any other distributed materials. They should be on all data sheets, packaging, instruction manuals, and even voice messages.

Fax Document Library

Documents are the underpinning of the fax-on-demand system. The first inclination is to use documents currently available such as catalogs or data sheets by scanning these into the fax library, but doing so usually gives poor results for a number of reasons:

- There is a loss of quality inherent in the scanning process. It is preferable to start with the computer-generated original and convert the document to fax format using conversion software.
- Photos and halftone images need to be processed in order to provide quality fax images. Scanned images may result in black blobs unless

these are converted using the photo setting. However the photo setting on a fax machine may make tint appear fuzzy. This problem is easily solved with image processing software.

- Some images take a long time to send as the design of the information on the page results in little or no compression when converted to fax format. Pages are compressed, and redundant information is removed during conversion to fax format. Poorly designed pages can take several minutes or longer to send.
- Some fonts and type sizes reproduce poorly when faxed.

Documents that can reproduce at a fax machine have been designed for the process. This process usually is one of trial and error as you experiment with fonts and font sizes and graphics. Software is available that will convert photos from grayscale or color to black and white halftones at the correct resolution for faxing. There are also desktop publishing services that are skilled in preparing documents for sending by fax. A properly designed document can be as crisp as one output on a laser printer at standard resolution. Success in this endeavor comes from knowing what works well with fax reproduction and using only those methods and techniques that work.

Planning a System or Service

Identifying and understanding a need for delivery of information by fax is the first step in planning any fax-on-demand application. There are many reasons to consider delivering information and documents by fax. Reducing costs, or keeping cost increases under control, is a common and obvious reason for turning to fax-on-demand. Other reasons are to improve service quality and to stay close to the customer.

Compression (image): Compression is a technique employed by fax and data processing equipment to code documents and other images in order to substantially reduce transmission time or storage requirements for the image. Group 3 fax uses two industry standard compression methods: Modified Huffman (MH), which is required by all Group 3 fax units (and all fax boards) and Modified Read (MR), which an optional feature with increased compression effectiveness (usually a 15 percent to 25 percent increase). MR is provided with most of the higher-priced fax transceivers.

Needs Assessment

The first step in planning a system of service is needs assessment. Consultants or internal planners should follow the same procedures whether they are working with a small company or a giant corporation. The intensity and extensiveness varies, but the steps are essentially the same.

In a typical project, the needs assessment phase often takes the most time as it involves planning sessions with a number of people within the organization. During these planning sessions, the current method of document distribution is determined along with the limitations and costs. Goals are usually defined for improved service and cost reduction, or constraints on the growth of personnel.

Another objective of the assessment is to define the computer and/or LAN and operational environment into which the system will fit. The document library, its formats, frequency of change, ownership, and responsibility for maintaining revision control, and the organization and person who will manage the system or service are all determined. Recommendations are made in the form of a needs analysis or white paper report for one or several plans to implement a new method of delivering information by enhanced fax.

Requirements Specifications

Before implementation begins, the needs assessment report should be reviewed by the project leader and other management. Once agreement on its contents are reached, it is then used as a basis for writing a requirements report that translates the company's needs into requirements that define the system or service. Management may choose to use either a service provider or to install their own system. The same report can be applied to either choice.

Implementation

Although the details of implementation will differ depending on the size, complexity, and cost of the system, the recommended process includes requesting quotations from suppliers, vendors, or resellers, and selecting and installing a system and training users and operators.

Planning and Delivery Process

A consultant or enhanced fax company should:

1. Define the current method of distributing information.
   a. Describe the limitations of this method.
   b. Suggest improvements.
   c. Identify the requirements for making these improvements.

2. Define the functions necessary to meet an enhanced fax method of delivering information.

   a. List the details of current and anticipated caller traffic.

   b. Identify requirements and write specifications for the system architecture and design to include:

   - Standalone or LAN connection
   - Number of ports to handle anticipated traffic
   - Functions to meet the needs
   - Telephone equipment

3. Write an RFQ to request quotations from suppliers.

4. Plan the installation and training.

5. Assist in the installation.

6. Evaluate system performance and suggest improvements if needed.

The following components should be included in the white paper or requirements report:

Purpose of the System or Service
Project Schedule

Anticipated start date
Installation schedule
Initial test and evaluation period
Projected date for full use of system

Service Requirements

Telephone service
Voice functions
Fax functions
Document database
Document preparation and input
Document access
Fax-on-demand traffic
Broadcast lists
Other functions
System activity reports

Backup and Reliability

> Fault tolerance
> Backup
> Site catastrophe

What's Coming?

With all the hype and success of the Internet and emerging intranets—the use of Internet technologies for intracompany communications—the use of fax for information delivery will not diminish. However, fax delivery will have to have connectivity with corporate networks and Internet/intranet technologies. Trends that are expected include:

More Connectivity with Corporate Resources

Access to corporate databases including data and image (document) files is currently being addressed by the leading systems-oriented fax-on-demand vendors. This trend will mean that more VARs and systems integrators will provide enhanced fax functionality in their systems. Greater connectivity will also mean that fax-on-demand services will use or work with other corporate resources including fax servers, e-mail gateways, Web servers, and common databases. Databases will include increased direct access to such software applications as Lotus Notes, Adobe Acrobat (PDF) files, and Internet HTML documents.

Trend: Compatible File Formats

Companies that are experimenting with various ways to make information available to their customers, prospects, employees, and associates are finding that it is a challenge to keep their databases up to date, which may be in dif-

> **Group 3 Fax:**   Group 3 facsimile is characterized by digital encoding using the Modified Huffman compression algorithm, by taking less than one minute to transmit a document, and producing 203 by 98 lines-per-inch resolution or, optionally, 203 by 198 lines-per-inch resolution. (Almost all fax units in use today are Group 3 or have Group 3 capability.)

Group 4 Fax: Group 4 facsimile are unit-defined to operate over digital telephone lines and other data networks. The compression algorithm is a modification of the Modified Read method used optionally by some Group 3 units. Most Group 4 units have optionally higher resolutions such as 400 by 400 lines per inch and operate at higher speeds, which allows them to operate over 56 Kbps or 64 Kbps networks such as ISDN. (Some Group 3 units also have similar capabilities, making it difficult to distinguish the advantages of units marketed as Group 4 types.)

---

ferent formats including ASCII, various word processor formats, Adobe PDF, Lotus Notes, standard (G3) or G4 fax (a more compact file used in image management systems). These companies want to eliminate as many of these different formats as possible and use one for all applications. Some companies have gone to PDF files as a master file that can be used to enter documents onto the Web or to generate fax documents in a batch process or, preferably, on-the-fly.

Information-on-Demand

People demand quick answers on their own schedules, and global commerce has made it more of a necessity. Integration of information delivery systems is key in electronic communication today. From standalone fax machines to corporate networks, telephone messaging, and e-mail/Internet access, the only solution is integration.

People will be able to obtain information in any form and over any medium they choose. It will be available 24 hours a day, 7 days a week, anywhere in the world where there is a telephone line, a cellular phone, or radio. Excluding low-end products, fax-on-demand may, before the year 2000, lose its identity as a separate technology and become just an application (but a major one) of information-on-demand services.

Fax-on-Demand Survey

To begin your preliminary needs assessment, answer the following questions:

If you are a marketer:

☐ 1. Do prospects call frequently for product information?
☐ 2. Are potential customers forfeited because they receive requested literature days or weeks after contact?
☐ 3. Does distributed information, such as brochures, specifications, and prices, change frequently?
☐ 4. Are customers dissatisfied or lost because the information provided is not up to date?
☐ 5. Is there a problem meeting demands for support; or is new support staff continually being hired and trained?
☐ 6. Are calls often made inquiring about the status of orders?

If you are a manager or executive:

☐ 1. Are you responsible for distributing up-to-date financial and other company information to stockholders, potential investors, and the press on a timely basis?
☐ 2. Do you need to distribute benefit and policy information to employees and contractors in a timely manner?
☐ 3. Do you need to provide data for inside and outside inquiries on potential company employment opportunities?

If you are a publisher and/or information provider:

☐ 1. Do you have an abundance of information you do not currently publish that could be sold?
☐ 2. Could you increase your revenue by selling information by fax that you currently advertise, sell, or distribute in other ways?
☐ 3. Can you generate more revenue from your current advertisers by augmenting their ads with promotional material by fax?
☐ 4. Will your readers pay for reprints of past articles or for background material on these articles?
☐ 5. Can you increase your circulation by making information, (recipes, results of sporting events, and so on) available by fax?

CHAPTER SEVEN

THE SMART CARD GAME

Margo Komenar

Card technologies today offer marketers significant options for promoting and expanding their businesses. Magnetic and optical cards, usually for a single account, that record retail, travel, and credit card account information; long-distance telephone personal identification numbers (PINs); and other data are now part of our everyday lives. Prepaid debit and smart cards have been prevalent in Europe and Asia for years, but are just entering the United States market in a number of aggressive pilot programs. These *stored-value* cards can be used almost anywhere cash or credit cards are accepted, including entertainment, retail, and travel venues, as well as in "smart" machines.

Smart or *chip* cards contain microprocessor-based electronics that make data storage and computation possible. Debit cards are less powerful because they do not support the embedded chip technology; instead, they use an optical PIN number or a magnetic strip to track debits. Debit and chip cards are revolutionizing the way personal and professional business is conducted. According to Visa International, industry observers predict one-half of all payment cards issued in the world will be chip cards by the year 2000. Some industry leaders believe smart cards will eventually replace money altogether. Marketers see enormous potential in the smart card's marketing capabilities, such as its ability to track individual buying patterns, which will result in promotions and marketing campaigns tailored to the individual.

In Germany, citizens carry smart health cards that contain their medical histories and health care information. All of the Visa and MasterCards in France have chips in them, and smart telephone cards are widely used outside of the United States. Ben Miller, chairman of the CardTech/SecurTech Conference, the largest smart card conference in the world, offers one reason why smart card technology has caught on more quickly in Europe than in the United

States: "In France, only eight banks had to decide to do smart cards for all 22 million cardholders in that country. We have over 10,000 banks in the United States, so it's harder to make that kind of decision, to get something pervasive across the market."

Another reason the United States has been slow to enter this market is because of its superior and comparatively inexpensive online telecommunications infrastructure. The U.S. banking industry invested billions of dollars in online automatic teller machines and credit/debit card authorization terminals, which now cover over 95 percent of all credit card transactions, and it needed to amortize that investment over a period of time, specifically the 1980s and early 1990s. Banks were not willing to invest additional billions to get smart card technology into the marketplace when they already had an online system that worked well.

However, the U.S. banking industry began to realize it didn't make sense to go online for low-dollar transactions such as buying a newspaper, or a hamburger at McDonald's. One reason is time—an online transaction takes up to 10 times longer than a debit or smart card transaction; another reason is overhead—the cost of flooding the online infrastructure with literally millions of these small transactions. Miller elaborates, "We're talking about 600 million transactions worth $3 trillion a year in those low-dollar (less than $10) [purchases]. [Banks] needed a mechanism that provided offline electronic funds transfer. That's where the smart card fits in nicely."

Smart cards and debit cards afford banks two major profit rationales: They can charge transaction fees for loading the cards, and they can use ("float") the money that the consumer pays up front for the credit, until it is actually debited from the card, which can be weeks or months after the credit has been purchased.

Miller predicts that these cards are going to be even more popular in the United States than elsewhere because he believes what drives America is laissez-faire economics, and the kinds of marketing benefits smart cards make possible are very appealing. "Governments can have health care programs, and governments can have national ID programs and things of that nature, but what really heats up is when you have open market competition driving applications. And that's what we're starting to see here in the United States."

Debit Cards

A debit card electronically stores and tracks credit that has been purchased in advance. It can be read by a computer or other dedicated machine. In the case of a telephone debit card, a PIN, either verbally given to an operator or digitally entered using the phone pad, activates debiting. With a debit card, services are prepaid and deducted, or debited, as they are used. Four years ago, debit cards were a practically unknown service but according to Tom Heaton, the director of Enhanced Services for Teltrust, Inc., a Salt Lake City operator service provider (OSP), "[the debit card industry] has grown to just under $1 billion dollars in 1995."

Prepaid cards are given as gifts, used in business promotions, and even serve as business cards. They are excellent for targeting a specific audience, since users of prepaid cards for a particular service are a well-defined population. A card may be carried around for weeks or months and used many times before the total value is consumed. As an advertising and marketing vehicle, this kind of continued exposure is highly desirable.

Telephone Debit Cards

Telephone debit cards are a convenient and secure way for managing the phone usage of employees who travel or do much of their work outside the office and of students away at school. They are often given as promotional or thank-you gifts. Since phone calls made with debit cards are not traceable, they are also ensure privacy. They can be useful when traveling in parts of the world where calling cards are not accepted. Telephone debit cards are very much a part of Asian and European lifestyles.

A telephone debit card user dials a toll-free service number from a Touch-Tone phone. When contact is made, a voice prompt lists the services, then asks for the user's name and PIN or authorization code. The user is told how much credit is still available on the card. If the card is being used for a long-distance call, the user is asked to dial the destination number; the credit used during the long-distance call is automatically tracked through the connection to the service number.

Calls can be made within the United States and from certain international locations, but access to debit services is not available everywhere in the world. Thus the card's calling parameters (options and limitations) should be considered before purchase, especially if it is intended for redistribution.

Telephone debit card credit is measured in currency, minutes, or units. The advantage to buying and storing in units is that they can be easily translated into different currencies. The number of units needed to call different destinations varies, and can be adjusted to the appropriate exchange rate for the country being called. For example, if units are purchased at a rate of 40 cents each, a call from the United States to Canada might cost two units per minute, while a call to Japan might cost four units per minute. It is also possible to purchase a card that is worth a specific dollar amount, such as $10 or $20. The dollars can be applied to almost anything a business offers as a prepaid product or service.

Advantages and Disadvantages of Debit Cards

The debit card provides convenience, privacy, and security, and its versatility in marketing and advertising applications is practically unlimited. Worldwide, especially in Europe as noted, debit cards are commonly used to make long-distance calls. The United States is probably the only country that still uses the talk now and pay later approach. With the telephone debit card, there are no service charges like those assessed on credit card phone calls. In fact, by using a credit card to load a debit card, these charges may also be avoided.

Debit cards provide what is essentially a throwaway service. You can buy the amount of credit that you want to use and throw the card away when it's used up. The potential for abuse is limited compared to credit cards, because the value of a debit card rarely exceeds $50. One disadvantage, however, is that a debit card is just like cash. If you lose it, it's nonreplaceable, because no record of the buyer's identity is linked to the card. It's also inconvenient if you discover you don't have enough credit on the card to finish a call or pay for the services you want.

Marketing Possibilities

Debit cards can be used to promote, advertise, and sell products and services. The greatest profit is not seen as much in the card's initial distribution as it is in the subsequent, ongoing purchasing of credit by consumers. Debit card vending machines are used by companies that want to make their specialty debit cards available in tourist areas, malls, terminals, and other places where people might do impulse buying. Consumers like cards with pictures on them, which can then serve as travel mementos, status symbols, or collector's items. For example, a San Francisco Bay tour and commuter ferry company, the Red and White Fleet, contracted with an independent marketing group to provide a card displaying a picture of its ship. The card was sold in vending machines along Pier 39 at Fisherman's Wharf.

> *Cross-Promotion:* As a holiday promotion, Hallmark included a telephone debit card in its Christmas cards; recipients were given five minutes of long-distance credit. By partnering with a long-distance company, Hallmark was able to leverage the benefits of cross-promotion. It was to the long-distance company's advantage to advertise Hallmark, and it was to Hallmark's advantage to offer the long-distance credit as a holiday gift idea that was as easy as purchasing a greeting card.
>
> *Business Cards:* Many companies double the use of debit cards by having them printed as customized business cards to give out. They are giving

something of redeemable value, and usually people keep these cards even after the credit is used up. It is a marketing tool for both the business that gives the card away as well as the service or product for which the card holds credit.

Events: Debit card handouts can help draw big crowds at trade shows and business functions. For example, they can be given away at grand openings to a predetermined number of customers who are either first to arrive or to make a purchase. At a McDonald's restaurant, a promotion was staged at which the first 200 people to order a Big Mac got a free debit card. It was very successful at bringing in large numbers of people, and it enhanced customer relations as well.

Collector's Items: Limited-edition cards are printed with art, sports figures, event souvenir images, famous or historical logos, and other types of memorabilia. The limited-edition status lends these cards added appeal and attracts collectors.

The PIC Entertainment/Info Network Card

The PIC Entertainment Card, a debit card developed by Partners In Communication (PIC), of Mill Valley, California, provides 800-number access to a range of entertainment services normally accessed by 900 numbers. The card has opened the door to a wide range of possibilities. In the past, debit card access to 900 numbers was practically impossible because those numbers connect to private networks that charge at different rates. For example, 1-900-Legal may charge the caller more per minute than 1-900-Psychic. Partners In Communication came up with a solution by creating business alliances with certain 900-number companies.

Through its research, PIC discovered that a significant number of people wanted access to entertainment services, such as psychics, lucky numbers, and astrologers. PIC also found that the majority of 1-900-psychic services had alternative 800 numbers. These services had set up their own 800 numbers in order to reach people who didn't have 900-number access; those callers paid by credit card. The PIC Info Network allows an individual to bypass home or business 900-number blocks by using the 800-number access on the card to make that connection. The time used on the 900 service is then monitored by the 800-number connection. According to PIC, this was the first time a service like this had been tried, and it was a challenge to set up, since there is no one service bureau or even a group of service bureau networks that handle 900 numbers.

PIC's exhaustive search for a combination of telephone entertainment services through a single network company led it to a group in Nevada that provides live astrology, psychic, and adult entertainment services. PIC and the network company worked out an arrangement so that PIC's 800 service, which is out of Utah, could call a local number in Nevada and use a special coding system to connect directly to a live psychic. Here's how it works. If you call the PIC Entertainment Card 800 number, you hear, "Welcome to the PIC Info Network. If you would like to make a long-distance call, please enter your PIN number." You are then told how much time you have left on the card and asked if you would like to talk to a psychic or an astrologer at a rate of $2.50 per minute. If you say yes, the system speed dials the prestored number of the live psychic or astrologer.

Since live information service is expensive to the debit card user, PIC decided to add automated services to its card. It selected a group called Tel-Trust, which offered automated sports update information, comedy, soap operas, daily horoscopes, music, and a wide range of other options, also available in Spanish. PIC decided to offer it to their end users at $1 per minute in order to create a standard rate.

World FM Network, a Hawaii-based radio syndication company, specializes in producing and marketing high-profile, American-style radio programs for the Japanese market. It contacted Partners In Communication to assist that firm in setting up a combination membership/debit telephone service/information and news card. WFN's president, Sakae Ross, proposed marketing the "Kamaaina Card" (kamaaina means local resident in Hawaiian) to the Japanese market using his radio stations in Japan and Hawaii. Interested Japanese and Hawaiian tourists pay a membership fee that includes the telephone services. Both the state government and the Hawaiian Department of Tourism enthusiastically support the program. What makes this card so innovative is the way it integrates membership, retail, and entertainment options. Kamaaina members are entitled to discounts in restaurants, stores, and entertainment venues. The telephone network advertises vendors, offers inexpensive dialing to and from Japan, and provides information and entertainment services, such as weather reports, world news, and psychic and astrological readings in Japanese.

PIC is also working with a telecommunications company in Las Vegas called Long Distance International, Inc. LDI has created alliances with major celebrities and is preparing to offer collector telephone debit cards to the general public. It has agreements with fitness guru Cory Everson and a well-known rap group that plans to include the debit cards with a CD purchase. The possibilities seem limitless.

Guidelines and Resources

If you plan to use a prepaid telephone debit card in a marketing or fund-raising campaign, it is advisable to use a marketing consultant who is familiar with the vendors and possible package configurations to get the best prices and services. The process involves finding the lowest rates for bulk telephone units, reliable, quality printers and card suppliers, and addressing a myriad of details. According to PIC, you should be prepared to answer the following questions:

- What is the nature of your project (such as fund-raising, event or product publicity, personal or business promotion)?
- How will the cards be distributed (through retail outlets, direct mail, vending machines, or at an event)?
- How many cards do you want produced? (Orders under 5,000 can run from $.80 to $1.50 per card for the printing alone.)
- How many units or minutes do you want on each card?
- What are the calling parameters (U.S. only or international origin)?
- Do you want to prepay for the telephone time upon the acceptance of the completed card, or do you want to pay a little more in order to be billed on a monthly basis?
- Do you want your card to be rechargeable?

The list of debit card-related businesses in Table 7.1 is not meant as an endorsement, but to provide sources of additional information on debit card promotional campaigns. All of the major long-distance carriers have some form of debit card service, including AT&T, MCI, Sprint, LDDS, LCI, and Frontier.

TABLE 7.1   Debit Card-Related Businesses

Marketing Consultants	Telephone	Fax Phone
Partners In Communication Shirley Ah Sing	415-380-9060	415-380-9329
International Communication Network Nakita Belton	916-332-0172	916-332-0172
ACMI	901-363-2100	901-363-9707
Printing Manufacturers		
Caulastics, Inc.	800-346-8643	
Combined Graphics	800-822-3971	
Custom Telephone Printing Company	800-753-5300	
Network Debit Platforms		
TelTrust, Inc.	800-530-3222	
Conquest	800-955-1313	
Enhanced Communications, Inc.	800-504-6040	

Cards Get Smart

Another type of card promises to revolutionize both personal and business modes of storing, tracking, transporting, and maintaining data. This card can store records, credit in almost any form, highly sensitive encrypted information and more. It's called a *smart* card.

A smart card looks just like a conventional credit card, with one exception: It contains a microcomputer chip, whose external electronic connections, or micromodules, appear on the surface of the card and act as contacts between the microcomputer inside the card and the external equipment that reads the card. Card-reading devices include public or cellular telephones, merchant point-of-sale terminals, ATMs, or other specially designed electronic equipment (Figure 7.1). The embedded computer chip may contain hundreds of thousands of transistors. The card is considered smart because of its sophisticated storage system, controlled access capabilities, and highly rated security features.

Like the debit card, the simplest type of smart card is used to electronically store and track credit that has been purchased in advance; also like the debit card, it is read by a computer or other dedicated machine. *Stored value* is the principle behind this type of smart card: Services or goods are prepaid, and then deducted or debited as they are used.

A reloadable smart card is called an *electronic purse.* When the prepurchased credit is used up on a reloadable card, it can be reloaded with more pre-

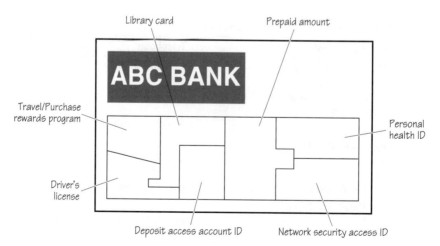

Figure 7.1 ABC Bank: hypothetical diagram of smart card information storage.

paid credit and used for another round of purchasing. Reloadable cards can be used in place of cash for a wide range of relatively small purchases. They can also be used in vending machines or other automated devices that are equipped with card readers.

The opportunities for marketers using smart cards are far-reaching, because these cards are closely tied to all aspects of commercial and personal information management. By acting as a *pocket billboard,* a smart card gives merchants with a unique opportunity to showcase products and enhance the image of the advertiser. Further, smart cards are capable of recording and tracking individual buying patterns, which has broad implications in the direct marketing arena. Smart cards can also be used in conjunction with the Internet, set-top boxes, TV, and interactive TV—and like these media, they will profoundly impact our lives as consumers.

Some of the Players

As noted earlier, the chip card industry has been active for many years in Europe and other countries. Pioneering companies eventually established offices in the United States to promote market expansion, and now many pilot programs are scheduled or under way across this country. In particular, the explosion of marketing opportunities and electronic commerce on the Internet finally woke up the banking industry to the potential of the new media and smart cards. Approximately 25 percent of the financial industry's net income is generated by transaction fees. If the major companies now doing business on the Internet support online transactions and collect those fees, the banks will lose a significant portion of their income, even though the banks' credit cards will still be utilized. This threat is significant enough to make the conservative U.S. banking industry move quickly. Ben Miller, chairman of the CardTech/ SecurTech (CTST) Conference, describes the situation:

> The banks realized—partially because Bill Gates called them dinosaurs— that their payment mechanisms were not adequate for the electronic world. They realized that they were totally out of position by being an isolated industry protected by regulation, which only moved when things got really hot for them. When Quicken proposed that Intuit be purchased by Microsoft, they realized, "Oh, my God, these people might set up a banking system; they might have their own credit cards! We have to make sure that the point of transaction initiation begins with our card, whether that point is a PC or some future set-top box environment." Therefore, in order for that to happen, their existing payment mechanisms needed to become part of the future financial streams. The possibility of losing that revenue stream scared them,

and moved them. Starting only in June 1994 did Visa and MasterCard commit to moving smart cards forward in the world and in the United States.

Hundreds of companies worldwide are active participants in the chip card industry. To give you an overview of the industry, a few of these companies are profiled here. Note that the companies presented do not necessarily reflect dominance in market share or superiority over those not mentioned.

Visa International

Visa is the largest consumer payment system in the world, with more than 12 million acceptance locations. Visa member financial institutions have issued more than 387 million cards worldwide. Visa also has one of the leading global ATM networks. Edmund P. Jensen, president and chief executive officer of Visa, said that demand for relationship-based products and services will skyrocket as consumers accept and embrace the offering. He is quoted as saying: "Consumers will drive the demand for future payment and financial services products when they are easy to use, convenient, and reliable. Our strategic direction for relationship-based products fulfills those requirements, and our member institutions are now poised to deliver."

Visa continues to participate aggressively in pilots globally. The following information, supplied by Visa, provides a brief history of this fast-moving industry, along with Visa's key contributions to it.

Visa Milestones in Chip Card Development

In 1988, the world's first sophisticated function chip card, the VISA SuperSmart Card, was launched in Japan as a pilot program. It was the beginning of a highly successful evolution. In 1982, the French banking community began developing early chip specifications that formed the basis of a nationwide launch of smart cards by Groupement des Cartes Bancaires. Between 1992 and 1994, nationwide chip-driven card programs and pilots for stored value were launched in a variety of countries around the world. By the end of 1993, 21 million banking cards in France had an integrated circuit that allowed cash withdrawal and payment.

The first and perhaps most influential of these is the Danmønt program in Denmark. Piloted in late 1992 and early 1993, and now fully operational on a national level, Danmønt—which means Danish coin—is a joint venture between PBS, the Danish Payment System representing more than 200 banks, and KTAS, an organization representing all of Denmark's telecommunications companies.

Following on the success of Danmønt, stored-value pilots have been launched in Finland, Indonesia, South Africa, Switzerland, Taiwan, and the

United States; and programs have been announced in Australia, Belgium, Estonia, Lithuania, Portugal, Singapore, Spain, and the United Kingdom.

At the end of 1993, Visa initiated a joint working group with MasterCard International and Europay International to develop a common set of technical specifications for integrating ICs in payment cards. This effort was followed in early 1994 with Visa's announcement that it would be the first payment systems organization to support the development of a global stored-value card. This announcement was soon followed by Visa's creation of a working group of 21 large payment systems organizations from 16 countries to ensure that stored-value card specifications support global systems that offer consumers worldwide utility for their electronic purses.

A Few Visa Milestones

March 1995: Visa stored-value cards are announced as the first product utilizing microchip technology. Pilot schedules are disclosed for Asia-Pacific, Canada, European Union, Latin America, and the United States.

May 1995: Visa, Europay, and MasterCard announce that joint EMV card and terminal specifications for microchip-based cards and card-reading terminals will be released, allowing industry participants to begin developing chip card applications that will work across borders and systems.

August 1995: Australia and New Zealand Banking Group (ANZ) and National Australia Bank begin piloting Visa disposable stored-value cards at their cafeterias in Melbourne. Credit Union Services Corporation, Westpac, and the Commonwealth Bank announce their intent to pilot Visa stored-value cards in Sydney.

October 1995: Visa International, Overseas Trust Bank (OTB), and Hutchinson Whampoa Ltd. offer the first smart card to be fully compatible with the Europay/MasterCard/Visa (EMV). Visa/OTB/Hutchison co-branded cards were in the hands of Hong Kong consumers by year's end. La Caixa Bank of Spain offers VISA Cash reloadable cards that customers can recharge at participating La Caixa banks or at compatible data phones.

November 1995: Bank of New Zealand announces a VISA Cash pilot. The First Union Corporation teams up to accept VISA Cash with Atlanta merchants including United Artist Theatres, Chick-Fil-A, Domino's Pizza, Baskin-Robbins, Taco Bell Corp., Crown Central Petroleum, Blimpies, BellSouth, and others. More than 150,000 stored-value cards are issued in Asia-Pacific's largest pilot of VISA Cash, started in Australia's Gold Coast region.

December 1995: Wachovia Corporation unveils a five-card series of VISA Cash cards. Called Salute to Atlanta, the card designs pay tribute to the world-class athletes who gathered in Atlanta in 1996. Marketed trials of VISA Cash in Toronto, Vancouver, and the province of Quebec mark a first for chip-based stored-value cards issued by Canadian financial institutions.

January 1996: Seven leading Argentinean financial institutions begin VISA Cash pilots in the capital city of Buenos Aires. Forty-two merchants, including Burger King and Pizzeria Romanaccio, welcome VISA Cash, which are included as a feature on electron cards.

February 1996: Bogota, Columbia, launches VISA Cash pilots. VISA Cash is accepted at vending machines, movie theaters, convenient stores, and such fast food places as Pizza Hut, Kentucky Fried Chicken, Presto Grilled Sandwiches, and CocoRico Grilled Chicken.

Experiments are also under way at Visa to develop Internet smart cards that use digital serial numbers to load digital coins and bills of various denominations onto computer hard drives. The serial numbers, which include a built-in expiration date, will help prevent counterfeiting. They also support an audit trail feature that can trace transactions back to would-be counterfeiters.

MasterCard International

On November 7, 1995, the first U.S. MasterCard smart card was launched at the PGA Grand Slam of Golf Tournament in Kauai, Hawaii. The famous 16th green at the Poipu Bay Golf Course was pictured on the card. Hundreds were given to guests for use at all the shops in the Hyatt Regency and the Poipu Bay Pro Shop.

H. Eugene Lockhart, MasterCard president and CEO, stated "Changes in technology are giving consumers more choices for accessing and managing their money. MasterCard's objective is to stay ahead of that change by delivering a broader array of payment options and value-added services to consumers whenever and wherever they use them." According to Mava K. Heffler, Master-Card senior vice president of Global Promotions and Sponsorships, "Major events, such as those connected to our sponsorships, enable MasterCard to showcase a new and very useful technology to a large audience and provide a convenience to our guests as well."

Chase Manhattan, Citibank, MasterCard, Visa

On April 10, 1996, Chase Manhattan Bank and Citibank, the two largest banks in the SmartCash group (made up of financial industry leaders), announced a partnership with MasterCard and Visa in an unprecedented initiative to launch a pilot program introducing chip-based, reloadable stored-value cards in the New York City market in the fourth quarter of 1996. The goals of the pilot are to test the dynamics of consumer and merchant acceptance of the new cards. There is no consensus on how the pilot program will affect the SmartCash program. (For more information on the SmartCash program, see the upcoming 'Gemplus' section.) Banks are realizing that they must move quickly to gain an advantage, and they appear to be willing to take some risks in the process. As the online and smart card technologies leap to the next level, they are rapidly forming alliances that cross industry lines.

The pilot program means merchants can accept either the MasterCard Cash or the VISA Cash smart cards at the same merchant terminal. Both cards are designed for purchases under $20, and will be accepted by approximately 500 merchants in a defined area of Manhattan. Chase and Citibank intend to issue about 50,000 of the smart cards for the pilot program.

First Union VISA Cash

Fred Winkler, executive vice president of First Union Bank in Charlotte, North Carolina, said in *USA Today* on December 22, 1995 that "Merchants like the cards. Cash transactions take 20 to 25 seconds versus less than 3 seconds for a card. Consumers won't want to be saddled with separate stored-value cards for every merchant. So First Union's VISA Cash card will be accepted by many merchants. And it comes in two types: One is disposable; another, with an embedded computer chip, lets bank customers reload value on it. Eventually, those reusable, chip-carrying 'smart cards' will serve as an ATM card, a stored-value card, a debit card, and a credit card—all in one piece of plastic."

The First Union VISA Cash card is available in $10, $20, $30, $50, and $100 increments. Cash, credit, or debit cards may be used to purchase the card, and there are no restrictions as to who may buy one, and there are no fees for purchasing or using one. As purchases are made, the value of the card is decremented. First Union Bank has teamed up with the following businesses:

Star Enterprise (an affiliate of Texaco)
MARTA
United Artists Theaters
Chick-Fil-A
Domino's Pizza
Baskin-Robbins
Crown Central Petroleum
Pollo Tropical
BLIMPIE
Bell South

Merchant installation of the stored-value technology began in the first quarter of 1996.

First Union Bank introduced a reloadable stored-value card in the second quarter of 1996. To purchase the reloadable card, a customer must have an account with First Union Bank, as the card is issued through a regular bank account or credit account. The card is reloadable at ATMs, card dispensing machines (CDMs), and screen phones.

Atlanta was selected for the launch because it is a large and diverse metropolitan community, and because of the huge influx of international visitors for the 1996 summer Olympic Games. If the card was deemed successful in Atlanta, First Union Bank plans to expand the program into other cities, most likely the 12 Eastern states in which they currently have branches, from Connecticut to Florida. First Union Corporation announced in March 1996, other future plans include using smart card technology for home banking, electronic ticketing, electronic loyalty, and couponing programs.

Mondex: Global Electronic Cash

Mondex is another leader in the electronic cash industry. Mondex UK, a partnership of National Westminster Bank and Midland Bank, defines itself as a "unique new payment scheme for the world's consumers, merchants, and banks." Its smart card enables its users to do the following:

- Carry electronic cash in a clean and convenient plastic card.
- Obtain electronic cash readily from the comfort of home.
- Make immediate and exact payments without the need to count change.
- Check a record of previous transactions.
- Store up to five different currencies on one card.
- Send electronic cash anywhere in the world.

Figures 7.2, 7.3 and 7.4 illustrate a number of Mondex applications for this technology. Mondex is one of many companies providing these types of services in various locations throughout the world. Its so-called electronic wallet, another great convenience of this technology, has a range of features that are described as follows:

- The Mondex wallet is a pocket-sized device with a keyboard and a screen. The wallet enables people to keep a separate store of value, for example at home or in a (relatively secure) hotel room, and only carry minimum funds on their card. This gives cardholders a degree of security because, if they lose their card, only a minimum amount of money is lost.

Figure 7.2 The Mondex wallet. (*Source: Mondex*)

• Transfers between individuals can be made by inserting the card into the electronic wallet and moving cash from the first person's card to the recipient's card. The wallet will enable families to manage their household finances by allowing transfer of value between cards. For example, parents could transfer an amount to a child's card as pocket money.

• The wallet can also be used by a service person, such as a taxi driver who is constantly on the move, as a simple POS terminal. Because the Mondex wallet has a keypad similar to an ordinary electronic calculator, the numeric keys can be used to enter the values of sums to be transferred between the "purse" in the wallet and the "purse" on the card inserted into the wallet. The screen of the Mondex wallet displays the current Mondex function and the status of the wallet at any time, including whether it is locked and whether the wallet itself or the inserted card is selected.

According to a Mondex spokesperson, in May 1995 the Royal Bank of Canada and Canadian Imperial Bank of Commerce signed a memorandum of agreement

Figure 7.3   A Mondex phone. (*Source: Mondex*)

to bring the Mondex electronic cash system to Canada, and they were the first to commit to join Mondex in North America. Other Canadian financial institutions will be invited to join them as members of Mondex. They are planning to pilot the Mondex system in a Canadian community in late '96. The Canadian pilot will last about one year and the national rollout of the Mondex system will begin sometime in 1998.

In October 1995, it was announced that the Hong Kong and Shanghai Banking Corporation Limited agreed to acquire rights to franchise Mondex in a number of countries in the Far East, including Hong Kong, China, Indonesia, Macau, the Philippines, Singapore, Sri Lanka, Taiwan, and Thailand.

Because Mondex cash is electronic, it can be transferred over a telephone line. Mondex cardholders can load money onto their cards at a new generation of cash dispensers, pay phones, and home phones . . . wherever the Mondex sign is displayed. Shops and service providers have their own cards on which Mondex value is accumulated, which can be paid into their bank accounts as a bulk value at any time of the day or night via a Mondex telephone. Figure 7.3 Mondex illustrates a Mondex phone.

With the Mondex wallet, it is possible for two people to transfer cash between their cards; and using a Mondex telephone will enable global person-to-person payments to be transacted as if cash were being exchanged. The

MONDEX AT A GLANCE

Mondex is electronic cash on a card
Instant cash is the preferred method of payment around the world accounting for between 60 and 90 per cent of all transactions. Now smartcards - storing electronic cash on an encrypted microchip - are set to revolutionise our spending habits.

Shopping with Mondex
Payments are made by slipping the Mondex card into a card reader in the retail terminal - funds are transferred immediately from the card to the terminal with no need for signatures or authorisation. Newspaper vendors and small shops can use battery-powered terminals.

Adding money to the Card
The card can be recharged with electronic money at specially adapted cash dispensers or by telephone - likely to become the main way of making bank deposits and withdrawals in the next ten years. Mondex-compatible mobile phones will be able to act as your own personal mobile cash dispenser. Specially adapted BT payphones will also be able to transfer funds. As well as loading up the card you can also lock it with a four-digit code to prevent misuse if stolen - money on a locked card can only be spent by first unlocking the card with the four-figure code.

Paying for a new era of electronic entertainment
Children, young people and adults will all be able to use Mondex to pay for the new generation of Video-on-Demand films and video games supplied down the phone line - without worrying about building-up debts on their phone-bill or bank account. With Mondex you can only spend what is on the card.

Paying on the Internet
You'll also be able to buy goods and services over the Internet 'Information Superhighway' using instant Mondex cash payments.

The electronic wallet
Using the Mondex wallet electronic cash can be moved from one card to another - as simply as one person can give another person physical cash. Parents will be able to use the wallet to give electronic pocket money to their children. The wallet also lets you see details of your last ten transactions - so you can finally find out just where your cash is going!

Balance Reader
A small electronic key-tag allows you to find out how much money is on your card.

Figure 7.4   Mondex at a glance. (*Source: Mondex*)

They've Enlisted

Marine recruits on Parris Island, the Marine training facility for the Eastern Recruiting Region, use the CP8 MICRO CARD smart card as electronic money. Their pay is entered onto the card, which they can then use to make purchases and withdrawals at all post exchanges. Each day, stored data from these transactions is relayed from point-of-purchase terminals to a micro-computer in the base comptroller's office. The advantages are clear: The built-in security of the smart card protects the recruits from theft or loss. This system also reduces personnel and material costs usually required to administer the paper coupon system previously in place.

Plastic Food Stamps

The Food and Nutrition Service (FSN) of the U.S. Department of Agriculture is using the CP8 MICRO CARD smart cards in a pilot test to replace food stamp coupon books. Approximately 10,500 households in the Dayton, Ohio, area are participating in the pilot, which began in February 1992. The pilot is a fully offline, electronic benefits system with the recipients carrying their benefits in the smart card's memory.

Counting Peanuts

The U.S. Department of Agriculture has issued more than 160,000 CP8 MICRO CARD smart cards and installed 1,000 terminals. Peanut farmers throughout the United States have been issued smart cards that are used to monitor and control crop sales. The card's memory stores crop quota and loan information, and allows the USDA to receive accurate, timely data about all crop sales for use in price forecasting.

implications for commerce are evident. In all other types of transactions, a third party is needed to clear or settle the transfer of funds or credit. Since there is no need for a bank to be involved, there is no need for authorization or PIN numbers. This is a direct transaction, and a retailer does not incur additional expenses that accompany third-party involvement.

According to Mondex, cash accounts for approximately 90 percent of all transactions in the global payments market. By providing an immediate transfer of cash value, Mondex believes it offers the best possible method for addressing this substantial market segment with a cash alternative. Visa International, in its article "Stored Value Cards—The Automation of Cash and Coins," February 1996, stated, "The $2 trillion market for small transactions remained untapped until now because it required a uniquely designed product." While Visa was referring to its VISA Cash stored-value product, it is clear that a large number of companies are entering this market with many viable products.

On July 3, 1995, Mondex launched a major pilot in Swindon, England. Mondex UK Chairman Tony Surridge describes the pilot this way: "The Swindon pilot is set to last up to two years. We're updating a form of payment that has been around for thousands of years. And whilst Mondex is essentially the same as cash, we've been able to add in a few important improvements, such as being able to send or receive money down a phone line. Swindon was chosen for the pilot as it has a population profile that is representative of the United Kingdom and has a wide retail and commercial base." Figure 7.4 shows several applications of the Mondex product.

Micro Card, Technologies, Inc.

MICRO CARD is the North American subsidiary of CP8 Transac. CP8 Transac, wholly owned by Bull SA, is a major computer company with over 30,000 employees worldwide; it has been a leader in the smart card industry from its inception. Its expertise includes chip architecture, design and production of terminals, security solutions, and a range of applications. CP8 is a division of Bull Groupe, and is a consolidation of four companies—Bull's Point of Customer Contact, Bull CP8, Bull Telesincro, and MICRO CARD Technologies—with headquarters in Louveciennes, France, near Paris. The combined revenues of these companies for 1994 were $130 million. Their core activities include automated banking transactions, microprocessor smart card technology and security, and payment and point-of-sale terminals. Considered the number one supplier in Europe in terms of smart card activity volume, revenues for smart card terminals and system solutions grew 25 percent, to $35 million between 1993 and 1994. Figure 7.5 shows a range of smart card hardware and applications. In the accompanying sidebar, MICRO CARD provides examples of the ways their cards are currently being used, adapted from the company's article "Smart Cards Are Solving Today's Business Problems."

Schlumberger Smart Cards & Systems

Schlumberger Smart Cards & Systems is part of Schlumberger LTD, an international organization with oil field services and measurements and systems businesses. The Smart Cards & Systems division participates in the entire range of smart card applications, from chips and cards to terminals and systems.

Card environment

Around the smartcard, CP8 Transac has risen to the challenges of the market with its technologically open offering comprising a wide range of products that can be sold separately, as secure solutions or as packaged security systems.

General purpose or customized masks (operating systems) for smartcards.

General purpose, multiple service smartcards for single or multi-service providers, cards for specialist applications.

Logical and graphical card customization systems, manual or automatic configurations.

Smartcard readers/encoders, transparent or programmable, with or without keypad, single or dual card slots.

Fixed station electronic payment terminals.

Handheld electronic payment terminals.

Workstation and network security systems.

EPOS systems for stores and supermarkets.

Cash dispensers and interactive terminals.

CP8-LOG for portables

CP8 Transac has designed the SecurLINK card reader for laptops with a PCMCIA interface. The PCMCIA card with its integrated chip then serves as both reader and access card. It can be left in the laptop without risk because access is conditional on knowing the chip's confidential code.

Figure 7.5 Card environment and laptop uses of smart cards. (*Source: Micro Card, Technologies, Inc.*)

Worldwide, Schlumberger claims to have installed more than 260,000 smart card-capable products and produced over 250 million smart cards, as of April 1996. The company predicts that there will be more than 2 billion smart cards in circulation by the year 2000. Schlumberger entered this industry back in 1978, and the following time line tracks its participation in the industry:

1972   First pay-and-display meter installed.

1974   Roland Moreno patents smart card.

1979   Schlumberger takes a 34 percent stake in innovation and commences research.

1982   France Telecom adopts Schlumberger's technology for new phone card; first smart cards in use.

1983   Schlumberger installs first smart card-based pay phones and memory-based smart phone cards in France.

1986   Schlumberger launches first French dual-technology Electronic Fund Transfer (EFT) system. France Telecom and Schlumberger work together to build the international credibility of smart card-based pay phones.

1988   Phone card shipments top 1 million per month.

1990   French banks decide to adopt chip card technology nationwide.

1992   Major South American pay phone deals are made, including Telmex Mexico and Telecom Argentina.

1993   Schlumberger ships its 200 millionth smart card. France begins work on national health card.

1994   Major card deals are made in the United States of America and China. BT, world's third largest telecom operator, selects Schlumberger's smart card pay phone technology. Visa, MasterCard, and Europay sign smart card development contract.

1995   Sixty countries have Schlumberger smart card pay phones. Schlumberger acquires Malco, the largest U.S. manufacturer of secure credit/debit cards, and Danyl, the leading manufacturer of self-service terminals for such traditionally coin-operated machines as vending and laundry machines.

1996   Schlumberger chosen as the sole supplier of the one million smart card–based electronic purses that First Union Bank issued in the period preceding the 1996 Olympic Games in Atlanta.

The need to curb fraud has been the driving force behind chip card technology in the finance industry. Smart cards are proving effective in this area: For example, eliminating the need for cash at pay telephones eliminates theft and reduces maintenance at these sites. Security research and development is a top priority at Schlumberger Smart Cards & Systems.

Schlumberger engineered a complete electronic purse system called Carte Crous, which was launched at the Universities of Strasbourg, Metz, and Nancy in France. The smart cards in this system can be used for meal plans, at libraries, and for controlled access to different campus areas. Reload terminals are located across campus, as well as at points of purchase. The Carte Crous system ensures university administrations better security and increased efficiency, while providing students with convenience and budgeting assistance.

In August 1995, First of America Bank issued 60,000 smart cards, supplied by Schlumberger Danyl, as part of a multiapplication smart card system in and around the University of Michigan and Western Michigan University. The cards support electronic purse, ID, and banking functions. They can be used to purchase books and food at off-campus restaurants and retail outlets, and for photocopying, in vending machines, and for laundry services on campus. "We believe this provides the student with the most versatile campus card in the country," said John Brecht, president of First America Services. "We are excited about installing the first major, all-encompassing chip card program in the country."

Gemplus

Gemplus, a relatively young French company, has become an international leader in the smart card industry over the past five years. In 1995 alone, its smart card sales reached approximately 180 million, more than one-third of the world market. Gemplus believes that in comparison to smart, magnetic, and optical cards, smart cards give the best global solution in terms of equipment and card cost, security, and reliability.

Telephones that support smart cards open up a new range of possibilities, including home billing from public pay phones and automatic dialing of pre-stored phone numbers. In addition to providing extensive graphic design and production services for these cards, Gemplus customizes direct-mail marketing campaigns, and works with clients to take full advantage of the far-reaching merchandising, cross-promotional, and advertising capabilities that these cards provide.

Gemplus sold 120 million smart phone cards in 1994, and delivered its 500 millionth phone card in October 1995, making Gemplus the world's largest manufacturer of these cards. Gemplus smart phone cards are compatible with the world's two main international standards: the French-designed GPM256 standard used by 60 percent of the world market and the German-designed GPM103 standard covering 40 percent of the world market.

The CashCard is a smart card that is expected to be in widespread use in Singapore by 1997, as the national Electronic Purse Program, promoted by the government, grows. It will enable citizens to pay for many everyday expenses usually purchased with cash, such as entertainment and convenience amenities. At this time, the CashCards are not linked to a bank or credit card, but this is an option for the future.

Smart cards can be protected by many layers of security, depending upon their use and means of distribution. They are protected by PIN numbers, and they will lock up if more than three incorrect attempts are made. Some cards are further safeguarded with a password that can be used by only one person on one particular machine; others may have more than one password and may require a second card or complex deciphering and authentication techniques to enable access.

This technology is not limited to cards. It can be applied to other objects, such as smart keys used for pay-TV access, or smart watches, glasses, jewelry, and objects commonly carried in pockets and purses. The smart card technology also lends itself to many creative possibilities for merchandising promotions.

According to a Gemplus Card International report, in 1995 the annual smart card market in the world exceeded 500 million units and could reach 4 billion units by the year 2000. Gemplus is aggressively expanding its global efforts, and enjoys an estimated 40 percent worldwide market share, according to its published figures. On January 22, 1996, it joined forces with Associated Construction and Trading Group (ACTG) of Abu Dhabi to set up its Middle East base for the marketing and manufacturing of smart cards.

Gemplus has also formed alliances with Hewlett-Packard (HP) and Informix to develop a secure infrastructure that uses a smart personal information card to facilitate the delivery of consumer services. The card supports unique features that will make it easier for consumers to manage personal information. Unlike single-transaction smart cards, the personal data stored on this card may be accessed by many service providers for a variety of tasks, such as purchasing airline tickets and storing frequent flyer transactions in the consumer's personal database. The personal information card will be more convenient than today's retail cards, since all transactions are captured on the card, thus showing current balances in checking, frequent-user, savings, credit card, and other types of accounts. Transactions are automatically posted to the correct place in the owner's personal accounting system. The information on the personal information card is fully accessible and viewable by the card owner, eliminating the need to call multiple firms or agencies to obtain or manage this information. All of this is accomplished with security that is controlled by the card owner.

Carte Plus Enfance

Analyses & Synthèses, a research and reporting agency based in France, developed another interesting application of smart cards. Carte Plus Enfance was created in 1993 by G.D.I.E. (Gestion Developement Etudes Integration) in partnership with Gemplus. The Carte Plus Enfance card makes it possible to automate child-oriented activities such as perischolastic services (food, school busing, aftercare, etc.), leisure, and nursery and day care services.

Each child carries a card that has his or her name on the back, along with instructions as to what to do in case the card is lost (the address of the issuing city hall, for example). If the card is used for school cafeteria services, the child inserts the card into a reader every morning as he or she arrives at school to validate his or her presence at the cafeteria for lunch.

Every morning, registrations are telecollected and processed. The list of children registered is transmitted automatically to the sites involved (central kitchens, cafeterias, schools, etc.) via fax or Minitel. The Carte Plus is not an electronic purse; it is linked to a family account. At the end of each month, parents receive a statement detailing each transaction for all of the family members' activities.

This system has several advantages:

- It provides for equality among the children by removing any discriminating signs (such as different-colored lunch tickets corresponding to parent income bracket).
- It gives the children a sense of importance (since they are using a means of payment usually reserved for adults).
- It provides security for parents (the card contains no actual money in case it is lost or stolen).
- It saves money (only meals eaten or activities participated in are billed).
- It saves time, and therefore money, for cities (through automation of operations).
- It simplifies financial management and reduces waste (the number of meals prepared corresponds to the number of meals actually ordered).

About a dozen cities have already adopted the card. The number in circulation today is reportedly around 20,000. For the operation, cards and readers are supplied by Gemplus, terminals by VeriFone, and operating systems by Microsoft.*

* Analyses & Synthèses-14, avenue de Corbéra, 75012 Paris, France

The cards being developed in the HP alliance will have a storage capacity that exceeds that of current smart cards and will support a highly sophisticated encryption system that provides enough security for international communication, thus making worldwide use possible. The implications for trade, advertising, marketing, and commerce are tremendous, and it is a significant venue to track. "HP is revolutionizing worldwide commerce as part of an alliance that will leapfrog any announced product or service in the area of international commerce," states Richard W. Sevcik, HP vice president and general manager of the System Technology Group of the Computer Systems Organization. "HP's open cryptographic structure is another example of HP's leadership position in developing open-systems technologies for the users of computer technology."

Gemplus is also a member of the partnership (discussed earlier in this chapter) called SmartCash, to roll out stored-value cards in the United States. Because one of the biggest barriers to implementation has been reluctance on the part of U.S. businesses to install smart card reading machines, this alliance was considered an important one. Things are moving so quickly in this industry, however, that constant regrouping takes place, and new alliances often blur industry lines. Only time will tell what form these various partnerships will ultimately take.

In public and mobile telephony, Gemplus supplies more than 90 countries, and more than 50 countries use Gemplus cards for a range of banking applications. In health care, the company provides smart cards that hold personal health data files, from immunization and medication records to specialized kidney dialysis information. Gemplus is also developing smart cards for a number of security applications for computers, personal identification, transportation, electronic entertainment and television program distribution, copyright protection, and electronic commerce over networks and the Internet. There are few industries in which these cards cannot be usefully applied.

Gemplus has also developed a *contactless* card that can be used wherever tickets are shown or stamped. Public transportation is a prime example of this type of application. With *teleticketing,* or contactless cards, a radio frequency makes it possible to communicate information within a few centimeters, thereby speeding up the process and saving money by reducing labor and time. This also allows for flexibility in fares, tariffs, and other variables inherent in travel and purchasing. Anonymity of the consumer is protected while valuable data is gathered that can be used in developing and marketing new products and services.

Giesecke & Devrient

Giesecke & Devrient GmbH (G&D) was established in 1852 in Leipzig, Germany, as the Typographic Institute for Banknotes and Securities. Today, G&D has several divisions, and the one in Munich is a worldwide leader in the development and manufacture of cards and card systems, including smart card applications in health care, banking, transportation, and telecommunications. It is the largest supplier of smart cards for pay phone, Global System for Mobile communication (GSM), and banking applications in Germany. G&D smart cards have a capacity of up to 8 kilobytes of memory, sufficient for multiple applications on one card, as well as advanced encyrption algorithms for high-level security. The microprocessors used in these smart cards comprise a complete central processing unit (CPU) controlled by an operating system (stored in ROM) with a working memory (RAM) and a memory sector for the application data (EEPROM) on a single chip.

G&D explains how its pay phone cards work: "[The] secure memory chips for prepaid telephone cards work on the principle of an irreversible counter. During card production, this counter is set to the specified prepaid amount, which is then decremented according to the usage in the card phone. The subscriber card for the frequent pay phone users allocates the debited units to a telephone account via the reference number stored in the chip."

In 1994, G&D launched an environmentally compatible card called ecard (ecological card). Made of a chlorine-free, polyester-based material that is recyclable, it satisfies the requirements determined by groups such as Greenpeace. The growing prevalence of plastic cards has become a great concern for the ecology-conscious, and several companies have made concerted efforts to produce environmentally safe cards that are made with nontoxic, biodegradable materials. Even though they are more expensive to produce, G&D felt it was important to include them in its mix of options.

In April 1995, Giesecke & Devrient announced the launch of its new contactless card. Developed for Lufthansa, this ChipCard was the first of its kind in the world. Deutsche Lufthansa AG and Lufthansa AirPlus GmbH offered the ChipCard as part of the test phase to certain frequent flyers who were currently using Lufthansa cards and who traveled the Frankfurt-Berlin-Frankfurt route within Germany. According to G&D, "The card contains a passenger's frequent flyer number, mileage information, ticket information for the current flight, and the customer's travel preferences. It allows passengers to skip the lines at the ticket and boarding check-in counters and simply hold their card (or even just their wallet) up to a Chip-In Terminal, which reads the passenger's information and then displays updated flight information on a touchable screen. The passenger can choose whether to continue on the reserved flight or change the flight depending on the circumstances and availability."

The card can be used to keep track of frequent flyer miles and reservations; it also supports a prepaid telephone utility. G&D adds, "Lufthansa even offers a Frequent Traveler ChipCard AirPlus VISA card with both telephone and credit card applications."

The uses for contactless cards are vast, and include public transportation and toll booth applications, ID applications, controlled access, and virtually any situation where efficiency and accuracy are enhanced by eliminating handling and manual processing. G&D reports that "the remote coupling technology allows for a communication between card and reader over distances between 10 and 30 cm. approximately." Further, these cards have multiple levels of security available, "including mutual authentication and encryption procedures. A powerful anticollision algorithm is capable of correctly identifying several cards presented simultaneously in the reader's range."

G&D also supplies the smart and ecard terminals, which provide the interface between the card and the host system. Figures 7.6 and 7.7 show examples of some of these terminals and cards. Terminals are constantly being updated, as is the card technology, and there is a range of styles and functions.

With this kind of advanced processing available on a single card, the possibilities for applications are as varied as a person's daily activities, from shopping to commuting, traveling, dining, banking, or bringing work home. The schemes being developed in pilot programs around the globe are creating opportunities for businesses to run promotions and make the overall experience of purchasing extremely convenient and efficient. Just as medical files may be stored on these cards, so can any type of product and automated remote ordering information. Used in conjunction with the pay phone capabilities, any number of innovative marketing and transaction programs can be designed. As these become more widespread, they will offer greater opportunities for innovative marketers and inventive entrepreneurs.

Figure 7.6   The intelligent smart card reader and the smart card terminal.

Figure 7.7   A variety of cards with different applications ranging from banking to traveling.

Danmønt

The Danish company Danmønt, introduced earlier, is a another leading stored-value card manufacturer. The Copenhagen Mass Transit System uses the company's ticket machines, and if the trial runs are successful, the transit authority will attempt to put the system in place in all stations by the end of 1996.

Notably, Danmønt has designed the first commemorative chip card with a likeness of Prince Joachim of Denmark and his wife, Alexandra Manley. Traditionally, a monarch's image appeared on commemorative coins that were specially minted for events of significance. It seems electronic cash is maintaining that tradition!

Danmønt has also broken new ground in the materials used in its latest cards. Like Gemplus, in an effort to come up with an ecologically sound solution to plastic, it has produced the first card made out of wood. Designers made the ECO-CARD AB out of birchwood laminates, embedding the chip just as in a plastic card. The company claims that it is just as flexible and strong as plastic, and that it meets all of the international standards. It is currently being tested by a limited number of users.

Mitsubishi and Sony

According to a French research firm, Analyses & Synthèses, Mitsubishi and Sony plan to supply 3 million contactless cards for Hong Kong's new mass-transit ticketing system. Creative Star Limited is a joint venture of Hong Kong's five largest passenger transit companies. The government set this company up in June 1994 to service all of the public transportation lines. A universal pass will be used for travel services provided by the different transit companies, which include trains, ferries, buses, and so on. Because it is a stored-value card, other services and functionality can be added in the future.

On the subject of smart card uses for entertainment venues, Ben Miller of the CardTech/SecurTech (CTST) Conference explains that Sony plans to take the Discovery Zone concept (recreational facilities for children with a wide variety of amusement games and activities) and focus it on adults. The plan includes building an entertainment center covering approximately 300,000 square feet on top of a major convention center in San Francisco, California. Miller explains that Sony needs about 2 million customers to break even. The company is looking at three revenue streams: one from visitors coming to San Francisco primarily to visit the facility, just as they might go to Anaheim to see Disneyland; one from convention attendees; and one from local San Francisco Bay Area residents.

This last revenue stream is a "make it or break it" factor—it requires a minimum of four visits per year from a significant number of local residents. Miller explains that Sony will make this happen by giving people smart cards that will "remember" things such as what level of Mortal Combat 9 you got to on your last visit, or what your Netscape bookmarks were when you stopped surfing the Internet, along with other discount and bonus points you may have earned. If you have a prepaid value on a card, you will have incentive to return and use it. That's just one more example of the potential these cards offer.

Smart Cards: A Loyalty Mechanism

Ben Miller of the CTST Conference believes that programs like Mondex's will look quite different a year or two from now. The banks are cooperating to test the consumer's willingness to use cards instead of cash for a broader range of transactions. But Miller explains that retailers don't really see smart cards as a replacement for cash. They see them more as a loyalty mechanism, as store or brand "membership" cards. This is a very real dilemma that the banks may have to face as merchants become more savvy about smart cards.

For example, nothing prevents merchants from cutting out the banks altogether and creating card affinity programs among themselves. Two or more merchants can issue their own cards to be used at any of the cooperating places of business. In this way, for every video you would rent at Blockbuster's, for instance, you would be eligible for a free milkshake or fries at McDonald's. There would be no transaction fees, no exchange of cash other than the purchase of the merchant's stored-value "membership" card. As an added incentive, a card could provide the purchaser with more value than the face amount; for example, a $50 card could provide $55 worth of services or goods. A single card could also be issued for a group of cooperating merchants. Consequently, merchants might end up telling banks that they do not want competing businesses on the same stored-value card, and could begin to dictate which merchants are on the same card.

Relationship Marketing

A number of promotional ventures are in progress where smart cards are used to store things such as points for retail or catalog purchases, travel, and other entertainment venues. For example, Safeway, Tesco, and Sainsbury's, three stores located in the south of England, are offering their customers points for purchases that are calculated at the checkout reader and are redeemable for cash credit toward future purchases, much the way frequent flyer miles are managed by airline reward programs.

The most successful marketing and loyalty campaigns have moved beyond the obvious long-term collection capabilities into highly targeted promotions with shorter-term but very potent results that actually lead to improved long-term relationship building. This is made possible by the sophisticated demographics, lifestyle, and purchasing pattern-tracking the smart card can provide. By linking specific purchases to individual consumers, buying patterns emerge, making it possible to tailor promotions so that a consumer's needs can be addressed directly, increasing the success and cost-effectiveness of any campaign.

The Casa Buitoni Club employs this kind of *relationship marketing* by utilizing purchasing information to invite the people collected in its database to join its club. The Club caters to its consumers' prequalified interest in its products by sharing regional Italian recipes, cooking tips, and information on Italian wines, pasta, and lifestyle; and by providing discount coupons, regular newsletters, and exclusive offers. It also uses a direct response vehicle linked to the ordering of a recipe booklet for Italian food.

The Microsoft Plus membership program allows members to accrue points on their cards whenever they buy Microsoft software. These points can in turn be redeemed against the purchase of another Microsoft product. There is an annual fee to join, which includes a magazine subscription and access to the Microsoft Plus Forum on CompuServe, so there is a good integration of incentive, reward, and tangible value.

Mobil is promoting its cards now as "gifts for all denominations." They are popular with parents who want to control the money they give teenage kids, says Marshall Reavis, Mobil's card manager.

Smart cards can help companies develop consumer loyalty. Blockbuster is giving a $5 stored-value card to customers who buy three videos during the holidays. The company soon will announce a program to share its cards with other businesses. "You could test-drive a car and receive a Blockbuster gift card," said Blockbuster's Brian Woods, as reported in *USA Today* on December 22, 1995.

Some programs offer special perks. For example, with Selfridge's Gold Card, a cardholder may be invited to have lunch with the CEO. Marks & Spencer cardholders may be invited to participate in late evening shopping, where refreshments are served. The Tandy Corporation, through its U.S. chain of consumer electronic stores, offers an Incredible Universe membership card that accrues points with purchases, redeemable in the form of $10, $25, $50, or $100 merchandise certificates. By tracking customers' purchases, its direct-mail campaigns are very specifically targeted using this information.

The ability to use technology to employ this kind of narrowcast marketing also brings with it the need to respect the voice of the customer to a greater degree than ever before, and responsiveness and flexibility are key. Marketers now have the power to have the right product at the right price, delivered in the right way for the right person. How well this power is used depends upon how well-rounded marketers are in their knowledge and understanding of these new vehicles and the value of relationship marketing over product marketing.

Smart Card Forum

The Smart Card Forum is a U.S.-based organization that was established in 1993 to bring industry leaders and active participants together to promote industry growth and success. The facts and statistics on the smart card industry in Figures 7.8 through 7.10 were gathered by the Forum in early 1996, based on information partially gathered at the 1995 CardTech/SecurTech conference. Jean T. McKenna, president of the Smart Card Forum, describes the purpose of the organization:

> *The Smart Card Forum was formed to accelerate the widespread acceptance of smart cards that support multiple applications by bringing together in an open environment leading users and technologists from both the public and*

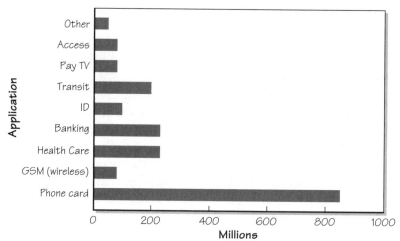

Figure 7.8 Forecast for the year 2000 by application. (*Source: MICRO CARD Technologies*)

private sector. Membership in the Forum has grown rapidly, doubling in the past year, and now exceeds 225 members from both the public and private sectors in North America and other geographic regions.

At its inception, the Forum's goal was to promote interoperability across appropriate business applications as well as to facilitate market trials. More recently, education in the marketplace and the development of business proposition and public policy issues have been added to these goals. Research on consumer and merchant interest has been undertaken, and we have published and made available to a wide audience positions on privacy and Regulation E. The market for smart cards is experiencing significant growth with the recognition that the technology provides a platform for organizations to package products and services that meet the needs of individual customers.

The Future

Dave Clauson of True North Communications Inc., the parent company and interactive media production arm of Foote, Cone & Belding Advertising, believes that between now and the next millennium, smart card technology is going to incorporate voice capabilities and intelligent agents. He offers the following predictions and insights:

Consumer Awareness

- U.S. consumers view multiple application cards favorably.
- A Smart Card Forum study revealed that 50% of U.S. households thought they were a good or excellent idea (Smart Card Forum).
- 44% of households surveyed were most likely to use smart cards for membership or ID card.
- 61.8% of households were likely to use at least one application (Smart Card Forum).

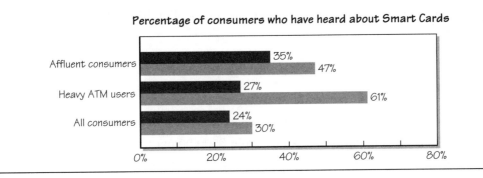

Figure 7.9 Consumer awareness. (*Source: Smart Card Forum*)

Instead of typing everything on a keyboard, I will pop my smart card into the side of my little digital appliance and speak to it; it will greet me and says, "Hello, Dave, where do you want to go today?" And I will say, "I want to check my bank balance," or "I'd like to see what's on the movie server tonight." And any issue with a transaction or any kind of data that it needs from me is in that card, and it's completely secure. In fact, it begins to take away the need for paper money.

The human voice is a far simpler user interface than a keyboard. Almost everybody has one [a keyboard] and most people know how to use them. It is not the technology that is the important piece here. It is the user's relationship to the content. And that technology, like an iceberg, in my opinion, should sink well below the surface, and it can be very broad and very deep below the surface of the user; but above the surface, there should be as little as possible between users and what they want to do. And right now we still make it very hard with our different operating systems and our different computers, our different standards, and so on.

Smart Card Facts

- France reduced fraud by 50% in two years when it converted form magnetic stripe cards to smart cards (Smart Card Forum).
- By the year 2000, smart cards sold worldwide will be sold in the United States (Electronics).
- The U.S. market will grow faster than the total Asian market (Electronics).
- By 1999, the third largest ATM network in the United States plans to have all its 28 million cardholders carry smart cards to operate its ATMs (VeriFone).
- In Germany, the entire population of more than 80 million people will be issued smart cards containing health insurance eligibility information (VeriFone).

Card Costs

- Card cost can range from $.80 for 1 Kbyte to $15.00 for 8 Kbytes.
- POS terminal upgrades cost banks about $500.00 per unit.
- Smart card prices will drop about 15% per year (Smart Card Forum).

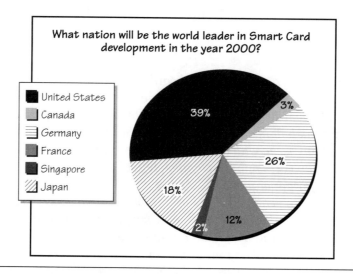

Figure 7.10 Facts, costs and global picture of future world leaders in smart card development. (*Source: Personal Identification News*)

What a lot of companies aren't aware of is that the consumer is a sleeping giant, and when you wake enough of them up, they will become incredibly forceful in how they want to see their world, and they're not going to wait for Bill Gates, you, or anybody else to tell them; they will tell you. And they will either vote with their cards or their feet or their money and make you pay attention that way.

Smart Card Resource List

CardTech/SecurTech Conference & Exhibition
Ben Miller, Chairman
12300 Twinbrook Parkway, Suite 300
Rockville, MD 20852
Tel: 301-881-3383
Fax: 301-881-2430
E-mail: cardsmarts@aol.com
Internet: http://www.ctst.com

First Union VISA Cash
P.O. Box 563967
Charlotte, NC 28256-3967
Customer Service Tel: 800-704-6923

Gemplus Card International
Marc Lassus, President and CEO
Hubert Giraud, Chief Executive
BP 100, 13881 GEMENOS Cedex
FRANCE
Tel: +33-42-32-50-00 or +33-42-32-50-03
Fax: +33-42-32-51-17

Giesecke & Devrient GmbH Germany
P.O. Box 80 70 29
D-81607 Muenchen
Tel: +49-89-4119-0
Fax: +49-89-4119-535

Giesecke & Devrient America, Inc., United States
11419 Sunset Hills Road
Reston, VA 22090
Tel: 703-709-5828
Fax: 703-471-5312

MasterCard International
Chip Card Business/Marketing
Tel: 914-249-2000
Internet: http://www.mastercard.com

MICRO CARD, Technologies, Inc.
Gerald Hubbard, Vice President
300 Concord Road
MS 849 A
Billerica, MA 01821-4186
Tel: 508-294-3670
Fax: 508-294-3671

Mondex
1st Floor, Podium, Drapers Gardens
12 Throgmorton Avenue
London, EC2N 2DL England
Tel: +44-171-920-5175
Fax: +44-171-920-5505
United States
Tel: 908-719-1251
Fax: 908-234-2866

Schlumberger Smart Cards & Systems, United States
Patrick Gathier
825-B Greenbrier Circle
Chesapeake, VA 23320
Tel: 804-578-7589 or 804-366-0593
Fax: 804-424-2236

Schlumberger Smart Cards & Systems, Europe
Isabelle Ferdane-Couderc
620-12, 50 avenue Jean Jaures
F92542 Montrouge Cedex
France
Tel: +33-1-47-46-62-47
Fax: +33-1-47-46-68-66

Schlumberger, Singapore
Sally Chew
Tel: +65-746-6344

Smart Card Forum
Bob Gilson, Executive Director
3030 Rocky Point Drive West, Suite 680
Tampa, FL 33607
Tel: 813-286-2339
Fax: 813-281-8752
E-mail: bob@smartcrd.com
Internet: http://www.smartcrd.com

Visa International
P.O. Box 8999
San Francisco, CA 94128
Tel: 415-432-3200
Internet: http://www.visa.com/visa.

CHAPTER EIGHT

INTERACTIVE KIOSKS

Margo Komenar

Kiosks are becoming more widespread as businesses realize the marketing potential they afford. The types of applications they can support are practically limitless, and the market has just begun to open up. With the high-speed connectivity now possible between a kiosk location and the online environment, kiosks offer almost everything a computer with a modem can, plus the customized deep database of information and/or entertainment made accessible by the kiosk provider. This is an important and growing marketing opportunity that can be adapted easily to almost any market segment.

The design of the kiosk housing is often as important as the interactive interface. Since kiosks can literally be "dressed up" (for example, spray-painted for a rock concert) to attract a range of tastes and ages, they are easily adapted to any environment or audience. For marketers, the cost to participate in this medium can begin as low as $5,000. And the best way to begin to grasp the potential of kiosks is through examples. The following descriptions provide a range of creative and practical applications for interactive kiosks.

Digital Levi's Fit!

Dave Clauson, of Foote, Cone & Belding's interactive company, True North Technologies, discusses an impressive global multimedia campaign for Levi's 501 jeans. The campaign required a skillful integration of media and cultures on all fronts: demographic, psychographic, and photographic.

We saw the emergence of the digital environment creating a terrific opportunity to weld a lot of Levi's messages together and do a lot of innovative tar-

geting and learning. In other words, gathering information to feed into the next cycle of development. So, for instance, we took the 501 advertising campaign, 501 Reasons, and developed the Web site, a key part of which was built around the 501 reasons. We took the ad campaign into an in-store kiosk, using the same sort of writing; advertising the different reasons that you'd want to purchase these kinds of products from Levi's.

[Kiosks] are in the Levi's-only stores. At this moment, they are available to other merchants who want to include them as part of their merchandising program for Levi's. So if J. C. Penney has a Levi's-only section of their store, they can have the kiosk in that area. The clients pay us and we make sure it happens . . . it's part of their merchandising credits. In other words, based on the volume of merchandise they order, they earn so many merchandise credits that they can apply to this.

In Levi's-only stores, [Levi's] pays for it. It's just part of the store cost. Initially, all of those were separate projects, and what we try to do is determine how we get something back across the brand from in-store to online in this situation. Look and feel is one thing. Tone and manner is another, and brand identity is a third. So we have to design for the experience of the person at the other end of the screen.

For instance, in the Levi's-only store on 57th and Fifth Avenue in New York, one of the things we knew about that store was that it would get a lot of international traffic, people from outside the United States. Two of the things that [the store's employees] would face were a language barrier and a sizing issue. European pant sizes run differently from U.S. sizes. One of the opportunities we saw with the kiosk was that we could design content that would address the language issue and the sizing issue, and minimize the salesperson's time with those folks; it could be used effectively, and yet let customers feel empowered, that they knew what they were doing.

We designed a kiosk with five languages built in. Every time [users] clicked on a piece of product, they could click on the international size for that product and on a button that would show them exactly where in the store the product was located. So if they didn't speak a word of English, they could still find exactly what they were looking for, all in a language that they could read and understand.

We created the Levi's Web site (http://www.levi.com). But, we wondered, "What if we created one big network where we could have the reach of a Web site, which is global, combined with the targeting of a local in-store environment, and how could we connect those two?" So we're developing an intranet, if you will, among all the Levi's-only stores where we can be in the store in New York and connect and see what's going on in Durban, South Africa, or in Santa Fe, New Mexico. At this point, we are going to have cameras on those kiosks. We have to be careful of what might go on at the other end, but that's part of the risk that we have to take.

The objective for Levi's in this instance was to connect with global youth culture. In other words, what is common to that 501 brand is that it is universal, it is driven by kids, and it's something they all share. You can be in any part of the world and be instantly recognizable wearing those jeans. The challenge was how to connect with global youth culture? Well, the Web is something that kids around the world are adopting rather quickly, so that was one path.

And then, ultimately, [the question was] how do we take all that and wrap it into the brand? Well, when you're in a Levi's-only store, you can buy that same pair of pants probably for four or five dollars less at a department store or some other location, but what you can't get is the experience of being in that store, part of which is the kiosk and what it allows you to see and connect with. It is part of the shopping experience. The store in a sense becomes the destination, and the brand is the way station, if you will. We're looking to give global youth a connection to the brand both overtly and covertly by serving up the kinds of content appropriate to the location of the screen, the individual we're speaking to, and what that individual wants to do at that location at that screen.

Take it one step further. You could be at home, and maybe you've gone to the Levi's Web site, and part of what you can do is to download a screen saver. So how do you give somebody a brand experience when they're not even [at the computer]? The 501 screen savers can be running on that PC, so a very subtle brand message is there in the home all the time. It's downloadable from the Web site, and it has a lot of the graphics from the 501 reasons campaign, which we created a lot of posters for. I think reason No. 257 is that they'll carry you into the next millennium; and when you use the screen saver, you can put some light animation in there and some sound, which is fun, connecting people to the brand. And so the media is part of the means to that connection.

The important thing that marketers like Levi's and agencies like Foote, Cone & Belding are going to have to deal with and are dealing with is the ability to strike an appropriate balance between traditional one-way media—television, radio, print, newspaper—and two-way, digitally driven media—online, CD-ROM, kiosks, screen savers, and a million and one other things.

We also created a CD-ROM that has everything from a product catalogue. We shot models wearing the product, every piece of product from every conceivable angle so we could put together a CD-ROM where the viewer could basically design his or her own catalogue content. Part of it was mailed, part *of it was given away, part of it was an in-store, over-the-counter kind of thing. [We wanted] to see who would be interested and what they'd do with that.*

The point at which the brand crosses over is that shift from one-way to two-way media. In other words, agencies have been talking about highly integrated campaigns for years, but most big agencies have fallen flat on their faces in doing it. More midsized and smaller agencies have had better success with integration because they did more of the work for those clients as entities.

Having to strike this balance between one-way and two-way media is forcing marketers and their agencies to come to grips with how to make it all work, because the one thing that we know is that clients' marketing budgets are not increasing; in fact, they're going the other way. So it behooves clients to ask those questions again: "Where can I get the most effectiveness? What should I do and in what order? How am I using the CD-ROM environment, the Web environment, the kiosk environment to complement what I'm doing in the television environment, the print environment, the in-store environment, and so on?"

Kathleen Brown Campaign Kiosk

Ross Gillanders, VP of Business Development for the Hypermedia Group, a full-service multimedia communications company, describes the first political campaign run with the support of kiosk technology (Figure 8.1) and a lot of ingenuity thrown in:

The Kathleen Brown kiosk project was really an entrepreneurial effort. We saw it as an opportunity to do something for Kathleen Brown that was unique. For the first time, multimedia kiosks would be used in a gubernatorial campaign. It was not something we were necessarily hired to do, but out of our entrepreneurial work came the acceptance and the final delivery of the software to the campaign.

We were able to get costs paid for. But the lights really went on when Kathleen Brown and her group were able to grasp what the delivery of her messages in this unique format would mean to her platform. It didn't help her, ultimately, [because] it was pretty late in the campaign when we rolled that out.

She made the decision to place the kiosks around California in strategic locations like Tower Records in Sacramento. The president and founder of Tower Records was a big endorser of Kathleen Brown, plus he was one of the very early success stories on the retail record side in California. The

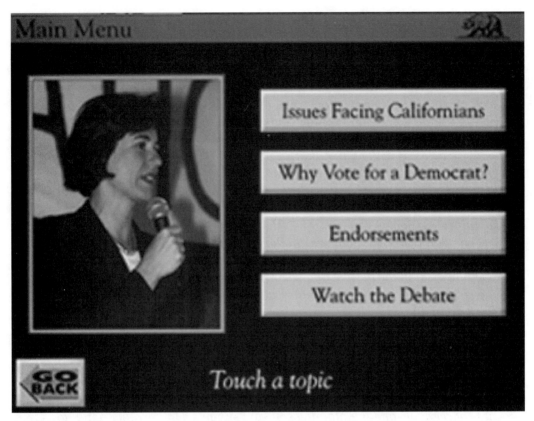

Figure 8.1   Kathleen Brown Kiosk campaign, main menu. (*Source: Hyper-Media Group*)

kiosks also were down in Los Angeles at a known coffee shop in Hollywood, and there were a couple of others around. It was not a wide distribution of kiosks.

We used very high-end graphics and full-motion video in an attract loop much like we would treat an intro in a trade show environment. The goal was to cut through the noise and have people engaged and pulled into the kiosk so that they could actually start working through the content. In fact, if users wanted to, they could go through the full Kathleen Brown/Governor Wilson debate. All of Kathleen Brown's platform positions were there as they related to Governor Wilson's platforms and positions. With animations and sound effects, we illustrated and annotated those positions.

[The kiosk] was CD-ROM delivered, with Macintosh hardware in the kiosk itself. In this case, we recommended and integrated the hardware ourselves. I think there was some discussion about repurposing the kiosk software to

other venues, but it was never used because of the late date. Real costs associated with the development of the software probably were around $30,000 to $50,000. We had a custom fabricator build the kiosks; they were custom-constructed.

Kathleen Brown certainly leveraged the kiosk rollout in her positioning statements concerning the utilization of technology. She used it to show that she was futuristic, in terms of her thinking and in terms of how she was utilizing technology—particularly multimedia technology—to help her campaign. The press really bit on that angle. It was widely publicized nationally that she was using multimedia technology to help her in her campaign. We received a lot of favorable press from it as well. It had never been done, as far as we know, at least in the kiosk form of interactive multimedia, to help a political campaign.

The additional cost really was in the kiosk itself, the physical structure. Kiosks can run anywhere from $1,000 on up to $10,000, depending on the complexity of it, the design, and so on. And then someone had to maintain the software and hardware, whether standalone or distributed. If the system went down, there was an infrastructure in place to take care of that, to get the system back up. However, in this case, there were so few kiosks out there that it wasn't a big issue.

Typically, a company like ours, which is really focused on developing the software, recommending the hardware system, and even training personnel to maintain it, would partner with a third-party provider who is in the business of servicing and maintaining software systems. On the other hand, low-level store employees with some training can be educated to maintain the system or fix minor problems with the hardware. These days, the hardware is much more solid than it used to be, and I think a client or a store can expect reliability. It may not be 100 percent, but the system itself [usually is] quite reliable and easy to maintain and upgrade, if designed appropriately.

The real opportunity for kiosks in particular is that you can link them via some kind of network, track demographics, and gather marketing research in real time, collecting that information back to a server. And that's exciting, because certainly we're starting to see that on the Internet. For a company, marketing firm, or advertising agency to be able to track usage and understand who the users are, and how they are moving through the content, then leveraging that understanding is a phenomenal opportunity.

Missouri Botanical Gardens

Another interesting project taken on by the Hypermedia Group required developing a set of six interactive touch-screen kiosks for the Missouri Botanical Gardens. Figure 8.2 shows the Missouri Botanical Gardens Global Views interactive kiosk, which links to the Web and pulls down satellite data from around the world in real time. Figure 8.3 shows an educational kiosk game of intrigue, and offers the opportunity to talk with the experts. Figure 8.4 shows another game called Canopy Climb. Ross Gillanders describes the project:

> *We were contracted to develop six different interactive touch-screen systems that would be placed in the new Missouri Botanical Gardens rain forest environmental exhibit. Actually, [the Gardens] constructed a new building for it, and the six kiosks provide information about different rain forest and environmental topics. They are distributed throughout the new building.*
>
> *One kiosk links to the Web and pulls down satellite data from around the world in real-time concerning temperature variations and variances in the rain forest around the world, which populates a graphical map of the world the user can interact with. That's a very interesting, exciting application of multimedia and online technology. Another one, for instance, talks about different flora and fauna and the animals that live at different levels in the canopy of the rain forest. Yet another kiosk allows the user to interview scientists on various issues. Each kiosk delivers different information and discusses a variety of topics depending upon where it is in the exhibit.*

Figure 8.2   Global views from the Missouri Botanical Gardens kiosk. (*Source: HyperMedia Group*)

Figure 8.3 Who Done It? A kiosk game. (*Source: HyperMedia Group*)

I don't know of any better medium in the exhibit or museum area to deliver large amounts of information that allows users to actually interact with it and be able to go wherever their interests take them. Certainly, if you view a diorama in a museum, it's a beautiful installation, and you can get a lot out of it, but you're not able to say, for instance, "I'm interested in an antelope as opposed to an elephant, so zero in on the antelope and tell me as much as I am able to absorb." Interactive multimedia has the power to make that kind of instant and individualized exploration possible.

We arrived at a variety of friendly and intuitive touch-screen interfaces that allow the user to navigate fluidly through the desired content. The interface approaches taken in the museum environment are much different from how we approach, for instance, an electronic catalogue interface or a marketing interface for Microsoft. Touch-screen systems—and I'm not the expert in this area—have come a long way. They have come down in cost considerably. They're much more reliable and accurate than they used to be. The standard screen size now is 16 inches.

Figure 8.4   Canopy Climb kiosk game. (*Source: HyperMedia Group*)

Pac Bell Kiosk

Pacific Bell asked the Hypermedia Group to develop beta software for a place-based advertising kiosk that would also deliver other kinds of information, including real-time news. The kiosks were to be rolled out in public areas, such as malls and airports. Ross Gillanders elaborates on the high-tech kiosks that he believes someday will be commonplace in malls around the country:

> *Pacific Bell partnered with KRON-TV Enterprises on this project and formed a company called BayVision. KRON and Pacific Bell were our clients. We built software that was to be located in public places like malls where people could go up to a touch-screen kiosk to get information concerning specials and sales that were going on in stores in the mall environment. The kiosk was video-based. It delivered very high-quality 640/480 commercial video that was hardware-assisted. Also, the kiosk delivered updated or real-time news, sporting event scores, and so on, which was KRON's primary interest.*

If you were visiting the mall, and your spouse was in the store shopping, and you wanted to catch up on the latest news or sporting events and scores, or get information like horoscopes, that content was available on the kiosk. [Initially,] it was going to be networked, and there was some talk about having a communications link with satellites. What was local was the interface and the rich video content. This was beta software, so it was never fully implemented, but we went through formal focus groups with Pacific Bell that looked at the software, the interface, and the kinds of content and information that could be provided to the kiosk user. Using the focus group findings, we modified the software appropriately.

Pacific Bell is a regional phone company and certainly its territory and focus is local. The issue that it was, and still is faced with, is that kiosks are a new channel for advertisers, and the concept behind this was to have the advertiser help pay for the advertising and defer the cost of the kiosk, including the software. So it still is early to know whether advertisers are going to buy off on this new channel, and whether it is an effective channel for the distribution of advertising messages.

Things have changed since we started that project, certainly with the Web heating up, and there are different considerations now than there were, say a year and a half ago. As far as I know, the BayVision kiosk project has been put on the back burner. We delivered a functional prototype. We used hypothetical advertising content; there was also real or alluded-to functionality like credit card swipes and ticketing functionality.

The software was very, very well received in limited field tests, focus groups, and Pacific Bell itself. But again, it was one of the multimedia areas that Pacific Bell and KRON were dabbling with. Pacific Bell is certainly getting its feet wet and spending a significant amount of money playing in a variety of areas, including interactive TV, kiosk systems, the Web, electronic catalogues—all kinds of things.

The same kind of thing happened with our financial services partners, as we started developing a business banking solution for them that was going to be rolled out on a proprietary network with dial-in access from the workplace to a back-end transactional system. During the development of that software, the Web heated up. So, after almost a year of working on the software development, everybody sat down and said, "Why are we going to roll this out on a proprietary network when the Web is a viable delivery platform?" Everybody shifted gears, and the application will finally be rolled out on the Web.

I think the issue around kiosks is capital investment. It requires a significant investment in hardware and kiosks and infrastructure to support, for instance, a distributed kiosk system.

Kiosks Go to School

As reported in *Business Wire* in April 1996, Comdisco Network, a provider of managed kiosk services, in collaboration with InterAction Media Corporation, an interactive content provider, rolled out 135 kiosks onto college and university campuses across the United States. Centrally located in student unions, and through an interactive interface, the kiosks provide campus maps; information on campus events, activities, and other school-related topics, as well as news, sports scores, merchandise incentives, and retrievable coupons from advertisers. The program is trademarked IKE, the Interactive Kiosk Experience.

With this kiosk system, marketers can run theme-based campaigns across the entire installation base, customize content and update each location remotely using high-speed telephone lines. Students can enter information about themselves and their preferences, feeding a database that is used by kiosk program managers and advertisers. The system includes a tracking component that measures usage on a daily basis. This is a great opportunity for businesses targeting the student market. Similar programs can be designed for any number of targeted location-based audiences.

On the Links

When 30 northern Ohio golf clubs installed multimedia kiosks in their pro shops in April 1996, it was considered a major milestone in sports marketing. According to *Business Wire* magazine, Interactive MultiMedia Publishers, Inc. (IMP) estimated that revenues from advertising for the "proof-of-concept" period (April to October) could reach between $450,000 to $650,000. The national market potential for all USGA clubs (approximately 8,000) is estimated to be between $75 and $150 million.

WorldWide Sports Marketing, a division of Interactive MultiMedia Publishers, Inc., is selling advertising space to a range of companies that focus on this particular market; airlines, automobile, sportswear, real estate, and resort companies are all targeted participants. It is likely that this kind of kiosk installation will begin to show up in many other niche markets soon.

Multimedia Kiosk Telephones

In April 1996, British Telecom (BT) announced a summer launch in London of its first color, multimedia, touch-screen telephone, the Touchpoint Kiosk. The kiosk features advertisers, and is equipped with a dedicated "Freefone" 800 number telephone line, for making purchases, and a printer so that customers can receive vouchers, coupons, and maps. Customers will be able to talk directly to the companies that interest them, inquire about products and services, and make purchases using the dedicated line. With the Touchpoint Kiosk, customers can also obtain area maps and guides, as well as arts, entertainment, sports, shopping, and ticketing information. BT plans to place approximately 200 of the Touchpoint Kiosks in high-traffic locations, such as travel terminals, shopping malls, recreation centers, and tourist areas.

The Touchpoint Kiosk represents a significant leap by interactive technology into "general public" applications. Incorporating multimedia into a commonly used medium, the telephone, and then placing those multimedia telephones in a broadly targeted consumer location, is giving the general public a crash course in some of the most advanced technology available. This will have tremendous impact on marketing products and services. It opens up a powerful channel to marketers who want to be a part of the Freefone 800 number group.

Driving Ketchum Advertising

Top advertising agencies are leading automobile manufacturers into interactive marketing in a big way. In addition to creating a very pervasive Internet presence, these agencies are employing a number of other electronic vehicles to reach their clients' audiences.

Ketchum Advertising ran a highly successful campaign using interactive place-based kiosks to "drive" potential buyers into their local Acura dealers. By designing award-winning media that showed the benefits of the Acura to thousands of prequalified potential buyers, they were able to entice 40 percent of this audience into dealerships for a test drive. They followed up with a series of computer screen savers based on Acura's top-of-the-line NSX sports car, and tied the release of the screen savers to the introduction of the NSX-T edition.

Medical Electronic Marketing

Kelly Stewart, director of Interactive Development for NewOrder Media, a company that combines advertising and software development, describes some interesting applications in the medical arena that incorporate information delivery with marketing and database development:

> We developed a trade show kiosk for clients from Medical Information Management Systems (or MIMS for short). They are software developers them-

selves. MIMS' flagship product is a system called PEARL, a medical records management suite for hospitals and physician practices. Instead of medical facility personnel storing their records in paper format, they scan all documents into the PEARL system for electronic storage and retrieval, by keyword, by date, by patient name, by illness, any of the stored criteria.

MIMS wanted some type of system to run in its trade show booth. When we begin working with a client on any project we usually start with these basic questions: Who is the audience? What are the goals of the project? What are the constraints (time, money, hardware)? How will we measure the success of the product after it is implemented?

Physicians and other medical professionals comprise the typical audience at [medical] trade shows. Hence, the kiosk system had to be simple to use. The number one goal of the product was to attract trade show attendees to the MIMS booth. Typically, you only have a matter of seconds to invite people into your booth at these events. To achieve this first goal, we used animated characters to host the kiosk, which played on large touch-screen monitors placed in the corners of the booth.

Figure 8.5 shows how NewOrder Media utilized cartoon characters to attract trade show attendees to this kiosk for Medical Information Management Systems (MIMS). The host of the kiosk, Dr. Pearl, walked users through answering questions and analyzing their medical records management costs.

Stewart continues: "Second, the kiosk had to communicate the potential cost savings to [medical practioners'] practices if they were to adopt the PEARL system. After asking a series of questions of the users, the kiosk presents cost comparisons that hopefully indicated they could be saving huge sums by adopting this automated system." Figure 8.6 shows how NewOrder Media's PEARL kiosk calculates cost comparisons based on user input at a trade show. "The third goal," said Stewart, "was to gather information about the people who interacted with the system so the client could have a record of prequalified sales leads.

Later, when MIMS wanted a CD-ROM-based interactive brochure with a more corporate look, but the same functionality as the kiosk, NewOrder Media was able to quickly change the graphic interface while retaining the back-end code structure. NewOrder's modular development techniques allow rapid modifications of interface or code elements, eliminating the need to reconstruct an entire product. Figure 8.7 illustrates this corporate adaptation.

Stewart, again speaking for NewOrder Media discussed another project:

Another kiosk project we did is in a totally different setting: the corporate headquarters of a medical manufacturer. Our client, Ethicon Endo-Surgery (a division of Johnson & Johnson), introduced a kiosk to enable visitors to look up educational offerings (classes the company sponsors) and to market

Figure 8.5 Cartoon used in a medical-oriented kiosk. (*Source: NewOrder Media*)

the company's products (endoscopic surgical equipment). The users of this kiosk are typically surgeons and nurses who are visiting the center and taking classes. This is a different surrounding from the trade show setting. The kiosks are placed in more relaxed lounge areas where people break in between classes. They have more relaxed time to explore the kiosk; they are not on their feet the entire time. The time people spend on a kiosk such as this is longer.

That's another thing we trap, the amount of time that the user interacts with the system. That's probably one of the most important benefits of electronic marketing: in the background you can collect any sort of demographic data in an unobtrusive manner. The other main benefit is that the material is audience-centered: users can explore the areas in which they are most interested. Certainly in the interactive learning environment, you absolutely have to trap user information. That is one of the main benefits of computer-based training.

Another question that we typically ask potential clients on the front end regarding any product that we create is how much will it cost to maintain and who will be responsible? There is going to be some maintenance in just about any product that we create, whether it be technical support on a standalone CD-ROM or collecting data or updating a Web site. We attempt

A1

Dr. Pearl's Report Card

Managing Patients	Your Practice	PEARL
Non-Physician Labor per Patient Visit	1.39 hrs	0.9 hrs
Cost of Non-Physician Labor per Patient Visit	$23.33	$15.14
Annual Non-Physician Labor	93600 hrs	60750 hrs
Annual Cost of Non-Physician Labor	$1,575,000.00	$1,022,235.58

PEARL could save you $552,764.42 per year, or $36,850.96 per doctor!

Figure 8.6   Using a kiosk to calculate costs. (*Source: NewOrder Media*)

to prepare our clients for the reality that a project is ongoing and dynamic, even after the software is rolled out.

We try to give the client as much control as possible in the case of kiosks, over updating and retrieving information. . . . For example, with the trade show kiosk, MIMS wanted to be able to go in and grab text files and import them into its own database for statistical analysis of the people using the kiosk: how long is the average person staying at the kiosk, [what are] the phone numbers of the people who interacted with the kiosk, and so forth. In [the Ethicon Endo-Surgery] case, there was little or no actual media change. Basically, [the company] just wanted to be able to retrieve the collected database on people who interacted.

With the Ethicon Endo-Surgery project, the class schedule changed regularly on at least a quarterly basis, so [the staff] wanted to have the capability of updating the course schedule very quickly and easily without having one of us fly to the site and make those updates. So, we built the software so that certain components could either be pulled out or put in, in a modular fashion, depending on whether the company wanted to retrieve the data or change the media."

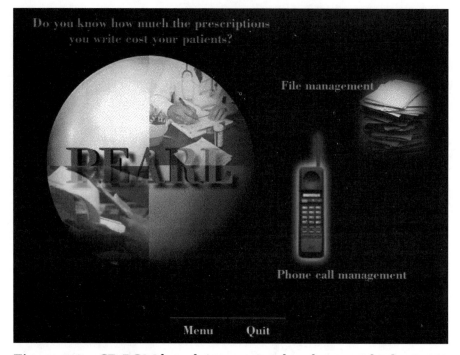

Do you know how much the prescriptions you write cost your patients?

File management

PEARL

Phone call management

Menu   Quit

Figure 8.7   CD-ROM-based interactive brochure with the same functionality of a kiosk but with a more corporate look. (*Source: NewOrder Media*)

Figure 8.8 shows the main menu for NewOrder Media's kiosk for Ethicon Endo-Surgery. Figure 8.9 allows users to look up course offerings by region, date, or specialty. The course information is stored as text files so that clients can update information quickly over their network. In Figure 8.10, high-quality graphics and video are used to market surgical equipment with NewOrder Media's kiosk for Ethicon.

Stewart explains the costs involved in producing such kiosk marketing projects:

> As far as cost goes, of course it depends on the size of the kiosk project. I would say a point of entry would be somewhere around $30,000–$80,000 with the average hovering around $50,000. That has been a scary number to some potential clients in the past. You have to be able to justify the long-term usage of the product. One trade show is not going to justify this expense.
>
> Much of the cost also depends on the hardware and furniture you use, of course. Since kiosks are—luckily—one of the product areas where we can fully

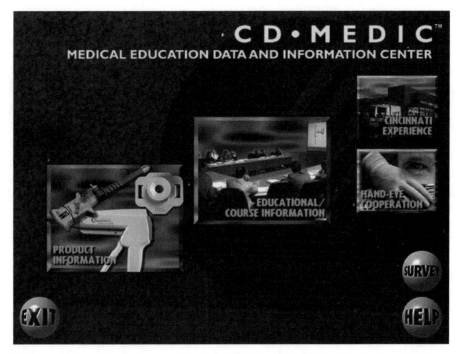

Figure 8.8   Main menu for NewOrder Media's kiosk for Ethicon Endo-Surgery. (*Source: NewOrder media*)

control the playback mechanism—we are not relying on end user's hardware— we tend to go with the higher-end systems in order to maximize the playback quality. MIMS, our trade show clients, wanted to supply all of the hardware and the touch-screen monitors, and just wanted us to write the software. And they were not going to build the furniture specifically to encase the kiosk; and it was going to be in a fairly controlled environment. They weren't afraid that people would come up and steal the monitor or try to damage something, so they felt confident that it was safe enough just to have a pedestal with a monitor, keyboard, and mouse, with the CPU hidden underneath at the trade show.

[In contrast,] Ethicon Endo-Surgery provided very, very detailed specs as far as the kind of furniture that [managers] wanted, in order to fit in with the interior design of their existing building. We ended up with their specifications and contracted the construction of the kiosk furniture; we managed the process of constructing the casing.

Usually, in the case of kiosks, it's a fairly controlled environment, fairly dedicated to the hardware and software, and we sell it as one package. Kiosks are one of the most popular uses of multimedia because people see kiosks in airports and malls and shopping centers and other corporate sites,

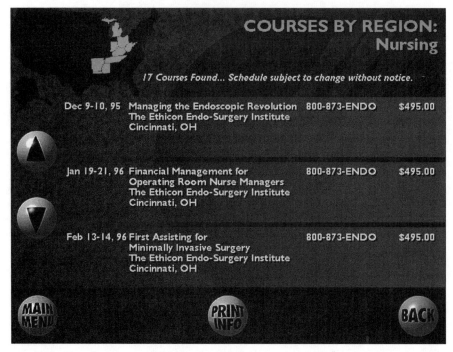

Figure 8.9 Selecting courses on the Ethicon Endo-Surgery kiosk by region. (*Source: NewOrder media*)

and quite often they come to us and they know they want a kiosk to begin with. Again, [kiosks] provide for a very controlled environment for playback. The client can control the hardware, lighting, how often the information is updated, and so on.

But clients sometimes do not realize the costs involved for ongoing maintenance, such as having a live modem connection going so that updates can be made frequently and quickly. They don't realize the cost in making a public kiosk as foolproof and damage-proof as possible with the hardware and the furniture. They don't realize the cost and the effort that goes into actually managing it once it has been rolled out.

Do-It-Yourself Kiosk Housing

21st Century Media, an interactive marketing and production company introduced earlier and featured in Chapter 10, The Internet: Marketing and Business Opportunities, is also in the business of designing and supplying kiosk hous-

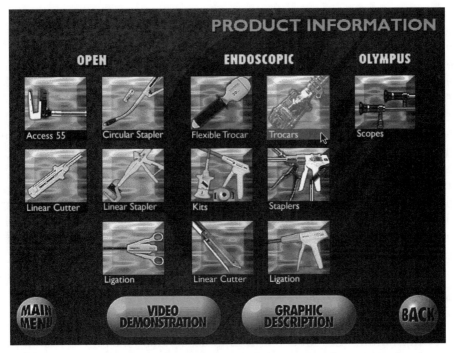

Figure 8.10   Using high-quality graphics and video to market surgical equipment. (*Source: NewOrder Media*)

ing. President and CEO Jim Baker explains that he has always liked the idea of a convenient "off-the-shelf" unit that can be assembled at a moment's notice, and that is also durable, lightweight, easy to ship, and adaptable to a variety of environments. Since most of the major kiosk manufacturers use heavy materials, such as plywood, chipboard, or formica, and often need a significant amount of lead time, 21st Century designers decided to create their own. They came up with a modular, lightweight steel housing that can be spray-painted and can accommodate any Mac or PC with a 14- or 17-inch monitor. They also designed sturdy custom flight cases for them. 21st Century sells and rents their kiosk housing to companies such as Microsoft. Baker describes how that software giant used the kiosks:

> [Microsoft] put enhanced CDs in the foyers of concert halls during a tour for a band called Sky Cries Mary. Microsoft had developed an enhanced CD in conjunction with [the band's] record company, and [the musicians] were on a U.S.-wide tour. They took our kiosks on tour with them in flight cases and demoed the enhanced CD in the foyer. And because [the kiosks] were sheet

*steel, they were hard wearing. The last thing you want is stuff that can
break. We do them in any color, and if you use a base color, you can spray-
paint them. And so [the band] just sprayed [their kiosks] with graffiti to
ensure that people didn't do their own spraying. We shipped them directly
to the band, which were already on tour. Microsoft put a Pentium and a CD-
ROM drive inside the kiosk.*

21st Century designs its other products (such as CD-ROMs) so that they are
easy to adapt to the kiosk environment. For example, designers use large buttons so that a touch screen can be substituted for a regular monitor. To support
keyboard input across venues, 21st Century developed a "soft," pop-up keyboard that appears on the screen of the kiosk and can be used like a regular keyboard. All of its products support an interactive help feature; as the user rolls a
finger or mouse over an object, a text message gives the name of the object or an
instruction.

Surf Plant Reebok

Reebok International Ltd. of Stoughton, Massachusetts, came to Planet Interactive, a full-service multimedia design firm in Boston, to develop a kiosk for
Reebok's 100th year celebration tour. When the tour was completed, the kiosk
was to be repurposed and used in-store for the grand opening of Reebok's Lincoln Center Concept store, Planet Reebok in New York City.

The kiosk had to satisfy three key objectives: to provide a fun, standalone,
interactive component of a traveling exhibit, designed to attract Generation X,
the MTV crowd; to provide a strong PR image piece; and to gather consumer
demographic information and other pertinent marketing research data. Joan
DeCollibus, a producer with Planet Interactive, describes the project:

*Originally, the kiosk served as a component in the traveling exhibit Reebok
100. To celebrate 100 years of Reebok, a Past, Present, Future time tunnel
exhibit traveled to eight worldwide locations including France, Spain, Australia, and Japan. Visitors could walk through the three areas. The Past was
[composed of] several cases of antique shoes with signage; the Present was
the three interactive kiosks; and the Future [contained] display cases of very
high-tech futuristic shoes.*

*The touch-screen kiosks were presented three in a row; the sound on the
two outside kiosks could be heard through headsets, while the center kiosk
had speakers. The content on all three was identical, but to the passerby it
appeared diverse, as different users would be at different points in the pro-*

gram. Our program, titled *Surf Planet Reebok*, invited users to explore current products such as 1995 shoes, Step Reebok exercise equipment, videos, apparel, advertising, and marketing messages, as well as currently used technologies which are proprietary to the brand.

The kiosk surveys the demographics of users, identifying them by age, gender, and sports/activity interest. Users are challenged to seek out a series of hidden objects and "hot" spots, which give them points toward a coupon, which is printed out automatically by the kiosk. Since the primary users of the kiosk are expected to be young, active, potential sport shoe consumers, the program is treated in a cutting edge style with a lot of animation, music, sound effects, and sometimes "elusive" interactivity.

Reebok gave Planet the opportunity to do "whatever we wanted" as long as it had the Reebok look and feel. Good news for us, as the existing marketing and advertising pieces were very diverse and cutting-edge. We did not have to restrain ourselves at all in the design. We were to design the interface and navigation to create an interactive environment that could showcase all of Reebok's products and video content. We ended up using over 800 megabytes of digitized video.

[Reebok] had 17 different areas of shoe categories. For instance, basketball, women's fitness, men's fitness, running, cleated, and so on. Together, we narrowed down the incredibly large array of products to the top of the line in each category. We approached the kiosk as a place or places users would visit—"Welcome to Planet Reebok, stay as long as you like." Each category became a landscape. On each landscape users could find hidden areas to gain points for a coupon, see the top shoes, explore technology, look at related video, or change their gender to see men's or women's products in the category.

We provided a large flowchart for approval of the content as we organized it. Flowcharts, though simple, are a great way to get the whole team, clients and producers, to come to an agreement on what the content will be. I recommend flowcharts and storyboards, however small or large the project. In this case, we would have been lost without them. We provided color comps for all of the category "landscapes" and screen comps for the user interface. Upon the approval of these key elements, we were able to launch into full production. Our production time was tight—eight weeks to completion. We had a team of about 12 people working some pretty long hours.

The team broke down into art director/producer, one writer, two lead designers, four production people creating graphics, four animators doing the animation for each landscape, one lead programmer with the four production people, who also provided roughed out areas, as well as composers to create the original music for each area and the opening interface.

Planet Interactive included a number of successful "attractors" in the product design. The video was eyecatching and and appropriate for the target audience. And by giving participants the opportunity to win something through embedded games and coupons, Reebok's brand affinity was heightened. The kiosk environment made it possible to use a lot of computing power, hidden in and protected by an aesthetic housing. The client's objectives were clearly well met.

Reebok-Thru Glass

Once the tour was completed, Planet Interactive repurposed the program so that it could become part of the Concept store launch at Lincoln Center, New York. The retail installation was called Reebok-Thru Glass. It was designed using technology developed by MicroTouch called *sidewalk interactive.* This technology allows passersby to interact with the screen through the store's glass display window, essentially turning the window into a touch screen. Planet Interactive describes it as follows:

> *Touch-sensitive pads are mounted on the inside of the window and wired to a CPU that runs the interactive program. On the outside of the window, decals cover the areas where the touch pads are mounted. The decals then serve as touch areas from which users make selections and navigate through the program.*
>
> *The program offers users three menu options: Store offers information on the store and featured product lines. Planet allows users to explore Planet Reebok by selecting from 12 full-screen video spots. Live-action video is controlled by the program and stored and played from a high-resolution video disc. Token gives users passwords with which they can receive merchandise discounts. All three choices feature animation and original music.*

This has been a highly successful program, and demonstrates an innovative and enticing use of these technologies. Figures 8.11 a, b, and c show different stages of the Reebok Thru-Glass images.

Conclusion

As this chapter demonstrates, kiosks have a wide range of applications. They can be effective and cost-efficient marketing, information-gathering, and communication tools. Marketing now extends into most areas of information delivery across all industries, and brand and product impressions are being made

Figure 8.11 a, b, c Visiting Planet Reebok via kiosk. (*Source: Planet Interactive & Reebok*)

whenever any product or service is used. Kiosks are especially good marketing vehicles because they can communicate brand on three fronts: the housing itself, the computer screen, and the printed material that the kiosk generates.

Kiosks make it possible to place powerful technology in locations previously untapped. This means reaching audiences who may not otherwise have access to computers and who may not otherwise be given information or be drawn to a given product or service. Kiosks are vehicles for information delivery and gathering that should be seriously considered when developing an electronic marketing plan.

CHAPTER NINE

MARKETING OPPORTUNITIES ON THE COMMERCIAL ONLINE SERVICES

Margo Komenar and Irene Graff

America Online, CompuServe, and Prodigy lead the commercial online industry today. CompuServe was founded in 1979 as a computer time-sharing service for fast and efficient data exchange. It quickly evolved into a rich information resource and efficient communication service used by millions of serious business professionals. CompuServe continues to expand its audience appeal to include a more general consumer base. America Online (AOL) launched in 1985 with an inviting user-friendly interface designed for a broad, general consumer audience. With an endless barrage of very aggressive marketing campaigns, the service quickly catapulted into a leading subscriber position.

Prodigy, the only Internet-based (designed in HTML) service, was launched by owners IBM and Sears in 1988, and at one time led the home-family market. However, while the other two services continued to grow and aggressively market their services, Prodigy did not invest as heavily in either marketing or evolving the appearance of the service. Prodigy gradually slipped from a leading position in the home market to third, behind AOL and CompuServe in subscriptions. With new ownership in 1996, Prodigy is expected to make significant changes.

Subscriptions to the commercial online services reached approximately 12.5 million by the end of 1995, double that of 1994. America Online was the leading consumer online service in 1995, finishing the year with over 4.5 million subscribers, adding 3 million in 1995 alone. The service continues to grow rapidly, passing the 5 million subscriber mark in February 1996 and the 6 million mark well before September 1996 (Figure 9.1). Not far behind is CompuServe at 4.7 million, Prodigy coming in third at just 2 million and MSN at 1 million. According to a September 1995 survey by Washington, D.C. based Information & Interactive Services Report, online service subscriptions soared 56 percent in the first nine months of 1995. The report estimates the 1995 online subscriber universe at 9.9 million. Other 1995 projections range from 9.4 million (Jupiter), to 8.2 million (Arlen) and 6.7 million (Inteco).

In spite of this overall growth, the concomitant explosion of the Internet and the World Wide Web is having a significant impact on these services. The number of World Wide Web users increased eightfold, to 8 million, in 1995 alone, according to International Data Corp. Although in April 1995, 47 percent of adults in America were unfamiliar with online services according to Virtual Media Resources, Natick, Massachusetts, by September 1995, FIND/SVP found that 8 percent of American households used online services.

Projections for growth vary greatly, however. Arlen Communications forecasts 13.5 million online subscribers by 1997, while Jupiter predicts 25 million. In 1995, Forrester Research predicted that online service subscribers would peak in 1997 at 10 million and gradually decline after that. Now the company claims that the popularity of commercial online services such as America Online and CompuServe will peak by 1998 at 16 million subscribers. That number will drop to about 15 million the following year, and will continue to fall as more businesses migrate to the Internet. (That's a change of heart of at least 6 million subscribers.) Dataquest estimates online services revenues will reach $3.3 billion in 1997.

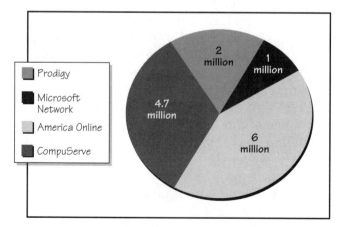

Figure 9.1 Commercial online services subscribers as of third quarter 1996.

Ironically, one of the key marketing strategies employed by all of these services has caused an unexpected drain on revenue, and plays havoc with the subscriber numbers. By offering free hours online with every subscription, the services have inadvertently encouraged "service-hopping;" Once the free hours are used up, the subscriber cancels, and signs up with the next service offering free hours. Since acquiring a new subscriber can be very costly, this is an issue of growing concern. According to Inteco Corp., subscriber churn (turnover) is a major problem. The company says that an estimated 8.4 million subscriptions to America Online, CompuServe, and Prodigy have already been cancelled. The services are combatting this problem with increased attention to customer service. After a member has subscribed, a customer service representative makes telephone contact to welcome the newcomer and to establish a connection. As a result of these efforts, retention has been increasing.

In addition, to address the shift in focus to the Internet, the major commercial services have launched separate Internet access divisions. Following a 5 percent acquisition of AOL by Bertelsmann in March 1995, AOL acquired Global Network Navigator (GNN) and launched a standalone Internet-based service on October 30, 1995. America Online spent $14.5 million for Virtual Places client/server maker Ubique. America Online reports that from October 1 to December 31, approximately 877,000 members were added. Other interesting statistics provided by Interstellar an online marketing and research agency, are:

- Total usage for the fourth quarter of 1995 exceeded 77 million hours.
- More than 28 million Web hits were processed daily.
- The Web accounts for 11 percent of total usage.
- More than 4 million pieces of e-mail are delivered daily, half of it via the Internet.
- AOL's own network, AOLNet, has bumped its share of network traffic to 40 percent.

AOL has also made cross-promotional agreements with AT&T's WorldNet and Microsoft's MSN online services to further its Internet alliances. AT&T will feature and promote America Online on AT&T WorldNet Service, and made the AOL software available to AT&T WorldNet service subscribers, as of summer '96. Access to AOL through WorldNet will be priced at a reduced rate. Customers of America Online who take advantage of the AT&T WorldNet Service offer will be able to retain their America Online screen names, e-mail addresses, and favorite places.

"This is the first integrated consumer offer between a leading online service and a major telecommunications provider offering Internet access," said Robert

E. Allen, chairman of AT&T. "With AT&T WorldNet Service, we are providing a high-quality, convenient, and financially attractive way for our customers to reach all the content and features of the Internet, plus all of the content and communities of America Online," Allen said.

Steve Case, chairman and CEO of America Online, added: "As we aim to reach the 89 percent of U.S. households who don't presently use any online service or have any Internet connection, we continue to believe simplicity is critical. AOL will continue to be offered as a simple, affordable, integrated, plug-and-play solution as we reach out to attract a mainstream audience. But as more consumers opt to use Internet access providers, such as AT&T WorldNet Service, we want to make it as easy and affordable as possible for them to also experience the magic of AOL."

AOL and Microsoft signed an agreement to make Microsoft's Internet Explorer the standard, built-in Web browser for its membership. At the same time, Microsoft will place a folder on the Windows 95 desktop that will give its users access to AOL. AOL agreed to seamlessly integrate Microsoft Internet Explorer into its client software for Windows 95, Windows 3.1, and the Macintosh and to transition its 6 million customers to the new software. The companies also agreed to conduct joint marketing and cooperative engineering activities. "We're committed to embracing the best technologies and tools for the benefit of our more than 5 million AOL members," said Steve Case. "That's why we're excited to make Microsoft Internet Explorer our standard integrated browser for AOL members."

"America Online has created the most successful consumer online experience, and we are excited about making this available to the millions of people who use Windows," said Bill Gates, chairman and CEO of Microsoft. "This agreement integrates Internet Explorer into AOL's client software, reaching more than 5 million users. . . . Our agreement with AOL is a tremendous win-win for consumers and the industry," said Gates. "Now, the two leading browsers will compete head-to-head to offer customers innovative Internet technology. And with the ActiveX Technologies we announced at the Internet Professional Developers Conference, independent developers and publishers can more easily create compelling active Internet content."

All of the commercial services realize that the only way they will be successful is by maximizing traffic. Each of the services and major Web sites bring different benefits to the table. The key is to make the Internet and the commercial services succeed as a whole so that consumers will find it a useful and interesting place to spend time and purchase goods and services.

Microsoft Network (MSN) quickly shifted its focus from building a proprietary commercial to an Internet-based network. The company has entered into an agreement with MCI that will offer Microsoft's Internet Explorer browser and a customized version of Microsoft Network. Similar agreements were made with AOL and AT&T.

Prodigy became the first service to offer access to the Web on January 17, 1995, and claimed to have signed up as many as 1 million Web surfers in the first three months. The company plans to upgrade its proprietary software with P2, which sports a Mosaic-like interface. Further, Prodigy has formed a partnership with three regional Bells to roll out ISDN services in Boston, San Jose, and Nashville. Moreover, the company has embarked on great ad campaign created by Cliff Freeman & Partners. Prodigy launched the Access Net Direct Service market trial on March 21, 1996, as an Internet-only access service in the New York metropolitan region. The service, still in successful market trials at the end of August, costs $1/per hour with no minimum fee; the Software includes Netscape 2.0 browser.

The Commercial Online Services

The following sections describe America Online, CompuServe, Prodigy, and Microsoft Network and give a brief overview of Bloomberg Financial Markets' online service, a very important and unique vertical market service. These overviews are intended to provide a sense of what each service has to offer to both consumers and marketers. In order to understand your audience as a marketer, it is of value to understand the features and nuances of the service(s) your customers use.

Advertising information is included to familiarize you with some of the marketing possibilities on each service. Then, information is given on areas other than those designated for sales and marketing, to help you see how an advertiser can begin to formulate creative ways to become a part of the community and make a contribution while building brand awareness. Interest groups and forums can provide excellent market research opportunities, and by taking part in these, a company can often learn a lot about how it and it's products are perceived.

Obviously, there is more to marketing than buying and selling. Marketing in today's electronic marketplace requires relationship building and an understanding of how to make that relationship mutually beneficial. The model is still "under construction" and all of the online services are very open to innovative ideas. The power has shifted to the consumer in the buyer/seller relationship, and it will behoove the marketer to respond creatively.

Intersteller provides the following market forecasts:

- Forrester expects online shopping to approach $5 billion by 1999 compared to The Yankee Group's estimate of $3.1 billion in "interactive consumer commerce."

- Jupiter says that $4.5 billion will be spent on the Web by 2000, plus another $2.4 billion via online services.
- ActivMedia believes that sales generated by the World Wide Web will grow from $436 million in 1995 to $46 billion by 1998.
- By 2000, International Data Corp. believes, electronic commerce will hit $150 billion.
- Killen & Associates believes all e-money transfers on the Internet will reach $600 billion by 2000.

Audience composition is transitioning from upper-middle class, predominantly male, married, Baby Boomers to a more diverse, generalized consumer base. By 1998, the number of married and unmarried users of consumer online services will be roughly equal (see Table 9.1). As Generation X ages, the types of products and services desired by this group will also evolve.

America Online

America Online, or AOL as it is commonly referred to, is the fastest growing, with the largest subscriber base of the three major commercial online services (America Online, CompuServe, and Prodigy). As of September 1996, the company had exceeded 6 million members. Previously, AOL's traditional target market had been restricted to the United States, although it has expanded internationally in the past year with the launch of localized Canadian and German services. The United Kingdom and France are expected to follow in the near future.

AOL's focus on the general consumer audience, rather than on one particular market segment, has resulted in a perception of AOL as more of an all-purpose

TABLE 9.1   Number of Married/Unmarried Users of Consumer Online Services

Segment	1994	1998
Business/Consumer	38%/62%	20%/80%
Male/Female	80%/20%	62%/38%
Single	40%	50%
Married	60%	50%
Children younger than 11 years	1%	5%
Children 12–18 years	4%	10%
18–34 years	25%	26%
34–49 years	60%	40%
50+ years	10%	19%

Source: Jupiter 1995 Consumer Online Services Report

service. Although AOL emphasizes personal and family interests and the home-based market, its user-friendly environment also attracts some corporate and small business usage, often for communication purposes and other amenities. Kathy Johnson, AOL corporate communications manager, states, "Basically, we are for everyone. We really run the gamut as far as who uses the service. We have seniors, kids, middle-aged, and young adults online."

Many users new to the online environment will sign up with AOL as their first online service. AOL knows that people are looking for a secure, community atmosphere that is easy to move around in and offers choices of interesting topics to explore. This focus on the customer has resulted in an online service that attempts to make the interactive experience more fun, friendly, and engaging—independent of the tools or technologies that are leveraged to accomplish it. Steve Case, AOL chairman and CEO states, "Our members have told us they want access to a broad range of content, presented in an engaging way, easy to use, affordably priced, and with a strong underlying sense of community. These factors are the underpinnings to our success, because our members have, in turn, brought other members online."

Who's on America Online

The America Online population is slightly less upscale than the other services as it includes a broader range of the general population geared toward home users. The AOL online user profile is:

- Average age: 40; more than 50 percent between the ages of 18 and 44.
- Home owners: 71 percent
- College graduates: 88 percent
- Employed full-time: 80 percent; with spouses who are employed: 66 percent
- In Executive or professional positions: 46 percent
- In Technical Positions: 16 percent
- In sales: 9 percent
- Self-employed: 22 percent
- Microsoft Windows users: 75 percent
- Own a CD-ROM drive: 71 percent
- Male: 79 percent
- Married with children at home: 67 percent

In addition, more than half of AOL users have two computers, and more than half have combined annual household incomes of more than $50,000. America Online members are located primarily in 20 major U.S. cities, including Portland, OR; Cleveland; New York; Los Angeles; Minneapolis; Washington, D.C.; San Francisco; Detroit; Dallas; Seattle; Philadelphia; Sacramento; San Diego; Denver; Atlanta; Houston; Boston; Chicago; and Miami.

AOL Service Features

Primarily operating its online services for personal computer owners, America Online offers communication services that include electronic mail, bulletin boards, and real-time chats. In addition, it offers computer enhancement services, including software downloading, and special interest groups that focus on hardware and software; entertainment services such as multiplayer games; business and financial information; educational, airline reservation, and shopping and discount brokerage services.

America Online's services are divided into departments each containing a wealth of information and resources. These departments include:

Today's News
Personal Finance
Clubs & Interests
Computing
Travel
Marketplace
People Connection
Newsstand
Entertainment
Education
Reference Desk
Internet Connection
Sports
Kids Only

A quick glance at AOL's Marketplace shopping mall and the Internet Connection area (Figure 9.2), which allows members access to the World Wide Web and other services, shows that AOL favors the family and soho (sole owner home office) market. These areas offer something for everyone in almost every age group with an emphasis on lifestyle.

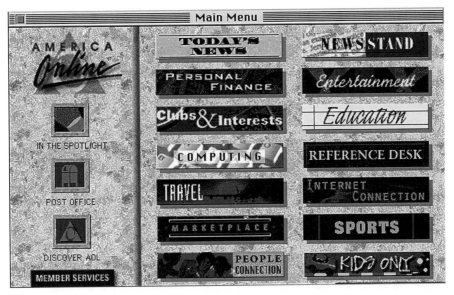

Figure 9.2 America Online Main Menu screen. (*Source: America Online*)

Computing

There is high interest in computer-related topics on AOL. In the Computing section, members find access to a variety of computing and software/hardware forums. These forums are used to exchange computing ideas, participate in discussions, and download software. More than 30,000 downloadable software/ shareware programs are available. Software libraries are grouped in categories, such as communications, desktop publishing, education, graphics, games, hardware, hypercard, utilities, and music and sound. There is also a help desk to guide users through the libraries. Computing conferences often host special guest "speakers" and allow interaction with editors of popular computer magazines such as *MacWorld Online.*

News & Finance

Another popular area is News & Finance, which gives members access to current national and world news. Participating newspapers include *Arizona Republic, The New York Times, Chicago Tribune, Orlando Sentinel,* and *San Jose Mercury News.* A keyword search function helps users find specific topics in these publications, as well as on ABC News On Demand, which offers daily news, money, and sports articles.

In addition, America Online has a Small Business Center to help organize, manage, and promote a small business. This area has its own message board and special software library. A Business and Markets section offers news, stock quotes, and portfolio management information. A special sports report area highlights all the major sports and other news. Entertainment News & Features offers movies, television, music, and book reviews. There are also 48 magazines available on AOL, listed here:*

American Woodworker	MacWorld
Backpacker Magazine	Mobile Office
Bicycling Magazine	National Geographic
Boating Online	Omni Magazine
Business Week Online	PC Novice/PC Today
Car and Driver	PC World
Christian Reader Magazine	Popular Photography
Christianity Online	Road & Track
Christianity Today Online	Saturday Review Online
Consumer Reports	Scientific American
Cycle World	Smithsonian Publications
DC Comics Online	SPINonline
Disney Adventures Magazine	Stereo Review
Elle Online	The Atlantic Monthly
Entertainment Weekly	The New Republic
Family PC Online	TIME Magazine
Flying Magazine	Today's Christian Woman
Home Magazine	Travel & Leisure Online
Home Office Computing	Travel Holiday
HomePC	Windows Magazine
Inside Media	Wired Magazine
Longevity Online	Woman's Day
MacHome Journal	WordPerfect Magazine
MacTech Magazine	Worth Magazine

*Source: Online Services: Review, Trends & Forecast, SIMBA Information Inc.

Education & Reference

The Education & Reference section on AOL includes a variety of sources for all ages:

- Compton's award-winning electronic encyclopedia from Britannica Software is easily accessible.
- Interactive Education Services includes real-time, online classes, including college preparatory assistance and general-interest courses.
- The Academic Assistance Center offers one-on-one tutoring for elementary through college level.
- The Career Center has new job listings and a database with information on thousands of careers.
- College Board Online provides general advice and information on admissions, placement, and financial aid for students who are making the transition from high school to college.
- The Teacher's Information Network is a resource/forum for teachers to exchange ideas and discuss current education issues.

Entertainment

The AOL Entertainment section offers information on the latest happenings in Hollywood. Many major music labels, such as BMG, Warner/Reprise, and Virgin maintain a presence here, along with dozens of independent labels. SPINonline, VH-1 Online, and MTV also sponsor online entertainment news and information.

Sports

The AOL Sports connection provides current information on sporting events all over the United States, with broadcast information from ABC Sports and Baseball Daily. Included in the Sports department is NTN Sport Trivia and STATS, Inc.

Kids Only

Kids Only is a specialized AOL department where children can find ABC Kidzine, The Cartoon Network, Club Kidsoft, Compton's Study Break, games, homework help, and Nickelodeon Online. America Online also offers several levels of parental control to prevent children from exploring areas that may not be appropriate for them.

People Connection

The AOL People Connection offers a variety of public and private chat rooms, and is the main place to gather to talk, debate, and meet people. There are chat rooms for almost any personal interest. The following are just a few:

Best Lit Chat House
Game Parlor
Hollywood Tonight
New Member Lounge
Over Forty
Red Dragon Inn
Romance Connection
Sports
Starfleet Academy
Starfleet Boot Camp
Tarot
Teen Chat
The Flirts Nook
The Meeting Place
Thirtysomething

Center Stage Auditorium

Another popular AOL area, the Center Stage Auditorium, is the hub of special events and interviews. In the last year, guests have included singers Luther Vandross and Michael Jackson, actors Martin Lawrence and Richard Greico, rapper Doug E. Fresh, and director Oliver Stone. In terms of hobbies and special interests, there are hundreds of clubs, special interest forums, conference rooms and message boards. The following is a sample list of America Online clubs and interest forums.

- AARP Online
- American Woodworker
- Astronet
- Astronomy Club
- Aviation Forum
- Baby Boomers
- Bernie Siegel Online
- BikeNet
- Black Voices
- Book Nook
- Cars
- Catholic Community
- Chicago Online
- Everything Edible
- The Exchange
- Family Life
- Focus On Family
- Food & Drink Network

- Games Channel
- Genealogy Forum
- Health Channel
- Hillary Rodham Clinton Forum
- Men are from Mars
- Mysteries from the Yard
- PetCare Forum
- Religion & Ethics Forum
- Science Fiction & Fantasy
- Star Trek Club
- Writer's Club

- Garden Spot
- Grateful Dead Forum
- Health Zone
- JOKES!
- Moms Online
- Parascope
- Photography
- Rogue
- SeniorNet
- Top Model Online
- XFiles

- Gay & Lesbian Forum
- Ham Radio Club
- Hecklers Online
- Kodak Photography Forum
- MusicSpace
- Parent Soup
- Public Safety Center
- Scuba Forum
- 60-Second Novelist
- Wedding Workshop

Travel and Shopping

AOL offers EAASY SABRE Travel Services so members can make airline and hotel arrangements online. The Marketplace, an electronic shopping mall, features dozens of vendors and hundreds of products from flowers to cars. Vendors include 1-800-FLOWERS, Fragrance Counter, Omaha Steaks, The Sharper Image, and the Online Bookstore.

American Express Travel-Related Services went live with ExpressNet in America Online's Marketplace, offering airline bookings through the Express Reservations program, which will also offer hotel and car rental reservations. ExpressNet lets American Express cardholders download their financial statements directly into several financial management software programs. It also allows cardholders to pay their bills and order customized travel guides, traveler's checks, and foreign currency online.

Marketing Options on America Online

When it came to member shopping and advertising options, in the past America Online trailed its competitors; however, it has made a determined effort to change its nontransactional image. Since 1995, America Online has upscaled its Marketplace to be a highly attractive and interactive marketing site (Figure 9.3). AOL has not prescribed rates for Marketplace partnerships. Agreements are made on a percentage-of-sales basis, and some vendors receive royalties on member's time usage in their stores. However, it depends on the contract; everything is negotiable. AOL will offer to design a marketing site for the vendor, and will charge an average of $20,000 to $50,000 to "build" a complete store. It is important to note that a Marketplace presence is not a Web site, but

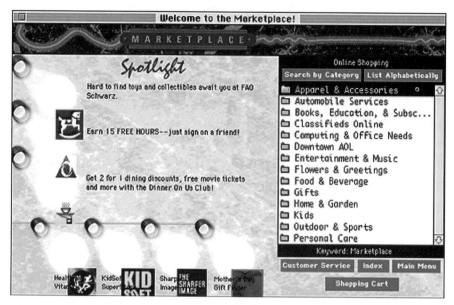

Figure 9.3   America Online Marketplace menu.

a "store front" in a closed environment, allowing online purchases without 800 numbers. Credit card orders go directly to the vendor.

America Online tracks the number of orders, the items ordered, and their prices, but not the identity of the member who placed the order. At the end of each month, vendors receive an Insight Report that tells them how many members went into their store area, plus member demographic information. This is intended to help vendors modify their product selection or create promotions that target certain types of consumers. In 1996, America Online hopes to strengthen vendor offerings in the apparel, accessory, and possibly discount store categories.

1-800-FLOWERS

One highly successful merchant on America Online is 1-800-FLOWERS (Figure 9.4). It was one of the first merchants with a presence in the Marketplace. The company worked closely with America Online's engineering and systems departments to develop the Marketplace, along with its own online presence, and everyone quickly began to see results. In its first few months online, 1-800-FLOWERS was receiving 500–600 orders a day, and in the thousands on special occasions. Donna Iucolano, 1-800-FLOWERS' manager of Interactive Services, states:

Figure 9.4 1-800-FLOWERS Marketplace main menu.

We've been live on America Online since November 1994, and it has been a wonderful ride. America Online has really proven the true potential for electronic shopping and electronic retailing. Our area was an overnight success, and we'll probably generate within this fiscal year [1996] about $10 million worth of sales just on America Online. It had a very, very active and interested subscriber base, and the Marketplace has really grown considerably in the year and a half since we first went live. Today America Online represents approximately 40 percent of our online business . . . which as a whole should generate about $20–25 million worth of business.

To be a successful merchant like 1-800-FLOWERS demands creating an effective interactive presence and continuously fresh promotions. Iucolano adds, "Our areas always have contests and games going on . . . people love them . . . we were the first to introduce the gift-reminder program three years ago and now just about every shopping area has one. We do chats, we have bulletin boards, we are constantly changing the areas and updating the products, the welcome sections, and what's new sections. We are very proactive online."

It is important to offer more than promotions when participating in the online community. Iucolano believes strongly in making a real contribution, and so her company began to build a floral reference and information resource. Gardening is a very popular hobby in the United States, and its bulletin boards are always packed with questions. 1-800-FLOWERS responded by becoming a publisher of its own information in order to make it more readily available.

One of the most valued aspects of 1-800-FLOWERS' relationship with AOL, according to Iucolano, is the exclusivity agreement. Because AOL has agreed to allow 1-800-FLOWERS to be the only company selling flowers on the service, it guarantees them strong volume levels and encourages the company to invest more into that profit center, adding more value to AOL. It also builds loyalty and a true partnership bond. AOL simply takes a commission on sales, which for a retailing platform is very desirable. States Iucolano, "The more we make, the more they make. The America Online relationship is very much a partnership."

Fragrance Counter

Another successful Marketplace merchant is the Fragrance Counter (Figures 9.5 and 9.6). A specialty store providing a selection of designer fragrances and cosmetics, this company positions itself between a traditional perfumery and a department store fragrance section. The company is primarily an electronic advertiser as opposed to print or any other medium, with a presence on other services, including CompuServe. Eli Katz, vice president of Sales and Marketing, explains that the reason they believe the online environment is appropriate for their products is because of the demographics:

Figure 9.5   The Fragrance Counter on AOL.

Figure 9.6 The Fragrance Counter's Shop the Store option.

The people online are usually educated, [have an] above-average income, and appreciate brands and are consumers of brands and can afford to buy them. In addition, they are people who value their time, which makes shopping online extremely convenient, especially when many of the brands that we carry are available only at certain department stores. Online shopping saves them the hassle of parking, searching for what they want in a busy store environment and paying full price.

Katz explained that AOL provided his company with a producer to develop the store presence. This same person continues to act as the technical liaison, to make sure the store run smoothly. According to Katz, America Online's strength is its flexibility and its partnership with its merchants. "The vendors on America Online are really committed to maintaining their stores. If you look at the way they're laid out and designed, you get the feeling that it's more like a community on AOL, and they [the vendors] are obviously committed to the Marketplace. AOL has a vested interest because its not charging us rent, and AOL makes money only when we make money."

Katz commented that he prefers the business model of AOL because the service really goes into partnership with its merchants, and build trust and loyalty. This is a very strong sentiment with AOL merchants. Although Katz does maintain a presence on other services, and is happy to see the others changing in their approach to merchant relationships, he feels strongly about how different the experience is when the service is not just charging rent, but playing more of a supporting role.

Windham Hill

Windham Hill was introduced to AOL through a company called 2Market. 2Market was originally an electronic catalogue on CD-ROM put out by Meteor, AOL, and Apple, which all owned a piece of it. At first, AOL ran a cross-promotion, providing a special 2Market area on the service where the merchants could sell their products. Then, in 1995, AOL purchased all of 2Market, and the merchants became part of Marketplace.

Gina Rayfield, manager of Special Markets for Windham Hill, explains that as much as her company is about selling music, its online presence has everything to do with branding. "It's building brand awareness and it's also building product awareness. We're able to talk a lot about the artists, and the releases, and spend more time with people to give them some real in-depth information and get them close to the artists."

Marketplace selects companies to participate in its program that will add value on a content level. Rayfield continues:

> If you spend some time there, it's actually very interesting. Most of the material in Marketplace is more than just merchandise; it's real community-driven; it's very specific to a hobby or a particular community, and when people get on there and look around, as they go from Tower to Windham Hill to Starbucks, they're visiting their favorite little neighborhoods.
>
> We actually do, from a vendor perspective, stay in contact a lot. We have these forums that we all get involved in, and we talk about what we want to see on AOL, what we think our consumers need from AOL. We talk cross-promotions with each other. We're always talking about different ideas and ways that we can work together.
>
> I'm trying right now to put together an auditorium for some of our specific artists, whereby they can get on and fans can really speak to them and ask them questions about their releases. On an ongoing basis we have promotions tied around our products and the seasons and holidays, which have done really well. For Valentine's Day, we were able to capitalize on AOL as a place where people go to look for gift ideas, and we were able to do really well with our romantic lines of music.

AOL offers its merchants many benefits. It will rotate a merchant in and out of different prime locations if it will be beneficial, especially for holiday promotions. AOL doesn't charge its merchants extra to be part of a holiday or special event promotion. Because it is in a partnership with its merchants, it has just as much to gain by promoting them. AOL is always looking for great content to present to its members, so its merchants are important content providers as well as storefront revenue sources. Rayfield explains how this partnership makes it possible for Windham Hill to be on AOL:

> We're a small company, even though we're actually owned by a larger one. We don't have a lot of online marketing dollars budgeted right now, and so a lot of the efforts that we make online are really on a shoestring. We try to cross-promote as much as we can. We don't spend a lot of dollars—we don't spend any money on advertising. You won't see us sponsoring a spot, because that's very expensive.

Rayfield says it really may not be as hard to negotiate as one might think, if a company has a great niche product. AOL is looking for products that add value to the service. Rayfield explained that she gets tracking reports by product that indicate exactly how many were sold, so during any given time period, she can determine whether promotions are doing well.

There are different levels of participation on AOL. Some companies are free to do their own content production and maintain their own look and feel. Rayfield explains that her company is still on a 2Market template with a set look for the area, similar to other former 2Market vendors. For those merchants, AOL does all of the production, which saves money and labor. Rayfield says Windham Hill is very happy with Marketplace. "When we first got online, we were selling anywhere from 50 to 100 CDs a month and, now, depending on the time frame, we'll sell from 600 to 1,000 a month."

KidSoft

KidSoft is a distributor and aggregator of quality software for kids. It is in both the OEM channels through direct relationships with Apple and Motorola, and in the retail channels with its own line of value-priced software for kids. Maggie Young, senior director of Corporate Marketing, states, "We are also online with America Online, and we will be launching a Web page sometime in '96, as well. On KidSoft on AOL, kids can have a sense of community while interacting with each other and talking about their favorite kinds of software (Figure 9.7). They can demo all the titles we sell in our online store. And it's through those channels that we provide parents and kids with an opportunity to review and preview the titles that we've prescreened to them before they make their purchasing decisions together, and then buy directly from KidSoft."

KidSoft's initial and core business was launched as Club KidSoft in May 1992. The company sent subscribers a print and CD-ROM magazine containing children's software product demos and reviews, plus a variety of educational

Figure 9.7   KidSoft Marketplace on AOL.

and entertaining activities. That magazine now is found in the Kids Only section on AOL. KidSoft provides rich content for AOL and maintains both an area just for kids and an online store in AOL's Marketplace. This has been a mutually successful partnership.

Rob Novotny, KidSoft's senior director of Digital Media explains some of the advantages AOL provides. "One of the things that AOL does, that does not happen on the Web, is bring the customers to you. It aggregates people to the mall and then AOL promotes you within the mall." One of the benefits of having access to such a large audience is the volume of instantaneous response when a merchant is promoting something new. You know right away if it is a good idea or not. Novotny elaborates, "An online service like this allows us to try something new, and immediately get a reaction from the kids, allowing us to then try something different. It's real time. We can react and change direction more quickly than in any other medium. We can do the same thing on the store side. We can run product specials, a week later see how it works, then change our merchandising accordingly. Another electronic venue, such as CD-ROM, has a much longer cycle and larger up-front costs. So to experiment online is less expensive."

The software products that KidSoft sells come from positive relationships with developers such as Broderbund, The Learning Company, MECC, Sierra, and Davidson. KidSoft prescreens the software; tests it with kids, parents, and teachers; and determines whether to represent it through its channels.

Direct Marketer Program

A fast-growing portion of America Online's Marketplace is its direct marketer program, which includes Tower Records, Hanes, Hallmark Cards, and Office-Max Online. Rather than charging start-up costs for this service, America Online collects 5–20 percent of vendors' transactions. The percentage is based on vendors' margins and/or sales volumes.

With a holiday scheduling option, Hallmark is one of the more innovative of these direct marketers. According to Judy Tashbook, manager of Public Relations for America Online, "An America Online member can, in the middle of the night on a Thursday in February, schedule birthday, anniversary, and holiday cards for the rest of the year, pay for them and then craft their messages. Hallmark will send the cards so that they get to the desired party on [the specified] day. These are real cards . . . and the advantage is that, if you never have time to go to a card store and stand there and pick out cards, when you're online, you have time. You can create a card or you can choose a card; we have every card you can imagine."

High-Ticket Visibility

If a company wants to create more of a presence on America Online than through the Marketplace, a program can be customized to enable a corporation to create its own interactive marketing area. The cost starts at around $240,000 annually for AOL to produce, develop, and maintain the area. For an additional $60,000 annually, AOL will create and maintain a complementary Web site. Some provisions are made for the advertiser to recoup the up-front costs through royalty and bounty payments based on traffic or for each new subscriber the client registers.

McDonald's has made use of this program in an interesting way. AOL says that "although [McDonald's is] not selling hamburgers online, it has an absolutely gorgeous area. It has created a content site for families." (Figure 9.8)

AOL Greenhouse

A specialized program developed by America Online called the America Online Greenhouse was founded in 1994 to gather and create new content. Of the initial 1,700 applicants, six companies were selected to become a part of the program. One of those companies was the electronic Gourmet Guide, commonly referred to as eGG. Since then, America Online has added 22 other partners, with a goal of 50 total. Although this is not an advertising option, it is a content-driven method of creating an online business or presence.

eGG   The electronic Gourmet Guide is the longest-running online digital publication dedicated to the professional chef and dedicated amateur. Established

Figure 9.8   McDonald's AOL main menu.

in 1994 as a bulletin board system, the system did not get much response at the time, and eGG did not have the marketing budget to promote the BBS. By December 1994, eGG decided to develop its own Web site. Within a week it had received more than 40,000 hits—a respectable number in 1994. Currently, eGG gets approximately 1 million hits per month.

Thomas Way, publisher of eGG explains the sequence of events. "In March 1995, the America Online Greenhouse contacted us and we joined the program. America Online gave eGG a small amount of seed money and a contract for three years. The first year we were exclusive to AOL, and didn't appear on any other service. AOL gives us a lot of technical support that we wouldn't ordinarily get if we were an outside partner."

Initially, eGG was a content provider for AOL. Then eGG asked to be in the Marketplace because it saw an opportunity to market quality food products along with the online magazine it produced. America Online thought the quality of the products was good enough to include eGG with the Marketplace merchants. Currently, eGG represents 11 vendors, including Indian River Gift and Fruit, which sells oranges and grapefruits from Florida, and a company that sells hand-made cheeses. eGG takes a commission from its vendors on products sold through its Marketplace store, and America Online takes a percentage of the sales.

The electronic Gourmet Guide sets itself apart from the other online companies by combining elements of a magazine and a merchandising area. Way explained, "I think one of the most important things about what we're doing is the fact that, unlike the normal (online) mall out there on the Internet or even on America Online, we're attaching this store to our magazine and there's content and credibility that you don't have in just a normal store or mall situation. The Web has grown at this astronomical rate and so has America Online. Prodigy has dropped a little bit. CompuServe is at about the same rate of growth that it was before. But America Online has leapfrogged everybody, and it's because of what we call community. There really is a community of people that we interact with, which is unlike what we have on the Net, simply because the tools on the Net haven't caught up."

2Market   2Market is primarily a transactional CD-ROM catalog, with each CD usually featuring 18 to 28 merchants. More than 2,000 products are featured on each CD, with most sold in the Marketplace as well. Vendors found in the Marketplace are often represented on 2Market's CD.

The advantages that CD-ROMs afford—video, audio, and other multimedia features—are valuable to companies such as music label Windham Hill. Even though the online technology doesn't support the immediate sampling of audio—something that is extremely helpful in music sales—Windham Hill has found success in Marketplace. Gina Rayfield, manager of Special Markets for Windham Hill states, "We can directly affect the music sale by having music online. If we do a direct mailing and it has an accompanying CD, it's amazing . . . the sales just blow the doors out."

2Market expects to distribute more than 1 million copies of the latest 2Market CD-ROM by doing away with a subscription fee and charging consumers only $3.95 to cover shipping and handling. Merchants are charged a $5,000 to $30,000 product fee by developer Medior, which is owned by America Online. It is important to be aware, however, that participation on 2Market does not necessarily guarantee participation in the Marketplace.

Downtown AOL

America Online has another service that is less expensive and enables smaller companies or entrepreneurs to be on the Web without making a significant investment. This service is called Downtown AOL. Downtown AOL is a virtual small business community where potential customers come to browse and shop for products and services of all types (Figure 9.9). Like any downtown business area, there are interesting activities, special events, contests,

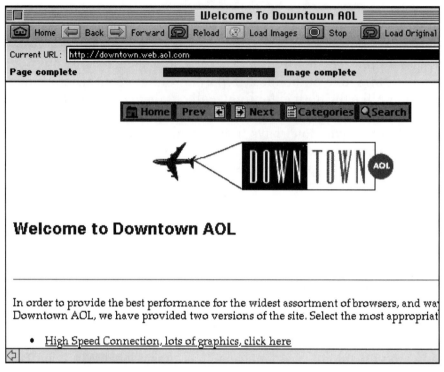

Figure 9.9   Downtown AOL main Web page.

and sometimes a sidewalk sale. It allows advertisers to reach both Internet users on the World Wide Web as well as 5 million-plus America Online subscribers. According to Judy Tashbook, "One of the neat things about a Downtown AOL ad is that it's a great way for a company to get onto the World Wide Web, because the ad exists on America Online and the Web. The benefit of being part of Downtown AOL is that we drive traffic to it. As a business, you'll get more hits through Downtown AOL than you would if you were just out there on the Web."

Downtown AOL offers more than three dozen product and service categories (Figure 9.10). Advertisers can place their materials in as many categories as they feel are appropriate. AOL also places paid advertisers in special promotional areas in addition to the regular ad space, at no additional charge. Company ad pages are automatically registered in the World Wide Web indexing service and search engines, such as Yahoo, WebCrawler, Lycos, and InfoSeek. Downtown AOL also features paid advertisers in its Wild, Wacky & Wonderful section and in What's New, which is an up-front view of the latest advertisers, complete with descriptions of products and services along with links to their Web pages.

Downtown AOL costs $495 for six months, or about $82 a month. As of March 1996, Downtown AOL showcased approximately 200 companies and was receiving about 50,000 visitors a month. An ad run is for six months, with at least one page of text and an e-mail link.

E-mail capability is essential if an advertiser is going to take full advantage of the interactive format. Advertisers with existing e-mail addresses are linked at no charge at the time the advertising contract is signed and the ad is placed. All advertising on Downtown AOL can feature color graphics within certain specifications, and the first page can include text, e-mail and a four-color graphic or company logo. Additional files such as catalogs or price sheets can be up to 15,000 characters in length and in electronic form for posting. They will be included in your paid advertising schedule of two or more pages at no extra charge. Table 9.2 shows the breakdown of rates and descriptions.

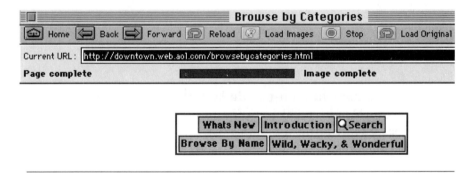

Figure 9.10   Downtown AOL Category screen.

TABLE 9.2   Downtown AOL Advertising Rates

Advertisement	Price	Description
Single Page Ad	$495	Includes text, logo or graphic & e-mail link
Additional pages to same ad	$275	Includes text, logo or graphic & e-mail link
Additional graphics (any ad)	$250	Per page, each graphic
Additional Ads	25% off	Must be placed at the same time as the original ad
Duplication of Ads	80% off	Same ad repeated in another category
Optional linking to external Web Site	$750	Per link
Direct link from Downtown AOL to a Web Site with no ad on Downtown AOL	$1,000	Per link
Minor text modifications to current ad	$100	Adding bold or italics, new address, promotional pricing etc. More extensive text/copy changes are evaluated and priced on a case-by-case basis.
Graphics Modifications	$250	Per change, per graphic

Web Link

If an advertiser has its own high-profile Web page, the company can opt for a simple Web link on America Online (Figure 9.11). This link would most often reside on America Online rather than on Downtown AOL. For example, if a member were interested in Computing and then clicked on Computing, a What's Hot icon would be available from the menu. When What's Hot was selected, the member would review a What's Hot page. This page would tell members about the new and interesting things in the computing section. It's on this page that an advertiser's Web link may reside. The advertiser would be one of (up to) three that may have a Web link posted there.

This link service costs $5,000 for four weeks, with America Online guaranteeing at least 90,000 "page views"—the number of individuals who will view the page on which the Web link resides. Web links can be placed in any of the America Online departments on the What's Hot screen. These include: Clubs & Interests, Computing, Education, Entertainment, Internet Connection, Marketplace, Newsstand, Personal Finance, Reference Desk, Sports, Today's News, and Travel.

Companies can also place a Web link on America Online's World Wide Web home page. The rate for this connection is $45,000, with 8.5 million guaranteed page views. The link runs for four weeks and companies receive a "traffic" report at the end of the period. In addition, America Online's Web site has an

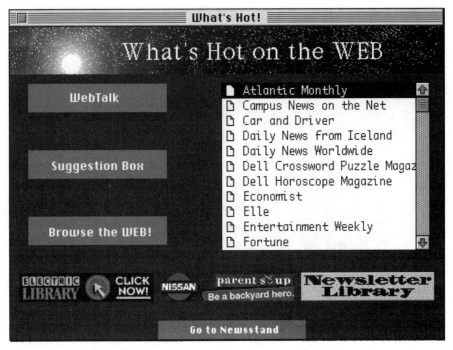

Figure 9.11   What's Hot page with three Web links.

Explore screen; the rate for a link on this screen is $30,000 for four weeks, with 1.5 million guaranteed page views. Likewise, a link on the What's Hot Internet Web site costs $9,000 for four weeks with 300,000 guaranteed page views. Both these options include an online traffic report at the end of the four weeks.

Classified Online

America Online Classifieds Online is a free service to members. Companies and individuals can also create their own home pages for the Web on America Online free of charge (Figure 9.12). Classifieds Online has a multimedia-style user interface and offers a variety of flea-market "swap and sell" bulletin boards, plus links to shipping vendors and related areas of interest across America Online. Unlike the other services, which charge users fees for posting their basic classifieds, there is no cost to members. A chat area is also included, in which members can have real-time discussions with other flea-market participants. Scheduled online discussions cover topics ranging from the best ways to assemble computer systems via the online channel to techniques for safe online buying and selling. AOL's Classifieds Online has the most active virtual flea market of the three major services, with tens of thousands of new ads posted every

Figure 9.12 AOL Classifieds Online.

week. Table 9.3 describes the eight clickable categories: Business, Collectibles, Computers, Employment, General, Habitats, People, and Vehicles.

There are no hidden charges for Classifieds Online; only regular AOL fees apply. America Online asks only that members abide by three guidelines:

- Ads should be posted only to folders that specifically match what is being advertised. (Just because people who buy cars might also be interested in buying a computer doesn't mean that the computer dealers should be listed in the vehicles folder.)
- Members may post a maximum of three different ads for three different items per folder per day in all folders of the Classifieds. Message folders are filled when they have 500 messages, and are reset each morning by 11:00 A.M. EST to the newest 300, leaving room for only 200 new ads per folder per day.
- Only ads should be posted in ad folders. All non-ad discussion postings should be posted to the Trading Talk area, which has been designed especially for that purpose.

There is a step-by-step procedure for posting new ads in Classifieds Online plus Safe Buy/Sell Guidelines. In addition, there are several shipping companies that will deliver parcels: United Parcel Service, Federal Express, the U.S. Postal Service, and Airborne Express. Some of these offer COD services to individual customers or small companies that ship often each month.

TABLE 9.3 Classified Advertising Categories

Category	Description
Business	Job offerings from various professional services, plus ads for investing, money management, consumer services, etc.
Collectibles	For buying and selling collector's items, from antiques to baseball cards.
Computers	For buying and selling computer-related products.
Employment	Job listings and related resources.
General	For locating items such as electronics, airplane tickets, books, pets, recipes, travel items, athletic gear, etc.
Habitats	For searching and listing available housing and furnishings.
People	For finding others, organizing reunions, placing people-to-people ads, plus a link to AOL's Romance Connection
Vehicles	Listings of cars, airplanes, boats, bikes, motorcycles, and accessories.

For companies that do not need access to the entire America Online community, AOL has initiated a new program called Digital City. This is similar to an affiliate program, and it organizes the classifieds by local area. Currently, there are three digital cities: Digital City Washington, Digital City London, and Digital City Boston.

Judy Tashbook states:

America Online wants to empower its members to become publishers; one of the hallmarks of cyberspace is that it's democratic. The idea is that anybody who knows how to program or design can have as gorgeous a home page as McDonald's; and if you're not very technologically adept, you can use our template, which is suited to a lot of people at this time. You don't have to know any HTML programming; members can just type in anything they want and create links to other home pages all over the Web. It just costs them the time on America Online.

People now have business cards that have a phone number, street address, fax numbers, and now e-mail addresses. In the same way that consumers have many ways of being reached, so do companies, and that's why so many are interested in exploring interactive advertising. . . . Whether it's going to be a classified ad or posting a message board or a very full site, like something in the Marketplace, this has become an important address.

CompuServe

In 1980, CompuServe became a wholly owned subsidiary of H&R Block, a diversified services company that is the world's leader in tax preparation and online information services. Since its introduction in 1984, CompuServe has become a leading worldwide provider of online information services for personal computer users, focusing primarily in the early days on business professionals, and extending its reach to a more general consumer audience over the past few years. Since 1994, CompuServe Information Service has remained one of the largest consumer online services with more than 4.7 million members, representing 150 countries and gaining nearly 60,000 new subscribers per month. The wealth of information available on CompuServe draws a large and diverse group of consumers. Keith Arnold, manager of Interactive Merchandising and Marketing states, "The CompuServe Information Service (CIS) is the oldest of the online services, so we are basically the grandparent of this industry. We are definitely the grandparent of content. We have aggregated a great deal more content than the other services, and definitely more business content."

Service Features

CompuServe was designed for instantaneous communication and information retrieval in the home or office (Figure 9.13). The service employs its own proprietary applications and operating system software and is one of the most efficient environments in the online industry.

Member Programs and Fees

CIS members pay a monthly fee of $9.95 for unlimited connect time access to more than 120 basic services in categories such as electronic mail, travel, shopping, investment, and games. Members also receive three free hours of Internet access with this flat monthly rate. Additional hours of Internet use are billed at $2.50 per hour, although members can participate in an Internet Club, which offers 20 hours of access to the Internet for a $15 monthly fee in addition to the basic monthly rate. Additional hours after the 20 for Internet Club members are billed at $1.95 per hour.

In addition to the basic group of services are the Extended Services, such as CompuServe's forums; they can be accessed for connect rates of $4.80 per hour for all baud rates up to and including 28.8 kilobits per second. About 10 percent of CompuServe's 3,000 online areas include Premium Services, which are usually made available by providers outside of CompuServe and are linked seamlessly. These charges are the same as the Extended Service rates.

International Reach and Multilingual Technology

CompuServe is one of the world's premier online information and network communications services, and it employs approximately 2,400 associates world-

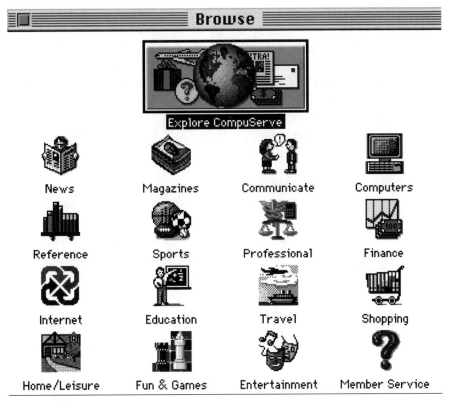

Figure 9.13 CompuServe main menu.

wide with headquarters in Columbus, Ohio. It also has offices in 29 other cities and offers customer service and support in more than 16 countries. CompuServe has affiliate relationships in Argentina, Australia, Chile, Hong Kong, Hungary, Israel, Mexico, New Zealand, South Africa, South Korea, Taiwan and Venezuela. It is the only information service that currently offers more than 100 local market products representing seven languages. CompuServe also provides a broad variety of services targeted to members in Canada and the United Kingdom, including computing support forums, business and financial information, and local weather, news, and sports. German-language services include a number of support forums sponsored by leading computer hardware and software vendors, such as Lotus, Microsoft, and Borland.

In addition to providing local language services, CompuServe offers the World Community Forum which is multilingual and makes use of machine translation technology to expand global communication. By utilizing automated translation software, the forum allows members worldwide to discuss news and politics, culture, dining, sports, and recreation in a common language. Four parallel versions of the forum exist today, with a home language of either English, French, German, or Spanish. Messages written in French, German, or Spanish are picked up and automatically translated into English. Members participating in the English forum have their messages automatically converted to French, German, or Spanish and posted in the appropriate location. This language translation capability also will be available via electronic mail before the end of '96.

One of the Largest Electronic Mail Systems

CompuServe has one of the world's largest electronic mail systems, with millions of mailboxes and 120 million messages sent on a yearly basis. More than 2 million messages per month are exchanged over the Internet, and tens of thousands of messages are exchanged each month between CompuServe and other commercial online/mail services.

Internet Access

Besides becoming the first major online information service to offer electronic mail exchange via the Internet, in March 1994 CompuServe announced its inbound access from the Internet. This ability to telnet from the Internet eliminated the need for a separate modem connection, and for some members, the need to dial long distance to reach CompuServe's network. CompuServe published its World Wide Web home page in May 1994, where Internet users who had not yet joined could find out more about the service.

USENET newsgroups were made available to CompuServe members in August 1994, and this access provided them with thousands of discussion groups. In April 1995, CompuServe announced a direct Internet connection open to any software or operating system using Point-to-Point Protocol from its service. This provided CompuServe's members with access to the Internet with unprecedented ease of use.

Premier Information Provider

One the most popular features on CompuServe is its forums. CompuServe offers over 1,320 forums on such diverse topics as humor, rock music, auto racing, and science fiction. Especially well-attended forums are devoted to a particular profession such as law or medicine, or to a specific personal computer product. Periodically, CompuServe hosts live, online conferences that feature distinguished guest speakers from both the entertainment and intellectual circles. The forums bring together literally thousands of members sharing ideas and information at one time.

Forum participants communicate either by posting messages on the electronic bulletin boards or by participating in live conferences. CompuServe provides libraries of downloadable software and information files for members, which include a comprehensive collection of public domain software and shareware. More than 1,000 computer hardware and software companies offer direct customer support on CompuServe forums, some of which are described here; more are listed in Table 9.4.

TABLE 9.4 Sample Forums on CompuServe

Categories and their Forum	
General	Hobbies & Interests (*Cont*)
Bacchus Wine & Beer Forum	Book Preview Forum
Cooks Online	Comics/Animation Forum
Consumer Forum	Crafts Forum
Consumer Electronics Forum	Dinosaur Forum
Family Handyman Forum	Dogs & Cats Forum
Homing Instinct Forum	Encounters Forum
Gardening Forum	Genealogy Forum
Time Warner Dwellings Forum	Issues Forum
Vegetarian Forum	Literary Forum
Under the Hood	Living History Forum
Automobile Forum	Mensa Forum
Automobile Information Center	Military Forum
Automobile Live	Model Aviation Forum
Automobile Magazine Forum	Pets Forum
Auto Vantage	Pet Product Forum
Cadillac Showroom	Photography Forum
Lincoln/Mercury Showroom	Outdoor Forum
Motorweek Online	Sailing Forum
New Car Showroom	Scuba Forum
Hobbies & Interests	Seniors Forum
AARP Forum	SF/Fantasy Literature Forum
African-American Forum	Space Exploration Forum
Animal Forum	Sport Illustrated Forum
Astronomy Forum	The Weather Channel Forum
Aquaria/Fish Forum	Trading Card Forum

- IBMNet is a group of forums designed for users of IBM PCs and compatibles, including IBM New Users, Hardware, Applications, Systems/Utilities, Programming, Communications, and Bulletin Boards.
- The Investor's Forum is an ideal place to share opinions on the direction of the stock market, learn more about all types of investments, and retrieve software that can assist with individual portfolios.
- The World Community Forum uses automated translation software and allows CompuServe members to communicate in other languages. This particular forum has areas where participants can discuss a wide array of topics such as world news, global politics, culture, travel, international cuisine, sports, and recreation.

CB Simulator   CompuServe has a very interesting service called CB Simulator. By "tuning in" to any of CB's three bands, members can chat electronically with others across the globe via "live" online dialogue. A diverse and sociable group of people can be found conversing on the 108 CB channels at anytime of the day or night. Although CB has practical applications, such as business conferences, most members log on to chat with old friends and to make new ones.

Beyond the forums CompuServe has several distinct areas that contain a wealth of information. These areas include Entertainment, Travel, Medical and Health Care Information, Investments, Small Business, Marketing, and Journalism.

Entertainment Drive   In terms of entertainment, one of CompuServe's newer features is Entertainment Drive. This is a global interactive entertainment magazine designed to encourage dialog among studios, networks, production companies, and entertainers. It also offers CompuServe members a chance to meet others in the industry (via interviews) and discuss aspects of the entertainment business. News releases, production notes, downloadable publicity photos, biographies, and behind-the-scenes information are available. Some of the interviews included on CompuServe are Home Improvement's Tim Allen, Oscar winner Marisa Tomei, Billy Crystal, TV's Superman Dean Cain, and horror movie director John Carpenter.

A complementary service is called Youth Drive, which is a children's version of Entertainment Drive. It provides downloadable files that include cartoon stills, photos and biographies of favorite teen stars, and the hottest games. There is an online entertainment database called Eliot Stein's Hollywood Hotline, where you can find Academy Award, Tony, and Grammy winners from the last several decades and TV schedules from as far back as 1948!

Travel Services   CompuServe's consumer reservation services include WORDSPAN's Travelshopper, EAASY SABRE, and the Official Airline Guide

Travel Service. Each offers 24-hour online rate and schedule information and reservation capabilities for more than 750 airlines worldwide. In addition to flight rates and schedules, EAASY SABRE offers hotel and car rental reservation capabilities. All three services enable members to order tickets online. When travelers elect to have tickets sent by mail or overnight delivery, credit cards are accepted for payment. The Zagat Restaurant Survey, which is searchable by restaurant name, location, or type of cuisine and price, features thousands of reviews of restaurants in more than 20 U.S. cities. International information gives regularly updated advice on visas, immigration laws, political environments, and hotel/motel availability.

Also found on CompuServe is MAGELLAN Geographix, which delivers information-rich maps detailing the seven continents of the world. Expert geographers, cartographers, computer specialists, graphic artists, editors, and map sourcing experts create the maps.

Financial Services Since 1974, CompuServe has provided extensive financial data to Wall Street brokerage firms and other financial institutions. A wide range of investment data is available on stocks, mutual funds, bonds, options, commodities, and the money market, along with other information services, and online databases. "CompuServe is part of the expanded information spectrum available to investors in today's electronic society," said Scott Gerber, CompuServe's financial services product manager. "Our members have 24-hour-a-day access to critical data when sorting through potential investments, looking up specific companies, and researching hot tips. They're taking control of their investment decision-making process. Once users have formed an investment game plan, the service offers a number of ways to put their decisions into action and monitor the results."

FundWatch Online by *Money Magazine* provides screening of more than 4,700 mutual funds by investment objective, performance versus the market of other funds, rate-of-return, load fees, expenses, dividend yields, and so forth. Investors interested in the leverage that options provide can price puts and calls for option contracts.

Income-oriented investors can get information on bonds, including maturity dates, coupon data, current yield, and price. Ratings from Moody's and Standard & Poor's are also available. Futures can be tracked daily, and price quotes go back more than 10 years. Besides giving investors the information, an online discount broker, Quick & Reilly, and deep-discounter E*TRADE Securities, Inc. provide timely and accurate trading of stock and options for members, 24 hours a day.

Business Services Entrepreneurs and small business owners can find a wealth of resources on CompuServe. They include:

• Biz*File, a yellow pages-style information source on more than 10 million North American businesses, searchable by geographic area, type of business, or name.

• Business Database Plus, which offers more than 500 full-text articles from publications including *Business America, Business Journal, Forbes, Nation's Business,* and hundreds of industry trade publications.

• Classified advertising, which allows members to advertise or respond to ads for employment/education, computers and software, business services, investments, and travel.

• Entrepreneur's Small Business Forum, which offers an information exchange for small business owners on topics including startup, marketing/promotion, financing, resources, management, planning, legal issues, franchising, international business, and home-based businesses.

Services for Journalists   The Journalism Forum offers professional and freelance writers a variety of services and libraries in the radio, TV, print, science, and business arenas. There are job listings, ethics discussions, Business News, and online newsletters. There is information on freelance opportunities, equipment exchanges, commentary, and a listing of names and phone numbers of proven resources.

The Electronic Mall

In 1984, CompuServe created The Electronic Mall. Previously, the concept of home shopping with a personal computer was virtually unknown. At first, many members were wary of buying items that they couldn't see or try out, and they tended to restrict their early purchases to items such as books or computer software. Today, however, CompuServe members shop for items such as fine art, professional-quality fitness equipment, and gourmet food, and sales are at an all-time high. Part of this is due to the fact that there is broader consumer acceptance of home shopping, which has resulted in the growth across many categories of direct marketing, including catalogue, direct mail and 800-number telephone ordering.

"In many ways, electronic shopping is the ideal medium for the '90s, from both the merchant and the consumer point of view," states Regina Brady, CompuServe's director of Customer Promotion. "Consumers, particularly those who work full time, appreciate the sheer convenience of being able to sit down at their computers, at any time of the day or night, and order top-quality merchandise from well-known retailers." As for merchants, Brady says services like The Electronic Mall help them to target their advertising dollars to an upscale audience and build stronger relationships with their consumers through interactive communications.

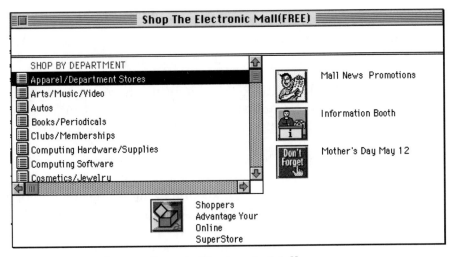

Figure 9.14   CompuServe's Electronic Mall screen.

The Mall has more than 160 merchants that range from Lands' End and JC Penney to specialty stores selling gourmet food, consumer electronics, pharmaceuticals, pet supplies, and much more (Figure 9.14).

Mall categories include: Apparel, Arts/Music/Video, Books/Periodicals, Clubs/Memberships, Computer Software, Gifts/Flowers/Gourmet Foods, Hobbies/Toys/Pets; Housewares, Sports/Fitness/Health, and others. Following is a partial list of companies that have stores on the CompuServe mall.

Adventures in Food	HarperCollins Online
Americana Cooking	Health & Vitamin Express
BMG Compact Disk Club	Honey Baked Hams
Book of the Month Club	Iams Dog and Cat Foods
Bose Express Music	JC Penney Online
Chef's Catalog	L'Eggs Hanes Bali Playtex Outlet
Coffee Anyone?	Lands' End
Colonial Video & Audio	New Country Music
Columbia House Music	Omaha Steaks
Contact Lens Supply	Patagonia
Critics Choice Video	Paul Frederick Skirt Co.
FTD Online	SDV Vitamins
Florida Fruit Shippers	Sears

Flower Stop	800-FLOWER & Gift Shoppe
Green Mountain Coffee Roaster	The Metropolitan Museum of Art
Hammacher Schlemmer	Zbest Electronics

The Mall is also available on CD-ROM, providing shoppers the opportunity to add audio, video, and animation to the experience (Figure 9.15). The CompuServe CD-ROM program was created in 1994 to encourage multimedia publishers to integrate access to the CompuServe Information Service into their CD-ROMs. In turn, the company launched CompuServeCD, a bimonthly multimedia title that highlights areas on the service as well as featuring its merchants. The CD is organized into six sections, including Technology and Trends, Entertainment, Personal Enterprise, Home and Leisure, and Shopping and Member Services. Comparison shopping is easy, and items are simple to locate. To make a purchase, members complete a short online order form and receive a confirmation number. Most merchants offer express delivery (within 72 hours).

Figure 9.15   The CompuServe Mall CD-ROM.

A subscription to *CompuServeCD* is priced at $7.95 per issue with a $5 dollar online credit per disk. CompuServe sends a full-color illustrated guide to the Mall to all members monthly as a supplement to *CompuServe Magazine*. This guide announces new merchants, alerts members to contests and special promotions, and includes photographs and descriptions of several featured items.

Despite the recession of the past few years, sales on the Mall have continued to grow. The number of member accesses increased over 75 percent during the last year, with the number of orders placed rising by over 45 percent. CompuServe, the pioneer in the concept of online direct marketing has also opened its collection of retail "storefronts" to the World Wide Web.

CompuServe—A Marketing Partner

CompuServe is like a big cosmopolitan city that never sleeps. People go there to work, plan, and research, or just shop. On CompuServe, they can catch up on the news, check investments, and answer and send messages to other members. The online lifestyle of this big "city" is attractive to a well-educated, well-informed and affluent group of consumers, and therefore makes it a very viable market for any merchant or vendor.

CompuServe members take home an average annual household income of $90,340, and they are the first to spend it on technology, high-quality products, personal and professional services:

95 percent attended college

72 percent are college graduates

90+ percent are professionals—managers, executives, and proprietors

92 percent buy from catalogues, direct mail, or TV

50+ percent belong to a frequent flyer club

43 percent have children

CompuServe members buy sporting goods, spend money on software for their homes, and own CD players. In short, they are the type of people who are computer-savvy and use online resources for business and purchasing.

The Metropolitan Museum of Art claims that CompuServe is almost always the source of its highest average orders, and in the museum's second year online, sales increased by approximately 300 percent. Simmons Market Research Bureau reports that households like those of CompuServe members respond better to direct marketing efforts. The survey and research firm, Erdos & Morgan, found that, as mentioned, over 92 percent of CompuServe members ordered merchandise from direct response marketers in '95 with the average Electronic Mall shopper spending $65 to $70 per sale.

The Fragrance Counter, an Electronic Mall specialty store that provides a selection of designer fragrances and cosmetics, advertises on several online venues, and feels that CompuServe's demographics are especially appropriate for the company's customer base, and that the Mall is a very cost-effective way to reach an extremely broad audience. Eli Katz, vice president of Sales and Marketing, states, "You can't beat the online medium for getting your feet wet, because to produce a 16-page catalogue in full color and mail it out to millions of people would far exceed what it costs to set up and maintain our online presence."

CompuServe offers customized 12-month plans that give merchants the following:

- Space to display products, with full descriptions, electronically.
- Opportunities to participate in various mall-wide promotions.
- Availability of store updates twice a month to those advertisers that supply copy in electronic format.
- Two store rebuilds per year.
- A complimentary user ID for CompuServe and 20 hours of free connect time per month.
- Coverage, where appropriate, in The Electronic Mall monthly print catalogue.

These features are packaged in four separate plans as detailed in Tables 9.5 through 9.8. Each plan is suited for a different level of advertiser commitment with some incentive to also advertise in *CompuServe Magazine* and *Compu-ServeCD*.

CompuServe encourages its merchants to participate in all of its advertising mediums such as the magazine or CD. The CD has a distribution rate of over 1.2 million, and the magazine is received by over 2 million members worldwide. Keith Arnold, CompuServe's manager of Interactive Merchandising and Marketing said, "CompuServe is the only online or Internet service that gives you the option to blend multimedia with online." Table 9.9 lists advertising rates for CompuServe magazine.

CompuServe feels that its magazine readers find the articles pertinent, because they include product reviews and industry news. Statistically, members spend nearly one hour with the magazine each month with over half of these members referring to an issue more than once. In terms of the CD, approximately 40 percent of the members have CD-ROM drives and sound boards, and utilize the CD's full capabilities; and that statistic is quickly rising. Therefore, when planning a marketing campaign on CompuServe, a media mix will pro-

TABLE 9.5 Minimum Level of Participation—Direct Marketers and Retailers

Annual fee	$50,000 + 2% of sales
Maximum number of products or screens	250
Minimum credit for advertising in *CompuServe Magazine*	$15,000
Number of online graphics if supplied in prescribed format	unlimited
Credit toward sponsorship of content	$10,000
Electronic Mall marquees	12
Kiosk (up to five screens); one issue of *CompuServe CD*	1

TABLE 9.6 Minimum Level of Participation—Advertisers

Annual fee	$50,000 + 2% of sales
Maximum number of products or screens	150
Minimum credit for advertising in *CompuServe Magazine*	$15,000
Number of online graphics if supplied in prescribed format	unlimited
Credit toward sponsorship of content	$15,000
Electronic Mall marquees	12
Credit toward advertising on CompuServeCD	$5,000

TABLE 9.7 Advanced Merchandiser Package—Direct Marketers and Retailers

Annual fee	$120,000 + 2% of sales
Maximum number of products or screens	1,000
Minimum credit for advertising in *CompuServe Magazine*	$30,000
Number of online graphics if supplied in prescribed format	unlimited
Credit toward sponsorship of content	$20,000
Electronic Mall marquees	26
Credit toward advertising on CompuServeCD	$15,000

TABLE 9.8 Advanced Advertiser Package—Advertisers

Annual fee	$120,000 + 2% of sales
Maximum number of products or screens	250
Minimum credit for advertising in *CompuServe Magazine*	$30,000
Number of online graphics if supplied in prescribed format	unlimited
Credit toward sponsorship of content	$40,000
Electronic Mall marquees	26
Credit toward advertising on CompuServeCD	$15,000

TABLE 9.9 CompuServe Magazine Advertising Rates

Ad Type	1×	3×	6×
Full Page	$13,000	$12,090	$10,925
⅔ Page	11,700	10,940	9,885
½ Island	10,140	8,575	7,675
½ Horiz	8,330	7,800	7,025
⅓ Page	6,380	5,985	5,465
¼ Page	4,815	4,550	4,160
⅙ Page	3,780	3,515	3,125

vide the most effective coverage. Ideally, that should include the magazine and CD-ROM, along with an online presence in the Mall and all appropriate forums.

CompuServe advertisers can also create downloadable catalogues of their goods for a yearly rate of $1,500, but catalogues have to be less than 50,000 bytes in size. Advertisers can also place software for free downloading in the Mall, where it is priced on a resource-used basis (based on file size). The annual rate for one download area is $3,000 plus $500 per 100,000 byte increments over an initial allowance of 750,000 bytes.

Beyond the bits and bytes advertisers can also conduct online surveys of their customers and offer usage credits to members that generate traffic in their stores. Usage credits come in $5 increments. Mailing lists of active, paying CompuServe members are also available to rent. These may be requested with highly targeted specifications for a particular advertising campaign.

One other option that an advertiser, especially a computer software or hardware manufacturer, should not overlook is the possibility of sponsoring a forum. The forum support area can be not only a great public relations tool for a company, but can also meet the immediate needs of customers. CompuServe, as mentioned earlier, has supported the online community of manufacturers of computer hardware, software, peripherals, and programming applications since 1979. Today, there are over 1,000 companies that rely on the forum for electronic support. With a forum, customers can search for information and get answers to their questions without waiting for telephone support, which also reduces the load on the phone services.

Forum sponsors have three tools: a message board, library, and conference room. The library is key because it can include product specification sheets, press releases, product upgrades, patches, documentation, commonly asked questions, customer success stories, demonstration software, graphic images, and sound and video clips. Message boards provide an opportunity to build rapport with customers, and conference rooms enable people to talk online, like a conference call. Whether the conference is impromptu or scheduled, it is both easy and economical to service prospective and current customers in this way. And today, when customer service is often the distinguishing factor between vendors, sponsoring a forum is a viable opportunity to demonstrate responsive customer care.

What makes forum sponsorship even more attractive is that there is virtually no cost required to put up a forum. "Basically, it's a revenue-sharing arrangement in which the people who host the forums share in the connect time revenue they generate," states Keith Arnold of CompuServe. However, "We control what forums go online, so it's not just a matter of running with any idea."

The money generated in consumer connect time while participating in a forum should not be considered a new profit center for sponsoring companies, but more a new source of revenue to complement what they are already doing. The hidden cost is the maintenance of the forum. Although it is easy to put up a forum, it does require maintaining the information, answering the messages, and corresponding daily with the consumer—not doing so would be detrimental to the overall marketing strategy, since the purpose is to serve and attract customers. Receiving some revenue relief through a program such as this really is just to offset the overall cost of maintaining it; the public relations benefits, for most companies, far outweigh the investment.

CompuServe has found that many companies that put up their own Web sites in an effort to create the same type of public relations/customer service effectiveness are not as successful as with forums. CompuServe helps to organize the Internet, and makes it a consumer application. In addition, CompuServe adds promotions and other events around Web sites that help advertisers or vendors build a bigger and better presence that can really have an impact. Keith Arnold of CompuServe states, "Just jumping around from page to page isn't going to make someone appreciate [being] online very much. Once we can get them into a community and communicating, that's when people become attached to the service and have a reason to come back."

WOW!

In March 1996, CompuServe launched its first family-based online service for home use, called WOW! The service licensed the Lycos cyberguide, the World Wide Web search engine that makes finding information on the Internet fast and efficient. (The service is available for Windows '95 users only.) "WOW! gives busy families an online service that is powerful, fast, and worry-free," said Scott Kauffman, vice president of CompuServe Consumer Markets, and general manager of WOW!. "Incorporating features from Lycos and Point helps our members quickly find high-quality information on the topics they choose, regardless of where the information resides—on the Internet or WOW!."

WOW! offers families access to a complete range of services from customized page views for adults and children, a very easy-to-use e-mail interface, multimedia with sound and motion, and seamless Internet travel. From any location within WOW!, access to the Internet is instantly available. And the Lycos engine can do category searches for Web sites and provide comprehensive content descriptions. Advertising packages are also available on WOW!.

CompuServe clearly offers diverse and content-rich services for both the consumer and the marketer. The service is constantly upgrading and broadening its scope of offerings. By the time this book is published, many more advertising options will be available, and technology upgrades will have improved and expanded the business and personal resources. Implementing a mix of promotional media packages leads to the greatest potential for success in the electronic marketplace. However, the most important aspect of any offering is the care of the consumer relationship once a connection has been made.

Prodigy

Prodigy is the country's largest dial-up access provider to the World Wide Web, and it was the first major online service with a link to this fast-growing area of the Internet. Although Prodigy currently trails CompuServe and America Online in membership, (Prodigy: 2 million, CompuServe: 4.5 million and AOL: 5 million), its change in ownership in May 1996, could also mean a change in membership numbers in 1997.

The three major commercial services offer the same basic fare, but each has its own image and appeal. CompuServe is considered to be the most business-oriented and global of the three, America Online offers a real sense of community, and Prodigy is the biggest Web site in the world. It offers the easiest and most reliable access to the Internet, and its Web browser is available to all members who have Windows-equipped computers (Figure 9.16). Members can also store their own personal Web pages on Prodigy. The service is designed 100 percent in the language of the Web. It is available at 2400, 9600, and 14,400 baud (modem speed), and is now being tested for 28,800 bps and ISDN services.

Prodigy information is well organized, catalogued, and very easy to access. Members can surf the Web by subject, point-and-click "hot lists" for storing and referencing favorite pages, and access software that makes screen capture as easy as saving a file. The Web browser also has special access controls, so parents can decide what to give their children access to on the Web. All USENET newsgroups are available through an easy newsreader service, and members can exchange e-mail-downloadable files online with anyone on the Internet. In addition, there are some 1,000 online bulletin board services (BBS), which generate 75,000 postings daily.

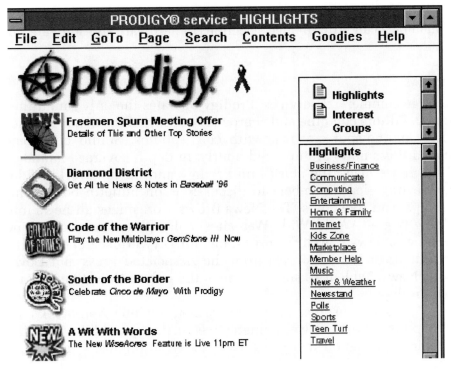

Figure 9.16 Prodigy main menu.

Prodigy intends to position itself as a content distributor, instead of a publisher, by relinquishing all of the in-house content creation and production to its third-party content partners. And while it plans to maintain its prominence as a family-oriented service, it also will expand its content offerings to attract a younger audience as well as business professionals.

Prodigy Services

Prodigy offers a range of informational and interactive features, including Computing, News & Weather, Homework Helper, Reference Databases, Financial Information, Investor Information, Small Business Information, Travel Services, Chat, Bulletin Boards, Sports, Kids features, Shopping, and Television.

Prodigy's Computing section affords members access to a broad range of computing news and resources. Features include, Living Digital, a Web-based magazine about the digital generation, the world of computing, multimedia, and cyberculture; downloadable libraries with thousands of programs from Ziff-Davis, C/Net, and other sources; Chatzone, a place to share thoughts and chat with the computer world's movers and shakers; and Computing Marketplace, where members can browse huge selections of hardware and software from top merchants.

24-Hour News

Of the three commercial services, Prodigy operates the only round-the-clock newsroom. Editors combine and sharpen reports from the major wire services to deliver on-the-spot coverage with color photos. Sound clips featuring Associated Press news are updated hourly. In-depth coverage includes links to related news magazine stories on Prodigy and on the World Wide Web. Interactive links lead members to discussions on bulletin boards, Internet newsgroups, and live chats. The News Browser organizes all news into files containing related World Wide Web sites, color photos, and magazine articles. Prodigy's news search features allow for keyword searches of all newsroom content, including stories from the Associated Press and Dow Jones Company News. Table 9.10 shows some of the publications that are available through Prodigy.

Prodigy's major consumer magazine partners include *Newsweek* and *Consumer Reports.* The Newsweek Interactive section provides a sophisticated multimedia presentation that gives users access to photos, sound and audio, graphics and text. *Consumer Reports* is a text-based section that lets users retrieve the latest product reviews and search archives by topic.

Homework Helper

Prodigy offers a search tool called Homework Helper that reviews more than 700 reference works including Compton's NewMedia, hundreds of newspapers and magazines, and television and radio stories. Students can launch a comprehensive search that encompasses over 100 newspapers, 500 magazines, plus atlases, major literary works, textbooks, 300 maps, and 1,500 pictures. In addition to these resources, Prodigy offers a variety of reference databases.

Consumer Reports helps members find information about thousands of products. Company News makes it easy to follow the fortunes of corporations around the world by organizing breaking stories according to company, industry, and news categories. ZD Net offers the latest in computer news, online editions of *PC Magazine, PC Week, Computer Life, Computer Shopper;* and the ZD Net Shareware Club that gives members access to the best shareware programs available.

Travel, Dining, and Entertainment Reference

City Guides on Prodigy tell members about events and activities in their cities. The service also offers expert columns with tips on family and business travel.

TABLE 9.10   Sampling of Newspapers and Magazines on Prodigy

Newspapers	Newspapers accessible through Prodigy on the Web	Magazines on Prodigy and Web Exclusives
Access Atlanta	Boston Globe	American Heritage
Gateway Virginia	Christian Science Monitor	Consumer Reports
Houston Chronicle	Daily Telegraphy (UK)	US News & World Report
Interactive	Detroit News	Newsweek Interactive
Newsday Direct	Miami Herald	PC World
Rhode Island Horizons	The New York Times	Playbill
SportsDay (Dallas, TX)	Newsday	Total TV
TampaBay Online	Philadelphia Inquirer	ZD Net
Los Angeles Times	San Diego Daily	Advertising Age
The Dallas Morning News	Transcript	George
Milwaukee Journal-Sentinel	San Francisco Chronicle	Bon Appetit
The Providence Journal	San Jose Mercury News	Sports Illustrated
	USA Today	Car & Driver
	The Wall Street Journal	Elle

The Flyer's Edge feature compares the frequent traveler programs, and EAASY SABRE is available for airline, hotel, and car reservations.

The Mobile Travel Guide is an easily searchable format with extensive information on restaurants, lodging, and vacation attractions in more than 3,000 recreation areas throughout the United States and Canada. The Zagat Restaurant Guide, which is based on extensive surveys of restaurants across the country, allows members to search the listings of restaurants based on their personal preferences in more than 25 cities or regions. The Movie Guide serves up film facts and more than 13,000 reviews of movies and new films.

Shopping

Prodigy's Marketplace includes several major catalogue merchants such as Hammacher Schlemmer, OfficeMax, Sears Shop at Home, and the Home Shopping Network (which alone offers over 1,000 products), along with smaller vendors selling everything from clothes and perfume to computers and cars.

Finance and Business

Prodigy provides 15-minute delay stock quotes and charts of the key economic indicators, updated throughout each day. Dow Jones Company News offers 21 days worth of past and present articles on publicly traded companies. In the Investment Center, members can use the research components including Strategic Investor, a powerful package enabling members to screen, select, and evaluate over 6,000 stocks and mutual funds. The PC Financial Network enables members to place orders to trade day and night in absolute privacy with the largest online discount brokerage service. Overall, the PC Financial Network has assisted in over 1.5 million trades on Prodigy.

Overall, Prodigy's campaign to attract small business owners and work-at-home professionals has been very successful. About 770,000, or 35 percent of Prodigy's 2 million-plus members, are small business owners.

Bulletin Boards

There are more than 1,000 Prodigy bulletin board topics on everything from archaeology to zoology. Prodigy also hosts interest groups, specialized sites that combine editorial content with interactive communications to link to related Web pages. Interest group sites are hosted by moderators who are passionate about their areas or are experts in the field. They maintain the editorial content of the interest groups, as well as ensure fresh and reliable links to related Web pages, USENET newsgroups, bulletin boards, and chat rooms.

Prodigy offers real-time chats on hundreds of topics, along with online chat "stadiums" that accommodate thousands of participants, and feature many celebrity guests, such as Aerosmith, Cybill Shepard, and even Santa Claus! There are also public and private, password-protected chat rooms available, which exist only as long as they are in use. Messages sent in a chat room are displayed in real time, and unlike on bulletin boards or in e-mail, members in chat rooms "talk" in brief sentences and await responses from others. The following partial list of Prodigy interest groups illustrates their range.

Accountants	Adoption	Adventure Traveler
Air Travel Unlimited	Alternative Medicine	America
Ancient Egypt Connection	Antiques & Collecting	Art & Technology
Artists Resource	Auto Racing	Automotive
Baseball	Basketball	Beer
Bicycling	Bipolar Disorder	Birding
Black Experience	Books	Boxing
Capitol Watch	Career Connections	Central States
Chocolate	Civil War	Classical Music
Coins	College Search	College Viewpoint
Comedy	Comics	Computer Programming
Computer Virus Help	Consumer Electronics	Contemporary Christian Music
Crafts	Creative Minds	Dads
Day Care	Disco Biscuit	Distance Learning
Early Child Education	Education K-12	Elder Care
Environment	Equestrian	Fashion

Feminism	Flyfishing	Food
Football Foreign	Language Concourse	Freebies Mall
French	Games	Gardening
Gay & Lesbian	Genealogy	Generation X
Girl Scouts	Go! Poetry	Golf
Gospel Music	Grief, Loss, & Recovery	Health & Fitness
HIV/AIDS	Hockey	Holiday Fun
Home Inspection	Homelife Pursuits	Homeschooling
Horse Racing	Housewives Club	Information Highway
Intergalactic Complaint Dept.	Internet Help	Investing
Jazz Kid's Money	Kool Kids	Latin America
Legal	Life Aid	Local BBS
Manners	Medical Center	Mid-Atlantic States
MIDI/Computer Music	Military & Veterans	Motorcycles
Movies	Musicians Resource	Mutual Funds
Native American	New Artist Spotlight	Northeast States
Old Car Garage	Olympics	Pacific & Southwest States
Paintball	Parenting	PC Network
Personal Connections	Pets on the Net	Philippines
Photography	Planet Teenager	Power Boating
Pregnancy	Psychology	Puppetry

Prodigy has educational and entertainment areas for children that include Sesame Street. National Geographic, Nickelodeon, NOVA, Pet Care Guide, and lots of games and other attractions. Members can check out program highlights for more than 30 television networks, take special viewer polls, chat with stars and producers online, and download video and sound clips. Networks online include; CBS, HBO, ESPN, CNBC, CNN, Lifetime, and the Comedy Channel.

Prodigy Membership Rates

Prodigy services are available for a membership fee of $9.95 per month for five hours of usage. Additional hours cost $2.95 each, and as many as six household members can use Prodigy under one membership. Members can send unlimited e-mail messages. A value plan, at $14.95 per month, is available for members who have been with the service for at least one month; they are given the first five hours free each month with additional hours charged at $2.95 each. A new 30/30 Internet pricing plan alternatively lets members pay $30/month for 30 hours of usage with additional hours at $2.95 per hour. This new pricing plan rivals other Internet service providers by offering excellent technical support and providing easy Internet access.

Advertising to Prodigy's Audience

The Prodigy audience enjoys cutting-edge technology, and purchases the latest products and services. They are educated, and express their opinions readily. They tend to be very active, and range in age from 18 to 49 years old; half of them are under 34. Most Prodigy users are married and have children. More than one-third are in professional/managerial positions, and almost half earn $75,000 or more per year. Their homes are valued at over $200,000, and they have three or more cars in the garage.

Prodigy consumers love to buy high-tech products such as cellular phones, CD players, video cameras, fax machines, games systems, and pagers. They travel for both business and pleasure, and approximately one-third of them take trips abroad. They listen to music and buy prerecorded audio records, tapes, and CDs much more than the average consumer. On the radio, they listen to adult contemporary and/or progressive road music, and they watch MTV and VH1. They love to entertain at home, and more than half enjoy fine food and drinks with their friends. As noted, most are working parents and thus their apparel ranges from suits and dress shirts to sneakers and jeans. They are investors, and they are most likely to have two times the amount of savings as the national average. These consumers tend to spend approximately $450 dollars a month in credit card purchases, and many made through direct sale venues.

Customized Advertising

Unlike its competitors, from its inception, Prodigy has included online advertising. Currently, however, Prodigy is undergoing a shift in its advertising strategies. Scott Schiller, vice president of Advertising Sales for Prodigy states:

> Prodigy will be moving away from a rate card to a customized media package based on personal needs. Advertisers discuss their marketing objectives with us and we develop content or activities that are consistent with those objectives . . . we work with the advertiser to sell specific products to a targeted customer base, and that is a benefit of working with Prodigy.
>
> We have over 2 million eyeballs that can also be directed to any Web site, and that's something that not a lot of people can do at the moment. We will have levels of pricing that are dependent on the types of packages [advertisers] want. They will consist of icons, banners, and links. How [advertisers] participate is based on the amount of money they want to spend and when they want to spend it. What we are hoping to do is very different from the

past. We want to develop relationships with marketers that can last a long time, that show that we are interested in learning about their product, not just in getting the sale and moving on.

For example, one Prodigy advertising experiment is based on compensation from advertisers on the number of inquiries or logons an advertiser receives rather than a flat fee per advertising screen. The model for this new ad approach is Toyota Interactive, a division of Toyota Motor Sales, which went live in 1994. The Toyota area was designed to ensure quality leads by letting only Toyota owners access the service, via their vehicle identification numbers. The section offers bulletin boards, input from Toyota mechanics about car problems, and full-color graphics of the newest models. Since its debut, Toyota has logged 1,000 requests for brochures.

Schiller states, "The medium is continuing to evolve to serve a number of purposes . . . you can advertise within an online service or on the Web because you want to be exposed there; you can advertise online and at the same time attract interest to your Web site, or you can work with the online service to communicate on a one-to-one relationship with users."

During the changeover period, projected to last through the end of '96, advertisers are given options that are a hybrid between the old Prodigy model, in which a general ad queue rotates through content and contextual advertising appears in certain popular content sections, and the new Prodigy model, in which GIF images (a graphic approximately 2″ × 1″ appear on popular screens and content pages. Table 9.11 details the different levels of involvement.

A single leader ad will rotate through the General Ad Queue, and a GIF ad is placed on selected high-traffic screens. General awareness advertising reaches the entire Prodigy audience, and can link either to sites on the Web or to sites on Prodigy. Premium positions such as Business News, Chat, Headline News, Market Watch, People News, and Sports News are seen by approximately 80 percent of the Prodigy population and can also link to Web sites or sites on Prodigy.

TABLE 9.11   Premium Positions Ad Rates on Prodigy

Product	Standard Price Per Week	Summer Price Per Week	Estimated Entrances Per Week
Business News	$7,500	$6,375	200,000
Chat	10,000	8,500	400,000
Headline News	20,000	17,000	300,000
Market Watch	12,000	10,200	350,000
People News	4,000	3,400	100,000
Sports News	6,000	5,100	150,000

TABLE 9.12   Prodigy Investment Center Ad Rates

Product	Standard Price Per Week	Summer Price Per Week	Estimated Entrances
Quote Track	$28,000	$23,800	1,400,000
Company News	17,500	14,900	700,000
Indicators	12,000	10,200	500,000

Advertisers specifically interested in the Prodigy Investment Center have a couple of options (Table 9.12). This area is viewed by approximately 80 percent of the members and can link to Web sites or sites on Prodigy.

Ad Packages

Prodigy ad packages can include sites on the World Wide Web or sites on the service itself. There is no fee for displaying an ad on the service; however, supplemental fees are charged based on activity levels involving database searches (more than 500 records), and downloading text, demos, video, and clips.

Advertiser's can send e-mail messages directly to targeted members, qualified by age, gender, household composition, geography, and interests. E-mail Direct rates are shown in Table 9.13).

Other Ads

Two types of ads are available on World Wide Web pages viewable exclusively by Prodigy members: banner ads and Marketplace ads (Figure 9.17). All ads are sold on a monthly basis and can link to any site on the Web. Banner ads appear near the top of a Web page right below the header, and they consist of three lines of copy and a clickable logo. The first line of copy identifies the sponsor when the logo is clicked. There is a limit of one banner ad to any page. Marketplace ads are text-only that appear near the bottom of the page. Standard ads consist of the advertiser's name, which is clickable, and up to 180 characters of copy. Table 9.14 describes these ad rates.

TABLE 9.13   E-mail Direct Rates

Mail Fees	Quantity	Cost Per Thousand
Prospect Mailings	20,000–149,999	$350 (35 cents/send)
Prospect Mailings	150,000–249,999	$300 (30 cents/send)
Prospect Mailings	250,000–plus	$250 (25 cents/send)
90-Day Hotline Buyers		$35
180-Day Hotline Buyers		$25
30-Day Direct Response Leads		$35
30-Day E-mail Users		$35
Customer Communications	1,000 and over	$250

Figure 9.17   Prodigy Marketplace example.

Computer Express: A Pioneer in Online Shopping   Computer Express is a computer mail-order company that sells hardware and software to the home and small business user (Figure 9.18). It has been selling online for over 10 years, and currently advertises on Prodigy, CompuServe, America Online, Delphi, E-Word, Interchange, and the Internet. At Computer Express, the company came before the technology. The founder, Philip Shear, a pioneer in online shopping, wrote the original code for the first cybermall, which was then on

TABLE 9.14   Banner and Marketplace Ad Rates

Page	Type of Ad	Price Per Month	Estimated Page Views
Main Home Page	Banner	25,000	2,100,000
Main Home Page	Marketplace	10,000	2,100,000
Search Tools	Banner	10,000	650,000
Interest Group Home Page	Banner	3,000	150,000
Business & Finance Web Site	Banner	1,000	25,000
Interest Groups	Banner	1,000	Varies
Interest Groups	Marketplace	400	Varies
Shopping Home Page	Marketplace	250	17,000

Figure 9.18   Computer Express shopping menu.

The Source in 1984. Computer Express believes that what sets the company apart from others that sell products online is that it specializes in customer support and satisfaction.

Operations Manager David Corman states, "Pricing is not as big an issue as far as being competitive with the other mail order companies as trying to satisfy my customers' needs . . . I get information every single day that I use to change my focus as far as the products that I am selling. Customer feedback has been one of the most valuable benefits of advertising in the online environment."

Computer Express has about 30 employees, and eight of them answer e-mail all day to take care of customer's needs. The company does about $15 million a year in sales. The advantage to selling online for Computer Express is that it can reach millions of computer buyers instantly. Corman states, "We are constantly making upgrades to our stores . . . on the Marketplace we are in the process of putting up graphics for over 5,000 items. We are constantly changing our database in ways to suit the members' and our customer's needs. We are upgrading our graphics to make them flashier and to keep people interested in coming to our site."

Computer Express also maintains its own Internet server and does a lot of cooperative marketing and talking with individuals at different sites over the Internet—linking and promoting its catalogue. Corman explains that in addition to straight sales, the company utilizes e-mail to communicate directly with customers. "I do a monthly e-mail to about 350,000 people. It's not just a selling vehicle; I also talk to them about new products that are coming out. I usually give them tips and hints on how to make the machine go faster or how to use their time online more effectively."

The key to online marketing, according to Corman, is to really take a look at what the end user needs online. "I have seen a lot of people try to sell different things online—contact lenses, seafood . . . you really need to sit back and ask, 'what is the average person online really interested in?' Listen to your customer's needs and the people hitting your sites."

Web Links and the Prodigy Web Browser Prodigy was the first commercial service to develop and freely release a Web browser, and since then, as noted earlier, it has become the world's largest Web access point with over 1 million members downloading the software and over 700,000 using it regularly. Daily usage of the browser is 50,000, and Prodigy's Web link ads increase traffic.

With over 80,000 commercial Web locations (an ever-increasing number), it is almost impossible for a Web site to stand out in the crowd without some type of viable link. Advertisers can take advantage of this by purchasing listings that link directly to their home pages on the Web. Prices range from as little as $19 dollars per week for an ad, (with a one-year commitment for placing ads on the Shopping page) up to $4,000 per week for an exclusive home page icon and ad.

Besides the browser home page, there are Best of the Net pages including categories such as Arts & Entertainment, Business & Finance, Career Center, Computers/Technology, Education & References, Law & Government, News, Science & the Environment, Shopping, Sports, and Travel. Premium home page listings are exclusive and hot-linked to the advertiser's Web page. The listing consists of an icon or log and 180 characters of text at a rate of $4,000 for one week. Standard Home Page listings, limited to eight per week and 60 characters of text, are $2,000 per week. Premium Best of the Net pages are composed of the same type of ad as on a home page and cost $1,000 per week; Shopping Best of the Net page listings are $250 per week.

Prodigy Promotions

Prodigy works closely with its media partners to develop innovative promotions. It has assisted cable networks, for example, in developing interactive online surveys for learning more about viewers' programming preferences. Cable networks often use Prodigy's online section to promote upcoming programming. In addition, Prodigy set up an exclusive area in which cable and television networks can advertise programming and maintain a dedicated bulletin board service. This area is furnished at no cost to these networks, and is equipped to handle up to 40 promotional areas.

Summary

Scott Schiller concludes, "The reality is, Prodigy has two million eyeballs and is the world's largest Web site. We are the leaders in Internet access, and the first to recognize the Internet as a viable medium. If you read anything about Prodigy now, every article mentions that we did embrace the Net first, and there is a vision, there is an aggressiveness. We are actively working with companies that are building Web sites, and we want to incorporate them into our network. We ultimately want to be representing Web sites, and hope to package it all together. We believe that only the early adopters are involved now and that there are going to be 20 or 30 million more folks in the next few years coming online. If we can position ourselves correctly, we will be able to take advantage of that because of our established brand name and our loyal members."

Microsoft Network

Microsoft, the world's leading operating systems and software developer, launched the Microsoft Network (MSN) in August 1995, bundled as a component in Microsoft's latest version of Windows 95. As of January 1996, there were more than 60 million units of Windows software distributed worldwide, and in six months from launch, membership to MSN reached over 1 million.

Microsoft has positioned MSN as an online service offering seamless integration with the Internet (Figure 9.19). Its initial approach was to build its system on an internal development platform, Blackbird, which is a robust multimedia tool that allows developers to implement full motion and sound. However, Microsoft shifted its focus from a service housed on a proprietary tool, similar to what AOL and CompuServe had done, to a completely Internet-based model. Microsoft developers realized that if they used a proprietary authoring tool, anyone who wanted to provide content or advertise on MSN would need to build at least two completely separate sites: one for Microsoft and one in HTML for the Internet. This was seen as a highly impractical, costly, and redundant approach, and counter-productive to establishing alliances with content and advertising partners. Steve Goldberg, manager of Advertising, Strategy, and Development, explains the Microsoft reasoning:

> *The HTML of the future stands a much better chance of success than any*
> *authoring tool that might be created by Microsoft, AOL, AT&T, or any of*

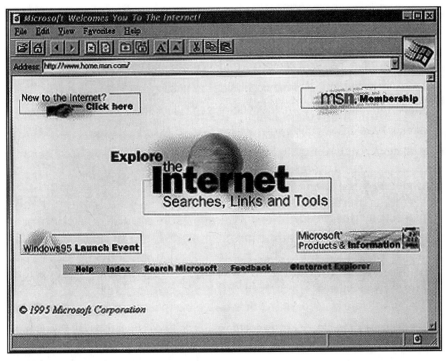

Figure 9.19   Microsoft Network main menu.

those companies. So looking at that first gate, which is the gate of flexibility, and understanding that if we had a proprietary authoring tool all the way into the future, it meant that anybody who wanted to publish with us would have to publish at least twice, once in HTML and once in our authoring tool; or even three times, once in HTML, once in our authoring tool, and once in America Online's authoring tool. We took a look at that and said, "You know, that's not good for our content partners' experience."

The next thing we looked at was the architecture and how it prevented us from giving our service to people around the world; and clearly, there is a larger potential audience with an open service. And so when we looked at all three of those things, we realized that it was vitally important to adopt and embrace what was clearly going to be the winning authoring tool and technological platform. We could achieve a better result overall from a standpoint of flexibility for content partners, navigation, and user experience with an authoring tool that is already a standard in the industry.

Microsoft has moved all of its content, member services, and communication functions, which include e-mail, BBS, and Chat, to the World Wide Web. Goldberg states, "We envision a future where people don't click on the MSN logo per se and go to a data center and end up as a member of our service, but instead enter the World Wide Web through the Internet Explorer, which is Microsoft's browser, and they find their way into Microsoft Network."

Goldberg believes that once a user customizes his or her MSN home page it will become the user's preferred launching pad for exploration of the Net (Figure 9.20). Creating the user's Web launch site is Microsoft's vision. "We've really tried to create an environment where people can spend their entire time on the Web, and that means offering search engines including Excite, Yahoo, and Magellan. There's a way to get stock quotes, sports scores, business news, computer news, weather information, all on [users'] custom home page. And we have some services areas in which they can look up different things like hotel information or 800 numbers. We also have an entire section of links so they can just surf and enjoy; and there's even an Internet tutorial so that people can spend time learning about more purposeful ways to use the Internet."

Content areas now offered by MSN include the following: Arts & Entertainment, News and Weather, Business & Finance, Sports, Health, and Fitness, Sci-

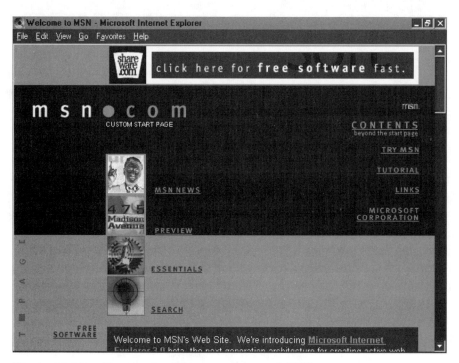

Figure 9.20 Customized home page on MSN.

ence and Technology, Computers and Software, Community and Public Affairs, and Home and Family. Table 9.15 describes a few of these areas in more depth.

A Jupiter Communications study concluded that the greatest barrier to adoption of the World Wide Web is a "perceived lack of usefulness." MSN is changing that perception and making it a great place for newcomers to the Web. MSN is available internationally and has built an impressive global network with localized Web sites. Goldberg states, "There's plenty of content to go around, and the real beauty of localized content is that it meets local needs. The Japanese subsidiary, for instance, can take content off of our Web forum and localize it." There are six global organizations: The Netherlands, United Kingdom, Japan, Australia, Germany, and Canada.

MSN Membership

MSN has four payment plans detailed in Table 9.16. The rates quoted are of course subject to change, as this service is evolving dramatically like everything else in the online universe. Pricing models for Microsoft Network also may vary depending upon the depth of the content. Goldberg says:

TABLE 9.15   MSN's World Wide Web Site Features

Feature	Description
Decision '96	A 24-hour interactive service from MSN and NBC News, that delivers continually updated insights and information about the candidates, issues, and elections of 1996.
MSN News	Up-to-the-minute information, including, news, weather, sports and financial information. MSN's dedicated news staff uses the major wire services to put it all in context with links to stories and other related information on MSN and on the Internet.
Car Source	An online buying guide that strives to be the premier resource for making informed automotive purchase decisions. It provides detailed automotive information and access to a community of car buyers (via chat and BBS) all in an entertaining and easy-to-use structure.
Microsoft Pregnancy and Early Child Care	An interactive online information service that offers easy access to quality, up-to-date consumer health information.
Guidebooks	A series of interactive multimedia program guides for content on the site. These guidebooks will help Web consumers find the best that the Net has to offer on topics like Computers and Software, Entertainment, and Science and Technology.
Slate Magazine	Michael Kinsley—former publisher of *The New Republic* and Co-host of CNN's *Crossfire*—has joined Microsoft to create *Slate*, a weekly online magazine of public affairs and culture, aimed at a general audience of intelligent Web users.

TABLE 9.16   Microsoft Network's Member Pricing Plans

Pricing Plans	Description
Standard Monthly	$4.95 per month for 3 hours of use with each additional hour at $2.50
Frequent User	$19.95 per month for twenty hours of use per month, each additional hour $2.00
Annual Plan	$49.95 per year for 3 hours of use per month with each additional hour $2.50

We always have believed that there is a body of content that subscribers can and should pay for. The best thing we can do is drive the subscription service price down low. . . . With an Internet platform, we can succeed in our vision of driving connect time as close to zero as possible. . . . So we are saying that a subscription will be a subscription, and [members] will get entry into a certain unique set of content that is available only on the Microsoft Network. Other online services do a lot to make sure that users stay online for a long time. We don't share that vision . . . we think that people should pay for the right to enter into certain areas of content or expose themselves to certain activities, but not to pay more because they are reading more slowly or because the activities they would expose themselves to are more graphically intense.

It seems that the world is moving toward a place where a very large portion of computing is done not just in the local environment but online, and if your company believes that a computer on every desktop should be getting as much utility as it can, then the best possible service won't be onerous; it won't be to the detriment of the user. Larger costs for longer times online is inconsistent with Microsoft's vision of full utility.

A competitor who does a great job is ESPN Net. A variety of really good content on ESPN is free. But there are certain aspects that [users] have to pay for, and I think that's an excellent model. And so we're going to pursue the same model. We have relationships with NBC, Paramount, and other content providers, and there's clearly information that should be available for free to everyone on the Internet, and we want to see that happen. If you think about Paramount and its franchise with Star Trek, or you think about NBC and some of the franchises that it has built up either in sports or in news or in commentary, clearly there's an opportunity to have certain content in a place where people will want to pay for it, the same way that ESPN or The Wall Street Journal or any of these other quality content providers are doing it. Those are really good models.

Advertising on Microsoft Network

Microsoft Network supports its advertisers by driving traffic to its Web sites. According to Goldberg, "We're not in the hosting business for advertisers. They want to host their own sites, and I think that's good. It allows them to place advertising on a company like C-Net, Pathfinder, the Microsoft Network. Basically what's changed with new media is the process of sending an ad to a person. [Advertisers] might send it in an envelope or on a TV show. They might send it in an in-flight magazine or wrapped inside a newspaper or on a radio commercial. The difference with online is that it's the first medium where you actually send the person to an ad. This changes the dynamic, and it makes the ad central. And that centralization really begs for advertisers not to host ads on servers like Microsoft's or AOL's or Prodigy's, but to host their own ads and have companies like AOL and Prodigy, and certainly the Microsoft Network, send people to their ads."

The international market, Goldberg explained, will be part of phase two. MSN will sell the U.S. Web server as a unit and then offer a separate buy from the top global units that have established a worthwhile number of impressions. The six global units, as just mentioned, are The Netherlands, the United Kingdom, Japan, Australia, Germany, and Canada. They will be offered as a separate piece of inventory to the advertiser. According to Goldberg, Microsoft believes that some of the international markets are going to emerge as their own stand-alone markets. Thus, MSN will be able to sell from either the United States or from an international sales office. Goldberg projects that they will begin to establish offices in "mid-1997 in Hong Kong, Sydney, or Singapore, or some combination thereof." He concludes, "We truly believe that's what's going to emerge, and we're going to have a really exciting opportunity to sell that kind of advertising to great global clients."

Cost to Advertise on MSN

Microsoft charges for advertising on an impression basis. The rates are between $2.50 and $4.75 per impression. Whereas Prodigy, CompuServe, and America Online function as advertising agencies in that they are building an actual advertisement or creating a sponsorship opportunity, Microsoft has established its program as a straight media buy. Microsoft will help the advertiser design a unique proposal that best achieves its media goals. Advertising rates (subject to change) for MSN are shown in Table 9.17.

MSN Sponsorship Opportunities

Building a Web site is like shooting a commercial or designing a print ad. Successful sites are compelling. The key to success is making sure that your marketing messages are seen and acted upon. Sponsorship opportunities assure value, flexibility, and tracking. Microsoft Network's planning model helps advertisers reach every content area of the network that fits the scope of their target audience. Banner advertising and premium placements are used to make sure the sponsor's messages are maximized (Figures 9.21 and 9.22), and Microsoft Network's track-

TABLE 9.17   MSN Web Site Advertising Rates March through June 1996

Content Zone	Cost Per Impression	CPM	Cost per CAD (10,000 Impressions)
Customized Home Page	.0375	$37.50	$375
Services Page	.0175	17.50	175
Shopping Guidebook	.0375	37.50	375
Links Section	.025	25.00	250
SiteSeeing Guide	.0175	17.50	175
Search Engines	.0175	17.50	175
TV-1	.025	25.00	250
Decision '96	.040	40.00	400
MSN News	.0375	37.50	375
Car Source	.045	45.00	450

ing system closely monitors impressions. Sponsors pay only for the impressions that they originally bought.

On many MSN sites, hard-wired banners are left on pages for days or months at a time. Dynamic rotation on Microsoft Network improves the user experience and helps the advertiser. Microsoft Network banners are delivered from a server that automatically generates a new advertisement each time a user accesses a

Figure 9.21   MSN standard banner from Virtual Vineyards.

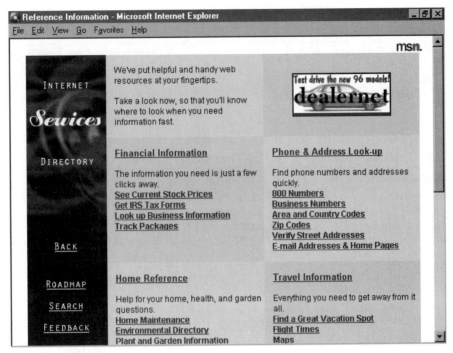

Figure 9.22 MSN small banner for DealerNet.

new page or refreshes a loaded one. This means that the user experiences a vibrancy typically not found on other sites. In addition, Microsoft limits the advertising opportunities to a single banner per page so that advertisers never have to share an impression with another marketer. Also, advertisers can purchase a predetermined number of impressions so that they don't have to guess or estimate what they are buying, and never have to pay unexpected over-delivery.

Advertising packages on MSN are designed on a case-by-case basis, so definitive costs are available only through consultation with Microsoft, but Tables 9.18 and 9.19 give an idea of the rates that Microsoft Network used in its initial launch in 1995. A February 1996 draft of a media proposal is shown in Table 9.20 as an example to be used as a reference point for the purpose of understanding the material in this section.

The system in the sample msn.com media proposal allows for short flights, front loading, back loading, and heavy-ups. It also allows for copy rotation and testing. Impressions are sold in small blocks to allow the advertiser to tailor the weight of delivery to meet specific needs.

TABLE 9.18   1995 MSN Advertising Rates prior to MSN's Transition to the Web

Ads	Description
Events, Sponsorships	$5,000–$50,000 per month
Guidebooks	$30,000 per month
Links	$2,500–$15,000 per month
Direct Electronic Marketing	$500 per thousand names

TABLE 9.19   1995 Revenue Deals prior to MSN's Transition to the Web

Revenue Deals, Storefront Rates	Description
Content Providers	70–80% share of revenues generated specifically from information downloading
Hard Goods Marketers	MSN gets 55% of revenues.
Soft Goods Marketers	MSN gets up to 35% of revenues.
Storefront rate	Starts at $50,000 per year.

TABLE 9.20   January 1996 Sample msn.com Media Proposal

Media Mix	Cost/Page View	% of Buy	Total Impressions	Zone Cost
Home Page	$.0375	20%	2,400,000	$90,000
Car Source	.0400	8%	1,000,000	40,000
Decision '96	.0400	62%	7,500,000	300,000
Link's Page	.0250	0%	—	—
Services Pages	.0160	10%	1,250,000	20,000
All-in-One Search	.0175	0%	—	—
		100%	12,150,000	450,000
Weighted Average Page Cost	.0370			
Annual Impressions & Expenditure	$12,150,000		$450,000	

Advertising and other marketing activities available on MSN will be evolving as the service does. There are a number of ways marketers and content providers can partner with MSN. Because of the number of desktops "owned" by Microsoft, it is an important venue to consider when designing an online marketing plan. Microsoft's Goldberg concludes, "Like every other online service and online company, we are in a share battle . . . we are trying as hard as we can to get great advertising . . . it is really important to us to provide a great service."

Bloomberg Financial Markets

Manhattan-based Bloomberg Financial Markets is a multimedia distributor of information services that combines news, data, and analysis for global financial markets and businesses (Figure 9.23). The Bloomberg, the company's core business, is composed of a dedicated, customized computer integrated with a secured online network. This integrated system delivers real-time financial information and links the world's markets and leading financial professionals. The Bloomberg's multimedia features include Bloomberg Information TV, Bloomberg Information radio, and a rich audio and video library.

The Bloomberg network combines timely pricing capabilities with inside dealer quotes; data on domestic and foreign bonds, stocks, futures, and options; and other publicly traded securities. It makes this information available 24 hours a day, 7 days a week. Bloomberg covers all key global securities markets and provides an advanced, reliable, online communications network worldwide, connecting the customers to their branches, clients, suppliers, exchanges, dealers, colleagues, and competitors. Research and financial statistics on over 52,000 companies worldwide can be obtained through the Bloomberg Financial Network. Bloomberg delivers the ability to research market sectors, track the competition, consider security alternatives, model investment scenarios, and conduct what-if scenarios. This information is delivered through 50,000 proprietary terminals used by over 200,000 financial professionals in 62 countries. Bloomberg is growing globally at an approximate rate of 1,000 terminals a month, with an average 3.5 users per terminal.

Figure 9.23 The Bloomberg terminal. (*Source: Bloomberg Financial Markets*)

Subscriber packages vary depending on the number of terminals and services desired, but the basic cost for The Bloomberg is $1,595 per month for a minimum two-year lease. The Bloomberg flat panel screen is available for an additional $250. Included in this price is all analytics, portfolio functions, monitors, long-distance communications, U.S. and international 24-hour/7-day-per-week general interest news wires, Bloomberg Business News, and 15-minute delayed exchange prices.

The Bloomberg Media Family

- *Bloomberg Magazine:* The *Bloomberg* Magazine is an award-winning publication sent automatically to all *Bloomberg* subscribers free of charge. The magazine supplements and enhances the online information and analytics. It is staffed by experts called applications specialists who were experienced traders, portfolio managers, analysts, and talented industry professionals. They travel around the world to conduct hundreds of Bloomberg client seminars. Articles range from practical market intelligence and current business and industry analysis to in-depth coverage of securities products.

- *Bloomberg Personal:* Bloomberg Personal is a monthly consumer finance magazine supplement to Sunday newspapers across America that focuses on family and personal financial issues. Some of the newspapers that carry the Bloomberg Personal supplement are *The Washington Post, Baltimore Sun, New York Daily News, Dallas Morning News, Houston Chronicle, Chicago Sun-Times, Denver Post, Arizona Republic,* and *The Alameda Group.*

- *Bloomberg Energy Newsletters:* Bloomberg offers a variety of newsletters for the energy industry that include *Bloomberg Oil Buyer's Guide* and *Bloomberg Natural Gas Report.*

- *Bloomberg Business News:* Bloomberg Business News is a global news service that appears weekday mornings on public and commercial TV stations throughout the United States. It is staffed by writers who previously contributed to publications such as *The Wall Street Journal, Forbes, Newsweek, TIME, U.S. News & World Report* and *Institutional Investor.* The Bloomberg Business News has over 350 reporters in 67 bureaus worldwide, and provides around-the-clock coverage of the world's governments, corporations, industries, and financial markets. It transmits over 3,000 staff-written stories daily to Bloomberg online customers. The Business News byline regularly appears in more than 800 flagship newspapers throughout the Americas, Europe, the Middle East, and the Pacific Rim, including *The New York Times, The Washington Post, International Herald Tribune, San Francisco Chronicle, The Globe & Mail, The European, Singapore Business Journal,* and *South China Morning Post.*

- *Bloomberg Forum:* The Forum provides multimedia presentations of in-depth interviews with corporate executives and industry experts. These presentations are distributed through The Bloomberg, Bloomberg Business News, videotapes, CEO/Analyst Roundtables, and national television. Bloomberg Conference Centers are located in New York, London, Tokyo, and Hong Kong, and are available for analyst and shareholder meetings held in conjunction with Forum interviews. Companies can participate in exclusive Forum executive interviews that are broadcast through the Business News service and the Bloomberg online terminal.

- *Bloomberg Information TV:* Bloomberg Information Television is a 24-hour news service that delivers the most current summaries of the world's major securities, commodities markets, and exchanges using a revolutionary satellite service, DIRECTV, and selected cable systems in the United States and a number of satellite services around the world. These news programs are presented live in 30-minute cycles, and are delivered directly to the Bloomberg terminal. Each program presents 50 of the top late-breaking stories, along with an analysis of how these events impact world financial markets. The multiscreen format used on the terminal allows for scrolling of live stock, bond, and commodity updates; sports scores; entertainment news; and horoscopes. Entertainment news and horoscopes appear on the upper left screen, while live market prices scroll across the bottom panel; reporters and graphics are shown in the upper right.

- *Bloomberg Information Radio:* The Bloomberg Information Radio reaches the New York metropolitan area on WBBR AM 1130, and is syndicated nationwide. It is available in multilingual audio and text formats on the Bloomberg network as well. Every 15 minutes, around the clock, the station reviews important business news and world events, and delivers local event and weather information. Bloomberg Forum interviews are featured, along with the top news stories and financial market updates. In addition to being able to tune to the radio station directly from the Bloomberg computer terminal, users can also listen to WBBR live on any computer by downloading the Streamworks player for Windows, Macintosh, or Unix from the Xingtech Web site.

- *Bloomberg Personal Online:* Bloomberg Personal Online is the newest addition to the Bloomberg Media family. This online site delivers information supplements on subjects covered by Bloomberg Personal on the Personal Finance television show. Viewers who watch the show are provided behind the scenes information on a private basis.

Advertising with Bloomberg

The Bloomberg audience is a highly targeted vertical segment that is a very desirable consumer group for certain types of product marketers. Bloomberg provides an attractive range of advertising venues for these marketers. Bloomberg does not rent or sell its customer list, so advertisers are provided with exclusive access to these elite customers.

Bloomberg Audience Profile

The Bloomberg audience is made up of high-income financial professionals, which include executives, managers, and traders. Bloomberg users are located in every country that boasts significant market activity, with approximately 67 percent in the United States, 22 percent in Europe, and 11 percent in Asia and Australia. Its customers fall primarily into six categories: executive management, investment management, traders, institutional and retail sales, research directors/security analysts, and cash managers (Figure 9.24).

More Bloomberg audience facts and figures show:

- The median age of Bloomberg customers is 35.8, with a mean age of 37.
- 81 percent are male and 19 percent are female.
- 91 percent are college graduates, with 48 percent completing a post-graduate education.
- 41 percent are single, and 59 percent are married, 41 percent with children.
- The average household income is $191,000 annually.
- The average value of investments is $494,000 and the average net worth is approximately $703,000.
- Bloomberg customers are active readers, with outside interests primarily in fitness, golf, skiing, and boating, and they spend money on

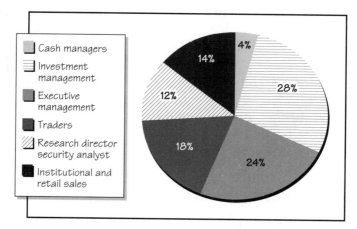

Figure 9.24 The Bloomberg audience. (*Source: Bloomberg Financial Markets Commodities News Brochure*)

art, antiques, vacations, wine, laptop computers, and personal home computers.

- 86 percent of the users feel that the Bloomberg terminal is an essential part of their business, and 40 percent of them use the terminal more than six hours a day.
- 88 percent of the *Bloomberg Magazine* readers read the magazine every month, over 40 percent for more than an hour; 78 percent feel the editorial content and featured products meet their needs.
- Over 73 percent of the Bloomberg audience say they have seen information from featured advertisers on the terminal, and 42 percent of them regularly respond to online advertising on the terminal.
- Over 75 percent of the Bloomberg terminal users are familiar with the Bloomberg Executive Shopper, and 56 percent use it.

Bloomberg Advertising Options

Bloomberg is selective when it comes to advertisers, to ensure that they and the Bloomberg audience are an appropriate match. Each advertising package is carefully customized to create a well-rounded media mix that is rotated through all of Bloomberg's venues over the course of a minimum one-year contract. If the Bloomberg advertiser account manager sees that a holiday or event is a timely opportunity for promotion of a certain product or bundle of products, the manager will work with the advertiser to take advantage of it at no additional charge. A promotion of this kind may mean appearing on the Bloomberg Notice Screen that all users see when they first log on to the terminal, or it may mean running a radio spot on Bloomberg Information Radio. One of the advantages to advertising with Bloomberg is that it owns all of the media, and can place ads at will in any or all of them. Bloomberg will do whatever will optimize the advertiser's success. As an added bonus, Bloomberg advertisers have access to all of the Bloomberg facilities, conferences, and seminars worldwide, free of charge.

Bloomberg Executive Shopper The Executive Shopper is an electronic shopping catalogue with products carefully selected to meet the particular needs of the Bloomberg audience. Users can see photo-like visuals, read product descriptions, access promotional tie-ins, and place orders directly over this closed, secure network. As a supplement to the online system, Bloomberg also offers *The Bloomberg Executive Shopper Catalogue* (print publication) featuring full-color offerings from online merchants. Bloomberg users receive the catalogue free with selected issues of the *Bloomberg Magazine.*

Bloomberg seeks to establish a long-term marketing partnership with its advertisers. Packages are designed to optimize both the advertiser's budget and use of the full range of venues available through Bloomberg. Even though some prices are suggested here, all advertising is completely negotiable and dependent upon the makeup of the total package and overall commitment.

With a $12,000 dollar investment, it is possible to advertise in the Bloomberg Executive Shopper, the online shopping catalogue, and receive 100 text pages with pictures that can be changed any time. Bloomberg sets up the marquee page and the interface for accessing the other pages. The advertiser supplies the chromes or photos, text information, and Bloomberg does the rest.

The Bloomberg Executive Shopper uses a nongraphical main menu that appears more reference-oriented than sales-oriented (Figure 9.25). This takes into consideration the way most financial professionals prefer to receive their information. Since the Bloomberg terminals usually reside on the desks of CEOs and other executive management; it is assumed it is these executives who will be doing the actual shopping. This is a unique and important distinction to note when targeting the Bloomberg consumer. In traditional office settings, lower management usually makes purchases requested by executive management, such as flowers, business gifts, and even personal items.

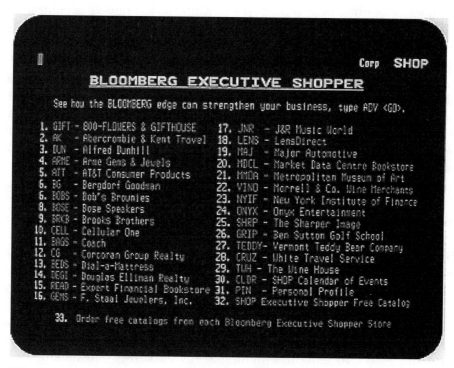

Figure 9.25 Executive Shopper main menu. (*Source: The Bloomberg Executive Shopper Brochure*)

The first time a Bloomberg user enters the catalogue to make a purchase, he or she fills out a personal profile (Figure 9.26) that includes credit card and demographic information. This profile is tied to a Personal Identification Number, or PIN, and is stored in a database so that with each subsequent transaction, the system knows who is placing the order and where it should be shipped. An electronic order form automatically lists the items ordered so that the shopper can review the total. Some advertisers have Bloomberg terminals, but they are not necessary. Bloomberg will fax to advertisers any orders and messages that are received three times a day.

Included in the initial $12,000 investment is the placement of an ad, usually one-third page in the *Bloomberg Magazine* at six-month intervals. Bloomberg encourages additional print advertising, and in fact prefers to sell the print ad program as the primary package initially, with the online as an added benefit. When advertisers enter the Bloomberg advertising program through the print media, they are automatically given 20 free pages in the online Executive Shopper. An advertiser can purchase three magazine ads at $4,000 each, placed at four-month intervals, and receive one year on the Bloomberg terminal at no

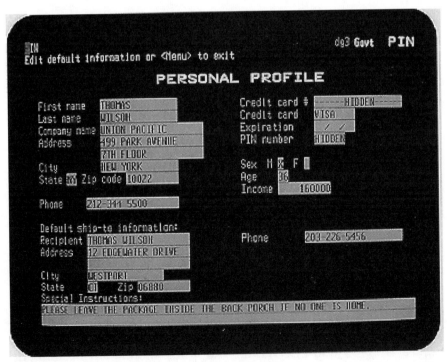

Figure 9.26 Bloomberg Personal Profile screen. (*Source: The Bloomberg Executive Shopper Brochure*)

additional charge. To advertise in the *Bloomberg Magazine* can cost about $12,000 a month for one page. The circulation, as reported in May 1996, is 84,000. The newer publication, the *Bloomberg Personal Sunday* newspaper insert has a circulation of over 6.7 million, in which quarter-page ads can cost between $7,000 and $8,000.

Some of the more successful advertisers on Bloomberg include 1-800-FLOWERS (Figure 9.27), Dial-A-Mattress, Vermont Teddy Bear, White Travel, Drake Hotels, Steuben Glass, and Bob's Brownstone Brownies. 1-800-FLOWERS has done very well because it appeals to the global marketplace and has a universally popular product. High-ticket items like mattresses also move very well because of the affluence of the audience, their desire for quality, and their preference for the convenience of the online transaction. A purchase by a Bloomberg user tends to be in a range higher than average—the $100 roses and top-of-the-line bed—which provides a healthy return on investment for the advertiser.

Bloomberg will often run contests or games online to promote an advertiser's product. For example, Metro Business Systems and Hewlett-Packard together ran a contest to give away a free digital camera to anyone who filled out their questionnaire. This promotion generated over 5,000 qualified leads.

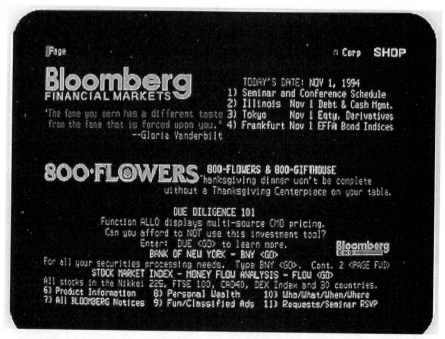

Figure 9.27 1-800-FLOWERS shopping menu on Bloomberg. (*Source: The Bloomberg Executive Shopper Brochure*)

Bloomberg encourages all its clients to do as much promotion as possible, and all ideas are considered. Every holiday, Bloomberg selects two or three items to highlight from each vendor, then creates a special menu for those holiday items along with special thematic graphics. It is very important to Bloomberg that the advertisers, are successful, and Bloomberg works diligently to make that happen.

Bloomberg Magazine Ad Rates   All the figures shown in Tables 9.21 and 9.22 are per-page advertising rates as of June 1996, for *Bloomberg Magazine*.

Placement on the magazine's cover is in high demand, so this is controlled by the Bloomberg management to allow fair access (see Table 9.23 for rates). Special consideration is given to long-term advertisers who utilize both inside-page and cover positions.

Bloomberg Financial Markets and all of its vast components form a unique entity and an excellent vertical market for advertisers. Bloomberg sees the advertiser as a full marketing partner, an ideal relationship from an advertiser's perspective.

Conclusion

The Introduction to this chapter presented several examples of collaboration among the various commercial and Internet-based services as one solution to

TABLE 9.21   Bloomberg Magazine Inside Page Rates—Worldwide

Frequency	Rate	Percent Savings
1×	$13,200	—
3×	12,240	5%
6×	12,144	8%
9×	11,800	10%
12×	11,220	15%

TABLE 9.22   Bloomberg Magazine Inside Page Rates—Targeted Circulation

Frequency	Regional Rate	Japan Only Rate
1×	$10,000	400,000¥
3×	9,500	380,000¥
6×	9,200	368,000¥
9×	9,000	360,000¥
12×	8,500	340,000¥

TABLE 9.23   Bloomberg Magazine Cover Rates

Cover Contracts	
2nd Cover	20% Premium
3rd Cover	20% Premium
4th Cover	33% Premium

the growing dominance of the Internet and the need for quality content. Another example of such collaboration is Project Open, where companies like AT&T, Microsoft, AOL, CompuServe, and Prodigy have aligned to set standards to make the Internet a safe, secure place from the perspective of families and educators. Still another alliance is being formed to set advertising and commerce standards to promote business online. The Alliance for Converging Technologies is an international research, education, and strategic consulting organization based in Toronto and New York. More than 30 major corporations and government agencies are members. Its current multimillion-dollar research program is entitled Interactive Multimedia in the High-Performance Organization: Wealth Creation in the Digital Economy.

According to PR Newswire, March 26, 1996, "Nearly 8 out of 10 telecommunications executives say their industries are being revolutionized by interactive multimedia, dramatically altering the way their companies market and sell products and services. These findings come from the largest-ever survey of North American (United States and Canada) executives regarding the use of interactive multimedia technologies by business, government, and other organizations. Conducted by the Alliance for Converging Technologies, the survey was based on responses from some 2,000 executives in 10 industries, including 145 leaders in telecommunications. "Telecommunications clearly is the torchbearer of online commerce," said David Ticoll, president of the Alliance. "But to fully exploit interactive multimedia business strategies, the telecom industry must present a consistent vision that fosters teamwork and decision-making within companies."

The findings show:

- 6 out of 10 telecom executives (60 percent) believe their organizations will rely on online services to sell products and services.
- 7 out of 10 telecom executives (65 percent) say their companies will rely heavily on online services to promote and advertise their services by the end of 1997.
- 3 out of 10 (34 percent) of all other executives from a variety of industries believe their companies will sell online by the end of 1997.

- 5 out of 10 (45 percent) executives saying their companies will market and advertise online.
- 34 percent of telecom executives value the Internet as a primary market, versus 29 percent of other industry leaders.

Table 9.24 is a subscriber survey chart that provides an overview of the wide range of online services, and the changing subscriber numbers between December 1994 and that same month one year later.

TABLE 9.24 Electronic Information Report's Year-End Online Subscriber Survey

Company (Parent)	Service	12/31/95	12/31/94	Change
Consumer	**Individual Passwords/ Subscriptions**			
America Online	America Online	4,500,000	1,500,000	200.0%
CompuServe Inc. (H&R Block)	CompuServe Information Svc.	4,000,000	2,660,000	50.4%
Prodigy Services Co. (IBM/Sears)[1]	Prodigy	1,400,000	1,200,000	16.7%
Ziff-Davis Interactive (Ziff-Davis)	ZD Net	300,000	260,000	15.4%
Telescan Inc.[2]	TIP, Billboard, CSN, AIA, Schwab	180,000	143,000	25.9%
Apple Computer	eWorld	130,000	65,000	100.0%
General Electric Info. Svc. (GE)[3,4]	GEnie	55,000	60,000	−8.3%
News Corp.[3,4]	Delphi	65,000	80,000	−18.8%
Microsoft Corp.[5]	Microsoft Network	600,000	0	—
AT&T	The ImagiNation Network	63,000	57,000	10.5%
Reality Online	Reuters Money Network	42,000	31,000	35.5%
Cox Newspapers, Prodigy	Access Atlanta	21,000	16,000	31.3%
Concentric Research Corp.[3]	CRIS, BBS Direct	19,000	10,000	90.0%
Whole Earth 'Lectronic Link	The WELL	12,000	11,000	9.1%
Ft. Worth Star-Telegram[3]	StarText	4,300	4,300	0.0%
SeniorNet	SeniorNet	4,500	2,500	80.0%
Reach Media LP	The Transom	3,000	2,200	36.4%
Subtotal		**11,398,800**	**6,102,000**	**86.8%**

(continues)

Company (Parent)	Service	12/31/95	12/31/94	Change
Business/ Professional	**Individual Passwords/ Subscriptions**			
Reed Elsevier	LEXIS-NEXIS	744,345	707,000	5.3%
Dow Jones Info. Svc. (Dow Jones)[3]	Dow Jones News/ Retrieval	233,000	220,000	5.9%
Knight-Ridder Information	Dialog Worldwide	200,000	158,000	26.6%
TRW Inc.	TRW Information Services	200,000	120,000	66.7%
Dun & Bradstreet Corp.[3]	D&B Information Services N.A.	135,490	120,000	12.9%
National Library of Medicine	MEDLARS	116,593	98,617	18.2%
Dow Jones & Co.	DowVision	110,000	100,000	10.0%
Individual Inc.	First!, Heads Up, iNews, NewsPage	90,000	35,000	157.1%
Desktop Data	NewsEDGE	80,613	51,548	56.4%
Apple Computer	AppleLink	60,000	60,000	0.0%
Official Airline Guides (Reed)	OAG Electronic Edition	52,000	50,000	4.0%
American Lawyer Media, LEXIS-NEXIS	LEXIS Counsel Connect	35,000	17,000	105.9%
CDB Infotek[3]	CDB Infotek	33,000	18,000	83.3%
West Publishing[3]	Information America	28,000	23,000	21.7%
NewsNet (Independent Pub.)[3]	NewsNet	26,000	22,000	18.2%
OCLC[4,6]	OCLC	21,821	20,508	6.4%
Ovid Technologies[3]	Ovid Online	19,000	14,000	35.7%
Orbit Questel Inc. (France Telecom)	ORBIT Search Services	12,000	11,000	9.1%
Questel (France Telecom)	Questel	11,000	10,000	10.0%
OCLC	FirstSearch	9,635	8,214	17.3%
OCLC	EPIC	4,525	4,739	−4.5%
M.A.I.D.[3]	M.A.I.D, Profound	4,500	4,000	12.5%
Southam Electronic Publishing[3]	Infomart Online	4,000	3,500	14.3%
Legi-Tech[3]	Legi-Tech	1,100	1,000	10.0%
Legi-Tech[3]	Florida Legislative Reporter	300	200	50.0%
Subtotal		**2,231,922**	**1,877,326**	**18.9%**

Company (Parent)	Service	12/31/95	12/31/94	Change
Financial	**Passwords/Terminals Teleprinters/ Workstations**			
Reuters Holdings plc[7]	Reuter's Real-Time Data Services	327,100	296,700	10.2%
Dow Jones Information Services[3]	DJ News Services (Broadtape)	143,000	140,000	2.1%
Telerate Inc. (Dow Jones & Co.)[3]	Telerate	98,500	90,000	9.4%
Automatic Data Processing (ADP)[3]	Brokerage Services	98,000	92,000	6.5%
Standard & Poor's (McGraw-Hill)	MarketScope	74,000	70,000	5.7%
Data Transmission Network Corp.[3,4]	DTN AgDaily, DTNiron, DTNStant DTN Produce, DTN Weather Center	75,500	65,000	16.2%
Bloomberg Financial	The Bloomberg Terminal	55,000	43,000	27.9%
Thomson Financial Services[3]	ILX	50,000	42,000	19.0%
Knight-Ridder Inc.[3]	Financial Information Services	43,000	38,000	13.2%
Data Broadcasting Corp.	Signal, QuoTrek, SporTRAX, SportSignal, RaceTRAX	33,000	22,100	49.3%
Global Market Information	Track OnLine Dial/Data, InfoVest	18,500	16,486	12.2%
Data Transmission Network[3,4]	DTN Financial Services: DTN Spectrum, DTN Wall Street, DTN GovRates	13,700	11,649	17.6%
Bridge Information Systems	Bridge	10,500	9,972	5.3%
Data Transmission Network[3]	DTNergy	6,700	6,400	4.7%
Data Broadcasting Corp.[3]	Bonneville	7,500	5,900	27.1%
Automatic Data Processing (ADP)[3]	Shark	6,200	5,900	5.1%
PC Quote Inc.[3]	PC Quote	5,000	4,700	6.4%
Subtotal		**1,065,200**	**959,807**	**11.0%**
Total		**14,695,922**	**8,939,133**	**64.4%**

[1]Figure is for households, not passwords. Each household has approximately two passwords. [2]An estimated 50% of Telescan's subscriber base is active. [3]Estimate. [4]Revised. [5]Launched in August 1995. [6]Number of library accounts. [7]User accesses or IDs.

Clearly, the online environment is a frontier; much of it is still undiscovered by the vast majority of businesses and general consumers. But through the collaborative efforts of the pioneering companies that are "settling the territory," challenges and obstacles are being are being overcome. Marketers today must also be pioneers, and look for innovative ways to utilize these new and unprecedented marketing opportunities.

CHAPTER TEN

THE INTERNET: MARKETING AND BUSINESS OPPORTUNITIES

Claudia Brenner and Tim Pearson

Day after day in the business press you can hear the call to Internet marketing: "Gold Discovered on the Cyberfrontier!" You can almost feel the ground shake as companies today rush in to stake their claim in cyberspace. These days, the Internet seems beset with a fever resembling the California gold rush of the mid-1800s, when the optimism, vigor, and confidence of a culturally diverse entourage more than a million strong reshaped the California landscape physically, economically, and spiritually in their lusty search for the riches that many actually found.

Yes, these *are* wild times on the cyberfrontier. New gold diggers arrive every day, a gleam in their eye, loaded with tools, and looking to hire a guide to the territory. They're ready to experiment with innovative approaches to marketing their wares in the new Internet medium and they want to get going now. Relative newcomers to the Internet, however, may find it difficult to discern the paydirt from the fool's gold. "For 50 years, stampeders would gamble their fortunes and their very lives on the strength of a whispered rumor, of an over-enthusiastic newspaper account, of a glittering nugget pulled from the pocket of a shabby, grizzled prospector," writes Paula Marks in her book *Precious Dust.*

These days, when marketers speak of using the Internet, they are usually referring to the part of the Internet called the World Wide Web, or just the Web, the interactive, graphical, multimedia part of the Internet (Figure 10.1). To navigate the Web, you simply enter the address of the place you want to visit, then click with your mouse on pictures and highlighted text to get more information or jump to other Web sites. The Web is so pervasive that most consumers think that it *is* the Internet.

Figure 10.1 *The New York Times* Web home page.

To make sound investment decisions and build successful business sites on the Internet, both newcomers and companies taking an existing Web site to the next level will want some help sorting the reality of the opportunity from the hype. This chapter is a guide straight from the cyberfrontier that will help companies achieve a new level of understanding about Internet marketing opportunities and how to maximize the return on investments in the Web.

The territory remains largely uncharted, and the landscape changes fast, but other, more experienced pioneers have contributed words of wisdom to this guide, based on their own adventures on the cyberfrontier. From them, newcomers can gleen valuable ideas about how to maximize the power of the Web for business benefit and gain some important insights on how to design commercial Web sites that actually meet significant business goals and objectives. This chapter is not, however, a step-by-step technical manual on setting up a business Web site. Plenty of those are available already. Rather, this chapter shows companies how to integrate business ideas with advanced Web technologies and interactive design to build a scalable and flexible blueprint for their own Web-based marketing gold mine on the cyberfrontier.

To do business successfully on the Web, companies must learn how to build and maintain new types of relationships with their customers by leveraging a key characteristic of the Internet: *interactivity*. The World Wide Web offers the potential for revolutionary win-win changes in the way that businesses interact with and serve customers. Customers win a much greater degree of control over the marketing process than ever before while companies gain major opportunities to realize significant economic benefits. The potential rewards are great, but the challenge lies in experimenting with interactivity on the Web to learn how to establish a *virtually personal relationship* with each customer.

Marketing on the Internet: Business as Usual—with a Twist

Doing business on the Web is really doing business as usual—with a twist. The twist is using the powerful capabilities of the Web to build virtual personal realtionships with customers. Building effective virtual personal marketing relationships on the Web begins with *effective marketing*. All marketers start with business goals that include:

- Increasing revenue.
- Advertising and promoting products and services.
- Keeping current customers happy and acquiring new ones.
- Increasing profitability.
- Reducing costs.
- Enhancing image and branding.

The Web provides powerful capabilities that can enhance and enable the efforts to achieve each of these business goals. Marketing efforts typically focus on seven key business areas:

- **Products and Services Marketing:** product marketing, pricing, positioning, demonstrations (demos), distribution, marketing programs, partnerships, and other strategic activities.
- **Fulfillment:** enabling ordering as well as acquisition, authorization, and authentication of customer funds; enabling the flow of goods and services from sellers to buyers through all wholesalers, jobbers, distributors, dealers, and representatives.
- **Advertising and Promotion:** development and dissemination of image and brand-enhancing persuasive information about products and services.
- **Customer and Business Tracking:** Market reseach to determine customer needs and evaluate business performance in meeting those needs.

- **Customer Service and Support:** Technical support, customer service, requests for information, product registration, and warranty service.

- **Corporate Communications:** product and service information, press releases, and related information for buyers, suppliers, contractors, dealers, representatives, shippers, and so on.

- **Customer Communications:** customer feedback and requests for information.

Each of these functions and activities can be enabled and enhanced on the Web with powerful interactive communications capabilites. To help you get a feel for the potential of the Web as a marketing platform, we'll look at how a few businesses are using their Web sites to market in several business areas mentioned to achieve important business goals and maximize their return on investments in the Web. In most cases, the featured companies present comprehensive, easy-to-use, easy-to-access information. They get customers involved by using interactivity. They utilize the power of advanced Web technologies.

Products and Services Marketing

For this chapter, products and services marketing includes product marketing, pricing, postioning, demos, distribution, strategic partnerships, advertising, promotions and marketing programs activities. Products and services marketing provides information pertinent to a product sale, therefore, adequate, easy-to-access, easy-to-use information is critical in helping customers help themselves.

Providing comprehensive product and service information directly enhances revenues. On the Web, significant opportunities to offer enhanced product and service information exist because the unique capabilities of the Web make giving customers information so easy. Gaining and keeping customer interest in a company and its products and services is always a challenge in any media. On the Web, multimedia can add visual and audio flair to a presentation of products. In addition to text, animation, graphics, and audio can all be utilized to interest and inform the customer. Companies can highlight a product by providing small clickable graphics linked to more information or even an animation. Customers can choose to click on a graphic to learn more.

A better informed customer makes better decisions. Better decisions lead to more satisfied customers, which in turn encourages repeat purchases with fewer returns. With the Web's ability to provide virtually infinite space, companies can post as much information as needed to fully explain a product and service. Explicitly telling customers what products are all about, how they are positioned, what they do, how they're used, and more, can make a big difference in sales revenues.

Let's see how Bank of America sells its services by helping customers calculate payments on an auto loan. Bank of America's Web site does a great job of providing comprehensive details about its products and services in an organized and creative manner (Figure 10.2). Bank of America includes a set of calculator tools on its Web site that help customers take advantage of the bank's services. For instance, customers interested in a car loan can estimate their monthly payment by entering the loan amount, duration, and interest rate (Figure 10.3). The Web site then calculates a monthly payment for the customer (Figure 10.4). Calculating car payments is fun for customers and it's helpful!

Both the bank and its customers benefit from the Web's ability to automate delivery of car loan and payment information, which in turn enables users to more quickly decide whether to apply for a loan; customers determine for themselves whether a particular model is affordable. The bank benefits by saving personnel costs for a support call that can easily cost $13–$35 per 15 minutes. In another part of the site, the bank has another more robust calculator for home equity loans. You can imagine the cost savings Bank of America is experiencing with its site!

At any point in the site, the information loop can be closed. Customers can always find the information they need or contact the bank with e-mail. Cus-

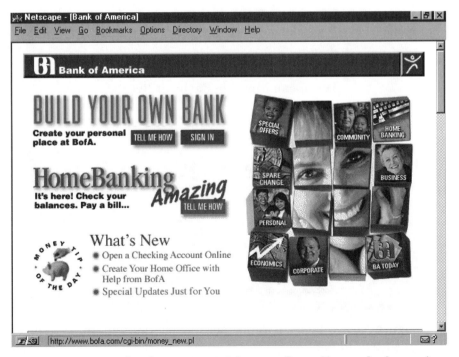

Figure 10.2   Bank of America Web page (http://www.bofa.com).

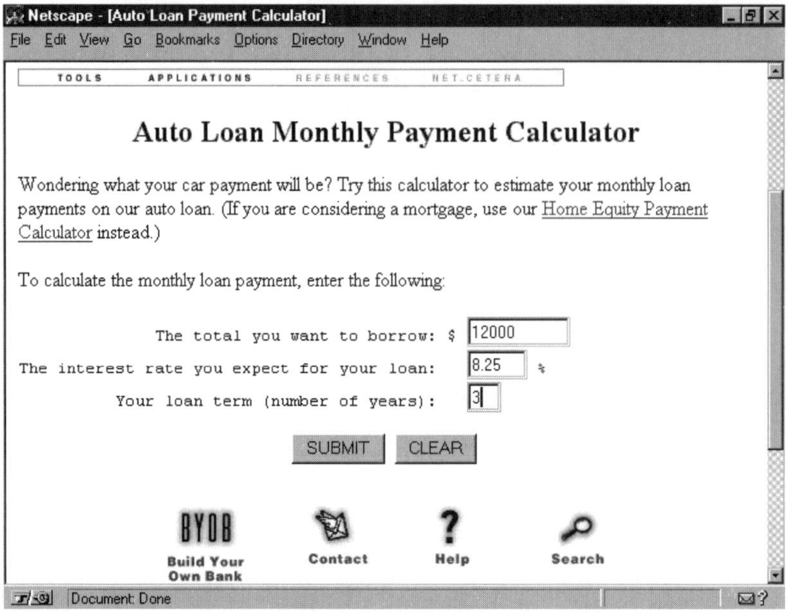

Figure 10.3   The customer enters financial information.

Figure 10.4   The customer sees what their monthly payment would be.

tomers are always serviced and never left hanging or "dropped." As a result, customers feel better served, thus more satisfied and more loyal.

Fullfilment: Enabling Partner/Distributor Relations

Partner/distributor relationships have long been essential to the sales cycle in many industries. With the ascent of the Web as an exciting new place to do business, distributors may worry that they will be left out as the marketing paradigm shifts and customers begin buying directly from manufacturers. The truth is, resellers can and will continue to play an important role in meeting customer needs. The personal touch will always be a clear advantage that resellers have over impersonal automated systems of distribution. By learning about doing business on the Internet and innovating new approaches to adding value, distributors will be able to thrive. In fact, some manufacturers, such as Saturn (http://www.saturncars.com), are promoting their dealers on the Web.

To find the nearest retailer in the United States, customers can click on a state (Figure 10.5) or fill in state and zip code information, and a listing of local retailers appears (Figure 10.6). They can then click on a retailer, get directions,

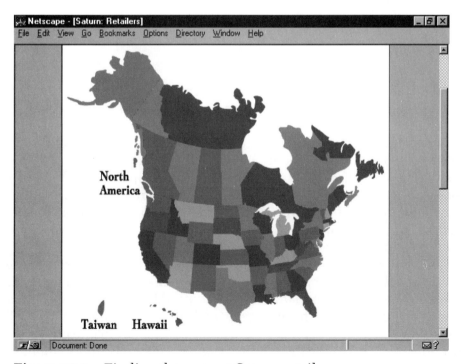

Figure 10.5   Finding the nearest Saturn retailer.

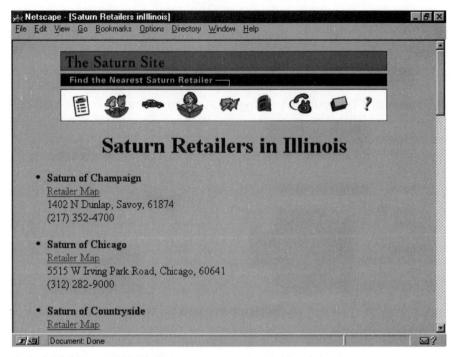

Figure 10.6   A listing of Saturn dealers in Illinois.

and find out about products and services. Being able to locate a dealer is a great service to the customer and a great time-saver. It also saves the company on costly phone calls to dealers, manufacturers, and customers so that more of a dealer's resources can be spent selling a car or focusing on customer service.

In this way, Saturn is enhancing its retailer relationships by including them in its site. The Web offers great ways to communicate in general. Hopefully, Saturn has also set up a secure internal Web site for its retailers offering the latest program and product information. An internal Web site can inform the retailers of product, price, inventory, promotional, and other changes. It also creates a two-way relationship for dialog, feedback, and suggestions.

Carrying out secure purchase transactions on the Internet is key to the success of companies doing business on the Web. Enabling transactions directly generates revenues for companies by utilizing the full potential of this new marketing channel to reach customers and close sales on the Web. Today, secure commerce servers and software from several companies have enabled transactions on the Web using credit cards and even electronic money. As a result, customers can complete the sales cycle by deciding to make a purchase with a simple click of a mouse. Transactions on the Web "close the loop" by enabling users to take immediate action by purchasing a product or service online without the need for any intervention from the seller.

Let's examine how Hawaii's Best Espresso Company (http://hoohana. aloha.net/~bec/) created a simple but effective approach to order transactions on the Web (Figure 10.7). Hawaii's Best Espresso Company's highly successful site is an inspiration to entrepreneurs who dream of owning their own business. After a year in business on an initial investment of just a $1,000, the site generates revenues of over $100,000 per year, and sales are increasing by as much as 25 percent per month!

The Place an Order section is very simply laid out with a one-line product description (Figure 10.8). All a customer needs to do is look at the variety of coffees and prices and insert a quantity in the empty text box. The form is very easy to understand and use. Hawaii's Best Espresso Coffee's co-founder, Bob Alexander's description is equally straightforward: "[We] simply describe the coffee and costs. That's it."

Once customers select and submit the quanities they want to buy, an Order Results page appears (Figure 10.9). Order Results presents an easy-to-read item-

Figure 10.7   Hawaii's Best Espresso Company home page.

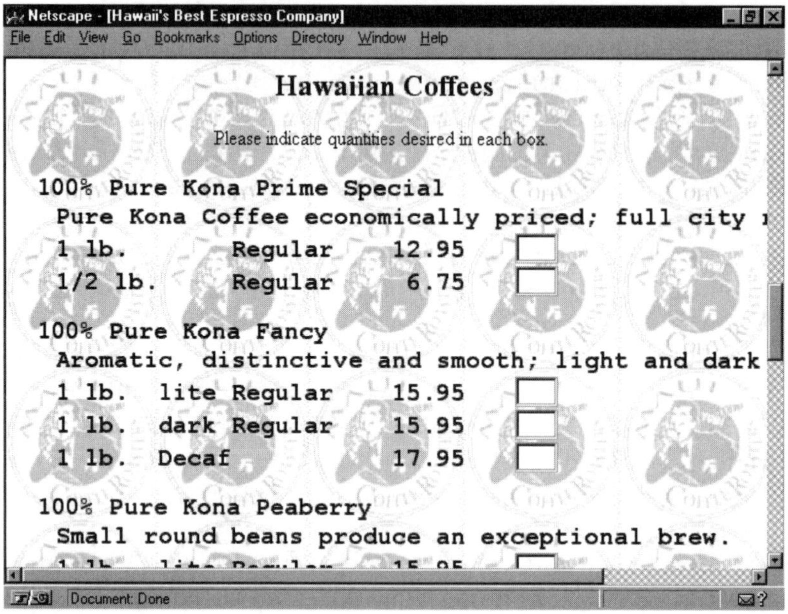

Figure 10.8　Purchasing coffee beans.

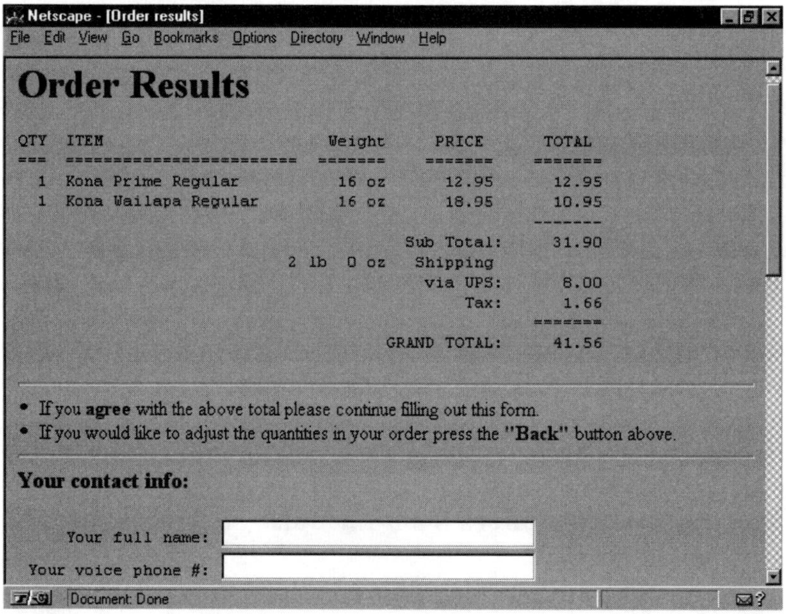

Figure 10.9　The Hawaii's Best Espresso Order Results page.

ization and total cost for the order. The only step left for customers is to enter contact, payment, and ship-to information. Once customers click on Submit, they're done! So easy, it's no wonder Hawaii's Best Espresso Company is so successful!

The best part of the site is that it requires minimal maintenance. The Alexanders now have a business that operates itself 24 hours per day. They "only check in a few times a day now, versus the 16 hours a day they used to work when they never had a chance to see each other."

Advertising and Promotion

In this section, the focus is on the most common type of advertising on the Web: banners. Advertising and promotions are two of the hottest areas of business activity on the Web. Through the Web, company logos and branding can get out to millions of users in a wide variety of places very cost effectively.

Remember, on the Web, it's up to the customer whether to click on an ad promotion, so encouraging interactivity becomes key to advertising and promotion. An interactive ad should attract interested customers, but it can do more. An ad can interest the customer in becoming involved with your product. With interactive advertising, the goal becomes getting customers to interact with a company's product by offering compelling interactive content, ideally, content that is targeted particularly to them. It can also get them to take an action.

Advertisers sponsor banners on a Web site, paying significant fees for the chance to attract interested customers. Presently, ad sponsorship is the major revenue generator on the Web and the driving force behind much of the content site development on the Web. Yahoo, a Web directory business, is trying to maximize the use of banners on its site by targeting customers according to their search activity. Yahoo divides sites into various categories such as arts, business and economy, computers and Internet, education, entertainment, government, health, news, and recreation. Such subject categorization Yahoo them a leg up on a lot of general-purpose content sites because advertisers can find the right audience among people interested in particular subject areas as determined by the search criteria users enter when they search.

"[Yahoo! is] a really good example of a site that has started to work on this," says John Danner, CEO of NetGravity whose AdServer software manages the placement, rotation, tracking, and reporting for Yahoo's 12,000 ad spots from 90 different advertisers. With 7 million hits from 1 million people per day, the number of impressions easily justifies the costs of advertising. AdServer lets Yahoo personalize its advertising by serving ads appropriate to the user, based on the search criteria or the subject category selected. For example, clicking on the Computer and Internet section in July 1996 brought up a banner from a computer-related company, IBM, which offered a free beta copy of its software called VisualAge for BASIC (Figure 10.10). IBM's ad gets the attention of interested users who are encouraged to "click here and get something free." In exchange, IBM brings the customer into its Web site and exposes them to more of the company's products.

Customer Service and Support

Keeping customers means survival to a company. Customer loyalty is forged by the positive experiences a customer has with a company (product, services, and support) over time. How a company deals with customer issues greatly influences whether that customer recommends a company's product or service or even buys from the company ever again.

The Web is becoming an increasingly important source of many kinds of information for millions of users. Web surfers primarily use the Web to access reference information. The Web's ability to provide interactive communication and robust information offers an excellent mechanism to provide customer service and support. Well-organized, easily accessible, and frequently updated cus-

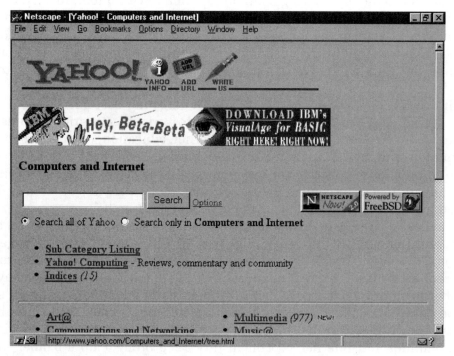

Figure 10.10   An IBM advertisement on the Yahoo! Web site.

tomer service and support features allow customers to help themselves to pertinent information by clicking through product and service reference sections.

Netscape Communications Corporation, known for its Netscape Navigator Web browser and other Internet software and services, offers extensive customer service and support on the Web and thus provides a strong example of how to meet customer needs online (Figure 10.11). Customers save time with comprehensive, up-to-date, instantaneous self-service. Netscape saves on supplies, personnel overhead, and time, freeing resources for other productive uses.

Netscape has the ability to service many of its customers' needs on the Web. Just looking at the contents of the Assistance section reveals the depth of information and services available. The site covers most of the information and resources necessary for customer service, technical support, and general assistance; for example, Customer Service, Netscape Online Support, Technical Education, About the Net, Creating Net Sites, and Helper Applications are all categories of customer support available from Netscape. Using these handy resources, customers learn about the Internet and how to develop for it. Information on Netscape's software is also available—such as general information; obtaining, using, and ordering; legal and licensing issues.

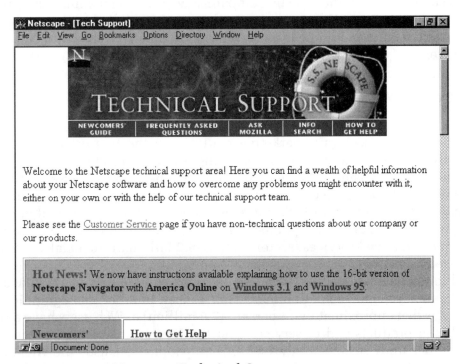

Figure 10.11   Netscape Technical Support page.

Corporate Communications

Corporate communications as a category on the Web includes all information generated by a company such as events and calendars, company information, and help wanted. Two key aspects of corporate communications that have become very common on the Internet are what's new and press releases.

What's New

C|Net uses an innovative interactive approach to "what's new" by sending comprehensive e-mail to its 250,000 registered member list who have requested to be kept informed of the latest information and activities on its Web site and other businesses. Recipients can quickly peruse the e-mail to determine whether there is anything of interest to them. Members can easily stay up to date on topics of interest and visit the site to follow up on features of interest.

Press Releases

Business press releases on the Web are common; however, most simply repurpose conventional media formats on the Web instead of utilizing its unique communications capabilities. All of these basic business functions and more can be carried out on the Web by companies wishing to maximize their return on investments in the Web. Marketers will want to carefully consider how these interactive features could be utilized on their company Web site to be equally effective.

How Big Is the Web Revenue Opportunity?

Depending on the source, you will get a range of answers about just how big the opportunity for electronic marketing really is on the Internet's World Wide Web. By the millennium, retail sales on the Net are projected to be $7 billion and business-to-business trade at $22 billion. The usually conservative Forrester Research, Inc. projects even more optimistic numbers: "By the year 2000, we expect $45.8 billion of U.S. Internet-related revenues to be created in [the computer, communications, publishing, retail, information services, entertainment, and financial services] sectors, and $46.2 billion of financial assets to be managed on the Net."

All indications are that the Web will become a vibrant new marketplace during the next several years. CommerceNet/Neilsen Internet Demographics Survey notes that approximately 14 percent (2.5 million) of Web users have already purchased products and/or services over the Internet, although a recent revision of that study says that only 1.51 million people have used the Web to purchase something.

Of course, all of these figures must be placed in the context of a new market channel that has been around only since 1994. Even if these figures were off by 50 percent, however, as a brand new channel, the Internet represents a significant marketing opportunity on a revenue basis alone. As the following lists show, Web demographics, according to Cyberatlas (http:www.cyberatlas.com/internet.html), present a significant, highly targeted market segment representing an important new channel opportunity.

Income Demographics of Web Users (Winter 1995)

Median income of Web users	$50,000–$60,000
Average income of all Web users	$63,000
Percentage of Web users with over $100,000 income	13%
Average age/Dominant age range	31/18–35

Web User Profile

Male Surfers	60%–71% (of all people on Web)
Female Surfers	29%–40% (of all people on Web)
Male Usage	77% (of all time spent)
Female Usage	23% (of all time spent)
Average Age	30–34 years
College Educated	64%
Average Income	$40,000–$63,000
Households with children	4 million

Savvy businesspeople already recognize the business potential of the Web. At a February 1996 conference, more than 75 percent of 200 top technology marketers said they expected the Internet to become an important medium for communicating business and marketing information during the next year; 40 percent reported either that the Internet was "exceeding their expectations," (24 percent) or that they were "betting the company on it" (16 percent). Interestingly, 42 percent also said that demonstrating marketing return on investment (ROI) was their biggest marketing challenge in 1996.

Clearly, Web marketing does offer significant opportunities to earn incremental revenues. Still, just as with any new venture, business success on the Web takes time and careful planning. Bill Rollinson, Co-founder and Vice President of Marketing at Internet Shopping Network (ISN), the world's largest retailer on the World Wide Web agrees. "All the hype about the Internet is setting expectations too high. Making money on the Web doesn't just happen overnight."

Founded in 1994, ISN is now growing as much as 100 percent a month. But Rollinson cautions, "You can't really expect to go into any industry and make money overnight. Just because company X is making money doesn't mean that you're going to make money." In this way, doing business on the Web is just like business as usual, in that, as he says, "It has to be a good business decision first. A good business plan specifies X investment over X time period for X return, and it requires capital and reinvestment of profits to achieve success."

There is a lot of hype about electronic commerce on the Internet these days, and it does set expectations high for entrepreneurs who hope to make a fortune. As we point out through out this chapter, though, doing business successfully on the Web begins with *doing business successfully*. If you have a good business plan and the ability to carry it out, the opportunity is there to succeed. But you will need to know a lot more to succeed as a Web marketer. Therefore, providing you with pointed insights on a range of the most important considerations for successful Web marketing is a primary goal of this chapter.

The Web Means Cost Efficiencies for Your Business

Despite the opportunity to earn incremental revenues, revenue generation has not, to date, been the primary driver behind the development of commerce on the Web. Instead, cost efficiencies have been the main contributor to an improved bottom line for companies doing business on the Web. While most companies look first to increased sales and revenues as their barometer of success on the Web, this approach overlooks the significant benefits of cost reductions in improving their bottom line.

Interestingly, surveys show that *information gathering,* rather than trade in goods and services, is the number-one activity of Web users. Likewise for companies, marketing communications is the number-one use of the Web. There are several reasons why the business use of the Internet so far has been almost exclusively limited to providing business information and promotions. First, besides its other powerful but less well-understood capabilities, the Web delivers attractive advantages in well-known business areas that companies understand and can take advantage of immediately such as:

- powerful communications capabilities
- an attractive user base
- cost efficiencies in business advertising, promotion, marketing, and distribution
- open access to globally distributed, multimedia information resources

By moving to establish domains on the Web, businesses so far have been able to quickly take advantage of significant efficiencies in the cost of:

- publishing information and advertisements on products and services
- enhancing corporate image and branding
- promoting products and services
- internal and external company communications

As a fundamentally new marketing channel, the Internet provides a new marketplace for sellers and buyers to exchange products and services. Existing businesses can *extend* onto the Internet, while new Internet-based businesses can be (and are being) created.

Pete Snell at CKS notes, "Smart smaller companies are using the Web very aggressively, and, in fact, establishing their entire brand and company around the Web without using any of the other media. Why? The Web is a very cost-effective [arena in which] to establish oneself, and very, very effective in delivering business value. For small to medium-sized companies, the Web becomes the leading channel of information, or the number-one place where they establish their brand. It can be the strongest weapon in their marketing arsenal."

Dan Janal of Janal Communications a Silicon Valley Internet public relations agency, adds, "The Internet is very important for large and small companies. The reason is that every company can increase their sales by reaching a world-wide audience that is available on the Internet. The best thing is that the Internet is the world's cheapest printing press. With the Internet, you can reach all these people at a fraction of what it would normally cost if you tried to reach them through traditional print or broadcast advertising." As early as November 1994, *Business Week* reported that direct marketing on the Net saved businesses about 25 percent of the cost of direct marketing through conventional media. Marketing discussion groups on the Web contain numerous reports from companies that have substantially reduced the cost of sales by doing business on the Net. Here are a few highlights:

- In 1995, Sun Microsystems reported (in the study *Internet-Based Secure Virtual Private Networks: The Cost of Ownership*), having saved more than $4 million since the company "reengineered information processes around the World Wide Web" by automating responses to frequently asked questions on its SunSolve Online site. More recently, Sun reported that companies can significantly cut costs by using the Internet as an internal data network, or intranet. Sun pointed to savings over four years of 23 percent ($240,000) to 50 percent

($1.3 million) of the cost of operating a traditional leased private-line network for small and large networks respectively.

• Cathay Pacific Airways reduced the costs of mailing promotional pieces to customers ($.75 and $1.00 per person) to just pennies per recipient by employing the Web.

• Broderbund, the software company, created an online product catalogue for one-fifth of *just the design cost* of its print catalogue, says Jason Everett, Broderbund Online marketing manager. And this didn't take into account the savings on production, printing, paper, and other distribution costs. Plus, changes can be made dynamically at any time on the Web so that the catalogue is always up to date.

• Tandem Computers reported the ability to keep workstation resellers around the world up to date with an immediacy never before possible by putting its print catalogues, spec sheets, price lists, and other resources up on the Web.

The reports go on and on, proving that there is gold in them thar sites and showing how companies utilizing the communication power of the Web are experiencing important successes. From public relations and personnel recruiting to internal corporate communications and project management, doing business on the Web is happening big time!

Space on the Internet is both dynamic and virtually infinite. There are no natural limits on the numbers of gold diggers who can drive a stake into the cyberfrontier, put up a shack, and seek their fortune. Still, not every business will see the need to join in the initial rush. True, significant benefits accrue from getting in early, making mistakes, and learning by doing, but there will always be room for newcomers to stake their claim on the cyberfrontier and possibly to find their fortune. Business pioneers blazing new trails into the future of electronic commerce are already harnessing the power of this virtually infinite space, as well as the many other natural features of the Internet, targeting solid business goals. In upcoming sections of this chapter, you'll gain valuable insights on how your company can maximize its marketing opportunities and achieve success on the Web by:

• Bringing products and services to customers worldwide.

• Advertising and promoting products to qualified buyers.

• Providing enhanced customer service to new and existing customers.

• Delivering a dynamic experience for customers and partners.

• Accessing rich new sources of customer data.

- Developing new collaborative relationships with customers and partners.
- Much, much more!

Building Better Customer Relationships

"Now is the time," says Snell, "for firms that have relied on traditional media to market themselves, to really be wrestling with the marketing potential of the Web, and figuring out if the Internet it is really applicable to their business goals." As more companies join the business pioneers on the cyberfrontier, the real benefits of doing business on the Web will start to match the level of the hype, and electronic commerce will really take off.

It is important to keep in mind that the Web is a fundamentally new media. It offers new, unconventional media capabilities that are unfamiliar to companies and their customers, who are comfortable with conventional broadcast media. Customers are used to being the passive recipients of ads, brochures, mailers, and other messages from conventional media; and companies are used to simply delivering one-way messages.

As with all new communications technologies, there is a steep learning curve associated with utilizing the Internet's capabilities, particularly interactivity. To understand this, recall the emergence of motion pictures and the pathbreaking efforts of such greats as Charlie Chaplin and D.W. Griffith. By comparison to today's films, those early features seem remarkably premature. Today, Internet pioneers are just beginning to understand the potential of interactive one-to-one communications, and only a few in the conventional media are beginning to recognize the importance of taking on the challenge.

As a result, today, many business Web sites bear a strong resemblance to the print collateral of the companies they represent. This first wave of business "brochureware" sites simply repurposed existing print collateral. In the heat of the Web-rush, most companies looked at their Web sites as another piece of promotional collateral rather than as the new marketing channel that it is. Few really stopped to consider how best to integrate their Web sites with their established business systems to maximize the benefit of one-to-one communication.

While many companies jumped in to achieve significant cost savings as well as important experience in the new media, it is still possible to get in on the ground floor of the Web marketing opportunity. Only a select few are recognizing and learning to use the power of interactive communications through experimentation. This *second wave* of business Web sites are beginning to take advantage of the Internet's ability to interactively gather, link, process, search, and deliver distributed multimedia information resources, *from* anywhere in the world *to* anywhere in the world, in mere seconds. These sites enable companies and their customers to make better, more complex choices, faster, cheaper, and easier than ever before.

To help people understand the importance of the Internet, Pete Snell draws a parallel to the impact of the personal computer on society. "You need to learn about the power of interactive marketing or it's going to blow past you. You're going to limit your ability to add value to your corporation if you don't understand the power of this medium." Interactive communications on the Web fundamentally enhance and enable new kinds of marketing relationships, altering the process of exchange and the future of marketing itself. Internet technology promises to revolutionize communication, and communication is central to building marketing relationships with customers. *Interactive communication* is both a key distinguishing characteristic of the Web and central to building and maintaining long-term business relationships on the Web.

Little wonder then that the Internet is of great interest to marketers. As a revolutionary new communications medium, the Internet enables a new marketing channel, which offers some very attractive capabilities and benefits when it comes to the exchange of business information, goods, and services. Customers benefit from Web marketing by:

- Gaining more control over the process of exchange.
- Building rich relationships with sellers they can trust.
- Accessing rich, diverse sources of information.
- Obtaining faster, easier access to the information they really want.
- Receiving better values for their money.
- Securing information tailored to their personal preferences.

Naturally, customers are attracted, engaged, impressed, and convinced to purchase the goods and services they need more quickly and easily by interactive marketing communications. Businesses benefit from Web marketing by:

- Helping customers make purchases more easily and quickly.
- Building rich long-term relationships with loyal customers.
- Enabling customers to access the information they really want.
- Gathering valuable customer and market data more easily.
- Targeting buyers with the right information, on the right products, at the right time.
- Reducing the cost of doing business.

- Enhancing company image and branding.
- Decreasing errors and overhead.
- Reducing the barriers to entry into new markets.
- Engaging in value rather than price competition.
- Much more.

By building virtual personal, one-to-one marketing relationships with buyers on the Web, companies can access a fundamentally new marketing channel, gain new revenue streams, and make more sales to motivated, loyal customers.

The Cyberfrontier: Maximizing the Power of the Web

In essence, marketing on the Web is really no different from marketing through any other channel. In any transaction, buyers and sellers establish a relationship based on an exchange of equal values based on what they each need and what they each bring to the table. It is in the *nature of the relationship* between companies and their customers that marketing on the Web distinguishes itself from other channels. A defining characteristic of the Web channel is that its customers exercise a much greater degree of control over the whole process of exchange than in any other channel.

As noted in the beginning of this chapter, to be successful in doing business on the Web, companies will have to learn new ways of interacting with customers by establishing virtual personal relationships based on understanding and meeting the unique preferences of each of their customers.

What the Internet Can Do for Your Business

As a fundamentally new communications technology, the Web distinguishes itself from conventional media by integrating seven key capabilities to enhance your business:

- global access
- Immediate real-time access
- virtually infinite space
- multimedia
- interactivity
- database driven information
- data mining and user tracking

Together, these powerful features offer companies on the Web important opportunities to enable and enhance marketing programs with unprecedented capabilities. This section defines and explores the business uses of each of these distinguishing properties of the Web. The objective: to help companies understand how investing in developing these powerful features on their Web sites can maximize the business benefits of the Web.

Surf Locally, Interact Globally

Never before in any medium have so many people all over the world been able to access and interact with the same information sources. Today, almost anyone with a computer and a modem anywhere on Earth can connect with diverse sources of information as well as other "wired" individuals. Understanding the Internet's capability for global communications offers companies important opportunities to bring their message to a worldwide audience and to maximize the benefits of their investment in the Web.

The Internet is designed to link distributed information resources through a worldwide network of computer *hosts.* Rather than storing data on a single central computer, the Internet serves information resources from more than 6.64 million different Internet host computers operating in more than 70,000 different interconnected networks around the world. As the first truly global network, more than 2.37 million of those hosts are located outside the United States in more than 150 countries. Beyond the confines of local, regional, and national borders, the Internet interconnects new people and organizations everywhere. Interestingly, so far more than 75 percent of these host computers are located in English-speaking countries, mostly in the United States (64 percent), as detailed in this list*:

	% of Total
United States	64.0%
Other English-speaking countries	12.7
Western Europe (Except Britain and Ireland)	16.9
Asia (Except Australia and New Zealand)	4.0
Eastern Europe	0.9
Africa/Middle East	0.9
Central and South America	0.6

In Europe, "the Internet has been a bit slow to develop because the perception is that there's too much content in English," says James Lewis, president of

*Source: Network Wizards, *Business Week*

Globalink Inc., a Fairfax, Virginia "localization" software company. Globalink is among the wave of new companies offering software that translates English e-mail and Web sites into an increasing number of local languages. "The Internet is the application that machine translation has been waiting for," says Glen Akers, president of Language Engineering Corp., a Belmont, Massachusetts company offering English localization software for Japanese, German, and French translation. Ecila, a new online search engine, retrieves information from all Web sites created in France, about 70 percent of which are in French.

While English is projected to be the Internet's dominant language through the millennium, the most rapid growth in Internet usage around the globe will come in non-English speaking countries. Table 10.1 shows projections for the number of people on the Internet in the United States, Asia, and Europe through the year 2000.

Today, business on the Internet must be viewed as a new global frontier. Rapid immigration and population growth fuels an Internet boom with an unprecedented expansion of 20 percent per month. Depending on which estimates you believe, the Internet already supports 18 to 30 million users representing nearly every country. Jupiter Communications reports that all but 23 countries have Internet access today. Some estimates project that one-third of all U.S. households (33 million) will have Web access, placing the total number of U.S. Web access accounts alone at 40 million by the year 2000.

Immediate, Real-Time Access

As marketing guru Tom Peters points out, on the Internet, anywhere on the planet is just six-tenths of a second away! Now, anyone who has tried to access the Net with a 14.4 baud modem knows that estimate *is* a bit of an exaggeration. Still, with a new wave of access modes expanding delivery capabilities, Internet access speeds for average users will increase, and Peters' optimistic assessment eventually will prove correct.

Today, the Web is accessible 24 hours a day, 7 days a week. Everyday, at every time of day, all over the world, Internet users access diverse sources of infor-

TABLE 10.1   People on the Internet: United States, Asia, and Europe

	1994 (mill.)	% of Total	1996 (mill.)	% of Total	1998 (mill.)	% of Total	2000 (mill.)	% of Total
U.S.	4.5	78.9	13.8	78.4	23.1	67.9	32.9	63.3
Asia	0.9	15.8	2.3	13.1	7.0	20.6	11.0	21.2
Europe	0.3	5.3	1.5	8.5	4.8	14.1	8.1	15.6
Total	5.7	100	17.6	100	34.0	100	52.0	100

Source: Forrester Research, Inc., September 1995

mation with an immediacy never before possible in any media. In the comfort of home or office, with the click of a mouse button, Internet users send digital signals to host computers in any part of the world, resulting in the near instantaneous delivery of desired information. E-mail, electronic file transfer, the World Wide Web, and other Internet capabilities enable virtually immediate access to people, data, images, sounds, animations, even video clips.

Such immediacy is called *real time* because, unlike conventional media, users themselves control when they send or receive these near-instantaneous information transfers. Likewise, information placed up on the Net can be changed and updated in real time as well. Product catalogues, pricing, sell sheets, and a host of other business materials can be kept fresh and up to date with an immediacy never before possible in any medium.

For business, real-time immediacy means that sellers can keep dynamically published information current without incurring the expense of printing and publication. In addition to accessing timely information on products and services, buyers can receive near-instantaneous answers to their questions, and sellers can substantially shorten the sales cycle by providing access to the information buyers need and by enabling online commerce capabilities on their Web sites. "I could be watching a commercial for a car on TV, but if I have questions, I have to wait for answers," says Dan Janal of Janal Communications. "I can't ask the commercial where's my nearest dealer? How much does it cost? How many miles per gallon, or anything else. I'd have to call the dealer the next morning. By the time the next morning rolls around, how many more commercials have I been exposed to? I don't even remember that car commercial."

On well-designed business Web sites, users will be able to find all the answers they need to make a purchase decision. If a user can't find the answer on the business site, he or she can easily and immediately send an e-mail message to a company representative and get an answer back in a very short amount of time. For example, Nando Times (http://www.nando.com) updates its news features every five minutes for its 5.5 million weekly users. Online catalogues are another example of how businesses can achieve efficiencies by storing data once and updating changes in real time at regular intervals.

Another business benefit of real-time immediacy impacts internal corporate communications. For intra-company communications, the Internet can provide highly secure, password-protected ways to keep employees updated on the latest product and policy information, completely replacing haphazard distribution of memos. Across all time zones, employees can access up-to-the-minute information about product features and availability without the expense of long-distance phone calls.

American Airlines takes advantage of the real-time immediacy and virtually infinite space on the Internet: "In the past we've downloaded all these graphics files and things from the host onto notebooks for sales reps to use in presentations," says Philip Holden at American Airlines. "Now we're going to house all that stuff on the Internet and let them grab those things as they need them; and that way, if we have to update something, we update it once instead of 500 times."

Today, by developing business features around the real-time capabilities of the Internet, companies can maximize the business benefits of their Web sites. A key is using the power of the Internet to provide immediate access to all the information resources buyers and employees need to take immediate actions in real time.

Virtually Infinite Space

"Let's imagine that you are a catalogue seller, and you normally print a 48-page catalogue that comes out four times a year," says Dan Janal of Janal Communications. "You can only put 100 to 200 of your top-selling products in that catalogue. And you only have about a paragraph of space to talk about each product. You send it out and hope that you make enough money to make it worthwhile."

"The Internet is the world's cheapest printing press," quips Janal. "There is virtually no cost for printing on the Internet. If you have a thousand products in your catalog, you can put all [of them] on the Internet. You can put as many pictures as you like on the Internet. You can have full descriptions about the products, not just one little paragraph."

Once you have a business Web site up, space in which to publish information resources is virtually free. Page after page of information can be posted on this site with no limitations, other than the amount of storage space you have connected to your host server. That's because space on the Internet is virtually infinite. By comparison, space in conventional media is limited and often costly. Unless you spend a fortune, it's impossible to tell customers everything they may want or need to know about products, services, the company, and so on. There's just too much to say. Instead, marketers must select the most important pieces of information and attempt to convey it in a print ad or a 30-second spot. And it may or may not be the information any particular customer needs to make a choice.

Using conventional media, marketers are restricted to attracting customers and sending a relatively simple message. Likewise, with direct mail, printing, paper, and postage expenses add up fast. On the Web, sellers can tell customers *everything* about all their products for a fraction of the cost. And customers can choose what most interests them. Companies only have to ensure that everything is there, ready to be easily accessed by customers.

In the Multimedia Development Group Bulletin, January 1995, Tim Pearson's article "Servers and Surfers: Electronic Commerce on the I-way" states:

The promise of cheap digital delivery of text, graphics, animation, video, and audio is a major factor pushing development of the Internet in general, and electronic commerce in particular. For the first time in the history of media, virtually infinite amounts of information can be made available and delivered to users at a minuscule cost per user compared to both broadcast and print media. In fact, information can be provided to 1 million users on the Web at a cost that is less than five-thousandths of 1 percent of the cost of delivering the same information via a newspaper, according to estimates by economist Arnold Kling. Combine this with the added values of user interactivity, flexibility of use, easy maintenance, and relatively low-cost hardware installations, and, clearly, the Web becomes a highly attractive, cost-reducing alternative to more traditional ways of reaching customers.

Multimedia Delivery

Describing a Web development project for a major automobile manufacturer, Pete Snell of CKS said, "The Web provides a place where you can get all the information you need, except for [being able to] physically walk up and touch the automobile." With advanced multimedia technologies, "You can virtually sit inside the car and see what it looks like," Snell says. "You're actually seeing what the dashboard looks like." Audio on the Web also lets buyers hear the door shut and an electric window open as a sales representative describes custom features. On the Web, multimedia lets buyers see the product and make a deal, all online.

Multimedia can be defined as communications and technology that integrates a variety of distinct media types into a single, hybrid presentation. Today, text, graphics, photos, audio, animation, video, broadcasts, and even 3D virtual reality spaces can be offered on the Web. For business, dynamic multimedia on the Web enables and enhances business communications capabilities in unprecedented ways. It enhances and expands the power of computer users everywhere to more intuitively know and understand the incredible diversity of the world we live, work, learn, and play in. For business, multimedia on the Web brings opportunities to communicate with buyers with an unprecedented power and immediacy. Product information, customer service, technical support, training, and many other aspects of business communication can be amplified on the Web. And that is exactly what is beginning to happen.

For example, customers might use a 3D environment to experience products before they buy. Interior decorators might display a 3D virtual reality showroom, in which customers could enter the dimensions of their living room and see how various pieces of furniture would look and fit from several different perspectives. Terry Jones, president of SABRE Interactive, producers of Travelocity, says:

Web technology with a combination of text, graphics, audio, and video allows us to bring travel to life in a way we couldn't do before. With hypertext we can let consumers wander and get as much information about the fare or destination they want. We can show them still images, we can play music, we can show them videos, and we can let them be very comfortable about their destination in a way we couldn't do before, and in a way that we think, over time, will substantially reduce the cost of marketing. There is a huge waste in the travel market. I ran a travel agency with seven people. We used to get a mailbag a day full of brochures. We had to sort them and put them away, and then we could never find them when [an interested customer] came in. Talk about non-one-to-one marketing! Here the consumers have the wheel, and they can really search out what they are interested in.

Interactivity

"On television you can buy a 30-second ad, and it's your time," says Dan Janal. "It costs a lot, but anyone watching during your time will be exposed to your broadcast message. However, they may or may not be interested in your message. On the Internet, customers are more qualified because they've chosen your site to look at. The beauty is, they're selecting you."

Perhaps the single most important, and arguably the least well-understood, capability of the Web is interactivity. Interactive communications on the Web are two-way communications during which users both provide and receive information. Depending on user choices, interactive communications can be:

- *one-to-one* interactions as in the case of a product purchase
- *many-to-many* as in a threaded technical discussion group
- *one-to-many* as in an online tour of a manufacturing operation
- *many-to-one* as in a user's request for assistance on a problem
- any combination of these general forms

For marketers who want to implement highly effective Web sites, understanding interactivity on the Web is key to unlocking the real power of the Internet as a fundamentally new marketing channel. To succeed on the Web, marketers must understand that, because of interactivity, their customers now have the ability to choose and control the content, timing, and pacing of their communications. As a result, interactivity enables and *requires* creation of new, enhanced, interactive relationships between sellers and buyers. Thus, designing highly interactive business features has become essential to maximizing the business benefits of a company's Web site.

Again, Internet users can *choose* the information they want and need rather than simply waiting to see and hear what information will be presented to them as on radio or television. The content broadcast on these "mass media" conform to a conventional model of communication called *one-to-many,* in which one content provider delivers highly edited media content to a mass audience of many spectators. In one-to-many communication, messages travel in one direction, from the provider to the spectator. Interest in one-to-many communications also tends to be random, since only a few people within a much larger audience of spectators are the targets of such programming. That's why such media messages may be referred to as "broad-cast" communications.

By contrast, user-selected information delivered on the Web can target an audience of one individual, and so is called *one-to-one* communication. One-to-one communication most closely resembles a conversation between two interested people, and is unconventional in mass media communication. One-to-one communications also travel in two (or more) directions: a user selects an information resource from a content provider, which delivers the requested information resource to the user. Because the information resource is selected by the user, interest in the information is prequalified and well targeted. Internet communications can therefore be referred to as "narrow-cast" or "point-cast" communications.

Ultimately, interactive, one-to-one communication on the Internet changes the nature of the relationship between information providers and information users, opening the door to enhancements of the relationship between buyers and sellers on the Internet as well. "The Internet is a great sales tool because people *select* your site and come to visit. They choose to browse and read your materials. They decide if and when they will look at your products to see and hear and feel everything about them," says Janal. "This is a complete twist from the traditional marketing methods where you have to go out and seek the customers. On the Internet, people come to your site because they want your product, or at least they're considering your product. Then you have to convince them that your product is better than the competitor's product."

Taking advantage of the interactive power of the Web for business benefit really means changing the way companies think about business communication. Because Web users can always select the information they want and need, as well as when and how they want it, the very nature of the traditional process of marketing communication via media changes in fundamental ways. "On the Internet, time is not something you, as a marketer, buy," says Janal. "Time is what your customers spend. Your customers choose to be there looking at your message because they have an interest in your products or services. On the Internet, your customer is prequalified. So the Internet is a totally different marketing paradigm."

Effective marketing on the Internet will acknowledge and enable customers' ability to control the flow of marketing communication. In any channel, the intent of marketing communications is to take customers through a complete sales cycle, and, with the support of sales and fulfillment personnel, "complete the loop" by ensuring that customers have everything they need to make a purchase decision or buy and use a product or service. On the Web, interactive marketing communications enable customers to complete the loop themselves, online, if the company has done a good job of design and providing easy access to information. Essentially, a company's marketing communications will take customers through a sales cycle by successfully getting the customer through the following processes:

- Attracting customers.
- Engaging customers' interest in the seller's marketing messages.
- Creating and reinforcing impressions of the seller's offerings.
- Convincing customers to take an action.

Conventional mass communications media have had relatively good, but limited, success in achieving these goals, but the one-to-many nature of conventional media has placed limits on the effectiveness of conventional marketing communications in taking customers through the entire sales cycle.

Marketing messages based on one-to-many communications inherently do not allow customers to immediately and easily complete the sales cycle, even if they fully succeed in attracting, engaging, and impressing the customer. This can mean lost sales and forgone opportunities. "In traditional marketing you're essentially broadcasting a message to passive recipients hoping to create impressions that attract customers. All of a sudden, a commercial comes on and they hear it, and five other commercials, then they're back to the TV program," says Janal. "By the next morning, they have forgotten all about the commercial because they have seen so many others."

In the broadcast model of marketing communications, sellers cast a wide net intent on catching a few good customers. The flow of information travels *from the seller to a pool of passive spectators.* Sellers expect that the spectator pool contains a small group of actual customers who can be convinced to complete the loop by being called into action. To reach actual customers and complete the sales cycle, a conventional broadcast campaign must first *attract* a potential customer's attention. Once attracted, the broadcast must *engage* the customer's interest in learning more about the product or service. If engaged, the broadcast must *impress* the customer enough to compel them to take further action.

Unfortunately, customers who are attracted, engaged, and impressed still have to make a sometimes costly effort to ask questions and obtain the additional information necessary to convince them, and then to provide any information necessary to actually make a purchase. Of course, this process requires significant extra time, effort, even expense, all of which should be viewed as hidden, and sometimes prohibitive, costs to customers.

By contrast, well-designed interactive marketing communications on the Web enable a customer to easily complete the sales cycle by providing all of the information customers need to make a decision, as well as convenient and simple interactive ordering and fulfillment features. One-to-one interactive communications on the Web can also enhance a company's marketing messages with all of the powerful communications capabilities of the Web. As we will see in the next section, on the Web, sellers have the ability to "pointcast" information to each user to attract, engage, and impress individuals with unprecedented power and immediacy.

The most effective marketing messages on the Web are those that really speak to people's need for information. Consequently, right now, Web demographics are skewed toward the "information seekers." Effective marketing sites fully understand and anticipate the information needs of their visitors, and make that information readily accessible. As discussed in the next section, effective Web marketers also use interactive communications technologies to "track" valuable market intelligence about customer preferences and behaviors, automatically. Companies use such customer data to provide key enhancements for future customer contacts and to enable creation of personal long-term relationships between buyers and sellers.

"It is getting more and more expensive [to build successful Web sites] because now people understand interactivity to some extent; they understand that they need to have things interactive; and as soon as you want anything interactive, or communications in the programming, the programming becomes expensive," says Karen Shapiro, Internet Channel Manager, Bank of America.

Some suggestions for building interactivity into your Web site are:

- Find ways for customers to communicate with the company.
- Find ways for customers to communicate with other customers.
- Find ways to draw people in and to participate with the site, products, and services.
- Hold activities and/or communications on an announced and ongoing basis.

Database-Driven Information

Steve Zocchi, director of Marketing at Spider Technologies, a Palo Alto California software developer that helps companies build applications to connect databases to the Web, points out a critical problem with many Web sites: "Everybody has rushed out to the Web and said, 'We are going to get our Web site out there. We're going to put up our brochures and a pile of information onto the Web.' And the poor users of the information get to these mammoth Web sites and they have no idea how to find anything or even if what they are looking for is there. And it could take them an hour to traverse through all the links to finally find it! My admonition is, if you're going to put your business up on the Web, make sure that you help your customers get to the right information really quickly."

To avoid the "brochureware" trap, companies new to the Web, as well as companies looking to take their existing site to the next level, should give serious consideration to investing in a database-driven Web site. Pretty pages with cool graphics and loads of content can be great, but there's so much more that a company can do with a database-driven Web site. A database linked to a company Web site can enable:

- efficient content management
- highly interactive value-adding applications
- user tracking and differentiation
- virtual personal relationships

Let's take a closer look at how Web marketers can utilize the power of database-driven networking on the Web to meet business needs. The Web offers marketers the opportunity to use powerful database-driven networking capabilities to enable and enhance existing business information systems. Highly efficient database-driven content management can deliver significant business benefits:

- Companies can make the right information available to the right users in the right format at the right time.
- Businesses can link vast corporate storehouses of information to employees, partners, and customers.
- Users can quickly and easily locate and interact with the people, information, and resources they need to succeed.

Pete Snell explains:

Prudential is a good example of where we've implemented some elements to increase the interactivity of a site. There are four separate databases on that site where people can look up information. Prudential sells insurance, but it also has real estate brokerage affiliates across the country. The site has geolocators where users type in their zip code, and they get information from a real estate or an insurance agent in their area.

There are also a couple of calculators on the site. We let visitors to the site calculate what their child's college education is going to cost them, projected forward, depending on whether it's a public school or private school and where it is in the country. We take data from the college board and do some calculations so people can realize: "I heard it was expensive. Now I can see that I'm going to have to start saving." There's a similar retirement planning calculator in there, as well.

So these are ways in which a company can deliver useful information to people visiting its site. The site is interacting with them. It's not just click, picture, click, picture. It's fill out some information and the calculator will do some homework for you and give you an answer and give it to you within a few seconds.

Delivering Pages on the Fly

One of the benefits of a database-driven Web site is that you don't have to organize all the content in advance for the customer. The customers can select what they want, and then a special Web page can be built for them on the fly. In this way your customers are automatically getting individual attention on a 24-hour basis. Illustra, a database company located in Oakland, California, offers a database with some powerful capabilities, including the ability to track user behavior and produce customized content based on that activity.

For example, the Illustra database enables the generation of a dynamic catalogue with customized pages generated especially for individual buyers. Customers can select from products, directly targeting their interests. They can also select related information via dynamic hyperlinks. Buyers unsure of a particular product name can search the contents of images, submitting queries such as, "Display all products in the database that resemble this laptop computer." Notably, the online catalogue can also automate management of product inventory levels, reorder schedules, account transaction histories, as well as the overall catalogue content itself, eliminating the need for manual updating when a product is added or dropped.

Clearly, database-driven content management offers significant business benefits, and the Illustra database does a great job of building Web pages on the fly. But building a complex database application that takes a user through a process of interacting with a database is completely different from dynamic content generation on the Web.

Custom Database-Driven Environments on the Web

Databases in the corporate environment already are good at allocating information differently to different classes of user. "Think about *database marketing* a hot phrase during the last five years; The Web is a tremendously easy-to-use conduit for the database marketing engine your company may have already created. No doubt, there is already a lot of intelligence in that database, but there is a lot more you could get," Zocchi points out. "The Web is an opportunity to get to those customers and provide a more interactive experience just by automating the whole thing."

"Let's take advantage of that infrastructure," says Zocchi. "I can create user classes that a database application will understand, and deliver different levels of information to different users on the Web. Somebody in the finance department using an internal Web site to get information should probably get a very detailed report while the marketing guys should get very general information about finances."

Databases connected to Web applications can do powerful content management for any class of user marketers want to define. But presenting different classes of users with different types of interfaces involves not just tailoring information; it also involves tailoring Web environments. Different users have varying preferences about how they like to receive information. Luckily, there *are* many different ways to communicate the same information.

For example, to consider the purchase of a new home, some users will want to fly through a 3D simulated house, or watch a time-lapse sequence as the sun moves across the living room to "get a feel for the place." Socially oriented buyers may want to see a video of the neighborhood and talk to some neighbors. Others will want to see a spreadsheet of the housing valuations and recent sales for similar homes in the district. The sound conscious will want to hear audio samples of street noise at different times throughout the day to identify the most quiet homes. The possibilities are as varied as the buyers themselves, and that is the point. Database-driven Web sites give marketers the opportunity to present information tailored to all user types.

Database-Driven Customer Service   "You can use the Web site to publish, and that's great," says Steve Zocchi, "That's one level. If you can make the site a little more interactive, that's super! You're already a step ahead of a lot of Web sites out there. But take it to the next level: How can you interact with your customer? Could you compress the sales cycle? Maybe. Maybe you could even give people an experience of what your product is like!" Corporate databases can already provide some of these functions, but the challenge is building custom applications that do it on a Web site.

Your company's database can be designed to deliver the information customers need as they need it. Simple database-driven features might include answers to frequently asked questions or regular updates and information on new product releases. Connecting text search engines to all your product and technical support documentation is a huge step forward.

Use your relational database, in conjunction with *data mining* technologies (discussed in the next section), to identify, store, analyze, and differentiate what matters to each customer. Find out what information is important to that person and how he or she prefers to receive it. Identify interests, preferences, needs, and personal background. The goal is to construct personal demographic and psychographic profiles that can inform delivery of future valuable products and services. Then you can begin to create features that feed them valuable information and really attract that customer to return again and again.

Keep in mind the responsibility that comes with access to a customer's personal information. Companies should consider writing a formal information policy to be posted on your site. For ease of use, users should have to enter information only once, to be accessed as needed anywhere in the site. Users should also maintain full control over the uses to which their information is being put. In revealing such personal information, users are relying on the integrity of your company to deliver better customer service, while not allowing unauthorized access.

Your company should strive for total integration of customer information with existing business systems to develop applications that better serve customers. For example companies could build an application front end that's essentially a mini expert system on the Web. In the case of a technical support application, the Web feature could lead users through a line of questions that result in a series of possible answers to a series of registered problems documented in a constantly updated database. The customer could enter: "My printer's not working," and then work with the database to distinguish likely from unlikely causes of the problem, such as: "It's not working because it's not plugged in" or, "It's not working because there are black streaks across the paper." In this way, database-driven technical support applications guide customers through the process of helping them help themselves solve problems, before you actually talk to them. Companies like Sun Microsystems and Cisco Systems have already saved millions of dollars a month with such database-driven applications running on the Web.

"There's a real strong sense of community on the Web. People want to share their information, and the easier it is for them to do that, the richer the information you are going to get," says Zocchi. "Our tools allow the many-to-many interactions to happen by enabling visitors to both browse archives and add input. The database becomes the key to bringing that kind of functionality to the Web, and that's what Spider Technologies is all about. Our Web site is the catalyst for information sharing by providing the mechanism and by encouraging our target community of users to participate."

By storing these kinds of discussions in searchable archives, you can begin to build a really valuable storehouse of information that will be of many uses and reduce costs by taking the company out of the loop as gatekeeper and maintainer of information. Providing database access on your digital outpost allows many-to-many interactions to happen without your direct involvement.

Encouraging customer input also generates valuable feedback for a company, revealing rewarding ideas for improving or building new products and services. "One of the great things about the Web is that ideas are coming in all the time," says Zocchi. "A customer says, for instance, 'You know, why don't we try building an application to do this on the Web?' We have this great infrastructure to reach people. The opportunities are infinite. We are just scratching the surface."

To go forward with designing advanced database-driven Web features capable of personalized interactive experiences for each user, companies will need to clearly identify and differentiate the needs of their target user segments. For this, databases integrated with Web tracking technology excel as well.

Data Mining: User Measurement and Differentiation

"With the rapidly declining cost and increasing power of information processing, companies are able to remember every detail of each relationship with each customer. Thus, they are able to offer tailored communications, personalized service, and mass-customized products. Simply put, the more I know about you, the better I'm able to meet your needs—better than someone who doesn't know you: Ultimately, if I do it right, it's a great advantage to both of us." So says Martha Rogers, co-author with Don Peppers of the best-selling *One-to-One Future: Building Relationships One Customer at a Time* (Doubleday, 1993).

"Think about it," says Steve Zocchi of Spider Technologies: "I rarely have the opportunity to watch somebody read my brochure. But if you put information on a Web site and you have tracking capabilities built in to applications, you can watch people move through the application. That gives me some very interesting marketing information. It helps me understand what they like on that Web site, helps me understand how they move from one topic to another, helps me understand where I want to put, let's say, my promotional announcement, or what kind of information certain people are looking for. So, as you move to the Web, you can begin to see opportunities to market much more intelligently and proactively. People are going to provide you with information by interacting with your application. You want to turn that information around and be a better marketer for it."

"I think that anyone who is going to be successful with marketing on the Internet is going to be successful because of the knowledge that they gain about their customers," says NetGravity's John Danner, speaking about the Web's potential for delivering custom, highly personalized products and services. "Tracking is the first step in trying to understand your customer base better through the Internet."

Tracking Web site users involves three phases in a recursive loop:

1. *Collecting* data provided by users themselves both actively and passively on the Web.
2. *Analyzing* the data to extract meaningful information about users' preferences as well as business processes and activities.
3. *Incorporating* that information into better services and products for users, and better business practices and enhanced business activities for you.

As customers navigate a site and make purchases, the market intelligence and customer data gathered can eventually form profiles of particular users, to be developed into templates for delivery of personalized information. Ideally, this data will shape new or improved products, services, and interactive features conforming to the needs of each user.

Analysis of collected data can define markets, identify individual consumers within each market, and differentiate purchasing behavior by demographic and psychographic cohorts, providing insight into why and how particular individuals make purchasing decisions. Tracking on the Web can also help identify the effectiveness of media spending, promotions, new product introductions technical support, and many other business activities by monitoring user response and choice.

Terry Myerson, president of Interse, a Web tracking and analysis software company, advises companies to think of tracking as "a way to determine what is working and what is not, so they can invest in those areas that provide the highest return." Myerson believes that companies should apply the results of tracking analysis to "all areas of business, not just the Web." During the next few years, tracking technology "will become far more integrated into the existing marketing and customer data infrastructure of a company," predicts Myerson.

Focusing on the overall return on business investments (ROI) by implementing user tracking techniques, we can uncover many other worthwhile business benefits as well. In particular, investing in Web tracking technologies can improve the ROI on a business Web site by enabling companies to:

• Understand and meet customer needs more effectively across all channels.

• Differentiate customers into highly targeted segments.

- Attract and retain target user/customer segments.
- Select high-margin users for extra-special treatment.
- Identify and reevaluate costly users.
- Offer highly targeted products, services, advertising, and promotions.
- Evaluate the success of business activities.
- Make more effective overall business decisions.
- Customize information, product, and service offerings for individual customers.
- Establish virtual personal relationships with every customer or user.

Of course, more effective tracking technologies also raise important and sensitive issues of business ethics, personal privacy, and data security that tracking companies and marketers must balance with their need for information about users.

There are two primary reasons why companies have only just begun to employ data-mining tools. First, data-mining technology on the Web is really in its infancy. Emerging in 1995, significant technical challenges still have to be overcome as advanced tools for highly effective user tracking are conceived. Likewise, defining appropriate business parameters for the collection and analysis of user data remains relatively uncharted territory. Tracking-savvy business experts have just started to identify the most basic formulas for generating the information marketers need to achieve the potential of the Web for business. During the next several years, tracking technology and methodology will evolve rapidly in response to the information demands of advertisers, marketers, and companies that want to maximize the potential of the Web for business benefit.

A second factor underlying the relative underutilization of tracking technology is that, so far, most companies have focused their investments on staking their claim on the cyberfrontier getting their sites up on the Web. As with other advanced Web capabilities, there has been a fairly steep learning curve, and, initially, only a few companies knew how to go about using Web tracking tools to collect user information for business benefit. Only after getting a site up have the majority of companies begun to consider enhancements like user tracking.

As companies move step by step up the Web learning curve, they will encounter several challenges. "First, there's getting something up that's interesting, and getting some people there," says John Danner of NetGravity. "The next step is to know who are those people? You want to start finding out something about those people and generating some interesting results." The third step involves creating processes for integrating the information collected with existing business systems. "You're just creating a big backlog of information, raw data, that needs to get into the other [business] systems," says Danner. "There are not many companies that are at the third step right now, but I think we'll see that very soon, especially for the sites that are really starting to collect a lot of information about customers."

To command the resources needed to get to the third step, Danner advises marketers to be ready to impress senior management with the quality of the data collected. "When you go to MIS, or to anyone else in the company, you've got to show them what you have learned about the customer. It could be just age, sex, and zip code. It's still very rough, but it does provide you some level of information. Then, you can say, 'Okay, we need to get this [information technology] integrated with our other business systems.' "

The Data to Collect from Customers

Measuring impacts and trends on a Web site can help marketers maximize the business benefit of their investment in the Web. Creating baselines of responses, purchases, requests, errors, problems, and other core business data can inform evaluations and improvements of business performance both on the Web and in other channels. By capturing baseline information, a company can measure the responses and effectiveness of various company activities and events such as marketing programs, new product announcements, and customer service programs.

Once users come to your site, your job is to figure out how to collect information about them in some structured way. Tracking users around the site can tell you how long they spent looking at different site features, and that gives a good general overview. But marketing effectively on the Web means collecting user information that helps you understand and communicate better with your customer base. One set of data is just raw demographics—age, sex, education, income, zip code, and so on. The next set is psychographic information—what do they like, what do they do, how do they play, what are their interests.

The third kind of information marketers want from each user is how they feel about your company and your products. For this, the more detail the better. "You need to figure out how to entice them to tell you more about what they think of you, and some people just love to do that," quips Danner. "If you could get everybody who comes to your site to fill out a complete questionnaire on each one of your products, that would be the best possible thing. You'll never get that, but your job is to get as close to that as you possibly can. Some people say, 'I used your product last week and it was this and that, and I didn't think it was good this way,' and that's great. Those are the people that you love to have. You also want the people who might not normally tell you what they think about your product giving you input because that creates a much better statistical sample of your user base than just the people who want to talk."

Tracking Business Activities

To date, most discussions of tracking have focused on the benefits of user tracking per se. In addition, though, companies that want to maximize the business benefits of the Web will also want to track the impact of general business activities. "Anything you can measure, you can improve," or so believed American industrialist Edward Deming. Deming would have loved Web tracking tools. The Web's unparalleled capacity for measurement and testing of business processes gives modern-day Demings the ability to observe and improve business activities with amazing immediacy and accuracy.

Product releases, promotional campaigns, public relations efforts, and many other activities both on and off the Web can all be tracked by establishing business activity baselines and measuring the impact of such dated business events on relevant features within your company's Web site. As tracking technologies evolve, the potential scope of such business process tracking efforts becomes limited only by the ability of companies to find innovative ways of integrating the Web into their business planning.

A company could, for example, measure Web activity and then track the number of visits to a product page following a new product announcement. The company could also monitor the number of purchases, the number of product information requests, and the number of overall visitors to the site, comparing data with average daily results. But beyond simply monitoring sales companies doing business on the Web can track and establish benchmarks for:

- sales leads
- profits
- responses
- errors on orders
- orders
- book-to-bill ratio
- number of support calls
- number of frequently asked question (FAQ) accesses
- types of customer support requested
- Web support requests
- phone support requests
- turn time on customer support

- file downloads for demo products
- product information requests

This list could go on for several pages. In fact, entire books probably will be written on this topic alone. Suffice it to say that no businessperson should be limited by this list.

Marketing to Individuals

Traditional marketers primarily considered customers in groups, and thus utilized mass-marketing techniques to reach a targeted market segment. In contrast, the distinctive communications capabilities of the Web make it possible to think about customers as individuals with unique needs and preferences, and to utilize one-to-one marketing techniques to establish long-term relationships with those individuals.

And, until recently, most analysis of market data stored in databases was carried out by statistical analysts rather than marketers. But new data-mining software technologies promise to automate that analysis, enabling businesses to develop accurate and sophisticated information about their customers and business activities. "You want to track users from the time they get on the Internet to the time they come onto your site to the time you're talking to them to the time they buy a product to the time they log off," says John Danner. "You're really trying to see where people are going so that you have that information and use it to tailor your message or to change the form of communication you have with the person."

To do so, marketers will need to incorporate both *active* and *passive* ways of learning about individual customers in great detail. Then, they'll need to find ways to use the information they gain to build mutually beneficial marketing relationships based on trust and fair exchange.

- *Active* approaches involve asking users direct questions about interests, preferences, needs, and experiences. User registration systems, customer surveys, and questionnaires are examples of techniques used to actively collect user data of importance to marketers.
- *Passive* approaches involve monitoring a user's clicksteam, file downloads, or purchase behaviors to construct a composite profile of the user.

Both approaches involve the transfer of data from users to tracking tools capable of collecting the information.

Today, many experts envision using powerful database-driven tracking technologies to collect hoards of information about individual customers as a way to develop one-to-one marketing relationships. Ultimately, the Holy Grail is creating full demographic and psychographic profiles of individuals based on extensive information provided by users themselves about all aspects of their lives. But obtaining reliable user information is proving to be a significant challenge for a number of reasons. At the minimum, marketers and site managers want to know:

How many people can see and have seen the information?

To which information did users pay attention?

How did users respond?

How did users navigate to the information?

Who are the users?

Interestingly, only a couple of these basic questions can be conclusively answered using passive tracking techniques based on the common log format standard most servers implement today to log user activity. On the other hand, active tracking techniques can provide the answers, but consumers have shown they want nonintrusive tracking technologies by demonstrating resistance to active tracking approaches. Cumbersome active registration and survey processes, for example, have proven annoying to users. HotWired, among others, launched its site with "registration required" before access to site content was allowed. A few months later, as consumers resisted the process, HotWired quickly made registration voluntary, offering users content incentives for participation.

Experience indicates that users will provide personal information if the process is easy, secure, and they receive some value in return. Ultimately, though, some consumers will object to any capture of their usage data, passive or active, and may insist on a way to block all such data capture. Nevertheless, basic user data is being captured passively today on the Internet. Each time a user clicks on a hyperlinked icon or text, the server automatically logs three pieces of information:

- the internet address of the destination user (client)
- the name of the file being sent (served)
- the time these events occur

Notably, in the world of tracking tools that analyze server logs to estimate the number and origin of "visitors," two plus two does not always equal four. Companies investigating tracking technology options should realize that significant problems must be solved before the data estimates delivered by passive tracking tools begin to be reliable. The following can all reduce the validity of data being collected passively using the common log format today:

- *Hits* measure files retrieved rather than individual users. Accessing a single page containing hyperlinks to, say, 10 other files would result in 10 hits being counted.

- Number of *visits* is typically an estimate routinely derived by dividing the number of hits by a factor representing the average number of links per page, for instance 10, a remarkably unreliable and potentially invalid methodology.

- Dynamically delivered content pages will have varying numbers of hits counted with each access depending on the number of hyperlinks present on each page.

- Site mirroring and page caching can significantly reduce the apparent number of measured hits a page receives because such accesses are not centrally logged.

- User IDs are not unique in many access situations, making accurate user identification impossible. Entire companies or online services sometimes share a single "unique" address for all users.

- "Rating," "share," "penetration," "reach," and "frequency" are at best highly unreliable terms since there is no way to know the total number of individuals who could be exposed to a message and no accurate way to measure the number of users actually exposed.

- "Unique sessions" by a particular user cannot yet be distinguished because user file requests involve connections and disconnections for specific servers, but lack a logon-to-logoff session.

- "High-use" files, which users regularly access, are difficult to distinguish reliably from other files.

- Proprietary tracking algorithms cannot always accurately distinguish between actual trend data and consciously manipulated data.

Current passive technologies based on the common log format seem able to deliver only relatively rough indications of individual user behavior. However, some server providers have begun to adopt extensions to the common log format to include additional data such as:

- the referring site, from which the user came
- the users "agent" or browser type
- "cookie" data, that is, an ID code written by servers to a user's hard drive as a file called cookie.txt and passed by the browser to the server each time a user accesses a Web site

Tracking Software Gold Pickers

Hybrid approaches combining passive data tracking with data actively collected from users seem to offer the greatest potential for useful tracking information for marketers today. As of May 1996, at least 10 companies have announced various software packages and services that combine passive and active tracking techniques (Table 10.2).

Each of these companies provides tools that deliver various reports estimating the number and origins of visitors, and identifying high-usage files and pages based on analysis of server logs. Most of these companies leverage databases of North American domain addresses indexed by city, region, and zip code to enrich reports on user visits. Most also offer proprietary algorithms and statistical models that perform processing operations on the server log data to enhance the usefulness of the information delivered. Likewise, the leading companies have partnered with leading audit firms. "As an advertiser you want to make sure that a stamp of approval comes from someone you trust or have worked with in the past, and so I think [forming] relationships with traditional media audit and research firms are an important piece of the picture right now," says John Danner of NetGravity.

One such company, I/PRO, offers a product called I/CODE, an active tracking system for nonsite-specific user registration that requires users to register only once for access to all I/CODE enabled sites. "Users really find it a hassle to have to repeatedly provide the same information over and over again, and to have to remember many passwords and many login names for all the sites," says Polar, CEO of I-Pro. His system allows end users to provide information once, get one code, and then leverage that across multiple sites. "Receptivity both from the end users and from the site [managers] has been really good." Polar believes

TABLE 10.2   Tracking Software

Company	Product	Audit Partner
I/PRO (http://www.ipro.com)	I/Count and I/Code	Nielsen
Interse (http://www.interse.com)	Market Focus 2	Arbitron
WebTrack (http://www.webtrack.com)	WebTrack	Audit Bureau of Circulations
Digital Planet (http://www.digiplanet.com)	NetCount	
Open Market (http://www.openmarket.com)	WebReporter	
Logical Design Systems (http://www.lds.com)	WebTrac	
BellSouth (http://bellsouth.com)	Interactive Information I	
W3.COM (http://w3.com)	Personal Website Toolkit	
Virtual Office (http://www.webwatch.com)	WebWatch	
DoubleClick (http://www.doubleclick.com)	DoubleClick	

registration has gotten a bad rap on the Web because it hasn't been done properly. His advice: "Make it seamless, and make it worthwhile for the user." Polar points to HotWired: "Today on HotWired, you can go in without registering. Nobody forces you to register, but [there are] incentives and benefits for registering, such as receiving personalized information."

I/CODE also reports user-specific demographic data to site managers. "Without registration, the level of information you can get about the user is minimal," says Polar. All you know is the user's Internet address. With I/CODE, you can cross-tabulate the IP address with consumer demographic information: age, sex, education, household income, and some business-to-business information." After paying a one-time $500 setup fee, pricing for I/CODE services ranges from $300 per month for up to 249 I/CODE visits per day to $1,500 a month for up to 2,499 I/CODE visits per day.

For site managers willing to pay to hand off tracking analysis to a service bureau, firms such as I/PRO stand ready to meet the need. For Web marketers who prefer to maintain internal control over their own user data and who want to create their own custom reports as often as they like without any monthly fees, other firms such as Interse in Sunnyvale, California, offer an attractive, Windows-based software alternative.

User Privacy and Data Piracy on the Cyberfrontier

"Cookies are starting to emerge as a simple but effective way to personalize a person's experience at any Web site (Microsoft's custom home page is a very effective example of this)," says Robert Ponce of I-Contact Media Inc. "Given that the real power of this medium is the ability to reach large numbers of people and make their experiences unique, I think that cookies will start to emerge very quickly as a powerful weapon in the arsenal of Web developers who are concerned with advertising and marketing." However, it remains unclear that security- and privacy-aware users will favor Web sites that write identification codes to their personal computers, thereby enabling any site to monitor their private clickstreams. To be viable, tracking tools must balance the competing needs of marketers with those of Web users.

Ponce calls for marketers to self-police abuses in order to avoid a backlash from consumers. "All it will take is one aggressive direct marketer who prequalifies Web consumers by checking for Quicken files and reviewing their bank accounts; or by sniffing hard drives for social security numbers, credit card information, and so on. Negative media attention to these types of privacy violations could threaten all development of commerce on the Web."

Marimba's Kim Polese says:

Gathering information about your customers is the Holy Grail in marketing or advertising, but it's a double-edged sword because people need to feel a level of trust. I think one of the reasons the Web and the Internet have really exploded is that people like being anonymous. They like being able to surf around and know they are not being tracked or that they're going to get 20 pieces of junk mail because they visited a site. And so the advertisers and marketers have to police themselves, and realize that if they start viewing this as just a way of targeting people and sending them information that they may not want, it's going to backfire. People will stop going to the Web because their mailbox clogs every time they visit a site. You should give people the option of receiving information, but you shouldn't require them to receive it.

Hackers don't take kindly to what they consider to be abusive "data piracy." Technologies to counter data pirates have been developed by university students and made freely available. Polese sees this as "another indication of the power of the Web. You don't necessarily have to go and buy a utility. If there's enough emotion behind it, a technology or utility will be developed and made available. We've seen that happen already. [Companies were] using very heavy-handed broadcast junk mail techniques. An early example was a law firm on AOL or CompuServe that started doing junk e-mailing. Instantly, somebody wrote a utility that screened it out or sent junk mail back. When you blow it on the Web in a big way, you feel the repercussions as a company."

There is general awareness of the need to protect against abusive data piracy if tracking technologies are to be made viable in the long run. And data piracy is not limited to junk mail or any particular tracking technology. "The medium gives you a lot more power to know more things about people," admits John Danner at NetGravity. "It is a responsibility not to abuse that information, because if it's abused, people will say, 'Forget it! I'm not going to tell anybody anything about myself.' There has to be a level of trust established between the corporate community and the users of the Internet. And if that's violated too many times, it's going to be a real problem. People will stop telling anyone who they are. And it's very easy to be anonymous on the Internet. It's really a privilege of corporations to learn things about people through the Internet, and that's how it should be treated."

"Privacy is very, very important," agrees Ariel Polar at I/PRO. "Users are very sensitive about it, and all of our systems are based on the premise that end users must control who gets access to their information. No information about a user reaches anybody without that user's permission." Unfortunately, some tracking firms may not be as committed to protecting end user privacy, says Polar. "There are companies who say, 'We retain the right to sell your data to anyone else,' and they will charge very little and make money by selling [customer] data elsewhere. That business model doesn't work, though, because the data is too valuable to sell and end up in a competitor's hands." Polar believes that "it's up to Web site [managers] to decide how to handle user information, who they share with, how they measure it, and so on."

Collecting user information in a way that protects and respects Web user's privacy remains a key issue that tracking service bureaus must address. Here are a few basic guidelines based on an assessment of the prevailing Internet cultural milieu:

- User information is private and belongs to the user.
- Users should volunteer to reveal their information.
- Users should be made aware of all information collection activity.
- Users should be able to refuse to allow collection of their user data.
- Under no circumstances should the privacy of a user be violated.
- No information about a user should reach a second party without explicit user permission.
- Users should be able to choose the type and timing of information they want to receive.
- Only information that the end user specifically says "I'm interested in and I want" should be sent.
- No junk mail should ever reach an end user.
- Users should remain in control of their information profile so that at any time they can say, for example, "I already bought my car. I don't want any more car information. Now I want camera information."

It is unlikely that Web tracking tools will ever be able to follow users as they surf from one Web site to another, reporting user clickstreams back to a central database log. "It's like the supermarket standard," quips Polar. "We help you find out everything that gets purchased. We can even walk down the aisles and observe what users are looking at. But if they walk out of your store and go to the grocery store next door, we can tell they went there but not what they did inside. That information belongs to the other grocery store. We are trying to provide information [services] without compromising the confidentiality and value of each organization."

One emerging approach to active tracking involves rewarding end users for providing information, making it worthwhile for them by giving them value in exchange for their information and their time. "We're working on systems that will allow Chrysler to tell end users, 'We realize your information and your time is valuable,' " says I/PRO's Polar. " 'We will pay for your connect time while you're surfing our virtual showroom, and, in exchange, we would like some information about you.' So far, as long as it's seamless, as long as they don't feel their privacy is being invaded, and you make it worthwhile for them, users take advantage of the value you give them back. They say, Great, I'll go for that."

How best to balance the needs of Web marketers for user information with the needs of Web users for privacy remains uncharted but important territory. Companies doing business on the Web will want to carefully consider their policies on these key issues. Successfully building virtual personal marketing relationships with customers will require both personal knowledge of customers and a bond of trust. Selecting a Web tracking technology able to ensure that both of these requirements are met will help companies maximize the power of the Web for business benefit.

Advertising on the Web

In 1995, companies of all sizes spent $43 million on Web advertising—real dollars but nothing compared to the growth that analysts are projecting. Estimates from the Forrester Research Corporation target 1998 ad spending on the Web at $700 million. But although major advertisers have accepted the Web as an important new media buying market, as indicated by ad spending in the fourth quarter of 1995 (Tables 10.3 and 10.4 show the analysis of Web advertising placement), Forrester estimates also showed that both Web ad spending and revenues are highly concentrated among a relatively few companies. Of total fourth-quarter (Q4) revenues, the top 10 Web ad publishers received $9.3 million (75 percent). Of total Q4 spending ($12.4 million), the top 10 advertisers spent $3.2 million (26 percent), and the top 20 advertisers spent $5.1 million (41 percent); 33 advertisers spent $100,000 or more.

Obviously, there is still plenty of room for others in this developing arena, and any company planning to maximize the Web's capabilities for business will want to consider the implications of interactive advertising for their site. Companies will also want to be sure and deploy systems capable of tracking the return on investments in advertising on the Web.

The Customer in Control

Because of its distinctive capabilities, interactive advertising on the Web has the potential to form new kinds of relationships between advertisers and customers. As stated previously, conventional advertising in print and on radio and television built relationships with target customers based on the one-to-many, broadcast communications model. Interactive advertising, conversely, involves one-to-one, *narrowcast,* communications, a whole new paradigm. Instead of being passive spectators, customers on the Web actively choose

TABLE 10.3   Top 10 Web Advertisers 1995 Q4—Based on Placement Spending

Rank	Advertiser	Spending 1995 Q4
1.	AT&T	$567,000
2.	Netscape	556,000
3.	Internet Shopping Network	329,000
4.	NECX Direct	322,000
5.	MasterCard	278,000
6.	American Airlines	254,000
7.	Microsoft	240,000
8.	C|Net	237,000
9.	MCI	231,000
10.	SportsLine	218,000

TABLE 10.4   Top 10 Web Ad Publishers 1995 Q4—Based on Placement Spending

Rank	Publisher	1995 Q4 Revenues
1.	Netscape	$1,766,000
2.	Lycos	1,296,000
3.	InfoSeek	1,215,000
4.	Yahoo	1,086,000
5.	Pathfinder	810,000
6.	HotWired	720,000
7.	WebCrawler	660,000
8.	ESPNET SportZone	600,000
9.	GNN	594,000
10.	C|Net	540,000

whether to participate. Web users can decide to click or not on an advertisement, as well as when and for how long.

Such increased buyer control over the process of exchange presents both challenges and opportunities for sellers. The opportunity is that prequalified buyers present themselves, asking to be convinced. On the Web, customers self-select: they either do or do not have an interest in a product or service advertisement. When customers select an ad for interaction, they prequalify themselves, and thus are far more likely to make an actual purchase. Investing resources in building relationships with these customers is also more likely to pay off.

Providing all the information a customer needs to make a purchase decision in an entertaining, compelling, and interactive format is the challenge. Luckily, as we have seen, the Web provides advanced capabilities that all play a role in helping advertisers design ads that can meet this challenge. Ads can be targeted to particular types of users, resulting in cost efficiencies by reaching the most likely buyers with the right messages.

Guidelines for Designing Interactive Ads

Well designed interactive ads must first attract user interaction because, on the Web, customers choose if and when to consider a company's products. But there's a lot more to effective advertising on the Web.

The first generation of advertising on Web pages consisted almost exclusively of "clickable banners," colorful but static miniature billboards, usually displaying a company's logo or an attractive caption. Clicking on a banner usually brought customers to the sponsor's Web page, where they were left to figure out by themselves what to do next.

Given the technical challenges of the Web, not to mention the lack of experience in designing interactive advertising, initially, little effort was put into creating compelling interactive advertising that targeted particular visitors. Today, a second generation of interactive Web advertising has begun to appear, enabled by:

- ad designers who understand how to build interactive relationships
- new ad management tools on the Web
- animation software for the Web

By working with one of the new breed of talented interactive designers and by giving careful attention to market-driven design, highly interactive ad experiences can be created that will do far more than simply attract users.

Compelling interactive ads can interest customers in a company's products, impress them with exciting features, reinforce impressions, and convince them to take an action such as "order now," all without any direct intervention by company employees. As we have said many times, the Web's powerful capabilities enable and enhance advertising with multimedia, virtually infinite space, and database technologies. "You can sell all the way through," says John Danner, CEO of NetGravity speaking of AdServer, the new interactive ad management tool his firm provides to companies like Yahoo! and Time Warner's Pathfinder. "NetGravity AdServer has already enabled Yahoo! to increase available ad space from 200 spots to over 12,000," says Anil Singh, the Yahoo! director of sales. Every day, Yahoo! uses NetGravity's AdServer product to manage ads from over 90 different advertisers, delivering 12,000 ad spots to over 1 million people during 7 million distinct visits to its more than 200,000 pages.

"Yahoo! is a really good example of a site that has started to work on ad personalization," says Danner. Amazingly, Yahoo! can automatically deliver ads related to a particular user's request. For example, while surfing Yahoo's Computer and Internet category, a colorful banner from a computer-related company appears:

> "CLICK HERE 'N SAVE $$. Rawspace.net $15.95 = 10 MB Why pay more?"

And clicking on the Internet category on this page brought up this Apple Computer ad:

> "Tech support costs for Mac approx. 25% lower than Windows. For more facts on Apple, visit us at http://always.apple.com."

True, these ad banners are not particularly stellar examples of creativity in interactive multimedia production, but Yahoo's ability to deliver them to targeted interest groupings is a big advance over static ad banners.

Personalization also enhances Yahoo's ability to sell advertising on its site because it can offer a potential advertiser specialized placement, "Your company wants to advertise tennis products. Let's put you in the tennis area. It's more likely that you're going to find the right audience among users who look in the tennis area." "Yahoo! has spent a good amount of time thinking about how to make its advertisers more effective," says Danner.

Notably, tools like AdServer also make it possible for advertisers to evaluate and increase the effectiveness of their Web advertising.

Targeting Ads

Targeting ads on the Web is just like targeting ads in any other media. But on the Web, the first rule is, make sure your audience is online. Travelocity's Terry Jones utilizes that strategy in advertising to attract visitors to the travel site. "Our's is a product for the do-it-yourself traveler," says Jones. "Our advertising right now, for example, is totally targeted at people who use the Net and who read *Wired* and *Digital World;* those kinds of magazines. We're not out to convert people [who] don't have that kind of money to run to the store and buy a computer and a modem. We're not going to do that. We say, 'If you're on the Net, come see us. If you're interested in travel, we're the place.' Eventually, we'll broaden that and target a wider audience of travelers as we expand the content in the system."

Travelocity's approach targets travelers already using the Web, a good lesson in understanding the target market. Presently, most of their advertising is online and in Web-related magazines. Wisely, they are not trying to sell people on Web access for now. Travelocity's flexible advertising strategy will also evolve with the changing marketplace.

Are Web Ads Working?

Ads on the Web expose many millions of viewers every month to commercial messages. But how can advertisers determine whether the ads are really working for them? Knowing how many potential customers see an ad is a good start, but what other kinds of information are important to an advertiser?

Until recently, advertisers simply received reports from individual sites providing basic statistics like the number of visitors who viewed and clicked on a particular ad during a certain period of time. Unless visitors also explicitly provided additional demographic information about themselves, advertisers only knew which domain a particular visitor came from. To draw comparisons about ad effectiveness, advertisers could only vary the timing of ad placements and place the same ad on different sites.

And there were all those statistical reports to evaluate. Dealing manually with literally thousands of reports on different ad placements gets ugly fast. Add to that the inability to manage ad content, to automatically rotate ads, or to target particular users and it's easy to understand why Mark Thomas, as quoted in "Start-Ups Plot to Make the Web Comfortable for Advertisers," *The New York Times,* February 13, 1996, said: "It's confusing to an agency and an advertiser." Thomas, the vice president and media research manager at Hal Riney & Partners, Saturn of America's ad agency adds, "We're working to make sure we're all reading from the same rule book." Fortunately, Web advertisers now have several new tools to help them access the information they really need and to effectively manage their advertising programs on the Web.

Web Advertising Tools

Ad management and analysis tools are in great demand as advertisers try to measure and understand the impact of their Web ads. In 1996, three California startups, Focalink, DoubleClick, and NetGravity became the first to provide such an ad management infrastructure for the Web. Each of these companies provides tools that deliver guaranteed numbers of impressions to advertisers, along with methods of scheduling, rotating, tracking, and generating reports. But that's where the similarity ends. These companies take two distinct approaches to managing advertising on the Web. These approaches can be understood by examining how they manage ad storage, data handling, and advertiser control.

Both Focalink and DoubleClick store ads from many advertisers together in a central warehouse server capable of automatically capturing user demographic data across multiple ad-sponsored Web sites. They also provide centralized statistical services for determining the success of ads across multiple sites, as well as within a single site. These Web sites become part of the firm's network, and they allocate space on their local sites for delivery of ads to customers. Advertisers simply select a set of criteria defining a target audience and the centralized server displays their ad on appropriate sites when a user matching those criteria accesses a site in the firm's network.

This centralized approach to ad management may offer real advantages for firms eager to contract out management of their ad placement and statistical capture programs. DoubleClick, for example, has the ability to manage millions of online spots simultaneously as well as the potential for triggering customized ads on the fly from user profile data. And Focalink President Ron Kovas reports that Netscape, TechWeb, and Global Network Navigator have all agreed to beta test its SmartBanner product.

Conversely, for those sites and advertisers not willing to hand over control of ad placement and monitoring to a centralized ad management intermediary, the disadvantages of the centralized Focalink/DoubleClick approach are significant. In particular, this approach ignores the power of the Web to deliver immediate, real-time information and control directly to Web advertisers and site managers.

With the centralized approach, Web site managers have no control over the central ad server, thus advertisers have no way of directly experimenting with ad content in real time to gain valuable experience in building effective interactive ads. Nor can advertisers remotely interact with users in real time, offering special deals or promotions as users navigate through an ad. Finally, analysis and evaluation of demographic data captured by the centralized system remains an arms-length matter of interpreting and integrating periodic reports into the ad program.

On the other hand, enabling such real-time advertiser control is a core advantage of NetGravity's decentralized approach to ad management. "We are building products to distribute control to each point along the advertising chain: from Web site to advertising rep firm to media buyer to advertiser," says President and Founder John Danner. "We enable different management decisions to be made at different places."

In general, larger sites will not allow intermediaries to control ad display. These sites prefer to maintain control over content and data collection at their sites. Internet Shopping Network (Figure 10.12), for example, requires that all ads are served from its own Web site.

"The NetGravity philosophy is that the Internet allows for decentralized control, and we provide products with the flexibility to let control be placed in the right place for a given relationship," says Danner. Today, NetGravity's AdServer 1.0 provides each Web site with a locally accessible advertising server and each advertiser with real-time remote control access to ad content and demographic data captured on the site. Advertisers can experiment with different approaches to advertising, while accessing demographic data on the site, all in real time.

AdServer is "a tool advertisers [can use] to figure out what's effective and what's not," says Danner. It's critical "to give the advertisers better information about where they should put their advertisements, what they should buy, what

Figure 10.12   The Internet Shopping Network home page.

happened, and how effective it was, in as close to real time as you can get," he adds. "The pot of gold for advertisers is being able to target different portions of the audience and put up the right ad for the right people."

AdServer delivers advertisements based on user selected keywords contained in the context of a search or other content. It also lets site managers define ad group categories to enable the sale of ad blocks. The product works with user data captured by four major data capture firms.

"Future products will allow the control to reside at any point along the ad management spectrum," says Danner. "These products will all interface with each other to allow AdServers to exist on Web sites as well as at rep firms, agencies, and advertisers. Control over data and management will be negotiated between these interests on a per-contract basis."

Whichever approach emerges as the market leader, advertisers and Web site managers all need ad management tools. "It's really a fundamental question of whether the industry is better served by centralized control," says Josh Bernoff, a senior analyst with Forrester Research Corporation.

Getting Started on the Internet

"One of the most important things to think about as a marketing director is how you are going to make your customer perceive value in your Web site and how you are going to differentiate the experience your customer has," says Steve Zocchi of Spider Technologies. "One of the most important things to do is to go on the Web yourself and visit lots of Web sites and experience them. See what it's like to get information from them. See if there is *real value* there. Providing real value for your customers is key to having a very successful Web site, and you won't be able to provide that without some first-hand experience."

"People really need to start looking at the Web as a way of providing new kinds of services," says Kim Polese. She says to ask yourself, "What new products can I offer on the Web, or what new ways can I enable people to find out about my products? Instead of just showing the picture of a product, give people information about it. In the case of a car, [for example,] there's instant information from what *Car and Driver* said [about it], and what the last 10 years' of safety records show for this car. This is data that you can't get just by looking at a traditional ad in a magazine, and that motivates people to come to that Web page."

"Interactivity," "multimedia," "data mining," "one-to-one relationship marketing," "interactive advertising" . . . Today, doing business on the Web immerses marketers in a new business paradigm. "It's kind of a brave new world, and it takes time to really grasp it. Be realistic," suggests Zocchi. "When you approach the Web, know that it's going to take you a few steps. Don't be afraid to take that first step. Then think about your Web site, and take it to the next level."

The bottom line is, the Internet isn't going away. "We estimate that 28.8 million people in the United States 16 and over have potential or actual access to the Internet; 16.4 million people use the Internet; 11.5 million people use the Web.

Depending on which statistics you believe, there are 5.8 million, 9.5 million, 16.4 million, or 24 million North Americans on the Internet; and the number of users are increasing at an unparalleled rate. Every day that passes that you do not maximize the opportunities on the Internet for your business is another day your company is behind. In fact, every day you wait costs you more to catch up. In addition to understanding the Web's unique properties as a new communications media, reaping the business benefits of your company's Web site also requires careful consideration of:

- your business goals and objectives
- the size of the market opportunity
- your target markets

- your competition
- your customers
- your company's strengths and weaknesses

Based on this market analysis, a detailed specification for site design can be developed, and interactive site features can be implemented.

Who's Doing Business on the Web?

Before making multimillion dollar investments in marketing on the Web, most companies want to know what other kinds of companies are betting on the Web and why. A recent study by Forrester Research Inc., titled "Brands on the Web," found that, "of the top 200 brands in America, more than 50 now promote themselves on the World Wide Web." Companies represented on the Web include both digital technology companies (computers, software, networking, telecommunications, and online retailers) as well as consumer goods manufacturers (beverages, automobiles, airlines, freight, entertainment, financial services, etc.). However, the study also showed that not all companies invest with the same objectives.

In the study, both technology and consumer goods companies listed "increasing brand exposure," "building customer relationships," and "gaining experience with the new medium" among their top Web marketing goals. But, technology companies seem better positioned to maximize the power of the Web for business than consumer goods companies listing "finding new customers" and "selling products" among their top Web marketing goals.

Technology Companies on the Web

For technology companies, target customer demographics closely match the demographics of Web users. Notably, target customers for technology companies tend to have Internet access, making the Web a natural place to do business. As a result, technology companies have been among the pioneers in cyberspace, making multimillion dollar investments in Web marketing.

But demographics are not the only reason technology companies have been among the first to jump on the Web bandwagon. Some digital technology companies can also sell and deliver digital products online. One software company executive explains in the Forrester study, "Some see the Web as a marketing channel, like all other media. Then there are people like us who see it as a place to create new business that is electronically based. It's a new way to market, sell, and distribute products. Of the 20 technology companies interviewed for the Forrester study, four already make million-dollar investments, and 14 others said they planned to spend more in 1996.

Consumer Goods on the Web

Because of its powerful information delivery capabilities, the Web is an ideal way to provide consumers with information-rich resources, and many consumer goods companies find it a cost-effective alternative to other conventional media. But many of these companies have approached the Web cautiously so far. As an entertainment company executive put it, "Our main goal is to create awareness and interest." As a result, until recently, relatively small budgets and staffs have characterized the commitment of consumer goods companies to Web marketing.

A perceived lack of tools and security for electronic transactions has kept many consumer goods companies from selling on the Web. But as more secure environments for electronic commerce are developed and the Web continues its record-setting growth, greater numbers of high-income, well-educated consumers are hopping on the Web. In addition, "major consumer brand sites like Saturn, Ragu, and Zima have succeeded in expanding awareness, delivering information, and encouraging consumer interaction," reported the Forrester study. Thus, consumer goods companies have begun to move more aggressively to expand marketing on the Web.

Where to Begin

Conducting business successfully on the Web is still, first and foremost, conducting *business* successfully; that is, you must pay careful attention to the following points of strategic and business planning, which are the foundation of all real success:

- goals and objectives
- business planning and project direction
- market opportunity
- target customers
- competitors
- Web business models

Business Structure

"Think outside the box. Think fantasy," says Kim Polese at Marimba. "If there were a tool that you could use to reach your customers and give them information faster and better and with more scope, along with the feeling that they were totally connected to your company, what would you want to do? Then look at what you can do on the Web; there is a very good chance that there is a pretty close match [to that fantasy] already today."

But before doing anything else, answer the question: What specific goals will my company accomplish by doing business on the Web? It may seem obvious that any company pursuing development of a business Web site should set clearly defined goals and objectives to steer a Web project in the right direction, but many companies have given apparently little consideration to business goals and how they impact Web site development. Unfortunately, as some companies have found out, such an approach fails to maximize the payoff to a company's investment in the Web. To avoid that, start with the following list of questions and jot down some answers:

- How quickly do you need to get a Web site up?
- Do you have an in-house staff capable of designing, implementing, and managing a Web site? Don't overlook employees who are interested in the Web and want to learn more.
- What amount of cash and other resources can be budgeted for site design, development, implementation, and maintenance?
- What business functions would you like to accomplish on the Web?
- Who are the customers you want to reach?
- Do you want to seek advertiser-sponsors?
- What business models do you want to consider?
- Do you want to do secure online transactions?
- Do you want to track users?
- Do you have a database that you want to link to your Web site?
- What information do your customers need?
- How often will information change? Which information is changed?

As you formulate your list of answers, picture yourself as a pioneer on the digital frontier blazing new trails into the unknown future of communication and commerce. You are an innovator ready to discover new solutions to new challenges, using new tools and even a new language with new inhabitants. Be prepared to accept certain hardships, as well as the rewards, for being among the early settlers in cyberspace.

Now reread your list of goals and prioritize it. The contents of this list will affect every other choice you make in the process. Don't forget to consider measurable objectives to target, types of market analysis to undertake, interactive features to design, the look and feel you want to create, and how much it will cost.

Based on your initial list, in particular your company should set specific, realistic objectives for each of the following:

- revenue generation
- business communications
- image enhancements
- customer service
- cost savings
- productivity enhancements
- and more

"One common error is to measure the effectiveness of the Web by 'how many widgets did I sell through the Web or how many leads did I get?,' " cautions Ariel Polar, founder and chairman of I/PRO. "For the majority of companies, the Web is a way of communicating with the rest of the world." As you work with your list, recall that business on the Web is not just about selling. It's about communicating and creating consensual marketing relationships. It's about providing easy access to information that potential customers need, and about saving staff time on customer support. Creating an ongoing, interactive conversation with customers that choose your company, as well as potential clients all over the world is your ultimate benefit.

Also remember that putting your site in place is only the beginning. Building relationships and ongoing conversations with your customers will make your site a work in progress.

How Much Will It Cost?

"There's such a low entry cost on the Internet," says Catherine Harding, IBM Internet consultant. "You can put up a decent Web site for a large company for $50,000, and that's not a lot of money. So companies are willing to rush right into it and go. But we found that there are a lot of hidden costs doing it that way. To build a good Web site, you need to be committed to keeping it refreshed and updated, and have a strategy behind it. All of that costs much more—[maintenance] is the most important cost, not the initial cost of the development." Depending on a company's goals, the costs of building a business Web site increase with every passing month, according to Josh Bernoff, senior analyst with market data company Forrester Research. Karen Shapiro, Internet Channel Manager, Bank of America confirms this: "It is getting more and more expensive, because now people understand interactivity to some extent." They understand that they need to have things interactive. Interactive communication is programming, and programming is expensive."

Although most first-generation Web sites have only begun to tap into the full power of the Web, building those sites has still involved significant investments. As of fourth quarter 1995, marketers from more than 50 consumer-oriented Web sites indicated in the aforementioned Forrester Research report that spending averaged between $300,000 and $3.4 million for launch and first-year costs to reach consumers on the Web. Forrester's Bernoff compares cost models (Table 10.5 concisely shows these cost) for three types of consumer-oriented sites: promotional, content, and transactions.

- *Promotional* sites create awareness, stimulate demand, promote brand awareness, and pursue other promotions-focused objectives. Typically, an outside Web development agency is hired to create, develop, and manage the promotional site project. Generally, promotional sites require two months to launch and feature "250 HTML pages, interactive forms, and e-mail but lacks a message area and transactional capability," according to Bernoff.
- *Content* sites entertain and inform users with content either designed especially for delivery on the Web or with content repurposed from conventional media. In many cases, content sites are database-driven. Forrester's archtypical content site "attempts to attract an audience with games, news, weather, or other information." Typically, content sites are developed in house with a staff of 10; in general, they take six months to launch, contain approximately 2,000 pages of content that are updated daily, and offer forms, e-mail, and a message area. A database delivers content to users, and advertising on these sites is the primary source of revenue.
- *Transaction* sites use powerful database technology to dynamically deliver information about products, prices or other resources in response to specific user requests. Typically, transactions sites take four months to develop in house, and require major investments in hardware, software, and information systems, as well as a staff of 30 to operate efficiently. Revenues tend to come primarily from advertising or from product sales and commissions.

The Forrester report further indicated that major expenses varied for each type of site. For promotional sites, launch costs were about one-third of the annual budget ($98,000). Nearly four-fifths ($237,000) of the annual promotional site budget went for creative work and support, and more than two-thirds ($206,000) was spent after the launch for site maintenance and additional cre-

TABLE 10.5   Average Web Site Launch and First-Year Costs

Promotional Sites	Image/brand enhancement	$304,000
Content Sites	Information and entertainment	$1,300,000
Transactions Sites	Database-driven information	$3,400,000

Source: Forrester Research, Inc. 1995

ative work. On the other hand, advertising and promoting the site soaked up a paltry $15,000.

For content sites, staff salaries and overhead accounted for more than 61 percent ($813,000) of the annual budget, with most spent after launch ($629,000). Print advertisements, public relations, and the marketing manager's salary absorbed another $247,000 annually. About a third of the total annual budget ($419,000) was spent on launching the content site.

For transactions sites, staff costs "including managers, content staff, customer service represantives, vendor relations staff, designers, programmers, marketers, and administrators" absorbed 61 percent ($1,910,000) of the budget, while hardware, software, and network connections accounted for another 20 percent ($675,000), and site promotion, roughly 23 percent ($783,000). Notably, transactions sites spent roughly 18 percent ($593,000) of their annual budget to launch and about 82 percent ($2,775,000) post-launch.

During the next two years, costs are projected to increase, from 50 percent to 200 percent as companies expand their Web offerings in response to increasing consumer expectations by investing in:

- new Web hardware and software technologies
- new content features that take full advantage of Web capabilities
- premium Web designers and programmers

Forrester predicts increasing development and launch cost trends will drive up the cost of promotional as well as content sites most dramatically in the next two years, especially for content development and site promotion. Transaction sites will also cost significantly more for technology platform, content and service, and site promotion and advertising, but existing technology platforms will scale up more easily.

From these figures, it's obvious that companies considering focusing on Web marketing would do well to get in sooner rather than later. The entry-level cost of a promotional site could easily move up to $1 million or more by 1998. At the same time, site developers should carefully set levels of expectations for senior management, apprising them of the great uncertainty associated with rapid change, which includes:

- emerging Web standards
- unpredictable consumer behaviors
- shortages of experienced Web developers

Ultimately, one of the most important decisions a company faces is determining which of the three kinds of Web site to build—promotion, content, or transactional. As this section iterated, the costs vary tremendously. Matching a company's goals and objectives with site type is critical. Optimally, the site should be built for scalability and future expansion, even if it starts simple. With careful planning, the type of site can change as the business evolves.

Finding clever ways to build flexibility into site development budgets will serve site managers well in such a rocky environment. Forrester agrees: "The best Web opportunities always appear on the way to somewhere else. Site managers must be prepared to reinvent their sites continually."

Web Business Planning, Project Direction, and Deliverables

To create a site that will maximize the benefits of the Web for business, companies need to form a site development team that combines expertise in business and marketing with mastery of interactive design and technology. Unfortunately, the cyberfrontier has its share of virtual snake-oil dealers, selling unwary pioneers digi-magical elixirs, in exchange for a few dollars. First-generation Web technologies made it easy for newcomers to hire full Web site development services complete with graphic designers and HTML programmers, but those days are gone forever. Likewise, broadsided by the explosion in interactive media on the Web, every ad agency and PR firm hastily created an "interactive media unit," and many still lack the expertise to direct the creation of marketing features that utilize the full power of the Web for business. More important, their experience is often gained at their clients' expense.

In the early days of the Web, many companies outsourced Web production to firms "specializing" in Web development. Many of these firms had a strong understanding of first-generation Web authoring tools but few had the business experience to really understand the requirements of developing an optimal business Web site. Companies intent on "just getting it up as cheaply as possible" precluded serious business planning and innovative, market-driven interactive design. As a result, with a few notable exceptions, most early business sites used first-generation Web technology to create "brochureware," which emphasized company and product promotion to the exclusion of other powerful business features. Even among the more advanced business sites on the Web today, only a few have begun to introduce database-driven features and to create market-driven interactive features.

To be fair, major obstacles confronted business pioneers on the Web. For one thing, upper management may have been skeptical or uninformed about the importance of the opportunities for business on the Web. In addition, many of the most exciting Web authoring technologies became available only at the end of 1995. Today, all that has changed and companies have begun to regard the Web as a serious business investment that requires careful business planning and the best available talent.

Interactive Design Expertise

To go beyond the limits of brochureware and begin taking advantage of interactive communications, companies will have to realize the need to take responsibility for ensuring that company goals drive the design of their Web site. Notably, to maximize the potential benefits of the Web, company officers—not outside contractors or designers—must insure that company goals are being met with the new Web site.

Though other business units, such as MIS and operations, will also be heavily involved in the design and implementation of a Web site, the primary responsibility for putting together a Web project team should ultimately rest with the director of marketing. The director of marketing understands better than anyone the strategic market analysis and business planning necessary to reach a company's most central business goals.

Directors will need to gain or hire project expertise in three essential areas:

- Web business planning and interactive marketing
- interactive media design
- advanced Internet technologies

Ideally, the director of marketing should appoint an in-house project director, or hire consultants with interactive marketing expertise, giving them the authority needed to coordinate and drive the Web site project and ensure that market factors drive the design for the Web site for the benefit of all business units.

To ensure that market intelligence drives the design of their Web project, marketers should seek individuals whose experience includes business planning, strategic market analysis including customer analysis, as well as interactive media design. Other valuable skills include expertise in database design, user tracking and analysis, media-communications project management, computer network integration, graphic design, and negotiation.

Support from Senior Management

Directors of marketing should take the lead to make sure their company's Web site addresses critical business objectives and has the full support of senior management. Many times, shortsightness, egos, and turf-wars can become obstacles to building an effective Web project team and implementing the business plan. According to the Forrester report, one beverage company manager puts it this way: "I have support from my bosses, but many people inside the company think this is all hype." An executive at a financial services company adds, "Some managers were resistant and some very supportive. A lot of enrolling and educating was needed. Senior management needed to enroll."

To open a wide trail into the cyberfrontier, Web projects should be "blessed" by senior management, especially at the CEO level. With the full and active support of upper management and the CEO, an effective plan for integrating existing business units into the planning and implementation of the Web site will go a long way toward overcoming opposition from reluctant managers and staff. A project director empowered to mobilize the resources of the company will then be able to build an in-house project team composed of representatives from all the affected business units, who will become Web champions within the company.

When upper management is skeptical, special efforts will need to be made to convince them of the benefits. As one pharmaceutical company manager put it, "The biggest obstacle for us is internal management. If we try to go through our normal channels, we'll react much too slowly. It has to be fast, responsive— that's hard to teach upper management."

Creative budgeting and scheduling will be necessary if a Web project is to have any chance of success under these circumstances. Creative managers have found resources to fund Web projects in advertising, customer service, market research and technical support budgets.

Implementing a market-driven interactive design employing the most appropriate Web technologies requires a deep understanding of interactivity. One-to-one communication requires different skills and a different attitude toward customers than the one-to-many communications paradigm.

To make the most of the Web's powerful capabilities for business, companies will have to work with the highest-caliber interactive design and programming talent available. Even though demand for the most experienced people has already outstripped supply, and wages are being bid up rapidly, success on the Web requires working with people who really understand interactivity. In some cases, directors of marketing will want to pursue development of their Web enterprise entirely in house or through existing agency partners. However, unless in-house people or agencies have a track record, this approach is risky and may result in "pot-luck" Web sites, as project teams learn interactive design on the job. Unless ad agencies can point to Web-experienced in-house personnel, their role should be limited to creating promotional media campaigns in the conventional media.

In other cases, outsourcing the entire Web site development to a specialist Web production house is the right answer. Marketers should carefully choose Web development firms with a demonstrated understanding of interactive design and business requirements in addition to Web technologies. But finding a Web specialist with all three types of expertise is not going to be easy. Today, most Web specialists have experience with one or two of the required areas of expertise.

In most cases, marketers will be wise to pursue a third, hybrid, approach to interactive design to optimize their chance for success. Companies can hire a permanent in-house expert, or bring in a consulting firm with expert resources in all three essential areas, to direct the Web project, coordinating closely with a company's in-house resource people. Internet marketing and design consultants have the requisite expertise in Web business planning, data tracking and analysis, and interactive design to help companies fulfill the potential of the Web for business.

As just stated, Web consultants with expertise in business, interactive design and Web technology are rare and in high demand. But a resourceful, interactive design expert will prove a worthwhile investment, and a well-connected project director will be able to tap the most appropriate talent for each phase of a project from a pool of experienced Web design and technology resource people including:

- interface/information designers
- interactivity designers
- art directors
- multimedia developers
- writers
- content providers
- project managers

Attracting top development talent isn't always a matter of money, although that helps. As in all projects, trade-offs will have to be made regarding scheduling and costs. The quality of the outcome will be tempered by the caliber of the talent your project director attracts to your project.

Web Technology Expertise

The Web offers powerful technological solutions that enable and enhance business capabilities online. Market-driven, interactive business features can and should integrate rich, high-tech features that give users access to all the enriched resources they need to take action.

That said, be forewarned that it is all too easy to become dazzled by the latest 3D, virtual reality holographic mirage that could, some day, become standard Web fare. Marketers should ensure that the Web project director is not so enamored with tools that technology itself, rather than market-driven design, becomes the focus of a company's Web site development.

Project directors should have a through understanding of the Web technology landscape and be able to pick and choose among the technology nuggets that will add the most desirable technology sparkle to the market-driven interactive features required for a successful business site. Project directors should also have access to a pool of technology resources and talent from which to select the most appropriate tools and staff for a given project. This pool should include:

- programmers of all kinds
- database specialists
- data capture, tracking, and analysis specialists
- security and firewall specialists
- intranet experts
- network integration and configuration specialists
- Internet service providers
- hardware, software, and server providers

It is particularly important that project directors have access to user data capture, tracking, and analysis expertise. This is one of the most essential, and most rare, skill sets. The ability of a company Web site to enable one-to-one marketing features depends on the inclusion of this expertise on Web design, implementation, and maintenance teams.

Project directors should also know how to plan for post-launch internal staffing and maintenance requirements that also will have a market-driven focus. The project director should provide companies with data tracking and analysis expertise to ensure that any user data that is captured will be, in the future, channeled back into custom features for the site. Since the Web is an interactive medium, customer representatives must be assigned to respond to queries; technicians must learn how to assist customers with technical solutions; and Web "champions" throughout the company should be trained and mobilized, in coordination with Web programmers, to keep content fresh and interesting. Selection and maintenance of the requisite hardware and software facilities, as well as determination of the most appropriate Internet service connections and configurations, is also among the technical responsibilities of the project director.

Changing site content frequently will encourage regular customer visits. Therefore, project directors should work with staff to determine how often content will change, and create a schedule for updating the site. Customers should be informed about what to expect and how often features will be updated. Clear staff responsibilities should be assigned, and the schedule should be strictly adhered to.

Once a project director is selected and empowered, business planning and market analysis are the next steps. To guarantee that a market-driven site design is generated and implemented, marketers should confirm that project directors provide resources for the deliverables discussed next.

Web Site Planning, Design, and Implementation

"Marketers should arm themselves with knowledge about the technology," says Kim Polese at Sun. [They should] find out about the capabilities of the technology and what other companies are doing—both companies in their area and not in their area; companies or research institutes on the leading edge that are doing interesting, innovative, compelling applications on the Web. And [they should] think about how that information applies to their particular businesses, and about services that they would like to offer customers whom they haven't been able to reach either because they haven't been able to access the broad customer base, or it has been too expensive, or there just hasn't been any way of getting live information out to people instantly."

To meet important company goals and objectives with your Web site, market intelligence must drive design of interactive business features. The process of Web site design requires having good answers to important questions concerning your company's readiness, your business model, the design specification for your Web site, a site launch plan, and a site implementation plan. The following lists provide an overview of the information you will need to ensure the success of your Web site project.

- *Company Readiness Assessment:*
  - executive backing
  - company (divisional) participation
  - funding and/or cash flow sources
  - clear goals and objectives
  - resources
  - project team

- *Web Business Plan:*
  - site mission, goals, and objectives
  - market opportunity
  - research and analysis
  - size, growth, trends, and convergences
  - target markets and segments
  - customer/user profile development

- segmentation and customer profiles
- buying behaviors, criteria, motivations
- customer/user needs assessment
- technology install base
- competitive analysis
- existing and potential competitors, target markets, and product offerings
- existing and emerging business models
- barriers to entry
- online business strategy development
- online business model recommendation
- initial site design; product and feature offerings recommendations
- interactivity and technology integration plan
- customer data capture and tracking plan
- site maintenance, content, and communications update plans
- marketing strategy and promotional plans
- branding and identity
- rollout plan recommendation
- distribution and promotion strategies
- public relations, online and direct marketing, advertising, trade shows
- strategy for integration with existing corporate infrastructure
- operations, finances, and budgets
- financial tracking plan
- revenue and expense projections
- balance sheet and cash flow
- financial forecasts
- costs of products, services, promotions, operations
- staffing and training requirements
- legal requirements
- success and funding requirements
- risk assessment
- areas for business development
- critical success factors

- *Market-Driven Site Design:*
  - information design and interface metaphor
  - interactive features
  - multimedia features
  - database-driven features
  - data capture and tracking
  - advertising
  - other Internet features

- *Site Launch Plan:*
  - site content, features, products, and services offered at launch
  - customer service, technical support planning
  - Web development team creation and management
  - operations requirements: hardware, software, Internet service
  - data management planning and implementation
  - launch schedule
  - operations budget and resource requirements
  - site marketing and promotion, PR strategies and materials
  - maintenance plan

- *Web Site Implementation:*
  - software technology selection, programming and authoring
  - database specification and programming
  - network system technology needs assessment
  - network system technology selection
  - Internet service provider selection
  - risk assessment and security implementation
  - site maintenance planning and procedures

As you can see, the market-driven site design document specifies all design features and becomes the "blueprint" for Web site implementation. A thorough assessment of the company's readiness for a Web site, as well as careful business planning and market analysis, should precede creation of the market-driven site design document. Some of the elements of this planning and analysis process and how they affect site design deserve special mention, including:

- market opportunity
- target customer profile
- competitive analysis
- business models

Market-Driven Site Design

To maximize the power of the Web for business, the requirements of the market should drive the design of a business Web site. A strong design will carefully integrate the results of a company's market analysis with the powerful capabilities of Web technologies to creative innovative, highly interactive business features, like many of those discussed previously.

The design team will also want to consider "look and feel" issues such as:

- information design
- interactivity mapping and file structure
- a unifying metaphor and interface design
- color, layout, and other Web design principals
- graphics, audio, and other multimedia integration

Information Design

Attracting customers to a Web site consistently requires valuable and relevent interactive features and high-quality information. Catharine Harding, IBM Internet services consultant, encourages her customers to help determine what information is on the company's Web site by asking them, "If we had a little device like a Geiger counter, and we could walk it around this company, and what would register is where information was of value, where would this thing start to blip? What parts of the company would we be walking in when it really went off?"

Information exchange between a company and its customers is a loop, and the sales cycle can be viewed as a series of such loops. If at any point in the sales cycle the customer cannot access the information requested, the loop breaks and the likelihood of a successful sale declines. Thus, good information design for a business Web site will prioritize "closing the loop" at every step in the sales cycle. Business site designers must be sure to provide customers with all the information they need to make decisions.

Similarly, customers should never be left hanging at a dead end, not able to find or access the information they want or need to take a next step. Users should be able to obtain the desired information they need to communicate to the company what they need. Providing an e-mail link to a company employee whose responsibility it is to respond to user requests should be an option of last resort, but, nevertheless, it should be an available option every step of the way. Naturally, companies should prepare to provide rapid responces to such inquirys.

Virtually infinite space, real-time immediacy and multimedia information, are all capabilities of the Internet that can be tapped to ensure that a customer's information needs are fully met. Similarly, Interactivity makes the Web a place where customers can help themselves, with or without intervention from the company. With the exception of having physical contact with a product or person, most aspects of the sale can be done over the Internet.

Designers can also help customers find information by:

- Offering an overall site map for navigation.
- Designing "wide and shallow" as opposed to "narrow and deep" file structures.
- Letting customers know when information was last updated, which information is new, and how often information will change.
- Using tracking data to tailor information to the preferences of various individual customers.
- Using databases to provide information on demand.
- Providing powerful, user-driven search tools on every major page.

Basic product marketing practices should also inform good Web information design. When you inform your customers about a product or service, make sure you cover all the:

- *Features:* objective capabilities of the product or service
- *Benefits:* qualitative and quantitative business reasons to use the product or service
- *Positioning:* when, how, and where to use it and who uses it
- *Strengths:* comparisons with previous versions and competitive products

Interactivity means that your customers can become actively involved with the information you present rather than remaining passive recipients of it. Therefore, always think about new ways to involve your customer in your product or service; ask if they:

- Want to hear about new products, or bug fixes on an older one.

- Know about complemetary products and want a usage comparison for their particular problem.
- Know how to more efficiently or effectively use the product or service.
- Know of other important applications for the product or service.
- Want to talk with other customers.

Effective information design that builds on interactivity helps companies establish productive, virtual personal relationships with customers.

Evan Schuman, editor-at-large at *CommunicationsWeek* points to the importance of graphics as part of content rather than as simple decoration, responding to a letter from one of his readers: "Normally I oppose excessive graphics, but only when used as decorations. Here the images are absolutely *content*. I wasn't clear on what the company was selling until I saw one of those images." Schuman suggests bringing important content to a prominant place in the site, such as the home page.

Interactivity Mapping and File Structure

If you've ever lost an urgently needed file somewhere seven or eight levels deep in your file directory and had to search for it manually on short notice, you know how it feels when effective interactivity mapping and file structures are lacking. By designing interactive file structures that are "wide and shallow" instead of "narrow and deep," you can enable your users to navigate more easily and avoid serious frustrations. A good rule of thumb is to never make your users backtrack more than one or two levels to reach their next destination. Ideally, users should be able to reach *any* other point in a site from any other point in fewer than two jumps. On large sites, of course, this can be a real challenge.

A site map, which provides a layout of labeled clickable icons for every major and minor menu page in the site and which is accessible with a single click on every page in the site, is one good solution.

A Unifying Metaphor and Interface Design

In a world where so much infomation is available, achieving brand recognition on the Web will prove to be an essential advantage. To do so, it must be eye-catching and memorable. Establishing brand and company identity on the Web is an uncharted territory in which to explore creative approaches using powerful multimedia integration capabilities.

Developing a "unifying metaphor" in which to envelope your business messages is a good way to begin thinking about branding and identity on the Web. As in any media, the selected metaphor should be consistent with the corporate identity and integrated with all other marketing, promotion, and advertising. Ideas for unifying metaphors range from the wacky and wild to the serene and sober.

Bank of America offers a good example of a well-done unifying metaphor. Like their print media advertising, their Web home page associates one of the largest banks in the world with everyday common people by depicting people from all walks of life. They carry this through on every page of the site.

Clickable *image maps* that embed links to all of the various features within the site have become a popular approach to establishing branding. Most sites use a simple and clean information layout, sometimes resembling news bytes in a newsletter. Others create a thematic room or other environment with clickable graphical icons linking to features. Some employ a mascot or caricature as a guide.

New authoring environments based on java, VRML, and Shockwave have just begun to hit the market. Look for serious enhancements to Web environments, including animation and 3D worlds, that will make a site's unifying metaphor come alive with motion, sound, and color.

A word of caution: Early in Web site development, many companies employed an "intro screen" without any links to the information the user came to the site to find. Users become impatient at sites where they find either a "cool" graphic (which takes forever to download) or the company logo (ditto on the load time) with a button that reads: "Click Here to Enter." This approach ignores the importance of real-time immediacy to users, who expect to link directly with the features they most need immediately. They do not want to wait for several screens to load before they reach the target information. "Narrow and deep" design such as this undervalues a user's time and discourages return visits.

The user also expects pages to include easily accessible menu bars at consistent locations on every page. Including Search, Site Map, and Company Contacts on the menu bar provides essential navigational capabilities for users. For a good example, see vivid studios at http://www.vivid.com.

Users also expect pages to be printable. Some backgrounds and color combinations do not allow users to print readable documents, and therefore, they should be avoided. Experiment with different combinations on a computer platform equivalent to the ones your target user segments employ.

Once a market-driven site design is nailed down, the launch plan can be operationalized, and site implementation can begin.

Site Promotion

After the site is built and launched, attracting customers becomes the priority. They won't just show up; they need to know your Web site exists. Karen

Shapiro, Internet channel manager at Bank of America noted that, initially, Bank of America "focused 95 percent on building the Web site and 5 percent on advertising," but that the focus is shifting. "You're going to have to spend 50 percent of your resources bringing people to you, and bringing them to the right place on your site."

Slowly, but surely, promoting company activities through the Web site will become a primary way to attract customers. Companies like Sun Microsystems are already reaping the benefits, as Kim Polese relates: "Recent examples have shown that conferences have been completely launched and successfully produced simply by advertising through the Web. That's the target audience, and you're getting them through the Web. I'm already seeing it translated into a cost savings in my industry. Of course, I'm in the software industry so it's natural that I have been in the first wave of marketing professionals taking advantage of this. But it's only a matter of time before everybody really takes advantage of these benefits."

Companies whose customers are using the Internet may consider promoting only through the Internet, but some, like Internet Shopping Network (ISN), experimented with promoting and advertising solely through the Internet and found that a combination of promoting through the Internet and traditional medias offered the maximum coverage.

Overall, the Internet offers a variety of opportunities for promoting sites, but traditional media remains crutial to reaching customers to let them know about your site, your products, and your business. Put your Web address on everything your company produces, both products and marketing communications. If you make it a big deal, they will come to see what's there. If you've done your job and designed a market-driven site rich in powerful interactive multimedia features, your customers will have good reason to return again and again.

There are more than 500 different places to announce your site to the Web community. Here are some Web resources—mostly free—and one newsletter to help you attract customers:

http://goldray.com/register.sht
http://www.shout.net/~whitney/html/gopublic.html
http://www.mmgco.com/top100.html
http://www.homecom.com/global/pointers.html
http://www.webcom.com/getagift/PressXpress.html
http://www.alco.com
http://www.novakint.com/announce.htm
http://www.samizdat.com/public.html
http://www.netcreations.com/postmaster/doit/index.html

http://www.soos.com
http://www.barnsides.com/links.htm
http://www.webpost96.com
http://www.tripod.com/~neon/index.html
http://www.grandcentralweb.com
email:scout@internic.net

Go for the Gold!

So there you have it: your business guide to the cyberfrontier. You've got sound advice from some of the best Web marketers in the business. You can get your company up on the Web or take your existing site to the next level. Go ahead, don't be shy, partner, go for the gold. There's gold in them thar Web sites if you're hankerin' to gather your team and hit the trail!

CHAPTER ELEVEN

How Businesses Use Electronic Marketing

Margo Komenar

The case studies in this chapter present a range of online business and advertising models and different approaches to utilizing current electronic venues for launching, marketing, and running a business.

AT&T has created an extensive array of services to meet the needs of consumers and marketers online. The reach and implications of these offerings are important to understand and consider when assessing the changing electronic consumer and marketing environment. Each of these new divisions as well as AT&T's overall online strategy is discussed by the top AT&T executives who are leading these business endeavors. Details concerning advertising and partnering opportunities are included, along with online screen shots to give the reader an idea of AT&T's approach to each division and to advertising placement.

AT&T Business Network contracted with **Network 1.0/SoftBank Interactive Marketing** to function as its advertising rep firm and bring on advertisers for the service. Network 1.0 was in business only a few months before it merged in early 1996 with SoftBank and two other major sales organizations to form SoftBank Interactive Marketing. This new entity combined Network 1.0's selling activities and site management responsibilities with Ziff Interactive, which represents the ZD-Net Technology Group of sites, and a company called Interactive Marketing based in Los Angeles, which represents Yahoo!, the NFL, NBC Intelecast, Playboy, and some other sites.

As a single sales organization, SoftBank Interactive Marketing now represents the largest group of sites and advertising inventory on the Internet. Ted West, president and COO, describes the company's evolution, activities, and strategies.

Womanhood, Inc. will officially launch The Solutions Network for Business Women online during the first quarter of 1997. Sophistocated agent technology, used for personalized search and retrieval, is one of the site's key features. Natalie L. Wood, founder and CEO takes the reader on a tour and describes the company's approach to providing customized information to a very targeted audience and creating a "home for women on the Web."

InfoStreet is a small electronic publishing and Internet marketing business both typical and unique among companies that are busily designing some of the most compelling sites on the Net. For companies or individuals that have neither the time nor dollars to invest, InfoStreet has a service called Instant Web, which along with a Web Weaving time estimate chart for deeper site development and a number of Project Briefs to illustrate several approaches to Web site design and functionality will be presented and discussed.

CAPP Company (Cary August Productions & Publishing), was launched in late 1993 by two ambitious entrepreneurs, Dominique Toulon and Marc J. Oshry, who wanted to create a music publishing company so that their band, Cary August, could retain all of the rights to their own music and legally submit and license it in their own behalf. They later formed CAPP Records as a subsidiary of CAPP Company to function as their promotional and sales arm. As a small, innovative startup with a very limited budget, CAPP launched itself with the help of several electronic vehicles, including CD samplers, faxing software, and the Internet. This case study illustrates how a lot of ambition, entrepreneurial spirit, and creative use of today's electronic venues can get a company onto the playing field alongside the majors. While the playing field has not been as leveled by the Internet as some have intimated, it at least allows small startups a chance to enter the lineup.

Great Escapes is another example of a small startup that has succeeded with the use of today's high-tech tools and unstoppable entrepreneurial spirit. Great Escapes, founded by Sandra Kretchmer and Debbie Poulton, is a home-based full-service travel agency that was launched by two women considered, at 60 years of age, to be "over the hill and headed out to pasture" by former employers. This case study is a lesson in what the ageless spirit of the true entrepreneur can accomplish with the willingness to gain a little high-tech know-how in order to build a successful business in the '90s.

Southwind Enterprises, Inc. is a direct e-mail company that was launched in July 1995 by Dave Fricke out of a small living room in Zion, Illinois, with one old computer, very little money, and two solid months of 18 to 20-hour work-days! The company's e-mailing databases now exceed 500,000 addresses. In addition to the e-mailing service, Southwind, as a Dun & Bradstreet-listed company, offers a check-faxing service to assist customers in getting relatively instant guaranteed payment if they are not using credit cards. This company is an innovative and highly successful example of the "overnight" success that is possible with the creative implementation of the new electronic vehicles at our disposal. In this case study, Fricke shares his wild roller-coaster ride plus some of the amazing successes his clients have experienced along the way.

Yinspire, Inc. has designed the FolksOnline web site as a "comfort zone" on the Internet for what the founder, Ruby Yeh, refers to as cyberfolks, the world's nontechnical majority, the company's target audience. This is not just another new Internet site going after a piece of the cyberspace pie, how-ever. Yinspire, Inc. is a new organizational concept. It is a virtual company model that extends beyond its own internal team to include its consumer community and vendor affiliates. In this unique model, both the internal team and the community have the opportunity to benefit from the overall financial success of the company. In addition to compelling content, the site offers creative ways to attract audience traffic and vendor alliances through participation rewards and profit bonuses. Yeh explains the premise, strategies, and evolution of her company. This is a case study well worth studying.

AT&T's Online Strategy

According to Tom Evslin, the vice president of AT&T WorldNet Services, AT&T is not interested in competing for the 6 to 8 percent of American families that are going online today, but intends to expand that market to at least everyone who has a computer at home. AT&T looked at what its competitors were doing, but looked even more closely at what it was not doing. The company researched the obstacles to people going online, and then designed a service that it believed addressed those issues, focusing attention on bringing everyone onto the Net, not just the technically adept.

Evslin explains what they did to set AT&T apart from the other services:

"We way over-invested in customer care to make sure that the phone gets answered in 30 seconds as it normally does when you call AT&T, rather than in 30 minutes as it can when you call some Internet service providers.

We over-invested in modems and network capacity so that people don't get a busy signal when they call during a peak hour. If they're going to make this an important part of their lives, then they want it to be there, just like when you pick up your phone, you want to get a dial tone.

We invested in redundancy so that we would have a highly reliable network. That's something we have a lot of experience with. We have a lot of experience with scale, with growing very quickly, and being able to handle surges in demand. So in an engineering sense, we built all of that in.

We built a lot of navigation into the front end of the service because we want to help all of the new people to find their way around the Internet. We announced that we would guarantee any transactions made with the AT&T Universal Card while they were using our services. And, finally, we offered a one-year free trial on the Internet with the first five hours of each month free.

AT&T's Disaggregated Business Model

AT&T has arrived on the Internet with a comprehensive strategy that currently focuses on three key areas: access, hosting, and content services. Using a disaggregated business model, the services are run as independent businesses, giving them the flexibility to become the "best of breed" in their respective categories. By creating separate entities, each is able to form strategic alliances with companies that may be competitors to one of the other AT&T services. AT&T is also evolving its Internet offerings to include private network solutions for businesses and standards-based Internet communications services.

Evslin explains AT&T's strategy: "Our online strategy is very much Internet-centered. We believe, as is graphically happening, that all online services will quickly become accessible from the Internet, and it's through these connections that people will get news, communicate with each other, get entertainment. Over time, there'll be a blend between traditional telephony services and the services we think of as online today."

AT&T sees the online service industry as having three parts. One of those parts is called value-added access. This means providing one connection from a home or business to the Internet that is used by the family or business to satisfy all of their online needs. This, says Evslin, will take the place of today's model where somebody might have one phone number for calling CompuServe, another phone number for calling AOL, a third to send faxes, a fourth number for sending e-mail, and a fifth for online electronic banking. Evslin predicts that there will be a single connection to the Internet through an Internet service provider and that all of those services will then be available through that Internet connection.

The second part of the online industry in which AT&T is participating is in the hosting business. This allows people to place the information on AT&T's computer network that they want to have available to its customers on the Internet. Evslin explains, "Customers for our hosting service want to have Web sites that are similar to stores, but they don't want to have to keep it up and running 24 hours a day 7 days a week, don't want to worry about having a big enough pipe available feeding into it for the five hours a month of peak time, and then have that be largely unused the rest of the time. So we sell our hosting services to people who want to have a presence on the Internet but don't want all the physical hassles of running that presence and connecting it to the Internet."

The third business is content aggregation services. This means integrating various content-rich sites into one deep Web site, and/or linking to them as seamlessly as possible. All of the older commercial services like AOL and CompuServe are repositioning themselves to adapt to the intensifying focus on the Internet. Evslin believes that these content-rich places on the Internet will begin to proliferate like magazines. Some will be very broad and some will be very narrowly focused. They will be supported, just as magazines are, by a mix of subscription and advertising revenue. The people who operate content services will not necessarily operate any computers, because they will receive worldwide hosting services from someone else. They won't operate access networks because their customers will get to them through the Internet. AT&T is in all three of those business segments.

AT&T WorldNet Services is a value-added Internet service provider. AT&T EasyCommerce Services provides Web hosting and a range of services for merchants and other people who want to do business on the Internet. And AT&T New Media Services is developing AT&T-branded content services, which both create and aggregate content from other sources, sell subscriptions to that content, and sell advertising that would appeal to the people who access the content. Business Network is the first of the New Media services and is aimed at the business and professional market. Personal Online Services is a separate set of services, focused on serving the residential, family market. Evslin explains the rationale for WorldNet's independence from the other services:

> WorldNet as an Internet service provider has to make sure that it's the best way for its users to get any kind of content that they want. If it restricted itself to providing good access to AT&T-provided content, then people who wanted access to non-AT&T content would go somewhere else. By having the separate business structure, we were able to lead the industry by closing deals to make AOL and CompuServe content available through their Internet connection to AT&T WorldNet users.

It's not just that we were able to play in the industry; we were actually able to lead it and to make business deals with companies that were to some degree competitive with AT&T's content services. If we bound the businesses more tightly together, then we wouldn't be able to make that kind of deal. We would not be as good an access service. Looking at it from the point of view of the content services—although they, of course, hope that all AT&T WorldNet subscribers will access their content—that's not enough. They really want people who get their Internet connection somewhere else to have access to the content as well, and so they need the independence to make sure that happens.

The organizations that support AT&T's three-pronged strategy—access, hosting, and content—are as follows:

Value-Added Access Services

- **AT&T WorldNet Services** Internet access for consumers and businesses
- AT&T WorldNet Service Dial-up Access—for consumers
- AT&T WorldNet Managed Internet Service—for businesses
- AT&T NetWare Connect Service—dedicated Internet access for medium-to-large-businesses

Hosting and Transaction Services

- **AT&T EasyCommerce Services** Web hosting and transaction service that helps businesses conduct electronic commerce under their own brand names.
  - AT&T Easy World Wide Web Services: Internet hosting platform that will allow businesses to publish information on the Internet without owning their own servers.
  - AT&T EasyLink Services: A family of electronic messaging offerings that expand customer's communication capabilities including:
    - AT&T Mail
    - AT&T Fax Solutions
    - AT&T Electronic Data Interchange
    - AT&T Telex
    - AT&T Professional Services

Content Aggregation Businesses

- **AT&T New Media Services** Chartered with developing a series of AT&T-branded World Wide Web-based content services for business and professional information markets

- AT&T Business Network: Provides business professionals, managers and entrepreneurs with easy access to the news, information and business services needed for management and growth.
- **AT&T Personal Online Services** Provides AT&T-branded content services for personal and family information markets, the first of which will focus on health and fitness.

AT&T WorldNet Services

AT&T's WorldNet Service organization offers comprehensive Internet access. The service is set up for both dedicated and dial access to the Internet. AT&T's WorldNet Managed Internet and NetWare Connect Services are specialized, managed subsets that provide dedicated high-speed access and optimize business applications.

WorldNet is positioned as an Internet gateway, the place to begin your Internet experience. It has directories and well-organized categories of information from which visitors can launch their explorations. At Home and At Work selection pages are provided to serve the whole person regardless of his or her purpose for being online. The At Home section will feature sites focused on leisure issues, education, children, and so on. The At Work area will point to business news sites, investment information, and other business or work-related issues. The goal is to be very broad-based in appeal, and extremely user-friendly so that those who are new to the online experience will feel well taken care of and considered in the interface design.

The service utilizes its own preconfigured version of Netscape Navigator browser, along with a directory for over 80,000 sites that helps users to preview and make informed decisions before they access these locations. The directory provides ratings, reviews, and descriptions of the sites. Its agent technology utilizes powerful search engines to assist the user in locating information quickly.

A series of theme areas can be found at the Harley Hahn Internet Exploration Station, focusing on family entertainment and education. Special themes are showcased each month such as gardening, modern art, games, and so on, and users are guided to Internet theme-related resources.

By March 14, 1996, when the service was launched, AT&T had been flooded with over 200,000 orders. It reported receiving calls at a rate of one every four seconds since it was introduced on February 27 with a year-long offer of five free hours a month for AT&T residential long-distance customers who signed up by December 31 and competitive flat fee rates for all customers. Robert E. Allen commented on his company's strategy: "AT&T is marketing AT&T World-Net Service to its 80 million residential and 10 million business customers as part of the company's strategy to offer innovative packages of services, including local, long distance, wireless, entertainment, and online services, tailored to customer's needs."

Another marketing strategy to benefit both parties was AT&T's announcement that customers who signed up for the service were eligible for the AT&T WorldNet Service Quality Inspector Program. The program awards points for each service improvement that users help them to make. This approach gives the users a feeling of control, participation, and ownership, and can lead to a greater sense of belonging and increased incentive to make WorldNet their home on the Internet. This strategy also gets users to function as an ongoing focus group, providing feedback that can be used to improve the service.

In an effort to encourage commerce on the Internet, and to allay consumers' fears of using credit cards in the online environment, AT&T WorldNet Service customers who charge the service to their AT&T Universal Card will not be held financially liable for fraudulent charges by unauthorized users if their account number is compromised while using the service to make purchases on the Internet. Evslin adds:

> We announced that we would guarantee transactions made with the AT&T Universal Card over WorldNet because our customers told us they were worried about fraud when they used their credit cards on the Internet. We could have explained to them the technology that minimizes that risk, but it was much simpler and much more effective just to say it's safe because we guarantee it.
>
> Finally, because a lot of people weren't sure whether they wanted to use the Internet or not, we put together a unique pricing plan that again said AT&T would take the risk rather than asking its customers to do so. We'll give you a year free trial on the Internet, the first five hours each month free, because we're convinced that most of you will like it and most of you will stay with it.
>
> Experienced users wanted reliability, accessibility, and a flat rate plan so they didn't have to watch the clock all the time they were online, and with the other part of our price plan, the $19.95 unlimited offer, they can afford to stay online as long as it's useful to them and not have to count the hours. What's happening is that people who would have used other Internet service providers, perhaps on a flat rate plan, perhaps even less than $19.95, said "I want the kind of quality that AT&T represents. It's now become not just a toy but an important part of my life, and so I want it to work like my phone, and I believe that AT&T will bring that kind of value to the service."
>
> And those are all things people took on faith because of our brand; almost a half-million people ordered it before they had a look at it. But now we're

very happy to see that, in things like the C-Net survey of Internet service
providers, we come in first in our own customer satisfaction surveys. We're
getting numbers that are close to the numbers that our long distance business
gets. So we're delivering on those things that people came to the service for.

According to Evslin, today, Internet service providers like NetCom and PSI
are the direct competitors to WorldNet. He adds:

MCI is also a competitor, although it hasn't been off to much of a start in the
consumer market. I think it got complacent, but with the early success of
WorldNet, that it will reverse and turn into a strong competitor. Each of the
regional Bell operating companies has said at one time or another that it
will offer an Internet service, and I expect that they'll do that. The way in
which World Net relates to the rest of the AT&T strategy is by providing
Internet access as a way of extending our relationships with our long-
distance customers, so we go from being just their long-distance provider to
being their provider of long distance, perhaps local service, direct TV, Inter-
net access, wireless communications.

A lot of our research and customer feedback tell us that [customers] prefer
to buy all of those communication services from one provider; and we know
that we can integrate those services technically so there are synergies in pro-
viding those services. As the whole industry deregulates and the local com-
panies are free to go after the long-distance business, and vice versa—like
the Bell operating companies, however many of them are left after they get
through merging—it makes sense that eventually our competitors end up
being the other interexchange carriers like MCI and Sprint.

In designing WorldNet as an organized gateway to quality content on the Net,
AT&T carefully selects locations in which it can build strong synergistic relationships. AOL provides, in addition to a very desirable consumer base, a complementary depth of content, and WorldNet can provide AOL, in addition to its
equally desirable consumer base, with reliable competency as an Internet partner.

Dan Hesse, senior vice president and general manager of the Online Services
Group, explains how the WorldNet/AOL agreement works:

Customer can subscribe to AT&T and get AT&T quality on their network
connections, and AT&T customer care. But, anytime they want to go to
AOL, there will be an icon to click on, and instantly they will be "hot
linked" directly to AOL. Customers can have their AOL experience and
then click back to WorldNet if they want to do something else there or go
out on the Web.

For a consumer, it's the best of all worlds because our pricing plans make it very attractive to bundle WorldNet access with AOL content. We make it a compelling offer. And it's great for AOL because it knows AT&T's core competence is providing a superior network experience, from both a technical and customer care perspective. AOL's expertise is in aggregating content and in creating online communities.

AOL could be considered a competitor to AT&T's consumer content aggregation business, Personal Online Services. Our AT&T HealthSite is targeted at the home or consumer market. While this could be considered a competitor to AOL, AOL does not offer the same kind of material we offer on HealthSite. CompuServe is perhaps a better example of a business-oriented service that could be considered competitive with AT&T Business Network, although we consider AT&T Business Network to be a very different service from CompuServe.

AOL is moving toward the content aggregation space, and I believe it will gradually focus fewer resources on the access business. You're going to see a disaggregation of these businesses—content aggregation and access—even among the traditional players like AOL and CompuServe, which now have both. For example, CompuServe created WOW! If AT&T WorldNet provides cost-effective, convenient access to the content customers want, more customers will sign up for AT&T WorldNet.

From an AOL perspective, it knows many millions of consumers will subscribe to AT&T WorldNet because of the WorldNet offer, and because of AT&T's relationship with its 90 million customers. It's a win-win relationship, and it's a confirmation of the disaggregation model, because AOL does not view WorldNet as a competitor. WorldNet, as an ISP, would occupy a market space more akin to a PSINet or a UUNet.

Advertising on AT&T WorldNet

WorldNet has several models for advertising. As of mid-April 1996, WorldNet had about 200 pages of content at the site. WorldNet is not meant to be an ultimate destination, but rather a place to peruse the possibilities for exploring the Internet by making use of the directory and information resources. What makes that appealing to advertisers is the tremendous amount of traffic browsing through those resources; and the numbers continue to grow substantially. Therefore, the first advertising model is based on the number of hits, or exposures, to an ad. This is the most standard form of advertising on the Net, and WorldNet gets paid on a per-hit basis.

The second model is based on shared revenue, driven by an advertiser's acquisition of new customers as the direct result of an advertisement. Since WorldNet is where people come to decide on a destination, those companies that have a presence on WorldNet's front pages are assisted in acquiring new customers. WorldNet has deals in place to share in the revenue derived by advertisers from acquiring those new customers.

Evslin states that while WorldNet is unique right now in its role as both a distribution mechanism and conduit for users, he believes that it will be copied. The kinds of deal AT&T struck with AOL and CompuServe to provide mutual access to each other's sites will become more common. He adds, "Up to this point the content services have stayed sort of distinct from the Internet and have their own access, but it was clear that we could bring enough users, so it made sense to make a deal like that with us."

A third kind of marketing opportunity is called *co-labeling*. For example, WCCO, a television station in Minneapolis, distributes a special version of WorldNet, which is co-labeled WCCO and AT&T WorldNet. WCCO becomes a distributor of WorldNet under its own brand name, but its customers become WorldNet customers as well. The only difference for customers is that when they use the WCCO version of WorldNet, the first page they come to is a WCCO page rather than the WorldNet home page. They still have all of the options and benefits that WorldNet customers enjoy, such as mail and AT&T connectivity.

Likewise, Prudential because it wanted all of its security customers to have access to its Web site, entered into a co-labeling agreement with AT&T. AT&T created a co-labeled Prudential Securities/AT&T WorldNet version for the insurance company. According to Evslin, that constitutes an ad because the default pointer inside AT&T WorldNet is what drives people to the site of that co-promoted, co-branded version.

As customers have surged onto WorldNet, AT&T's business customers have become increasingly interested in investing in their own Web presence. Evslin says that this may mean more companies will be interested in buying connections to the Internet or even hosting services. AT&T is harnessing the power of its relationship with its business customers by encouraging them to make attractive offers to their customers to entice them online. Evslin states, "One of the things that we have to do in order to succeed is make sure that those people who are new to the Net find this a useful experience; and when they don't find something useful the first time, we want to make sure they come back until they do."

One way he suggests that can happen is through direct (paper) mailings done by WorldNet on behalf of a business partner, offering special deals if the recipient comes online through AT&T WorldNet that month. Evslin adds, "I think we'll do a lot in using our business customers to stimulate and satisfy the consumer market, at the same time we help those businesses introduce themselves to that audience. You'll certainly see many more bundles of Internet access with basic LD (long-distance) service, and perhaps with local service as well, as AT&T goes into that market. We're offering, rather than a series of discrete services, a bundle of as many communication services as people want to buy. That might include their wireless or direct TV. Bundles are certainly a trend for us."

Charter Advertising Package   A charter advertising package was made available for AT&T WorldNet Service through the end of April 1996. Charter advertisers had banner ads placed in a sequential queue on the At Home or At Work home page throughout the charter period. The charter advertisers were also given exclusive sponsorship of one of the 22 targeted content category pages as they become available. The home page queue allowed a maximum of 22 advertisers. The charter package, competitively priced at $30,000, guaranteed 1 million impressions over the display period from April 29 through July 28. Advertisers who signed up in March had the opportunity to display their ads during the month of April without charge. Other charter advertiser benefits included special discounted rates through 1996, unique advertising and co-marketing opportunities, and sponsor index inclusion.

Post-Charter Advertising Opportunities   AT&T WorldNet Service provides advertisers with a wide variety of placement categories, which include 14 At Home and 7 At Work category pages covering a broad spectrum of subject areas for targeted advertising (see Figures 11.1 to 11.8). Other advertising opportunities include content category logos; box/banner combinations for tertiary pages, and box/banner combinations for premium space, which includes placements in Today's Features, Celebrity Spotlights, Search, Directories, and My World.

Sample Advertising Opportunities on WorldNet

At Home Categories

Arts & Entertainment	Home & Lifestyles	Shopping
Health & Wellness	News	Travel
Learning & Reference	Computing	Door No. 3
Personal Finance	Kid's Corner	Weather*
Sports	Local & International	

At Work Categories

Employment	Mobile Office	Technology
Finance	Politics & Government	Business Life
Global Vision	Sales & Marketing	Weather*

* Single site available on both At Home and At Work sections.

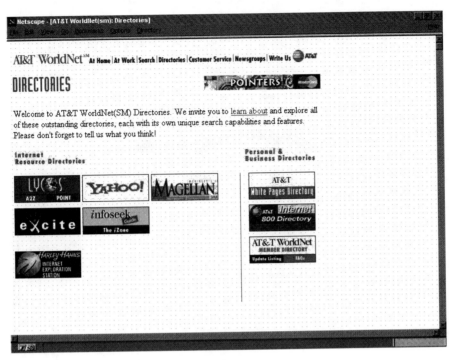

Figure 11.1   WorldNet Directories.

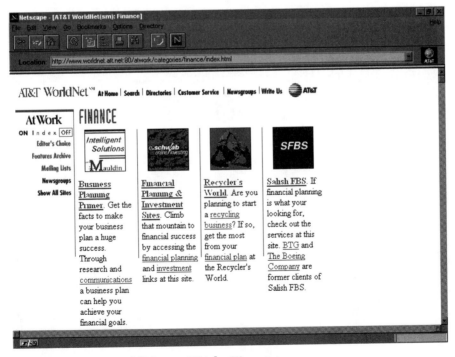

Figure 11.2   WorldNet at Work: Finance.

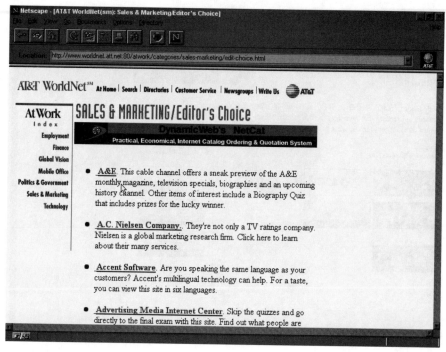

Figure 11.3 WorldNet at Work: Sales & Marketing Editor's Choice.

Figure 11.4 WorldNet at Home: Health & Wellness.

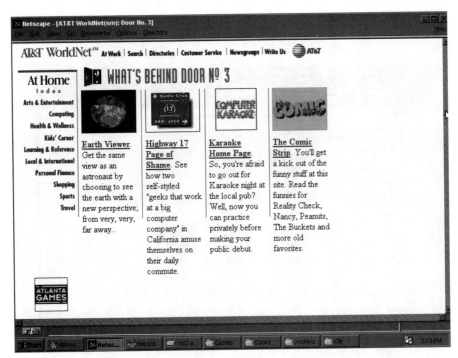

Figure 11.5 WorldNet at Home: What's Behind Door No. 3.

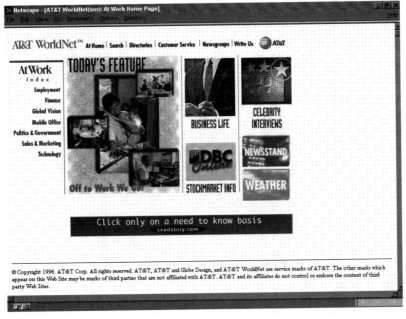

Figure 11.6 WorldNet at Work: Today's Feature.

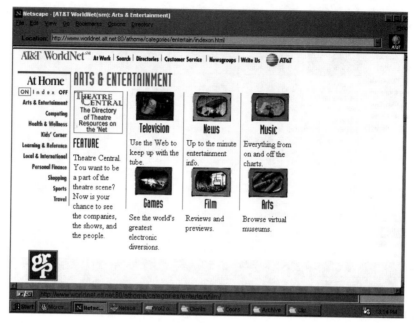

Figure 11.7 WorldNet at Home: Arts & Entertainment.

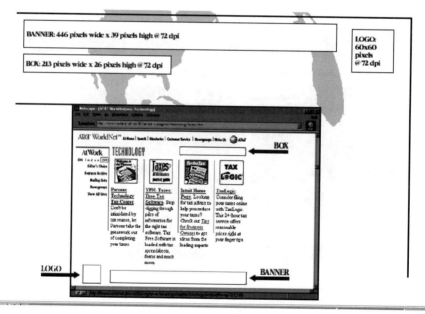

Figure 11.8 WorldNet Advertising Spec Sheet.

Content Category Logos

$5,000 for a one-month period

250,000 guaranteed page views

Location: Lower left corner of the page below index, as per content categories listed.

Tertiary (Third Level)

Box/Banner Combination or Upper Banner

$10,000 for one-month period

250,000 guaranteed page views

1. Box/Banner—30 locations within At Home
2. Upper Banner—7 locations within Editor's Choice at Work and 7 locations within Mailing Lists at Work

Logo/or Lower Banner

$7,500 for a one-month period

250,000 guaranteed page views

- 30 within At Home
- 14 within At Work

Premium Space

Box/Banner Combination

$25,000 for a one-month period

500,000 guaranteed page views:

- Search
- Directories
- My World
- Celebrity Feature at Home
- Celebrity Feature at Work
- Today's Feature at Home
- Today's Feature at Work

Thirteen companies are participating in an AT&T WorldNet Service advertising preview in connection with the advertising program. They are Delta Air Lines, JC Penney, and MasterCard International, represented by Modem Media, a leading interactive marketing and advertising company; The Discovery Channel, Duracell, and The Cox Communications Atlanta Games site, represented by i-traffic, Inc., a leader in media planning tools and services for Internet advertising; Adobe Systems, Inc., The HomeArts online network from Hearst New Media & Technology, a division of The Hearst Corporation; National Basketball Association, Sony Electronics, Personal Information Co., 1-800-FLOWERS, Frontier Technologies, and MCA/Universal.

WorldNet plans to keep advertising rates highly competitive. One of the greatest advantages to advertisers is the guaranteed audience of AT&T's customer base, many of whom will be long-distance customers. AT&T also has a strategy for bringing all of its 800-number customers onto the Internet. The results promise to be significant in increasing WorldNet customer numbers.

AT&T WorldNet Managed Internet Service

Officially launched in September 1995, this service is sold jointly with BBN Planet, one of the leading managed Internet access providers in the industry. This service offers companies dedicated access speeds ranging from 56 Kbps to 45 Mbps, and options such as bulk provisioning, redundant configuration, and security features. Some of the features include:

- Implementation: support site planning, registration, provisioning, testing training
- Network management: monitoring, access link management, configuration, equipment maintenance
- Customer care: 24-hour, 7-day software/configuration support, fault isolation, security support, secondary Domain Name Service (DNS)
- Managed access speeds up to T3: critical elements for developing networked applications

Some of the companies utilizing this service are Promus Hotel Corporation, owners of Embassy Suites; Hampton Inn and Suites; and Homewood Suites hotels; McCann-Erickson, the world's largest advertising agency; and the Associated Group, one of the largest insurance companies in the United States.

AT&T NetWare Connect Service

This service uses the AT&T network and Novell NetWare to connect local area networks while providing robust directory services, network security, and access to the Internet. LAN environments are extended into the wide area networks both within and outside of the company, opening up new ways of working electronically. The service provides a single point of network administration, scalability of platform, and reduced capital investment to allow smooth, manageable growth of existing environments.

AT&T EasyCommerce Services

AT&T EasyCommerce Services provide advanced electronic solutions that make it easier for companies to market, advertise, and run their businesses. EasyCommerce Services contains AT&T Easy World Wide Web Service and AT&T EasyLink. The Easy World Wide Web Service is an Internet hosting platform that allows businesses to easily establish Web sites on the AT&T network. AT&T EasyLink is a family of standards-based electronic messaging subscription services such as e-mail, fax, and electronic data interchange (EDI), which provide various electronic functionality for businesses.

Kathleen Earley, vice president of AT&T EasyCommerce, explains that the entire business vision, mission, and strategy are dedicated to delivering a platform environment in which electronic commerce can take place. From AT&T's perspective, the 1-800 call centers carry out a form of electronic commerce. AT&T has 1 million customers who conduct their business electronically using the telephony network. Earley explains the EasyCommerce strategy as it relates to this customer group:

> We're extending the Web hosting capability of the Internet so that our over 1 million, 800 and 888 toll-free number customers will be able to have an electronic storefront on the Internet. If you think about the Internet and its strengths today, it is really a worldwide marketing and distribution medium. It is a giant infomercial in real time. And while people are talking about conducting business on the Net, in reality, there's a very small portion of actual ordering, purchasing, payments, and transactions currently taking place there. Most of those transactions take place in an offline or a store-and-forward environment where people pick up the phone and make an 800 call or they transact in another way. Our goal in EasyCommerce is to help our businesses put up an electronic storefront that will drive traffic to their door.

Beginning in the summer of 1996, EasyCommerce began offering progressively more sophisticated transaction services along with the Web hosting capability. It "commerce-enables" a marketing site only when it is appropriate, to accommodate those people who use the Internet primarily for publishing or marketing, and for whom it may not make sense to actually conduct commerce online. For other businesses, it is entirely appropriate to utilize the Internet to take orders and deliver goods and services.

EasyCommerce provides any required transaction capability in what Earley calls a "vendor-neutral" environment. AT&T acts as a trusted third party and does not become involved in determining mode of payment or which credit card or smart card company wins the business. AT&T simply makes it possible for its merchants to conduct commerce any way they choose.

Earley emphasizes that it is very important from a strategic standpoint to allow businesses or consumers to select their payment mechanism on a going-forward basis as they grow into the need for a particular feature. AT&T will work with all of those providers in order to make them competitive, because she believes that a lot of the physical world will be replicated on the Internet over time, and that there is no one payment stream.

The AT&T vision is to provide these electronic storefronts, and to help their customers learn how to effectively market and merchandise on the Internet. Earley believes this is just another marketplace and that with time and experience, the most effective ways will be found to capture and hold a customer's attention and to generate loyalty. Figure 11.9 illustrates why electronic commerce is so important and the direction it is moving in.

AT&T Easy World Wide Web Services (EW3)

AT&T's EW3 Services provide an end-to-end solution for businesses that want to create their own branded Internet presence but do not want to be burdened with building or owning their own servers (Figure 11.10). Companies are given complete control over their design and the content they publish, while EW3 takes care of connectivity issues, bandwidth requirements, server capacity, routing, and disaster recovery.

Through an AT&T online university, EW3 provides training in the creation and setup of a Web site on the hosting service. In-person two-day classes are also held as part of the program for customers. By course completion, customers have a functioning Web site. Earley explains that EW3 trainers have a content creation and staging space "in the sky" where EW3 keeps multiple versions of the Web site. Therefore, all customers need is a PC so they can run the front page and work on it from their own location. EW3 uses the Microsoft Vermeer Front Page tool, which is tightly integrated into EW3. The WorldNet dialing service is used to load content into the network.

It is possible to prestage by day and time when a site goes "live" or when a production version of a Web site goes live. This is especially useful for merchants running promotions or managing price changes. Another benefit of the system is its default capability that causes the site to revert to the previous version if the newest one is not completed in time for an "opening." EW3 is working very closely with its merchants and other business clients to take the fear out of utilizing the technology and managing the complex details.

Earley reports that more than half of EW3's customers bring someone from their advertising agency to the class. The customer, whether alone or with an agency consultant arrives with storyboards and graphics, is given assistance in placing them in the site, and is trained in how to make updates. For an average cost of $1,500 for the class, a customer ends up with a fully functional site and an understanding of how to maintain it. The monthly hosting charge ranges from approximately $300 to $500, plus usage for AT&T 800 or 888 customers, and $600 for other businesses. These prices are targeted at a level below what it would cost someone to run and manage this technology independently. Included in the package are 100 megabytes of server storage for Web pages, and up to 300 megabytes per month of usage (data downloaded from the site by users).

Earley explains that another big advantage AT&T has in targeting its 800-number customers is that not only does AT&T own a packet-switched network and data centers, but it also is a very big circuit-switched company. For 800 businesses, AT&T intends to tightly integrate those two network capabilities. Earley explains how that might manifest:

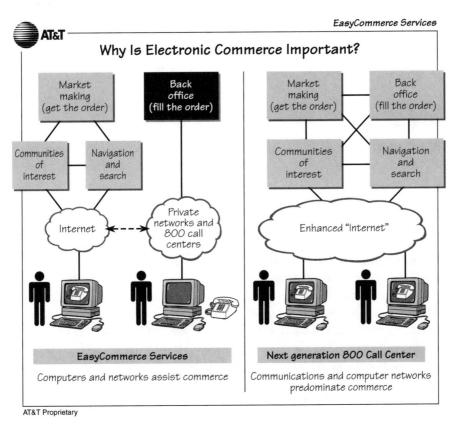

Figure 11.9 Why Is Electronic Commerce Important?

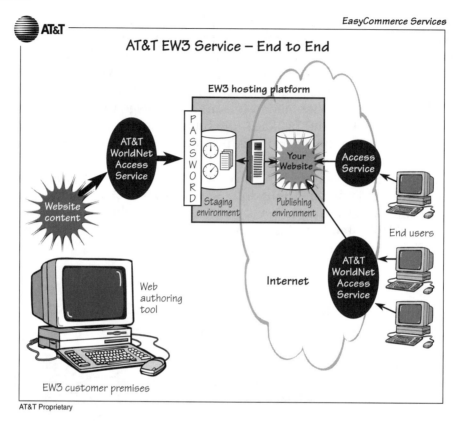

Figure 11.10   AT&T Easy World Wide Web Services: End to End.

Down the road there may be a button on the Web page that says, "Call me now." How we implement that is to be determined, but whether it's the customer calling the business or the business getting a signal to call the customer, it will be a very powerful integration of these two technologies. Since automatic number identification is approved, we will provide inter-activity on multiple levels, because we truly believe that if we really want to penetrate the next segment of the market beyond the heat seekers, we have to enable people to do business the way they want to do business. We believe that there will be a tremendous amount of voice transactions in the near term when people will still want to complete their transactions by voice, because no matter how secure the Internet becomes, they'll never trust it.

EW3 is also investing heavily in improving tracking capabilities. Tracking not only how many times a page is looked at, but where those visits are coming from is important market research information that many companies are working very hard to capture. EW3 supplies detailed reports to its customers and knows that the information must be expanded to include origination data.

In addition, Earley points out, the target customer is the 800 business, so the company provides hot links to its 800 services directory, which is currently up on the Internet.

> *If you go to that services directory and you look up flowers, you'll find every flower business with an 800 number. If you find the one you want and double-click on it, you will be taken to that Web site. We provide those kinds of links between the online 800 services directory and their Web sites if they happen to be 800 customers and AT&T Web-hosted customers.*
>
> *We would also consider doing what MiniTel did, which is co-market and co-advertise, so that wherever you see an 800 number advertised, there ought to be a Web site address. There is no incremental cost to a company to drive traffic to its site. AT&T does not own the entire 800 market, but we do own contractually and have responsibility for the 800 directory. We list all 800 numbers in the industry. That's nonexclusive. People can copy it, but ours is the official 800 directory. We've been out there since October 1995.*

Disney Online AT&T EasyCommerce Services state-of-the-art data center in Virginia provides the environment to host Disney.com, the first in a series of family online products from Disney Online, a Disney Interactive division founded in September 1995. The following are excerpts from AT&T's press release announcement of April 30, 1996: "The Disney.com server facility is on one of the most robust Web hosting platforms on the Internet and introduces the world of all things Disney in an exciting new way."

The special Virginia facility focuses on emerging customer applications that require higher degrees of reliability, availability, and scalability. The site is equipped with the latest comprehensive network analysis and performance tools, and is designed with fault tolerance that provides continuous customer service. During the first week of operation, the AT&T servers handled an unprecedented 18.5 million visitors. Since then, the Disney.com site has received an average of 2 million hits each day.

In developing a Web server and network system with massive capacity and storage capability, AT&T EasyCommerce Services had to ensure that the site would accommodate millions of hits each day with unimpeded operation.

Redundancy was built in at every level—site, staging, network, backbone—for the highest reliability. Leading-edge software and state-of-the-art technology were applied for the site's interactive multimedia requirements, including the use of several of the highest-capacity servers.

The site is graphically rich and includes games, puzzles, stories, and downloads. To ensure reliability, AT&T built a high-speed connection from the AT&T backbone to the Internet for unparalleled uptime performance as well as a redundant backbone to ensure high network reliability. Other AT&T innovations in support of Disney.com are:

- bandwidth on demand that allows millions of hits on the Disney site each day
- redundant Web servers for continuous availability of content
- firewall security
- domain name servers outside the firewalls to facilitate user access
- a set of facilities tools to manage and monitor the running of the hosting platform

Too Much of a Good Thing   "One of your best dreams and worst nightmares," states Earley, "is waking up and being one of the hot spots on the Net. Because while you're excited to be one of the hot spots on the Net, the terror is that all of a sudden you're going to get a bill from your hosting entity that is unaffordable because you're getting a couple million hits a day, and yet you have no revenue to pay the higher expense.

"And so we tell [these customers], 'You can either risk your brand because your own server can't handle the capacity, or you can come and be hosted on our site, and we'll offer you tiered levels of services in terms of how many hits you get a month or how much data you use. But we're going to do it over a 30-day running average, so that if you become the hot spot on the Net, the only way you get bumped up into a higher price point is when, for 30 consecutive days, you are operating at that higher level."

EW3 Services Summary   AT&T EW3 summarizes its services as follows:
- A secure, reliable network-based hosting environment managed by AT&T professionals 24 hours per day, 7 days per week.
- A single point of contact—one phone call for all customer needs.
- Bandwidth capacity on demand for peak and nonpeak periods.

- Microsoft FrontPage Web design software that makes it easy to create a home page.
- Online administration tools for ongoing site management. Customers control their own content, Web design, and updates. Additionally, the administration tools give customers access to site and usage reports.
- A staging server behind a firewall that enables customers to preview and make changes to their Web pages before they are published on the Internet. Customers use AT&T's WorldNet Service Dial Access to connect to the staging server. This service is an additional $19.95 per month for unlimited access to the Internet.
- Hot links from AT&T's Internet-based Toll-Free Directory (www.tollfree.att.net) for AT&T toll-free customers. Web surfers can click from a customer's listing on the AT&T toll-free directory and jump to the customer's Web site.
- Registration of one vanity domain name with InterNIC.
- 100 MB of server storage for Web pages and up to 300 MB per month of usage, data downloaded from the site by visitors.
- An optional two-day, hands-on training program.

Table 11.1 shows sample rates for these services.

AT&T EasyLink Services

EasyLink Services are value-added network services that include a fax, EDI, and message-enabled application provider, which can deliver messages to over 160 countries with data centers in seven locations around the world including the United Kingdom, Australia, Japan, Hong Kong, Israel, and the United States. It supports electronic commerce, by making it easier to integrate some of the more widely used marketing tools with the Internet.

AT&T launched its Internet business in Japan 1994. According to Earley, AT&T has their own backbone down the center of the islands where they aggregate traffic and then provide connectivity to the Internet backbone in the United States. AT&T also is a Web hosting entity in Japan, where custom systems integration is done for customers, such as Web-based interactive catalogues.

In December 1995, AT&T also put up a Web server in Hong Kong to complement its EasyLink business. This follows basically the same concept of electronic storefronts, but extends it around the world. Credit cards preclude the

TABLE 11.1   EW3 Sample Rates

	Monthly	One-Time Charge
EW3 registration		$1,000.00
EW3 registration with a one-year contract		500.00
EW3 service fee for AT&T customer	$295.00	
EW3 service fee for non-AT&T customer	395.00	
EW3 data downloaded by end user		
0	200MB	Included
201	500 MB	155.00
501	800 MB	$380.00
801	1,400 MB	605.00
1,401	3,500 MB	1,055.00
3,501	7,000 MB	1,505.00
7,001	15,000 MB	2,005.00
EW3 Storage Charge, per MB over 100*	1.0	
Toll-free Internet Directory Link	50.00	
EW3 domain name registration (per add'l vanity name)		$200.00[+]
EW3 domain name maintenance (per add'l vanity name)	$100.00	
EW3 Premium Customer Care	85.00	
EW3 Training, first attendee		$995.00
EW3 Training, second attendee		$495.00[‡]
Microsoft FrontPage for AT&T, add'l copies each		$149.00[§]

The plan includes the following at no extra charge: EW3 initial vanity domain name registration and maintenance, first copy of Microsoft FrontPage at AT&T and EW3 toll-free Internet Directory link.

* First 100 MB storage included in monthly service fee.

[+] Billed one month in advance, proratable for partial months.

[‡] Training for second attendee, same company, same session, using shared terminal. Additional attendees, same company, same session will be charged full first- and second-attendee rates.

[§] First copy of Microsoft FrontPage for AT&T included with EW3 registration.

Sample Provided by AT&T EW3: U.S. only costs as of July 1, 1996 (subject to change)

necessity to use a country's currency in order to buy goods and services. But the governing rules of taxation in commerce—who is taxed and how, and who collects, is a very complicated subject when it comes to electronic storefronts on the Internet.

Earley suggests that the tax laws and the importing laws will never keep up with the rate and pace of the innovative merchants on the Internet. She refers to them as innovative because, while the big name brands will not want to be tied up in courts with lawsuits, the smaller companies can move their servers virtually from Bermuda to the Bahamas to the Cayman Islands. Thus transactions could be made to look as if they were occurring in the United States. Earley states:

> *One of the things that I challenged our Hong Kong team to do was to set up a personal importing business. I told them to go to all of the little shops in Hong Kong that sell items like the Pan Am pearls that everyone buys for $7 to $12 but that they pay $97 in the United States for as Carol Lee pearls. By doing nothing more than creating a form that turns into a fax, people would be able to fax orders, literally order on the Web, and do personal importing. AT&T will work very aggressively not only with the transaction platforms and the different payment mechanisms, but equally with the freight companies, whether Federal Express, UPS, or DHL.*
>
> *The merchants will negotiate with shippers, but our hope is that we can provide the end-to-end service so that you literally do personal importing. Rather than calling Shannon Catalogue for your Waterford crystal—which is just an 800 storefront for an Irish importing business—you just do it on the Web.*

For example, a directory search using any of the Internet search engines could be conducted to find the Hong Kong storefront because it's got a URL. Earley describes the process: "I just hot link to that site in Hong Kong, and I fill out the form, which is all in English, and I order my pearls, and [the merchant will] ship them to me. Right then and there I'll find out how long it'll take, approximately, to get them. Another option is that we will move that site electronically to the United States to have better performance. Or if its an AT&T customer, for the really hot sites, we could cache those in multiple locations around the world, depending on from where people are trying to get to them. It's pretty hard to cache a site the size of Disney, but it's not that hard to cache a site the size of electronic storefronts in order to be able to guarantee availability and reliability."

Resellers   One of EasyCommerce's important value propositions is to use resellers for its services. These resellers tend to be the companies that are designing Web sites, and include such innovative companies as U.S. Web and Clement Mok's newest company, Net Objects. As a reseller, Net Objects would provide the Web site design services to a client, and then place that client's site on the Easy Commerce service for hosting. It would be as easy as pushing a button according to Earley. Earley adds, "And then it's up to the customer whether or not Net Objects does the continual updates and refreshments of the site, or if it is just a one-time design. That's a whole separate industry that I think is going to spring up."

The Smart Card Link   AT&T is one of the largest card distributors in the world. In addition to its telephone calling cards, the company also offers pre-paid telephone cards, and a Universal Credit Card. AT&T plans to participate aggressively in the smart card technology base because of the broad applications in customer and personal customer information management. This technology is seen as a potentially integral component in the transporting of information when linked into the online environment, still very much in its infancy at this point.

The Legacy Write-Offs   Businesses are going to need to develop programs that will interface directly with the technology on the Internet, if they hope to conduct commerce there. (A legacy system is any system that already is in place when a new one is installed.) With the rate and pace of technological advances, corporate America has been very busy writing off its legacy systems even if they are only two years old. Earley gives a good example of some of the issues facing a business conducting commerce on the Internet:

> [Let's say], I call up Lands' End today. I'm looking at the catalogue. I tell [the operator] I want the red sweater that's $42 on page 24, which is such and such a number. The Lands' End operator immediately inventories his or her database, comes back, and tells me whether that sweater can be shipped today or has to be back-ordered. There is a law that says a company cannot debit your credit card until [the product] ships. It has everything to do with cash flow in a business.
>
> If I move to the Internet environment, there's now a picture of a red sweater, and I decide to purchase it, and I fill out the order form that says, "Buy now." How do I learn whether the sweater is available and when it will ship? So there's this interface in today's inventory management and purchasing systems that needs to be created in order to have online commerce, if you're running a physical business today like Lands' End.
>
> And that's difficult, because now you have multiple systems going into that same inventory database. You've got the 800 operator as well as the Internet. So you have synchronization issues between your inventory and who's debiting your inventory when. There are lots of business issues to be resolved here.
>
> Meanwhile, think about people who decide to go into business. They don't have the 800 call center or they don't have the very complex database system, whether it's Oracle or CICS, already installed. And they decide to

create something today from scratch. They will create a service based on Web technology that will be inherently tightly linked to a brand new inventory system. So your marketing system on the Net is your ordering system, your inventory management system, in real time. It's all one system tightly linked.

There are tremendous challenges for today's businesses to compete with the new ones that will be created. I'm in the business of creating the platform so that if you're Lands' End and you want to aggregate your orders on your Web site and put them in what we call an electronic data interchange wrapper—an envelope that goes to your database to check it out and then comes back—we will put in those kinds of connections. But somebody else is going to be writing that application.

We have a small professional services unit focused on electronic commerce implementation. We want to work very aggressively with other professional services companies because there's a lot of integration here. Think of all the companies that sprung up around client-server integration. They'll now all evolve to Internet-centric systems integration for legacy systems. We have the raw capability with the EDI links and the real-time links. If [these companies] want a dedicated T-1 link, aside from their database, we have it. If they want a fax link to their home fax machine, we have it. And if they want just an EDI link, we have that, too. There's a whole continuum of choices a current business has to make.

AT&T New Media Services

The mission of AT&T New Media Services, based in Cambridge, Massachusetts, is to develop a series of AT&T-branded, World Wide Web-based content services for business and professional information markets. AT&T Business Network, offered on the World Wide Web, is the first of such services, Michael E. Kolowich, president of New Media Services explains that with the strong relationships AT&T has with 80 million consumer customers, 10 million business customers, 15 million credit card users, and 5 million cellular telephone customers, it has the wherewithal to not only enable but also to drive markets.

Kolowich states that AT&T's philosophy of building these services is based on the concept that people approach an online session in one of four or five different modes. "One is very mission-oriented—'I want to find this.' Another is browse-oriented—'I want to look around.' Another is follower-oriented—'I trust Larry Magid to take me somewhere really interesting, so let's see what he has to say.' Another is community-oriented—'I want to connect with other people and interactively figure out where I want to go.' "

These were all taken into consideration as the first of New Media's products, AT&T Business Network, was launched. The charter for this service is to organize the resources of the Web and to create new Web tools for business professionals. The goal is to turn the diffuse collection of Internet resources and capabilities into an efficient, effective, daily utility for business, and create a place where professionals want to go each day. New Media Services refers to that as developing "the home page business," aggregating business information and services.

The range of quality, depth, and currency of business information on the Internet is all over the map, leaving room for people to organize, repackage, and redistribute it. Kolowich explains that most of the organization tools, whether they be directory services or search engines, spend the majority of their time addressing consumer services.

> By focusing on solving the problem of what businesspeople do every day, how they can use the Internet, and what are the best resources for doing that, we're in the process of building a very unique type of service. From a commercial standpoint, it really is all about building a traffic concentration point for businesspeople on the Internet. Its target is business managers, professionals, and entrepreneurs with an emphasis on smaller companies and on individuals in larger companies, as opposed to the enterprises themselves.

Kolowich believes that the Internet is all about individual decisions and individual choices, and in many ways it eliminates the intermediation of many of the middle people in the purchasing process. It's about giving individuals the information they need to do their jobs, information that is highly customized to them, not to their organizations. Every individual in an organization has a different set of information needs.

From an economic model standpoint, AT&T Business Network is designed to concentrate traffic of business managers, entrepreneurs, and professionals. The top business sites are selected by professional editors and reviewers, and the best ones are invited to become affiliates of Business Network. This stimulates the use of the Internet and of the top business sites by making those sites stand out. What places this service a level above most resources is that it is not just a directory of site names; it is designed to reach inside the sites and extract and highlight the most relevant information. Users can then make informed decisions before they visit, saving valuable time and legwork.

AT&T Business Network Service Features

Business Network was originally delivered over AT&T Interchange Online Network, a next-generation publishing platform, based on Internet protocols, hosting a collection of specialized services from independent publishers and media companies. In mid-1996, the transition was complete, and Business Network was made available commercially on the World Wide Web.

Lead Story (Figure 11.11a) is Business Network's first site (http://www. leadstory.com.). It is only the surface layer of the information road map, and its purpose is to keep business professionals abreast of the most important, late-breaking news stories from around the world that have an impact on the business environment. Lead Story delivers the top story of the day, the one story that the editorial staff believes business professionals need to know about. It provides an in-depth analysis using links to many other frequently visited news sites like CNN or The New York Times, and it includes sites like the Jerusalem Press and the Singapore Times.

The staff editors visit a large number of sites and find the ones that they believe are most relevant and most appropriate for a particular story and their business audience and weave them into a coherent, compelling story. Michael Kolowich, explains the process:

> We have a staff of seven people who spend all night essentially studying and reading the Web as it's updated for the next day, and studying it around a particular theme, that is, what everybody's talking about. By noon Eastern time, 9:00 A.M. Pacific time, we have a full package that goes up. It contains the original writing of our staff, but it also provides the most thorough briefing possible on that top story. This, more than any other source, is the deepest briefing anyone could get on a particular subject. One of our philosophies is to float content up into the navigational layers of the Internet so that we're not only giving [readers] a bunch of categories that take them to the next level, but we're also giving them examples of things from deep inside those sites so they can start to see what's new and what information is important in those areas.

Search engines usually index every one to three weeks, says Kolowich, and so nothing in a search engine is current. There is a tremendous amount of news on the Internet, and if you are a businessperson and want to be well informed about what your customers or employees are talking about, or if you want a "little snippet" that might add to a luncheon speech that you're making, search engines aren't going to help you. Lead Story plays off of that fact (Figures 11.11b and c). Kolowich states:

> You can go to individual media sites, but generally you will only get one or two or at most three stories about the subject that you're interested in. And as a number of our colleagues who run news sites will readily tell you, journalists are genetically incapable of pointing to another news organization's work.

Figure 11.11a AT&T's Lead Story is the first site from AT&T Business Network on the Web. It features a different major news story each day, a complete, multiperspective package of information, including news, analysis, background, and opinion from leading sources.

Figure 11.11b The analysis page of a Lead Story featuring the increasing controversy over cigarette manufacturers' practices. Note the "infographic" to the left of the screen that Lead Story editors produce to help users get quick access to information.

Figure 11.11c The news page of a Lead Story topic covering the housing market. Lead Story often examines specific markets that have larger implications and indicators for the overall economy.

*Now along comes AT&T, which has made a commitment not to get into
the content business, per se—we don't have a news-gathering organization,
we don't build content databases, and the like. But we step in and say
we'll organize around the story that everybody's talking about that day; we'll
organize the resources of the Web around that story or that theme, and we'll
do it not just by pointing at the individual sites, like the Charlotte Observer
home page or the Detroit News or CNN, but we'll point at the actual stories
within them, in context.*

Business professionals, in addition to their specific needs for vertical information from industry-specific newsletters, legislative updates, or pricing analyses also need a daily source of general business information and indexes to a
broader set of resources. In the print world there are actually three tiers of information in the business market. There is very vertical, very exclusive high-end
information, generally contained in newsletters, which can cost anywhere from
$295 to $900 and up a year. There are industry trade publications, which are
broader in their category of industry coverage, and are sometimes controlled-
circulation publications that attempt to cover that entire industry. And then
there are general business resources like *The Wall Street Journal* or *Business
Week* that provide a much broader foundation of information that cuts across
industries and across professions.

Business Network occupies the last space, but edges into the industry trade
publications category with the quality of focused information and pointers
leading to specific industries. Kolowich states that it is a good place to start if
you're just getting on the Web and you want to learn what's going on in your
particular industry. From an information provider standpoint, companies that
are providing high-end information—for example a Dun & Bradstreet—are considering ways to open up the next tier of distribution without collapsing their
core price structure. By licensing next-level data sets to AT&T Business Network, this information can be packaged as a more general business resource
that provides very useful information but is down market from the more highly
targeted information.

Business Network provides a combination of free and subscription-based
areas. Lead Story is free, and is advertiser supported. Some of the subscription-
based areas are filled in by the staff, and some are partnerships with individuals or companies in the industry that have an expertise in a particular area. This
eliminates the need for multiple IDs and passwords now needed to access various information sources. It is all together in one place.

The service eventually also plans to offer secure transactions, commercial
services, and Java applets to assist users in getting additional utility from the
site's information and services. AT&T Business Network on the Web is opti-

mized for Netscape's Navigator browser, as well as browsers offered by Microsoft and America Online.

Rather than creating its own content for AT&T Business Network, Lead Story aggregates independent content into one information package. In addition to the business resources of the Web, some of the information providers featured in AT&T Business Network include Dow Jones, Dun & Bradstreet, CNN Interactive, Standard & Poor's, Thomas Register, and TRW Business Information Services. The service provides news, directories, and reference information for most major industries, as well as tools and resources for different professional areas such as sales and marketing, finance, and human resources. A search engine is also featured so that users can go beyond the sites that Business Network editors have selected and recommended as valuable and useful.

AT&T Business Network on the Web offers a mix of ad-supported/free content (such as Lead Story and a basic level of information in each of the major areas of the services), pay-as-you-go content, and monthly or yearly subscription-based information from premier information providers.

AT&T Business Network Marketing and Advertising

Kate Margolese, vice president of AT&T Marketplace Development, explains that she is responsible for creating a "vibrant" electronic marketplace for business information, services, and products for the Business Network. In that role she brings together buyers and sellers and creates the demand for merchants' products on the Web.

Although there are a lot of companies "building" electronic malls and bringing merchants to the Web, there has not been equal emphasis on creating the demand for purchasing online. Margolese feels that demand is growing, but that the barriers to commerce will not come down until people feel comfortable and understand what is available and why it is more efficient and effective to use the online venue for buying and selling. That is a key focus of Business Network. Addressing the specific needs of the business professional, Margolese explains, is the driving impetus for the service, and she will be working not only with the merchants to build that side of the business, but also on the consumer side to stimulate pull-through by creating consumer demand and acceptance.

By making the most current information available to consumers on topics such as electronic commerce, they can gain more knowledge about the nature of secure online transactions, cybercash and what it means to do business on the Web from a buyer's standpoint. For merchants, it's a little more straightforward because they have less at risk. As a result of AT&T's trusted position, they can broker multiple transactions without being tilted toward one particular supplier or one particular buyer. That puts them in a very unique position, states Margolese, in establishing a vibrant electronic marketplace and creating a vibrant community.

Three valuable benefits that AT&T brings to this marketplace, notes Margolese, are the AT&T brand, the bundling possibilities with that brand, and the position of neutral, trusted broker. Once the access providers get business professionals online, Business Network plans to be the home page for those professionals. At that point, Business Network's advertising campaign will make extensive use of interactive media and explore a number of bundling options. One possibility for the future might be bundling the billing of online transactions with long-distance phone bills. Another bundle might be resources for new business with access into a particular mall.

Margolese points out that this is a very compelling value proposition for the business professional, as well as for the advertiser and the merchant. The Business Network can offer a very targeted, very well-qualified business audience to advertisers that can sometimes be difficult to reach, in a targeted manner, through other kinds of media. She highlights the unique nature of AT&T's relationship with its customers:

> We have a strong relationship with our businesses. We write to them every month, and they generally send a check back to us every month, and we know exactly who they are. That is a claim that very few other companies can make. And that market access is an additional benefit that we bring as AT&T in setting up this Business Network. By knowing who those people are, I can then, on the e-commerce side, package them and offer them to advertisers who are looking for different types of individuals, whether it's a particular demographic or a particular type of vertical business that an advertiser might be interested in targeting."

Even though AT&T has very rich customer information, New Media Services must develop its own interpretation of that data, and apply it to the online environment and its own business model. One of the pieces of information not available in the typical physical world database is where a person is spending time online, and that's precisely the kind of information that a merchant and an advertiser want to know. While tracking an individual's journey around the Internet is still a concept, tracking volume of traffic in a particular area is how services decide what to charge for advertising visibility in those areas. Eventually, when an individual can be tracked in detail, it will be possible for advertisers to target their consumer audience even more precisely.

As of May 1996, the advertising product is based on a guaranteed number of impressions in a one-month period. For that, an advertiser is assigned a space in the Business Network, and the ad rotates through the entire service. As noted, the first site is Lead Story, so that is the only place the ad can rotate through until the next site is built. The ads are left on the service until they reach the number of impressions for which they signed up.

Advertisements appear on both horizontal and vertical banners, which run down the right side of the page (Figures 11.12a and b). With browsers, when users leave a page and come back, they come back at the place in the page where they left. So, in the case of a horizontal banner ad at the top of the page, a user may scroll down past it, leave, and return to the place they left off, and not be exposed to anything else commercial. With a vertical banner ad, the commercial opportunity need not be lost, as it provides continuous exposure all the way down the page.

Contracts are sold on a cumulative exposures basis in 200,000, 500,000, 1 million, and 5 million exposures over a particular period of time. As of May 1996, the cost for 200,000 impressions was $7,200, and for 500,000, $17,500. Both the rates and ad packages change continuously as the service expands and new opportunities develop.

Margolese estimates that the rates for other online ad products are generally in the range of $33 per thousand impressions, which is higher than the run-of-the-mill Web site, where the users are a lot less targeted, and lower than a very focused site like a C-Net. Business Network also provides its advertisers with a monthly usage report that shows how many impressions were generated. The sample advertiser report in Table 11.2 illustrates how usage is reported to a Business Network client.

Initially, the ads will rotate through the site, but just as in print, over time, premium positions will no doubt make themselves evident. Advertising works better when it is juxtaposed with relevant content material. If you have a certain columnist or a specific type of information that is particularly suited to the content of the ad, then that location becomes premium positioning for that advertiser.

Margolese states that since they are in the content as opposed to access business, there are three elements Business Network tries to create. "First of all, we want habituation. We want people to keep coming back to our site. Then we want duration. We want people to stay in the site for long periods of time, because that way they will see more ads and they will conduct more commerce and they will be more satisfied with the service. And then we want to be able to escalate them to subscription levels of service, premium levels of service. Time in the service is definitely important to us as a product developer online. If someone's there longer, that person's more valuable to us."

Kolowich explains a concept he developed called the Habituation Ladder, which he is applying to the marketing of New Media Services and Business Network:

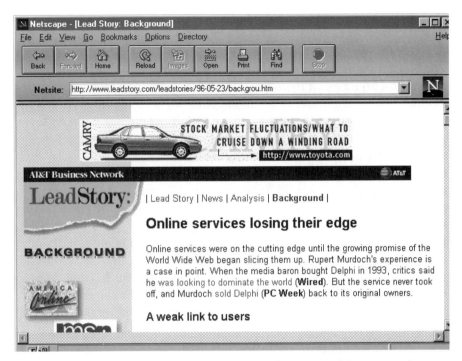

Figure 11.12a   Sample of a Lead Story horizontal banner ad.

Figure 11.12b   Sample of a Lead Story verticle banner ad.

There is accelerating value as you go up: from somebody visiting your site to somebody registering at it to bookmarking it to earning the place of the first bookmark to hooking it up to your home page button to having it open as wallpaper on the screen. A product called PointCast creates a screen saver that pulls information off the Internet that's relevant to the user and throws it up there when the screen has nothing else on it.

But if you believe, for example, as I do, that an average page review is worth something like 2 cents, $20 per thousand, I believe that there is almost an order of magnitude of difference in the value of the customer for every rung up on the habituation ladder. Somebody who visits your site once and doesn't come back is worth 2 cents. Somebody who registers but does not do anything else might be back 10 times on average, and he or she is worth 20 cents. Somebody who bookmarks it might be worth $2.00. Somebody for whom it's a first bookmark, indicating that he or she will be back a lot, might be worth $20. Somebody who hooks up to their home button

TABLE 11.2   Sample AT&T Business Network Advertiser Report (4/1/96)

Impression Package: 300,000
Ad Live Date: 3/19/96
Ad Removal Date: 6/31/96

Advertiser Summary

AD	Impressions	Click-throughs	Click through Yield
Girls	40,000	1,000	2.5%
Commit 2000	35,000	700	2.0%
Total for month ending 3/31/96:	75,000	1,700	2.2%

Month ending			
3/31/96	75,000	1,700	2.2%
4/30/96			
5/31/96			
6/30/96			
Total to date:	75,000	1,700	2.2%

Impressions to deliver: 225,000

Week	Name	Impressions	Click-throughs	Click Yield
3/19–3/26	Girls	30,000	700	2.3%
3/27–3/31	Girls	10,000	300	3.0%
Total for month ending 3/31/96		40,000	1,000	

Week	Name	Impressions	Click-throughs	Click Yield
3/19–3/26	Commit 2000	20,000	400	2.0%
3/27–3/31	Commit 2000	15,000	300	2.0%
Total for month ending 3/31/96		35,000	700	2.0%

might be worth $200 in advertising. And if it's wallpaper, that's a gold-plated customer, worth $2,000.

It's important to know that we will be measuring the company on the distribution of our customers over the business—over this Habituation Ladder. We'll be contacting customers and asking, "Where are you; [is the company] wallpaper yet? Have you got us bookmarked?" That kind of thing. And I think measuring the company by how high we drive our customer base up that ladder is really important.

The stronger the magnet to draw people of like interest together and the stronger the sorting, the higher the value of every page view. Currently, the range is from 1 to 1½ cents per page view or per banner for a completely undifferentiated casual audience to 3-½ cents in serious business markets to 6 to 10 cents in very focused industry-specific markets to people charging as much as $1 dollar or more per page view for highly targeted exposures.

Tracking plays a key role in determining the effectiveness of ads in attracting users. Tracking click-throughs on ads can detect whether a banner or a leader ad is starting to wear out. According to Kolowich, the click-through levels have been much higher than anticipated. They were ranging between 2 percent and 4+ percent, which are higher ratios than the response rates on direct-mail advertising. And the delivery price is much lower. Once there is click-through, it then becomes the advertiser's responsibility to carry through with the cycle and close a sale or achieve the goal of the ad.

Business Network intends to bring the advertiser much closer to closing that sale. The Web opens up the opportunity to go through the full cycle from creating the impression, closing the sale, to delivering and supporting the product, all in one place. Business Network's vision is to be able to match the business customer with the business resource supplier, whether that's an office supply or a package delivery service.

Currently, the focus is at the top layer of that cycle. An ad is primarily designed to create an impression. Where Business Network expects to evolve, and where they believe the entire industry is heading, is further down that spectrum, to the point where it is closing the sale, delivering the product, and supplying the support online.

That has already happened in software. Software is unique in two ways: one, it can be transmitted online; and, two, the people who happen to be developing the product are also the people who are developing the online market industry, so they're already in the forefront.

There are significant advantages to allowing a purchaser to make the customer service link online. Margolese states several of them:

For one, you can do it at your leisure, and you have more information available to you directly. It's not like you're talking to a representative on the phone, although you may need to talk to a person, and at some point we will have voice commonly used on the Internet. It's already there, but it will become more common. And you will be able to look at other styles or other sizes or other colors, which you wouldn't be able to do over the phone. A lot more information is there, and it's a lot more efficient, and it can be more easily delivered online.

Fed Ex and UPS are both leaders in this. Fed Ex already has an incredible site. And it allows you to track your package. You can now request a pickup online.

Even though, currently, most online advertisers are the large conglomerates, telecommunications, entertainment, catalogue, and car companies, Business Network will be providing advertising products for a broad spectrum of businesses. As more people develop personal Web sites for their office supply or computer furniture store, Business Network plans to offer affordable and effective products to them. The small- and home-office market is an excellent opportunity for Internet commerce, because most of those businesses are already on the Internet, or are close to making the move, and they can more easily grasp the possibilities for online marketing and advertising.

What business professionals really need, in order to conduct business online, says Margolese, are services like MasterCard, because that's how they conduct business with their consumers. They also use package delivery services, software, and office supplies. So those are the primary advertiser targets Business Network is pursuing. They also add value to the service Margolese says. "FIND/SVP, a research company, did a survey showing that the majority of Internet users actually appreciate advertising on the Net when it adds value to what they're looking for."

According to Margolese, Business Network intends to branch out to a broad spectrum of business needs and create compelling services that deliver timely information. It plans to build the Business Network by adding multiple sites, similar to Lead Story, and provide a spectrum of solutions to the business professional.

[Users] come to the AT&T Business Network as a home page, and they can learn about how to buy and use the latest technology, build their own Web site, and find new customers or learn how to find them, and then market to those customers. We'll help them do that. We want to be the place on the Web where business professionals go to conduct business, and that I think is our short-term vision; beyond that, we keep expanding

because the technology will continue to allow us to do more with the Web as a tool."

AT&T Business Network has contracted with SoftBank Interactive Marketing to function as its advertising rep firm, and bring on advertisers for the service. The company was launched as Network 1.0 just months before it merged with SoftBank and two other major sales organizations. As a single sales organization, SoftBank Interactive Marketing now represents the largest group of sites and advertising inventory on the Internet. It is discussed more fully later in this chapter.

AT&T Personal Online Services

The mission of this division of AT&T is to bring personalized content to individuals and families through the Internet. Caroline Vanderlip is the president of Personal Online Services. She states:

> *AT&T believes customer expectations for online services have moved far beyond the need for the basics, and meeting those expectations is key to growing this industry to 50 million Net users by the year 2000. It would be naive, even self-destructive, to sit back and profess otherwise. . . . The structure of the industry has shifted from companies providing access, browsers, and content to a model adopted by AT&T that endorses these areas as distinct, but allows them to be combined as the market demands. AT&T believes this new, open model will be the template from which successful online services will be molded by the year 2000.*
>
> *By making our businesses customer-focused and letting users drive content, we'll find the missing pieces to the puzzle of how to increase usage, retain customers, and build viable business models. If we deliver customized content, organized in a way that makes it easy to find, anticipates users' needs, and makes getting help easier than ever, we'll give users what they say they want—value-added services that enrich their lives.*

Dan Hesse, senior vice president and general manager of the Online Services Group, explains that on the consumer side, AT&T is creating a portfolio of consumer-oriented, highly targeted, and segmented online services. It is similar to AOL in that it is like a magazine, but it is much more targeted and focused, and very deep in content within that focus. It will feel, according to

Hesse, even more like a contained and complete environment than AOL. The content will be a combination of purchased material, some of it exclusive, with links to carefully selected, high-quality Web locations.

Personal Online Services

Personal Online Services is devoted to lifestyle and life stage content for families and the individual. It launched the AT&T Health Beta testsite, a focused, content-rich site in mid-1996. The subjects include dieting, nutrition, workouts, yoga, first aid, mental health, and the origins, effects, and treatment of medical conditions. Also available are the names of local, regional, and national specialists, support groups, spas, health clubs, pharmacies, and other resources. Figures 11.13 and 11.14 show pages from the site.

IVI Publishing, Inc., based in Minneapolis, Minnesota, was the service's first content provider. IVI is the digital publisher of the Mayo Clinic Family Health Book CD-ROM and HEALTHNEWS, the sister publication to *The New England Journal of Medicine.* It is valued as a highly credible source in the medical field.

The next content provider to come on board was Rodale Press, publisher of *Prevention,* the largest health magazine in the country focusing on health and lifestyle issues for consumers. With a monthly readership approaching 12 million, it has been first over all other consumer magazines nationwide for growth in newsstand sales for the last 10 years, according to Vanderlip. Rodale intends to develop exclusive interactive applications for AT&T's online health and fitness service based on information from its premier line of health publications, which, in addition to *Prevention,* includes *Men's Health* and *Heart & Soul.* Figures 11.15 through 11.19 show sample pages from the site. The service will also draw from Rodale's broad-based series of books, including the popular *Doctor's Book of Home Remedies* and *The Women's Encyclopedia of Health and Emotional Healing.* Vanderlip reports "*Men's Health,* launched with a circulation of 250,000, has grown to 1.3 million in only 10 years, with bonus circulation topping 5.5 million. *Heart & Soul,* one of the newest members of Rodale's family, has a total readership of 1.5 million, and increased its circulation 60 percent in just one year."

Vanderlip believes that the combination of IVI and Rodale will create a perfect balance of rich resources on the service. Even though both are print publishing companies, they do not simply move printed material directly into the online environment. Original interactive applications will be designed so that the information is presented in a very user-friendly and efficient interface design. Vanderlip explains that the content of the magazines will be only a jumping-off point for developing online media. She adds:

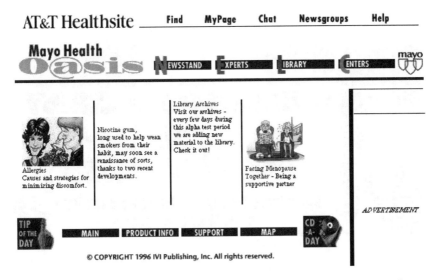

Figure 11.13 AT&T Healthsite Mayo Health sample page showing the location for a verticle ad banner.

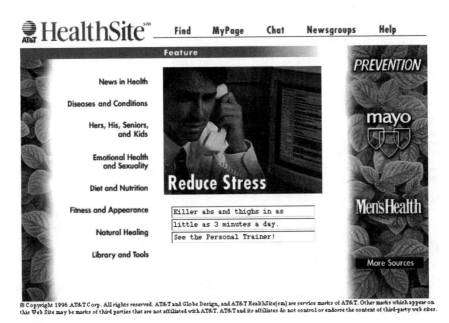

Figure 11.14 AT&T Healthsite feature page.

Figure 11.15   AT&T Healthsite, Men's Health page.

It will be new, interactive content, designed to be user-specific. If you need a personal trainer, personal dietitian, personal sports consultant, or whatever your specific health or fitness need, you'll be able to get it online. . . . Irrespective of the models we use—and I do believe we will see every business offer a variety of pricing models—there is a single truth: If we are to make online services part of the consumer's everyday activities, we must deliver value-added content and not just a repackaging of what exists in other media.

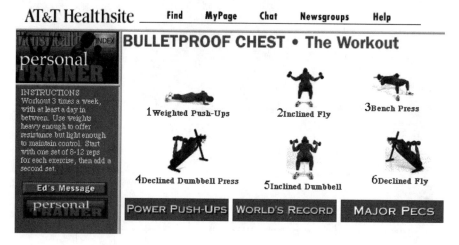

Figure 11.16   AT&T Healthsite Personal Trainer: The Workout page.

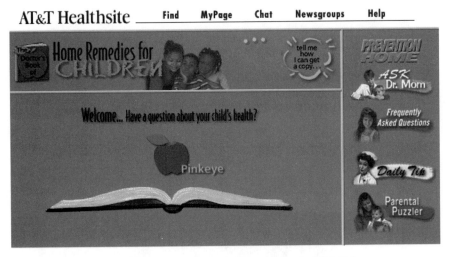

Figure 11.17   Healthsite's Home Remedies for Children page.

The trend toward finer targeting of niche interests, exemplified in print media by the hundreds of new vertical interest magazines published each year, is a valuable lesson to apply to the online environment. It is on that premise that Personal Online Services is developing its products. It is apparent that consumers want vertical channels of information and entertainment, says Vanderlip, to supplement the more generalized overload they must sort through daily.

Figure 11.18   AT&T Healthsite Prevention page.

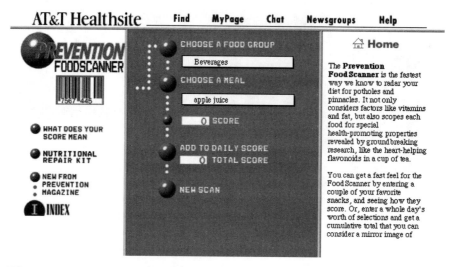

Figure 11.19   AT&T Healthsite Prevention Foodscanner.

Localizing that content is the next level of targeting niche interests, and it is a challenge that Personal Online Services intends to meet.

Vanderlip gives an example of the value of localized content on local resources: "In the online world, if you're looking for a nursing home for an elderly parent, you probably don't want lists of those several states away. You'd find value in a shorter list with names of nearby homes so you could visit often, just as you'd find value in knowing about local organizations who could help with other aspects of elder care. All of the AT&T online products completely integrate national, generic information with local products that deliver relevancy, immediacy, and, ultimately, value."

According to Vanderlip, the service also provides space for chat services, bulletin boards, and open forums for both general and local communities of interest. The goal of Personal Online Services is "... to aggregate content to give consumers the most complete, up-to-date, brand-name information they can use, rather than pages of data that hold no value for them. We recognize all this may sound good, but if it means being tied to a PC to get the information you need, the service won't really meet your needs anytime, anywhere. So, AT&T's Personal Online Services will give users multiple delivery options—cellular, voice mail, fax, CD-ROM, and, of course, online."

The answer to being profitable, says Vanderlip, is through an open business model, with multiple streams of revenue offered to the content providers, such as shared subscription fees, advertising, and income from transactions. On the content side, AT&T is exploring a number of options such as pay-per-view and subscriptions. She believes that consumers will be just as willing to buy an online package as they are a magazine or cable subscription.

Vanderlip concludes, "Beyond information, content is a magnet attracting customers with similar interests, which answers a basic human need to belong. Sociologists talk about the 'retribalization of America' as they see more people joining groups around shared interests. In the past, people congregated in the town square. In the present-future, they do it on the Net. The Internet is changing the definition of America's retribalization from geographic to electronic—a shift that holds the promise of changing the very fabric of our society, if we act wisely."

AT&T Update: Nets Inc. Buys AT&T's New Business Services

AT&T is a minority partner in Nets Inc.; it holds a seat on the board, and has licensed the use of the AT&T brand to Nets Inc. for the AT&T Business Network service. The AT&T Business Network (www.bnet.att.com) and Industry.Net (www.industry.net) services will remain separate but will link to each other, and the new company will develop vertical market electronic commerce services. Industry.Net brings together more than 200,000 buyers and 4,500 sellers of industrial products in an electronic market.

AT&T Swaps Healthsite for HomeTown Network

In August, AT&T discontinued the beta test of AT&T HealthSite in order to focus on content services that are more closely aligned with its core business. One such service is AT&T HomeTown Network, a communications-rich service that aggregates content in the local community. AT&T is currently providing links to the sites by the former AT&T HealthSite content providers, IVI Publishing, Rodale Press, and MediLife Inc.

The HomeTown beta test was launched in Sacramento, CA, and will focus on local content providers such as KOVR-TV, a CBS affiliate, *Sacramento* magazine, Sacramento News & Review, Sacramento Public Library, and the Sacramento Chamber of Commerce. AT&T is evaluating different business models such as subscriptions, transactions, and advertising.

Mergers and innovative enterprises alter the face of the electronic marketplace daily, and present creative challenges to marketers and entrepreneurs trying to keep pace with the changes and new opportunities they provide.

Network 1.0/SoftBank Interactive Marketing

Network 1.0 was formed in the beginning of 1996 to provide marketing services and sales representation to Internet sites seeking interactive advertisers. They were set up to focus on accounts or sites that have a business-to-business commercial and technology orientation. Network 1.0 assembled a group of sites to represent that reflect that focus. These sites, or companies, include AT&T Business Network; IDG's Netscape World, which is a Web zine, or Web magazine; Who Where?; and Netscape itself. The Netscape representation is shared with another firm in the industry so that Network 1.0 was given responsibility for about 50 percent of the advertising market.

Network 1.0 provided consulting services to help develop the advertising product and then represent that product to clients and agencies across the country. Their mission is to provide the market leadership and essential services to help both clients, or Web sites, and accounts, or advertisers, realize the full potential of interactive marketing. Market leadership means establishing standards and a professional standard of doing business in this new media system. Essential services includes writing rate cards, trafficking ad programs and providing customer service. The focus is on providing those two things to both clients and advertisers to help them fulfill the potential of interactive marketing.

In the second quarter of 1996, Network 1.0 merged its sales operations and site management relationships with SoftBank Interactive Marketing. SoftBank Interactive Marketing will incorporate or combine the selling activities and the site management responsibilities of Network 1.0, Ziff Interactive, which represents the ZD-Net Technology Group of sites, and a company called Interactive Marketing based in Los Angeles, which represents Yahoo, the NFL, NBC Intelecast, Playboy, and some other sites. Together the three sales organizations will be integrated to a single sales organization and represent the largest group of sites and advertising inventory on the Internet.

Just months after launching Network 1.0, the company was catapulted into a leading position in the industry. SoftBank Interactive Marketing will represent over 1 billion advertising impressions on the Internet a month, according to Ted West, former president and CEO of Network 1.0, and now the president and COO of SoftBank Interactive. "We'll be fielding the largest combined interactive media sales organization in the industry, and as we add a few more carefully selected sites to the portfolio, we expect to be in a position to lead the development of the interactive media business."

SoftBank Interactive will do premarket, market, and postmarket work for sites. Premarket work refers to the consulting and professional service provided in developing and marketing advertising products on the Internet. A product must be clearly defined. The rate card, marketing, and collateral materials need to be designed along with traffic building and promotional programs to support the development of the site.

The second set of services SoftBank Interactive provides is sales representation in taking the site to market and to the appropriate or targeted potential advertising accounts and their ad agencies. For some clients, the company also provides custom design services for promotional programs. As of May 1996, its small staff of just over 30 was projected to grow considerably, as a significant part of the service will be to call on accounts and handle leads and inquiries regarding the site. The sales representatives will need to develop recommendations and programs, present proposals to those accounts, sell, close, and process the orders.

The third set of services that SoftBank Interactive offers is fulfilling what they have sold, and providing back-end customer service. This service ranges from handling complaints and queries to providing research information and backing, to support the returns and the results that are generated by the advertising programs.

According to West, SoftBank Interactive Marketing has developed a couple of business relationships as an initiative to integrate with the software companies that provide database management and add program management services to the sites. West feels that it is an important dimension to include in providing a more effective advertising program and more efficient management of both the sites and the inventory on the sites.

Currently, the company is primarily recommending that its site clients contract directly with the software companies that provide the services. However, SoftBank Interactive anticipates developing a much closer relationship with those software companies, which may include a licensing arrangement, a joint marketing arrangement, or possibly an acquisition of the appropriate software tools to incorporate into a full service turnkey or full-service model. At present however, SoftBank Interactive's business is to define placement programs with the sites it represents. It plans to be working closely with the ad agencies that are representing individual clients, matching the objectives of those clients to the traffic characteristics of the advertising placement options.

With respect to the economics of advertising on the Internet and the pricing models that exist there, most of the business to date has been modeled around cost-per-thousand, borrowing liberally from traditional media. West explains that within the CPM model, the pricing has settled into the range of $15 on the low end up to $80 per thousand for advertising that reaches a highly targeted market segment. Now some advertisers are buying on a cost-per-click-through or conversion, basically paying the equivalent from the print media world of a per-inquiry program. Some have actually taken the next step and have programs priced out on a cost-per-transaction or cost-per-sale basis.

There are a wide range of objectives being carried out on the Internet. Some are advertisers who find the brand impression is sufficient and the cost-per-thousand valuation is a decent methodology for pricing. Others use a merchandising model and measure success by percent of sales or by the conversion rate of visitors to their catalogue or shopping site. It really depends on the marketing objectives that the client is holding for the Internet.

The typical sales process involves first understanding what the client is trying to accomplish and then matching that objective to the characteristics of the sites SoftBank represents. Some sites are better suited to some advertisers than others, and it is the firm's job to sort through that and make recommendations. Its objective is to sell the right sites to the right clients.

When SoftBank Interactive Marketing develops a program, it combines a number of sites that together accomplish much of what the advertiser or the agency is looking for. SoftBank works to combine a number of different sites that are complementary and constitute what the company calls a "foundation buy" on the Internet. West explains:

> The foundation buy is a concept that helps to get clients focused on how the group of sites that we represent can meet a large portion of their objectives on the Internet. But we end up tailoring those programs pretty substantially, once we understand their objectives and understand their budget limitations.
>
> For example, we worked with a company in the plug-in software business, looking for a technical audience, an audience of Web developers and other Web technicians. It was looking for a cost-effective reach to that audience of users, but not necessarily all users on the Internet. And so we put together a program that included placement on the Netscape site, placement on the Netscape World site, and a couple of other sites we recommended, which in the end were not included because of some budget limitations, but we took the approach of identifying those portions of the Netscape, the Netscape World, sites where the audience that the client was looking for could best be reached.
>
> [The client] had a product and was looking for three-month coverage. Through those two sites we put a proposal together that totaled about $80,000 gross, for a three-month period. We ended up selling it at that level, the $80,000. Netscape offers a couple of discounts, so with those discounts the program actually came in at about $68,000 for the client. The program purchased on Netscape ran through the same part of that site throughout the three-month period. The program on Netscape World involved placement in different parts of the site during that period.
>
> If [the client] had chosen to buy the whole original package, it would have cost in the vicinity of $125,000 for three months. By going for a less expensive buy, some new coverage was lost but mostly repeat coverage. In other words, the notion in the foundation buy is to provide multiple impressions in the normal course of trafficking through a variety of sites, and what our client lost in backing down to a couple of sites was the opportunity to achieve repeat impressions for a number of users.

The interactive media business today has been characterized by inbound inquiries, people calling sites wondering how they can advertise on those sites, and the majority of those inquiries that actually end up in business being written are from companies that are looking to experiment on the Internet. These companies will typically end up buying programs in the vicinity of $10,000, $20,000, and sometimes $30,000.

West describes these last as "one-off" programs, experiments just to see how they work. Yahoo and Netscape generate 50 to 100 inquiries a day from people expressing interest in their advertising programs. Not all of them buy, but that kind of inquiry stream currently exists.

More frequently, as interactive media budgets are being developed, they are typically managed by agencies, not the clients directly. Those budgets can exceed $1 million, although according to West, there are a couple of budgets out there over $2 million, and those are just placement dollars, exclusive of creation. He states, however, that he will write as much business at the $20–$30,000 level as at the $200,000 level.

Softbank Interactive Marketing has international ambitions as well because of the global reach of the Net. Many of the sites that the company represents, such as Netscape, are establishing international language editions, including Japanese, German, and French. There are also potential relationships through the parent company in Japan, and West expects to begin to leverage some of the advertising sales and agency relationships there. He also plans to open up a sales presence in Europe in the near future. West anticipates that three key factors will influence the growth of this market over the next 12 to 18 months. "If we see a good development of understanding of what interactive media is and does, that's the education piece. If we see the sites doing a better job of defining and tracking and providing the research to support what's going on in their sites—which really gives us, the sellers, a better product to sell—that's the second piece. And third, [we need to see] developing techniques for advertisers to better target their audiences on those sites. If we make good progress in those three areas, I think we'll see great impact on the market's growth in the next year or so."

Womanhood, Inc: The Solutions Network for Business Women on the Web

The questions uppermost in the minds of women beginning to use the Internet are, "Why should I go online? What's in it for me?" With good reason. Until recently very little on the Internet was personalized and/or tailored to help women in their daily lives.

The founder of Womanhood, Inc., Natalie L. Wood, wanted to create a value-added resource that would be helpful to herself as well as to other women. Wood had a successful sales career before she started her own multi-media production company six years ago. Her experience as a successful executive producer led her to understand the importance of managing time efficiently and getting value from the extensive professional networking required in her business.

In December 1994, Wood decided to develop The Solutions Network for Business Women Web Site. Her goal was to provide herself and other women with an easier, more efficient way to make contacts, research information, and build a knowledge base. Her vision for the site is to make a material difference in women's personal and professional lives.

Just Ask Amelia!

"There are two themes I hear over and over again from women who are starting to use the Internet." says Wood. "First, they say they want quality information served in a way that is easy to digest so that they can make good decisions in their personal and professional lives. Second, these women tell me they want someone they can turn to who will help them find the information they require. In other words, they want a 'personal assistant.'

"So, when [a visitor] first enters the Womanhood site, they are greeted by Amelia, [the namesake] of a special feature we call Ask Amelia! (in honor of the fearless aviator). Amelia provides a wide variety of personal assistance services. Registered site visitors can ask Amelia for assistance anywhere on the site. Amelia even conducts customized search and retrieval services. Amelia gives our site that kind of personal service and amiability that we believe makes it a welcoming place to visit."

This web site specializes in providing time-saving access to information that helps visitors take care of business quickly and easily. In fact, that is the key purpose for the site. Wood knows that any Web-savvy woman can go to AltaVista, (an Internet search directory), and seek out subjects that interest her. But that doesn't mean she has the time and energy to sift through the 3,000 possible responses to find the specific information she may want on a vital topic like, parental leave policies. Visitors (both male and female) want to get right to the meat of the matter, and Wood created this network of solutions to address that need.

The site provides two different types of information resources. The first is a series of solution-oriented resource databases that contain stores of information useful to professional and business women. These databases are quick and easy to use, and they give visitors the information they need, when they need it—without having to pay a research firm. For example, they offer women:

- consultants to fit their specific business needs
- pertinent financial planning strategies
- salary ranges by career
- tax information and tips based on salary range
- the highest-rated careers for women
- women role models and heroines, by profession
- pension and retirement plan information
- books and resources on all of these topics, and more

Solutions Network

The site is made up of a network of top business and professional women. These professionals provide information and services for women who want credible and reliable sources. This network offers information and advice from seasoned professionals on such topics as:

- parental leave policies
- the most effective ways to approach your boss for a raise
- hiring and firing techniques
- making successful presentations
- organizing trade shows
- the latest management techniques
- sales tips and strategies
- selling overseas

The site has many opportunities for personal and professional networking, brainstorming, and learning from the experience of other women who have similar decisions to make. Wood states, "We know that women also like to 'take a reading' of other women's experiences and concerns when they are making decisions of importance in their lives and careers. We also offer our visitors incentives to give us their feedback. This way we are able to keep track of new areas that need to be added and new services that might benefit our visitors."

On Tour with Linda

Wood conducts the following tour through the site to give the reader a better idea of how it works:

Let's follow Linda on her first visit to The Solutions Network for Business Women. Linda is in her mid-30s and works in sales for a small telecommunications company. One of her responsibilities is to plan a mini-trade show overseas. She works one day a week from her home. Linda heard about the Web site from a friend, and has also seen banners advertising the site on Yahoo!

When Linda first logs on, she is personally greeted by Amelia, who introduces her to the site. As a result, Linda chooses to register as a new member. When Linda indicates she works in sales for a telecommunications company, Amelia suggests she visit the Business and Career Section to find information specific to her career.

Linda goes into the Business and Career section. She wants valuable information to help her get ahead in her career, but she doesn't have a lot of time to waste searching on the Net. Since she works from home one day a week, she clicks into the Working from Home section. She is given several reading options: original articles on setting up an ergonomic home workstation, what tax issues to be aware of when working from home, and a humorous piece on avoiding distraction in the home office. Linda marks a couple of these articles that she wishes to have sent to her via e-mail so she can read them at a later date.

Linda is also eager to find a consultant to help her organize her overseas trade show. So she asks Amelia for a list of consultants who specialize in trade shows. She immediately gets back a list and prints it out. She then posts a notice to the Consultants Network detailing her needs. (Within days, her request is answered, and she receives an additional list of names of consultants in her city that can be of assistance.)

Linda clicks into the The Solutions Network Calendar section to see if there are any events, conferences, speakers, or trade shows taking place in her city relevant to her interests and needs. She then marks that she would like to be notified of any updates to the site on the following topics: telecommunications, public speaking, working from home, and financial planning.

Linda decides to fill out a feedback form detailing her impressions of the site. This automatically enters her in a raffle for a vacation. She wants (and needs) to win a trip to Hawaii.

She logs off after 15 minutes. Miraculously, she wins the raffle!

"Linda and our other visitors come to us from a number of different places, says Wood. "We have attracted them through strong branding and market awareness campaigns conducted both online and with traditional media. Ask Amelia! plays a large role in our branding efforts. She represents the fearless aviator who will do what needs to be done to solve problems and accomplish her goals."

According to Wood, on the site, "We have taken particular care to make the environment easy to use and understand, while at the same time making it visually appealing and comfortable. We want our visitors to feel that this is a place dedicated to helping them take care of business and getting something done! We use Internet technology to make their lives easier, not to confront them with the latest "gizmos" that are essentially "cool" but take up a lot of time and energy. Amelia helps us to personalize each visitor's experience."

Womanhood offers an additional convenient feature. After a visitor's initial visit, she doesn't need to come to the site to get new information on topics that interest her. She can request what she wants and have it e-mailed to her. This works to mutual advantage. Visitors get the information they want, and are constantly reminded that the site is available for their benefit. In e-mails, that must be requested by the visitor, updates about new features and services are provided. The recipient is thereby encouraged to return to the site and check out what's new.

A Virtual Community

According to Wood, a recent survey of women online found that they want their own virtual communities. The Solutions Network site *is* a virtual community that provides opportunities for personal and professional networking, sounding out of ideas, and learning from the valuable experiences of other women. "One of our main goals," states Wood, "is to provide a homebase for women so that we can help them help themselves and support each other! These community-building activities create visitor loyalty." Wood elaborates:

Since women constitute 73 percent of primary shoppers across all product categories, we are particularly aware of offering our visitors only products and services that women are known to need and want. Our advertisers are clearly very important to us. We give them the ability to customize their ads to women's wants and needs, since we do not expect that level of customization on their standard Web pages. They can also sponsor surveys on the site to learn more about their customer's specific needs and interests.

Our vitality depends on our ability to listen, respond personally, and follow up with requested site features and offerings. This is also of extreme importance, because, over time, more women will be coming online. These new visitors will have new sets of interests that will be crucial for us to integrate into our site.

Our mission is to be the preeminent site for women on the Web by providing the finest value-added network of personalized resources, contacts, and opportunities for women online.

InfoStreet: Paving the Web

InfoStreet defines itself as an electronic publishing and Internet marketing business. The company is committed to "harnessing the Internet as a dynamic tool" for its clients. It was founded in October 1994 by Siamak Farah. Farah spent a number of years working for Next, Steve Job's company in Redwood City, California, and combines his understanding of Unix technology with a sales and marketing background to work with clients to design, maintain, and host Web sites.

InfoStreet is purposefully small, asserts Farah, "We have a saying that only 10 percent of our employees are human, 90 percent is technology. We employ technology to deliver quickly at a reduced cost and with highest possible quality."

The following project briefs illustrate several InfoStreet approaches to Web site design and functionality:

Information Access Company

Client   One of InfoStreet's bigger clients is Information Access Company (IAC), an aggregator of information from approximately 7,000 magazines and newspapers (Figure 11.20). IAC creates searchable databases of abstracts and full-text of articles from these publications and then resells them to the major research houses like Dialog or Lexus Nexus as well as public, academic, and corporate libraries. These organizations in turn resell or provide that information in the form of reports or database access to end users. InfoStreet was hired to create a Web site for IAC that provides background information on the company and lists files and databases that it sells. IAC is using the Internet to provide additional information directly to the end users. It is this kind of direct access that is reshaping the publishing and distribution channels in many industries.

URL   http://www.iacnet.com (hosted at IAC)

Goals   The IAC Web site was designed to:
- Promote IAC product and services.
- Provide information about IAC and each of its divisions.
- Assist existing customers (tips, journals list, etc.).

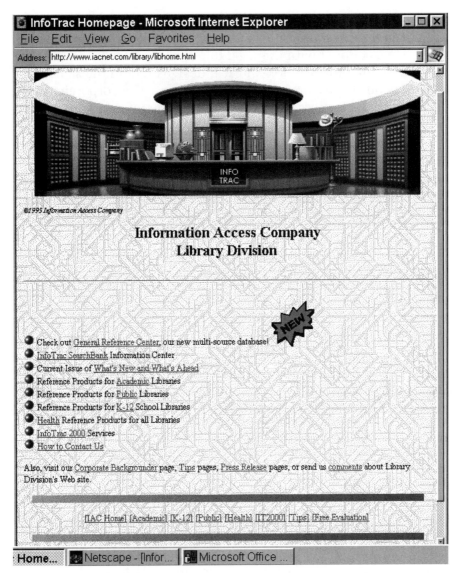

Figure 11.20   Information Access Company main menu screen.

Interface Design   IAC has multiple divisions catering to various demographic groups, ranging from librarians and corporate clients to the at-home consumer. This, coupled with the need to reflect the corporation's brand identity, resulted in multiple look-and-feel designs within the same site. The three divisions target three different audiences. The corporate division describes products geared toward the corporate information user, and is presented in a more reserved and straightforward style; the library division is targeted at the librarian market, and uses brighter colors and is organized in a style that will feel familiar to librarians; the third division is geared to the home market, and is designed in a casual, playful style that incorporates a number of on-screen visual help features.

Length of Time to Build Site   The initial site was designed over a three-month period using five people to develop the corporate and library divisions. Exact data for the development of the At Home division is not available, but it is a successful site, and maintained with daily updates, ensuring that visitors return.

Biggest Challenge   By any Internet standard, this site is very large. The sheer volume of pages and the variety of look-and-feel requirements made it a challenge to organize so that it remained informative, aesthetically pleasing, quick and easy to use. The interface had to consider preferences for accessing information. People search for information in different ways, and it was a real challenge to accommodate those variations.

Outcome   This site is very successful. IAC has received substantially more Product Evaluation Requests than it originally anticipated.

Lessons Learned   InfoStreet learned the importance of educating the client as to the necessity for constant updating and maintenance of a site after it is created. Sites go stale rapidly and must be updated frequently in order to encourage return visitors. Backing up a site with adequate human resources to keep a site fresh is vital. The lessons IAC learned in this regard are common to all early adopters on the Net.

The Idea Cafe

Client   By far the most successful site that InfoStreet has helped design and maintain is the Idea Cafe (Figure 11.21). The Idea Cafe is the brainchild of Rhonda Abrams and Francie Ward. Abrams is America's leading business planning expert and the author of the best-selling business plan

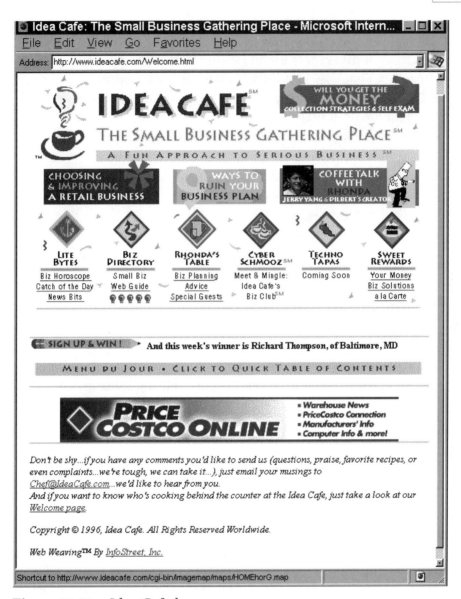

Figure 11.21 Idea Cafe home page.

book *The Successful Business Plan: Secrets and Strategies.* There are lots of "dishes" on the Cafe menu—everything from vital business info and advice to light diversions for an Online Coffee Break. Among many other features, the Idea Cafe regularly updates these features:

- Business Directory: If you're looking for business info on the net, come here first.
- Techno Gossip: Who's doing what to whom in interactive media.
- Self-Exams: To discover your business abilities.
- Dr.Matt's Business Horoscope: The first horoscope created especially for business.
- CyberSchmooz: Meet and mingle with other biz folks.
- Rhonda's Roundtable: the central area for business planning and advice.

URL http://www.ideacafe.com (Hosted at InfoStreet)

Goals The Idea Cafe Web site was designed to:

- Be the entry point to the Web for the small business community.
- Be a place where entrepreneurs can find the information, resources, and advice they need.
- Enable small businesses to make contacts with others in similar situations.
- Encourage small businesses in their efforts to take control of their own business destiny.
- Have some fun.

Interface Design The concept and the graphic design for the fun atmosphere was created by Francie Ward and Connie Nygard, and the site development was developed by InfoStreet. Many of Idea Cafe's clients access the Internet via modems as opposed to high-speed direct lines that are common to large corporations and universities. As a result, download time was a major consideration. This was successfully addressed by breaking up large images into smaller portions that are repeated throughout the site. This ensures that visitors download the images once, and from then on use the cached version from their local disk. The overall result is a very fast-loading and easy-to-explore site.

Length of Time to Build Site The initial site was developed in two months utilizing four people. Two-plus people are dedicated to maintaining the

site on an ongoing basis. The site also has a number of automated programs that constantly add freshness.

Biggest Challenge   From a Web design point of view, the challenge was to
present a fun and colorful site within the limits of modem download times.
Another major challenge was to keep the content constantly fresh, which is
costly and extremely time-consuming. That challenge has been partially
addressed through the development of a number of automated processes.

Outcome   This site is extremely successful, exceeding every expectation. The
site's traffic has sustained a healthy volume since its launch a year ago.

Lessons Learned   Lesson 1: Try to automate through programming those
areas that you are going to update frequently.
Lesson 2: It's harder than it looks!

Fabrik Communications, Inc.

Client   InfoStreet specializes in developing marketing-oriented sites. A good
example is Fabrik's Web site (Figure 11.22). Fabrik Communications, Inc.
is a value-added Internet e-mail service provider for business-to-business
communications. The Fabrik service enables users of Lotus cc:Mail,
Lotus Notes, Microsoft Mail, and other LAN-based e-mail systems, to
connect existing LAN mail clients to the Internet, X.400, and commercial
online services such as AOL and CompuServe. The Fabrik Service currently hosts over 150,000 registered users.

URL   http://www.fabrik.com (Hosted at InfoStreet)

Goals   The Fabrik Web site was designed as:
- an information source for customers, press, and partners
- a support medium for existing customers
- a demand-generation tool
- a distribution mechanism where prospective customers can
  actually download software files that allow them to "test drive"
  the Fabrik service

Interface Design   Fabrik's entire product and corporate philosophy is based
on ease of use. Its product provides a quick, reliable Internet connection
with no effort. InfoStreet wanted its site to reflect the same no-hassle environment. As a result, a very friendly site has been designed, equipped

Figure 11.22   Fabrik Communications, Inc. home page.

with quick jumps to points of focus within pages. Site Search is also provided so visitors can jump to specific points with two mouse clicks.

Length of Time to Build Site   The initial site was developed over a one-month period, utilizing 2.5 people. One person keeps the site updated with press releases, information on products, the industry, and job opportunities.

Biggest Challenge   In order to convey Fabrik's corporate motif, which is very chic, state of the art, and elegant, great care had to be taken to represent the brand identity with a look of quality and sophistication that was not compromised by the limitations of the technology. It was crucial to the success of the project to work with one key decision maker in the company who could provide decisive guidance and resolution during the design phase.

Outcome   The Fabrik site has been very successful, exceeding all expectations. In its debut week, 10 percent of the people who asked for a "test drive" became clients.

Lessons Learned   The Web is an excellent vehicle for sensing the pulse of the market. Fabrik visitors must fill out a small registration form prior to downloading the test-drive software. This form asks some very simple survey questions, such as "Which LAN do you have?" or "Where did you hear about this site?" The results of those questions have proven invaluable.

Trans-Act

Client   Trans-Act is an international organization specializing in leadership and team-building programs. Recognizing the need in today's competitive environment for leaders and teams to consistently perform at the highest level, Trans-Act offers a unique learning experience to develop world-class leaders and performing teams.

URL   http://www.trans-act.com (Hosted at InfoStreet)

Goals   The Trans-Act site was developed to:
- Generate leads.
- Be informative.
- Allow teams and leaders to evaluate their performance.

Interface Design   InfoStreet modeled the Trans-Act site after the company's training seminars (Figure 11.23). A lot of white space was used, to convey openness. Teal, purple, and blue colors were used to create a soft, comfortable, and relaxing atmosphere. The amount of text per page was kept to a minimum so that the user is not inundated or overwhelmed with information.

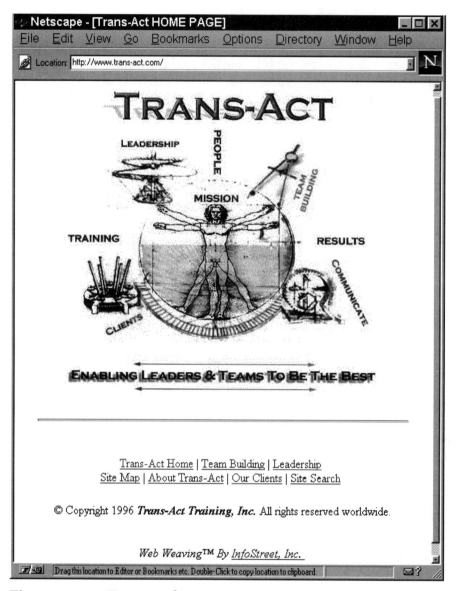

Figure 11.23   Trans-Act home page.

Length of Time to Build Site   This site was developed in two weeks utilizing 1.5 people.

Biggest Challenge   Getting the word out about this site. InfoStreet used special HTML tags (keywords that search engines recognize) to increase

Trans-Act's hit rate. InfoStreet also registered Trans-Act on over 200 search engines, and has encouraged the company to add the Web site address to all print and other promotional materials.

Outcome   The site was launched May 15, 1996, and is enjoying steady traffic to date.

Farah explains InfoStreet's approach to determining the time it will take to design a particular Web site, and, thereafter, the cost. "InfoStreet has developed a tool called the WebWeaving Time Estimate Sheet (Figure 11.24). For instance, we say that every site has four hours of plain design, one hour of presenting that to the customer, and two hours of touchup for all customer comments. So even if [customers] want to do a three-page site, we take seven hours right off the bat and make sure we understand what they want to present, because this is their brand identity on the Net. This has to convey their company's mission. At InfoStreet, we treat every Web site as a business. It has to have a valid business model, not limited to but including, the project scope, its budget, and the corporate commitment. The WebWeaving Time Estimate Sheet is an excellent tool for gauging the commitment and resources required."

On this sheet, InfoStreet has listed the approximate times (in hours) for each task. This amount is then multiplied by quantity to achieve the total time for each category of tasks. For instance, if three forms need to be created, and each fully tested form takes 4.5 hours, the total time spent on forms is 13.5 hours.

For companies or individuals with neither the time nor the dollars, Info-Street provides a way to create a Web site instantly. InfoStreet has taken its experience in creating, serving, and maintaining numerous client Web sites, streamlined it, and packaged it for ease of use (Figure 11.25). This service is called Instant Web (http://www.InstantWeb.com). "We automated every step necessary for having a successful Web site," Farah asserts, "and all this automation is at the user's disposal in less than a minute. Visitors just fill out a form, and, within seconds, they have their own Web presence. It is literally that easy." Here's the process:

1. Visitors fill out a sign-up form, with their name, address, and chosen Web site name. Seconds later, they have their very own Web site and address.
2. Visitors use a form to create their first Web page online.
3. Using the login name and password they chose, visitors can upload/download images and files. They can tap into a vast library of help files to grow their site. In addition, a customized help file is created automatically to assist those who visit the site.

			Hours				
Item	**Qty**	**Description**	**Setup**	**Test**	**Touchup**	**Total**	**Estimated Hours**
1		Initial site design consultation	2.0				
2		General site design	4.0	1.0	2.0	7.0	
3		Basic text to HTML conversion (per 8.5″ × 11″ page)	0.5	0.25	0.25	1.0	
4		Forms/back-end scripts (per 8.5″ × 11″ page)	3.0	0.75	0.75	4.5	
5		Scanning and treatment of existing graphics	0.5	0.25	0.25	1.0	
6		Graphics creations	3.0		1.0	4.0	
7		Final test and touchup	6.0			6.0	
8		Publicizing the Website	3.0			3.0	
9		Other					
						Total:	

WebWeaving Time Estimate Sheet

- The above is an *estimate*. Billing will occur based on actual hours.
- Actual hours are kept at quarter-hour increments.
- Graphic creations vary upon the complexity of the artwork. Simple artwork can be completed within 2–4 hours.

Figure 11.24   InfoStreet's Time Estimate Sheet.

Farah states, "We found that many individuals and organizations still believe that the barrier to entry in creating a World Wide Web site outweighs the benefits of developing one, therefore the goal of Instant Web is to eliminate, or at least reduce, some of the inhibitors." Instant Web does so by providing a service with no startup cost, a low monthly charge (starting at $9.95 per month), and a host of automated tools to manage the sites.

Figure 11.25   Instant Web Site guide page.

Farah concludes, "From a sales and marketing point of view, what the Internet does is bring a totally new price performance curve to the company. It allows people to reach the masses with a substantially lower amount of investment. We have dubbed the Internet as 'the silent salesperson' to either filter the tire-kickers or allow customers to self-qualify. This will ensure that when a customer reaches a person who is drawing a paycheck, it's a substantially more qualified lead."

CAPP Records Mixes Music and Electronic Marketing

CAPP Company was launched in 1993 with a combination of new electronic and traditional marketing vehicles. The founders, Dominique Toulon and Marc J. Oshry, originally created CAPP as a music publishing company for their band, Cary August. CAPP Records was later formed as a subsidiary to manage the sales and marketing functions. Electronic vehicles used for marketing include a CD-ROM Sampler, faxing software and search engines, and Web sites on the Internet.

First Break: Network 40 and AEI

In the beginning of 1994, with an initial investment of $7,500, the band Cary August recorded a CD single and demo tape. Band members aggressively publicized it and used it as an effective tool for marketing their live performances. Following contacts made at the music industry's NARM (National Association of Retailers & Merchandisers) convention, CAPP was able to get its single on a CD sampler called Network 40 for a little over $1,000.

This was a major achievement for a small independent, because the Network 40 is composed of all of the major labels with their artists' newest material before it's available in the stores. Thus, Network 40 can prerelease, test-market, and promote the music on over 1,000 top-40 network stations across the nation. Without CAPP's knowledge, its sampler was picked up by AEI, a music service company that creates six-hour cassette cartridge tapes used for background music in an estimated 120,000 different businesses throughout the United States. Some 17 million people hear this music in hotels, airplanes, restaurants, malls, and offices. CAPP got phone calls from all over the country as a result. (However, CAPP is still waiting for royalties earned from its music performing rights organization, BMI, (Broadcast Music Inc.)!) Since that time, CAPP developed a direct relationship with AEI and is licensing its newest releases to AEI.

Faxing on a Shoestring

One of the ways CAPP gets the word out on both performances and available CDs is with a software faxing program called WinFax Pro. This is a very economical alternative to fax-on-demand systems. With this program, as well as some others on the market, it is possible to send "broadcast" faxes to hundreds of recipients at one time, and program them to go out when the lowest phone rates are in effect, leaving the computer available for other uses during the workday. Oshry explains:

We design a cover page, and the program automatically drops the appropriate recipient name and address into the header of the fax. If a fax doesn't go through, the software detects it and will retry up to a specified number of times and then provide a reason why it was not able to go through, such as an incorrect number, in the fax log. By creating different directories or phone books for different types of recipients, we can send one kind of fax to record companies in Europe on one schedule, another to all of the domestic record companies, music publishers, and record pools, and still others to licensing firms, movie producers, and the press. We can also fax directly out of a program where we keep all of our addresses and phone numbers like Database, ACT, or Word.

Toulon adds:

One of the big advantages WinFax offers is the ability to receive faxes directly into our computer and, using the OCR feature, translate a fax into a document that can be manipulated and edited in a word processor, unlike paper faxes received in a machine. Also, faxes can be forwarded from the home office to other satellite offices or anywhere else, instantaneously and without the use of paper.

Some modems that are compatible with WinFax make it possible to transfer whole files from one computer to another. For example, if we don't want to convert a WordPerfect document into a fax, we could send the actual file, and the recipient would be able to make any necessary changes in his or her own word processing program.

We send sound files for people to download so they can listen to small samples of our music. We zip them up so they're compressed, and it only takes three to four minutes to download a 20-second excerpt of a song. I think that, in the future, we'll be able to pitch our music this way to companies abroad so that they don't have to wait for "snail" mail. We can literally fax our music to them, and they can convert it and listen to it through their computer speakers!

Oshry adds:

These days, it's very difficult to reach people, so fax or e-mail is probably one of the most efficient and convenient ways to get information in front of them. Most of our contacts are overseas, so if we fax them at night here, they receive the document in the morning their time and have the whole day to prepare a response. The alternative, before faxing, was sending an unsolicited letter or tape. We found that sending an unso-

licited fax is more accepted, and we are more likely to get a return fax within 24 to 48 hours. Another advantage of using programs like WinFax is that whenever we send or receive faxes, they are stored as memory in our computer. This is especially useful during contract negotiations and other interactions that require detailed records of all communications.

Low-Budget Surfing

CAPP has also made good use of advertising and marketing opportunities on the Internet. Oshry, who took the lead in this endeavor, explains:

> The first thing we did was use a service called IUMA (Internet Underground Music Archive), which started in 1994. It provides storage space on its World Wide Web server where we can put sound clips of our songs, text, and pictures of our band. There is a comment section where [listeners] can give feedback on what they thought of the band and music. It's quite a popular service. A benefit for us is not only great exposure but also the use of IUMA's hard drive storage space for our sound clips. It also provides e-mail services so that people can communicate with us right from our page on IUMA. I think the reason we didn't receive much response when we subscribed to the America Online and CompuServe services, using their forms to upload our sound clips and pictures, is because those services are more geared toward the well-known, popular artists.
>
> We discovered that Internet companies like Slipnet, based locally in San Francisco, offered a superior combination of services that met our needs better than the larger commercial ones. With the Web and the hard drive space I was allotted, I taught myself the HTML language and created the company's web site consisting initially of over 20 pages of interactive sound clips, downloadable photos, and forms for ordering merchandise from the band (Figure 11.26). All I pay is $20 a month for my Internet service. With IUMA, we had to pay a $300 fee, but we feel it was worth the exposure.
>
> The Internet is definitely the wave of the future, especially for small start-up companies, because of the accessibility and low entry cost, as well as the great new features like animation that programs like Java make possible. My main job is to publicize our site on search engines and other music services, and get links added to related pages. That's the way to get the word out on the Web. The Ultimate Band List is a really excellent spot for us because it links to almost all of our pages."

Toulon advises:

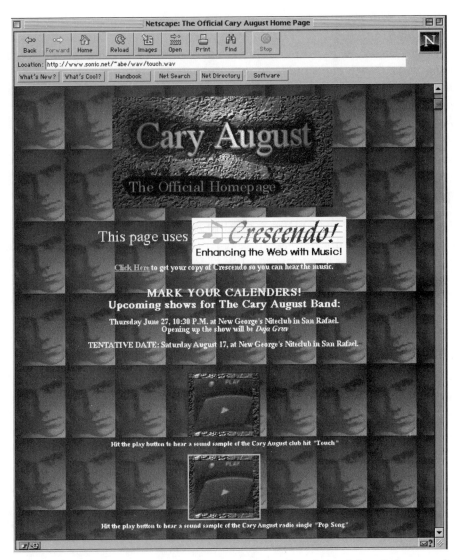

Figure 11.26 Cary August home page, developed by Oshry and Toulon, features animated graphics, important links, user feedback and request e-mailing function, (not all visible here), and embedded MIDI sound files that play songs by the artists.

It is important to add your pages to search engines such as Yahoo! and Web Crawler, and you should look up your category in those and all of the other search engines. Call up these other pages, e-mail their creator, and get your Web site linked or written up on those pages so they can go from that Web page to your Web site. Advertise on the USENET newsgroups, which are like bulletin boards over the Internet, but these are Internet-wide and they're uncensored, and free.

Another means of advertising our Web page and band is through the home pages of local nightclubs publicizing our upcoming performances. For example, in San Rafael, California, New George's nightclub has its own home page listing all the local bands and a calendar of who's playing. It is advertised in the local papers throughout the San Francisco Bay Area. The Web sites are also listed on all of its flyers and calendars, which are available in stores and restaurants around the Bay Area, and are passed out nightly at the club.

More Than a CD

CAPP also participated in CD-Direct, a CD-ROM sampler bundled with the *E2* and *PC Electronic Entertainment* magazines. CAPP provided some background music to the games and pages described on the CD. It managed to get that spot free of charge, which was an excellent opportunity. Over 200,000 units were distributed throughout the United States. Interested parties can e-mail CAPP Records and place orders for the music and other products directly from the CD-ROM.

Phone Music

CAPP also contributed to the Payne Catalogue which is a music catalogue of independent record companies. People can call up Payne and sample CAPP's music over the telephone. The cost for that service was $150, and the results are negligible to date.

In early 1995, CAPP started production on its Impact CD and pressed about 1,000 vinyl records and 1,000 CDs, with a combined production and promo budget of about $16,000. Currently, CAPP's focus is on live performances, pre-production on its new CD, and making the most of the Internet. Response and sales are steadily growing as CAPP is able to expose more people to its music through all of the available electronic media.

Newest Offering

CAPP has started a new service for bands in the San Francisco Bay Area. Oshry explains, "We provide a low-cost Web page service to design and promote Web pages. It is a less-expensive alternative to some of the other services on the Internet. We have the ability to allow Web surfers to download music and video clips of the band on their own pages. With the new Netscape 3.0, they will be able to see and hear video right on the page, and all of the multimedia features will be easier to enjoy."

Great Escapes: Over the Hill and Still Climbing

On October 7, 1994, two long-time employees were fired from the largest travel agency in Northern California. Rather than investing time and hard-earned dollars in lawsuits claiming age and health discrimination, these two women decided to pool their experience and their determination and launch a travel agency of their own. Within 32 days of leaving their former jobs, they had launched a unique home-based business called Great Escapes.

The founders were both over 60 when they took the entrepreneurial plunge, and they were forced to learn about and utilize some of the latest technology in order to carve out a niche for their new company. With the use of cellular phones and laptop computers, fax machines and fax software, this boutique travel agency was able to provide a personal touch to making travel plans. The company has been profitable from the very beginning, partially because the overhead is so low.

Sandra Kretchmer, one of the founding partners explains, "We basically provide the same services as all travel agencies; that is, air tickets, tours, and cruises. Because we're so small, we can be highly attentive to our clients. We have independent contractors on laptops, which gives them the flexibility to make reservations at the clients' convenience. We also have pagers and are on call for our clients. We often do things after normal business hours, and answer our phones and pagers on weekends and evenings in case of emergency. So it's not just a cut-and-dried, 9:00-to-5:00 job."

The Launch

The initial efforts to get Great Escapes rolling involved simple word of mouth, a direct-mail campaign, and a fortunate write-up in the newspaper. Kretchmer adds, "We told everyone the truth about how we'd been fired. We felt it was important to be honest. That, of course, made certain corporations, particularly female-owned corporations, very incensed, and they wanted to support us in our new endeavor."

The two women then decided it was time to explore the Internet as a marketing venue. They signed on for a 12-month program in November 1995 that would allow up to 3 megs of information on a Web site with 12 updates, for a cost of $635. When they compared that to the cost of $119 for a nonproductive ad in the yellow pages, they chose the Internet. They added an e-mail address and an 800 number, and included this information in print ads they had been running in a needlepoint magazine. (Needlepoint can be a very expensive hobby, so this audience generally has money to spend on travel.) Great Escapes also was listed on the Internet search engines and sites such as Senior Net to gain as much exposure as possible. The company has experienced a steady increase in business as a result of promotional efforts and the team plans to exploit their presence on the Net fully.

Great Escapes is growing rapidly, and is building on to the home office space to accommodate more people, although the women plan to remain small. (Just 10 months after launch, Great Escapes was so profitable that it was necessary to invest in the building expansion to lower tax liability.) They find that the lifestyle of running a home-based business lowers stress and makes it possible to deliver personalized service.

Kretchmer concludes, "The whole idea that a bunch of old birds can go out and start a business, and, not only that, be successful, is important for people to know." It is also important that people know that the entrepreneurial spirit is not only ageless, it is well suited to the benefits of electronic vehicles. By utilizing a combination of portable computers, fax machines and fax software, cellular phones, an 800 number, print advertising, and the Internet, Great Escapes has been able to run a very successful home-based business. It demonstrates values that are the hallmark of the new customer-centric marketing model. The firm relies heavily on word-of-mouth, puts customer care first, and provides personalized, responsive service. At 60, these women entered the world of high-tech, incorporated a highly personal value system, and are now well on their way to the next millennium with a bustling new business.

Southwind Enterprises: Riches to Rags to Riches to Riches

Southwind Enterprises, Inc., a direct e-mail Internet company launched in July 1995, and officially incorporated in October 1995, was founded by Dave Fricke with one old computer, very little money, and two months of round-the-clock workdays! Fricke describes his rocky road to success:

> When I started, I managed nightclubs, and was doing very well at that. I had a nice house in Illinois, three cars, a boat, and everything I could want. I was a very successful nightclub manager; very good with promotions and advertising. Then I tried to switch nightclub positions, and one thing led to another, and there was just nothing left. I lost the house, lost two of the three cars, but kept the boat, of all things!
>
> I started doing some advertising online to get design business, but it was slow. I was playing around on the Internet and the online services just trying to figure out how to incorporate my design business there. I was placing ads in the newsgroups, placing ads on some of the online services and classified sections, and on forums and such. I was advertising for graphic artwork and merchandise specialties, too, like pencils, keychains, lighters, and hats where companies can have messages or business logos imprinted. I got to

the point of selling all my computer equipment and going back to work. I wasn't sure how I was going to pay the rent.

Then, like a bolt of lightning, one day the direct e-mail idea just hit! Another company was doing a similar type of thing, and it just dawned on me the amount of money that could be made from it. It's just extending what's going on now with postal mail to the new technology of e-mail, which is expanding rapidly:

The whole idea was to cut advertising costs for the consumer and get their ads out to more people faster. With a regular direct-mail campaign, it may take up to two months to get something out and get a response. The cost of a direct-mail print campaign is also astronomical in comparison. I can get it done using e-mail in 48 hours for a fraction of the cost.

I did searches and pulled names out of classified sections, out of ads placed for business opportunities, [looking for] people who had business-type keywords that matched words used in their online membership profiles, or anywhere on the Internet that had to do with business. I also went through the phone book front to back looking for different kinds of businesses and professional positions, and pulled the names and organized them.

I had to do a lot of manipulation of the basic software, so the first two months I was up at 6:00 A.M., to bed at 3:00 A.M., and then three hours of sleep, and back up again. Seven days a week. I didn't break. I alienated all my friends, and at that point had no money to do anything, so I was going off of what we had, doing the best I could."

When Southwind had 100,000 names compiled, Fricke did a small 5000 name test mailing, just to explain the advertising opportunity. Nothing came of it. For the next mailing, Fricke decided to include some ads, rather than just explaining it like he did in the test mailing, hoping that by doing what he was offering, people would understand and respond. He called up friends, friends of friends, anyone who might be willing to place an ad. That first big mailing to all 100,000 names took two days to send out. Half-way through the first day the phone was ringing off the hook.

In the beginning, Southwind used two full-time employees to do the mailing. Then Fricke began automating all of the processes and was able to manage with one employee plus himself working on the mailing, which averaged 20 minutes per 100,000. At last count Southwind's mailing database had over 600,000 addresses.

Southwind also takes the time each day to eliminate those people who have requested to be removed from the list. This was an important feature to automate in order to keep up with the growing volume and be respectful to those who do not want these kinds of mailings.

Fricke says:

It was a hard first two or three months, then all of a sudden it took off. With over 600,000 names now, we e-mail on a regular basis to 100,000 a day, and a different 100,000 the next day, so people are getting only one to two messages a week. We keep them really short, 10 to 15 messages per mailing so people don't get sick of them.

We keep our rates very affordable. A line is considered 70 characters, including spaces. A three-line ad is $49; a five-line ad is $89; and a 10-line ad is $139. That's one shot to 100,000 people, which sits in their mailbox until they read it. That's with 10 to 15 other ads; what we call a co-op ad. A fourth way to go is an individual mailing, where you can have a 25-line ad, just your ad, going out to 100,000 people. That's $499. And I have customers who do higher-number packages, too, like 25 ads. It's basically like getting 10 free. Buy 15, get 10 free. We'll be coming out with a lot of advertising packages for the small businessperson, too.

It's possible to make a huge impact on your business with just one mailing. It is important to be prepared for a high response, rather than risk creating bad PR and losing business as a result of an inability to answer all inquiries in a timely and adequate way. It's easier to take away resources at the last minute than to add them. The following are a few examples of some success stories shared by Fricke:

One advertiser, for example, had a pager service. He placed a three-line ad. Spent $49. The first day, he had 90 phone calls. There was no e-mail address in this ad. It was just an 800 number. He ended up with about 300 phone calls from that one $49 ad. Most of them turned into sales. That's about a 90 percent rate of sell-through.

A few days later, I started getting calls from people who didn't even have computers. When I asked how they heard about us, since we do no outside advertising, they said, "Oh, this guy from the pager shop photocopied Southwind's ad, and ran down the shopping mall and handed it to every single store."

Another customer, a private investigator, did an individual mailing. He has mailed to all 500,000 already, and was overjoyed from his first mailing. He spent $500 on the ad, and has easily made it all back through resulting business. He ended up getting 10 or 15 corporate accounts, three or four collection agencies, and a lot of other major, major accounts. And he's done it four times, and each time he gets more and more accounts.

A company called Software Source offers discount software to educational institutions, students and teachers. The first time the company ran an ad to 100,000 people, it had over 500 e-mail responses. And about a month later, the company had an 800 number listed in the ad, so the response went up even higher.

Southwind provides a check-faxing service to expedite business transactions when credit cards are not available. Fricke describes the service:

We offer a check-faxing service to our customers to assist them in getting relatively instant guaranteed payment if they are not using credit cards. We're a Dun & Bradstreet-listed company, and the federal government has allowed us to have customers fax us their checks. The customer holds on to the original. We take the faxed check and re-create a legal draft of the check with our computer. We have software that does this—with the routing numbers, the magnetic ink, the whole nine yards. We take that check and deposit it in our account. It appears on the customer's statement just like we had the original check. The customer keeps that original check as his or her receipt.

A lot of customers ask, "How do I know you're not going to write a check for $10,000?" I answer, "You have that original check as your receipt. You'll go to your bank and tell them that you only wrote it for $49, and you're safe. It's called CheckFax, by the CheckFax Development Company of Arizona. We will also print checks for other companies that want to accept checks by fax. Their customer faxes them the check, they fill out the information on a form, and fax it to us. We print the check and mail it to them. As soon as they have that fax in hand, that's payment in hand.

For companies that can't afford the $300 to $400 price tag for the software, Southwind Enterprises will do the check processing for them for $.75 per check, an affordable alternative. There's no start-up fees or monthly cost. They pay for it as they use it.

"This business is ideal for me," states Fricke. "I love it. I love the computers. I love the challenge. I love talking to people. I get the greatest satisfaction from running a high-technology business. I'm offering people a service, and it makes me feel really great when they send me a letter saying, 'Dave, thanks a lot. We got an excellent response.' I've made a lot of new friends from some of the regular advertisers.

"A whole world of business contacts has opened up; products, things I never knew existed. People are coming to me with invention ideas, and we're advertising those for them. It's amazing to realize that in just a few months I went from trying to figure out how I was going to pay the rent to trying to figure out where I wanted to go on vacation!"

FolksOnline.com: Home for the Nontechnical Majority

Yinspire, Inc. was formed in the summer of 1995 to use new media technologies to help America's nontechnical consumers join the digital revolution. Founder Ruby Yeh, a hopeless technophobe herself, recognized that most people are a little intimidated by computers, and, even if they have one, often use it for only one or two applications such as word processing and spreadsheets. Her original vision was to create a CD-ROM featuring inspirational real-people stories about how certain underrepresented population segments, such as women, senior citizens, and mom-and-pop proprietors, have used various software applications to support and enhance their lifestyles.

When the CD-ROM prototype was completed during the fall of 1995, it became apparent that a Web strategy should be added, given the pace of Internet growth. So Yinspire put up an online test site to supplement the concept of the CD-ROM, which was to provide a resource for the "Net newbies," computer novices and technophobes who were coming online in droves. The informal test site was launched in February 1996, and the theme was "people helping each other to use new technologies to reach for our dreams."

Yeh states, "I originally had the opinion that the Web was only for social misfits who had nothing better to do than hang out with their computers. I never even looked at a Web site until October when all the hoopla about the growth of the Internet forced me to take my head out of the sand. I discovered an incredible new world and quickly became a convert. My eyes were really opened when our site began generating responses. People told us what they liked and what they wanted. I immediately saw that the Internet is truly a creative marketer's dream. People were writing to us for advice and help when we didn't even solicit such requests."

Within a couple of months, the decision was made to drop the CD-ROM and pursue an Internet-only strategy. Yeh explains the decision: "It became apparent that, technically, we could accomplish what we wanted to do through the Net at about one-third of the cost of the CD-ROM, plus reach a much larger audience and provide a more diverse program."

So, armed with the feedback from its audience, Yinspire totally overhauled the site so it would be more professionally designed. The redesigned site added information databases and a content program based on the test site audience input regarding the type of help and support users want. There are four main sections to the site (Figure 11.27):

Real People Stories
Helping Hands

Figure 11.27   FolksOnline.com
home page.

Resource Leads

Cyberfolks' Software

There is also a weekly comic strip called *The Revenge of the Non-Technical Majority*. FolksOnline.com is not meant to be a source of technical tutorials for newbies. Rather, its mission is to offer a friendly and fun place for people to learn and get inspired about the practical things they can do with their computers. It is "the place for today's cyberfolks—the world's nontechnical majority."

FolksOnline.com is unique in that most of the site's content comes from its audience, following the company's theme: *People helping each other to use new technologies to follow their dreams*. In this way, the boundaries between company and audience become diffused. The audience is providing content and forging the evolution of the site with their input and needs; the company plays the role of conduit to serve and support the directives of the audience. Yeh elaborates:

> *The idea of audience contribution evolved because people were writing to tell us they supported the concept of the site and wanted to help in any way that they could. I got excited after I started to get audience feedback and offers of help and participation in the Yinspire vision. Now, audience contributors receive a $50–$100 thank-you for their content contributions. I began to understand the interactive and virtual nature of the Net and realized that these qualities allow me to further support the fundamental vision of why I had formed Yinspire, Inc. in the first place.*
>
> *I wanted to create a collaborative virtual corporation or a network of independent entrepreneurs who come together to implement a shared vision. That idea includes collaborative profit sharing among the core team members, a profit bonus to the software vendors who are affiliated with Yinspire and who feature their products on the site, and a profit allocation for charitable community organizations. With FolksOnline.com's strategy of audience participation, it became a natural to include this group as part of the collaborative team. So, in addition to receiving the $50–$100 thank-you for their published content, audience contributors also qualify for the Yinspire profit bonus.*
>
> *Because the audience has the opportunity to share in the financial success of FolksOnline.com as a result of their participation, the distinction becomes further blurred between the company and the audience. I believe the most valued assets for any business are the commitment, loyalty, and creativity of its customers, the internal team, and business affiliates. It makes sense to win their hearts by inviting them to participate in the "collaborative virtual mission" and by including them in the financial success of that shared vision. And the boundless nature of the Net is making this approach possible.*

Yeh elaborates on the profit bonus plan for Yinspire's software vendor affiliates: "Part of my original vision was to build a bridge between the independent software developers who have created great, easy-to-use software and the Cyberfolks audience who generally don't know about the availability of these products. There are over 15,000 multimedia titles, and most of these are totally unknown because of the distribution channel limitations. I wanted to provide a means for consumers to find out about some of these wonderful offerings, which could increase the usefulness of their computer investment.

"Therefore, in the Cyberfolks' Software section of our site, we have developed a really fun and interesting way for our audience to learn about some of these unknown titles and what the software can do for them. And we are creating an expanded market base for these developers by driving business directly to them. But besides the incremental revenue we are generating for these developers, I want to further motivate these business partners to support our overall success so I am including them as part of Yinspire's virtual team, and giving them a share in the bounty of the company's profits."

Another unique aspect about Yinspire is its revenue strategy. It is not based on advertising, sales transactions, or subscription fees but instead follows an innovative referral sales model. Yinspire offers a 10–50 percent price rebate when a user buys a service or product seen on the FolksOnline site. A system has been devised to track such Yinspire-referred purchases. The vendor then pays Yinspire a commission, plus the rebate amount, and that rebate is then passed along to the consumer.

Yinspire draws a significant community of Cyberfolks because it offers a place of inspiration, guidance, and help for this audience. From this foundation of genuine support and added value, the audience can check out products and services that have been identified as useful resources. All software products promoted by Yinspire in the Cyberfolks' Software section include this price rebate. Thus, Yinspire has crafted several compelling reasons for its audience to take advantage of products and services presented at the site.

Yinspire does not handle sales transactions or order fulfillment. Interested buyers are referred to the third-party vendor's Web site or 800 number. Once a purchase is made directly from a software or other product/service vendor, Yinspire receives a referral commission for that sale. This is Yinspire's basic revenue model. Its benefit to Yinspire's vendor partners is that they pay only a referral commission when a sale has actually been made. And the benefit to Yinspire, in addition to making a commission on sales, is that it is able to give the 10–40 percent price rebate back to its audience buyers.

FolksOnline.com (http://www.FolksOnline.com) was launched in August of 1996. Here is a glimpse into FolksOnline's content sections:

- *Real People Stories:* Inspirational vignettes about regular folks who have changed their lives or pursued a dream using computer technology. One story is about the Southern Baptist minister who taught himself how to use a computer and is now a multimedia designer. Another story tells of a 13-year-old from a low-income neighborhood who learned Web programming in a free kids computer training center and now makes $5 an hour making Web sites for small businesses. A third story is about a 60-plus-year-old woman who used to be a "certified computerphobe," and, once she learned how to use the computer, ended up with several dozen clients during her first year as a "certified cyber-coach."

• *Helping Hands:* An area filled with practical guidance regarding new technology and the Web. The section called The Real Scoop About the New Technologies presents a weekly topic such as Audio on the Web, Internet Phone, or What Virtual Reality Is All About. FolksOnline does not approach these subjects with the journalistic authority of a magazine. Instead, the tone is like having your neighbor or cousin explain the ins and outs of some new technology and what it can do for you. Another section is titled Look Ma, I Did Something Useful on the Web Today. The one called Evolve Existing Skills to the Web guides people on how they can take a talent such as writing and adapt it to publishing on the Web. There is a technical advice column and forum, and a business advice column and forum where people trade entrepreneurial ideas for the Web. There is even a section called First Day on the Web to offer a helping hand to people who venture onto the Web with no prior orientation about any of the basic conventions.

• *Resource Leads:* A place filled with links, regional resources, and referrals to helpful products and services for Cyberfolks. Users can search for a computer consultant who makes house calls, a computer training class, or an Internet Service Provider (ISP) in their local area by inputting their telephone area code. There are also pointers to computer magazines and direct mail catalogues appropriate for Cyberfolks and other useful products and services referrals.

• *Cyberfolks' Software:* A section that presents dozens of useful, consumer-friendly software products through entertaining vignettes about how each product can be used by various cyberfolk audiences. Each product is categorized into one of three levels, based on technical sophistication. An application labeled Proud Technophobe is for people who only want to point and click. Trainable Newbie is a product category for people who are willing to learn something a little more advanced, and Adventurous Cyberfolks titles are for individuals who enjoy exploring new application innovations. If a particular title looks appealing, the person is referred to the software vendor's Web site to directly purchase the software application via the Web or an 800 number. The bonus for the FolksOnline community is that when a product is purchased because of the referral, the buyer automatically receives a 10–50 percent purchase rebate from Yinspire. Accompanying this section is a Toaster Award, which cites cyberfolks' nominations of products that are "as easy to use as a toaster." Toaster Award nominations are culled from the community's review of FolksOnline-presented software, plus other titles nominated by the audience.

Clearly, the FolksOnline site aims to address a segment of the population that will be entering the online world in droves over the coming years. By making this entry a positive experience, and adding a business model in which everyone who participates is able to benefit beyond standard expectations, Yinspire leads the way to revolutionizing the way business is conducted. The company embraces the tenets of relationship-based business, which include every point of contact with the company from product vendor to online visitor.

Conclusion

These case studies have presented a range of experiences, insights, and innovative approaches that can prove helpful to readers who may be considering "jumping into the Net" and/or into other electronic vehicles. Before taking the leap, it is worthwhile considering carefully whether the media you have chosen to invest in is the most appropriate for your audience. Good marketing principles apply to any medium, and although it is more difficult to compete in today's marketplace without the use of these various electronic vehicles, this industry is still in its infancy, and realistic goals are recommended. When the Internet and other media are used well, however, the benefits to a business can exceed all expectations.

CHAPTER TWELVE

INDUSTRY LEADERS:
THE ROAD AHEAD

The following interview excerpts were taken from over 70 conducted in the course of doing research for this book. Three others, Paul Saffo, Bill Gates, and Michael Bloomberg, were generously contributed by Eric Nee, editor in chief of *Upside* Magazine. A short article on the intranet was also contributed by *Upside.* These excerpts are presented to give the reader an opportunity to hear from a range of industry experts directly, who share their opinions, concerns, and predictions about the impact of present and emerging technologies on both marketers and consumers on the road ahead.

Paul Saffo
Institute for the Future

Paul Saffo has the kind of job many people would kill for. He travels around the globe talking to some of the brightest minds in business and science, in an effort to figure out what the future will bring. Saffo has a solid grounding in history, a deep fascination with new technologies, and a dollop of skepticism that keeps him from flying off into fantasy. He calls himself a forecaster, and says his views are agnostic, unlike futurists such as George Gilder. Saffo has been with the Institute for the Future in Menlo Park, California, for 11 of its 28 years.

> *The Internet will allow for a myriad number of ways to intermediate all kinds of interactions. That has been the biggest change between the mass-media age of the '60s and the personal-media age that we're solidly into today. All of our thinking today is infused with theories that there is one way to do things. What is the one optimum way to do things? What is the one outcome?*

Will other cultures find this technology as interesting and compelling as we do? Yes, but they're going to reinvent it for their own ends. Several decades ago, Marshall McLuhan observed that the whole world was becoming a global village because of the impact of mass media. Well, McLuhan hit a large nail not quite on the head, as was his wont. In fact, the world is not becoming a single global village. It is becoming multiple, interlinked global villages. That is the difference between mass media and personal media.

Japan's Great Surprise

. . . But the real surprise is going to be [that] there is this large population of single women in Japan who have great-paying jobs, but because they're single, they are still living at home with their parents, and thus have enormous amounts of [discretionary] income. They're very enthusiastic purchasers of items from American mail-order catalogues. So this becomes the "cybershop until you drop" vehicle for Lands' End and L.L. Bean to sell stuff to Japan, delivered by some specialized Federal Express prepositioned system. . . .

The Web will evolve to a place where, instead of connecting people to information, it connects people to people in information-rich environments. The people who construct those information-rich environments are going to be the ones who get rich three, four, or five years from now.

An *Upside* magazine article by Kora McNaughton reports that according to a December 1995 report by Zona Research Inc., Redwood City, California, the intranet market presents a much greater opportunity than the Internet in the next few years. By 1998, the report predicts, intranet server revenue will reach $7.8 billion, while Internet server revenue will amount to just $1.9 billion.

Internet security is synonymous with firewalls, a segment The Yankee Group of Boston expects to grow at a 66 percent compound rate, reaching $924 million in 1999. One company that's making it simpler to build and deploy enterprisewide applications with a Web browser as the common GUI is Spider Technologies Inc. of Palo Alto, California. Spider, says Kevin Fong of Mayfield Fund, Menlo Park, California, is helping open up information more rapidly to Internet access, and is set to play a key role in the development of corporate intranets.

Bill Gates
Microsoft Corporation

According to Gates, "Many debates in our industry just have to do with people using words in different ways, with nothing of substance being argued. Client-server is greatly aided by low-cost connectivity, because the clients can be anywhere in the country, connected to the Internet.

Will Diskless PCs Sell?

. . . Say diskless PCs caught on tomorrow. How does that change the world? Well, maybe for disk manufacturers it changes. If anybody comes to you with this "Internet terminal," just write down on a piece of paper where it's different from a PC. People will take PCs and configure them in a variety of ways. The lesson of 1995 is that low-end PCs don't sell very well. It's very difficult to get anywhere close to the high-quality display and sound that the PC industry is able to get.

. . . So why don't people buy $800 PCs? Are those people confused? In the future, innovation may go more toward price reduction. The greatest problem that the PC market has had, remember, is that demand has been too high. What has this meant? It has meant that every component in the PC has been in short supply. Actually, the disk-drive guys have done such a good job that that's not a problem. But for CD-ROM drives, graphics cards, you name it, we've suspended Moore's Law. Memory prices have been the same over the last two or three years. Do you realize what an impact that is? If Moore's Law hadn't been suspended, the typical PC today, for the same price, would now have 24 Mbytes instead of 8 Mbytes.

Now that means there's a wonderful thing going on in the PC market. You have people investing heavily in capacity for RAM and all the parts of the PC. We can grow the PC industry and get out of this shortage thing, which will bring the price of the PC back down that Moore's Law curve. So there's no doubt that we'll have $500 PCs. The question is, will anybody buy them? So whenever you talk about these [Internet terminals], you're just saying that Acorn is better than Intel. Or that some different operating system is better than the Microsoft operating system. Or that nobody wants a sound card, nobody wants motion video, or nobody wants a mouse. Anyone is welcome to project sales of machines connected to the Internet. Let's just take the next three years. Do whatever you want to PC sales and look at that installed base. What percentage of machines connected to the Internet will be Internet terminals?

. . . The question is, is there any value added in some sort of device that has a Web browser in it and doesn't really run any other software? It doesn't have an operating system.

Software Is More Valuable, Not Less

. . . We're writing server software. We're writing client software. So in cases where people actually want to run code on the client, we'll provide value. If

they want to actually run code on the server, we'll provide value in that case. I happen to think that, even as you move into this [Internet] world, software will be more valuable. Somebody could take the position that because of low-cost connectivity, software's not important anymore. But I don't.

I don't care where it runs. The user doesn't even have to know where it runs. That's the whole point; it doesn't matter. But the question is: Is this a world where we want more tools, better server software, and a broader range of applications? Or one where you don't need software anymore?

Clement Mok
NetObjects

Clement Mok is the president and CEO of NetObjects. NetObjects is a software company developing a family of products that will enable Web site builders to dramatically improve the design, authoring, publishing, and updating of Web sites. NetObjects was formed in November 1995 by Rae Technology Inc. and Clement Mok designs Inc., and is a privately held company headquartered in Woodside, California, funded by Norwest Venture Capital, Venrock Associates, and private investors.

Clement Mok shares his views on the future and the relevance of the Net. "As the Web grows into a commercial medium, the key to making businesses viable is to use all aspects of interactivity design—information architecture, information design and information arts—to find order and opportunity in the chaos of the new medium. Interactivity design may seem complex and difficult to master, but the truth is that it is social science, not rocket science."

Michael Bloomberg
Bloomberg Financial Markets

At a time when tiny Internet startups are being heralded as the model media companies of the future, Michael Bloomberg has already "been there, done that." He has built his namesake firm into one of the largest business information providers in the world, rivaling the likes of Dow Jones, Reuters, and Nikkei. And he did it by being one of the most innovative and aggressive users of computer, communications, and recording technology. He has also brought together the frenetic energy of a Silicon Valley startup with the panache of a New York media company.

The bulk of Bloomberg L.P.'s estimated $700 million in annual revenue continues to come from the tens of thousands of Bloomberg terminals leased to financial traders throughout the world. But the company is quickly moving beyond that, supplying its growing collection of business news to a range of other outlets and markets, including a 24-hour news channel on DirecTV, a business magazine, a radio station, a news service and, of course, a World Wide Web site. Bloomberg states:

> Clearly you're going to see a combination of the PC and the TV. They're even both two-lettered products, and it's easy to combine them. Most people don't want to sit there and look up facts on ancient Mesopotamia. They want TV listings that they can scan. That's a nice application. They want video on demand. They want it digitally so they can look at five different places in the interview show and pick out the place they want to start.
>
> You can do that now at your terminal. It's just that you've got to make it simpler for the average person to use. Whether it's done from a very fancy chip or whether it's downloaded with Java is immaterial to the user. The user is not going to know the difference. Every television is going to be the average person's PC, not the other way around. That doesn't mean that the PC guy isn't going to make it, but you will sell a lot more PCs when you change the two letters to TV. [Users] will think of it as a television and they will like thinking of it as a television, and they will buy it a lot easier. So I think that you will see a lot more of the video-on-demand kinds of things. Most people are very comfortable watching the same thing that everybody else watches—250 million people a week watch Baywatch.
>
> They might prefer to be able to watch it when they want, don't you think? I think they do. I have always argued that the reason people do not time-shift with VCRs is that VCRs are tape-based, so you can only time-shift something a minimum of the length of the program. In other words, I can't time-shift a three-hour football game because it's going to be at least three hours if I want to watch it in its entirety, and then in the next three hours invariably someone is going to break in and tell me who won.
>
> If I could take that football game and time-shift it two minutes, which is the length of time that it took me to answer that phone call, or get a beer, or change the diaper, it's as good as real time. Shifting a football game two minutes is okay. Shifting Roseanne 10 minutes is okay. If you could just get a VCR that is disk-based—and those are very close. We use them as editing stations [at Bloomberg]. There just has to be a mass market and a cheap product. That will let you do some things with television that have nothing to do with how that television gets to your home. Nobody tunes in to NBC or CBS or ABC to see a particular type of programming.
>
> People do say that Fox has a certain character. Fox, CNN, and CNBC are worth something. But ABC, NBC, and CBS—those are the networks that trade for billions, and I don't think their brand names are worth much of anything. It doesn't give me much of an advantage. So what you are left with is saying that networks are guaranteed low-numbered positions on the dial.

And, in fact, if you remember what happened when [Rupert] Murdoch took a number of affiliates away from CBS, CBS scrambled and had to go on UHF channels, and its ratings went way down. Nobody goes to UHF channels. Well, a navigator built into your television ends that problem. You pick a program by participant or by title or by genre and [the navigator] figures out what station it is on; it sets your VCR or tunes you directly to the station. But if it changes to channel 5 or to channel 55, you don't know the difference; you don't care. And when the programming is done, it brings you back to the navigator. Why? Because the [person] selling you the navigator wants to sell advertising. [They] want you back on [their] page.

That's like Netscape. When you buy its browser, the default is that you come in through Netscape. Most people don't know that you can change the default. Absolutely. So my question is, what is the value of a network? Why would you spend $5 billion for CBS if it's only a production company, no brand name, and you can't guarantee the positions? Now, what Michael Jordan [chairman of CBS parent Westinghouse Electric Corp.] or Bob Wright [CEO of NBC] or Bob Iger [president of Capital Cities/ABC] would say is, "We still deliver an audience for a while." And it is true that for a while not every television is going to have a navigator. But two or three years from now, they will. The average life of a television is very short, and they make them in the millions.

Michael Rogers
Newsweek InterActive

Michael Rogers, VP PostNewsweek New Media and managing editor of Newsweek InterActive states, ". . . A few years ago, I used to say that if people really wanted to make money online, the two things to work on were security and privacy. Secure transactions and privacy, because there would always be the market. Now I would add tracking hits to that. Tracking demographics. And obviously everyone's working on that. But if you could really come up with a good way of tracking it, you'd have an incredible business, because I don't think anybody knows how to do it yet." He continues:

Paul Saffo at the Institute for the Future has pointed out that it's "context," not "content" that's really important. There is so much content out there that the real service is helping people find it, which is, of course, the directory business, the Yahoos, the Excites, Lycos, and they all sell advertising. But for now that's basically just pure search and retrieval. The second level of that is really not just providing a blank search but providing information that is, as the phrase goes, vetted by Newsweek. In other words, this is information that Newsweek believes to be true.

I remember a year or so ago I was at a conference and someone asked why we will ever need Newsweek *or* The New York Times *again because they said when they want to know what's going on in Bosnia they just get on the Net and they have a conversation with someone in Bosnia. I said, "Well, who are you talking to in Bosnia? Which side are they on? Who pays them? What are their interests?" And that's what you get* Newsweek *or* The New York Times *for. We know who we're talking to. So that value is what in the long run we will need to transmit into this new medium.*

Michael Kolowich
AT&T Business Network/Nets Inc.

"I still believe that right now and for the next five years, the most intelligent agents are human beings or human editors. The first kind of agenting that we'll actually have is people developing a following for particular editors or packagers of information on the Web. . . . I think the key to our business and to any of these businesses is habituation, and so I believe that we are going to be seeing many, many new habituation devices, such as presentation of information through screen savers."

Amanda North
Studio Archetype (formerly Clement Mok Designs)

Amanda North, Studio Archetype's identity architect, states, "What is really going to be exciting in creating the buyer/seller relationship is the way in which technology will make it possible to track individual preferences. A store will know that you like a size 4 dress from Calvin Klein, for example, and if anything special comes in or goes on sale in that department, they'll immediately flag that for you as you enter the Web site. So the site's going to become very customized and very targeted."

Tom Evslin
AT&T WorldNet Services

Tom Evslin, vice president of AT&T WorldNet Services, states, "World Net and the Internet will succeed in becoming true broad-based communication services when they're used for both communication and commerce, the way the telephones are. There has been a lot of attention paid lately to the role of the Internet in commerce. Of course, we think that's very important and you think it's very important, but the success of the Internet in commerce depends on its success in person-to-person communication, because that's what will in large degree give people the motivation to learn to use and to install Internet access."

Ben Miller
CardTech/SecurTech

Ben Miller, chairman of the CardTech/SecurTech Conference, the largest smart card conference in the world, offers his view of smart card technology as we move into the next century. "We're going to have literally dozens of places where you're going to basically plug into the worldwide information system to do things. And the smart card is ultimately going to be a way of identifying who you are if you're willing to give that up. It's also going to be a way of making it easier for you to navigate where you go and find what you're looking for.

"Since you're not just sitting at your set-top box or your PC at work, but might be on your cell phone, at your PC in your home office, or 30,000 feet up in an airplane, that knowledge base needs to move with you. That's what the smart card does for you or will in the long term. At some point, if you lose your smart card, you can get a new one issued with the push of a button. You identify your-self and the data can be pulled in from a variety of sources."

The WEBster and the TransPhone

Computer Life magazine's Greg Kizer reported on two new products in April 1996 that provide a peek down that road to the future. WEBster was created by a company called ViewCall America. The $300 box hooks up to your TV for display and into your phone in order to transmit data. It looks like a set-top cable box and contains both TV and PC elements. The WEBster has a 32-bit micro-processor, 4 megabytes of RAM, 2 megabytes of ROM, and a 28,800-bit-per-second (bps) modem. It comes with a handheld, TV-style infrared remote control that has four colored buttons for navigation. (An infrared keyboard is optional.) WEBster's custom browser works with HTML 3.0 and Netscape, and lets users go all over the Net. But ViewCall's home page offers services such as e-mail, news, sports information, and shopping.

The TransPhone is about the size of a notebook computer and folds out to display an LCD screen (in monochrome for $350 or passive-matrix color for $500) and a keyboard.

Features include two PC card slots intended for smart card use; a pair of phone jacks; a 14,400-bps modem; a credit-card swipe strip; and ports for a monitor, printer, and mouse. With only 512 K of RAM and a 286 chip, Trans-Phone relies on remote servers for almost everything, which means that its look and feel could swing from graphical to textual depending on the Internet server you call. With its card-ready design, TransPhone seems well prepared for online shopping. You could, for instance, dial an 800 number, surf a company's site, and then swipe a credit card through the machine to complete a purchase.

Track the evolution of communication and transaction technologies, and you will have a good indication of the trends and growth in the electronic market-place. Industry leaders may have a bit more vision and basis for making predictions than the average consumer, but it is clear that no one has this market too tightly wrapped. Partnerships, software, and hardware are changing faster than press announcements can be released. One thing is certain, however; this global electronic marketplace impacts all of our lives every day. Whether you work in a large corporation or run a sole proprietorship, the road ahead is rich with opportunity.

3PCO Network
P. O. Box 16223
San Francisco, CA 94116-0223
J. P. Morgan, Owner
Tel.: 415.647.5102
Fax: 415.647.8226
E-mail: jp@3pco.net
Home Page: http://www.3pco.net/

3PCO Network provides Internet hosting and development services for small businesses that include: Web site hosting and maintenance, virtual domain name registration, FTP, DNS, and e-mail and Web server and network installations for Internet and intranets.

ABConsultants
3234 McKinley Drive
Santa Clara, CA 95051
Bill Austad & Paul Brobst, Senior
    Partners
Tel: 408 243-2234
Fax: 408 243-2236
Fax-on-Demand: 408-243-2275
E-mail: Compuserve 71732,2776;
    pbrobst@ix.netcom.com
Home Page:
    http://www.abconsultants.com

ABConsultants, formed in 1989, is dedicated to helping organizations plan, install, and reap the benefits of enhanced fax and image management systems.

AT&T
32 Avenue of the Americas
New York, N.Y. 10013-2412
AT&T WorldNet Service: 1-800 WorldNet
Easy Link Services 1-800-242-6005
AT&T Easy World Wide Web & Creative
    Alliance Program (Site Designers):
    (Site Hosting) 1-800-746-7846
AT&T Business Network: 1-800-285-5551
AT&T Personal Online Services:
    1-800-809-1103
AT&T Toll-Free Directories:
    1-800-426-8686
AT&T International Helpline:
    1-888-ATT-INTL (1-888-288-4685)
From non-AT&T Direct countries
    1-810-262-6644
Home Page: http://www.att.com

AT&T is the world's networking leader, providing voice, data, and Internet services to businesses, consumers, and government agencies.

Attitude Network Ltd.
1421 El Miradero Avenue
Glendale, CA 91201
Annie Van Bebber, Vice President
Tel: 1-818-548-5076
Fax: 1-818-548-5162
E-mail: anynerd@aol.com
    labiche@happypuppy.com
Home Page: http://happypuppy.com

Attitude Network's Happy Puppy is the number-one games site on the Internet, reaching more game enthusiasts than any other media and featuring the largest content area of game-related information.

BC Publishing Services

2227 Filbert Street, #5
San Francisco, CA 94123-3426
Brian Cooke, Director
Tel: (415) 771-4171
Fax: (415) 771-0151
E-mail: Bcpub@aol.com

BC Publishing Services, a San Francisco-based consulting firm, provides editing, writing, desktop publishing, and market research consulting services.

CAPP Company

P.O. Box 150871
San Rafael, CA 94915-0871
Dominique Toulon or Marc J. Oshry
Tel: 415-457-8617
Fax: 415-453-6990
E-mail: capp@wco.com
HomePage: http://www.wco.com/~capp/index.shtml

CAPP Company is an independent music publishing and production organization as well as a Web site design business based in San Rafael, California.

Chalice Productions

252 Frederick Street
San Francisco, CA 94117
Tel: 415-731-7924
Fax: 415-731-7924
E-mail CHALICE@MSN.com

Chalice's immediate agenda is to develop and produce low budget feature films and interactive multimedia products of exceptional content and quality.

Computer Express

Tel: 508-443-6125
Fax: 508-443-5645
CompuServe: 70007,1534,Delphi: COMPEXO,
Prodigy: UCSS27B, America Online: CEXPRESS,
Internet: INFO@CEXPRESS.COM

Computer Express is a computer mail order company that sells hardware and software to the home and small business and sells online on Prodigy, CompuServe, America Online, Delphi, E-Word, Interchange, and the Internet.

CKS Interactive

10260 Bandley Drive
Cupertino, CA 95014
Pete Snell, Vice-President, General Manager
Tel: 408 366-5177
Fax: 408 342-5420
E-mail: pete@cks.com
Home Page: www.cks.com

CKS Group, Inc., headquartered in Cupertino, California, specializes in offering a wide range of integrated marketing communication services that help companies market their products, services, and messages.

Dimension X

181 Fremont St., Ste. 120
San Francisco, CA 94105
Munjal Shah, Director of Marketing
Tel: 888 DNX-Java, 415-243-0900
E-mail: lr-sales@dimensionx.com,
lm-sales@dimensionx.com

The Dimension X business model addresses the frantic pace of Internet technology by leveraging the synergy between the development of Java tools and cutting-edge Web site production.

electronic Gourmet Guide
P. O. Box 3407
Thomas Way & Katherine Heyhoe,
    Publisher & Editor
Tel: 909-338-7040
Fax: 909-338-5510
E-mail: egg@2way.com
Home Page: http://www.2way.com/food
    or America
Online keyword: eGG

The electronic Gourmet Guide, Inc., also known as the eGG, was created in 1994 as the very first food and cooking electronic magazine, and is an award-winning e-zine with separate publications on both America Online and the World Wide Web.

FutureLink
2400 Pacific Avenue, Suite 135
San Francisco, CA 94115
Claudia Brenner, Director of Marketing
Tim Pearson, Director of Technology and
    Design
Tel: 415-441-4407
E-mail: tim@futurelink.com
    and claudiab@sirius.com
Home Page: www.futurelink.com

Consult FutureLink for comprehensive CyberSavvy marketing services designed to maximize the power of the Web for business. FutureLink combines expertise in business, interactive design, and advanced Web technologies.

GartnerGroup, Inc.
56 Top Gallant Rd.
Stamford, CT 06904
Contact: Gartner Direct

Tel: 203-316-1111
Fax: 203-316-1100
E-mail: inquiry@gartner.com e-mail
Home Page: http://www.gartner.com

Gartner Group is the world's premier provider of technology advisory services. Research and consulting is provided on a broad array of trends relating to the direction, management, and application of technology.

GeoSystems MapQuest
227 Granite Run Drive
Lancaster, PA 17601
Joan Blake, Corporate Communications
    Manager
Tel: 717-293-7559
E-mail: jblake@geosys.com
Home Page: http://www.mapquest.com
    and http://www.geosys.com.

GeoSystems' MapQuest is the first consumer-oriented interactive mapping service for the Internet, designed with highly detailed and expertly compiled cartographic information.

Global Vistas
1133 Douglas Ave., Suite 103
Burlingame, CA 94010-3994
Kathryn Swafford, President & CEO
Tel: New #'s 415-347-2901
Fax: New #'s 415-347-5709
E-mail: swafford@ix.netcom.com

Global Vistas provides interactive media and global market consulting to Internet and high technology companies.

GolfWeb
10001 N. De Anza Blvd., Suite 220
Cupertino, CA 95014

Bob Vieraitis, Vice President, Marketing and Sales
Tel: 408-342-0460
Fax: 408-342-0455
E-mail: bobv@golfweb.com
Home Page: www.golfweb.com

GolfWeb is the Internet's premier golf Web site and winner of the 1995 GNN (Global Network Navigator) Best of the Net Award for Best Professional Sports Site.

Great Escapes, Inc.
85 Montecito Rd.
San Rafael, CA 94901
Sandra Kretchmer, Debbie Poulton, Jan Toulon
(415-456-6284)
Tel: 415-459-6800; 800-459-6818
Fax: 415-453-2037
E-mail: Greatescps@AOL.com
Home Page: http://www.iscweb.com/getravel.html

Great Escapes, Inc., a Global Destination Company, offers the traveler the benefits of 60 years of experience in cruises, tours, and airline reservations.

Hawaii's Best Espresso Company
3510 S. Chicago St.
Seattle, WA 98118
Bob & Arminda Alexander, Owners/Operators
Tel: 206-725-9330
E-mail: bobalex@concentric.net
Home Page: http://planethawaii.com/bec

Hawaii's Best Espresso Company & Maui Coffee Roasters are offering the best coffees from paradise at the best prices.

HyperMedia Group, Inc.
5900 Hollis Street, Suite O
Emeryville, CA 94608-2008
Jeff Najar, Business Development Executive
Tel: 510-601-0900 x304
Fax: 510-601-0933
E-mail; info@hmg.com

The HyperMedia Group, Inc. custom-creates multimedia software solutions to meet client specifications.

INFINITY Marketing Group
2658 Bridgeway, Suite 206
Sausalito, CA 94965
Solange Van Der Moer, Senior Partner
Tel: 415-331-7256
Fax: 415-331-2050
E-mail: infinitymg@aol.com

INFINITY is a full-service marketing and research firm comprised of innovative professionals who have been involved in imaging, interactive media, and Web-based interactive marketing since the inception of these technologies.

InfoStreet, Inc.
4533 Van Nuys Blvd., Suite 202
Sherman Oaks, CA 91403
Phillip Conrad, Sales Manager
Phone: 818-788-8488
Fax: 818-788-8558
E-mail: info@InfoStreet.com
Home Page: http://www.infostreet.com and http://www.instantweb.com

InfoStreet, Inc. is a consulting and development company dedicated to publishing information electronically. It assists companies in establishing their presence on the Internet as well as publishing multimedia titles.

Internet Profiles Corporation (I/PRO)
785 Market Street, 13th floor
San Francisco, CA 94103
Deirdre Polson, Product Manager
Tel: 415-975-5800
Fax: 415-875-8617
E-mail: deirdre@ipro.com
Home Page: http://www.ipro.com

I/PRO provides online interactive deci-sion support systems that enable mar-keting and business professionals to optimize marketing programs on the Web.

Internet Shopping Network
3475 Deer Creek Rd.
Palo Alto, CA 94304
Bill Rollinson, VP Marketing
Tel: 415-842-7400, 415-846-7413
Fax: 415-846-7409, 415-842-7415
E-mail: bill@internet.net
Home Page: http://www.isn.com,
    http://www.internet.net

The Internet Shopping Network (ISN), a division of the billion-dollar television retailer Home Shopping Network, Inc., is the first large-scale enterprise to embrace the Internet as a new medium for con-ducting commerce worldwide.

Interstellar Management Consulting
Michael Tchong
Tel: 415-931-2921
Home Page: http://www.cyberatlas.com

Interstellar is a trend-setting marketing agency that specializes in the new disci-pline of information architecture.

Jupiter Communications, LLC
627 Broadway
New York, NY 10012

Yvette DeBow, Editorial Director
Tel: 212-780-6060
Fax: 212-780-6075
E-mail: yvette@jup.com
Home Page: www.jup.com

Jupiter Communications, LLC, is a New York City-based research, consulting, and publishing firm specializing in emerging consumer online and interactive tech-nologies to produce research reports, newsletters, multiclient studies, and industry seminars.

Ketchum Interactive
55 Union St.
San Francisco, CA 94111
Bob Johnson, SVP/Director
Tel: 415-984-6105
Fax: 415-982-5861
E-mail: bob_johnson@ketchumst.com.
11755 Wilshire Blvd.
Los Angeles, CA 90025
Paul Ratzky, VP/Director
Tel: 310-444-5023
Fax: 310-477-3118
E-mail: paul_ratzky@ketchumla.com
Home Page: http://www.ketchum.com

Ketchum Interactive is part of Ketchum Advertising, a wholly owned agency within Omnicom Group, Inc., that pro-vides clients with advertising, public relations, sales promotion, direct market-ing, and directory advertising support.

Komenar Production & Marketing Group
2143 Centro East
Tiburon, CA 94920-1906
Margo Komenar, President
Tel: 415-435-9470
Fax: 415-435-6143
E-mail: komenar@komenar.com

Komenar Production & Marketing Group provides consulting in electronic marketing strategies, project management, and media production services for entrepreneurs and large corporations.

Ladera Press
3130 Alpine Rd., Suite 200-9002
Menlo Park, CA 94028
Dianne Brinson, Publisher
Tel/Fax: 415-854-0642
Order: 800-523-3721
E-mail: Laderapres@aol.com

Ladera Press publishes the Multimedia Law and Business Handbook, a comprehensive, practical guide to the legal and business issues in developing, publishing, and protecting multimedia and on-line products.

MAW Transcribing Service
1320 Pacific Avenue
Crescent City, CA 95531
Maryann Woodruff
Tel: 707-464-4659
Fax: 707-464-9460
E-mail: mawtrans@aol.com

A transcribing service since 1980, it provides professional word processing and transcription, specializing in focus groups, interviews, and legal transcription from mini and regular cassettes, deliverable on floppy disc, hard copy or e-mail.

Multimedia Development Group (MDG)
2601 Mariposa
San Francisco, CA 94110
Tel: 415-553-2300
Fax: 415-553-2403
E-mail: MDGOFFICE@aol.com

MDG is a trade association for professionals in the multimedia industry.

Medius IV
52 Colin P. Kelly St., Suite 101
San Francisco, CA 94107
Kevin McCarthy, Director of Business
     Development
Tel: (415) 905-6959
Fax: (415) 243-9281
E-mail: info@Medius-IV.com
Home Page: http://www.Medius-IV.com

Since 1987, Medius IV, an interdisciplinary design firm, has combined information architecture with creative and engaging designs to meet every type of communication need, from print to interactive media.

NetObjects, Inc.
2055 Woodside Road
Redwood City, CA 94061
Priti Khare, PR Coordinator
Tel: 415-562-0285
Fax: 415-562-0288
E-mail: priti@netobjects.com
Home Page: www.netobjects.com

NetObjects is a software company developing a family of products that will enable Web site builders to dramatically improve the design, authoring, publishing, and updating of Web sites.

New Jersey Online
26 Academy Drive East
Whippany, NJ 07981
Evan Schuman, Facilitator, Business
     and the Net
Tel: 201-993-9117
E-mail: eschuman@cmp.com
Home Page: http://www.nj.com/forums/
     get.cgi/groups/business.html

New Jersey Online, an editorial product owned by the Newhouse newspaper chain, offers a Dear Abbey for the Internet Business User service.

NewOrder Media
209 10th Avenue South, Suite 450
Nashville, TN 37203
Kelly Michael Stewart, Director of
    Interactive Development
Tel: 615-248-4848
Fax: 615-248-6833
E-mail: Kelly_Stewart@nom.com
Home Page: http://www.neworder.com

NewOrder Media is an award-winning multimedia developer specializing in interactive training, presentations, CD-ROM, kiosk, and World Wide Web site development.

Newsweek InterActive
251 W. 57th St.
New York, NY 10019
Peter McGrath, Executive Editor
Tel: 212-445-4000
Fax: 212-445-5327
E-mail: pmcgra@aol.com

Newsweek InterActive is the electronic publishing group of Newsweek *magazine, which has produced award-winning, advertiser-supported CD-ROMs and online areas featuring and expanding upon the editorial content of* Newsweek.

Niehaus Ryan Group Public Relations, Inc.
601 Gateway Blvd., Suite 900
South San Francisco, CA 94080
Ed Niehaus, President
Tel: 415-615-7900
E-mail: ed@nrgpr.com
Tim Smith, Project Leader, Online
    Services
Tel: 415-827-7059

E-mail: tim@nrgpr.com
General:
Tel: 415-615-7900
Home Page: http://www.nrgpr.com

Niehaus Ryan Group offers public relations and strategic communications services to high technology clients.

Organic Online, Inc.
510 3rd Street, Suite 540
San Francisco, CA 94107
Cimeron Dunlap, New Business
    Development
Tel: 415-278-5516
Fax: 415-284-6891
E-mail: Cimeron@organic.com
Home Page: www.organic.com.

Founded in 1993, Organic Online has grown to become one of the premier full-service World Wide Web development companies.

Partners In Communication
234 Shoreline Hwy.
Mill Valley, CA 94941
Shirley Ah Sing, Principal
Tel: (415) 380-9060
Fax: (415) 380-9329

Partners In Communications (PIC) is owned and operated by JSJ Services, a Mill Valley telecommunications consultancy. PIC provides two specialized services, Prepaid Debitcard service/consultant and Operator Services Providers (OSP).

Pat Meier Associates
120 Broadway
San Francisco, CA 94111
Tel: 415-392-4200
Fax: 415-392-4205
E-mail: patmeier@patmeier.com
Home Page: http://www.patmeier.com

Pat Meier Associates Public Relations specializes in PR and marketing services for companies involved in online, consumer multimedia, development tools, and other technology products.

Phase Two Strategies
170 Columbus Avenue #300
San Francisco, CA 94133
Christine Boehlke, President
Tel: 415-772-8400
Fax: 415-989-8186
E-mail: chris_boehlke@p2pr.com
Home Page: http://www.p2pr.com

Phase Two Strategies is a San Francisco-based public relations and marketing firm that helps companies build loyalty among the people who determine their success.

Pocket Shop, a division of Pop Rocket
1320 7th Avenue
San Francisco, CA 94122
Joe Sparks, President
Tel: 415-731-9112
Fax: 415-731-9112
Home Page: http://www.poprocket.com

Rocket Shop focuses on the development of interactive advertising, custom games, and Web sites, and other contract work for advertising agencies, corporate clients, Web developers, and interactive media publishers.

PostLinear Entertainment, Inc.
2650 18th Street
San Francisco, CA 94110
Robin Nakamura, VP of Market
    Development & Operations
Tel: 415-487-1100
Fax: 415-487-1180
E-mail: Nakamura@postlinear.com
Home Page: http://www.postlinear.com

PostLinear Entertainment is an interactive entertainment software company and multiple media entertainment studio.

Red Sky Interactive
50 Green Street
San Francisco, CA 94111
Tel: 415-421-7332
Fax: 415-421-0927

Utilizing an expertise in both film production and software development, Red Sky Interactive creates finely crafted products for advertising, business, education, and entertainment applications.

Sage Interactive
257A Miller Avenue
Mill Valley, CA 94941
Steven Kirk, Partner
Tel: 415-381-4622
Fax: 415-381-0581
E-mail: sage@sageinteractive.com
Home Page: http://www.sageinteractive.
    com

Sage Interactive is an instructional design and development firm that uses technology to enhance the learning process.

SIMBA Information Inc.
213 Danbury Road
Wilton, CT 06897
Tel: 203-834-0033
Fax: 203-834-1771
Home Page: http://www.simbanet.com

With nearly 15,000 client companies worldwide, SIMBA's information network provides key decision makers with timely news, analysis, exclusive statistics, and proprietary forecasts on developments in the media and information business.

Reports published by SIMBA include Online Services: Review, Trends & Forecasts; The Electronic Marketplace 1996: Strategies for Connecting Buyers & Sellers; Electronic Marketplace Report (newsletter); Electronic Information Report (newsletter); Online Tactics (newsletter).

Southwind Enterprises, Inc.
8600 Sheridan Road
PO Box 4055
Kenosha, WI 53143
Dave Fricke
Tel: 800-939-8188 or 414-942-0479
Fax: 414-942-0503
E-mail: dave@vcity.net
Home Page: http://www.southwindent.
    com

Southwind Enterprises is an electronic advertising company, specializing in direct e-mail and custom Web site development.

Spider Technologies
185 Constitution Drive
Menlo Park, CA 94025
Nancy Colwell, VP Marketing
Tel: 415-462-7600, 415-462-7637
E-mail: nancy@w3spider.com
Home Page: www.w3spider.com

Spider Technologies is the leading provider of open software tools for developing Web/database applications.

Spin Interactive
783 Rodney Drive
San Leandro, CA 94577
Irene Graff, Producer/Writer
Tel: 510-929-2318
E-mail: IMGraff@aol.com

Spin Interactive provides technical writing, multimedia, and Web site development services.

SpiralWest Interactive
325 Pine Street, 2nd Floor
Sausalito, CA 94965
Jeff Neugebauer, President
Tel: 415-332-6797
Fax: 415-332-6796
E-mail: jeffn@spiralwest.com
Home Page: www.spiralwest.com

SpiralWest Interactive is a full-featured service company with experience in virtually every aspect of multimedia.

Symantec Corporation
895 Don Mills Road
500-2 Park Centre
Toronto, Ontario
Canada M3C 1W3
Vicki Ziegler, Online Business Dev.
    Manager
Tel: 416-446-8000, 800-441-7234,
    541-334-6054
Fax: 416-446-8726
E-mail: vziegler@symantec
Home Page: http://www.symantec.com

Symantec Corporation develops, markets, and supports a complete line of application and system software products designed to enhance individual and workgroup productivity as well as manage networked computing environments.

Tavel/Gross Entertainment
9171 Wilshire Blvd., #406
Beverly Hills, CA 90210
Barry Layne
Tel: 310-278-6700
E-mail: barryl@earthlink.net

Layne is a veteran media, entertainment, and interactive consultant and new business executive. His focus is on the intersection of marketing and content in the linear and digital worlds.

TN Technologies

1255 Battery Street
San Francisco, CA 94111
Dave Clauson, Managing Director
Tel: 415/772-8606
Fax: 415/677-3455
E-mail: dclauson@truenorth.com

TN Technologies assists clients in achieving maximal marketing value from their investment in digital media.

Torme & Kenney

545 Sansome Street, 6th Floor
San Francisco, CA 94111
Margaret Torme, Creative Director
Tel: 415-956-1791
Fax: 415-954-0952
E-mail: Torme123@aol.com

Since 1983, Torme & Kenney, a San Francisco-based marketing and public relations firm, has served clients in a broad range of industries, including leading companies that market products and services nationally.

Transcape Systems, Inc.

215 2nd Street
San Francisco, CA 94105
Jeffrey Cahn, Vice President
     of Multimedia Development
Tel: 1-888-CLUB-ICE
Fax: 1-415-357-1998
E-mail: info@transcape.com
Home Page: http://www.transcape.com

Transcape Systems creates interactive fitness equipment and services for a market of more than 30 million affluent, educated health club members worldwide.

Upshaw & Associates

250 Via Barranca
Greenbrae, CA 94904
Lynn B. Upshaw, Principal
Tel: 415-461-8583
Fax: 415-461-9302
E-mail: Upshaw@ix.netcom.com
Home Page: http://www.brandbuilding.
     com

Upshaw & Associates is a brand and marketing consulting firm providing brand development consulting, brand team building, and motivational speaking.

Upside Magazine

2015 Pioneer Court
San Mateo, CA 94403
Tel: 415-377-0950
Fax: 415-377-1961
E-mail: info@upside.com
Home Page: http://www.upside.com

The editorial mission of Upside *is to interpret the high-technology industry in a sophisticated, in-depth yet humorous fashion.*

Womanhood, Inc.

San Francisco, CA
Natalie L. Wood, President & CEO
Tel: 415-771-6126
E-mail: NWood@Womanhood.com
Home Page: http://www.SNBW.com

The Solutions Network for Business Women on the Web uses sophisticated agent technology to provide customized resources and information for business women.

Yahoo!
635 Vaqueros Avenue
Sunnyvale, CA 94086
Linda Buckel
Tel: 408-328-3388
Fax: 408-328-3301
Home Page: http://www.shop.yahoo.com
Now open: Yahoo! Surf Shop

Yahoo! Inc., offers a globally-branded Internet navigational service that is among the most widely used guides to information and discovery on the Web.

Yinspire, Inc.
6020 Shelter Bay Ave.
Mill Valley, CA 94941
Ruby Yeh, Founder
Tel: 415-508-0622
Fax: 415-508-1622
E-mail: Ruby@Yinspire.com
Home Page: http://www.folksonline.com

Yinspire, Inc. has designed the Web site FolksOnline.com as the "online home for today's cyberfolks—the world's non-technical majority." FolksOnline.com targeted net newbies, computer novices, technophobes, and the general non-technical consumer audience.

INDEX

Y